Guatemala and Belize

THE ROUGH GUIDE

There are more than eighty Rough Guide titles covering
destinations from Amsterdam to Zimbabwe

Forthcoming titles include
China • Corfu • Jamaica • New Zealand • South Africa
Southwest USA • Vienna • Washington DC

Rough Guide Reference Series
Classical Music • The Internet • Jazz • World Music

Rough Guide Phrasebooks
Czech • French • German • Greek • Italian • Mexican Spanish
Polish • Portuguese • Spanish • Thai • Turkish • Vietnamese

Rough Guides on the Internet
http://www.roughguides.com/
http://www.hotwired.com/rough

Rough Guide credits

Editor:	Samantha Cook
Series editor:	Mark Ellingham
Editorial:	Martin Dunford, Jonathan Buckley, Jo Mead, Amanda Tomlin, Alison Cowan, Annie Shaw, Lemisse Al-Hafidh, Catherine McHale, Vivienne Heller, Paul Gray
Online editors:	Alan Spicer (UK), Andrew Rosenberg (US)
Production:	Susanne Hillen, Andy Hilliard, Judy Pang, Link Hall, Nicola Williamson, Helen Ostick
Cartography:	Melissa Flack, David Callier
Finance:	John Fisher, Celia Crowley, Catherine Gillespie
Marketing & Publicity:	Richard Trillo, Simon Carloss (UK), Jean-Marie Kelly, Jeff Kaye (US)
Administration:	Tania Hummel, Margo Daly

PETER: Thanks again to Maureen for her support during all the absences this work entails. In **Guatemala** thanks to all at *Inguat*, especially Marco Tulio Ordoñez, Migdalia de Barillas, and Carmen Adler and Hector Solis in Panajachel; Tammy Ridenour and all at *Maya Expeditions*; Judith Strong at the *Europa Bar*; Frank Galán of *Continental*; Gabriel Delgado of *Aviateca*; Raul Molina of *Tikal Jets*; in Antigua to Ramelle Gonzales, Bill Wynegar and Laura Woodward; in Flores to everyone at the *Doña Goya* and *Posada Tayazal*, to *ProPetén*, especially Carlos Sosa Manza Nero and Daniel Irwin, to *Cahui*, and finally to David and Rosa at El Remate. In **Belize** many thanks to Kevin Gonzales at the *Belize Tourist Board* and Iraida in San Pedro; to Homer Leslie and Jean Shaw; Bob Jones of *Eva's*; the various computer experts who helped when all seemed lost, especially Alex Arnesen, Dave Cryer, Santiago Mendoza and Bart Mickler; John and Martha August; Martin Galvez, the mayor of San Ignacio; Anton Holmes and Wende Bryan in Placencia; Ann Miles, her brother Derek and his wife Debbie; Wade Bevier; *Classifieds Review*, and to the many people throughout Guatemala and Belize, some whose names I never knew, who have given so much help over the years. Fulsome apologies to those I've missed.

Back in the **UK**, thanks to all at *Rough Guides*, especially Sam Cook, whose expert and patient editing, often at long distance and at the mercy of communication gremlins, has made the book into what it is today; the staff and fellow students of SLAS at Portsmouth; the staff of Chamberlain Ward, Hospital for Tropical Diseases, especially Dr Peter Chidioni; Angelyne Rudd, and Alan Godwin, Anne Barrett, Jo Clarkson and Hamish McCall for help and travel advice.

NATASCHA: The Guatemalan section of this third edition could not have been researched and updated half as well without the help of the following, listed in no particular order. A big thank you to them all: Marco Tulio Ordónez (Head of Marketing), Carolina Gonzalez, and Sandra Morales at *Inguat*; Lissa Hanckel; Richard Branson; Alfredo Toriello of *Izabal Adventure Tours*; Carlo Roesch of *Camino Real Hotel*; Evelyn Búcaro de Altamirano; Ana Lucia Asensio and Julio Alvarado of *Panamundo Tours*; Francisco Florian; Claudio Angeletti; Leslie Fairhurst; Séan N Acuña of *Epiphyte Adventures*; *Tikal Jets*; *Jungle Flying*; and the following hotels and guest houses: *Hotel Camino Real* (Guatemala City); *Hotel Cayos del Diablo* (Puerto Barrios); *Hotel Tucan Dugú* (Livingston); *Hotel Marimonte* (Río Dulce); *La Posada* (Cobán), and *Johnny's Place* (Monterrico).

The **editor** would like to thank the Rough Guide team: Andy Hilliard, Helen Ostick and Nicola Williamson; Melissa Flack, Andy Burgess and Mike McCambridge for maps, and Elaine Pollard. for proofreading. Also Jeanne Muchnick and Narrell Leffman for work on *Basics*; Alan Godwin; *Cubola Productions*, Belize; Steve Houston; Krystyna Deuss and Jamie Marshall of the Guatemala Indian Centre, London, and Angelyne Rudd for the Bay Islands.

The publishers and authors have done their best to ensure the accuracy and currency of all the information in *The Rough Guide to Guatemala and Belize*; however, they can accept no responsibility for any loss, injury, or inconvenience sustained by any traveller as a result of information or advice contained in the guide.

This third edition published October 1996 by Rough Guides Ltd, 1 Mercer Street, London WC2H 9QJ.

Distributed by The Penguin Group:
Penguin Books Ltd, 27 Wrights Lane, London W8 5TZ
Penguin Books USA Inc., 375 Hudson Street, New York 10014, USA
Penguin Books Australia Ltd, 487 Maroondah Highway, PO Box 257, Ringwood, Victoria 3134, Australia
Penguin Books Canada Ltd, 10 Alcorn Avenue, Toronto, Ontario, Canada M4V 1E4
Penguin Books (NZ) Ltd, 182–190 Wairau Road, Auckland 10, New Zealand

Typeset in Linotron Univers and Century Old Style to an original design by Andrew Oliver
Printed in the UK by Cox & Wyman Ltd, Reading, Berks

Illustrations in Part One and Part Four by Edward Briant
Illustration on p.1 by Mark Whatmore and on p.435 by Henry Iles

544pp includes index.

A catalogue record for this book is available from the British Library.
ISBN 1-85828-189-X

Guatemala
and Belize
THE ROUGH GUIDE

Written and researched by
Mark Whatmore
and Peter Eltringham

with additional research
and accounts by
Natascha Norton

THE ROUGH GUIDES

LIST OF MAPS

MAP SYMBOLS

═══ Main road	✈ Airport
─── Minor road	ⓘⓟ Immigration post
── Unpaved road	⌂ Ruin
▬▬▬ Railway	Ⓟ Gas station
── ── Ferry route	★ Bus stop
▬-▬-▬ International border	ⓘ Information office
▨▨▨ District border	Ⓒ Telephone
── ── Chapter division boundary	⊠ Post office
∧∧ Mountain range	■ Building
▲ Mountain peak	⊞ Church
⋌⋌ Escarpment	⊹⊹ Cemetery
⋑ Coral reef	▨ National Park
⌒ Cave	▨ Park
⎊ Waterfall	⋯ Beach
⋎ Lighthouse	

CONTENTS

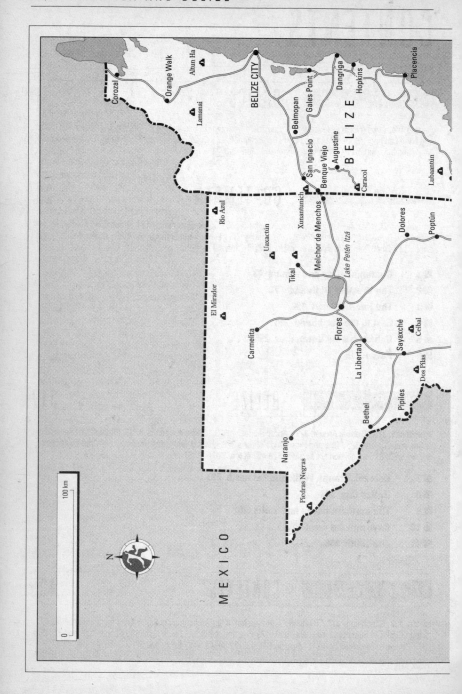

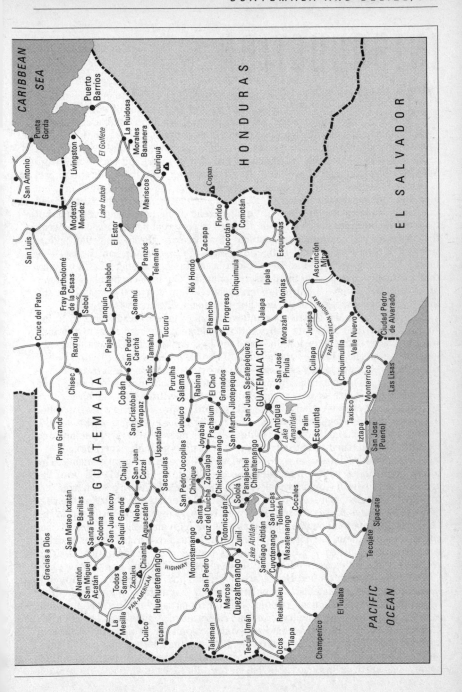

INTRODUCTION

Guatemala and Belize, spanning the narrowing Central American isthmus, don't take up very much space, but they make the most of what they have with a range of scenery, wildlife, cultural traditions and archeological remains that would do justice to an entire continent. They also have a way of defying your expectations at every turn. The two countries are very different from each other – not only in language, but also in mood and pace – and from anywhere else you might have been. If you're coming from the north, the impact is perhaps greatest: you're an awfully long way from the United States here, but also a surprising distance from Mexico. The serene beauty of the Guatemalan highlands undermines the violent image created by newspaper reports, but beneath the surface, and clearly felt at times, a very real tension exists between the two sharply contradictory cultures that coexist throughout the nation, between Western values and indigenous ones, *Ladino* and Indian. Belize feels more easy-going, with wild scenery and a breathtaking coastline. It's a country that, especially compared to the densely populated Guatemalan highlands, sometimes feels half empty – until you reach Belize City, no longer the capital but still the centre of all activity, a rough, bustling and decidedly streetwise town.

Both Guatemala and Belize offer an astonishing range of **landscape**, from the volcanic cones and sweeping valleys of the Guatemalan highlands to the lush tropical forests of the Petén lowlands and the Belizean interior. One of the world's longest and loveliest **barrier reefs** runs off the Caribbean coast of Belize, dotted with islands – known locally as cayes – that provide divers, snorkellers and fishermen with access to an amazingly rich marine environment. Both at sea and inland Guatemala and Belize support a tremendous array of **wildlife**. The rainforests are among the best preserved in Latin America, affording protection to a huge number of species including jaguars, tapir, toucans, howler monkeys, jabiru storks, and the elusive quetzal, national symbol of Guatemala. The forest itself is spellbinding, and for both the uninitiated and the expert a visit is an unforgettable experience.

The region also boasts an exceptional wealth of archeological remains. The **Maya civilization**, which dominated the area from at least 2000 BC until the arrival of the Spanish – but above all during the so-called Classic period, from 300 to 900 AD – has left its traces everywhere. Both Guatemala and Belize, at the very heart of *El Mundo Maya*, are scattered with ruins, rising mysteriously out of the rainforest and marking out the more fertile of the highland valleys. These ancient cities – some of them, like **Tikal**, well known, others, like Caracol, just as exciting yet hardly ever visited – are a fascinating testament to a civilization of great complexity and with a tremendous enthusiasm for architectural grandeur.

Culturally, Guatemala and Belize are quite distinct. **Indigenous groups** still make up half of the Guatemalan population. Their language, costumes and crafts, which dominate the highland regions, remain remarkably distinct, setting them entirely apart from the country's *Ladino* rulers. In the cities and lowlands it's *Ladino* culture, an aggressive blend of Spanish colonial customs, native American traditions and North American enterprise, that sets the less relaxing pace. Belize, on the other hand, seems to sit uneasily in Central America, its past as a British colony still much in evidence: English is the official language and the wooden clapboard buildings are similar to those in the West Indies. Its tiny population includes Lebanese, Chinese, Afro-Caribbeans, indigenous Indians, Mestizos and even a community of Mennonites. But it's the rhythm and pace of the Caribbean that characterize the country: relaxed and easy-going on a steady diet of rum, reggae and superb seafood.

As for **where to go**, each country has its established attractions. In Guatemala it's the Indian-dominated highlands that most people head for, and rightly. The colour, the markets, the culture shock, and above all the people make it an experience wholly unique. And it seems almost an unfair bonus that all this is set in countryside of often mesmerizing beauty: for photographers, it's heaven. **Guatemala City** is not somewhere you'll want to hang around and most people head instead for one of two centres: **Antigua**, the former capital, now thriving again but still featuring a ruined colonial building on every corner; or **Panajachel** on Lake Atitlán, a growing resort in a setting of exceptional beauty. Either makes a good base from which to visit markets and villages around – or to learn Spanish – but there are plenty of more adventurous options covered in detail in the guide. Certainly you should try to get to the rainforest. **Tikal**, by far the most accessible of the great Maya cities, lies right in its midst, and conveniently on the way to Belize.

In Belize it's the water that's the main draw, and many people arrive and head straight out to the **cayes**, without even spending one night on the mainland. Certainly the cayes are the chief attraction, with crystal-clear waters, diving and snorkelling as good as any in the world, and an atmosphere where time simply stops. But the country deserves more than this, and if you use **San Ignacio** as a base to discover the rivers, ruins and rainforest of **Cayo** district you'll have some of the best experiences that the Belizean interior has to offer.

Climate – when to go

Guatemala and Belize lie in **subtropical** latitudes, so the weather is always warm by European standards and can often be hot and humid, though rarely to the point of being uncomfortable.

The immediate climate is largely determined by **altitude**. In the highlands of Guatemala the air is almost always fresh and the nights cool, and despite the heat of the midday sun humidity is never a problem. In the lowlands, particularly in the rainforests of Petén, the **humidity** can be exhausting. Both coasts can also be sweltering, but here at least you can usually rely on a sea breeze. Humidity is most marked in the **rainy season**, which officially lasts from May to November, when clear mornings are soon obscured by gathering cloud and afternoons are often drenched by downpours. The worst of the rain falls in September and October, when these cloudbursts are often impressively dramatic, though still usually confined to the late afternoon. However, the November deadline is vague, at best, and there's certainly a chance of rain until the end of January, especially in Petén. Fortunately the rainy season is never serious enough to disrupt your travels too badly. In the more out of the way places, such as the Cuchumatanes in Guatemala or the remote south of Belize, rain may slow you down by flooding dirt roads or converting them to a sea of mud, but it rarely puts a stop to anything. However, if you intend visiting remote ruins in Petén, north of Tikal, you'd be well advised to delay a trip until after January; the mud can be thigh-deep at the height of the rains. In the middle of the rainy season, usually in August, there's a mini dry season, when a couple of weeks of clear, fine weather interrupt the rains.

The very best **time of year** to go is from November to Christmas, when the hills are still lush with vegetation but the skies are clear. The tourist season, which is perhaps more marked in Belize, runs from December to April, though there are also plenty of people taking their summer holidays here from July to September.

Perhaps the most serious weather threat is from **hurricanes**, which occasionally sweep through the Caribbean in the late summer and autumn. If you're on the cayes or in the coastal area of Belize, which are really the only areas in any danger, you'll hear about it long before the storm hits. Wind speeds can exceed 119km per hour but the country has an efficient system of warning and a network of shelters. Elsewhere, particularly in the highlands of Guatemala, there's some danger from **earthquakes**, which shake the country on a regular basis. Minor tremors are not uncommon and you'll probably only recognize them after they've passed. You're highly unlikely to experience anything more serious, and there's really nothing you can do to guard against the threat.

AVERAGE TEMPERATURE (°C), HUMIDITY AND RAINFALL

Guatemala City

	Jan	Feb	Mar	Apr	May	Jun	Jul	Aug	Sep	Oct	Nov	Dec
Maximum temperature	23	25	27	28	29	27	26	26	26	24	23	22
Minimum temperature	12	12	14	14	16	16	16	16	16	16	14	13
Humidity (%) at 2pm*	69	62	51	51	55	70	67	72	71	72	71	70
Rainfall (mm)	8	3	13	31	152	274	203	198	231	173	23	8
Number of rainy days	4	2	3	5	15	23	21	21	22	18	7	4

Belize City

	Jan	Feb	Mar	Apr	May	Jun	Jul	Aug	Sep	Oct	Nov	Dec
Maximum temperature	27	28	29	30	31	31	31	31	31	30	28	27
Minimum temperature	19	21	22	23	24	24	24	24	23	22	20	20
Humidity (%) at 7pm*	89	87	87	87	87	87	86	87	87	88	91	90
Rainfall (mm)	137	61	38	56	109	196	163	170	244	305	226	185
Number of rainy days	12	6	4	5	7	13	15	14	15	16	12	14

*Humidity is always greater in the early morning, when the wind is usually calm, decreasing to the lowest level at mid-afternoon, then rising in the early evening.

HELP US UPDATE

We've gone to a lot of effort to ensure that this third edition of *The Rough Guide to Guatemala and Belize* is completely up-to-date and accurate. However, things do change — places get "discovered", opening hours are notoriously fickle — and any suggestions, comments or corrections would be much appreciated.

We'll credit all contributions, and send a copy of the next edition (or any other *Rough Guide* if you prefer) for the best letters. Please mark letters "Rough Guide Guatemala and Belize Update" and send them to:

Rough Guides, 1 Mercer Street, London WC2H 9QJ

or Rough Guides, 375 Hudson Street, 9th Floor, New York, NY10014

or guatemala@roughtravl.co.uk

THANKS

Thanks to all those who have written in and otherwise offered assistance since the last edition, including, in no particular order: Brett Stewart, Joe Lembo, Barton Thomas, Ian Signer, Lindsay A Frantz, G M G Parsons, Blandford, Helen White, Eveline Sievi, Bruce Young, Jenny Mainland, Joan Forest, G H Percival, John Clark, Chuck Hutton, Jean Wagoner, Lin Tobin, David Younger, Mark de Salis and Karen Davis, Francoise Donovan, David Oved, John Whidden, Kathy Griffiths, Cathy Tavel and Peter Brown, Yvonne and Dennis Speakman, Beatrice Segal, Erica Schultz, Sulay Burns, Ed Carter, Robert Pierce and Jeannie Park, Ken Meyer, Clare Kirkman, Hilary Dennison, Mark and Martin Walters, John and Tanya Hortop, Ian Fraser, Anabel Gammidge, Reno Marioni, Mr and Mrs Henley, Annie and Fred, Alfreda and Yvonne Villoria, Dave Wright, Paul Vandegrift, Sulay Burns, Helle Regine Hansen, Frieda Verbrece, Verna Samuels, Paul Stevenson, Major Ned Middleton, Norman Hammond, John Estephan and Medleine Lomont, Maria Svenningsson, Luigi Fiorino, Hannah Makilligin, Barbara Van Ham, Ken and Phyllis Dart, Lawrence Breslauer, Tim Burford (something of an expert himself), Camilla Geels, Peter Kugerl, Aya Boye, Jerry Makransky, Ana María Pellecer, Peter Wiegand, Frank Schaer, Maria Bauer, Michael Niman.

PART ONE

THE

BASICS

GETTING THERE FROM NORTH AMERICA

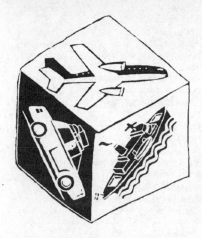

Unless you have time to spare, or are keen to travel overland through Mexico, getting to Guatemala or Belize is simplest and cheapest by plane. If you want to visit both, it makes little difference in terms of cost which you choose to fly out to first, and once there travel between the two countries is easy and relatively inexpensive.

BY AIR

Most bargain flights to Guatemala and Belize leave from **Miami, Houston or New Orleans**, and you'll generally have to fly to one of these hubs to connect from elsewhere in the US. There are **no "off-season" fares** but flying midweek costs less.

To **Guatemala City** there are direct flights with *American* (Miami), *Continental* (Houston), *United* (Miami), *Sahsa* (Miami, Houston, New Orleans), *Avieteca* (Houston, Miami), *Iberia* (Miami), and *Taca* (Miami, Houston, New Orleans). Any of these carriers can organize a connecting flight from elsewhere in the US. As an example of fares, from Miami *American* charge around $430 return, from New York around $645. With *Avieteca*, expect to pay around $500 from Houston and $250 more from LA. *United* flights from Miami are around $345 return; from New York around $600.

Direct flights to **Belize City** leave from LA, Miami, Houston and New Orleans. *Taca* – which

also flies direct from San Francisco – stop in Belize before heading on to San Salvador and Guatemala City; return fares start at $400. You can also fly with *American* (daily from Miami) and *Continental* (daily from Houston); again, expect to pay around $400 return.

It can be cheaper and easier to fly to **Mexico City**, served by daily flights from most major US cities. The cost of a flight from, say, New Orleans works out around $350 return, and from there you can fly with *Mexicana* (who also fly from Chicago, New York and Miami) or *Aviateca* to Guatemala or Belize. It's often cheaper to fly on a package or charter to **Cancún**, from where you can fly to Belize City, Chetumal (near the Belize border), or Flores, or continue overland to Belize. Chetumal is also connected to **Mérida** by air.

Travelling from **Canada**, there are no direct flights. You have to go via the US and connect with one of the carriers mentioned above, though *Canadian Airlines* fly from Toronto to Belize via Miami for around $860 return. Flying from Toronto to Guatemala costs around $980; the Montreal fare is similar. If you're leaving from Vancouver, you're in for a long haul (around two days), flying to LA and picking up *American* to Belize after overnighting in Dallas. The fare for this route is more than $1300. It is also possible to fly with *Canadian* from Toronto to Puerto Vallarta in Mexico, from where it's a pleasant journey overland.

You can normally cut costs further by going through a **specialist flight agent** – either a **consolidator**, who buys up blocks of tickets from the airlines and sells them at a discount, or a **discount agent**, who in addition to dealing with discounted flights may also offer special

AIRLINE NUMBERS
American ☎1-800/433-7300
Aviateca ☎1-800/327-9832
Canadian ☎1-800/665-1177
Continental ☎1-800/231-0856
Iberia ☎1-800/772-4642
Mexicana ☎1-800/531-7921
Taca ☎1-800/535-8780
United ☎1-800/538-2929

NORTH AMERICAN DISCOUNT TRAVEL COMPANIES

Airtech, 584 Broadway, Suite 1007, New York, NY 10012 (☎1-800/575-TECH or 212/219-7000). *Standby seat broker; also deals in consolidator fares and courier flights.*

Canada 3000 (☎416/259-11180). *Inexpensive charter flights from Toronto to Belize (Dec–April).*

Council Travel, 205 E 42nd St, New York, NY 10017 (☎212/822-2700); branches in many US cities. *Student/budget travel agency.*

Educational Travel Center, 438 N Frances St, Madison, WI 53703 (☎1-800/747-5551 or 608/256-5551). *Student/youth and consolidator fares.*

Now Voyager, 74 Varick St, Suite 307, New York, NY 10013 (☎212/431-1616). *Courier flight broker and consolidator.*

Skylink, 265 Madison Ave, 5th Fl, New York, NY 10016 (☎1-800/AIR-ONLY or 212/599-0430) ;

branches in Chicago, Los Angeles, Toronto, and Washington DC. *Consolidator.*

STA Travel, 10 Downing St, New York, NY 10014 (☎1-800/777 0112 or 212/627-3111); branches in the Los Angeles, San Francisco and Boston areas. *Worldwide discount travel firm specializing in student/youth fares; also student IDs, travel insurance, car rental, rail passes, etc.*

Travel CUTS, 187 College St, Toronto, ON M5T 1P7 (☎416/979-2406); branches all over Canada. *Organization specializing in student fares, IDs and other travel services.*

Travelers Advantage, 3033 S Parker Rd, Suite 900, Aurora, CO 80014 (☎1-800/548-1116). *Full-service travel club.*

Worldtek Travel, 111 Water St, New Haven, CT 06511 (☎1-800/243-1723 or 203/772-0470). *Discount travel agency.*

student and youth fares and a range of other travel-related services. Bear in mind, though, that penalties for changing your plans can be stiff. Remember too that these companies make their money by dealing in bulk – don't expect them to answer lots of questions. Some agents specialize in **charter flights**, which may be cheaper than anything available on a scheduled flight, but again departure dates are fixed and withdrawal penalties are high (check the refund policy). If you travel a lot, **discount travel clubs** are another

option – the annual membership fee may be worth it for benefits such as cut-price air tickets and car rental.

PACKAGES AND ORGANIZED TOURS

Several companies operate **tours** to Guatemala and Belize, the majority of which include visits to wildlife preserves, hikes in the jungle, birdwatching and Maya ruins. Trips average at around ten days, for which you'll pay about US$2000.

SPECIALIST TOUR OPERATORS IN CANADA

Belize Eco-Adventures, Uniglobe Castaways Travel, 1089 Marine Dr, N Vancouver, BC V7P 1S6 (☎604/984-8727).

Eco-Summer Expeditions, 1516 Duranleau St, Vancouver, BC V6H 3S4 (☎604/669-7741).

Fun Sun Adventures, 10316-124 St, #201, Edmonton, Alberta T5N 1R2 (☎403/482-2030).

Gap Adventures, 264 Dupont St, Toronto, Ontario, M5R IV7 (☎1-800/465-5600 or 416/922-8899; fax 922-0822).

Island Expeditions, 368–916 W Broadway, Vancouver, BC V5Z 1K7 (☎1-800/667-1630; ☎ & fax 604/325-7952).

Journeys of Discovery, 1516 Duranleau St, Vancouver, BC V6H 3S4 (☎604/669-7741; in US:

☎1-800/688-8605). *Sea kayaking and rainforest exploration in Belize.*

Mountain Travel-Sobek Expeditions, 159 Main St, Unionville, Ontario L3R 2G8 (☎416/479-2600; fax 510/525-7710).

Pacific Sun Spots Tours, 202-1768 W Third Ave, Vancouver, BC V6J 1K4 (☎713/737-1667).

Quest Nature Tours, 36 Finch Ave W, Toronto, Ontario, M2N 2G9 (☎416/221-3000). *Nature tours to Belize.*

South Wind Tours, 4800 Dundas St West, Ste 206, Toronto, Ontario M9A 1B1 (☎416/234-9176).

Winter Escapes, PO Box 429, Erikson, Manitoba, R0J 0P0 (☎204/636-2968; fax 636-2557).

SPECIALIST TOUR OPERATORS IN THE US

Belize Adventure Travel, 336 S State St, Ann Arbor, MI 48104-2412 (☎1-800/878-8747; fax 313/761-7179).

Belize Eco-Tours, 9424 Canton Loop, Anchorage, AL 99515 (☎1-800/349-7830; ☎ & fax 907/349-7830).*Sea kayaking*.

Belize Tradewinds, 8715 W North Ave, Wauwatosa, WI 53226 (☎1-800/451-7776 or 414/258-6687).

Best of Belize, 672 Las Galinas Ave, San Rafael, CA 94903 (☎1-800/735-9520 or 415/479-2378).

Castle Rock Center for Environmental Adventures, 412 Rd 6NS, Cody, WY 82414 (☎1-800/356-9565). *Rafting, mountain climbing and biking tours to Central America.*

Clark Tours, 310 Lynnway, Suite 304, Lynn, MA 01901 (☎1-800/223-6764 or 617/581-0844).

Far Horizons, PO Box 91900, Albuquerque, NM 87199-1900 (☎505/343-9400; fax 343-8076). *Superb archeological and cultural trips.*

Global Travel Club USA, 12633 Hwy 6, Santa Fe, TX 7510 (☎1-800/673-8813; fax 713/332-7942).

Great Trips, PO Box 1320, Detroit Lakes, MN 56502 (☎1-800/552-3419; fax 218/847-4442).

Guatemala Travel Representatives, 5 Grogans Park, Suite 102, Woodlands, TX 77380-2190 (☎1-800/451-8017 or 713/688-1985).

Guatemala Unlimited, PO Box 786, Berkeley, CA 94701 (☎1-800/733-3350; fax 415/661-6149).

Imagine Travel Alternatives, PO Box 13219, Burton WA 98013 (☎1-800/777-3975; fax 206/463-9372).

International Zoological Expeditions, 210 Washington St, Sherborn, MA 01770 (☎1-800/548-5843 or 508/655-1461). *Ecologically oriented safaris, birdwatching and hiking tours.*

Journeys International, 4011 Jackson Rd, Ann Arbor, MI 48103 (☎1-800/255-8735).

Laughing Heart Adventures, PO Box 669, Willow Creek, CA 95573 (☎1-800/541-1256 or 916/629-3516). *Canoeing tours in Belize.*

Magnum Belize, 718 Washington Ave, PO Box 1560, Detroit Lakes, MN 56501 (☎1-800/447-2931 or 218/847-3012).

Monkey River Expeditions, 1731 44 Ave SW, Seattle, WA 98116 (☎206/660-7777). *Specialists in archeology, bird-watching, cultural tours, diving, fishing, marine life studies and jungle safaris.*

Mountain Travel-Sobek Expeditions, 6420 Fairmount Ave, El Cerrito, CA 94530 (☎1-800/227-2384).

Paradise Bicycle Tours, PO Box 1726, Evergreen, CO 80439 (☎303/670-1842).

Sea & Explore, 1809 Carol Sue Ave, Suite E, Gretna, LA 70056 (☎1-800/345-9786 or 504/366-9985).

Slickrock Adventures, PO Box 1400, Moab, UT 84532 (☎1-800/390-5715; fax 801/259-6996). *Sea kayaking.*

Summit to Seas Adventures, PO Box 5045, 302B East Elkhorn Ave, Estes Park, CO 80517 (☎1-800/896-2398; fax 970/586-3041). *Diving and caving in Belize.*

Temptress Voyages, 1600 NW LeJeune Rd, Suite 301, Miami, FL 33126 (☎1-800/336-8423; fax 305/871-2657). *Cruises to Belize.*

Timeless Tours, 2304 Massachusetts Ave, Cambridge, MA 02140 (☎1-800/370-0142).

Toucan Adventure Tours, PO Box 1073, Cambria, CA 93428 (☎805/927-5885; fax 927-0929).

Tour de Caña, PO Box 7293, Philadelphia PA 19101 (☎215/222-1253). *Biking tours to Central America.*

Travel Belize, 637B S Broadway, Boulder, CO 80303 (☎1-800/626-3483 or 303/494-7797).

Tread Lightly Limited, 1 Titus Rd, Washington Depot, CT 06794 (☎1-800/643-0060; fax 860/868-1718). *Natural history and cultural travel in Guatemala, Belize and Honduras.*

Victor Emanuel Nature Tours, PO Box 33008, Austin, TX 78764 (☎512/328-5221; fax 328-2919).*Bird watching tours led by experts.*

White Magic Unlimited, PO Box 5506, Mill Valley, CA 94942 (☎1-800/869-9874 or 415/381-8889). *Canoe and kayak trips in Guatemala and Belize.*

ROUTES THROUGH MEXICO

It's a long haul **overland** to Guatemala and Belize from the US and not something to be recommended if you're in a hurry. However, if you want to see something of Mexico on the way, it might be worth considering. There are numerous possible routes through Mexico, combining bus and train travel or taking an internal flight if the distances get the better of you. Almost all the routes pass through Mexico City along the way.

From every border crossing there are constant **buses to the capital** (generally at least 24 hours away) and it's also possible to take the **train** – more comfortable but less convenient. Beyond Mexico City the train is not recommended, but there are good bus connections to all the main Guatemala and Belize border crossings. Probably the best route into Guatemala takes you along the Pan-American Highway through Oaxaca to San Cristóbal de las Casas, and then on to Huehuetenango in Guatemala. The other main road crossings are on the Pacific coast, through Tapachula, and on the Caribbean coast, from Chetumal into Belize. A more exotic option is to visit the Maya site of Palenque, and from there travel via the River San Pedro to a remote border crossing that brings you into the department of Petén in Guatemala. If you do decide to go all the

way by bus, then you should realistically expect a journey of three days from New York to the border, a couple of days from there to Mexico City, and two more to reach Belize or Guatemala.

Travelling south by **car** may give you a lot more freedom, but it does entail a great deal of bureaucracy. You need separate insurance for Mexico (sold at the border) and again for Belize or Guatemala. You and the car will also require separate entry permits, often valid for different lengths of time – you may be allowed to stay for just a month while the car gets three months. Cars are usually granted between thirty and ninety days, and you'll need to show the registration and your licence. If necessary the permit can then be extended at a customs office. Everywhere there are strict controls to make sure

VOLUNTARY WORK IN BELIZE

Several organizations in **Belize** accept volunteers, who have to raise a substantial sum for the privilege. If you find the cost a deterrent, you could always volunteer independently. Contact directly the *Belize Audubon Society* or the *Belize Center for Environmental Studies* – see *Contexts* – or just ask at any of the country's reserves. You'll need to be self-motivated and self-supporting – no funding will be available – but you'll probably get accommodation in the field and it's a highly rewarding experience.

Earthwatch matches volunteers with scientists working on a particular project. Recent expeditions to Belize have studied marine ecology from Tobacco Caye and researched Maya coastal trade routes on Wild Cane Caye. The cost per two-week stint is around US$1700. For more information contact *Earthwatch Headquarters*, 680 Mount Auburn St, PO Box 403, Watertown, MA 02272-9104, USA (☎617/926-8200; fax 926-8532); *Earthwatch Europe*, Belsyre Court, 57 Woodstock Rd, Oxford OX2 6HU, UK (☎01865/311600; fax 311383); *Earthwatch Australia*, PO Box C360, Clarence St, Sydney 2000 (☎008/251327; fax 02/290 1017).

Coral Cay Conservation sends teams to Belize to research into proposed protected marine areas. Approximate cost is £750 for two weeks to £3000 for three months. For information contact *Coral Cay Conservation*, 54 Clapham Park Rd, SW4 7DE (☎0171/498 6248; fax 498 8447); Suite 124, 230 12th St, Miami Beach, FL 33139, USA (☎ & fax 305/534-7638); c/o *Australian Marine*

Conservation Society, PO Box 49, Moorooka, QLD 4105, Australia (☎07/848 5235; fax 892 5814).

Voluntary Service Overseas (*VSO*) takes suitably qualified UK volunteers for long-term commitments (1–2 years), frequently working in remote parts of the country. There are currently 31 *VSO* staff in Belize; about half are involved in teaching (including training teachers) and there are requirements for specialists in agriculture, plant pathology, entomology and soil science. You don't have to raise money to be a volunteer and you get a small allowance. For more information contact *VSO*, 317 Putney Bridge Rd, London, SW15 2PN, UK (☎0181/780 2266; fax 780 1326).

The US **Peace Corps** sends volunteers to Belize (and Guatemala), to work in education, conservation and agriculture. Write to them at 1990 K St NW, Washington DC 20526 (☎703/235-9191).

Trekforce Expeditions' first project in Belize is to undertake a survey of remote Maya sites in the west, near Gallon Jug. Later plans include a manatee census and other wildlife surveys. Volunteers need to raise £2600 for a six-week expedition. Contact 134 Buckingham Palace Rd, London SW1W 9SA (☎0171/824 8890; fax 824 8892).

The British-based **Raleigh International** run 10-week expeditions for young volunteers (who must be able to swim) working on demanding community and environmental projects. Applicants are expected to raise £3000. Contact Raleigh House, 27 Parsons Green Lane, London SW6 4HZ (☎0171/371 8585; fax 371 5116).

you're not importing the vehicle – if you attempt to leave without it (even if it's been destroyed in a crash) you'll face a massive duty bill. The shortest route from the US to Guatemala and Belize sets out from Brownsville in Texas, heading south along the Gulf of Mexico. You could try to **hitch** your way down through Mexico, although this is certainly not an easy option.

Obviously the simplest way to get to Guatemala or Belize from Mexico is to fly. There are two or three daily **flights** from Mexico City to Guatemala and to Chetumal, on the Belizean border (around $170 one way). There are also flights from Cancún and Mérida: the former is the best connected, with flights to Flores on *Aerocaribe* and to Belize City on *Aerocozumel* or *Aerocaribe*. If you're thinking of doing a number of journeys by air, it may be worth contacting *Mexicana/Aerocaribe/Aerocozumel* in advance about their **air passes**, which must be bought from outside the country.

BETWEEN BELIZE AND GUATEMALA

There are two border crossings between Belize and Guatemala. The first joins **Benque Viejo** (in Belize) and **Melchor de Mencos** (in Guatemala), and takes you fairly directly between Belize City and Petén (the crossing is well connected to Belize City, and to Flores in Guatemala, by a regular bus service). The second option is the twice-weekly ferry or daily skiffs between the town of **Punta Gorda** (in southern Belize) and **Puerto Barrios** in Guatemala.

It's also possible to **fly** between Belize and Guatemala: *Aerovias*, a Guatemalan airline, flies between the capitals four days a week, calling at Flores. *Aerocaribe* flies Flores–Chetumal (5/6 days a week high season, 3 days a week low season; $96) while *Tikal Jets* fly Guatemala City – Flores, with a connecting flight on *Tropic Air* to Belize (Mon–Fri). In the opposite direction the *Tropic Air* flight from Belize connects with *Tikal Jets* to Guatemala; each of these is arranged so you can spend a day at Tikal.

GETTING THERE FROM THE UK AND IRELAND

There are no direct flights from London to Guatemala or Belize, so it's not all that cheap to fly there, although with a little creative routing it's possible to bring the price down. Fares to Guatemala and Belize are always a little higher than those to Mexico City, so you might want to consider travelling down overland from there, or even from the USA if you want to see some of Mexico along the way.

For a **scheduled flight** from London to Guatemala City or Belize City you should expect to pay between £500 and £560 return, if you book through a travel agent or "bucket shop". Official fares, quoted direct by the airlines, are generally much higher. Prices rise slightly in the **high season**, which is July, August, December and during carnival. There's always some deal available for young people or students, though don't expect massive reductions. Tickets are usually valid for between three and six months, and you'll pay more for one that allows you to stay up to a year. The cheapest tickets are fixed-date returns, but for a little more you can either change the date once you arrive or decide when you'd like to come home once you are there.

Scheduled flights to **Guatemala City** are operated from Europe by *Iberia* via Madrid, *KLM* via Amsterdam, *Avianca* via Paris and Bogotá and *Continental* via Houston, with other airlines, such as *British Airways*, offering deals that connect in the US with American airlines. As yet there are no scheduled flights from Europe to **Belize City**: you have to fly to Miami or Houston and change there (this usually costs about the same as flights to Guatemala City). For the cheapest deals, on these or any others, you'll need to go through an agent, and the more specialized they are the better – see the list of operators for details. It's also worth looking through the classified ads in magazines and newspapers. In London the most comprehensive lists are in *Time Out* and the *Evening Standard*, and nationally in the *Guardian*, the *Independent*, and the *Observer*. *LAW* and *TNT*, two magazines distributed free in London, also have useful lists of flights and travel agents.

An alternative is to fly to **Mexico City, Mérida** or **Cancún** and continue overland or by

AIRLINES

Aeroflot ☎0171/355 2233
Air France ☎0181/742 6600
American Airlines ☎0181/572 5555
Avianca ☎0171/437 3664
British Airways ☎0181/897 4000

Continental ☎01293/567711
Delta ☎0800/414 767
Iberia ☎0171/830 0011
KLM ☎0181/750 9000

To contact the Central American airlines, call the Central America Corporation on ☎01293/553330.

FLIGHT AGENTS

Campus Travel, 52 Grosvenor Gardens, London SW1W 0AG (Europe ☎0171/730 3402; North America ☎0171/730 2101; Worldwide ☎0171/730 8111); 541 Bristol Rd, Selly Oak, Birmingham B29 6AU (☎0121/414 1848); 61 Ditchling Rd, Brighton BN1 4SD (☎01273/570226); 39 Queen's Rd, Clifton, Bristol BS8 1QE (☎0117/929 2494); 5 Emmanuel St, Cambridge CB1 1NE (☎01223/324283); 53 Forest Rd, Edinburgh EH1 2QP (☎0131/668 3303); 166 Deansgate, Manchester M3 3FE (☎0161/833 2046); 105–106 St Aldates, Oxford OX1 1DD (☎01865/242067).
Student/youth specialists, with branches also in YHA shops and on university campuses all over Britain.

Journey Latin America, 14–16 Devonshire Rd, London W4 (☎0181/747 3108).
Some of the best prices on high-season flights.

Nouvelles Frontières, 11 Blenheim St, London W1 (☎0171/629 7772). Offices throughout Europe.

STA Travel, 86 Old Brompton Rd, London SW7 3LH, 117 Euston Rd, London NW1 2SX , 38 Store St London WC1 (Worldwide ☎0171/ 361 6262; Europe ☎0171/ 361 6161); 25 Queens Rd, Bristol BS8 1QE (☎0117/929 4399); 38 Sidney St, Cambridge CB2 3HX (☎01223/366966); 75 Deansgate, Manchester M3 2BW (☎0161/834 0668); 88 Vicar Lane, Leeds LS1 7JH (☎0113/244 9212); 36 George St, Oxford OX1 2OJ (☎01865/792800); and branches in Birmingham, Canterbury, Cardiff, Coventry, Durham, Glasgow, Warwick Loughborough, Nottingham and Sheffield.
Student/youth specialists.

Steamond Travel, 23 Eccleston St, London SW1 (☎0171/730 8646).

Trailfinders, 42–50 Earls Court Rd, London W8 6FT (Long haul and RTW ☎0171/938 3366; European flights ☎937 5400); 194 Kensington High St, London, W8 7RG (☎0171/938 3232); 58 Deansgate, Manchester M3 2FF (☎0161/839 6969); 254–284 Sauchiehall St, Glasgow G2 3EH (☎0141/353 2224); 22–24 The Priory, Queensway, Birmingham B4 6BS (☎0121/236 1234); 48 Corn St, Bristol BS1 1HQ (☎0117/929 9000).

SPECIALIST TOUR OPERATORS

Aztec Diving Holidays, 2 Wharf Row, Aylesbury, Buckinghamshire HP22 5LJ (☎01296/630845).

Cox and Kings, 45 Buckingham Gate, London SW1E 6AF (fax 0171/630 6038).

Dragoman, Camp Green, Kenton Rd, Debenham, Suffolk IP14 6LA (☎01728/861133; fax 861127).
Overland camping expeditions through Mexico and Central America.

Exodus, 9 Weir Rd, London, SW12 0LT (☎0181/673 0859).

Explore Worldwide, 1 Frederick St, Aldershot GU11 1LQ (☎01252/344161).

Global Travel Club, 1 Kiln Shaw, Langdon Hills, Basildon, Essex SS16 6LE (☎01268/541732; fax 542275).
Range of tours; specialize in diving holidays on the cayes off Dangriga.

Journey Latin America, 14–16 Devonshire Rd, London W4 (☎0181/747 3108).
High-standard tours start at £1400 for 21 days.

Reef and Rainforest Tours, Prospect House, Jubilee Rd, Totnes Devon TQ9 5BP (☎01803/866965; fax 865916).
Belize and Honduras specialists.

Trips, 9 Byron Place, Clifton, Bristol BS8 1JT (☎0117/987 2626; fax 987 2627).
A number of tailor-made itineraries in Latin America.

Wildquest Expeditions, 31 Laneside, Low Leighton, New Mills, Derbyshire SK12 4LT (☎01663/741578).
Budget hiking and camping in remote jungle locations.

air (see p.5). Several airlines fly from Europe to Mexico City, although only *British Airways* goes direct, several times a week. *Aeroflot*, via Moscow, is usually the cheapest, but more comfortable and straightforward routings include *Continental* from Gatwick via Houston, *KLM* via Amsterdam, *Air France* via Paris and *Iberia* via Madrid. To Mérida or Cancún you travel via Miami or Houston. Flying to Mexico you should expect to pay between £50 and £100 less than you would for a flight to Guatemala or Belize, through much the same agents. Bear in mind, if you're intending to head overland, that Guatemala City and Belize City are two days' bus journey from Mexico City, while Mérida and Cancún are less than a day from the border with Belize.

If you want to travel through several countries in Central America, or continue into South America, then it's worth considering an **"open jaw"** ticket, which lets you fly into one city and out of another. Engineering one of these can be a little complex, but on some routes you can end up paying not much more than you would for a normal return. For example, a flight from London to Mexico City, returning from Quito and valid for a year, should cost around £500. *Journey Latin America* is the best first call to sort out the possibilities.

Yet another option is **flying to the USA**, which might well work out cheaper, particularly if you decide to head south overland. From London, **New York** is the cheapest destination, but hardly the most convenient, unless you're planning a tour of the entire continent. **Los Angeles** or **Houston** makes more sense if you plan to continue overland, and **Miami** if you want to fly south, either to Mexico or directly to Belize or Guatemala.

Also worth checking out are US **air passes**, which can cover Mexico and are often cheaper if bought in Europe along with a transatlantic ticket. *Continental* and *Delta* are the most likely candidates.

PACKAGES AND INCLUSIVE TOURS

Many companies offer **package tours** to Guatemala and especially Belize. If your time is short, some of the offers can be exceptionally good value. Among the more interesting operators are *Trips* and *Reef and Rainforest Tours*, who are able to offer a pretty reasonable degree of comfort on tours that take in wildlife and archeology, and the offerings of the likes of *Journey Latin America* and *Explore Worldwide*, whose overland tours are relaxed and friendly, and

which are known for making use of local transport and taking in most of the main sites. *Nouvelles Frontières* also have several tours of Guatemala in varying degrees of luxury, with departures from points all over Europe.

All the above tours do provide company and a degree of security, but it's worth remembering that there are a large number of local travel agents who regularly operate day or overnight trips to all the main places of interest, and are especially useful for the ones that are hard to get to on your own.

FROM IRELAND

No airline offers direct **flights from Ireland** to Guatemala or Belize. The cheapest way to get there is to take one of the numerous daily flights from Dublin or Belfast to London and then connect with one of the transatlantic flights detailed in the previous section. A return ticket is likely to cost around I£600 in total. From Dublin the other option is to fly direct with *Aer Lingus* to New York and pick up an onwards flight from there (see p.3). To sort out the various possibilities, contact a reliable travel agent, such as *USIT*.

USEFUL ADDRESSES IN IRELAND

Aer Lingus, 46 Castle St, Belfast BT1 1HB (☎01232/314844); 40 O'Connell St, Dublin 1 (☎01/844 4777); 2 Academy St, Cork (021/327155); 136 O'Connell St, Limerick (☎061/474239).

British Airways, 9 Fountain Centre, College St, Belfast BT1 6ET (☎0345/222111); Dublin reservations (☎1800/626747).

British Midland, Belfast reservations ☎0345/676676; Nutley, Merrion Rd, Dublin 4 (☎01/283 8833).

Britannia Airways no reservations office in Ireland – bookings from Luton Airport, Luton, Beds (☎01582/424155).

Maxwell's Travel, D'Olier Chambers, 1 Hawkins St, Dublin 2 (☎01/677 9479; fax 679 3948).

Ryanair, 3 Dawson St, Dublin 2 (☎01/677 4422).

USIT, Fountain Centre, Belfast BT1 6ET (☎01232/324073); 10–11 Market Parade, Patrick St, Cork (☎021/270900); 33 Ferryquay St, Derry (☎01504/371888); Aston Quay, Dublin 2 (☎01/679 8833); Victoria Place, Eyre Square, Galway (☎091/565177); Central Buildings, O'Connell St, Limerick (☎061/415064); 36–37 Georges St, Waterford (☎051/72601).

GETTING THERE FROM AUSTRALIA & NEW ZEALAND

There are no direct flights from Australasia to Guatemala or Belize, and consequently you've little choice but to fly via the US. The best deals are on *Qantas–Continental* and *United*, who fly via LA. Average fares from Sydney or Auckland to Guatemala City are A\$2500/NZ\$2600 on both airlines. Fares to Belize are marginally higher.

Otherwise you're looking at a fare to Mexico City, combined with an add on fare to Guatemala or Belize. This is pricey, and usually involves a stopover in the carrier's home city. Typical fares are A\$1880/NZ\$2295 to LA or Mexico City; add on fares from LA range from A\$620/NZ\$650 to A\$900/NZ\$950; from Mexico City A\$430/NZ\$475 to A\$700/NZ\$800.

You could also visit Guatemala and Belize on a **Round the World** fare. *Cathay Pacific–United's Globetrotter* (from A\$2350/NZ\$2700) allows six stopovers worldwide with additional stopovers for around A/NZ\$100 each; *UA*, in conjunction with a number of airlines, offer an unrestricted RTW fare for around A\$4500/NZ\$4800.

AIRLINES IN AUSTRALASIA

Air Caledonie–Corse Air (☎09/373 2605).
Auckland to LA via Papeete

Cathay Pacific, Level 12, 8 Spring St, Sydney (☎02/9931 5500); 11f Arthur Andersen Tower, 205–209 Queen St, Auckland (☎09/379 0861).
Sydney, Brisbane and Cairns to LA via Hong Kong

Garuda, 55 Hunter St, Sydney (☎02/9334 9900); 120 Albert St, Auckland (☎09/366 1855).
Sydney, Brisbane, Melbourne, Cairns, Adelaide and Darwin to LA with a stopover in Asia or the Pacific

JAL, Floor 14, Darling Park, 201 Sussex St, Sydney (☎02/9283 1111); Floor 12, Westpac Tower, 120 Albert St, Auckland (☎09/379 9906).
Sydney, Brisbane, Melbourne, Cairns, Adelaide and Auckland to LA and Mexico City via Tokyo

Korean Airlines, 36 Carrington St, Sydney (☎02/9262 6000); 7–9 Falcon St, Parnell, Auckland (☎09/307 3687).
Sydney and Brisbane to LA and San Francisco via Seoul; Auckland to LA via Seoul

MAS Malaysian Airlines, 16 Spring St, Sydney (local-call rate ☎13 2627); Floor 12, Swanson Centre, 12–26 Swanson St, Auckland (☎09/373 2741).
Sydney, Brisbane, Melbourne, Cairns, Adelaide and Auckland to LA and Mexico City via Kuala Lumpur

Air New Zealand, 5 Elizabeth St, Sydney (☎02/9223 4666); Quay St, Auckland (☎09/357 3000).
Sydney, Brisbane, Melbourne and Adelaide to LA.

Air Pacific, 129 Pitt St, Sydney (☎02/9957 0150; toll-free 1800/230 150); cnr Mayoral Drive and Queen St, Auckland (☎09/379 2404).
Auckland to LA via Fiji

Philippine Airlines, 49 York St, Sydney (☎02/9262 3333). No NZ office.
Sydney, Brisbane and Melbourne to LA via Manilla

Qantas, Chifley Square, cnr Hunter and Phillip streets, Sydney (☎02/9957 0111); Qantas House, 154 Queen St, Auckland (☎09/357 8900).
Sydney, Brisbane, Melbourne, Cairns and Auckland to LA and Mexico City; Sydney, Brisbane and Melbourne to Belize City via LA; Auckland to Belize City via Sydney and LA

Singapore Airlines (☎02/350 0129).
Sydney to Singapore via LA

United Airlines, 10 Barrack St, Sydney (☎02/237 8888); 7 City Rd, Auckland (☎09/307 9500).
Sydney, Brisbane, Melbourne, Cairns and Auckland to Guatemala City via LA

TRAVEL AGENTS IN AUSTRALASIA

Accent on Travel, 545 Queen St, Brisbane (☎07/3832 1777).

Anywhere Travel, 345 Anzac Parade, Kingsford, Sydney (☎02/9663 0411).

Brisbane Discount Travel, 260 Queen St, Brisbane (☎07/3229 9211).

Budget Travel, 16 Fort St, Auckland; other branches around the city (☎09/366 0061; toll-free 0800/ 808 040).

Destinations Unlimited, 3 Milford Rd, Milford, Auckland (☎09/373 4033).

Flight Centres *Australia*: Circular Quay, Sydney (☎02/9241 2422); Bourke St, Melbourne (☎03/9650 2899); plus other branches nationwide. *New Zealand*: National Bank Towers, 205–225 Queen St, Auckland (☎09/209 6171); Shop 1M, National Mutual Arcade, 152 Hereford St, Christchurch (☎03/379 7145); 50–52 Willis St, Wellington (☎04/472 8101); other branches countrywide.

Harvey World Travel, 631 Princes Highway, Kogarah, Sydney (☎02/9567 6099); branches nationwide.

Northern Gateway, 22 Cavenagh St, Darwin (☎08/8941 1394).

Passport Travel, Kings Cross Plaza, Suite 11a, 4010 St Kilda Rd, Melbourne (☎03/9824 7183).

STA Travel, *Australia*: 855 George St, Ultimo, Sydney (☎02/9212 1255; toll-free 1800/637 444); 256 Flinders St, Melbourne (☎03/9654 7266); other offices in Townsville, state capitals and major universities. *New Zealand*: Travellers' Centre, 10 High St, Auckland (☎09/309 0458); 233 Cuba St, Wellington (☎04/385 0561); 90 Cashel St, Christchurch (☎03/379 9098); other offices in Dunedin, Palmerston North, Hamilton and major universities.

Thomas Cook, *Australia*: 321 Kent St, Sydney (☎02/9248 6100); 330 Collins St, Melbourne (☎03/9602 3811); branches in other state capitals. *New Zealand*: Shop 250a St Luke's Square, Auckland (☎09/849 2071).

Topdeck Travel, 65 Glenfell St, Adelaide (☎08/8232 7222).

Tymtro Travel, 428 George St, Sydney (☎02/9223 2211).

UTAG Travel, 122 Walker St, N Sydney (☎02/9956 8399); branches throughout Australia.

SPECIALIST AGENTS

Adventure Associates, 197 Oxford St, Bondi Junction (☎02/9389 7466; toll-free 1800 222 141).
2–12 day jungle, archeological and cultural tours.

Adventure Specialists, 69 Liverpool St, Sydney (☎02/261 2927).
Variety of adventure travel options.

Adventure World, 73 Walker St, N Sydney (☎02/956 7766) with branches in Perth and Auckland.
Variety of tours, including reef-river cruises.

Contours, 466 Victoria St, N Melbourne (☎03/9329 5211).
Specialists in packages to the Caribbean, Central and South America. Range from short stays to a 27-day cultural and archeological tour including Mexico.

Padi Travel Network, 4/372 Eastern Valley Way, Chatswood, NSW (toll free ☎1800/678 100) with agents throughout Australasia.
Dive packages to the prime sites of the Belize coast.

RED TAPE AND ENTRY REQUIREMENTS

GUATEMALA

US and Canadian citizens need a **visa** to enter Guatemala. In the US you can apply by mail, sending passport and SAE; the process takes about 24 hours and is free. Canadian citizens, however, must apply in person, taking passport as ID. The fee is $10. **British citizens** no longer require a tourist card to enter Guatemala, just a valid passport. Citizens of other European countries and **Australasia** need to get hold of a visa. Coming from Australia and New Zealand, where there is no consulate or embassy, you'll have to wait until arriving at Guatemala's international airport (where a visa costs US$5); others would do better to arrange things at home.

You'll also need a visa if arriving **overland** (including British citizens, for whom they are free). **Business visitors** are required to obtain business visas, for which you need to pay a small sum and provide two photographs, two application forms and a letter from your employer.

Visas are valid for at least thirty days, and can allow you to stay in the country for up to ninety days, depending largely on the mood of the border guard. They can be extended at the immigration department in Guatemala City (41 C and 17 Av, Zona 8). The process takes a full day, so you may choose to use the services of a *tramitador:* an

GUATEMALAN REPRESENTATIVES ABROAD

USA 9700 Richmond Ave, Suite 218, Houston, TX 77042 (☎713/953-9531); 2500 Wilshire Blvd, Suite 820, Los Angeles, CA 90057 (☎213/365-9251); 300 Sevilla Ave, Oficina 210, Coral Gables, Miami, FL 33134 (☎305/443-4828); 57 Park Ave, New York, NY 10016 (☎212/686-3837); 180 N Michigan Ave, Chicago, IL 60601 (☎312/332-1587); 10405 San Diego Mission Rd, Suite 205, San Diego, CA 92108 (☎415/282-8127); 2220 R St NW, Washington DC 20008 (☎202/745-4952).

Canada 130 Albert St, Montréal, Canada (☎613/233-7188); 294 Albert St, Suite 500, Ottawa, Ontario KIP 6E6 (☎613/237-3941; fax 230-0492).

UK 13 Fawcett St, London SW10 9HN (☎0171/351 3042; fax 376 5708).

Australia and New Zealand no representative.

Belize 1 St John St, Belize City (☎02/33150; fax 35140).

Mexico Av Esplanada 1025, Lomas de Chapultepec 11000, Mexico D.F. 4 (☎05/520 2794); Alvarado Obregon No. 342, Aptdo Postal 226, Chetumal Q.R. (☎0052/98321365); 2 Av Poniente Norte No. 28, Comitán, Chis; 2a C Oriente No. 33, Tapachula, Chis (☎61252).

BELIZEAN REPRESENTATIVES ABROAD

USA Embassy of Belize, 2535 Massachusetts Ave NW, Washington, DC 20008 (☎202/332-9636); honorary consuls throughout the US.

Canada Consulate General of Belize, Suite 904, 1112 West Pender, Vancouver BC V6E 2S1 (☎604/683-4517; fax 683-4518).

UK Belize High Commission, 22 Harcourt House, 19 Cavendish Square, London W1M 9AD (☎0171/499 9728; fax 491 4139).

Australia British High Commission, Commonwealth Ave, Yarralumla, Canberra (☎06/257 1982).

New Zealand British High Commission, 44 Hill St, Wellington (☎04/495 0889).

Guatemala Embassy of Belize, Av Reforma, Edificio El Reforma 1–50, Zona 9, 8 Floor, Suite 803, Guatemala City (☎3345531).

Mexico Embassy of Belize, Bernado de Galvez 215, Col. Lomas de Chapultepec, Mexico DF 11000 (☎52-5/203-5642).

agency that, for a fee, will deal with the red tape. Check the *Classifieds Revue* and noticeboards in Antigua or the capital. Staying any longer than three months is extremely problematic and requires proof of funds and a Guatemalan sponsor – most people simply leave the country for a few days and enter on a new visa.

It's always worth a phone call to an embassy or consulate to check up on what's required of you. If you travel down through Mexico, there are Guatemalan consulates in Mexico City, and in Comitán and Tapachula close to the major crossings.

Arriving in Guatemala you must go through immigration (*Migración*) and customs (*aduana*), where your passport is stamped. After this you should keep your passport with you at all times, or at least carry a photocopy, as you may be asked to show it.

BELIZE

Getting into **Belize**, visas are not needed by citizens of the US, Canada, Britain, all EU and most Commonwealth countries – notable exceptions are Austria, Switzerland and all East European countries. If entering on a one-way air ticket, providing the airline lets you board, you'll have to prove your intention to leave the country. Officially, visitors are also required to prove that they can afford to stay in Belize – estimated at a cost of US$50 a day – but rarely, if ever, are you asked to show proof at the border.

For details of **entry and departure taxes** for both countries, see p.15.

COSTS AND MONEY

By **European or North American standards the cost of living in Belize and Guatemala is low, and by Latin American standards their currencies, the Belizean dollar and the Guatemalan quetzal, are surprisingly stable.**

However, fluctuations can and do take place, particularly in Guatemala, so prices quoted in the *Guide* are in US dollars (for Guatemala) and Belizean dollars (worth exactly US$0.50) for Belize. The **US dollar** is the most widely accepted foreign currency in both countries, and by far the easiest to take. Travellers' cheques are the safest way to carry your money, but it's also a good idea to have some dollars in cash, in case you run short of local currency a long way from the nearest bank. Credit cards are also widely accepted.

PRICES

Under any circumstances, life in Guatemala and Belize is cheaper than in North America and Europe. **Costs** in Guatemala are on the whole about half those in Belize, where prices have increased with the recent introduction of VAT. To an extent, what you spend will obviously depend on where, when and how you choose to travel. Peak **tourist seasons**, such as Christmas and Holy Week, tend to push up hotel prices, and certain towns, most notably Belmopan, San Pedro, Guatemala City and the tourist centres of Antigua and Panajachel, are more expensive.

In Guatemala it's quite possible to get by on around $100 a week, and in Belize on around $150, if you're travelling as a couple. Solo travellers should reckon on $140 a week in Guatemala, and $200 a week for Belize. On the other hand, for $25 a day in Guatemala – say $35 in Belize – you can expect to live well.

The following prices should give you a rough idea of what you might end up paying in **Guatemala**; in Belize you'll find things are between one and a half and two times as expensive. Basic **rooms** cost anything from $2 to $8 for a single, $3 to $10 double. **Food** prices vary tremendously, but in a simple *comedor* you can always eat for a couple of dollars. Processed food, often imported, is expensive, but fresh produce from the market is very good value – although local prices fluctuate in accordance with the growing seasons. A bottle of Guatemalan **beer** costs a little over $1, but local fire-water, such as the ubiquitous *Quezalteca*, is a lot cheaper. **Travel** is probably the greatest bargain in Central America, providing you stick to the buses, which charge around 30¢ an hour, or 3¢ per kilometre, although again prices vary throughout the country. Pullman buses charge almost double this, and in general the more remote the area the cheaper it is to get around. Travelling by car is expensive, and the cost of renting a car is higher in Belize and Guatemala than it is in the USA, as is the cost of fuel – although this is still cheaper than in Europe.

As a general rule locally produced goods are cheap while those that have been imported are overpriced. This applies to most tinned food, American clothing – although plenty of imitations are produced inside Guatemala – and high-tech goods such as cameras, film and radios. Almost everything is available at a price, from French wine to canned baby food, but unless it's made in Central America you'll have to pay over the odds. **Cigarettes** cost $1 a pack for local brands, and $1.50 for North American imports.

A **student card** is worth carrying, as it sometimes opens the way for a reduction, but it won't save you a great deal.

CURRENCY

The **Guatemalan quetzal**, named after the endangered, sacred bird, is one of the most stable currencies in Latin America, defying the nation's inherent instability. A quetzal is divided into 100 centavos. Bank notes come in denominations of Q0.50, Q1, Q5, Q10, Q20, Q50, and Q100. One quetzal is often called simply a *billete* (bill) or *sencillo* (single). Coins include the 5 centavo, the 10 and the 25, which is sometimes called a *choco* or *choca*.

At the time of writing the **exchange rate** stands at Q6 to $1. Cash and travellers' cheques can be changed easily at banks in the main towns and with street traders in Guatemala City, who can be found around the main post office, sometimes offering a better rate than the bank – but they're reluctant to exchange travellers' cheques.

Outside the main towns, it can be hard to change money at all.

The US dollar is the best currency to take, but in Guatemala City you should be able to **change** other currencies at the main branch of the *Banco de Guatemala* – the state bank. All the other banks are privately run and most of them will exchange dollars, although in small towns it's always simplest to make for the local branch of the *Guatemala*. ATMs at all banks take foreign cash and credit cards. If you end up with an abundance of quetzals it is possible to change them into dollars at the *Bancoquetzal* at the airport or at *Banco Continental* in Guatemala City, at 5 Av 12–46, Zona 1.

Banco de Guatemala **opening hours** are Monday to Thursday 8.30am to 2pm, with an extra half-hour on Friday, while the private banks tend to stay open into the early evening and on Saturday mornings.

BELIZE

Even more than the quetzal, the **Belizean dollar** has remained remarkably stable: firmly fixed at two to one with the US dollar (Bz$2=US$1). US dollars are again much the best foreign currency to carry and you don't even have to change them; most banks will change pounds sterling, but at a worse rate. Travellers' cheques are easily exchanged at banks in all the main towns, and you'll even find branches of the English *Barclays Bank* in Belize City, Dangriga and Belmopan. If you bank with *Barclays* you can use your regular cheque book or credit card to withdraw Belizean dollars and a limited amount of US dollars if you can prove you're about to leave the country. At the moment the recently installed ATMs in Belize don't accept foreign cards but this could soon change. Again there's a small black market for cash, operated by street dealers in Belize City, but as always you run the risk of being ripped off.

Opening hours for most banks in Belize are Monday to Friday from 8am to 1pm, with an additional session on Friday afternoons.

PLASTIC, CHEQUES & MONEY PROBLEMS

Credit cards are widely accepted in Guatemala and Belize, even in smaller hotels and restaurants. You can also use them to get cash (except when crossing land borders, which is where travellers' cheques and US$ cash come in handy). *Visa* is the most useful, enabling you to get cash advances from several banks, but both *American*

Express and Mastercard are also accepted fairly widely. All branches of Banco Industrial have working ATMs that accept Visa (with PIN), while ATMs at almost all Banco G&Ts accept Mastercard.

Travellers' cheques are a safe way to bring money, as they offer the added security of a refund if they're stolen. To facilitate this you want to make sure that you have cheques issued by one of the big names, which are also more readily accepted. Thomas Cook, with offices at the Banco Nacional de la Vivienda (6 Av 1-22, Guatemala City) or American Express (Av La Reforma 9-00, Zona 10, Guatemala City, and Belize Global Travel, 41 Albert St, Belize City), are probably the most widely recognized. **Personal cheques** are useless in Guatemala, but Barclays Bank customers can use their cheques and Connect cards in branches in Belize.

If you manage to run out of money altogether, then it's not too hard to get someone back home to **send money**, and in a real emergency you just might persuade your embassy to lend you some. Having **money wired** from home is never convenient or cheap, and should be considered a last resort. From the US and Canada, funds can be sent via Western Union (☎1-800/325-6000) or American Express MoneyGram (☎1-800/543-4080). Both companies' fees depend on the destination and the amount being transferred, but as an example, wiring $1000 to Europe will cost around $75. The funds should be available for collection at Amex's or Western Union's local office within minutes of being sent. It's also possible to have money wired directly from a bank in your home country to a bank in Guatemala and Belize, although this is somewhat less reliable because it involves two separate institutions. If you go this route, the person wiring the funds to you will need to know the routing number of the bank the funds are being wired to.

TAX

There's a current level of 10 percent value added tax on all goods and services sold in **Guatemala** – you'll see it marked on bills as I.V.A. Market goods are exempt from tax.

In **Belize**, hotel rooms and restaurant bills are subject to a 7 percent tax. The 15 percent VAT, which applies to most goods and services does not yet apply to hotel rooms, though some package operators will slap it on illegally – always check carefully what you're paying for.

When leaving Guatemala by air you have to pay a Q50 **exit tax**, payable in US$ or quetzals. At land borders the official charge is Q3, but you may be asked for up to Q5 or Q10; if you feel up to it, arguing can sometimes bring the price down. Leaving **Belize** you must pay a Bz$22.50 exit tax at the international airport. There is also a new tax, the PACT (see Contexts), which costs Bz$7.50, and is payable at all exit points.

HEALTH

There are no obligatory inoculations for either Guatemala or Belize, but there are several that you should have anyway. Always check with your doctor or a travel clinic (see box on p.17) before you set off: many clinics also sell travel-related accessories, malaria tablets and the like.

Cholera/typhoid is a sensible precaution, and you should check that you're up-to-date with **polio**, **tetanus** and **smallpox**. Gamma-globulin, which protects against **hepatitis A**, is recommended, although the protection wears off in about two months. For this reason it's best to leave it until just before you set off, and if you stay longer to arrange for a booster locally. If you've got the cash, it may be worth investing in the new vaccine against hep A (havrix in US or havrax in UK). All these inoculations, and gammaglobulin boosters, are available from the Centro de Salud in Guatemala City at 9 C 2–64, Zona 1, or from any doctor in Belize City or Belmopan. If you're arriving from a country where **yellow fever** is endemic, you'll also have to have a vaccination certificate for this (only available from specialist centres).

If you plan to visit the Pacific coast, the rainforests of Petén, or almost anywhere in Belize, then **malaria pills** are a good idea. You have to take them for at least a week before you arrive and stick with it for another month after you leave the

WATER PURIFICATION

Contaminated water is a major cause of sickness in Guatemala and Belize, and even if it looks clean, all drinking water should be regarded with caution. That said, however, it is also essential to increase fluid intake to prevent dehydration. Bottled water is widely available, but always check that the seal is intact.

If you plan to venture off the beaten track, you'll need an appropriate method of treating water, whether your source is tap water or natural groundwater such as a river or stream. **Boiling** it for a minimum of five minutes (longer at higher altitudes) is sufficient to kill micro-organisms, but is not always practical and does not remove unpleasant tastes.

Chemical sterilization is cheap and convenient, but dirty water remains dirty, and still contains organic matter and other contamination. You can sterilize using chlorine or iodine tablets, but these leave a nasty after-taste (which can be masked with lemon or lime juice) and are not effective in preventing such diseases as amoebic dysentery or giardia. Tincture of iodine is better; add a couple of drops to one litre of water and leave to stand for twenty minutes. Pregnant women, babies and people with thyroid problems should avoid using iodine-based products.

Water filters remove visible impurities and larger pathogenic organisms (most bacteria and cysts). The Swiss-made *Katadyn* filter is expensive but extremely useful (available from outdoor equipment stores, or direct from *Water Works on Wheels*, Oughterard, Co. Galway, Ireland; ☎353/ 918 2479). However, bear in mind that however fine the filter, it cannot remove viruses, dissolved chemicals, pesticides and the like.

Purification, a two-stage process involving filtration and sterilization, gives the most complete treatment. Portable purifiers range from pocket-size units weighing 60g up to 800g. Some of the best water purifiers on the market are made in Britain by *Pre-Mac*. For details of stockists contact *Outbound Products*, 1580 Zephyr Ave, Box 56148, Hayward, CA 94545-6148 (☎1-800/663-9262); 8585 Fraser St, Vancouver, BC V5X 3Y1 (☎604/ 321-5464); *Pre-Mac (Kent) Ltd*, 40 Holden Park Rd, Southborough, Tunbridge Wells, Kent TN4 0ER (☎01892/534361), or *All Water Systems Ltd*, Unit 12, Western Parkway Business Centre, Lr Ballymount Rd, Dublin 12 (☎01/456 4933).

country; but it's worth it. The prophylaxis for both countries are *Proguanil/Paludrine* or *Chloroquine*. Obviously, it's best to avoid getting bitten by insects altogether: cover up arms and legs, burn mosquito coils containing pyrethrum (available everywhere) and use insect repellent containing a high percentage of *Deet*.

Once **in Guatemala and Belize** you're far more likely to experience a dose of **diarrhoea**, which is endemic and all too easy to contract. Its main cause is simply the change of diet: the food in Belize and Guatemala contains a whole new set of bacteria, as well as perhaps rather more of them than you're used to. Everyone has their own ideas about which particular ingredient should take the blame, whether it's the water or the salads, but in truth you can pick it up almost anywhere. Standard remedies may have some effect, but the best cure is the simplest one: take it easy for a day or two, drink lots of bottled water, and eat only the blandest of foods – papaya is good for soothing the stomach and also crammed with vitamins. Only if the symptoms last more than four or five days do you need to worry.

More serious is **amoebic dysentery**, which is also endemic in many parts of the region. The symptoms are more or less the same as a bad dose of diarrhoea but include bleeding. On the whole, a course of *flagyl* (metronidazole or tinidozole) will cure it; if you plan to visit the far-flung corners of either country then it's worth carrying these, just in case. If possible get some, and some advice on their usage, from a doctor before you go.

To avoid the worst stomach problems it's advisable to exercise a degree of caution, particularly during the first week or so, when your system is still adjusting. You should be especially careful with **water**: see the box above. **Altitude and sun** can also be a cause of illness; if you're struck down by either there's little you can do other than take it easy and wait to acclimatize.

PHARMACIES, DOCTORS AND HOSPITALS

Local pharmacists can sell drugs that in Europe are available only on prescription, but you may not get correct instructions on dosage and the like. For simple medical problems head for the **farmacía**, where you'll find some common brand names and reasonably knowledgeable advice.

MEDICAL RESOURCES FOR TRAVELLERS

USA

Canadian Society for International Health, 170 Laurier Ave W, Suite 902, Ottawa, ON K1P 5V5 (☎613/230-2654).
Distributes a free pamphlet, "Health Information for Canadian Travellers".

Medic Alert, 2323 Colorado Ave, Turlock, CA 95381 (☎1-800/432-5378; in Canada ☎1-800/668-1507).
Sells bracelets engraved with the traveller's medical requirements in case of emergency.

Travel Medicine, 351 Pleasant St, Suite 312, Northampton, MA 01060 (☎1-800/872-8633).
Sells first-aid kits, mosquito netting, water filters and other health-related travel products.

Travelers Medical Center, 31 Washington Square, New York, NY 10011 (☎212/982-1600).
Consultation service on immunizations and treatment of diseases.

UK

British Airways Travel Clinic, 156 Regent St, London W1 (Mon–Fri 9am–4.15pm, Sat 10am–4pm; ☎0171/439 9584 or 434 4700), no appointment necessary; appointment-only branches at 101 Cheapside, London EC2 (☎0171/606 2977) and at the BA terminal in London's Victoria Station (☎0171/233 6661). Regional clinics throughout the country (call ☎0171/831 5333).
Inoculations, travel associated accessories, including mosquito nets and first-aid kits. Charges start at £8 for the basic injections to £20 and up for the more exotic ones.

Hospital for Tropical Diseases, St Pancras Hospital, 4 St Pancras Way, London NW1 (Mon–Fri 9am–5pm; ☎0171/530 3454).
Travel clinic; recorded message service on ☎0171/530 3429 gives hints on hygiene and illness

prevention as well as listing appropriate immunizations.

MASTA (Medical Advisory Service for Travellers Abroad), London School of Hygiene and Tropical Medicine (☎0891 224100).
Operates a Travellers' Health Line 24 hours a day, 7 days a week, giving written information tailored to your journey by return of post.

*British travellers should also pick up a copy of the free booklet *Health Advice for Travellers*, published by the Department of Health; it's available from GP's surgeries, many chemists, and most of the agencies listed above.

IRELAND

Travel Medicine Services, P.O. Box 254, 16 College St, Belfast 1 (☎01232/315220).

Tropical Medical Bureau, Grafton St Medical Centre, Dublin 2 (☎01/671 9200); Dun Laoghaire Medical Centre, 5 Northumberland Ave, Dun Laoghaire, Co. Dublin (☎01/280 4996).

AUSTRALASIA

Auckland Hospital, Park Rd, Grafton (☎09/797 440).

Travel-Bug Medical and Vaccination Centre, 161 Ward St, N Adelaide (☎08/8267 3544).

Travel Health and Vaccination Clinic, 114 Williams St, Melbourne (☎03/9670 2020).

Travellers' Medical and Vaccination Centre, Level 7, 428 George St, Sydney (☎02/9221 7133); Level 3, 393 Little Bourke St, Melbourne (☎03/9602 5788); Level 6, 29 Gilbert Place, Adelaide (☎08/8212 7522); Level 6, 247 Adelaide St, Brisbane (☎07/3221 9066); 1 Mill St, Perth (☎08/9321 1977).

Travellers Immunization Service, 303 Pacific Hwy, Sydney (☎02/9416 1348).

If you need the services of a **doctor**, you'll find that many of them, in both countries, were trained in the US and speak good English. Your embassy will always have a list of recommended doctors, and some are included in our "Listings" for the main towns. Belize has a reciprocal health agreement with Britain, meaning that doctors' consultations and public hospital treatments are free (though you still have to pay for drugs and x-rays and the like). However, in both countries, if you have insurance (and it would be madness not to) it's probably better to go to a **private hospital**; Guatemala City,

Quezaltenango, Belize City and Belmopan have good ones. Even the smallest of villages has a **centro de salud** or *puesto de salud* (health centre) where health care is free, although you can't rely on finding an English-speaking doctor.

If you suspect something is amiss with your insides, it might be worth heading straight for the local **pathology lab** (all the main towns in both countries have them), as they can generally detect what's causing your symptoms. In many cases it's better to go to a lab before seeing a doctor, as the doctor will probably send you anyway.

INSURANCE

Medical insurance is a must. Public health care in both countries is very basic, and the private hospitals are expensive. The British High Commission in Belmopan stress that you should not travel to Belize without insurance, including provision for repatriation by air ambulance.

Bank and credit cards (particularly *American Express*) often have certain levels of medical or other insurance included, especially if you use them to pay for your trip. This can be quite comprehensive, anticipating anything from lost or stolen baggage and missed connections to charter companies going bankrupt; however, certain policies (notably in North America) only cover medical costs.

If you plan to participate in **water sports**, you'll probably have to pay an extra premium; check carefully that any policy you are considering will cover you in case of an accident. Note also that very few insurers will arrange on-the-spot payments in the event of a major expense or loss; you will usually be **reimbursed** only after going home. In all cases of loss or theft of goods, you will have to contact the local police to have a **report** made out so that your insurer can process the claim.

NORTH AMERICAN COVER

Before buying an insurance policy, check that you're not already covered. **Canadian provincial health plans** typically provide some overseas medical coverage, although they are unlikely to pick up the full tab in the event of a mishap. Holders of official **student/teacher/youth cards** are entitled to accident coverage and hospital in-patient benefits – the annual membership is far less than the cost of comparable insurance. **Students** may also find that their student health coverage extends during the vacations and for one term beyond the date of last enrollment. **Homeowners' or renters'** insurance often covers theft or loss of documents, money and valuables while overseas.

After exhausting the possibilities above, you might want to contact a specialist **travel insurance** company; your travel agent can usually recommend one, or see the box below. **Policies** vary: some are comprehensive while others cover only certain risks (accidents, illnesses, delayed or lost luggage, cancelled flights, etc). In particular, ask whether the policy pays medical costs up front or reimburses you later, and whether it provides for medical evacuation to your home country. For policies that include lost or stolen luggage, check exactly what is and isn't covered, and make sure the per-article limit will cover your most valuable possessions.

The best **premiums** are usually to be had through student/youth travel agencies – *ISIS* policies, for example, cost $48–69 for fifteen days (depending on level of coverage), $80–105 for a month, $149–207 for two months, $510–700 for a year. If you're planning to do any "dangerous sports" (skiing, mountaineering, etc), be sure to ask whether these activities are covered: some companies levy a surcharge.

Most North American travel policies apply only to items lost, stolen or damaged while in the custody of an identifiable, responsible third party

---

TRAVEL INSURANCE COMPANIES IN NORTH AMERICA

Access America ☎1-800/284-8300

Carefree Travel Insurance ☎1-800/323-3149

Desjardins Travel Insurance (Canada only) ☎1-800/463-7830

International Student Insurance Service (ISIS) – sold by *STA Travel* (☎1-800/777-0112).

Travel Assistance International ☎1-800/821-2828

Travel Guard ☎1-800/826-1300

Travel Insurance Services ☎1-800/937-1387

– hotel porter, airline, luggage consignment, etc. Even in these cases you will have to contact the local police within a certain time limit.

BRITISH COVER

Comprehensive **travel insurance schemes** are sold by almost every travel agent (many will offer insurance when you book your flight or holiday) or bank, and by specialist insurance companies. Other than *Campus Travel* or *STA* (see p.8), you can try any of the companies listed below.

If you have a good "all risks" home insurance policy it may well cover your possessions against loss or theft even when overseas, and many

> **TRAVEL INSURANCE COMPANIES IN THE UK**
>
> **Columbus Travel Insurance**, 17 Devonshire Square, London EC2M 4SQ (☎0171/375 0011). *Offer an annual multi-trip policy which gives twelve months' cover for £125.*
>
> **Endsleigh Insurance**, 97–107 Southampton Row, London WC1B 4AG (☎0171/436 4451).
>
> **Frizzell Insurance**, Frizzell House, County Gates, Bournemouth, Dorset BH1 2NF (☎01202/292 333).
>
> **Marcus Hearn**, 65–66 Shoreditch High St, London E1 6JL (☎0171/739 3444). *Good-value policies for long-term travellers.*

private medical schemes also cover you when abroad – make sure you know the procedure and the helpline number.

AUSTRALASIAN COVER

Travel insurance is put together by the airlines and travel agent groups (see box below) in conjunction with insurance companies. They are all comparable in premium and coverage. Adventure sports are covered – except mountaineering with ropes, bungee jumping (some policies), and unassisted diving without an Open Water licence. Always be sure to check the policy first. Typical costs for Guatemala and Belize are A$150/NZ$170 for one month, A$220/NZ$250 for two months and A$280/NZ$320 for three months.

> **TRAVEL INSURANCE COMPANIES IN AUSTRALASIA**
>
> **AFTA** 144 Pacific Highway, N Sydney (☎02/9956 4800).
>
> **Cover More**, Level 9, 32 Walker St, N Sydney (☎02/9202 8000; toll-free 1800/251 881).
>
> **Ready Plan**, 141–147 Walker St, Dandenong, Victoria (toll-free ☎1800/337 462); 10th Floor, 63 Albert St, Auckland (☎09/379 3399).
>
> **UTAG**, 347 Kent St, Sydney (☎02/9819 6855; toll-free 1800/809 462).

MAPS AND INFORMATION

Information about Guatemala and Belize is relatively easy to come by, both inside and outside the countries. In addition to the tourist organizations listed below, you can try specialist travel agents (see our "Getting There" sections) and even the embassies (see p.12), though at the last you have to struggle to get any real help.

GUATEMALA

You could try writing to **Inguat**, the Guatemalan Tourist Board, at 7 Av 1–17, Centro Civico, Guatemala City, although communication will inevitably take a week or two: you might as well

TOURIST OFFICES

USA *Guatemala Tourist Commission*, PO Box 144196, Coral Gables, FL 33114-4196 (Mon–Fri 9am–5pm; ☎305/442-0651 or 1-800/742-4529).

Belize Tourist Board, 421 Seventh Ave, 11th Floor, New York, NY 10001 (Mon–Fri 9am–5pm; ☎212/563-6011 or 1-800/624-0686; fax 563-6033).

Canada *Consulate General of Belize*, Suite 904, 1112 West Pender, Vancouver BC V6E 2S1 (☎604/683-4517; fax 683-4518) provide the excellent publication *Belize Report*.

UK *Guatemala Tourist Service*, 47 Causton St, London SW1 (Mon–Fri 9.30am–5.30pm, Sat 10am–12.30pm; ☎0171/976 5511).

Belize High Commission, 22 Harcourt House, 19 Cavendish Square, London W1M 9AD (☎0171/499 9728; fax 491 4139), will provide a list of tour operators.

Australasia No tourist offices

wait until you arrive. In addition to the office in Guatemala City, *Inguat* also have branches in Antigua, Quezaltenango, and Flores. Their information varies highly in quality, though generally the main office, Panajachel and Antigua branches are the most reliable.

For more contextual information in the UK, the **Guatemalan Indian Centre** (94a Wandsworth Bridge Rd, London SW6; ☎0171/371 5291) is a useful resource. This cultural and educational centre allows access to its extensive reference library, video archive and textile collection, all for an annual membership fee of £5. There are also a number of ongoing free exhibitions on various aspects of indigenous life and crafts.

MAPS

The **best map of Guatemala** (1:500,000) is produced by *International Travel Map Productions* (PO Box 2290, Vancouver, BC, V6B 3W5, Canada) and is available in London and in Guatemala from the *Casa Andinista* (4 C Oriente 5A, Aptdo Postal 343, 03901 Antigua). Specialist map shops may have copies. *Inguat* is another good source. Their "tourist map" (1:1,000,000), which includes a map of the whole country (also covering Belize), a detailed map of the central area and plans of the main cities, is the easiest to get hold of. It's sold for $1 from *Inguat* offices and some shops in Guatemala. Some map shops sell a simple four-sheet version (1:500,000), which is produced for use in Guatemalan schools and includes the national anthem in one corner.

The only **large-scale maps** of Guatemala (1:50,000) are produced by the *Instituto Geográfico Militar*, Av de las Americas 5-76, Zona 13, Guatemala City (Mon–Fri 7.30am–4pm, bring passport). These cover the country in 250 sections and are accurately contoured, although some aspects are now out of date. You can consult these at the offices of the *Instituto*, and most can be bought for around US$6 without special permission from the Ministry of Defence. A cheaper option, however, is to buy photocopies of most of them from the *Casa Andinista* in Antigua.

MAP OUTLETS

USA

Adventurous Traveler Bookstore, PO Box 577, Hinewburg VT 05461 (☎1-800/282-3963).

Central American Infocenter, PO Box 50211, San Diego, CA 92105 (☎619/583-2925).

The Complete Traveler Bookstore, 199 Madison Ave, New York, NY 10016 (☎212/685-9007); 3207 Fillmore St, San Francisco, CA 92123 (☎415/923-1511).

Forsyth Travel Library, 9154 W 57th St, Shawnee Mission, KS 66201 (☎1-800/367-7984).

Map Link Inc, 25 E Mason St, Santa Barbara, CA 93101 (☎805/965-4402).

Phileas Fogg's Books & Maps, #87 Stanford Shopping Center, Palo Alto, CA 94304 (☎1-800/233-FOGG in California; ☎1-800/533-FOGG elsewhere in US).

Rand McNally,* 444 N Michigan Ave, Chicago, IL 60611 (☎312/321-1751); 150 E 52nd St, New York, NY 10022 (☎212/758-7488); 595 Market St, San Francisco, CA 94105 (☎415/777-3131); 1201 Connecticut Ave NW, Washington, DC 20003 (☎202/223-6751).

*For other locations, or for maps by **mail order**, call ☎1-800/333-0136 (ext 2111).

Sierra Club Bookstore, 730 Polk St, San Francisco, CA 94109 (☎415/923-5500).

Travel Books & Language Center, 4931 Cordell Ave, Bethesda, MD 20814 (☎1-800/220-2665).

Traveler's Bookstore, 22 W 52nd St, New York, NY 10019 (☎212/664-0995).

MAP OUTLETS (cont)

CANADA

Open Air Books and Maps, 25 Toronto St, Toronto, ON M5R 2C1 (☎416/363-0719).

Ulysses Travel Bookshop, 4176 St-Denis, Montréal (☎514/289-0993).

World Wide Books and Maps, 1247 Granville St, Vancouver, BC V6Z 1E4 (☎604/687-3320).

UK

Daunt Books, 83 Marylebone High St, London W1 (☎0171/224 2295).

John Smith and Sons, 57–61 St Vincent St, Glasgow G2 5TB (☎0141/221 7472).

National Map Centre, 22–24 Caxton St, London SW1 (☎0171/222 4945).

Stanfords,* 12–14 Long Acre, London WC2 (☎0171/836 1321); 52 Grosvenor Gardens, London SW1W 0AG; 156 Regent St, London W1R 5TA.

The Travel Bookshop, 13–15 Blenheim Crescent, London W11 2EE (☎0171/229 5260).

*For **mail order** maps call the Long Acre branch.

IRELAND

Easons Bookshop, 40 O'Connell St, Dublin 1 (☎01/873 3811).

Fred Hanna's Bookshop, 27–29 Nassau St, Dublin 2 (☎01/677 1255).

Hodges Figgis Bookshop, 56–58 Dawson St, Dublin 2 (☎01/677 4754).

Waterstone's, Queens Bldg, 8 Royal Ave, Belfast BT1 1DA (☎01232/247355).

AUSTRALASIA

Bowyangs, 372 Little Burke St, Melbourne (☎03/9670 4383).

The Map Shop, 16a Peel St, Adelaide (☎08/8231 2033)

Perth Map Centre, 891 Hay St, Perth (☎08/9322 5733).

Specialty Maps, 58 Albert St, Auckland (☎09/307 2217).

Travel Bookshop, 20 Bridge St, Sydney (☎02/9241 3554).

BELIZE

Several maps of Belize are available from specialist map shops; and it's wise to try to get one before you go. The best map, widely available, is *Travellers Reference Map Belize*, published by *International Travel Map Productions*, at a scale of 1:350,000. Ordnance Survey also produces **topographic maps** of Belize: two sheets at 1:250,000 cover the whole country, with 44 sheets at 1:50,000 providing greater detail, though it has to be said these are out of date and and not all are readily available. In Belize they're available from the Ministry of Natural Resources in Belmopan and from the Lands Office, above the post office in Belize City.

METRIC WEIGHTS AND MEASURES

1 ounce = 28.3 grams	1 pint = 0.47 litre	1 inch = 2.54 centimetres	1.09 yards = 1metre
1 pound = 454 grams	1 quart = 0.94 litre	1 foot = 0.3 metre	1 mile = 1.61 kilometres
2.2 pounds = 1 kilogram	1 gallon = 3.78 litres	1 yard = 0.91 metre	0.62 miles = 1 kilometre

Guatemalan Indians also use the **legua**, a distance of about four miles, which is roughly the distance a person can walk in an hour. **Yardas** are yards.

Indigenous fabrics are often sold by the **vara**, an old Spanish measure of about 33 inches, while land is sometimes measured by the **cuerda**, a square with sides of 32 *varas*. The larger local units are the **manzana**, equivalent to three-quarters of a hectare or 1.73 acres, and the **caballeria** (45.12 hectares).

Belize uses imperial measurements.

PART TWO

GUATEMALA

Introduction

Guatemala is a physical and cultural micro-cosm of Latin America, incorporating an astonishing array of contradictions in a country roughly the size of Ireland. Uniquely, it still has a population which is at least half Indian, and the strength of indigenous culture is greater here than perhaps anywhere else on the American continent. More than anywhere, Guatemala is the product of the merger of sophisticated pre-Columbian cultures with Spanish colonialism and the consumerist influences of modern America.

Today, **Indian society** is a hybrid of pre-conquest pagan traditions and more recent cultural and religious influences, which combine – above all in the highlands – to form perhaps the most distinctive culture in all of Latin America. At the other end of the scale, *Ladino* Guatemala supports a culture of equal strength, a blend of Latin machismo that is economically aggressive and decidedly urban. At the edges there is a certain blurring between the two cultures, but the contrast between the urban hustle of Guatemala City and the murmur of village markets could hardly be more extreme.

All of this exists against the nagging background of Guatemala's turbulent and bloody **history**. Over the years the huge gulf between the rich and the poor, between indigenous and "Western" culture, has produced bitter conflict, and even today this is a violent country where political killings are commonplace. As a visitor, however, you're as safe in Guatemala as in almost anywhere else in Latin America. The victims of violence are clearly defined political targets, and to outsiders the country seems relaxed and peaceful. Highland culture remains essentially introspective but this is still a varied, easy, enjoyable and friendly place to travel.

Physically, too, Guatemala is defined by extremes, and by regular earthquakes and volcanic eruptions (though you're most unlikely to encounter either of these). In the south, the narrow, steamily hot Pacific coastal plain rises towards a string of magnificent volcanic peaks. These mark out the southern limit of the central highlands, and beyond them lies a series of rolling hills and larger granite peaks that form the country's heartland – and are home to the vast majority of the Indian population. The scenery

here is astonishingly beautiful with unfeasibly picturesque lakes, forests and lush green hills. Further to the north the peaks of the last great mountain range, the Cuchumatanes, drop off into the lowlands of Petén – a huge, sparsely populated area of virgin rainforest that was once the centre of Maya civilization.

◼ Where to go

The attractions of each area are discussed at greater length in the relevant chapter introductions but the following, briefly, are the highlights.

The **Pacific coast** (usually taken to mean the entire coastal plain) is hot and dull. The coastline is a single strip of black volcanic sand, and behind this a smattering of mangrove swamps rise into the country's finest farmland. The area is devoted to commercial agriculture and dotted with bustling urban centres such as **Escuintla**, **Mazatenango** and **Retalhuleu**. Points of interest are thin on the ground, confined mainly to the **pre-Columbian ruins** near Retalhuleu and around the town of Santa Lucía Cotzumalguapa (which can't compare with the ruins in Petén), the **beaches** (scrubby and desolate for the most part, and not how you imagine a Pacific beach ought to be), and the wildlife reserve at **Monterrico**, where you can explore the maze of mangrove swamps.

It is in the **central highlands** that things really get interesting, particularly to the west of Guatemala City, where Indian culture dominates. Not only is the scenery wildly beautiful, but the Indian villages, with an endless array of fiestas and markets, are fascinating. Among the highlights are **Lake Atitlán**; **Antigua**, the old colonial capital, devastated by earthquakes but still scattered with superb architecture and the remains of huge churches, and the vast market in **Chichicastenango** (though this is just one of literally hundreds of markets that are worth visiting). The ideal way to explore the highland area is to base yourself in one of the larger towns – **Antigua, Quezaltenango, Huehuetenango**, or even the lakeside village of **Panajachel** – and set out on day trips to the smaller places. If you want to explore the more remote regions, such as the **Ixil triangle** or the **Cuchumatanes** to the north of Huehuetenango, you'll need to stay in the small villages along the way. In the highlands you'll also find pre-Columbian ruins, the capital cities of the various tribal groups. Among the best of these are **Iximché, Utatlán and Zaculeu**.

None of these, however, can compete with the archeological wonders of **Petén**. This unique lowland area, which makes up about a third of the country, is covered with dense rainforest – only now threatened by development – that is alive with wildlife and dotted with superb Maya ruins. The only town of any size is **Flores**, from where you can easily reach **Tikal**, the most impressive of all Maya sites, rivalling any ruin in Latin America. There are hundreds of other smaller sites, though many take some effort to reach. From **Sayaxché**, for example, you can take river trips to the ruins of **Ceibal** or **Yaxchilán** (just across the border in Mexico); from Flores and Tikal you can hike through the jungle to **El Mirador** or **Uaxactún**, both of them largely buried in the forest.

Finally, the **east** of the country includes another highland area, this time with little to offer the visitor, though in the **Motagua** valley you'll find the superb Maya site of Quiriguá, and it's possible to cross the border into Honduras and visit the ruins of Copán or head further off into the Bay Islands. You can also travel up into the rain-soaked highlands of the **Verapaces**, similar in many ways to the central highlands, though fresher and greener. Here also Lake Izabal drains, via the Río Dulce, through a dramatic gorge to the **Caribbean**. At its mouth is the town of **Lívingston**, an outpost of Caribbean culture that is home to Guatemala's only Black community. Yet again, however, the Caribbean beaches are a disappointment – if it's white sand and blue seas you want, head north from here into Belize.

Getting around

Travel within Guatemala is as diverse as the country itself. Buses ply the Pan-American Highway every half-hour or so – some of them quite fast and luxurious – but once you leave the central routes and head off on the byways, things are sure to slow down. The only really long journey is to Petén, and for this one you might want to consider flying. Otherwise you can rely on the bus system almost exclusively: despite occasional frustrations it's a pleasure to use and offers a real insight into the country. Details of travel schedules and bus company offices are given in the relevant sections of the *Guide.*

■ Buses

Buses are, without doubt, the best way to get around: they're cheap, convenient and can be wildly entertaining. In Guatemala private cars are still owned only by the privileged few, and for the rest of the population, along with their possessions and livestock, buses are the only mode of transport. For the most part the service is extremely cheap and comprehensive, reaching even the smallest of villages.

There are two classes of bus. The so-called **pullman** is usually an old *Greyhound*, and is rated as first-class: each passenger will be sure of a seat to him- or herself, and tickets can generally be bought in advance. These "express" buses are about 40 percent more expensive but considerably faster than regular buses, not only because the buses themselves are better, but also because they make fewer stops. Pullmans usually leave from the offices of the bus company – addresses are listed in the text – and on the whole they serve only the main routes, connecting the capital with the Mexican border, Huehuetenango, Quezaltenango, Puerto Barrios, Esquipulas and San Salvador. This does mean, though, that most long journeys can be done at least part of the way by pullman. Note that tickets are sometimes (always in Petén) collected by conductors at the end of the journey, so make sure not to lose yours.

Second-class buses, known as *camionetas*, are open to all and stop for every possible passenger, cramming their seats, aisles and occasionally even roofs. These are often old school buses from the US, their seats designed for the under-fives, so you're liable to have bruised knees after a day or two's travel. Nevertheless, travel by second-class bus offers you a real taste of Guatemalan life, and if many trips are uncomfortable and frustratingly slow, they are never dull. There are hundreds of small bus companies, each determined to outdo the next in the garishness of the paint jobs of their vehicles. Almost all of them operate out of **bus terminals**, usually on the edge of town, and often adjacent to the market; between towns you can hail buses and they'll almost always stop for you. Be warned, though, that bus traffic is almost nonexistent after dark. Tickets are bought on the bus, and are always a bargain.

■ Trains

Until relatively recently, **trains** provided an essential link between the capital and the two coasts, but these days only freight trains remain operational, and there are no passenger services. The service is in rapid decline and before too long the state rail company, steadily accumulating hefty debts, may close down altogether.

■ Planes

The only **internal flight** you're at all likely to take in Guatemala is from the capital to **Flores**. The flight costs about $110 return and takes only 45 minutes (as opposed to some 12–14 hours on the bus), with four rival companies offering services. Their addresses and other details can be found in our Petén chapter; tickets can be bought from any travel agent in Guatemala City and several outlets in Flores and Antigua. There are also flights to Poptún and Playa Grande, and charters to Cópan; again, details are given in the *Guide*.

You might also want to fly **between Belize and Guatemala**: planes connect Belize City with Flores or Guatemala City several times a day.

■ Driving

If you've succeeded in getting your car to Guatemala (see p.7), any further problems you face are likely to seem fairly minor. On the whole, **driving** inside the country is straightforward and it certainly offers unrivalled freedom – traffic is rarely heavy outside the capital, although local driving practices can be alarming at times.

Most of the main routes are paved, but beyond this the roads are often extremely rough. **Filling stations** (*gasolineras*), too, are scarce once you venture away from the main roads: fuel is extremely cheap by European standards, though marginally more expensive than in the US. Should you break down there'll usually be an enthusiastic local mechanic, but **spare parts** can be a problem, especially for anything beyond the most basic of models. *Toyota*s, *Dodge*s, *Ford*s and *VW*s are all fairly common in this part of the world, so you might be able to find someone who has some spares, but for other makes you'd be sensible to bring a basic spares kit. Tyres in particular suffer badly on the burning hot roads and rough dirt tracks. If you plan to head up into the mountains or along any of the smaller roads in Petén then you'll need high clearance and four-wheel drive.

Parking and security constitute a further problem, particularly in the cities where theft and vandalism are fairly common. If possible you should get your car shut away in a guarded car park – there are plenty in the centre of Guatemala

City. Some hotels also have protected parking space.

Local **warning signs** are also worth getting to know. The most common is placing a branch in the road, which indicates the presence of a broken-down car. Most other important road signs should be fairly recognizable: you'll see many *Alto* ("stop") signs marking the military checkpoints from more troubled times. Locals usually know which to ignore, but if in doubt it's safest to stop anyway. *Derrumbes* means "landslides", *frene con motor* "brake with motor" (meaning a steep descent) and *tumulos* "bumps in the road", a favourite technique for slowing down traffic.

Renting a car takes some of the worries out of driving but is expensive: generally at least $50 a day (or around $220 a week) by the time you've added the extras. Nonetheless, it can be worth doing if you can get a few people together – even better value if you get a larger group and rent a minibus. If you do rent, make sure to check the details of the insurance, which often does not cover damage to your vehicle at all. Local rental companies are listed in the *Guide* for the main towns.

■ Hitching

It's possible to **hitch** around Guatemala, and on the main routes this can be a good way to get around, though you might well end up on a bus as these are almost as frequent as private cars. Off the main highways private cars are rare, and many of those that do take hitchers run as a bus service, charging all passengers. So under most circumstances you should anticipate paying for the ride, and it's polite to offer. If you face a long wait for the next bus then it's almost always worth a try – lots of locals hitch rides (again they usually expect to pay) and the occasional discomfort of riding in the back of a pickup or truck is worth it for the time saved and the contact with fellow passengers.

■ Taxis

Taxis are available in all the main towns and their rates are fairly low. Meters are a rarity so you should try and fix a price before you set off, particularly in Guatemala City. Local taxi drivers will almost always be prepared to negotiate a price for a half-day or day's excursion to nearby villages or sites, and if time is short this can be a good way of seeing places where the bus service is awkwardly timed. If you can organize a group this need not be an expensive option, possibly even cheaper than renting a car for the day.

■ Bikes and motorbikes

Bikes are very common indeed in Guatemala, and cycling has to be one of the most popular sports. You'll be well received almost anywhere if you travel by bike, and if you've got the energy to make your way through the highlands it's a great way to see the country. Since cycling is so popular, most towns will have a repair shop where you can get hold of spare parts, although you still need to carry the basics for emergencies on the road. Mountain bikes make the going easier, as even the main roads include plenty of formidable potholes, and it's a rare ride that doesn't involve at least one steep climb. Second-class buses will carry bikes on the roof, so if you can't face the hills then there's always an easy option. In case you didn't bring you own bike, you can **rent** them in Antigua or Panajachel: mountain bikes can be rented by the day (about $20), week ($35) or month ($75).

Motorbikes can also be a good way of getting around and since many locals ride them it may not be too hard to locate parts and expertise. There are rental outlets in Guatemala City, Panajachel and Antigua, charging around $20 a day or $100 for a week.

■ Boats and ferries

Ferries operate on several different routes inside Guatemala. The two major routes take you across Lake Izabal, from Mariscos to El Estor, and between Puerto Barrios and Lívingston. Both of these are daily passenger-only services and very reasonably priced. From Puerto Barrios there's also a twice-weekly service to Punta Gorda in Belize. Once again the precise details of schedules are given in the *Guide*.

Smaller boats run a regular service along the Río San Pedro, from El Naranjo in Petén to the Mexican border and beyond, and you can hitch a ride, or rent a boat on the Río Salinas from Sayaxché to Benemerito on the Mexican bank of the Río Usumacinta; on the Río Usumacinta from Bethel to Frontera Corozal, Mexico, and on Lake Petén Itzá between Flores and San Benito to San Andrés. You'll also find plenty of boats offering to take passengers along the Río Dulce to and from Lívingston. On almost any of the other navigable waterways you should be able to rent a boat somewhere.

Along the Pacific coast the Chiquimulilla canal separates much of the shoreline from the mainland. If you're heading for a beach you'll find that a regular shuttle of small boats takes people across the canal. If the village is also on the other side then arriving buses are met by boats.

Accommodation

Guatemalan hotels come in all shapes and sizes; on the whole, it's not hard to find somewhere reasonable, and it doesn't take long to find yourself in tune with what's on offer and able to recognize the style that suits your needs. Accommodation comes under a range of names: *hotels, pensiónes, posadas, hospedajes* and *huespedes*. The names don't always mean a great deal: in theory a *hospedaje* is less formal than a *hotel*, but in practice the reverse is almost as common.

Prices for rooms vary as much as anything else. On the whole you can expect the cheapest places to charge $2–5 per person (although most of these are out in the countryside, away from the main tourist centres), and to get a reasonable but basic room with its own bathroom for under $10. But price and quality are not always as closely linked as you might expect, and despite the fact that rates are officially regulated you'll find both bargains and rip-offs at almost every level. It's often worth trying to haggle a little, or asking if there are any cheaper rooms. You can also ask to see the official prices, which should be set by *Inguat*, the national tourist board, and are meant to be displayed in the room. If you've been overcharged you can register a complaint with *Inguat*, although it's unlikely that much will happen. If travelling in a group you can often save money by **sharing** a larger room, which almost all of the cheaper hotels can offer.

Prices are at their highest in Guatemala City, where the cheapest rooms cost around $5, and here it's sometimes difficult to find a single room at all. Most hotels insist on charging solo travellers for the cost of a double regardless. Costs are also higher than average in Antigua and Flores. At fiesta and holiday times, particularly Holy Week and Christmas, rooms tend to be more expensive and harder to find, and the summer tourist season can also be crowded. At these times, particularly if you're going to arrive in Guatemala City at night, it's worth booking a room by phone or fax, but in other parts of the country it's hardly worth it.

When you arrive at a hotel you should always insist on seeing the room before any money changes hands, otherwise they'll dump you in the noisiest part of the building and save the good rooms for more discerning customers. In general the cheaper hotels recommended in this book are not the very cheapest – which are often genuinely squalid, although we do list some notable bargains – but one step up. Rooms in these places will be simple, with a shared toilet and bathroom usually at the end of the corridor. In the bracket above this ($5–10) you can expect a private bathroom, although you may have to pay more if you're determind to have reliable hot water, which is considered to be something of a luxury. For more than $20 you can expect international standards of comfort and luxury.

A major problem in all but the most expensive, air-conditioned hotels is the **insects**, usually fleas in the highlands and mosquitoes in the lowlands. You can often spot the worst places by the remains splattered on the wall. There's not a lot you can do about this, although anti-mosquito devices (either pyrethrin coils which burn all night, or the more modern electric equivalents), sold widely and cheaply throughout Guatemala, are reasonably effective. Ceiling fans can also help to keep flying insects at bay. Mosquito nets are never provided, but are only really essential if you're going to be sleeping out in Petén.

■ Camping and towns without hotels

Youth hostels are nonexistent in Guatemala but in a country so heavily populated you rarely need to **camp**. The main cities certainly don't have campsites, and the only places with any decent formal provision for camping are Panajachel and Tikal.

If you decide to set off into the wilds, then a **tent** is certainly a good idea, although even here it's by no means essential. Hiking **in the highlands** usually takes you from village to village,

and everywhere you go it's possible to find somewhere to sling a hammock or bed down for the night. In villages that don't have hotels you should track down the mayor (*alcalde*) and ask if you can stay in the town hall (*municipalidad*) or local school. If that isn't possible then you'll almost certainly be found somewhere else. If you do take a tent along, the Guatemalan countryside offers plenty of superb spots to camp, although you should take care in politically sensitive areas and also try to ask the landowner. In some places, such as Semuc Champey and the ruins of Mixco Viejo, there are thatched shelters where you can sling a hammock or bed down out of the rain.

When it comes to **hiking in the jungle** you'll need to hire a guide. They usually sleep out in the open, protected only by a mosquito net, so you can either follow suit or use a tent. At most of the smaller Maya sites there are guards who will usually let you sleep in their shelters and cook on their fires. If you plan to use their facilities then bring along some food to share with them.

The other occasion for which a tent is useful is climbing **volcanoes**, which often entails a night under the stars. On the lower cone of Acatenango there's a small hut that provides shelter for sleeping out, but it sometimes fills up at weekends. Tents, sleeping bags, stoves and backpacks can be rented from the *Casa Andinista* in Antigua (see p.86).

Communications – mail, phones and media

Keeping in touch with home shouldn't be a problem in Guatemala, although outside the capital the mail and phone services are a bit thin on the ground. International phone calls, however, are expensive and in the long run it may work out cheaper to reverse the charges/ call collect.

◼ Mail

Guatemalan postal services are fairly efficient by Latin American standards, and you can **send mail** easily from even the smallest of towns – though it's probably safer to send anything of importance from the capital. Letters generally take around a week to the US, a couple of weeks to Europe. To ensure that it won't take any longer make sure that you send your letters *express*, which costs twice the normal fee but is still cheap, and mark them *correo aereo* (air mail). The **main post office** (*Correo Central*) in Guatemala City is open from Monday to Friday from 7.30am to 6.30pm, but most local branches close at 4.30pm.

Receiving mail is also straightforward. You can have it sent to any post office in the country, and to a number of privately owned communications offices (see below) although once again Guatemala City is the safest bet. Letters to be picked up from the post office should be addressed to you at the *Lista de Correos*, Guatemala City, Central America, and it's important to use only one initial before your surname. Otherwise you should check under all your initials as letters are all too easily mislaid. A small fee is charged by the post office and you'll need ID in order to pick up your mail. Letters are only kept at the post office for one month, after which they're returned to the sender.

Alternatively, you could have your mail sent to the **American Express** office, which offers a much more efficient and reliable service and keeps letters for several months. They will also receive and keep faxes for you. The address of the office is Av Reforma 9–00, Zona 9, Guatemala City, Central America. You need to show either an *American Express* card or travellers' cheques: in the end it's unlikely that they'll actually refuse to hand over any letters.

Sending parcels is less easy, as there are complex regulations about the way in which they should be wrapped. Normally this entails cardboard boxes, brown paper and string, although you can also pack things in a flour sack. (Boxes and sacks can be bought in shops and markets.) The parcel has to be taken to the post office for inspection by the customs department, and is then sealed. Rates for shipment are reasonable, but parcels sent by air are fairly expensive. In the end the whole process is so time-consuming and frustrating that you're almost invariably better off using one of the agencies in Antigua or Panajachel. The better of them is *Get Guated Out*

in Panajachel; it's slightly more expensive than Antigua's longer-established *Pink Box*, but considerably more reliable.

Telegrams are a much used and very cheap mode of communication within the country, and once you get into the swing of it they are a good way to get in touch with misplaced travelling partners – by addressing them to assorted hotels – and to book hotel rooms. Telegrams within the country are handled by the post office and cost next to nothing; **international telegrams** have to be sent from *Guatel* (the phone company) and cost far more.

◼ Phones

Local phone calls in Guatemala are cheap, but outside Guatemala City there are hardly any payphones: where you do find one you'll need 10, 15 or 25 centavo coins. Some shops, bars and restaurants will allow customers to use their phones, and international calls can also be made from upmarket hotels, though usually at a considerable premium. Otherwise, all calls have to be made from the offices of **Guatel**, the national phone company. At a *Guatel* office you tell the operator who it is that you want to phone, wait until your name is announced and go to the booth they point out. Afterwards they present you with the bill. *Guatel* offices are open daily from 7am to 10pm, with some staying open until midnight.

For **long-distance and international calls** the procedure is pretty much the same. International calls can be direct dialled or you can use the international operator; if you're calling the US you can also use AT&T, MCI and Sprint, to make regular, collect or credit card calls, avoiding the complications and uncertainties of the Guatemalan phone system. There are similar services for Canada (☎198). Calls to Europe cost around $20 a minute, with a three-minute minimum call. From Guatemala you can only make **collect calls** (reverse charges) to the USA, Canada, Mexico and other Central American countries – not to Britain.

RINGING THE CHANGES

In 1996 all **telephone numbers** in Guatemala were changed to seven digits. Although we have taken these changes into account in the *Guide*, you should be prepared to encounter a certain amount of teething problems – if in any doubt double check with the tourist office or at *Guatel*.

USEFUL PHONE NUMBERS

Telephoning overseas from Guatemala

AT&T ☎190   MCI☎189   Sprint☎195

International operator   ☎171

Telephoning Guatemala from abroad, the international direct dialling (IDD) code is ☎502.

Faxes can be sent from *Guatel* offices, or from a number of offices, hotels and shops in Guatemala City, Antigua, Flores, Panajachel and Quezaltenango – their names and numbers are listed in the *Guide*. Several **privately owned phone and fax offices**, some of which offer e-mail, will also let you receive mail for no charge. *Conexion*, which has branches in Antigua, Panajachel, Xela and Flores, is one of the most reliable.

■ Media

For finding out what's happening both inside and outside the country, Guatemala is equipped with several daily papers, a handful of TV channels, and more than enough radio stations. The nation's press is expanding in both volume and coverage and in theory there is little restriction on its freedom, although pressures are exerted and journalism remains a dangerous profession.

Of the **daily papers** the most widely read are *La Prensa Libre* and *El Grafico*, both available in the early morning throughout the country and published in tabloid format. Their stance on national issues is well to the right of centre. *La Prensa Libre* is the country's most popular paper, with a circulation of 70,000. Founded in 1951, it represents the interests of the right-wing military and economic elite. Its main rival *El Grafico* sells some 60,000 and is owned by Jorge Carpio, an unsuccessful presidential candidate who uses it to promote his cause – despite the fact that his campaign is said to have left him bankrupt.

For a more balanced view you need to read the "marginal" papers. *La Hora* is the oldest and best of these; it comes out in the afternoon, sells a mere 7000 and is available only in Guatemala City and Antigua. The *Siglo Veintiuno*, set up in 1991, has been widely praised for its even-handed coverage and liberal editorial line. It is also published in several indigenous languages, as is the weekly *El Regional*, based in Huehuetenango, which takes a very strident and progressive approach. Finally, the *Diario de CentroAmerica* is a daily government publication

and unashamed in its propaganda, filling many pages with official announcements.

The left remains largely unrepresented in the Guatemalan media. In 1989 the left-leaning *La Epoca* newspaper survived for a mere month before its offices were bombed and its editor driven into exile. The latest attempt to confront this pressure is *Tinamit*, a bold weekly magazine which launches bitter attacks on leading political and social figures. The magazine is privately owned and accepts no advertising, and although its offices have been bombed on a number of occasions, the journalists defy such pressure, even publishing small pictures of themselves alongside their articles.

Several other **periodicals** have substantial sales: none more so than *Extra*, which catalogues the horrors of the previous week and includes graphic pictures of mutilated corpses. More respectable journalism is peddled by *La Cronica*, a monthly magazine that deals with regional issues from a politically central standpoint, and *Guatemala Weekly*, the main locally produced **English-language** paper. It's actually more of a newssheet, taking an aggressively free-market line while criticizing governmental corruption and human rights abuses. It is published every Saturday and is available free. You can pick up copies at the major hotels and many restaurants in Antigua, Guatemala City and Panajachel, as well as other tourist centres around the country.

Its rival is *The Guatemala News*, also free and published on Fridays. Less contentious, it caters largely to the concerns of the growing North American expatriate community in Guatemala. Also in English are *Central America Report*, a long-established publication, available from their offices at 9 C A 3–56, Zona 1, Guatemala City; and *Viva Guatemala*, a bi-annual magazine published by *Fundesa*, a local business organization, to encourage foreign investment. It does this by consistently singing the praises of the country and the stability of its economy. Copies are available for free from their office at Ruta 6, 9–21, Zona 4, Guatemala City.

As for **foreign publications**, *Newsweek, Time* and *The Economist* are all sold in the streets of Guatemala City, particularly around the main plaza. Some American newspapers are also available, in particular *USA Today*, the *Miami Herald*, the *New York Times* and the *Wall Street Journal* – all sold at the *Pan-American Hotel*, the *Camino Real*, and the *Sheraton* in Guatemala City. Some are also available in Antigua, and you can read them at the *Instituto Guatemalteco Americano* library at Ruta 4, 4–05, Zona 4, Guatemala City. No British papers are sold in Guatemala although the British Embassy has recent copies.

Guatemala has an abundance of **radio stations**. There are 43 of them in Guatemala City alone, with another 105 in the rest of the country. Some of them are religious stations, but most transmit a steady stream of Latin rock, and whether you have a radio or not you're certain to hear plenty of it. Two of the best are *Radio Conga* (99.7FM) and *Radio Fiesta* (98.1FM). If you yearn for the voice of the BBC, the World Service transmits a good daily service, as does the Voice of America (see box).

Television stations are also in plentiful supply, and in Guatemala City viewers can choose from five local channels and ten satellite

channels, all of them dominated by American programmes. In other parts of the country the local channels are rivalled by regional cable networks. Many upmarket hotels and some bars in tourist areas (Antigua, for example) also have direct satellite or cable reception of US stations, which can be handy for catching up with the news on *CNN*.

Eating and drinking

Food doesn't come high in the list of reasons to visit Guatemala, and although Guatemalan cuisine does have its high points they're not easy to come by. But at least you're unlikely to go hungry: there's plenty of international food on the menu and, given enough time, you may even end up liking the beans.

■ Where to eat

The most important distinction in Guatemala is between the **restaurant** and the **comedor**. The latter translates as an "eatery", and in general these are simple local cafés serving the food of the poor at rock-bottom prices. In a *comedor* there is normally no menu, and you simply ask to see what's on offer, or look into the bubbling pots. Restaurants, in general, are slightly more formal and expensive. As usual, however, there are plenty of exceptions to this rule: many a restaurant has a very *comedor*-like menu, and vice versa. On the whole you'll find restaurants in the towns, while in small villages there are usually just one or two *comedores*, clustered around the market area. *Comedores* generally look scruffier, but the food is almost always fresh and the turnover is fast.

In the cities you'll also find **fast-food** joints, modelled on the American originals and often owned by the same companies. When you're travelling you'll also come across the local version of fast food: when buses pause they're besieged by vendors offering a huge selection of drinks, sweets, local specialities and complete meals. Many of these are delicious, but you do need to treat this kind of food with a degree of caution, and bear in mind the general lack of hygiene.

Traditionally, Guatemalans eat a **breakfast** of tortillas and eggs, accompanied by the inevitable beans – and sometimes also a sauce of sour

BBC World Service		
All times are Greenwich Mean Time (GMT):		
00.00–06.30:	5.975MHz	50.21 metres
00.00–03.30:	7.325MHz	40.96 metres
	9.915MHz	30.26 metres
00.30–02.30:	9.590MHz	31.28 metres
05.00–06.30:	9.640MHz	31.12 metres
11.00–14.00:	15.220MHz	19.71 metres
14.00–16.15:	17.840MHz	16.82 metres
23.00–00.00:	5.975MHz	50.21 metres
	8.325MHz	40.96 metres
	9.915MHz	30.26 metres

Voice of America		
All times are Greenwich Mean Time (GMT):		
10.00–02.00:	6.030MHz	930 metres
	6.165MHz	1580 metres
	9.59MHz	
00.00–02.00:	5.995MHz	
	9.775MHz	
	9.815MHz	

cream. **Lunch** is the main meal of the day, and this is the best time to fill up as restaurants often offer *comidas corridas*, a set two- or three-course meal that sometimes costs as little as a dollar. It's always filling and occasionally delicious. Sometimes the same deal is on offer in the evenings, but usually not, so **evening meals** are likely to be more expensive.

Vegetarians are hardly catered for specifically, except in the tourist restaurants of Antigua and Panajachel and at a couple of places in Guatemala City. It is, however, fairly easy to get by eating plenty of beans and eggs, which are always on the menu (although you should check, as beans, especially, are often fried in lard). The markets also offer plenty of superb fruit, and tortillas, which are the basic ingredient of most Guatemalan diets.

There are three distinct **types of cooking** in Guatemala, and although they overlap to an extent it's still clear enough which one it is that you're eating.

■ Maya cuisine

The first and oldest style is **Maya cooking**, in which the basic staples of beans and maize dominate. **Beans** (*frijoles*) are the black kidney-shaped variety and are served in two ways: either *volteados*, which are boiled up, mashed, and then refried in a great dollop; or *parados*, which are boiled up whole, with a few slices of onion, and served in their own black juice. For breakfast, beans are usually served with eggs and cream, and at other times of the day they're offered up on a separate plate to the main dish. Almost all truly Guatemalan meals include a portion of beans, and for many highland Indians beans are the only regular source of protein.

Maize is the other essential, a food which for the Maya (and many other American Indians) is almost as nourishing spiritually as it is physically – in Indian legend, humankind was originally formed from maize. It appears most commonly as the **tortilla**, a thin pancake. The maize is traditionally ground by hand and shaped by clapping it between two hands, although these days machines are equally common. It's cooked on a *comal*, which is a flat pan of clay placed over the fire, and the very best tortillas are eaten while warm, usually brought to the table wrapped in cloth. While beans may be part of many a Guatemalan meal, it's tortillas that are the country's staple, and for Indians it's the

tortilla that forms the hub of a meal, with beans or the odd piece of meat as accompaniments to spice it up. Some people never get to like them, but the burnt, smoky taste of tortillas will become very much a part of your trip; and the smell of them is enough to revive memories years later. Where there's an option local people often serve gringos with bread, assuming they won't want tortillas.

Maize is also used to make a number of traditional **snacks**, which are sold on buses, at markets and during fiestas. The most common of these is the *tamal*, a pudding-like cornmeal package sometimes stuffed with chicken. It's wrapped in a banana leaf and then boiled. Slightly more exciting is the *chuchito*, which is similar but tends to include a bit of tomato and a pinch of hot chilli. Other popular snacks are *chiles rellenos*, stuffed peppers, and *pacaya*, which is a rather stodgy local vegetable.

Chillies are the final essential ingredient of the Indian diet, usually placed (raw or pickled) in the middle of the table in a jar, but also served as a sauce – *salsa picante*. The strength of these can vary tremendously, so treat them with caution until you know what you're dealing with.

Other traditional Maya dishes include a superb range of **stews** – known as *caldos* – made with duck, beef, chicken or turkey; and *fiambre*, which is the world's largest salad, a delicious mix of meat and vegetables traditionally served on the Day of the Dead (November 1), when you can usually find it in restaurants. The best chance to sample traditional food is at a market or fiesta, when makeshift *comedores* serve freshly cooked dishes. A highland breakfast often includes a plate of *mosh*, which is made with milk and oats and tastes rather like porridge. It's the ideal antidote to an early morning chill.

■ Colonial cuisine

Guatemala's second culinary style is *Ladino* **food**, which is indebted to the great range of cultures that go to make up the *Ladino* population. Most of the food has a mild Latin American bias, incorporating a lot of Mexican ideas, but the influence of the United States and Europe is also strongly felt. At its most obvious *Ladino* food includes *bistek* (steak), *hamburguesa* and *chao mein*, all of which are readily available in most Guatemalan towns. But you'll also find a **German** influence in the widespread availability of frankfurter-type sausages, and plenty of

A LIST OF FOODS AND DISHES

Basics

Azucar	Sugar	*Mantequilla*	Butter	*Queso*	Cheese
Carne	Meat	*Pan*	Bread	*Sal*	Salt
Ensalada	Salad	*Pescado*	Fish	*Salsa*	Sauce
Huevos	Eggs	*Pimienta*	Pepper	*Verduras/Legumbres*	Vegetables

Soups (*Sopas*) and starters

Sopa	Soup	*Caldo*	Broth (with bits in)
de Arroz	Plain Rice	*Ceviche*	Raw fish salad, marinated
de Fideos	with noodles		in lime juice
de Lentejas	Lentil	*Consome*	Consomme
de Verduras	Vegetable	*Entremeses*	Hors d'oeuvres

Meat (*Carne*) and Poultry (*Aves*)

Alambre	Kebab	*Codorniz*	Quail	*Pato*	Duck
Bistec	Steak	*Conejo*	Rabbit	*Pavo/Guajalote*	Turkey
Cabrito	Kid	*Cordero*	Lamb	*Pechuga*	Breast
Carne (de res)	Beef	*Costilla*	Rib	*Pierna*	Leg
Carnitas	Stewed	*Guisado*	Stew	*Pollo*	Chicken
	chunks	*Higado*	Liver	*Salchicha*	Hot dog or
Cerdo	Pork	*Lengua*	Tongue		salami
Chorizo	Sausage	*Milanesa*	Breaded	*Ternera*	Veal
Chuleta	Chop		escalope	*Venado*	Venison

Specialities

Chile Relleno	Stuffed Pepper	*Pan de Coco*	Coconut bread
Chuchitos	Stuffed maize dumplings	*Quesadilla*	Cheese-flavoured sponge
Enchilada	Flat, crisp tortilla piled	*Taco*	Rolled and stuffed tortilla
	with salad or meat	*Tamale*	Boiled and stuffed maize pudding
Mosh	Porridge	*Tapado*	Fish stew with plantain and vegeta-
Pan de Banana	Banana bread		bles, served on Caribbean coast

Vegetables (*Legumbres, verduras*)

Aguacate	Avocado	*Hongos*	Mushrooms
Ajo	Garlic	*Lechuga*	Lettuce
Casava/Yuca	Potato-like root vegetable	*Pacaya*	Bitter-tasting local vegetable
Cebolla	Onion	*Papas*	Potatoes
Col	Cabbage	*Pepino*	Cucumber
Elote	Corn on the cob	*Tomate*	Tomato
Frijoles	Beans	*Zanahoria*	Carrot

Fruit (*Fruta*)

Ciruelas	Greengages	*Limon*	Lime	*Piña*	Pineapple
Coco	Coconut	*Mamey*	Pink, sweet,	*Pitahaya*	Sweet, purple
Frambuesas	Raspberries		full of pips		fruit
Fresas	Strawberries	*Mango*	Mango	*Platano*	Banana
Guanabana	Pear-like	*Melocoton*	Peach	*Sandia*	Watermelon
	cactus fruit	*Melon*	Melon	*Toronja*	Grapefruit
Guayaba	Guava	*Naranja*	Orange	*Tuna*	Cactus fruit
Higos	Figs	*Papaya*	Papaya	*Uvas*	Grapes

Eggs (*Huevos*)

a la Mexicana	Scrambled with mild tomato, onion and chilli sauce	*Rancheros*	Fried and smothered in hot chilli sauce
Fritos	Fried	*Revueltos*	Scrambled
con Jamon	with ham		
con Tocino	with bacon	*Tibios*	Lightly boiled
Motuleños	Fried, served on a tortilla with ham, cheese and sauce		

Common terms

A la Parilla	Grilled	*Empanado/a*	Breaded
Al Horno	Baked	*Picante*	Hot and spicy
Al Mojo de Ajo	Fried in garlic and butter	*Recado*	A sauce for meat made from garlic, tomato and spices
Asado/a	Roast		

Sweets

Crepas	Pancakes	*Helado*	Ice cream
Ensalada de Frutas	Fruit salad	*Platanos al Horno*	Baked plantains
Flan	Crème caramel	*Platanos en Mole*	Plantains in chocolate sauce

Italian restaurants offering pasta and pizza. In the main tourist towns, Antigua and Panajachel, you'll also come across some more unusual additions, such as Tex-Mex, Thai, plenty of Chinese, French, Swiss, vegetarian, and even a European-style deli.

■ Creole cuisine

The final element is the **Creole cooking** found on Guatemala's Caribbean coast. Here it's **bananas**, **coconuts** and **seafood** that dominate the scene, all of them, if you're lucky, cooked superbly. You have to hunt around to find true Creole cooking, which incorporates the influences of the Caribbean with those of Africa, but it's well worth the effort. Some of the more obvious elements have also penetrated the mainstream: you'll get fried plantains everywhere (*platanos fritos*) as well as *ceviche*, a delicious dish of raw fish marinated in lemon juice and onions.

■ Drink

To start off the day most Guatemalans drink a cup of hot **coffee**, **chocolate** or **tea** (all of which are usually served with plenty of sugar), but in the highlands you'll also be offered *atol*, a warm, sweet drink made with either rice or maize and sugar. Some travellers swear by it. At other times of day **soft drinks** and beer are usually drunk with meals. *Coca-Cola*, *Pepsi*, *Sprite* and *Fanta* are common, and bottled mineral water (*agua*

mineral) is almost always available. In many of the larger towns the tap water is safe to drink, but it's still a good idea to stick with the bottled version, especially in light of the regular outbreaks of cholera (for more on water, see p.16). There are also two main varieties of bottled beer on sale in Guatemala: *Gallo* (Cockerel) and *Dorada Draft*. If you venture into the more upmarket bars you may also come across some premium brands, including *Moza*, the country's only dark beer.

As for **spirits**, rum (*ron*) and *aguardiente*, a clear and lethal spirit, are very popular and correspondingly cheap. Hard drinkers will soon get to know *Quezalteca* and *Venado*, two local *aguardientes*, sold and drunk everywhere, whose power is at the heart of many a fiesta. If you're after a real bargain then try locally brewed alcohol (*chicha*), which is practically given away. Its main ingredient can be anything: apple, cherry, sugar cane, peach, apricot and quince are just some of the more common varieties.

Wine is also made in Guatemala, from local fruits or imported concentrates. It's interesting to try, but if you hope to find anything drinkable it's best to stick to the more expensive imports.

Opening hours and holidays

Guatemalan opening hours are subject to considerable local variations but in general many places, including shops and museums, open between 8 and 10am, close for a siesta of an hour or so between noon and 2pm, and stay open until around 7pm. Others, including most offices, work a standard nine to five. In general opening times are stricter in the capital, where you need to check up on museums and banks before you set out.

Museums and **galleries** are usually open from 9am to noon and from 2 to 6pm. They stay open at weekends but tend to close on either Monday or Wednesday. **Banks** are mostly open from 9am, closing any time between 3pm and 8pm, and government offices close at around 3.30pm. Outside the main towns, branches of the *Banco de Guatemala* are open 8.30am to 2pm from Monday to Thursday, with an extra half-hour on Friday afternoon, while some private banks now open on Saturday morning. **Archeological sites** are open every day, usually from 8am to 5pm. For **post office** hours, see p.30.

Principal public holidays, when almost all businesses close down, are listed below, but each village or town will also have its own fiestas or saints' days when everything will be shut. These can last anything from one day to two weeks.

Fiestas and entertainment

Traditional fiestas are one of the great excitements of a trip to Guatemala, and every town and village, however small, devotes at least one day a year to celebration. The date is normally prescribed by the local saint's day, but the party often extends to a week or two around that date, although the main day is always marked by a climactic event. On almost every day of the year there's a fiesta in some forgotten corner of the country, and with a bit of planning or a stroke of luck you should be able to witness at least one. Most of them are well worth going out of your way for.

The **format** of fiestas varies between two basic models. In towns with a largely *Ladino* population, fairs are usually set up and the days are filled with processions, beauty contests and perhaps the odd marching band, while the nights are dominated by dance halls and salsa rhythms. In the highlands, where the bulk of the population is Indian, you'll see traditional dances, costumes and musicians, and a blend of religious and secular celebration that incorporates elements which predate the arrival of the Spanish. What they all share is an astonishing energy and an unbounded enthusiasm for drink, dance and fireworks: all three of which are virtually impossible to escape during the days of fiesta.

One thing you shouldn't expect is anything too dainty or organized: fiestas are above all chaotic, and the measured rhythms of traditional dance and music are usually obscured by the crush of the crowd and the huge volumes of alcohol consumed by participants. If you can join in the mood there's no doubt that fiestas are wonderfully entertaining and that they offer a real insight into Guatemalan culture, *Ladino* or Indian.

Many of the best fiestas include some specifically local element, such as the giant kites at **Santiago Sacatepéquez**, the religious processions in **Antigua** and the horse race in **Todos Santos**. The dates of most fiestas, along with their main features, are listed at the end of each chapter in the *Guide*. At certain times virtually the whole country erupts simultaneously: Easter Week is perhaps the most important, particularly in Antigua, but both All Saints' Day (November 1) and Christmas are also marked by partying across the land.

PUBLIC HOLIDAYS

January 1 New Year's Day

Semana Santa The four days of Holy Week leading up to Easter

May 1 Labor Day

June 30 Army Day, anniversary of 1871 revolution

August 15 Guatemala City fiesta (Guatemala City only)

September 15 Independence Day

October 12 Discovery of America (banks only closed)

October 20 Revolution Day

November 1 All Saints' Day

December 24 From noon

December 25 Christmas

December 31 From noon

◼ Dance

Dance is the subject of yet another cultural divide. In the nightclubs of Guatemala City it's Latin rock and salsa that get people onto the dance floor, and once they're there they dance a mixture of disco and Latin styles. Outside the capital, dance is usually confined to fiestas, and in the highland villages this means traditional dances, heavily imbued with history and symbolism.

The drunken dancers may look out of control, but the process is taken very seriously and involves great expense on the part of the participants – who have to rent their ornate costumes. The most common dance is the **Baile de la Conquista**, which re-enacts the victory of the Spanish over the Indians, while at the same time managing to ridicule the conquistadors. According to some studies, the dance is based in pre-Columbian traditions. Other popular dances are the **Baile de los Gracejos**, the dance of the jesters, the **Baile del Venado**, the dance of the deer, and the **Baile de la Culebra**, the dance of the snake; all of them again rooted in pre-Columbian traditions. One of the most impressive is the **Palo Volador**, in which men swing by ropes from a thirty-metre pole. Today this is only performed in Chichicastenango, Joyabaj and Cubulco.

◼ Music

Guatemalan **music** combines many different influences, but yet again it can be broadly divided between *Ladino* and Indian. For fiestas bands are always shipped in, complete with a crackling PA system and a strutting lead singer.

Traditional music is dominated by the **marimba**, a type of wooden xylophone that may well have originated in Africa (although many argue that it developed independently in Central America). The oldest versions use gourds beneath the sounding board and can be played by a single musician, while modern models, using hollow tubes to generate the sound, can need as many as seven players. The marimba is at the heart of traditional music, and marimba orchestras play at every occasion, for both *Ladino* and Indian communities. In the remotest of villages you sometimes hear them practising well into the night, particularly around market day. Other important instruments, especially in Indian bands, are the *tun*, a drum made from a hollow log; the *tambor*, another drum traditionally covered with the skin of a deer; *los chichines*, a type of mara-

cas made from hollow gourds; the *tzijolaj*, an Indian piccolo; and the *chirimia*, a flute.

Modern, or *Ladino*, music is a blend of North American and Latin sounds, much of it originating in Miami, Colombia, the Dominican Republic and Puerto Rico, although there are plenty of local bands producing their own version of the sound. It's fast-moving, easy-going and very rhythmic, and on any bus you'll hear many of the most popular tracks. It draws on merengue, a rhythm that originally came from the Dominican Republic, and includes elements of Mexican mariachi and the cumbia and salsa of Colombia and Cuba.

Finally, on the Caribbean coast, you'll hear the sound of **reggae**, which reaches Lívingston from island radio stations. Much of this music comes from the Caribbean islands and is sung in English, although there is also a thriving reggae scene in Central and South America, with the most important bands coming from Belize, Costa Rica, Panamá and Colombia. Reggae has also made it to Guatemala City, where there are a couple of nightclubs run by people from the Caribbean coast.

◼ Sport

Guatemalans have a furious appetite for spectator sport and the daily papers always devote four or five pages to the subject. **Football (soccer)** tops the bill, and if you get the chance to see a major game it's a thrilling experience, if only to watch the crowd. Otherwise North American sport predominates – **baseball**, **American football**, **boxing** and **basketball** are all popular.

On a more local level **bullfights**, which are staged in Guatemala City in October and December, draw large crowds. The *matadores* are usually from Spain or Mexico, and entry costs are high. The main bull ring is beside the Parque Aurora in Guatemala City.

Hiking is perhaps the most popular sport among visitors, particularly volcano climbing, which is certainly hard work but almost always worth the effort – unless you end up wrapped in cloud. Guatemala has some 37 volcanic peaks; the tallest is Tajumulco in the west, which at 4220m is a serious undertaking. Among the active peaks Pacaya is an easy climb and a dramatic sight, although as it has been the scene of much violent rape and robbery, it should not be attempted alone. Volcano climbing trips are organized by a number of tour groups in Antigua.

As a participatory sport, **fishing** is also popular. Good sea fishing is available on either coast. On the Pacific side the coastal waters offer sierra mackerel, jack cravelle, yellow and black tuna, snappers, bonito and dorado, while further offshore there are marlin and sailfish; the Caribbean side also offers excellent opportunities – see the section on Belize for more information. In Petén the rivers and lakes are packed with sport fish, including snook, tarpon and peacock bass, and lakes Petexbatún, Izabal and Yaxjá all offer superb fishing, as do the Usumacinta and Dulce rivers. Fishing trips to both coasts and on the inland waterways are organized by *Tropical Tours*, 4 C 2–51, Zona 10, Guatemala City (☎3393662). These trips are expensive, though, and if you just want to dabble around then you should be able to sort something out with local fishermen in the coastal villages or perhaps in Sayaxché or El Estor.

Guatemala's dramatic highland landscape and tumbling rivers also provide some excellent opportunities for **white-water rafting**, particularly on the rivers Cahabón and Motagua. Three-day trips down the Río Cahabón are organized by *Tropical Tours* (see above), while *Maya Expeditions*, 15 C 1–91, Zona 10, Guatemala City (☎3634955; fax 3634164) arrange trips on the Usumacinta, Naranjo, Motagua and Cahabón, giving you the chance to see some really remote areas and visit some of the country's most inaccessible Maya sites. *Area Verde Expeditions*, in Antigua at the *Hotel San Jorge*, 4 Av Sur 13, are also worth contacting. *Maya Expeditions* organize Guatemala's only **bungee jump**, every weekend from one of the ravine bridges near the capital or on the Río Dulce bridge.

Diving is another up-and-coming sport in this part of the world, although again Guatemala really has little to offer compared to the splendours of Belize's coastal waters. Nevertheless, there are some diving curiosities here, including Lake Atitlán, the Ipala Lagoon and Lake Izabal, as well as some good Pacific and Caribbean dive sites. Dive trips and courses are offered by *Prodiver*, 6 Av 9–85, Zona 9, Guatemala City (☎3312738; fax 4782286).

There is also some **surfing** in Guatemala, on the Pacific coast, although if you've come all this way for the waves you may be disappointed; you'll certainly find a better break in El Salvador or Costa Rica.

Crafts, markets and shops

Guatemalan craft traditions, locally known as *artesania*, are very much a part of modern Indian culture, stemming from practices that in most cases predate the arrival of the Spanish. Many of these traditions are highly localized, with different regions and even different villages specializing in particular crafts.

■ Artesania

The best place to buy Guatemalan **crafts** is in their place of origin, where the quality is usually highest, the prices reasonable, and above all else the craftsmen and women get a greater share of the profit. But if you haven't the time or the energy to travel to remote highland villages then there are plenty of places where you can find a superb selection from all around the country. The markets in Chichicastenango (Thursday and Sunday) are always good, but you'll also find good-quality *artesania* in Guatemala City, Antigua, Panajachel and Huehuetenango. In all of these places it's well worth shopping around – and bargaining – as prices can vary wildly.

The greatest craft in Guatemala has to be **weaving**, with styles and techniques that have developed consistently since Maya times and are now practised at an astonishingly high standard throughout the western highlands. Each village has its own traditional designs, woven in fantastic patterns and with superbly vivid colours. One thing to bear in mind is that for the Indians clothing has a spiritual significance and the pattern is specific to the weaver and the wearer, casting them in a particular social role. If you go into a village and buy local clothing you may well cheapen the value that's placed on it, and it is deeply insulting to offer to buy the clothes that someone is wearing. Having said this there are plenty of Indian weavers who are very keen to expand their market by selling to tourists, and for them you offer an ideal supplement to a meagre income. All the finest weaving is done on the backstrap loom; the quality and variety are so impressive that you'll be spoilt for choice. Antigua's *Kaslan Po't*, 4 C Oriente 14, sells some of the finest weaving in the country, and is more accessible than the emporia in the capital. It's a veritable museum of styles and designs, and worth a visit even if you're not interested in buying.

Alongside Guatemalan weaving most **other crafts** suffer by comparison. However, if you hunt around you'll also find good ceramics, baskets, mats, silver and jade. The last two are easiest to come by in Antigua, although most of the silver is mined in Alta Verapaz. The others are produced by Indian craftsmen and women in the villages of the highlands, and sold in local markets throughout the country.

▣ Markets

For shopping – and simply sightseeing – the **markets** of Guatemala are some of the finest anywhere. Most towns and villages, particularly in the highlands, have weekly markets – some of the larger ones are held twice a week, although one day is always the more important. Traditional markets are the focus of economic and social activity in rural Guatemala, and people come from miles around to sell, buy and have a good time. You really should make the effort to see a few: the mood varies tremendously, from the frenetic tourist markets in Chichicastenango to the calm of San Juan Atitán, but all markets have an air of fiesta about them and incorporate a great deal of chaotic celebration as well as hard-nosed business deals. Above all else markets offer a real glimpse of Indian culture, as they are at the heart of the village economy and social structure.

Prices are almost always lower in markets than in shops or on the streets in tourist areas (although in Chichicastenango bargains are becoming increasingly scarce), but you'll still need to **haggle**. Everyone claims to have perfected a bargaining technique, but few stand a chance against the masters of the market: obvious tips are to have an idea of the shop price of similar items before you start, and always offer way below what's asked and expect to meet somewhere in the middle.

▣ Everyday goods

When it comes to everyday **shopping**, you can buy just about everything in Guatemala that you can in the States or Europe – at a price. For **food** you need to look no further than the market, where things are fresh and prices are low, but you should stick to the shops for other things. Basic items are always cheaper but imported goods command a higher price and luxuries, like electrical goods and cameras, are often very expensive. **Film** is available – colour and monochrome but nothing beyond 64–400 ASA. Video

film can be bought in Guatemala City but Video 8 is very hard to come by, as is cine film. English-language **books** – a rather limited selection – are sold in Guatemala City and Antigua, but prices are high. For anything out of the ordinary it's a good idea to do your shopping in the capital, where there's a much greater range on offer.

Trouble and sexual harassment

The problem of personal safety in Guatemala is part of a strange contradiction. The country does have a horrific record on human rights and Guatemalans are shot, robbed, mutilated and killed on a daily basis. Political violence is still widespread and death squads do operate throughout the country, but targets in this war of intimidation are clearly defined and you are unlikely to get caught up in political incidents.

However, though Guatemala is still one of the safer countries in Latin America, particularly compared to the horrors of Peru and Colombia, there are still serious **dangers** for visitors. Incidents of mugging, attacks, robbery and rape have increased in recent years, particularly in the main tourist areas of Antigua and Lake Atitlán, as well as in the capital.

▣ Crime

Despite the alarmingly high murder rate visitors are unlikely to run into that kind of trouble in Guatemala. However, theft and violent crime are on the increase. Theft is most common around bus stations in Guatemala City and the main tourist centres. **Petty theft** and **pickpockets** are likely to be your biggest worry. Again the risk is highest in the capital, where there has been a recent rash of backpack theft: the pack is sprayed with dirt and a "passer by" offers to help clean it; the bag can then be snatched by an accomplice. Markets and fiestas are also favourite haunts of pickpockets – large gangs sometimes descend on villages for such events. It's never a good idea to flash your money around, and you should avoid leaving cameras and cash in hotel rooms: most hotels will have somewhere to lock up valuables, although even this may not be too secure. You are also particularly vulnerable when travelling, so try and keep your bag, or at least your most valuable stuff, with you in the bus, and keep an eye on anything that goes up top. Be careful in restaurants, too, where leaving your belongings unattended for even a second is a risk. The best place to keep passports and vital papers, including air tickets and travellers' cheques, is in a cotton moneybelt under your clothing.

Muggings and **violent crime** are on the increase in Guatemala City. There's little to worry about during the day, providing you don't visit the slum areas, but you should think twice before wandering outside the centre after dark. Stick to the main streets and use buses and taxis to get around. There have also been some cases of armed robbery in Antigua and in some very specific rural areas. The Pacaya volcano has been the scene of several robberies and rapes, and barely a week passes without some incident – if you're planning to climb it, check out the wisdom of this with people in Antigua. The other dangerous area, the backroads from Godínez to the Pan-American Highway, is best avoided.

Drivers are perhaps the most likely to run into trouble, and cars left unattended are often relieved of a wing mirror or two. To avoid this it's a good idea to search out hotels that can accommodate your car as well as you.

If you are robbed you'll have to report it to the police, which can be a very long process and may seem like little more than a symbolic gesture. In the end it's worth it, though, as many insurance companies will only pay out if you can produce a police statement.

Bear in mind that **drug offences** are dealt with severely. Even the possession of marijuana could land you in jail, a sobering experience in Guatemala.

■ Police and soldiers

For Europeans and North Americans expecting to enter a police state, Guatemala may come as something of a surprise. Though there are a lot of police and soldiers on the streets there's rarely anything intimidating about their presence, and if you do have any dealings with them you'll probably find them gratifyingly helpful. If anything the country is really surprisingly lawless and in most areas there is little effective law enforcement.

Travelling in Guatemala you'll inevitably pass through many **road blocks** and **checkpoints**, though these are by no means an intimidating experience and in almost all cases it's a routine process. At some you may be asked to get out of the bus and line up, with men and women separ-

ated. If this happens you'll be frisked and have to show your passport, but again it's a routine procedure that Guatemalans have learned to live with. It's also possible that your bus will be stopped by the guerrillas, and though this is a little unnerving it's again nothing to worry about. Under normal circumstances you'll hear a short lecture on their aims and be allowed to go on your way.

It's important to **carry your passport** at all times, as you never know when someone might demand to see it. If for any reason you do find yourself **in trouble with the law**, be as polite as possible and do as you're told. Remember that bribery is a way of life here, and that corruption is widespread. At the first possible opportunity get in touch with your embassy and negotiate through them: they will understand the situation better than you. The addresses of embassies and consulates in Guatemala City are listed on p.67.

■ Sexual harassment

So many oppressive limitations are imposed on women travellers that any advice or warning would seem only to reinforce the situation. However, it has to be said that **machismo** is very much a part of Guatemalan culture. The hassle is usually confined to comments on the street and perhaps the occasional pinch or grab, and unless your Spanish and nerve are up to a duel it's a good idea to ignore such things.

The worst areas are those dominated by *Ladino* culture: the Pacific coast, Guatemala City and the eastern highlands. Indian society is conditioned into being more deferential so you're unlikely to experience any trouble in the western highlands.

Though there's a strong and growing **women's movement** in Guatemala, compared to other Latin American countries, Mexico, say, there are as yet few places that travellers can depend upon making contact with local feminists.

Directory

ADDRESSES Almost all based on the grid system that's used in most towns, with avenidas running in one direction and calles in the other. The address specifies the street first, then locates the block, and ends with the zone. For example, the address Av Reforma 3–55, Zona 1 means that house is on Avenida Reforma, between 3 and 4 calles, at no. 55, in Zona 1.

Almost all towns have numbered streets, but in some places the old names are also used. In Antigua calles and avenidas are also divided according to their direction from the central plaza – north, south, east or west (*norte*, *sur*, *oriente* and *poniente*).

AIRPORT TAX Has to be paid before departure on all international flights. It's currently set at $10 (Q50), payable in either currency.

BAGS If you're planning to travel around by bus – and certainly if you're going to do some walking with your gear as well – then a backpack is the best option. But you might also bear in mind that there is some prejudice against "hippies", and backpacks are often seen as their trademark. Whatever you decide to pack your stuff in, make sure it's tough enough to handle being thrown on and off the top of buses. It's a good idea to buy an old sack and string net in a local market, to enclose your bags and make them less of a target for thieves. Better still carry something small enough to fit inside a bus, on the luggage rack, which is both more convenient and safer.

BEGGARS Fairly common, particularly on the streets of the main towns and around church entrances, though they rarely hassle anyone. Local people tend to be generous, and it's worth having some change handy.

CONTRACEPTION Condoms are available from pharmacies (*farmacías*) in all the main towns, although it's safest to get them in Guatemala City, where shortages are less common. Some makes of the Pill are also available, mostly those manufactured in the States, but it's obviously more sensible to take enough to last for your entire stay. Bear in mind that diarrhoea can reduce the reliability of the Pill (or any other drug) as it may not be in your system long enough to be fully absorbed.

DRUGS Increasingly available as the country is becoming a centre for both shipment and production. Marijuana, which mostly comes in from South America and Mexico, is readily available and cheap – especially as in recent years Petén has become an area of production, and there is a plentiful supply across the border in Belize. Cocaine is available as it is shipped to the States through Guatemala, and heroin, now produced here, is also to be found on the streets. The drugs problem is viewed increasingly seriously by the government and users will be dealt with harshly. If you're caught, expect to go to jail, or at least pay a hefty fine/bribe in order to avoid it.

ELECTRICITY Theoretically 110 volts AC, although the nature of the supply varies from place to place. In some smaller towns the current is at 220 volts, so ask before you plug in any vital equipment. Anything from Britain will need a transformer and a plug adaptor, as may US appliances. Cuts in the supply and wild fluctuations in the current are fairly common, while in some isolated villages, where they have their own generator, the supply only operates for part of the day (usually the early evening and morning).

EMBASSIES AND CONSULATES Listed in the *Guide* in the account of Guatemala City, where almost every country, except Belize, is represented. In addition there are Mexican consulates in Quezaltenango and Retalhuleu, and a Honduran consul in Esquipulas.

GAY GUATEMALA There is a small gay community in Guatemala City but few clubs or public meeting places. Homosexuality is publicly strongly frowned upon – although not theoretically illegal. Macho attitudes incorporate an overwhelming prejudice against gays and the newspapers occasionally include accounts which might read "the arrest of prostitutes and gays". Discretion is the only answer.

LAUNDRY Hotels occasionally offer a laundry service, and most inexpensive places will have somewhere where you can wash and dry your own clothes. In Guatemala City, Quezaltenango, Panajachel, Huehuetenango and Antigua there are self-service laundries, and several places that will do your washing for you – on the whole these are much easier and cost about the same.

ODD ESSENTIALS Insect repellent is a must – you can buy it in markets, particularly in Petén, which is where you'll really need it. You can also buy coils that burn through the night to keep the beasts at bay, although if you plan to sleep out then there's no substitute for a mosquito net – which you can also buy in the markets in Petén. A torch and alarm clock are worth having for catching those pre-dawn buses, and it's always a good idea to carry toilet paper with you. It's easy enough to buy in Guatemala but it's never there when you need it.

STUDENT CARDS can get you discounts from time to time, particularly in the expensive private museums in Guatemala City. But it's hardly worth struggling to obtain one as there are few discounts available outside the capital.

STUDYING SPANISH Guatemala is a great place to study Spanish, with popular language schools in Antigua, Guatemala City, Huehuetenango and Quezaltenango among other places. Antigua's branch of the American organization *Amerispan* (in US: ☎1-800/879-6640; fax 215/985-4524), which matches potential students with schools throughout Latin America, is a very useful information and resource centre.

TIME ZONES Guatemala is on the equivalent of Central Standard Time, six hours earlier than GMT. There are no seasonal changes and it gets light around 6.30am, with sunset at 7pm.

TIPS In upmarket restaurants a 10 percent tip is appropriate, but in most places, especially the cheaper ones, tipping is the exception rather than the rule. Taxi drivers are not normally tipped.

TOILETS Vary greatly throughout the country, but in general the further you are from the city the lower the standard. Public toilets are few and far between, and mostly filthy. Toilet paper is usually sold by the attendant, who also charges a small entrance fee. The most common name is *baños*, and the signs are *damas* (women) and *caballeros* (men).

TOURIST OFFICES are to be found in Guatemala City, Panajachel, Antigua, Flores and Quezaltenango. They are all very friendly and making genuine efforts to improve the level of information they give out.

WATER Tap water in the main towns is purified and you can usually taste the chlorine. However, this doesn't mean that it won't give you stomach trouble, and it's always safest to stick to bottled water – widely available – at least until your body has begun to adapt. For more on water see p.16.

WORK is generally badly paid, and unless you have something very special to offer your best bet is to teach English. All the English schools in Guatemala City (listed in the phone book) are always looking for new teachers, and there are also schools in Antigua. If you'd like to work as a **volunteer** for a relief agency in Guatemala, get hold of a copy of the government-published directory of voluntary organizations in the country, which can be borrowed from the *Casa Andinista* in Antigua.

CHAPTER ONE

GUATEMALA CITY AND AROUND

Guatemala's capital is splayed out across a sweeping highland basin, surrounded on three sides by low hills and volcanic cones. Cosmopolitan and congested, **Guatemala City** has an atmosphere that seems somehow ill-suited to the country as a whole. The capital was moved here in 1776, after the devastation of Antigua, but the site – on a natural trade route between the Pacific and the Caribbean – had been of importance long before the arrival of the Spanish. In its early years the capital grew slowly, and it wasn't until the beginning of this century that it really began to dominate the country. These days its shapeless and swelling mass, ringed by shanty towns, ranks as the largest city in Central America. It's home to around two million people, a quarter of Guatemala's population, and is the undisputed centre of politics, power and wealth.

The city has an intensity and vibrancy that are both its fascination and its horror, and for some travellers a trip to the capital is an exercise in damage limitation, struggling through a swirling mass of bus fumes and beggars. The centre is now run-down and polluted – and the affluent middle classes have long since fled to the suburbs – but it does have its share of "sights", including some impressive architecture, old and new, and a couple of good museums. Beyond this the real attraction has to be the sheer energy of life on the streets, where the calm of the highlands is long forgotten. The city's population is truly cosmopolitan, its aspirations firmly rooted in the United States, and incorporates an aggressively commercial outlook – two of the essential components of *Ladino* culture.

Like it or not – and many travellers don't – Guatemala City is the crossroads of the country, and you'll certainly end up here at some time, if only to hurry between bus terminals or negotiate a visa extension. Once you get used to the pace, though, it can offer a welcome break from life on the road, with decent restaurants, cinemas, hot showers and good hotels. And if you really can't take the city it's easy enough to escape; buses leave every few minutes, day and night.

The hills that surround the city have somehow managed to remain unaffected by it, and within an hour or two you'll find yourself back in the highlands. The basin is hemmed in on three sides by a horseshoe of hills, while to the south, in a narrow gap between the volcanic peaks of Agua and Pacaya, the Río Michatoya and the Pacific Highway cut through to the ocean. Heading out this way you pass **Lake Amatitlán**, a popular weekend resort for those who don't have their own *fincas*. Beyond here a branch road leads up to the village of **San Vicente Pacaya**, from where you can climb the **Pacaya volcano**, the most active of Guatemala's volcanic peaks. The cone's size and appearance aren't particularly impressive, but

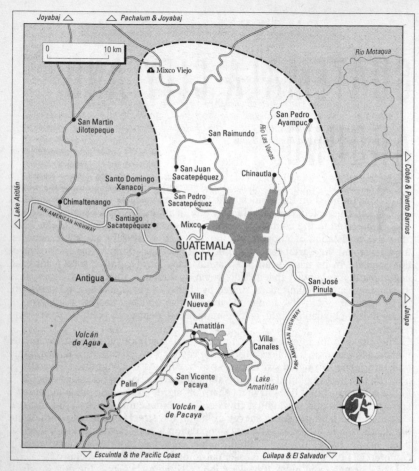

for the last few years it has been spewing a fountain of sulphurous gas and molten rock that glows red in the night sky. Further down the valley is the village of **Palín**, beyond which you emerge at Escuintla and the Pacific coast, with Puerto San José and the chance of a dip in the ocean just three or four hours from the capital (see *The Pacific Coast*).

Leaving the city from the opposite side, to the northwest, you travel out through rolling hills and pine forests to the villages of **San Pedro Sacatepéquez** and **San Juan Sacatepéquez**. Both were badly hit by the 1976 earthquake but are now returning to normal and are well worth visiting for their weekend markets. To the north of the villages the road divides, one branch heading north-east over the mountains to **Rabinal**, and the other northwest towards Pachalum, passing the ruins of **Mixco Viejo**, a well-restored but rarely visited site in a spectacular, isolated setting.

GUATEMALA CITY

Guatemala City, an extremely horizontal place, is like a city on its back. Its ugliness, which is a threatened look (the low morose houses have earthquake cracks in their facades; the buildings wince at you with fright lines), is ugliest on those streets where, just past the toppling houses, a blue volcano's cone bulges. I could see the volcanoes from the window of my hotel room. I was on the third floor, which was also the top floor. They were tall volcanoes and looked capable of spewing lava. Their beauty was undeniable; but it was the beauty of witches. The rumbles from their fires had heaved this city down.

Paul Theroux, *The Old Patagonian Express*

While much has changed since Theroux was here, Guatemala City, though by no means as black as he implies, is certainly not somewhere you visit for its beauty or architectural appeal, although there are some notable exceptions. The city has been built in a massive highland basin, on a site that was a centre of population and political power long before the arrival of the Spanish. The pre-conquest city of **Kaminaljuyú**, with its ruins still scattered amongst the western suburbs, was well established here two thousand years ago. In early Classic times (250–550 AD), as a result of an alliance with the great northern power of Teotihuacán (near present-day Mexico City), Kaminaljuyú came to dominate the highlands, and eventually provided the political and commercial backing that fostered the rise of Tikal. The city was situated at the crossroads of the north–south and east–west trade routes, and also controlled the obsidian mine at El Chayal, giving it a virtual monopoly of this essential commodity. To further ensure its wealth, Kaminaljuyú also had access to a supply of quetzal feathers, another highly valued item.

At the height of its prosperity Kaminaljuyú was home to a population of some 50,000. However, following the decline of Teotihuacán and its influence, around 600 AD, it was surpassed by the great lowland centres that it had helped to establish. Soon after their rise, some time between 600 and 900 AD, it was abandoned.

Seven centuries later, when Alvarado entered the country, the fractured tribes of the west controlled the highlands and preoccupied the conquistadors. The nearest centre of any importance was the Pokoman capital of **Mixco Viejo**, about 60km to the northwest. Mainly because of the need to keep a close watch on the western tribes, the Spanish ignored the possibility of settling here, founding their capital instead at Iximché, and later at two sites in the Panchoy valley.

In the early years of Spanish occupation the only new building in this area was a church in the village of La Ermita, founded in 1620. For over a hundred years the village remained no more than a tiny cluster of Indian homes, but in 1773, following months of devastating earthquakes, Captain Mayorga and some 4200 followers, fleeing the disease-ridden ruins of Antigua, established a temporary headquarters in the village. From here they despatched envoys and scouts in all directions, seeking a site for the new capital, and eventually decided to settle in the neighbouring Valley of the Virgin.

By royal decree the new city was named **Nueva Guatemala de la Asunción**, in honour of the Virgin of the Ascension, whose image stood in the church at La Ermita. On January 1, 1776, the city was officially inaugurated, and the following day its "fathers" held their first council to administer construction. The plan was typical of the Spanish colonial model, and identical to that used in the two previous, ill-fated cities. A main plaza was boxed in by the cathedral, the Palace of the Captains General and the town hall, and around this, on a strict grid pattern, was a city fifteen streets long and fifteen wide. Early development was slow: the people of Antigua were reluctant to leave, despite being bullied by endless decrees and deadlines, although waves of smallpox and cholera eventually persuaded some. By 1800, however, the population of the new capital was still only 25,000.

The splendour of the former capital was hard to re-establish and the new city's growth was steady but by no means dramatic. An 1863 census listed the main structures as 1206 residences, 7 warehouses, 130 shops, 28 churches, 1 slaughterhouse, 2 forts, 12 schools, and 25 fountains and public laundries. The author, Enrique Palacios, concluded that it was "a delightful city and a pleasant place to live". Boddam-Wetham, on the other hand, living here in 1877, claimed that it was "gloomy and dull; owing to the uniformity of the houses . . . the regularity of the streets . . . and the absence of traffic", adding that "the few signs of life are depressing". When Eadweard Muybridge took some of the earliest photographs in 1875, the city was still little more than a large village with a theatre, a government palace and a fort.

One of the factors retarding the city's growth was the existence of a major rival, Quezaltenango. Stimulated by the coffee boom and large numbers of German immigrants, Quezaltenango competed with the capital in both size and importance. However, when in 1902 it too was razed to the ground by a massive earthquake, many wealthy families moved to the capital, finally establishing it as the country's primary city. Guatemala City's population had, by then, been boosted by two major **earthquakes** – in Antigua and Quezaltenango – and inevitably its turn had to come. On Christmas Eve 1917 the capital was shaken by the first in a series of devastating tremors, and not until early February, after six long weeks of destruction, did the ground stabilize and the dust settle. This time, however, there was nowhere to run; and spurred on by the need to celebrate a century of independence, and the impetus of the eccentric President Ubico, reconstruction began.

Since 1918 Guatemala City has grown at an incredible rate, tearing ahead of the rest of the country at a pace that still shows little sign of letting up. The flight from the fields, characteristic of all Third World countries, was aided and abetted here by the chronic shortage of land or employment in the countryside, and has in the past been swollen by rural violence (though in practice it's far more dangerous to live in the city than anywhere in the highlands). According to some estimates an additional six hundred agricultural peasants arrive in the city every day. In some ways the capital is becoming a city of refugees, as the streets fill with displaced Indians, most of whom feel unwanted and unwelcome here. The deep ravines that surround the city, thought by the original Spanish planners to offer protection from the force of earthquakes, are now filling rapidly with rubbish and shanty towns, while street crime increases daily.

In today's Guatemala City the streets, choked with jet-black bus fumes, tunnel beneath neon signs; while the wealthy, as ever, have abandoned the scramble of the city centre to take refuge in relaxed suburbs. Glass skyscrapers rise alongside colonial churches, and while the rich bask in the joys of an all-American lifestyle, the poor struggle to earn a living on its fringes. The contrasts of poverty and extravagance are extreme.

STREET CHILDREN IN GUATEMALA CITY

One of the most disturbing manifestations of the deteriorating situation for the capital's poor is the increasing number of **street children** and the way in which they are treated by the authorities. Around five thousand children live on the streets of the capital, scratching a living from begging, prostitution and petty crime, and many sniff glue to combat boredom, hunger, cold and depression. Faced by a rising crime wave, the city's police have directed much of the blame towards these children, who are regularly attacked and beaten. In June 1990, eight children were taken from the streets by armed men in plain clothes. A few days later their bodies were found, some bearing the marks of **torture**. Similar cases have become disturbingly common, although journalists and **human rights** workers are now taking a strong interest in the plight of street children and putting pressure on the authorities.

The main group offering protection and help to the children is *Casa Alianza*, run by the British-born Brian Harris, who has received countless death threats for his work and now spends much of his time in Mexico. The organization, which runs a refuge for the children, is always looking for **volunteers**. Their office is at 10 C 6–37, Zona 1 (☎2323646 or 2327716).

Arrival, orientation and information

Arriving in Guatemala City for the first time, it's easy to feel overwhelmed by its scale, with suburbs sprawled across some nineteen **zones**. In fact, once you've got your bearings, the layout is straightforward and you'll find that the central area, which is all that you need to worry about, is really quite small. Like almost all Guatemalan towns it's laid out on a strict grid pattern, with **avenidas** running north–south and **calles** east–west.

Broadly speaking, the city divides into two distinct halves. The northern section, centred on **Zona 1**, is the old part of town, containing the central plaza or **Parque Central**, most of the budget hotels, shops, restaurants, cinemas, the post office, and many of the bus companies. This part of the city is cramped and congested, but bustling with activity. The two main streets are 5 and 6 avenidas, both thick with street traders and neon.

To the south, acting as a buffer between the two halves of town, and on the border of Zona 1 and Zona 4, is the **Centro Cívico**, around which you'll find all the main administrative buildings, the **tourist office**, the central market and the National Theatre. The avenidas of Zona 1 are brought together at several junctions in this section before fanning out into the southern city.

The southern section, starting in **Zona 4**, is the modern city, where the streets are broad and tree-lined. To complicate matters slightly, this southern half of the city is itself divided into two halves, split down the middle by 7 Avenida. On the eastern side is the main **Avenida La Reforma**, which leads on into Avenida las Americas. Here the wealthy dominate the scene, with expensive offices, private museums, banks, travel agents, smart hotels and embassies. The other half of the modern city, to the west, is the hub for trade and transport, notably the **airport** and the Zona 4 **bus terminal**. The **railway** line to the coast runs out through this area, as does Avenida Bolívar, one of the main traffic arteries bringing buses from the western highlands into the heart of the city.

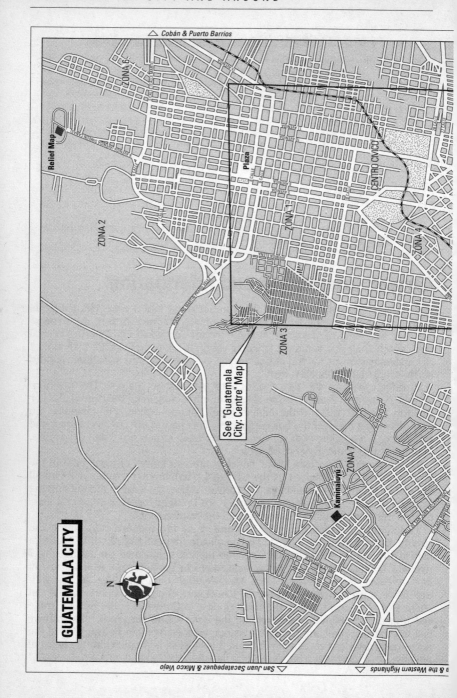

GUATEMALA CITY

△ Cobán & Puerto Barrios

Relief Map

ZONA 6

ZONA 2

Plaza

ZONA 1

CENTRO CÍVICO

ZONA 4

ZONA 3

See "Guatemala City: Centre" Map

N

ZONA 7

Kaminaluyú

▽ San Juan Sacatepequez & Mixco Viejo

▽ a & the Western Highlands

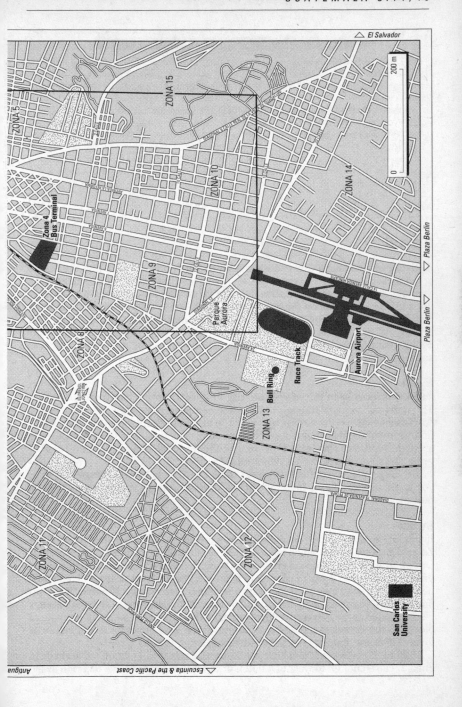

ADDRESSES IN GUATEMALA CITY

The system of **street numbering** in the capital may seem a little confusing at first as the same numbers are given to different streets in different zones. However, once you get the hang of things there is a degree of method to this apparent madness.

When it comes to finding an address, always check for the **zone** first and then the street. For example "4 Av 9–14, Zona 1" is in Zona 1, on 4 Avenida between 9 and 10 Calle, house number 14. Be warned that the same calles and avenidas exist in several different zones.

You may see street numbers written as 1a, 7a etc, rather than simply 1, 7. This is technically more correct, since the names of the streets are not One Avenue and Seven Street, but First (*primera*), Seventh (*séptima*) and so on. A capital "A" used as a suffix indicates a smaller street between two large ones: 1 Calle A is a short street between 1 and 2 calles.

Arrival

Arriving in Guatemala City is always a bit disconcerting, but most of the hotels are bunched together in central Zona 1, so you'll find that settling in isn't as daunting as it might at first appear. If you're laden with luggage then it's probably not a good idea to take on the bus system, and a taxi is well worth the extra cost. For details on using the transport terminals to **move on** from the capital, see p.68. Note that **trains** to and from Guatemala City were once an important component in the national transport network, but these days only cargo is carried.

By air

Aurora airport is on the edge of the city in Zona 13, some way from the centre. The domestic terminal, though in the same complex, is separate, and entered by Av Hincapié. Much the easiest way to get to and from the airport is by **taxi**: you'll find plenty of them waiting outside the terminal. The fare to or from Zona 1 costs around $10. Buses also leave from outside the terminal, across the open patch of grass, dropping you in Zona 1, either on 5 Av or 9 Av.

The *Banco del Quetzal* at the airport (daily) gives a better **exchange** rate than you'll get outside the country, and takes most European currencies as well as dollars.

By bus

If you arrive in the city by second-class bus prepare yourself for the jungle of the **Zona 4 bus terminal**, which has to rate as Guatemala City's most chaotic corner. On the whole it's only second-class buses from the western and eastern highlands that arrive here, so if you're coming in from the Pacific coast or from Petén you'll be spared, arriving instead at the Zona 1 terminal (see below). However if you do find that you've ended up in Zona 4, and decide not to take a taxi – there are always plenty around at the entrance to the terminal – then you'll need to walk a couple of blocks to the corner of 2 C and 4 Av, from where local buses go to the centre of town (#17 is one, but always ask if the driver is going to *Zona Uno*).

Most of the buses that don't use the Zona 4 terminal will end up somewhere in Zona 1, close enough to walk to a hotel, or at least an inexpensive taxi ride away.

The main **bus companies**, their addresses and departure times, are all given in "Travel Details", at the end of this chapter on p.74.

The Zona 1 bus terminal is at 18 C and 9 Av, but many companies, especially first-class ones, have their own offices.

Information

The **tourist office**, *Inguat*, is at 7 Av 1–17, Zona 4 (Mon–Fri 8.30am–4.30pm, Sat 8.30am–1pm; ☎3311333). The information desk is on the ground floor and here you can buy **maps** of the country and the city, or put your questions to the staff – usually someone there speaks English. For a really detailed map of Guatemala try the *Instituto Geografico Militar*, Av las Americas 5–76, Zona 13 (Mon–Fri 7.30am–4pm). To buy maps, which cost around $6, you will need to show your passport. #65 bus gets you nearest, or take a taxi. (Photocopies of these maps, including restricted sheets, are sold in Antigua at the *Casa Andinista* bookshop.)

The **post office** (Mon–Fri 7.30am–6.30pm), at 7 Av and 12 C has a *lista de correos*, where they will hold mail for you, at the back on the ground floor. *American Express*, Av La Reforma 9–00, Zona 9, runs a more efficient service for receiving mail. You can make long-distance phone calls and send international telegrams from *Guatel* (daily 7am–midnight), one block south of the post office.

City transport – buses and taxis

One of Guatemala City's greatest nightmares is the **bus system**; even local people who've lived in the city all their lives remain baffled by it. One major complication is that the city authorities regularly re-route the buses in order to control traffic congestion, and another is that each route, or bus number, includes many possible variations. The easiest way to handle it is to accept that getting on

#2 Runs along 10 Av and 12 Av in Zona 1, goes past the train station at 18 C and 9 Av, through Zona 4 along 6 Av, and then all the way down Av La Reforma to the Parque Independencia. This route is particularly handy as it takes you past many of the embassies, the office of *American Express*, the Popol Vuh and Ixchel museums, and to within walking distance of any address on Av las Americas.

#17 Marked *Kaminaljuyú* – runs along 4 Av in Zona 1, and will take you out west into Zona 7, and to the ruins of Kaminaljuyú.

#83 The only bus in the city that goes to and from the airport.

Terminal Any bus marked *terminal*, and there are plenty of these on 4 Av in Zona 1, will take you to the main bus terminal in Zona 4.

Bolívar or Trébol Any bus with either of these written on will take you along the western side of the city, down Av Bolívar and to the Trébol junction.

the wrong bus isn't the end of the world, and that you can always get off, cross the road and go back to where you started. Above all else the buses are cheap, so you'll need some small change to hand. A number of new "Metro Buses" cover some routes: these are clean, modern, and more expensive (around Q1) than the ordinary buses. In Zona 1 all the main avenidas are one-way; buses going south towards the newer parts of the city run down 4 Av and 10 Av; those coming up into Zona 1 run along 5 Av and 9 Av.

Buses **run** from around 6 or 7am until about 10pm; **minibuses** serve similar routes but tend to be a little more expensive. After 10pm, the minibuses effectively operate as taxis, running along vaguely defined routes until around 1am.

Taxis

If you can't face the complexities of the bus system then **taxis** are always an easier option and not necessarily that expensive, providing you arrange a deal beforehand (meters are nonexistent). There are plenty around any of the bus terminals and in the Parque Central and the Parque Concordia, 6 Av and 14 C, Zona 1.

Accommodation

Hotels in Guatemala City come in all shapes and sizes. The majority of the budget choices are conveniently grouped on the eastern side of Zona 1; there are also a few in the area of the two main bus terminals, but these are really for emergency use only (or for very early starts) as the neighbourhoods are neither pleasant nor safe. Bearing in mind that the city is not a great place to be wandering around in search of a room, you might want to call ahead and book.

El Aeropuerto Guest House, 15 C A 7–32, Zona 13 (☎3323086), five minutes' walk from the international airport. Cross the grass from the terminal and follow the road to the left. Pleasant, convenient and very comfortable hotel, all private showers and hot water. ⑤.

Camino Real, Av La Reforma and 14 C, Zona 10 (☎4484633; fax 3374313). The favoured address for visiting heads of state and anyone on expenses, this hotel continues to lead in the luxury category in spite of increasing competition from newer places. ⑦.

La Casa Grande, Av Reforma 7–67, Zona 10 (☎ & fax 3320914). Elegant villa set slightly back from the road, with very attentive service. ⑥.

Hotel del Centro, 13 C 4–55, Zona 1 (☎2382281; fax 2300208). Large modern building, decorated in dark, colonial-style wood. Formal but comfortable; all rooms have private bathroom and cable TV. ⑥.

Hotel Colonial, 7 Av 14–19, Zona 1 (☎2326722; fax 2328671). Smart and somewhat formal, with wrought iron and dark wood decor, but clean and comfortable. All rooms have private bathroom. ④.

ACCOMMODATION PRICE CODES

All accommodation reviewed in the Guatemala section of this guide has been graded according to the following **price scales**. These refer to the cost of a double room in US$. For more details see p.28.

① Under $2	③ $5–10	⑥ $35–55
② $2–5	④ $10–20	⑦ Over $55
	⑤ $20–35	

Hotel Cortijo Reforma, Av La Reforma 2–18, Zona 9 (☎3322713; fax 3318876). Convenient first-class hotel near the American embassy. ⑥.

Hotel Costa del Sol, 17 C 8–17, Zona 1 (☎2321296). Opposite the terminals for Petén, this is really only an option if you're just off the bus and cannot face more travelling. It's basic, but has hot water, and is secure – one of the only places round here that isn't a brothel. ③.

Crowne Plaza Las Americas, Av Las Americas 9–08, Zona 13 (☎3390676; fax 3390690 or 4489071). The newest luxury hotel in town, the latest in design and modern services, but you need your own transport or taxi to reach the *Zona Viva*. ⑦.

Hotel El Dorado, 7 Av 15–45, Zona 9 (☎3317777; fax 3321877). In the same category as the *Camino Real*, charging the same prices. ⑦.

Hotel Excel, 9 Av 15–45, Zona 1 (☎2532709). Clean and safe hotel near the red light district, which has the advantage of secure parking. ④.

Hotel Fenix, 7 Av 15–81, Zona 1 (no phone). Dingy, rather run-down hotel in an old, warped wooden building, but still perfectly reasonable, clean and comfortable. Some rooms have private bathroom. ③.

Hotel Fiesta, 1 Av 13–22, Zona 10 (☎3322555; fax 3322569). First-class hotel within walking distance of the city's best upmarket shops, bars and restaurants. ⑦.

Hotel Fortuna Real, 12 C 8–42, Zona 1 (☎2303378; fax 2512215). Spotless, Chinese-owned hotel in the heart of Zona 1. All rooms have TV and private bath. ④.

Hotel Hernani, corner 15 C and 6 Av A, Zona 1 (☎2322839). Comfortable old building with good, clean rooms, all with their own shower. ③.

Hotel Hincapié, Av Hincapié 18–77, Zona 13 (☎3327771; fax 3374469). Under the same management as the *Airport Guest House*, conveniently located for the domestic airport. Rates include local calls, continental breakfast, and transport to and from the airport. ⑤.

Hotel Lessing, 12 C 4–35, Zona 1 (☎2513891). Simple budget hotel: small, central, friendly and good value, though just a touch grubby. ③.

Pensión Meza, 10 C 10–17, Zona 1 (☎2323177). Infamous budget travellers' hang-out: cheap and laid-back, with plenty of drugs and 1960s-style decadence. Back in the good old days Fidel Castro and Che Guevara stayed here – the latter in room 21, although his bed is now in room 10. No private showers; many rooms are shared. There's music all day and a cheap restaurant next door – and the owner, Mario, is delightful. ②–③.

Hotel Monteleone, 18 C 4–63, Zona 1 (☎2382600). Clean and extremely safe, all rooms with private bath. Right by the terminal for buses to Antigua, it's handy if you need to catch a bus out the next day. ④.

Hotel PanAmerican, 9 C 5–63, Zona 1 (☎2326807; fax 2326402). The city's oldest smart hotel, very formal and civilized, with a strong emphasis on Guatemalan tradition. ⑤.

Hotel Posada Belen, 13 C A 10–30, Zona 1 (☎2534530; fax 2513478). In a beautiful old building, tucked down a side street. Supremely quiet and safe and very homely, with its own restaurant, although you have to order evening meals in advance. No children under five. ④.

Hotel Posada Real, 12 C 6–21, Zona 1 (☎2381092). A little rough, musty and dark, but still safe, cheap and central. ③.

Hotel Princess, 13 C 7–65, Zona 9 (☎3344545; fax 3344546). Pleasant mid-sized hotel with pool, sauna, gym and tennis facilities. ⑦.

Hotel Ritz Continental, 6 Av A 10–13, Zona 1 (☎2512115; fax 2324659). Huge modern block in the city centre. More than 200 rooms with all the luxury you'd expect. ⑦.

Hotel Spring, 8 Av 12–65, Zona 1 (☎2326637). The best bargain in town, though usually full with Peace Corp volunteers. Rooms are set around an open courtyard. Breakfast available; some rooms have private bath. ②–③.

Hotel Stofella, 2 Av 12–28, Zona 10 (☎3346191; fax 3310823). Immaculate business-oriented hotel, though the rooms are a little dark. ⑥.

Chalet Suizo, 14 C 6–82, Zona 1 (☎2513786; fax 2320429). Friendly, comfortable and certainly very safe. Spotlessly clean, all very Swiss and organized, with left luggage and a new café that's open all day and also overpriced. ④.

The City

Though few people come to Guatemala City for the sights, there are some places that are worth visiting while you're here. Quite apart from the Ixchel and Popol Vuh **museums**, which are particularly good, much of the city's **architecture** is impressive and unusual, with the older buildings huddled together in Zona 1 and some outlandish modern structures dotted across the southern half of the city.

Zonas 1 and 2: the old city

The hub of the old city is **Zona 1**, which is also the busiest and most claustrophobic part of town. Here the two main streets, 5 and 6 avenidas, are still the city's principal shopping area, despite the fact that the really exclusive places have moved out into Zona 10. Nevertheless, the old city remains the most exciting part of the capital, throbbing with activity as it falls steadily into disrepair.

The Parque Central and around

Zona 1's northern boundary runs behind the Palacio Nacional, taking in the **Parque Central**, the square that forms the country's political and religious centre, dominated by the palace and the cathedral. This plaza, currently concealing a large underground car park, was originally the scene of a huge central market, which now operates from a covered site behind the cathedral (see below).

Most of the imposing structures that face the plaza today were put up after the 1917 earthquake, with the notable exception of the **Cathedral**, which was completed in 1868. For years its grand facade, merging the Baroque and the Neoclassical, dominated the plaza, dwarfing all other structures. Its solid, squat design was intended to resist the force of earthquakes and, for the most part, it has succeeded. In 1917 the bell towers were brought down and the cupola fell, destroying the altar, but the central structure, though cracked and patched over the years, remains intact. Inside there are three main aisles, all lined with arching pillars, austere colonial paintings and intricate altars supporting an array of saints. Some of this collection was brought here from the original cathedral in Antigua when the capital was moved in 1776.

These days, however, the most striking building in the plaza is the **Palacio Nacional**, a solid stone-faced structure facing south towards the neon maze of Zona 1. The palace was started in 1939 under the auspices of President Ubico – a characteristically grand gesture from the man who believed that he was a reincarnation of Napoleon – and completed a year before he was ousted in 1944. Today it houses the executive branch of the government, and from time to time its steps are fought over by assorted coupsters. The interior of the palace is open to the public, and once you've offered the security guard a glimpse of your passport you can simply wander in and stroll around the two courtyards, on any of three floors. It's astonishingly relaxed inside, the various ministries housed in the chambers around the courtyards, their doorways guarded by waiting journalists. Most impressive are the **Salas de Recepción** (state reception rooms), at the front of the second floor. Unless they're being prepared for use you're allowed to go in; if they're closed, ask the guards to let you take a look. Along one wall is a row of flags and the country's coat of arms, topped with a stuffed quetzal. The stained glass windows represent key aspects of Guatemalan history. Back in the main body of the building the stairwells are decorated with murals, again depicting historical scenes, mixed in with images of totally unrelated events: one wall shows a group of idealized pre-conquest Indians, and another includes a portrait of Don Quixote.

Opposite the cathedral, on the western side of the plaza, is the **Parque del Centenario**. The Palace of the Captains General used to stand here, a long single-storey building, finished at the end of the nineteenth century, that was intended to function as the National Palace. It was promptly destroyed, however, in the 1917 earthquake. For the 1921 centenary celebration a temporary wooden structure was set up in its place, but once this had served its purpose it went up in flames. After that it was decided to create a park instead, with a bandstand, gardens and a fountain. Sited on the other side of the Parque del Centenario the fairly unattractive modern **Biblioteca Nacional** (National Library), holds the archives of Central America.

Around the back of the cathedral is the **Mercado Central**, housed in a couple of layers of sunken concrete. Taking no chances, the architect of this building, which replaced an earlier version destroyed in the 1976 earthquake, apparently modelled the structure on a nuclear bunker, sacrificing any aesthetic concerns to the need for strength. The top level is given over to a car park, and beneath that are the **handicraft** sellers. Unexpectedly, this is a good spot to buy traditional weaving, with an astonishing range of cloth from all over the country. The market is only visited by a trickle of tourists so prices are reasonable and the traders very willing to bargain. On the bottom layer, beneath the handicrafts, is the market proper, a great spread of food stalls and *comedores*. This was once the city's main food market but these days it's just one of many, and by no means the largest. Two blocks east of the market and one block south along 9 Av, you reach one of the city's less well-known museums, **Museo Nacional de Historia**, 9 C 9–70, Zona 1 (Tues–Sun 9am–noon & 2–4pm), which features a selection of artefacts relating to Guatemalan history, including documents, clothes and paintings. Probably the most interesting displays are the photographs by Eadweard Muybridge, who, in 1875, was one of the first people to undertake a study of the country.

South along 6 and 7 avenidas

Heading south from Parque Central are **6 and 7 avenidas**, thick with clothes shops, restaurants, cinemas, neon signs and bus fumes. What you can't buy in the shops is sold on the pavements, and *McDonalds*, *Wimpy* and *Pizza Hut* are all very much part of the scene. It's here that most people head on a Saturday night, when the traffic has to squeeze between hordes of pedestrians. By 11pm, though, the streets are largely deserted, left to the cigarette sellers and prostitutes.

Sixth Avenida is the more overwhelming of the two main streets. Halfway along, strangely out of place at the corner of 13 C, is the **Iglesia de San Francisco**, a church famous for its carving of the Sacred Heart, which, like several other of its paintings and statues, was brought here from Antigua. Building began in 1780, but was repeatedly interrupted by seismic activity – it's said that cane syrup, egg whites and cow's milk were mixed with the mortar to enhance its strength. For the most part the church fared well, but in 1917 a tremor brought down one of the arches, revealing that the clergy had used the roof cavity to store banned books.

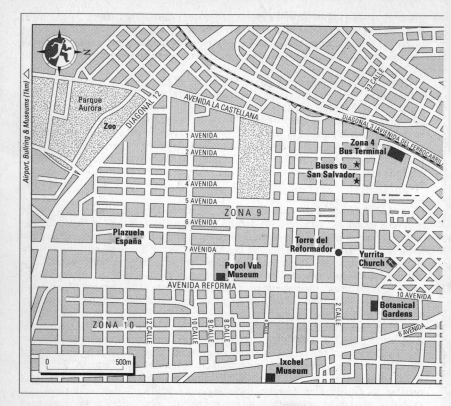

Another block to the south is the **Police Headquarters**, an outlandish-looking castle built in imitation of medieval battlements. The next block is taken up by **Parque Concordia**, a leafy square, one of whose sides is lined with cheap *comedores*. Plenty of people spend their time hanging out here, and there's always a surplus of shoeshine boys, taxi drivers and lottery tickets – the prizes, usually cars, are sometimes on display in a corner of the park. Concordia is also a favourite spot for street performers and travelling preachers, and at weekends you can see the snake charmers, clowns and rabid evangelicals all competing furiously for an audience.

Over on 7 Avenida, there are also a couple of buildings worth noting. The **post office** is a spectacular Moorish building with a marvellous arch that spans the road; the *Guatel* office is nearby (see p.51). A few blocks to the east, you come across the very impressive churches of **La Merced**, at 11 Av and 5 C, and **Santo Domingo**, 12 Av and 10 C. Not impressive, though it ought to be, is the **Museo Nacional de Artes y Industrias Populares**, 10 Av 10–72, Zona 1 (Tues–Sun 9am–noon & 2–4pm), a collection of painting, weaving, ceramics, musical instruments and Indian masks. Again the museum is sadly neglected and very small, and it's not really worth going out of your way for.

Returning to 6 Avenida, heading south from the Parque Concordia, things go into a slow but steady decline as the pavements become increasingly swamped by

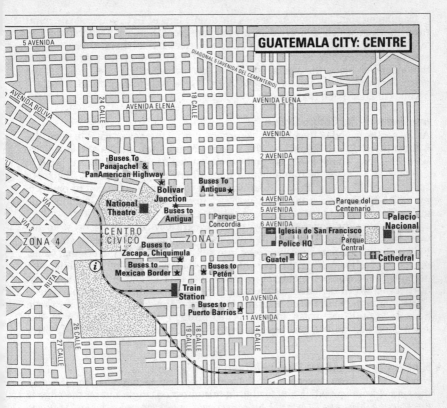

temporary stalls, and the commercial chaos starts to get out of control. At this southern end of 6 Avenida there is a predominance of electrical shops, gradually giving way to clothes stalls, and finally emerging in the madness of 18 Calle. On the other side of 18 C is the **Tipografía Nacional**, the government's printing press and media centre: a wonderful, crumbling building, where bureaucrats beaver away at their task of disseminating information and propaganda.

To the left, beneath the trees, **18 Calle** becomes distinctly sleazy, the cheap food stalls and shoeshine boys now mixed in with grimy nightclubs and "streap-tease" joints. By night the streets are patrolled by prostitutes and the local hotels are protected by prison-like grilles. In daylight it's a grubby but otherwise harmless part of town – though you may still have the odd encounter with the occasional highly skilled pickpocket – with a collection of the very cheapest restaurants and hotels. At the corner of 18 C and 9 Av is the **eastern bus terminal**; the surrounding streets are home to a number of bus company offices. On the east side of the open square is the **train station**, an inconspicuous whitewashed wooden building from where trains used to leave for Tecún Umán and Puerto Barrios. Inside, amidst all the dust and rubble, is a carefully preserved Baldwin Locomotive, built in 1897. If you ask nicely they'll probably let you take a look. Further east, past the station, lies **Zona 5**, a run-down residential suburb.

Continuing south along 6 Av, across the deadly flow of 18 C, you pass the **main food market**, which is housed in a vast, pale-green hangar. Traders who can afford it pay for a space inside, while those who can't spread themselves along the streets, which are littered with rubbish and soggy with rotten fruit. At the end of this extended block the character of the city is radically transformed as the ageing and claustrophobic streets of Zona 1 give way to the broad tree-lined avenues of Zona 4 and the new city.

Into Zona 4 – the Centro Civico

At the southern end of the old city, separating it from the newer parts of town, the **Centro Civico**, also known as the **Centro Municipal**, marks the boundary between zones 1 and 4. At this point the avenidas from the north are brought together at a couple of roundabouts, from where they fan out into the more spacious southern city. Bunched around these junctions a collection of multistorey office blocks house the city's main administrative buildings, including the main office of *Inguat* (see p.51).

Overlooking the concrete sprawl of the Centro Civico, a block or so to the west, is the **National Theatre**, the city's most prominent and unusual structure. Built on top of the **San José Fortress**, and still surrounded by the original battlements, it's designed along the lines of a huge ship, painted blue and white, with portholes as windows. Finding an entrance that isn't locked is not always easy, but it's well worth the effort for the superb views across the city. The building is also home to the little-visited **Military Museum** (Mon–Fri 8am–6pm), a strange homage to the Guatemalan army. Reached through the main theatre gate, this small collection of weapons and uniforms is really only of interest to military buffs.

North to Zona 2 and the Parque Minerva

North of the old city centre is Zona 2, bounded by a deep-cut ravine that prevents the sprawl from spreading any further in this direction. Right out on the edge is the **Parque Minerva**, a scruffy little park and sports complex where fairs are held on public holidays and fiestas. The main point of interest at other times is a **relief map of the country**, which covers 2500 square metres and has a couple of special viewing towers. The map was finished in 1905 and designed to have running water flowing in the rivers, although the taps are usually shut off. Its vertical scale is out of proportion to the horizontal, making the mountains look incredibly steep. It does nonetheless give you a good idea of the general layout of the country, from the complexity of the highlands to the sheer enormity of Petén. To get to the Parque Minerva take bus #1 from anywhere along 5 Av in Zona 1.

The new city

The southern half of the city is far more spacious, but though you may have more room to breathe, the air is no less noxious. Roughly speaking, the new city divides into two, split down the middle by 7 Avenida. The eastern half, centred on Avenida La Reforma, is the smartest part of town, with the banks, hotels, restaurants, boutiques and walled residential compounds that belong strictly to Guatemala's wealthy elite. The western half of the new town is rougher, incorporating the bus terminal, zoo and airport.

The east: 7 Avenida and Avenida La Reforma

Heading to the south of the Centro Civico and into Zona 4 proper, 6 Av runs into the modern city, with Ruta 6 branching off to the east, towards Av La Reforma, crossing 7 Av beside the landmark **Edificio El Triangulo**. From here, 7 Av heads south beneath the **Torre del Reformador**, Guatemala's answer to the Eiffel Tower, at the junction of 7 Av and 2 C. The steel structure was built along the lines of the Parisian model, in honour of President Barrios, who transformed the country between 1871 and 1885; a bell in the top of the tower is rung every year on June 30 to commemorate the Liberal victory in the 1871 revolution.

Pushing its way southeast, Ruta 6 passes the **Iglesia Yurrita**, an outlandish building designed in an exotic neo-Gothic style that belongs more to horror movies than to the streets of Guatemala City. It was built as a private chapel by a rich philanthropist; his house, in the same style, stands alongside. The church is also known as **Nuestra Señora de las Angustias**, and is usually open to the public. It's well worth taking a look as the inside is just as wild.

Ruta 6 meets Av La Reforma at a busy roundabout marked by the *Cine Reforma*, which has been both a cinema and an evangelical church, but is now a theatre and music venue. On the opposite side of Av La Reforma are the **Botanical Gardens** (Mon–Fri 8am–noon & 2–6pm) of the San Carlos University; the entrance is on 0 C. Inside you'll find a beautiful, small garden with quite a selection of species, all neatly labelled in Spanish and Latin. There's also a small, but not terribly exciting, **Natural History Museum** with a collection of stuffed birds, including a quetzal and an ostrich, along with geological samples, wood types, live snakes, some horrific pickled rodents and a small library that includes books in English.

Far more worthwhile is the **Museo Ixchel** (Mon–Fri 8am–4.50pm; Sat 9am–12.50pm; $2), in its own purpose-built cultural centre on the campus of the University Francisco Marroquin. Following 6 C Final off Av La Reforma, heading east, you will easily recognize the building, which is designed along the lines of a Maya temple. Probably the capital's best museum, the Ixchel is dedicated to Indian culture, with particular emphasis on traditional weaving. You'll see a collection of hand-woven fabrics, including some very impressive examples of ceremonial costumes, with explanations in English. There's also information about the techniques used, and the way in which costumes have changed over the years. Despite the fact that it's by no means comprehensive, and that the costumes lose much of their impact and meaning when taken out of the villages where they're made, this is a fascinating exhibition. A private institution dedicated to the study and preservation of traditional Indian culture, the museum also possesses a large library together with collections of textiles and pictures.

Heading south on Avenida La Reforma you pass the *Politecnica*, a school for the training of young military officers, built in the style of a toy fort. Beyond this is the smart part of town, with boutiques, travel agents, the American Embassy, banks, office blocks, sleek hotels and the offices of *American Express*, at Av La Reforma 9–00. While there's a steady flow of traffic along Av La Reforma, the surrounding streets are quiet and the lawns mown. This part of town has clearly escaped the Third World. A little to the east, around 10 C and 3 Av, is the so-called **Zona Viva**, a tight bunch of upmarket hotels, restaurants and nightclubs.

It's in this part of town, at the southern end of Av La Reforma, that you'll find the city's other private museum, the **Popol Vuh Archeological Museum**, at Av

La Reforma 8–16, Zona 9 on the sixth floor of the black office building (Mon–Sat 9am–5pm; $2). Standards here are just as high as at the Ixchel, but this time the subject is archeology, with an outstanding collection of artefacts from sites all over the country. Among the best pieces are some incredible ceramics and several ball-court markers. The museum also goes beyond the Maya to the colonial era with a few musty Spanish costumes and Indian exhibits.

Out to the west side of Av La Reforma, **Plaza España** occupies the junction of 7 Av and 12 C. Now marked by a fountain, this crossroads was once the site of a statue of King Carlos III of Spain, torn down when independence was declared. At the four corners of the plaza you can still see some superb tiled benches dating from colonial times, although they're now in a state of some disrepair.

To get to Av La Reforma from Zona 1, take bus #2, which runs along 8 and 10 avenidas in Zona 1, past the Yurrita Church, and all the way along Av La Reforma. La Reforma is a two-way street, so you can return by the same means.

Zona 14

Heading further south into Zona 14, the end of Av La Reforma is marked by the **Parque Independencia**, at the junction with 20 C. Beyond this point it continues as the **Avenida las Americas** and things become even more exclusive, many of the large walled compounds belonging to embassies. At the southern end of the avenida, behind a statue of Pope John Paul II, is the **Plaza Berlin**: a filthy park that was once worth visiting for the view of Lake Amatitlán and the Pacaya volcano, but new building has obscured the view. Running parallel to Av las Americas, 14 C – better known as **Avenida Hincapié** – gives access to the **domestic airport**, opposite the junction with 18 C.

To the east, the main highway to the border with El Salvador runs out through Zona 10. As the road leaves the city it climbs a steep hillside and passes through one of the most exclusive and expensive residential districts in the country, where every house has a superb view of the city below, and most are ringed by ferocious fortifications. Out beyond this, at the top of the hill, is Guatemala's main (if not only) motor-racing track.

West of 6 Avenida

Out to the west of 6 Av it's quite another story, and while there are still small enclaves of upmarket housing, and several expensive shopping areas, things are really dominated by transport and commerce. The **railway** to the coast, its tracks lined with bedraggled slums, runs out this way, and the airport, the bullring, the zoo and the infamous Zona 4 bus terminal all rub shoulders. Of these, the one you're most likely to be going to is the **Zona 4 Bus Terminal**, at 1 C and 4 Av. This is certainly the country's most impenetrable and intimidating jungle, a swirl of petty thieves, bus fumes and sleeping vagrants.

Around the terminal the largest **market** in the city spreads across several blocks. If you can summon the energy it's a real adventure to wander through this maze of alleys, but don't carry too much money as it's a relatively risky part of town. To get to the bus terminal from Zona 1, take any of the buses marked *terminal* from 4 Av or 9 Av, all of which pass within a block or two.

Behind the bus terminal, railway tracks head off towards the coast, and behind these is **Avenida Bolívar**, an important traffic artery that runs out to the **Trébol junction**, where it meets the main highways from the western highlands and the Pacific coast. Up above the bus terminal here, just off Av Bolívar, is the **Santuario**

Expiatorio, also known as the Iglesia Santa Cecilia de Don Bosco, a superb modern church designed (by a then unqualified Salvadorean architect) in the shape of a fish. It's part of a church-run complex that includes clinics and schools, and is well worth looking at, above all for the fantastic mural running down the side of the interior, which depicts the Crucifixion and Resurrection with vivid realism.

Further to the south, in Zona 13, the **Parque Aurora** houses the city's **zoo** (entrance free), with a collection that includes lions, crocodiles, monkeys and wild boar. As you might expect, it's a cramped and vaguely depressing gathering of beasts. The zoo's main gate is marked by a huge statue of Tecún Umán, the great Quiché warrior.

On the other side of the Parque Aurora, reached along 7 Av, is a collection of state-run **museums** (all Tues–Fri 9am–4.30pm, Sat & Sun 9am–noon & 2–4pm; Q1). The best of these is the **Museum of Archeology and Ethnology**, with a selection of Maya artefacts to rival the Popul Vuh. The collection includes some fantastic stelae, as well as a display on Indian culture, with traditional masks and costumes. There are several vast pieces of Maya stonework on show, some of them from the more remote sites such as Piedras Negras. In comparison, the city's **Museum of Modern Art** is a little disappointing and seems rather neglected. It's not worth a special trip, but if you're in the area you might as well drop in to see some impressively massive murals as well as an abundance of new images of Indian life. The works cover the last couple of centuries of Guatemalan art, taking in most of the modern movements. Suffering from a similar neglect, the **Museum of Natural History** features a range of mouldy-looking stuffed animals from Guatemala and elsewhere and a few mineral samples. Beside the park there's a **bullring** (Oct–Dec), and a running track, while to the south is the **Aurora airport**. To get to Parque Aurora from Zona 1, take bus #5 from 4 Av.

The final point of interest in the southern half of the city is the **Ciudad Universitária**, the campus of San Carlos University, in Zona 12. A huge, purpose-built complex, it is heavily decorated with vivid political graffiti. The San Carlos University, originally founded in Antigua by Dominican priests in 1676, is probably the best in Central America; it has an autonomous constitution and is entitled to 5 percent of the government's annual budget. The university also has a long history of radical dissent and anti-government protest and students here have been victims of repression and political killing on several occasions – many right-wing politicians still regard the campus as a centre of subversion. Buses marked *Universitária* travel along 4 Av through Zona 1 to the campus.

Zona 7: the ruins of Kaminaljuyú

Way out on the western edge of the city, beyond the stench of the rubbish dump, is the long thin arm of Zona 7, a well-established but run-down part of town that wraps around the ruins of **Kaminaljuyú** (Mon–Fri 8am–4pm, Sat 8am–1pm). Archeological digs on this side of the city have revealed the astonishing proportions of a Maya city that once housed around 50,000 people and includes more than three hundred mounds and thirteen ball courts. Unlike the massive temples of the lowlands, these structures were built of adobe, and most of them have been lost to centuries of erosion and a few decades of urban sprawl. Today the archeological site, incorporating only a tiny fraction of the original city, is little more than a series of earth-covered mounds, a favourite spot for football and romance. A couple of sections have been cut into by archeologists, and by peering through the fence you can get some idea of what lies beneath the grassy exterior, but it's virtually impossible to get any impression of Kaminaljuyú's former scale and splendour.

To get to the ruins take bus #17, #13 or #63 from 4 Av in Zona 1. These all have several different destinations so be sure to get on one with a small *Kaminaljuyú* sign in the windscreen.

A history of Kaminaljuyú

Despite their nondescript appearance, the ruins are those of a particularly important site, once the largest Maya city in the Guatemalan highlands. The history of Kaminaljuyú falls neatly into two sections: a first phase of indigenous growth, and a later period during which migrants from the north populated the site.

In the Late Preclassic era, 400 BC to 100 AD, the city had already grown to huge proportions, with some two hundred flat-topped **pyramids**, the largest reaching a height of about 18m. Beneath each of these lay entombed a member of the nobility; a few have been unearthed to reveal the wealth and sophistication of the culture. The corpses were wrapped in finery, covered in cinnabar pigment and surrounded by an array of human sacrifices, pottery, jade, masks, stingray spines, obsidian and quartz crystals. A number of carvings have also been found, proving that the elite of Kaminaljuyú were fully literate at a time when other Maya had perhaps no notion of writing. Many of the gods, the ceramic styles and hieroglyphic forms from these early days at Kaminaljuyú are thought to prefigure those found in the flowering of Maya art at later centres such as Tikal and Copán. But the power of the city, pre-eminent during the Late Preclassic era, faded throughout the second and third centuries, and the site may even have been abandoned.

Kaminaljuyú's renaissance took place shortly after 400 AD, when the Guatemalan highlands suffered a massive influx of migrants from the north and fell under the domination of Teotihuacán in central Mexico. The migrants seized the city of Kaminaljuyú and established it as their regional capital, giving them control of the obsidian mines and access to the coastal trade routes and the lowlands of Petén. With the weighty political and economic backing of Teotihuacán the city once again flourished, as the new rulers constructed their

own temples, tombs and ball courts. Numerous artefacts have been found from this period, including some pottery that's thought to have been made in Teotihuacán itself, along with endless imitations of the style. Kaminaljuyú's new-found power also played a crucial role in shaping the lowlands of Petén: it was only with the backing of the great Teotihuacán-Kaminaljuyú alliance that Tikal was able to grow so large and so fast. This role was considered of such importance that some archeologists suggest that Curl Nose, one of the early rulers at Tikal (who ascended to power in 387 AD), may actually have come from Kaminaljuyú. The fortunes of Kaminaljuyú itself, however, were so bound up with those of its northern partner that the fall of Teotihuacán around 600 AD weakened and eventually destroyed the city.

Eating, drinking and entertainment

Despite its role as the country's economic centre, Guatemala City isn't a great place for indulging. Most of the population hurry home after dark and it's only the very rich who eat, drink and dance until the small hours. There are, however, **restaurants** everywhere in the city, invariably reflecting the type of neighbourhood they're in, most concentrating on quantity rather than quality. Moviewatching is hugely popular, with a good selection of cinemas; nightclubs and bars are concentrated in Zona 10.

Restaurants and cafés

When it comes to eating well and cheaply in Guatemala City, stick to **Zona 1**, where the restaurants tend to reflect the cosmopolitan side of the capital's population – and the fact that most people have little money to spare. There's a cluster of **Chinese** restaurants on 6 C, between 4 and 3 avenidas, a patch that ranks as the city's Chinatown. **Italian** restaurants have also established themselves in the city and a couple of specifically **vegetarian** places have sprung up, despite the fact that this is a city obsessed with meat eating. If you're trying to cut costs, cheap and filling food is sold from stalls around all the bus stations and markets, and on many of the streets in the centre. In Zona 1 you'll also find a concentration of cheap *comedores*, around 18 C and 9 Av. In the smarter parts of town, particularly Zonas 9 and 10, the emphasis is more on upmarket cafés and overpriced hamburgers, and inexpensive places are hard to find.

Fast food is perhaps at the heart of life in Zona 1, and there's plenty to choose from, the vast majority of it imported directly from the States. There's a *McDonald's* at 10 C 5–56, Zona 1, and 7 Av 14–01, Zona 9, and a *Pizza Hut* at 6 Av between 12 and 13 calles, Zona 1. Home-grown breeds include *Burger Shop*, 6 Av 13–40, Zona 1, and the slightly cheaper *Pollo Campero*, the Guatemalan version of *Kentucky Fried Chicken*, with branches throughout the city.

Restaurants

Altuna, 5 Av 12–31, Zona 1. Spanish food in a subdued but wonderfully civilized atmosphere. Not cheap, but affordable.

Los Antojitos, Av La Reforma 15–02, Zona 9. Good, moderately priced Central American food – try the *chile rellenos* or guacamole.

Antro's, 4 Av 15–53, Zona 10. Excellent vegetarian restaurant with some Middle Eastern dishes. Not too puritanical, with "unhealthy" drinks like beer and espresso. Closed Sun.

El Arbol de la Vida, 7 Av 13–56, Zona 9. The city's best veg restaurant; reasonably priced

Café de la Libre, 7 Av and 13 C, Zona 13. Pleasant, if pricey, vegetarian place next to *Libreria del Pensativo*. The daily lunch specials are good value.

Delicadezas Hamburgo, 15 C 5–34, Zona 1. A hybrid of Guatemalan and German food; the set meals are particularly good value. They also do a good deal on a set breakfast, offering a number of menus from cornflakes to beans and eggs.

Estro Armonico, 15 C 1–11, Zona 10. Fancy food at fancy prices; rare delights such as lamb and duck in unusual sauces.

Europa Bar, 11 C 5–16, Zona 1. The most enduring gringo hang-out in Zona 1, which combines full restaurant services with being a bar, complete with *CNN* and North American sports coverage. Prices are moderate for anything from pasta to burgers, and owner Judy is a mine of local information. You can trade US$ here, and make local calls. Closed Sun.

Fu Lu Sho, 6 Av and 12 C, Zona 1. Popular, inexpensive Chinese restaurant with Art Deco interior, opening onto the bustle of 6 Av.

El Gran Pavo, 13 C 4–41, Zona 1, 6 C 3–09, Zona 9 & 15 Av 16–72, Zona 10. Massive portions of genuinely Mexican, moderately priced food in a decidedly Mexican atmosphere.

A Guy From Italy, 12 C 6–23, Zona 1. Part of a citywide pizza and pasta chain. Slightly more upmarket than *Piccadilly*.

Jake's, 17 C 10–40, Zona 10. Lunch and dinner from an international menu, very strong on fish and with terrific sweets. Pleasant, candle-lit atmosphere, excellent service, and correspondingly high prices. Closed Sun and Mon.

Long Wah, 6 C 3–75, Zona 1, west of the National Palace in the main Chinese area. Good Chinese restaurant, not at all expensive.

Luigi's Pizza, 4 Av 14–20, Zona 10. Very popular, moderately priced Italian restaurant, serving delicious pizza, pasta and baked potatoes.

Mundial, 6 Av and 15 C, Zona 1. Good, quiet Chinese restaurant, with low prices.

Café Penalba, 6 Av 11–71, Zona 1. Inexpensive set meals.

Piccadilly, 6 Av and 11 C, Zona 1 & Plaza Espana, 7 Av 12–00, Zona 9. One of the most popular Italian restaurants with tourists and Guatemalans alike. Delicious range of pastas and pizzas, served along with huge jugs of beer. Moderate prices.

Puerto Barrios, 7 Av 10–65, Zona 9. Excellent, pricey seafood in a boat-like building.

Selecta, 14 C 6–24, Zona 1. Inexpensive set meals – better than *Café Penalba*.

Sol Rey, 8 C, near corner of 5 Av, Zona 1. Very good selection of vegetarian dishes, opposite the Parque Centenario. The shop sells wholewheat bread and veggie snacks.

Sushi, 2 Av 14–63, Zona 10. Very popular new Japanese restaurant, which rather bizarrely advertises itself as a "rock café" too. Reasonable prices.

Tao Restaurant, 5 C 9–70, Zona 1. The city's best value three-course veggie lunch. There's no menu; you just eat the meal of the day at tiny tables round a plant-filled courtyard.

Tu Tu Tango, 2 Av 14–74, Zona 10. International menu covering everything from fish to pasta, steak to mango mousse. Welcoming atmosphere, and excellent service. Closed Sun.

Vesuvio Pizza, 18 C 3–36, Zona 10. Huge pizzas cooked in traditional, wood-burning ovens with plenty of mouth-watering toppings.

Cafés and delis

Los Alpes, 10 C 1–09, Zona 10. A haven of peace, where superb pastries and a fine range of drinks make for the best place to relax in the city. Closed Mon.

Café Astoria, 10 C 6–72, Zona 1. Very German deli and café – excellent sausages and ham.

Maitreya's Deli, 13 C 4–44, Zona 10. Top quality, delicious sandwiches, freshly prepared in house. Wide range of drinks and full meals also offered. Expensive.

Palace, 10 C 4–40, Zona 10. Pasta and snack bar dishes with cakes and pastries in a cafeteria atmosphere.

Patsy, Av La Reforma 8–01, Zona 10. Very handy after visiting either the Popol Vuh, diagonally across the street, or the Ixchel Museum. A full range of sandwiches, burgers and pastries.

Pumpernik's, 2 Av 13–17, Zona 10, inside the Vivacentro building. Good for early breakfasts (from 7am), but also American-style snacks and meals.

Señor Tenedor, 15 C 3–52, Zona 10. Expensive gourmet deli, for those who crave imported food and don't mind paying for it.

Drinking and nightlife

Despite appearances, Guatemala City quietens down very quickly in the evenings, and **nightlife** is certainly not one of its strengths. The best plan is to

drink in one of the restaurants on 6 Av, and perhaps move on later in search of a **club**. What little nightlife there is divides into two distinct parts: in the southern half of the city, particularly in the so-called **Zona Viva** (Zona 10), there are a handful of western-style nightclubs and bars, while in Zona 1 strip clubs and sleazy bars are all that's on offer. If you crave the low life then stroll on down 18 C, to the junction with 9 Av, and you're in the heart of the Zona 1 **red light district**, where there are plenty of truly sleazy bars and clubs. As you head towards the newer part of town, the nightclubs take on a more Western flavour.

The city's greatest **reggae club** is a nameless place on Via 4 between 6 Av and Ruta 6, Zona 4. Radiating rhythm, it's relaxed, but not as worn out as the clubs of Zona 1. It's a favourite haunt of Guatemalans from Lívingston and the Caribbean coast, and well worth a visit.

Bars and clubs

La Bodeguita del Centro, 12 C 3–55, Zona 1 (☎2302976). Large, leftish venue with live music, comedy, poetry and all manner of arty events, many of them free. Food also.

Camino Real Hotel, Av La Reforma and 14 C, Zona 10. The bar and *El Jaguar* disco in this *Zona Viva* hotel, just off Av La Reforma, have more of a Western flavour than other clubs.

Crocodilo's, 16 C and 2 Av, Zona 10 in the *Gran Centro Los Próceres* shopping mall. A restaurant that doubles up as a cocktail bar, with happy hour daily 6–9pm.

Danny's Mariscobar, Av Las Américas 8–24, Zona 13. A new bar to liven up this posh residential area. Live bands every Sat.

Dash Disco, basement at 12 C and 1 Av, Zona 10. Popular spot with young, wealthy Guatemalans.

El Establo, Av La Reforma 14–34, Zona 9. Cosy bar with polished wood interior and pool tables round the back.

Le Pont Disco, 13 C 0–48, Zona 10. Dance spot popular with the capital's young and trendy.

La Quinta, 5 Av between 13 and 14 calles, Zona 1. A club in the centre of Zona 1, *La Quinta* typifies this part of town – weary and middle-aged. But at least there's usually live music, and you can buy (overpriced) food and drink.

Shakespeare's Pub, 13 C 1–51, Zona 10. Small basement bar catering to middle-aged North Americans, most of them ex-pats.

Sheraton Hotel, Via 5, 4–68, Zona 4. Another hotel bar and yet another hotel disco in the *Zona Viva*.

El Zócalo, corner of 18 C and 4 Av, Zona 1. Slightly rougher than *La Quinta*, but very much in the same mould, with blasting marimba.

Cinemas

Most movies shown in Guatemala City are in English with Spanish subtitles. Often they're the very latest releases from the States, which tend to arrive in Central America before they reach Europe. There are four **cinemas on 6 Av** between the main plaza and the Parque Concordia, and the following is a selection of the others scattered throughout the city. Programmes are listed in the two main newspapers, *El Grafico* and *Prensa Libre*.

Cine Las Americas (2 screens), 8–9 C and Av las Americas, Zona 13.

Cine Bolívar, Av Bolívar and 28 C, Zona 8.

Cine Capitol (6 screens), 6 Av and 12 C, Zona 1.

Cine Capri, 8 C and 3 Av, Zona 1.

Cine Lido, 11 C 7–34, Zona 1.

Cine Lux (3 screens), 11 C and 6 Av, Zona 1.

Cine Palace, opposite the *Capitol*.

Cine Plaza, 7 Av 6–7 C, Zona 9.

Cines Taurus, Leo and Aires, 9 C and 4 Av, Zona 1.

Cine Tropical, Av Bolívar 31–71, Zona 8.

Listings

Airlines Airline offices are scattered throughout the city, with many along Av La Reforma. It is fairly straightforward to phone them and there will almost always be someone in the office who speaks English.

Aerolineas Argentinas, 10 C 3–17, Zona 10 (☎3311276); *Aeronica*, 10 C 6–20, Zona 9 (☎3325541 or 3317683); *Aerovias*, airport, 2nd floor (☎3345386 to 90); *Air France*, Av La Reforma 9–00, Zona 9, 8th floor (☎3311952; fax 3320286); *American Airlines*, Av La Reforma 15–54, Zona 9 (☎3347187; fax 3346940); *Aviateca*, Av Hincapié 12–22, Zona 13 (☎3318222; fax 3317401), *Camino Real Hotel* , and 10 C 6–39, Zona 1 (☎2511791); *British Airways*, 1 Av 10–81, Zona 10, 6th floor of Edificio Inexa (☎3327440; fax 3327401); *Continental*, airport (☎3312051; fax 3353444); *Copa*, 7 Av 6–53, Zona 4 (☎3366256); *Iberia*, Av La Reforma 8–60, Zona 9 (☎3370911; airport ☎3325517; fax 3343715); *KLM*, 6 Av 20–25, Zona 10, Edificio Plaza Maritima (☎3370222; airport ☎3319247); *Lacsa*, 7 Av 14–44, Zona 9, Edificio La Galeria (☎3310906; fax 3312284); *LanChile*, Av La Reforma 9–00, Zona 9, Edificio Plaza Panamericana (☎3312070; fax 3312079); *Lufthansa*, 20 C 6–20, Zona 10, Edificio Plaza Maritima (☎3370113; fax 3336906); *Mexicana*, 13 C 8–44, Zona 10, Edificio Edyma (☎3336001; fax 3336096); *Sahsa*, 12 C 1–25, Zona 10 (☎3352671); *Taca*, 7 Av 14–35, Zona 9 (☎3322360; airport ☎3364613; fax 3342575); *Tapsa*, Av Hincapié, 18 C, Zona 13 (☎3314860; fax 3345572) and airport, 2nd floor; *Varig*, Av La Reforma 9–00, Zona 9, Edificio Plaza Panamericana, 8th floor (☎3311912; fax 3320286).

American Express Main office in the *Banco del Café*, Av La Reforma 9–00, Zona 9 (☎3340040; fax 3311928; Mon–Fri 8.30am–4.30pm). The office, which includes the mail service, is in the basement, and the bank on the first floor. Take bus #2 from 10 Av, Zona 1.

Baggage If you want to leave a bag then you'll have to trust it to your hotel as there's no central left luggage facility.

Banks and exchange Opening hours vary wildly, with some banks shutting as early as 3pm, and others staying open until after dark. The bank at the airport is open every day, including Sundays and public holidays, and gives a good exchange rate. For cashing travellers' cheques, try any of the following: *Banco Industrial*, 7 Av 11–52, Zona 1 (Mon–Fri 8.30am–7pm, Sat 8.30am–5.30pm; gives *Visa* cash advances); *Banco del Quetzal* (Mon–Fri 8.30am–8pm, Sat 9am–1pm) and *Banco Promotor* (Mon–Fri 9am–4pm), opposite each other on 10 C, between 6 and 7 avenidas, Zona 1; *Banco de Guatemala*, in the Civic Centre on 7 Av, Zona 1 (Mon–Thurs 8.30am–2pm, Fri 8.30am–2.30pm) and *Lloyds Bank*, 8 Av 10–67, Zona 1 (Mon–Fri 9am–3pm). At *Credomatic*, in the gallery of shops next to the *Europa* bar on the corner of 5 Av and 11 C, you can get *Visa* and *Mastercard* cash advances (Mon–Fri 8.30am–7pm, Sat 9am–1pm); you'll need to show your passport. Back in Zona 1, on 7 Av between 12 and 13 calles, there's a legal **black market** which at times offers a better rate than the banks – although only for cash. Here you can also exchange other Central American currencies.

Books The best place for fiction in English and German is *Arnel*, a musty old bookshop in the basement of the Edificio El Centro on 9 C, corner of 8 Av, in Zona 1 – but it keeps irregular hours and seems to open briefly at around 3pm. *Librería del Peusativo*, 7 Av and 13 C, Edificio La Cúpula, Zona 9 (Mon–Fri 10am–7pm, Sat 10am–1.30pm) and *Geminis*, 6 Av 7–24, Zona 9. Otherwise the bookshops in Antigua are probably better. An impressive selection of secondhand English books can be bought from *Europa Bar*, and *El Establo* café, Av La Reforma 14–34, Zona 10.

Camera repairs *Foto Sittler*, 12 C 6–20, Zona 1, offer a three-month guarantee on their work, or *La Perla*, 9 C and 6 Av, Zona 1.

Car rental Renting a car in Guatemala is expensive and you should keep a sharp eye on the terms, particularly when it comes to insurance. All the companies listed below rent jeeps for a little under $100 a day, and also have slightly cheaper cars (for around $70) and minibuses. *Avis*, 12 C 2–73, Zona 9 (☎3312734; fax 3321263); *Ahorrent*, Bvd Liberacion 4–83, Zona 9 (☎3320544; fax 3320548); *Budget*, Av La Reforma 15–00, Zona 9 (☎3322591; fax 3312807); *Dollar*, Av La Reforma 6–14, Zona 9 (☎3348285; fax 3326745); *Hertz*, 7 Av 14–76, Zona 9 (☎3322242; fax 3317924); *National Car Rental*, 14 C 1–24, Zona 10 (☎3370221); *Rental*, 11 C 2–18, Zona 9 (☎3341416) – the only company to rent **motorbikes**; *Tabarini*, 2 C A 7–30, Zona 10 (☎3319814; fax 3341925); *Tally*, 7 Av 14–60, Zona 1 (☎2514113; fax 2329845); *Tikal*, 2 C 6–56, Zona 10 (☎3324721).

Dentist *Central Dentist de Especialistas*, 20 C 11–17, Zona 10 (☎3371773) is the best dental clinic in the country, and superb in emergencies. Prices are reasonable.

Doctors Your embassy should have a list of bilingual doctors, but for emergency medical assistance, there's the *Centro Medico*, a private hospital with 24-hour cover, at 6 Av 3–47, Zona 10 (☎3323555). They can also provide booster vaccinations.

Embassies Most of the embassies are in the southeastern quarter of the city, along Av La Reforma and Av las Americas, and they tend to open weekday mornings only. If the opening time isn't listed below then it might be worth phoning ahead. All embassies and consulates are listed in the blue pages of the phone book, which often also lists opening hours.

Argentina, 2 Av 11–04, Zona 10 (☎3326419; Mon–Fri 9am–1pm); *Belgium*, Av La Reforma 13–70, Zona 9 (☎3315608; Mon–Fri 9am–2pm); *Belize*, Av La Reforma, Edificio El Reforma 1–50, Zona 9, 8th Floor, Suite 803 (☎3345531); *Bolivia*, 7 Av 15–13, Zona 1 (☎2326156); *Brazil*, 18 C 2–22, Zona 14 (☎3370949; Mon–Fri 9am–1pm & 3–4pm); *Canada*, 13 C 8–44, Zona 10, Edificio Edyma Plaza (☎3336102; Mon–Thurs 8am–4.30pm, Fri 8am–1.3pm); *Chile*, 14 C 15–21, Zona 13 (☎3321149; Mon–Fri 8am–1pm); *Colombia*, 12 C 1–25, Zona 10 (☎3353602; Mon–Fri 8am–2pm); *Costa Rica*, Av La Reforma 8–60, 3rd floor, Zona 9 (☎ & fax 3320531; Mon–Fri 9am–3pm); *Denmark*, 7 Av 20–36, Zona 1 (☎2381091); *Ecuador*, 4 Av 15–67, Zona 14 (☎3372902; Mon–Fri 9am–5pm); *El Salvador*, 12 C 5–43, 7th floor, Zona 9 (☎3325848; Mon–Fri 8am–2pm); *France*, 16 C 4–53, 11th floor, Zona 10 (☎3373639; Mon–Fri 9am–1pm); *Honduras*, 15 C 3–20, Zona 10, 8th floor (☎3374344; Mon–Fri 8.30am–1.30pm); *Italy*, 5 Av 8–59, Zona 14 (☎3374578; Mon, Wed & Fri 8am–2.30pm, Tues & Thurs 8am–1.30pm & 3–6pm); *Mexico*, 15 C 3–20, Zona 10 (☎3337254; Mon–Fri 9am–1pm & 3–6pm); *Netherlands*, 12 C 7–56, 4th floor, Zona 9 (☎3313505); *Nicaragua*, 10 Av 14–72, Zona 10 (☎3680785); *Norway*, 6 Av 7–02, Zona 9 (☎3310064); *Panama*, 5 Av 15–45, Zona 10 (☎3337182; Mon–Fri 8.30am–1pm); *Peru*, 2 Av 9–42, Zona 9 (☎3318409; Mon–Fri 8.30am–1.30pm); *Spain*, 6 C 6–48, Zona 9 (☎3343726); *Sweden*, 8 Av 15–07, Zona 10 (☎3336536); *Switzerland*, 4 C 7–73, Zona 9 (☎3313726); *United Kingdom*, Torre II, 7 Av 5–10, 7th floor, Zona 4 (☎3321604; Mon–Thurs 9am–noon & 2–4pm, Fri 1.30–5pm); *United States*, Av La Reforma, 7–01, Zona 10 (☎3311541; Mon–Fri 8am–noon & 1–5pm); *Venezuela*, 8 C 0–56, Zona 9 (☎3316505; Mon–Fri 9am–3.30pm).

Emergencies Police ☎120, Fire ☎123.

Film Colour transparency and both colour and monochrome print film is easy to buy, though expensive. There are several camera shops on 6 Av in Zona 1.

Immigration Main immigration office (*Migración*) is at 41 C 17–36, Zona 8 (Mon–Fri 8am–4pm). Come here to extend your tourist card up to a maximum total of ninety days, or extend a visa for a month.

Language courses At least five different schools in Guatemala City teach Spanish; the best is probably the *IGA* (the Guatemalan American Institute) on Ruta 1 and Via 4, Zona 4. If you're coming specifically to learn Spanish, though, you're better off in Antigua.

Laundry Best is *Lavandería Obelisco*, Av La Reforma 16–30, next to *Samaritana* supermarket (Mon–Fri 8am–6.45pm, Sat 8am–5.30pm), which charges around $3 for wash and dry yourself. *Lavandería Internacional*, 18 C 11–12, Zona 1, is another good bet, although they may insist that you pay for a complete service including ironing. *Lavandería Pichola*, 18 C

11–60, Zona 1, is cheaper and more basic; or there's a do-it-yourself place at 4 Av 13–89, Zona 1, which costs much the same and takes a lot longer.

Libraries The best library for English books is in the *IGA*, the Guatemalan American Institute, at Ruta 1 and Via 4, Zona 4. There's also the national library in the Parque Central, another big library alongside the main branch of the *Banco de Guatemala*, and specialist collections at the Ixchel and Popol Vuh museums.

Newspapers Guatemalan newspapers are sold everywhere on the streets, but European ones are hard to come by. Copies of *Time, Newsweek* and *The Economist* are usually on sale in the main plaza, and the British Embassy usually has copies of the *Times, Independent* and *Guardian*. American papers are fairly readily available. The *Hotel Panamerican*, 9 C 5–63, Zona 1, and *El Dorado*, in Zona 4, both sell US papers, as do some of the street sellers in the centre. *Central American Report* is available from 9 C A 3–56, Zona 1.

Police Main police station is in a bizarre castle on the corner of 6 Av and 14 C, Zona 1. In an emergency dial ☎120.

Travel agents There are plenty in the centre and along Av La Reforma in Zonas 9 and 10. Flights to Petén can be booked through all of them. *Clarke Tours*, who run tours of the city and many parts of the country, 7 Av 6–54, Zona 4 (☎3310213; fax 3315919); *Discovery Tours*, 12 C 2–04, Zona 9 (☎3392281; fax 3392285); *Maya Expeditions*, 15 C 1–91, Zona 10 (☎3634955; fax 3634164); *Mesoamerica Explorers*, 7 Av 13–01, Zona 9 (☎3325045), who specialize in nature and archeological trips around Petén and Alta Verapaz, and *Tropical Tours*, 4 C 2–51, Zona 10 (☎3393662). For flight tours to Copán/Honduras as well as to Quiriguá, Caracol, Tikal, Ceibal, Yaxchilau, Zaculeu or Palenque, try *Jungle Flying*, Av Hincapié and 18 C, domestic airport, Hangar 21, Zona 13 (☎ & fax 3314995). Their speciality is day-trips to Copán/Honduras–excellent for those with little time but plenty of money (around $200 per person).

Credit cards Cash advances from *Credomatic*, 7 Av 6–26, Zona 1 (☎3318027; Mon–Fri 8am–7pm, Sat 9am–1pm).

Work Hard to come by; the best bet is teaching at one of the English schools, most of which are grouped on 10 and 18 calles in Zona 1.

MOVING ON FROM GUATEMALA CITY

During the day the #83 **bus** goes past the **airport**. Remember that there's a $10 (Q50) **departure tax** on all international flights, payable in either quetzales or dollars.

For the **domestic terminal** take the #65 bus from Zona 1, which heads south on 6 Av in Zona 9 and down Av Las Americas. Alight at the corner of 18 C, easily recognized by the large globe and sculpture of Christopher Columbus on your left. The easiest way to get to the airport, however, is by taxi (around $10 from Zona 1); if you're **leaving** for Petén you'll certainly want to do this as departures are mostly in the early morning, when the bus service is poor.

To get to the **Zona 4 bus terminal** from the centre of town, take any bus marked *terminal*: you'll find these heading south along 4 Av in Zona 1. From here second-class buses run to all parts of the country, with departures every minute of the day. If you're setting out to find a bus, remember that only some of them leave from the terminal itself, while others park in the streets around. There's no real pattern to this, but people are always keen to help, and if you look lost someone will eventually point you in the right direction.

At the corner of 18 C and 9 Av is the **eastern bus terminal**, from where pullman buses head to Puerto Barrios, Esquipulas and the Mexican border (via the Pacific coast); the surrounding streets are home to the offices of several bus companies, including *Monja Blanca* for Cobán, and *Fuente del Norte* who will take you to Petén and Puerto Barrios. For a rundown of bus companies, routes and frequencies, see the "Travel Details" at the end of this chapter.

AROUND GUATEMALA CITY

Leaving the capital in any direction you escape its atmosphere almost immediately. There are just two destinations suited to excursions from the city, while the rest of the surrounding hills are easily visited using other towns as a base.

To the south the main road runs to Escuintla and the Pacific coast, passing through a narrow valley that separates the cones of the Pacaya and Agua volcanoes. Out this way is **Lake Amatitlán**, a popular weekend resort just half an hour from the capital. A few kilometres to the south of the lake is the village of **San Vicente Pacaya**, from where you can climb Pacaya itself, one of Guatemala's three active cones and currently the most impressive, spouting a plume of lava.

To the northwest of the capital, the villages of **San Juan Sacatepéquez** and **San Pedro Sacatepéquez**, both have impressive markets. Further northwest are the ruins of **Mixco Viejo**, the ancient capital of the Pokoman Maya.

South of the city

Heading out through the southern suburbs, the **Pacific highway** runs past the clover-leaf junction at El Trébol and leaves the city through its industrial outskirts. The land to the south of the capital is earmarked for new housing projects, but as yet the skeletal ground plan has drawn only one or two takers, and elaborate advertising posters on empty lots sing the merits of suburban life. Further south lies the small town of **Villa Nueva**, a place a lot older than its name might suggest, and beyond this the valley starts to narrow, overshadowed by the volcanic cones of Agua and Pacaya.

Lake Amatitlán

A few kilometres east of the highway, **Lake Amatitlán** nestles at the base of the Pacaya volcano, encircled by forested hills. It's a superb setting, but one that's been sadly undermined by the abuses the lake has suffered at the hands of holidaymakers. In the not too distant past its delights were enjoyed by a handful of the elite, whose retreats dotted the shoreline, but since then the bungalows have proliferated at an astonishing rate, and the waters of the lake are grossly polluted. The wealthy have moved on, seeking their seclusion at Lake Atitlán, while here at Amatitlán the weekends bring buses from the capital every ten minutes or so, spewing out families who spend the day eating, drinking, barbecuing, boating and swimming. If you'd like to enjoy the view then come during the week, but if you want to watch Guatemalans at play drop by on a Sunday.

Where the road arrives on the lakeshore the beach is lined with grimy *comedores* and *tiendas*. Taking a **boat trip** across the lake is a popular pastime, as is a dip in the thermal baths that are said to cure rheumatism and arthritis. Considerably less healthy are the black waters of the lake, and although the brave (or foolhardy) still swim in them, the pools, where you can pay to take a dip in cleaner waters, are safer bets. High above the lake, to the north, is the **Parque de las Naciones Unidas** (the United Nations Park, formerly the Parque El Filón), reached from the lakeside by an Austrian-made bubble-lift that looks strangely out of place so far from the ski slopes. The trip up there, and the park itself, offer incredible views of the lake and the volcanic cones. The lift operates on Saturday and Sunday only, from 10am to 12.45pm.

A kilometre or so from the lake but closer to the highway is the village of **AMATITLÁN**, where you'll find restaurants and hotels, as well as a seventeenth-century church housing El Niño de Atocha, a saintly figure with reputedly miraculous powers.

Buses run from the capital to Lake Amatitlán every ten minutes or so, from 20 C and 3 Av in Zona 1 and returning from the plaza in Amatitlán and the lakeshore. The journey takes around 45 minutes.

The Pacaya volcano

Heading further down the valley towards the Pacific coast, a branch road leaves the main highway to the left (east), heading into the hills to the village of **SAN VICENTE PACAYA**. From here you can climb the **Pacaya volcano**, one of the smallest and most impressive of Guatemala's peaks. At a height of just 2250m Pacaya is the country's most dramatically active volcano, spitting out clouds of rock and ash. The current period of eruption began in 1965, although colonial records show that it was also active between 1565 and 1775. Today it certainly ranks as the most accessible and exciting volcano in Central America.

The route

Whether you decide to go with a guide or not, you'll follow the track from the main highway, winding up through lush coffee plantations and clouds of dust to the village. San Vicente itself is a fairly miserable place, but if you're planning to climb the cone and make it back down the same day then you might be able to find somewhere to stay. There's no hotel in the village and people don't seem particularly friendly, but it's worth asking around for a room anyway – if you don't succeed you can always try one of the villages higher up.

To climb the volcano you need to rejoin the dirt road (which actually bypasses San Vicente) and then turn left at the fork after 100m or so. You'll come to a second bedraggled village, **Concepción El Cedro**, where you want to keep straight on, walking up the track to the right of the church. This track heads around to the left as it leaves the village, and then climbs in a narrow rocky gully, coming out at the village of **San Francisco**, the last settlement and the highest

---

SAFETY ON THE PACAYA VOLCANO

Before setting out on the climb to the peak of Pacaya, you should bear in mind that the volcano has been the scene of a number of **attacks**, rapes, murders and robberies. The most serious incidents to date took place in early 1991, since when things have quietened down, although robberies are still regularly reported, and weekend tours now come complete with armed guards. While plenty of people climb the volcano without encountering any trouble, it is worth checking the current situation with the tourist office in Guatemala City or Antigua and having a look on Antigua noticeboards, where recent incidents are usually publicized. You might also think about climbing Pacaya with one of the teams of guides who operate out of Antigua, which does make it a lot safer (see p.95) – that said, even with a guide, safety is by no means guaranteed.

point accessible to motor vehicles. Here, about an hour from the start, you'll pass the last *tienda* and your last chance of finding a bed for the night – ask in the *tienda* and they'll point you towards someone with a room to rent.

From San Francisco the path is a little harder to follow, but it's only another couple of hours to the top. After you pass the *tienda* the path goes up to the right, beside an evangelical church, above which you need to head diagonally across the open grassland – bearing to the left. From this left-hand corner a clear-cut path heads on towards the cone, and where it first forks you should go left, along a path that climbs diagonally. After a while this meets a barbed-wire fence, where you turn sharply to the right and continue up through a thickish forest. From here you head straight on for a kilometre or so (moving diagonally across the hill) until the path goes over a hump, and then down the other side. On the second hump you turn to the left, onto a smaller path, which you follow up through the woods, scrambling up the slippery cinder until you reach the top.

Scrambling up through the forest you suddenly emerge on the lip of an exposed ridge from where you can see the cone in all its brutal glory. In front of you is a massive bowl of cooled lava, its fossilized currents flowing away to the right, and opposite is the cone itself, a jet black triangle that occasionally spouts molten rock and sulphurous fumes. From here you can head on around to the left, across lava fields and between the charred stumps of trees. The path runs around the lip of the bowl to a concrete post, and then up the side of the dormant cone, which is a terrifying but thrilling ascent, eventually bringing you face to face with the eruptions – hang back to watch them for a while beforehand to ensure that you won't be hit.

The best time to watch the eruptions is at night, when the sludge that the volcano spouts can be seen in its full glory as a plume of brilliant orange. But to see this you need either to camp out at one of several good sites near the top (tents can be rented from the *Casa Andinista* bookshop in Antigua) or to find somewhere to stay in one of the villages, which is possible but not that easy: you just have to ask around.

A **bus** leaves Guatemala City for Concepción daily at 7am, and returns from there at noon; a later service runs to San Francisco at 3.30pm, coming back at 5am the following day.

On towards the coast: Palín

Continuing towards the coast the main highway passes through **PALÍN**, where the road is lined with restaurants and *tiendas*. Palín was once famous for its weaving, but these days the only *huipiles* you'll see are the purples of Santa María de Jesus, to which the village is connected by a rough back road. The original Palín *huipiles* were particularly short, exposing the women's breasts when they raised their arms, and it's said that President Ubico, witnessing this when a woman tried to sell pineapples to his train, ordered that they be lengthened.

The best time to visit Palín is for its Wednesday market, which takes place under a magnificent ceiba tree in the plaza. Buses pass through every ten minutes or so, heading between the capital and the coast, so it's worth dropping in even if you just happen to be passing on a Wednesday morning. The name Palín derives from the word *palinha*, meaning water that holds itself erect, a reference to a nearby waterfall.

Northwest of the city

To the northwest of the capital lies a hilly area that, despite its proximity, is little tainted by the influence of the city. Here the hills are still covered by lush pine forests, and heading out this way you'll find a couple of interesting villages, both badly scarred by the 1976 earthquake but with markets well worth visiting. Further afield are the **Mixco Viejo** ruins, impeccably restored but seldom visited.

San Pedro Sacatepéquez and San Juan Sacatepéquez

Leaving the city to the northwest you travel out through the suburb of Florida. Once you escape the confines of the city the road starts to climb into the hills, through an area that's oddly uninhabited. To the south of the city the high ground has been colonized by the rich, but here there are only one or two mansions, lost in the forest.

The first of the two villages you come to is **SAN PEDRO SACATEPÉQUEZ**, where the impact of the earthquake is still painfully felt. The market here – which takes place on a Friday – is by some way the smaller of the two. Another six kilometres takes you over a ridge and into the village of **SAN JUAN SACATEPÉQUEZ**. As you approach, the road passes a number of makeshift greenhouses where flowers are grown: an industry that has become the local speciality. The first carnation was brought to Guatemala by Andrés Stombo some sixty years ago. He employed the three Churup brothers, all from San Juan, and seeing how easy it was they all set up on their own. Since then the business has flourished, and there are flowers everywhere in San Juan.

By far the best time to visit is for the Friday market, when the whole place springs into action and the village is packed. Keep an eye out for the *huipiles* worn in San Juan, which are unusual and impressive, with bold geometric designs of yellow, purple and green. **Buses** to both villages run every half-hour or so from the Zona 4 terminal in Guatemala City.

Mixco Viejo

Beyond San Juan the road divides, one branch heading north to El Chol and Rabinal (one bus a day takes this route, leaving the Zona 4 terminal in Guatemala City at 5am), the other branch going northwest towards **Mixco Viejo** and **Pachalum**. Heading out along this western route the scenery changes dramatically, leaving behind the pine forests and entering a huge dry valley. Small farms are scattered here and there and the *Politecnica*, Guatemala's military academy, is also out this way. Several hours beyond San Juan, in a massive valley, are the ruins of Mixco Viejo.

The ruins

MIXCO VIEJO was the capital of the Pokoman Maya, one of the main pre-conquest tribes. The original Pokoman language has all but died out – it's now spoken only in the villages of Mixco and Chinautla – and the bulk of their original territory is swamped by Cakchiquel speakers. The site itself is thought to date from the thirteenth century, and its construction, built to withstand siege, bears all the hallmarks of the troubled times before the arrival of the Spanish. Protected on all sides by deep ravines, it can be entered only along a single-file causeway. At the time the Spanish arrived, in 1525, this was one of the largest highland centres, with nine temples, two ball courts and a population of around nine thousand.

The Spanish historian Fuentes y Guzmán actually witnessed the conquest of the city, so for once there's a detailed account. At first Alvarado sent only a small force, but when this was unable to make any impact he launched an attack himself, using his Mexican allies, two hundred Indians from Tlaxcala. With a characteristic lack of subtlety he opted for a frontal assault, but his armies were attacked from behind by a force of Pokoman warriors who arrived from Chinautla. The battle was fought on an open plain in front of the city, and by sunset the Spanish cavalry had won the day, killing some two hundred Pokoman warriors, although the city remained impenetrable. According to Fuentes y Guzman the Pokoman survivors then pointed out a secret entrance to the city, allowing the Spanish to enter virtually unopposed and to unleash a massacre of its inhabitants. The survivors were resettled at a site on the edge of the city, in the village of Mixco Viejo, where Pokoman is still spoken.

Today the site has been delicately restored, with its plazas and temples laid out across several flat-topped ridges. Like all the highland sites the structures are fairly low – the largest temple reaches only about 10m in height – and devoid of decoration. It is, however, an interesting site in a spectacular setting, and during the week you'll probably have the ruins to yourself, which gives the place all the more atmosphere.

Getting there

Mixco Viejo is by no means an easy place to reach, and if you can muster enough people it's worth **renting a car** or trying to arrange for a travel agent to ferry you to and from the ruins. If you're determined to travel by bus there are several, leaving the Zona 4 terminal in Guatemala City before noon, and passing the site on their way to Pachalum. (Make sure that the one you take will pass *las ruinas*, as there are buses that go to the village without doing so.) If you opt to travel by bus then you'll have to stay overnight at the ruins unless you can be back at the road junction where the buses pass by at 2.30pm. You could try to hitch out again in the afternoon, but there's desperately little traffic except at weekends.

fiestas

Despite its modern appearance Guatemala City has some firmly established traditions, and accordingly one or two fiestas. Also listed below are some of those in the surrounding villages, which aren't necessarily covered in the text but may well be worth visiting if you're around at fiesta time.

JANUARY

The fiesta year around Guatemala City starts from the 1st to 4th in the village of **Fraijanes**, and there's also a moveable fiesta in **San Pedro Ayampuc** at some stage in the month.

MARCH

Villa Canales has its fiesta from the 6th to 14th, and **San Pedro Pinula** has its fiesta from the 16th to 20th, with the main day on the 19th. **San José del Golfo** has a fiesta from the 18th to 20th, with the main day on the 19th.

APRIL

The only April fiesta is in **Palencia**, from the 26th to 30th.

MAY

May 1, Labor Day, is marked in the capital by marches and protests, while the fiesta in

Amatitlán is from the 1st to 7th, with the main day on the 3rd.

JUNE
Again there's only one fiesta in this month, in **San Juan Sacatepéquez**, from the 22nd to 27th, with the main day on the 24th.

JULY
Palín has its fiesta from the 24th to 30th, a fairly traditional one which climaxes on the final day.

AUGUST
Mixco, an interesting Pokoman village on the western side of town, has its fiesta on the 4th,

while the main **Guatemala City** fiesta, involving all sorts of parades and marches, is on the 15th.

NOVEMBER
The end of the year sees very few fiestas in this part of the country but there is one in **San Catarina Pinula**, from the 20th to 28th, with the main day on the 25th.

DECEMBER
The year ends with a fiesta in **Chinautla**, from the 4th to 9th, with the main day on the 6th, and **Villa Nueva**, where they have a fiesta from the 6th to 11th, with the last day the main day.

travel details

Guatemala City is at the transport heart of the country and even the smallest of villages is connected to the capital. Hence there are literally thousands of buses into and out of the city. Most of these are covered in the "Travel Details" of other chapters; following are the main services.

BUSES
The main **bus companies**, their addresses and departure times are as follows.

The western highlands

San Marcos *Transportes Marquensita*, 21 C 12–41, Zona 1, runs direct pullmans (4.30am, 6.30am, 8.30am, 10am, 11am, noon, 1.30pm, 3.30pm & 5pm).

Antigua Every half-hour or so from 15 C between 3 and 4 avenidas in Zona 1 (every 30min; 6am–8pm).

Chichicastenango and Santa Cruz del Quiché Second-class buses leave from the Zona 4 terminal (every hour or so) .

Lake Atitlán and Panajachel *Transportes Rebuli* runs direct buses from 21 C 1–54, Zona 1 (hourly; 6am–4pm); or you can go to the Zona 4 terminal and board any bus going to the western highlands, and then change buses at the Los Encuentros junction.

Quezaltenango Several pullman companies run buses: *Lineas Americas*, 2 Av 18–74, Zona 1 (5.15am, 9am, 3.15pm, 4.40pm & 7.30pm); *Rutas Lima*, 8 C 3–63, Zona 1 (5.15am, 7.15am &

2.15pm). Avoid *Galgos* whose pullmans are on their last legs and who have had some horrific accidents recently.

Huehuetenango There are only a few regular pullman services, the best being *Los Halcones*, 7 Av 15–27, Zona 1 (7am & 2pm). *Rapidos Zaculeu*, 9 C11–42, Zona 1, also runs buses (6am & 3pm); *Transportes El Condor*, 2 Av and 19 C, Zona 1, runs second-class buses (4am, 8am, 1pm & 5pm).

Cobán and the Verapaces

Salama, Rabinal and Cubulco *Rutas Verapacenses*, 19 C and 9 Av, Zona 1, runs buses (hourly; 5.30am–4pm). Heading for Baja Verapaz from Cobán or Guatemala City, you can also take any bus between Cobán and the capital and get off at La Cumbre de Santa Elena, from where minibuses run to Salamá.

Cobán services, calling at all points between, including the Biotopo and Tactic, are run by *Transportes Escobar Monja Blanca*, 8 Av 15–16, Zona 1 (hourly; 4am–5pm; in Cobán at 4 Av and 0 C). If they're full try *Express Verapax* across the road.

The Pacific coast and the Mexican border

The bus service to this part of the country is one of the best, and most bus companies are also conveniently sited on the edge of Zona 1, outside the train station at the junction of 19 C and 9 Av. Buses to **Tecún Umán** and **Talisman** (hourly; 5am–5pm) pass through all main towns in the coastal region between Escuintla and the border, where you can change buses for smaller places off the main highway.

The Motagua Valley, the Caribbean and Petén

Buses for Petén are run by *Fuente del Norte*, 7 C 8–46, Zona 1 (☎2513817), close to the main area of budget hotels. There are three or four buses a day and you need to get a ticket in advance in either direction. A newer service (4pm, 6pm & 8pm), is operated by *Maya Express*, 17 C 9–36, Zona 1 (☎2321914).

Puerto Barrios, Zacapa, Chiquimula and Esquipulas Hourly buses, most of them pull-mans, leave from the train station terminal at 19 C and 9 Av in Zona 1. *Litegua* provide the best service to Puerto Barrios (hourly; 5.30am–5pm), while *Rutas Orientales* run buses to Esquipulas (hourly; 4am–6pm), calling at Zacapa and Chiquimula. There is also a private tourist shuttle-bus operating between the capital, Río Dulce and Puerto Barrios, which is faster, air-conditioned and not unreasonably expensive. Contact *Izabal Adventure Tours*, 7 Av 14–44, Zona 9, Edificio La Galeria, 2nd floor (☎3340323; fax 3343701).

The eastern highlands and San Salvador

For all towns between the capital and the border with El Salvador, second-class buses leave from the terminal in Zona 4. If you're heading across the border then several bus companies run a direct service to **San Salvador**: *Melva*, *Taca Internacional*, *Mermex*, *El Condor* and *Transcomer* are the main ones, all around the junction of 1 C and 4 Av, a block or so from the main Zona 4 terminal. Between them they offer an hourly service (5.30am–3.30pm; 8hr). Buses take you directly to the *Terminal Occidente* in San Salvador. To other parts of the eastern highlands there are regular departures from the Zona 4 terminal and to **Jalapa** (hourly; 4am–6pm) from 22 C 1–20, Zona 1.

To central American countries, except Belize

Tica Bus, 11 C 2–38, Zona 9 (☎3318996; Mon–Sat 8am–4pm, Sun 8am–2pm) has daily departures at 12.30pm to Panama City, via San Salvador, Tegucigalpa, Managua and San José. The whole trip takes three days and two nights, the first night spent in Salvador, the second in Managua.

PLANES

There are frequent **international flights** from Guatemala City's Aurora airport to Mexico, Central America and North America, and four daily flights to **Flores** in Petén. Three of these leave at around 7am, and one at about 4pm. Tickets can be bought from virtually any travel agent in the capital (see p.68). It's a 50min flight, and return tickets cost around $110.

TRAINS

There are no longer any passenger trains.

CHAPTER TWO

THE WESTERN HIGHLANDS

Guatemala's **western highlands**, stretching from Guatemala City to the Mexican border, are perhaps the most fascinating and beautiful part of the entire country. The area is defined by two main features: the string of volcanoes that runs along the southern side, and the mountain ranges that mark out the northern boundary. The greatest of these are the **Cuchumatanes**, whose granite peaks rise to some 3600m. Strung between the two is a series of spectacular, twisting ridges, lakes, sweeping bowls, forests, gushing streams and deep valleys.

It's an astounding, brooding landscape blessed with tremendous fertility but cursed by instability. The hills are regularly shaken by earthquakes and occasionally showered by volcanic eruptions. Of the thirteen cones that run through the western highlands, three are still active: **Pacaya**, **Fuego** and **Santiaguito**, all oozing plumes of sulphurous smoke and occasionally throwing up clouds of molten rock. Two major **fault lines** also cut through the area, making earthquakes a regular occurrence. The most recent major quake was centred around **Chimaltenango** in 1976 – it left 25,000 dead and around a million homeless. But despite its sporadic ferocity the landscape is outstandingly beautiful and the atmosphere is calm and welcoming, with irrigated valleys and terraced hillsides carefully crafted to yield the maximum potential farmland.

The highland landscape is controlled by many factors, all of which affect its appearance. Perhaps the most important is **altitude**. At lower levels the vegetation is almost tropical, supporting dense forests, **coffee**, **cotton**, **bananas** and **cacao**, while higher up the hills are often wrapped in cloud and the ground is sometimes hard with frost. Here trees are stunted by the cold, and maize and potatoes are grown alongside grazing herds of sheep and goats. The seasons also play their part. In the rainy season, from May to October, the land is superbly green, with young crops and lush forests of **pine**, **cedar** and **oak**, while during the dry winter months the hillsides gradually turn to a dusty yellow.

The Indian highlands

The western highlands are home to a substantial percentage of Guatemala's population, of whom the vast majority are Maya Indians. Their life and culture are strongly separate from the world of *Ladinos*, and their history is bound up with the land on which they live. In the days of Classic Maya civilization (300–900 AD) the western highlands were a peripheral area, with the great developments taking place in the lowlands to the north. Apart from the city of **Kaminaljuyú**, on the site of modern Guatemala City, little is known about the highlands at this time, and there are no archeological remains that date from the Classic period.

Towards the end of the eleventh century the area was colonized by **Toltec Maya**, who moved south from what is now central Mexico and conquered the Maya of the western highlands, installing themselves as an elite ruling class. Under Toltec rule a number of rival empires emerged, each speaking a separate language and based around a ceremonial centre. (For a detailed rundown of the different groups, see *Contexts*.)

Even today the highlands are divided up along traditional tribal lines. The **Quiché language** is spoken by the largest number, centred on the town of Santa Cruz del Quiché and reaching into the Quezaltenango valley. The highlands around Huehuetenango are **Mam-speaking**, the **Tzutujil** occupy the southern shores of Lake Atitlán, and the **Cakchiquel** are to the east. **Smaller tribal groups**, such as the Ixil and the Aguateca, also occupy clearly defined areas in the Cuchumatan mountains, where the language and costume are distinct.

The Spanish highlands

Though pre-conquest life was certainly hard, the **arrival of the Spanish** was a total disaster for the Maya population. In the early stages Alvarado and his army met with a force of Quiché warriors in the Quezaltenango basin and defeated them in open warfare. The defeated Quiché took the Spanish to their capital, Utatlán, hoping to negotiate some kind of deal. Alvarado, however, was not to be seduced by such subtlety and promptly burnt the city along with many of its inhabitants. The next move was made by the Cakchiquel, who formed an alliance with the Spanish, hoping to exploit the newcomers' military might to overcome former rivals. As a result the Spanish made their first permanent base at the site of the Cakchiquel capital Iximché. But in 1527 the Cakchiquel, provoked by demands for tribute, rose up against the Spanish and fled to the mountains, from where they waged a campaign of guerrilla war against their former allies. The Spanish then moved their capital into the Almolonga valley, to a site near the modern town of Antigua, from where they gradually brought the rest of the highlands under a degree of control.

However, the damage done by Spanish swords was nothing when compared to that of the **diseases** they introduced. Waves of smallpox, typhus, plague and measles swept through the indigenous population, reducing their numbers by as much as 90 percent in the worst hit areas. The population was so badly devastated that it only started to recover at the end of the seventeenth century, and didn't get back to pre-conquest levels until the middle of the twentieth century.

In the long term the **Spanish administration** of the western highlands was no gentler than the Conquest, as Indian labour became the backbone of the Spanish empire. Guatemala offered little of the gold and silver that was available in Peru or Mexico, but there was still money to be made from **cacao** and **indigo**. Maya labourers were forced to travel to the Pacific coast to work the plantations, while priests moved them from their scattered homes into new villages and attempted to transform them into devout Catholics. At the heart of all this was the colonial capital of **Antigua**, then known as Santiago de los Caballeros, from where the whole of Central America and Chiapas (now in Mexico) was administered. In 1773 the city was destroyed by a massive earthquake, and the capital was subsequently moved to its modern site.

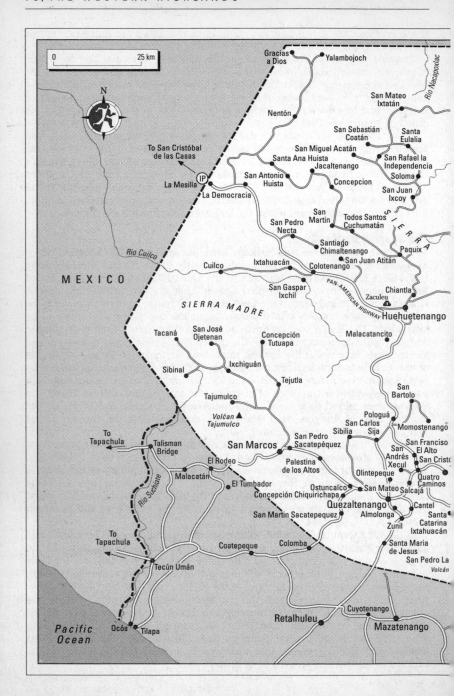

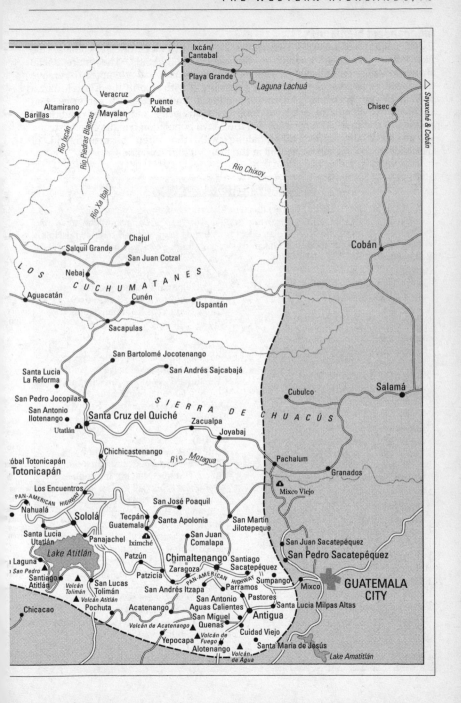

Independent highlands

By the time the Spanish left Guatemala, in 1821, three centuries of colonial rule had left a permanent imprint on the western highlands. The entire social structure had been radically transformed. The Spanish had attempted to remove the power of large regional centres, replacing it with that of the Church, but a lack of clergy, particularly in the seventeenth and eighteenth centuries, had enabled the villages to establish their own authority and allowed traditional religion to continue. As a result of this the Maya population had developed strong village-based allegiances: these, along with the often bizarre hybrid of Catholicism and paganism, are still at the heart of highland life.

MARKET DAYS

Throughout the western highlands **weekly markets** are the main focus of economic and social activity, drawing people from the area around the town or village where they're held. Make an effort to catch as many market days as possible – they're second only to local fiestas in offering a glimpse of a way of life unchanged for centuries.

Monday
Antigua; Chimaltenango; Santa Barbara; San Juan Atitán; Zunil.

Tuesday
Acatenango; Comalapa; Chajul; El Tejar; Olintepeque; Patzún; Salcajá; San Andrés Semetabaj; San Antonio Ilotenango; San Lucas Toliman; San Marcos; San Pedro Jocopilas; Totonicapán; Yepocapa.

Wednesday
Almolonga; Chimaltenango; Colotenango; Cotzal; Huehuetenango; Momostenango; Palestina de Los Altos; Patzicia; Sacapulas; San Sebastián.

Thursday
Aguacatán; Antigua; Chichicastenango; Chimaltenango; El Tejar; Jacaltenango; La Libertad; Nebaj; Panajachel; Patulul; Patzite; Patzún; Sacapulas; San Juan Atitán; San Luis Jilotepeque; San Mateo Ixtatán; San Miguel Ixtahuacán; San Pedro Necta; San Pedro Pinula; San Pedro Sacatepéquez; San Rafael La Independencia; Santa Barbara; Santa Cruz del Quiché; Soloma; Tajamulco; Tecpán; Totonicapán; Uspantán; Zacualpa.

Friday
Chajul; Chimaltenango; Jocotenango; San Francisco el Alto; San Andrés Itzapa; San Lucas Toliman; Santiago Atitlán; Sololá; Tacaná.

Saturday
Antigua; Almolonga; Colotenango; Cotzal; Ixchiguan; Malacatán; Nentón; Palestina de los Altos; Patzicia; Santa Clara La Laguna; Santa Cruz del Quiché; Sumpango; Todos Santos; Totonicapán; Yepocapa.

Sunday
Acatenango; Aguacatán; Cantel; Chichicastenango; Chimaltenango; Cuilco; Huehuetenango; Jacaltenango; Joyabaj; La Libertad; Malacatancito; Momostenango; Nebaj; Nahualá; Ostuncalco; Patzite; Nentón; Panajachel; Parramos; Patzún; Sacapulas; San Bartolo; San Carlos Sija; San Cristóbal Totonicapán; San Juan Comalapa; San Luis Jilotepeque; San Martin Jilotepeque; San Mateo Ixtahuacán; San Miguel Acatán; San Miguel Ixtahuacán; San Pedro Necta; San Pedro Sacatepéquez; Santa Barbara; Santa Cruz del Quiché; Santa Eulalia; Sibilia; Soloma; Sumpango; Tacaná; Tecpán; Tejar; Tucuru; Uspantán; Yepocapa; Zacualpa.

At the village level **independence** brought little change. *Ladino* authority replaced that of the Spanish, but Indians were still required to work the coastal plantations and when labour supplies dropped off they were simply press-ganged (or more subtly lured into debt) and forced to work, often in horrific conditions. It's a state of affairs that has changed little even today, and remains a major burden on the Indian population.

In the last few decades fresh pressures have emerged as the Maya have been caught up in waves of political violence. In the late 1970s **guerrilla movements** began to develop in opposition to military rule, seeking support from the Indian population and establishing themselves in the western highlands, particularly the departments of Quiché, Huehuetenango, Sololá and Totonicapán. The Maya became the victims in this process, as they were caught between the guerrillas and the army. A total of 440 villages were destroyed; thousands died and thousands more fled the country, seeking refuge in Mexico. Indian communities have also been besieged in recent years by American **evangelical churches**, whose influence undermines local hierarchies and threatens to destroy indigenous culture.

Today the level of violence has dropped off significantly although the fighting is still dragging on in some remote areas. Despite intense pressure and bitter racism, **Maya Indian society** remains largely intact: traditional structures are still in place, local languages still spoken, and traditional costume still worn. It is this, above all else, that is Guatemala's most fascinating feature. Maya Indian society is inward-looking and conservative, operating, in the face of adversity, on its own terms. Rejecting *Ladino* commercialism, they see trade as a social function as much as an economic one. They live in a world centred on the village, with its own civil and religious hierarchy. Subsistence farming of maize and beans remains at its heart, and the land its life-blood. Today Guatemala's indigenous peoples are facing immense cultural and economic pressures, which may even come to threaten their survival; however, it is their culture, moulded by centuries of struggle, which shapes the western highlands and gives them a totally unique atmosphere.

Visiting Maya **villages** during the week you'll find them almost deserted – their permanent populations are generally small, though they may support five or ten times as many scattered rural homesteads. This wider populace is regularly brought together by markets and fiestas, and at such times the villages fill to bursting. This is when you can most clearly sense the values of the Indian world – in the subdued bustle of the market or the intense joy of celebration.

Where to go

Travelling in the western highlands you're spoilt for choice, with beautiful scenery and interesting villages at every turn. It's the villages that are the main attraction, but there are also **historical sites**: the pre-conquest cities of **Iximché**, **Utatlán** and **Zaculeu**, as well as the colonial ruins in **Antigua**, which is certainly the most impressive colonial city in Central America. The ancient cities don't bear comparison to Tikal and the lowland sites, but they're nevertheless fascinating in their own way.

The **Pan-American Highway** runs through the middle of the western highlands so it's easy enough to get around. There's a constant flow of buses along this main artery, some branching off along minor roads to more remote areas. Travelling in these can sometimes be a gruelling experience, particularly in northern Huehuetenango and Quiché, but the scenery makes it well worth the discomfort. The most practical plan of action is to base yourself in one of the larger places and then make a series of day trips to markets and fiestas, although even the smallest of villages will usually offer some kind of accommodation.

Travelling west from Guatemala City the first place of interest is **Antigua**, where it's easy to settle into the relaxed pace of things, visiting the surrounding villages, climbing the volcanoes, or taking in the colonial ruins. Further west is the department of **El Quiché**, with the famous market at **Chichicastenango** and the ruins of **Utatlán**, near the departmental capital of **Santa Cruz del Quiché**. To the south of Quiché, **Lake Atitlán** is the jewel of the western highlands, ringed by volcanoes and villages, and reached through **Sololá** and **Panajachel** – now a booming lakeside resort. To the north are the wildly beautiful peaks of the **Cuchumatanes**, between which are the towns of the **Ixil triangle**, in a superb world of their own. Heading on to the west you pass the strongly traditional town of **Nahualá** and go up over the mountains to **Quezaltenango**, Guatemala's second city, an ideal base for visiting local villages or climbing the **Santa María volcano**. Beyond this the border with Mexico is marked by the departments of **San Marcos** and **Huehuetenango**, both of which offer superb mountain scenery, dotted with isolated villages.

ANTIGUA AND AROUND

At the base of a broad U-shaped valley, suspended between the Agua, Acatenango and Fuego volcanoes, lies Guatemala's colonial capital, **ANTIGUA**. In its day this was one of the great cities of the Spanish empire, ranking alongside Lima and Mexico City and serving as the administrative centre for the entire *Audiencia de Guatemala*, which encompassed all of Central America and Chiapas.

Antigua was actually the third capital of Guatemala. The Spanish settled first at the site of **Iximché** in July 1524, so that they could keep a close eye on their Cakchiquel allies. In November 1527, when the Cakchiquel rose up in defiance of their new rulers, the capital was moved into the Almolonga valley, to the site of **Ciudad Vieja**, a few kilometres from Antigua. In 1541, however, shortly after the death of Alvarado, this entire town was lost beneath a massive mud slide. Only then did the capital come to rest in Antigua, known in those days as *La Muy Noble y Muy Leal Ciudad de Santiago de los Caballeros de Goathemala*. Here, despite the continued threat from the instability of the bedrock – the first earth-

---

TOURIST CRIME IN ANTIGUA AND LAKE ATITLÁN

While there is no need to be paranoid, visitors to the heavily touristed areas around Antigua and Lake Atitlán should be aware that **crime against tourists** – including robbery and rape – is a problem. Pay close attention to local security reports, and follow the usual precautions for your personal safety and belongings with extra care. In particular, avoid walking alone, especially at night or in isolated spots during the day, and be wary of strolling to popular viewing points such as the *cruce* in Antigua or on footpaths around the lake. Both are regularly the scene of armed attacks on tourists, involving robbery and sexual assault. If you do want to walk in the countryside, then head out into the more remote highlands, where such crimes are rare.

quake came after just twenty years – it settled and began to achieve astounding prosperity.

As the heart of colonial power in Central America, Antigua grew slowly but steadily. One by one the religious orders established themselves, competing in the construction of schools, churches, monasteries and hospitals. Bishops built grand palaces that were soon rivalled by the homes of local merchants and corrupt government officials. The city reached its peak in the middle of the eighteenth century, after the 1717 earthquake prompted an unprecedented building boom, and the population rose to around 50,000. By this stage Antigua was a genuinely impressive place, with a university, a printing press, a newspaper, and streets that were seething with commercial and political rivalries.

When the English friar Thomas Gage visited Antigua in 1627, he was shocked by the wickedness of Spain's empire:

> Great plenty and wealth hath made the inhabitants as proud and vicious as are those of Mexico. Here is not only idolatry, but fornication and uncleanliness as public as in any place of the Indies. The mulattoes, Blackamoors, mestizos, Indians, and all common sort of people are much made on by the greater and richer sort, and go as gallantly apparelled as do those of Mexico. They fear neither a volcano or mountain of water on the one side, which they confess hath once poured out a flood and river executing God's wrath against sin there committed, nor a volcano of fire, on the other side, roaring with and threatening to rain upon them Sodom's ruin and destruction.

But as is so often the case in Guatemala, **earthquakes** brought all of this to an abrupt end. For the best part of a year the city was shaken by tremors, with the final blows delivered by two severe shocks on September 7 and December 13, 1773. The damage was so bad that the decision was made to abandon the city in favour of the modern capital: fortunately, despite endless official decrees, there were many who refused to leave and Antigua was never completely deserted.

Since then the city has been gradually repopulated, particularly in the last hundred years or so. As Guatemala City has become increasingly congested, many of the conservative middle classes have moved to Antigua, where they've been joined by a large number of foreigners attracted by its relaxed and sophisticated atmosphere.

In recent years concern has mounted for the fate of the city's ancient architecture. Antigua was the first planned city in the Americas, originally built on a rigid grid pattern, with neatly cobbled streets and superb architecture. Of this, some now lies in shattered ruins, some is steadily decaying, and yet more is impeccably restored or relandscaped. Local laws protect the streets from the intrusion of overhanging signs, and every effort is made to re-create the architectural splendour of the past.

Antigua

Once regarded as the cultural and religious centre of the country, these days **ANTIGUA** is a haven of tranquillity. Offering a welcome break from the unrelenting energy of the capital, it has become the country's foremost tourist destination, the great meeting and resting place for travellers in Central America, where you're sure to bump into someone you met in a bar in Mexico City or on a beach

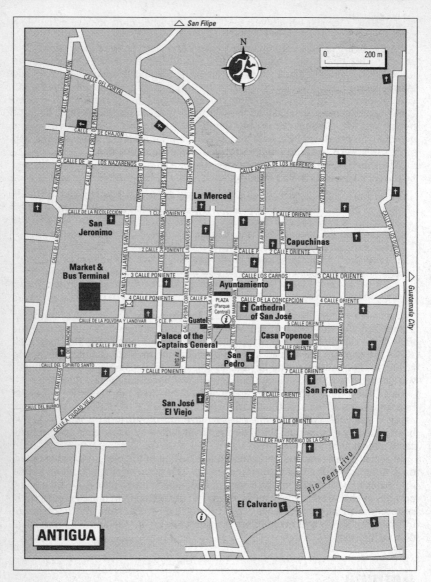

ANTIGUA

in El Salvador. Apart from the good food and relaxed lifestyle, the city's main attraction is its **language schools**, some of the best and cheapest in all Latin America, drawing students from around the globe. The expats, including English, Italians, Americans, Colombians, Swiss and Germans, contribute to the town's cosmopolitan air, mingling with locals selling their wares in the streets and the middle-class Guatemalans who come here at weekends to eat, drink and enjoy themselves. The downside of this settled, comfortable affluence is perhaps a loss of vitality – it's a great place to wind down and eat well for a few days if you've been travelling hard, but after a while it can come to seem too smug. Still, it's certainly somewhere you should visit, and the surrounding **countryside** is superbly beautiful – though do take into account our warnings about the increase in **crimes against tourists** on p.82.

Arrival and orientation

Antigua is laid out on the traditional grid system, with avenidas running north–south, and calles east–west. Each street is numbered and has two halves, either a north and south (*norte/sur*) or an east and west (*oriente/poniente*), with the plaza, the **Parque Central**, regarded as the centre. To complicate matters the old names for some streets have been revived and are occasionally used instead of the number system. The town is small, and it's all a lot simpler than it sounds; if you get confused, remember that the Agua volcano, the one that hangs most immediately over the town, is to the south. The only problem with finding your way around is that overhanging signs are outlawed in a bid to preserve the colonial ambience, so specific places can be a little hard to locate.

Arriving by bus, whether from Guatemala City or Chimaltenango, you'll end up in the main **bus terminal**, a large open space behind the market, three long blocks to the west of the plaza. To get to the centre of town, cross the broad tree-lined street outside the terminal and walk straight up the street opposite, which will bring you into the plaza.

Information

The **tourist office** (daily 8am–noon & 2–6pm) on the south side of the plaza dispenses reasonable if overcautious information. Benjamen Garcia Lopez, who

---

BUSES

The bus terminal is beside the market at the western end of 4 C Poniente (also known as C del Ayuntamiento). The main bus schedule is as follows:

To Guatemala City (45min) buses leave every fifteen minutes or so from 3am to 7pm, except on Sunday, when the first one leaves at 6am.

To Chimaltenango (50min) every twenty minutes from 5am to 7pm.

To Escuintla (via El Rodeo) 7am and 12.30pm.

To Yepocapa and **Acatenango** buses leave in the late afternoon, around 3 or 4pm.

Local buses, to the villages within the valley, also leave from the terminal. The times are listed in the relevant sections below.

The shuttle

Bus services between Antigua, Guatemala City, Panajachel and Chichicastenango are supplemented by several "tourist shuttle" services, the best of which is run by the *Turansa* travel agency. Although a lot more expensive than the bus, the shuttle does travel direct. It runs twice daily to the airport, leaving Antigua at 4.30am and 3pm, returning at around 8am and 5pm. The service to Panajachel is less frequent. Details are widely published in Antigua but for more information contact *Turansa*, 5 Av Norte 17 (☎8322928).

heads the team, speaks good English and, having worked in the office for thirty years, knows the area extremely well. The most comprehensive and up-to-date **guidebook** to Antigua and the surrounding area is *Antigua For You*, by Barbara Balchin De Koose, which gives detailed information on the town's history and colonial ruins. If you can't get hold of that, then *Antigua Guatemala* by Trevor Long and Elizabeth Bell ranks alongside it. Both are available from bookshops in town (see p.98). Though **guides** of the human variety are often to be found in the plaza, hustling for business, it's better to ask the tourist office to recommend someone.

Noticeboards in various popular tourist venues advertise everything from private language tuition to apartments, flights home and shared rides. Probably the most read are at *Doña Luisa's* restaurant, 4 C Oriente 12; *Casa Andinista*, 4 C Oriente 5A, and *Rainbow Reading Room*, 7 Av Sur 8. It's also a good idea to drop into the Antigua branch of the American organization *Amerispan*, 6 Av Norte 40 (☎ & fax 8320164). Predominantly geared towards fixing students up at language schools (see p.92), this is a great resource centre with good maps and general information; you can also use their **phone** and **fax**.

For other telecommunication services, including **e-mail**, try *Maya Communications*, *Hotel San Francisco*, 1 Av Sur 15 (24hr); at *Conexion*, 5 C Poniente 11B (☎3323316; fax 3320602) you can type out your fax beforehand. Also worth checking is *Eco-Intertel*, 5 Av Norte 30 (☎ & fax 8322440). The **Guatel** office is in the corner of the plaza at the junction of 5 Av Sur and 5 C Poniente (daily 7am–10pm).

Accommodation

Hotels in Antigua are in plentiful supply, although like everything else they can be a bit hard to find due to the absence of overhanging signs; and be warned that rooms get scarce (and prices increase) around Holy Week (see p.88). Would-be guides often hassle arriving bus passengers with offers to take you to a hotel (or language school) and at busy times it can be worth taking one of them up – you can always move later. The **luxury hotels** listed below start at around $80 for a double room – at the opposite end of the scale the **cheapest place in town**, basic but clean, is the unmarked guest house at 6 C Poniente 48 (①–②).

Luxury hotels

Hotel Antigua, 8 C Poniente 1, 5 Av Sur (☎8320288; fax 8320807). Antigua's oldest and finest luxury hotel. Tasteful colonial decor with a ruined church practically on the premises; a pool, excellent restaurant, beautiful gardens – and pleasant rooms with open fires to ward off the chill of the night. ⑦.

ACCOMMODATION PRICE CODES

All accommodation reviewed in the Guatemala section of this guide has been graded according to the following **price scales**. These refer to the cost of a double room in US$. For more details see p.28.

① Under $2	③ $5–10	⑥ $35–55
② $2–5	④ $10–20	⑦ Over $55
	⑤ $20–35	

Casa Santa Domingo, 3 C Oriente 28 (☎8320140; fax 8320102). Colonial convent, converted to a hotel and restaurant at a cost of several million dollars. There's no lack of luxury and the entire place has the air of a colonial museum. Certainly the town's most unusual and luxurious hotel. ⑦.

Hotel Posada de Don Rodrigo, C del Arco, 5 Av Norte 17 (☎8320291). In the same league as the *Hotel Antigua*, this well-established classic Antiguan hotel has rooms set around courtyards, a good restaurant, daily marimba music and two beautiful macaws. The central location means it tends to get swamped by day-trippers, though. ⑦.

Quinta Maconda, 5 Av Norte 11 (☎ & fax 8320821). Immaculate colonial house with just three guest rooms, each unique and with its own fireplace. Undoubtedly the most exclusive and heavenly place to stay. Worth every dollar if you can afford it. ⑦.

Hotel Ramada, 9 C, south of town on the road to Ciudad Vieja (☎8320011; fax 8320237). Although it looks like an army base from the outside, this large concrete structure holds 119 rooms with every luxury, including two tennis courts, a pool and a disco. ⑦.

Other accommodation

Albergue Andinista, 6 Av Norte 34 (☎ & fax 8323343). Secure rooms and apartments; luggage storage, plus volcano tours run by Guatemala's most experienced volcano guide (see p.95). ③.

Pensión El Arco, 5 Av Norte 51. Pleasant, friendly and clean. ②–③.

Hotel Aurora, 4 C Oriente 16 (☎ & fax 8320217). Attractive colonial building with rooms set around a lovely courtyard; good breakfasts. ⑤.

El Carmen, 3 Av Norte 9 (☎8323850). The most comfortable and best equipped hotel in town at this price. Rates include continental breakfast, and there's an international phone and fax service. ⑥.

Casa de los Càntaros, 5 Av Sur 5 (☎8320674; fax 8320609). American-owned colonial house with modern conveniences, including library and TV room. ⑤.

La Casa de Santa Lucía, Alameda Santa Lucía 5. Gorgeous small place, built in dark wood around a leafy courtyard. Not only very safe and spotless but also has hot showers and some private bathrooms. You'll have to ring the bell to get in; guests are given a key. ③.

Hotel Casa Santiago de los Caballeros, 7 Av Norte 67 (☎8320465; fax 8325858). Restored colonial mansion, very peaceful. ④.

Hotel del Centro, 4 C Poniente 22 (☎8320657). Bright new hotel, a little overpriced. ④.

Hotel Confort, 1 Av Norte 2 (☎8320566). Family-run guest house with pleasant garden. No private baths. ④.

Hotel de Cortez y Larraz, 6 Av Sur 3 (☎8230276). Very decent choice for the price. Clean and friendly. ③.

Hotel Cristal, Av del Desengano 25. Good value family-run hotel with pleasant balcony around flowering courtyard. Hot water and use of kitchen included. Only drawback is its site on the main road out of town: the noise doesn't penetrate to the back rooms as much, but the whole building shakes as buses thunder past – not the place to stay if you're worried about earthquakes. ②–③.

Hotel Convento Santa Catalina, 5 Av Norte 28 (☎8323080; fax 8323079). Scruffy rooms, made up for by the beautiful courtyard. Neighbouring bar means it can be noisy. ④.

Hotel El Descanso, 5 Av Norte, just off the plaza (☎8320142). Very central, clean and comfortable, with a rooftop terrace. ④.

Posada de Doña Angelina, 4 C Poniente 33. Newish and pleasant sort of place, large and a little chilly. Some rooms with private bathroom. ②–③.

Posada Doña Marta, 7 Av Norte 100 (☎8320261). Very secure, with clean rooms and good views from the first floor. ④–⑤.

Posada La Merced, 7 Av Norte 43A (☎8323197). A touch grubby, but very quiet. ③.

Mesón Panza Verde, 5 Av Sur 19 (☎ & fax 8322925). Small, quality hotel in a colonial-style building that specializes in personal service and top class meals in its restaurant. In the

SEMANA SANTA IN ANTIGUA

Antigua's **Semana Santa (Holy Week) celebrations** are perhaps the most extravagant and impressive in all Latin America. The celebrations start with a procession on Palm Sunday, representing Christ's entry into Jerusalem, and continue through to the really big processions and pageants on Good Friday. On Thursday night the streets are carpeted with carefully drawn patterns of coloured sawdust, and on Friday morning a series of processions re-enact the progress of Christ to the cross. Setting out from La Merced (the most spectacular), Escuela de Cristo and the village of San Felipe, teams of penitents wearing peaked hoods and accompanied by solemn dirges and clouds of incense carry images of Christ and the Cross on massive platforms. The pageants set off at around at 8am, the penitents dressed in either white or purple. After 3pm, the hour of the Crucifixion, they change into black.

It is a great honour to be involved in the procession, but no easy task as the great cedar block carried from La Merced weighs some 3.5 tons, requiring eighty men to lift it. Some of the images displayed date from the seventeenth century and the procession itself is thought to have been introduced by Alvarado in the early years of the Conquest, imported directly from Spain.

Check the exact details of events with the tourist office. During Holy Week hotels in Antigua are often full, and the entire town is always packed on Good Friday. But even if you have to make the trip from Guatemala City or Panajachel, it's well worth being in Antigua for Good Friday.

southern quarter of town, away from the main tourist drag, you can be sure of peace and quiet. Excellent value. ⑤.

Hotel El Pasaje, Alameda Santa Lucía 3. A touch chaotic, but friendly and cheap, with a laundry and hot water; 1am curfew. ②.

Hotel Placido, 3 C Poniente 33. Small, quiet budget hotel run by Doña Esmeralda, who managed the *Cristal* for many years. No private baths. ②.

El Refugio, 4 C Poniente, just across from the bus terminal. Vast, laid-back place with a variety of rooms; avoid the ones out the back – "decency" is included in the price of a room. Strict 1am curfew, after which you sleep in the plaza. ②–③.

Hotel San Francisco, 1 Av Sur 15 (☎8323383). Simple budget hotel on the eastern edge of the town centre. ③.

Posada San Sebastian, 3 Av Norte 4 (☎ & fax 8322621). A very strange combination of antique shop and guest house, very conveniently located. ④.

Posada San Vincente, 6 Av Sur 6 (☎8323311). Friendly guest house in a quiet part of town, away from the main tourist bustle. ④.

La Tatuana, 6 Av Sur 3 (☎8320537). Quiet, beautifully decorated small hotel, with rooms (private bath) opening onto a little courtyard. Good, fresh coffee always available. ④.

The City

In accordance with its position as the seat of colonial authority in Central America, Antigua was once a centre of secular and religious power, trade, and above all wealth. Here the great institutions competed with the government to build the country's most impressive buildings. Churches, monasteries, schools, hospitals and grand family homes were spread throughout the city, all with tremendously thick walls to resist earthquakes. Today Antigua has an incredible number of ruined and restored **colonial buildings**, and although these constitute only a fraction of the city's original architectural splendour, they do give an idea of its former extravagance. Mentioned below are only some of the remaining examples; armed with a map from the tourist office you could spend days exploring the ruins (most charge a small entrance fee). However, the prospect of visiting the lot can seem overwhelming; if you'd rather just see the gems, make La Merced, Las Capuchinas, Casa Popenoe and San Francisco your targets.

The Parque Central
As always the focus of the colonial city was its central plaza, the **Parque Central**. Old prints show it as an open expanse of earth, which in the rainy season turned into a sea of mud. For centuries it served as the hub of the city, bustling with constant activity: a huge market spilled out across it, cleared only for bullfights, military parades, floggings and public hangings. The calm of today's tree-lined Parque Central is relatively recent, and the fountain, originally set to one side so as not to interfere with the action, was moved to the centre in 1936.

The most imposing of the surrounding structures is the **Cathedral of San José**, on the eastern side. The first cathedral was begun in 1545, using some of the vast fortune left by Alvarado's death. However, the execution was so poor that the structure was in a constant state of disrepair, and an earthquake in 1583 brought down much of the roof. In 1670 it was decided to start on a new cathedral worthy of the town's role as a capital city. For eleven years the town watched, the Indians laboured and the most spectacular colonial building in Central America took shape. The scale of the new cathedral was astounding: a vast dome, five naves, eighteen chapels, and a central chamber measuring 90m by 20m. Its altar was inlaid with mother-of-pearl, ivory and silver, and carvings of saints and paintings by the most revered of European and colonial artists covered the walls.

The new cathedral was strong enough to withstand the earthquakes of 1689 and 1717, but its walls were weakened and the 1773 earthquake brought them crashing to the ground. Today, two of the chapels have been restored as the **Church of San José**, which opens off the Parque Central, and inside it is a figure of Christ by the colonial sculptor Quirio Cataño, who also carved the famous Black Christ of Esquipulas (see p.232). Behind the church, entered from 5 C Oriente, are the remains of the rest of the structure, a mass of fallen masonry, rotting beams, broken arches and hefty pillars, cracked and moss-covered. Buried beneath the floor are some of the great names of the Conquest, including Alvarado, his wife Beatriz de la Cueva, Bishop Marroquín and the historian Bernal Díaz del Castillo.

Along the entire south side of the Parque Central runs the squat two-storey facade of the **Palace of the Captains General**, with a row of 27 arches along each floor. It was originally built in 1558, but as usual this first version was destroyed by earthquakes and in 1761 it was rebuilt, only to be damaged again in 1773, and finally restored along the lines of the present structure. The palace was home to the colonial rulers and also housed the barracks of the dragoons, the stables, the royal mint, law courts, tax offices, great ballrooms, a large bureaucracy, and a lot more besides. Today it contains the local government offices, the headquarters of the Sacatepéquez police department and the tourist office.

Directly opposite, on the north side of the plaza, is the **Ayuntamiento**, the city hall, also known as the *Casa del Cabildo* or town house. Dating from 1740, its metre-thick walls balance the solid style of the Palace of the Captains General.

Unlike most others this building survived earlier rumblings and wasn't damaged until the 1976 earthquake, although it has been repaired since. The city hall was abandoned in 1779 when the capital moved to its modern site, but it later housed the police headquarters; now that they've moved across the plaza the building is again used by the city's administration.

The Ayuntamiento also holds a couple of museums. The first of these is the **Museo de Santiago** (Tues–Fri 9am–4pm, Sat & Sun 9am–noon & 2–4pm), which holds a collection of colonial artefacts, including bits of pottery, a sword said to have been used by Alvarado, some traditional Maya weapons, portraits of stern-faced colonial figures, and some paintings of warfare between the Spanish and the Maya. At the back of the museum is the old city jail, beside which there was a small chapel where condemned prisoners passed their last moments before being hauled off to the gallows in the plaza. Also under the arches of the city hall is the **Museo del Libro Antigua** (hours as above), in the rooms that held the first printing press in Central America. This arrived here in 1660, from Puebla de los Angeles in Mexico, and churned out the first book three years later. A replica of the press is on display alongside some copies of the works produced on it.

South and east of the plaza

Across the street from the ruined cathedral, in 5 C Oriente (Calle de La Universidad), is the **Seminario Tridentino**, one of the great colonial schools. It was founded at the start of the seventeenth century for some fifteen students, and later expanded to include the Escuela de Guadalupe, a special school for Maya Indians of high birth, so that local people could share in the joys of theology. The structure is still in almost perfect condition, but it's now divided up into several separate homes, so the elaborate stucco doorway is all you'll get to see.

A little further up the same street is the **University of San Carlos Borromeo**, which now houses the **Museo de Arte Colonial** (Tues–Fri 9am–4pm). The founding of a university was first proposed by Bishop Marroquín in 1559, but met with little enthusiasm as the Jesuits, Dominicans and Franciscans couldn't bear the thought of a rival to their own colleges. It wasn't until 1676 that the plan was authorized, using money left by the Bishop, and classes began in 1681 with seventy students applying themselves to everything from law to the Cakchiquel language. For a while only pure-blooded Castilians were admitted, but entry requirements were later changed to include a broader spectrum of the population. After the 1751 earthquake the university's original building was beyond repair and the rector of the Seminary donated the house next door to his own. Since then the university has moved to Guatemala City, and in 1832 this building became a grammar school, and then, in 1936, a museum. The deep-set windows and beautifully ornate cloisters make it one of the finest architectural survivors in Antigua. The museum contains a collection of dark and brooding religious art, sculpture, furniture, murals depicting life on the colonial campus, and a seventeenth-century map of Antigua by the historian Antonio de Fuentes y Guzmán.

Further up 5 C Oriente, between 1 and 2 avenidas, is the house that once belonged to **Bernal Díaz del Castillo**, one of the soldiers who served under Alvarado in Mexico and Guatemala and, in his later years, wrote an account of the Conquest. Just around the corner, on 1 Av Sur, is the **Casa Popenoe** (Mon–Sat 2–4pm), a superbly restored colonial mansion, which is not only a welcome break from church ruins, but also an interesting insight into domestic life in colonial times. The house, set around a gorgeous courtyard, was originally built in 1634 by the Spaniard Don Luis de las Infantes Mendoza, who came to Antigua to act as the supreme court judge. Needless to say it was badly damaged over the years and eventually abandoned, until its comprehensive restoration in 1932 by Doctor Wilson Popenoe, a United Fruit company scientist. Dr Popenoe and his wife Dorothy painstakingly sifted through the rubble and, piece by piece, restored the building to its former glory, filling it with an incredible collection of colonial furniture and art. Among the paintings are portraits of Bishop Marroquín and the fierce-looking Alvarado himself. Every last detail has been authentically restored, down to the original leather lampshades painted with religious musical scores and the great wooden beds decorated with a mass of accomplished carving. The kitchen and servants' quarters have also been carefully renovated, and you can see the bread ovens, the herb garden and the pigeon loft, which would have provided the original occupants with their mail service. Dr Popenoe died in 1972, but two of his daughters still live in the house.

A block to the south, on 6 C Oriente, two churches face each other at opposite ends of a tree-lined plaza. At the western end is the **San Pedro Church** and hospital. Originally built in 1680, and periodically crammed full of earthquake victims, the church was finally evacuated in 1976 when one of the aftershocks threatened to bring down the roof. Reconstruction was completed in 1991 and the facade now has a polished perfection that's strangely incongruous in Antigua. At the other end of the plaza is the convent and church of **Santa Clara** founded in 1699 by nuns from Puebla in Mexico. In colonial times this became a popular place for well-to-do young ladies to take the veil, as the hardships were none too hard, and the nuns earned a reputation for their cooking, selling their bread to the aristocracy. The huge original convent was totally destroyed in 1717, as was the second in 1773, but the current building was spared in 1976 and its ornate facade remains intact.

Walking around the front of the church down 2 Av Sur and then left, along 7 C Oriente, you arrive at **San Francisco** (daily 8am–6pm), one of the few churches to have come back into service. The latest phase of its reconstruction, recently completed, began in 1960 and is still the subject of much controversy. The nave has been restored in its entirety, but the ornate mouldings and sculpture have been left off, so although you get a rough idea of its former splendour, it would actually have been considerably more decorative. One of the oldest churches in Antigua, the earliest building on this site was begun in 1579 by the Franciscans, the first religious order to arrive in the city. It grew into a vast religious and cultural centre that included a school, a hospital, music rooms, a printing press and a monastery, covering four blocks in all. All of this, though, was lost in the 1773 earthquake. The **ruins** of the monastery, which are among the most impressive in Antigua, are open daily from 8am to 6pm.

Inside the church are buried the remains of **Hermano Pedro de Betancourt** (a Franciscan from the Canary Islands who founded the Hospital of Belén in Antigua), and pilgrims from all over Central America come here to ask for the benefit of his powers of miraculous intervention. Hundreds of little plaques and photographs, as well as a handful of disused crutches, all clustered around the shrine, give thanks for miracles performed. Hermano Pedro's remains have been moved around several times over the years, most recently in October 1990, some 323 years after his death, when he was put into a newly built Chapel of the True Cross, on the north side of the altar. Across the nave, on the south side of the

STUDYING SPANISH IN ANTIGUA

Antigua's **language school** business is currently booming, with more than thirty schools in operation and new ones cropping up on a weekly basis. Most visitors stop off for a week or two to learn the basics or revitalize their grammar, while others settle in for several months in pursuit of total fluency, among them US military personnel (though they're always reluctant to admit it), aid workers, missionaries and businesspeople. There can be no doubt that this is one of the best places in Latin America to learn Spanish: it's a beautiful, relaxed town, lessons are cheap and there are several superb schools. The only major drawback is that there are so many other students here that you'll probably end up spending your evenings speaking English. If this worries you then you might want to consider studying in either Quezaltenango or Huehuetenango, both of which have excellent schools and fewer visitors (see p.146 and p.166).

Before making any decisions, drop into Antigua's branch of the American organization **Amerispan**, which selects schools throughout Latin America to match the needs and requirements of students, and provides advice and support. If you arrange your study through them you get a discount card for many restaurants and services in the city. They're at 6 Av Norte 40 (☎ & fax 8320164; in USA ☎1-800/879-6640; fax 215/985-4524.).

CHOOSING A SCHOOL

Most schools offer a weekly deal that includes up to eight hours' one-on-one tuition a day and full board with a local family. Prices vary tremendously: top schools can charge as much as $140 a week for the above deal, while the smaller schools offer a similar programme for as little as $70; you can, of course, sign up for tuition only. Generally speaking you get what you pay for, the more expensive and established schools offering the best programmes and most professional teachers. However, if you're only interested in learning the basics or simply practising your conversational skills, then this may not be so important. Prices are negotiable, particularly in the low season and at the smaller, cheaper schools.

It's important to bear in mind that the success of the whole exercise is totally dependent on hitting it off with your teacher, so a school that works superbly for one student may be a disaster for another. Some programmes offer a change of teacher at the end of each week, and it is also common for students and teachers to go

church, there is a new museum to Hermano Pedro, featuring clothes, sandals and a moneybag that belonged to him.

Heading out of town to the south, in the direction of the Agua volcano, you can follow the **stations of the Cross**, signifying Christ's route to crucifixion at Calvary. Twelve little chapels, all of them now in assorted states of disrepair, represent the stations. Along the way you pass the cracked remains of **Nuestra Senora de Los Remedios** and at the far end is **El Calvario**, a small functioning church with magnificently thick walls. Outside the church, sunk in the middle of the road and looking oddly out of place, there stands a beautifully carved stone fountain.

North of the Parque Central

Setting out northwards from the Parque Central, along 4 Av Norte, you'll find the hermitage of **El Carmen**, down to the right past the first block. This was originally one of the city's great churches, first built in 1638 and rebuilt many times since: the top half of the facade finally collapsed in 1976 but the remains private, having met through a school – this brings the price down and enables the teacher to earn more, although it should only be done with the utmost discretion.

The tourist office in Antigua has a list of fifteen "approved schools", but this is as much a product of bribery and influence as a reflection of professional integrity. Two schools that should be avoided are the *Centro Linguistico* and the *Centro Internacional Español.*

The most respected, established and expensive schools are:

Tecún Umán Linguistic School, 6 C Poniente 34 (☎ & fax 8312792).

Projecto Linguístico Francisco Marroquín, 4 Av Sur 4 (☎8320406).

Centro Linguístico Maya, 5 C Poniente 20 (☎ & fax 8320656).

Instituto Antigueno de Español, 1 C Poniente 33 (☎8322685).

Christian Spanish Academy, 6 Av Norte 15 (☎ & fax 8320367).

The following are not in the big league, and so a touch cheaper, but still very professional and recommended:

Sevilla, 6 C Oriente 3 (☎8323609). Quality teaching with a friendly atmosphere and lively cultural programme that consistently gets good reports from students.

San José El Viejo, 5 Av Sur 34 (☎8323028; fax 8323029). Small, tranquil and accommodating school, where you can also learn French, German and Portuguese.

The really **inexpensive schools** tend to use untrained and inexperienced teachers. Don't expect a ruthless structure to the course but if you simply want to spend a few hours every day chatting away in Spanish then two reasonable schools in this league are *Panchoy*, 7 Av Norte (☎8322646), and, possibly the cheapest of the lot, *Don Pedro de Alvarado*, 1 C Poniente 24 (☎8322266).

PRIVATE TUITION
Finally, if you'd rather not get involved with a school but would like to study with a private teacher, then contact one of the following. At the time of going to press the standard rate for private tuition was $2–3 an hour.

Julia Solis – see noticeboard in *Doña Luisa's* at 4 C Oriente 12.

Rossalinda Rosales, 1 C Poniente 17.

Gladys de Porras, next door to the *Rainbow Reading Room* at 7 Av Sur 8.

hint at its former glory and you can look in at the rubble-filled nave. Back on 4 Av and another block to the north lies the church and convent of **Santa Teresa**, originally founded by a Peruvian philanthropist for a group of Carmelite nuns from Lima. These days it serves as the city jail.

A block further to the east, at the junction of 2 C Oriente and 2 Av Norte, is the site of **Las Capuchinas**, the largest and most impressive of the city's convents, whose ruins are some of the best preserved but least understood in Antigua. The Capuchin nuns, who came from Madrid, were rather late on the scene, founding the fourth convent in the city in 1726. They were only granted permission by the colonial authorities because the women would not need dowries to pay their way into religious life. The Capuchin order was the most rigorous in Antigua. Numbers were restricted to 25 with nuns sleeping on wooden beds with straw pillows. Once they had entered the convent the women were not allowed any visual contact with the outside world, food was passed to them by means of a turntable and they could only speak to visitors through a grille.

The ruins are the most beautiful in Antigua, with fountains, courtyards and massive earthquake-proof pillars. The two-storey tower or "retreat", however, is the most unusual point. On its top floor eighteen tiny cells are set into the walls, each with an independent sewage system, while the lower floor is dominated by a massive pillar that supports the structure above and incorporates seventeen small recesses, some with stone rings set in the walls. Theories about the purpose of this abound: as a warehouse, a laundry room, a communal bath, a pantry, or even a torture chamber.

A couple of blocks to the west, spanning 5 Av Norte, is the arch of **Santa Catalina**, which is all that remains of the original convent founded here in 1609. By 1697 it had reached maximum capacity with 110 nuns and 6 novices, and the arch was built in order that they could walk between the two halves of the establishment without being exposed to the pollution of the outside world. Somehow it managed to defy the constant onslaught of earthquakes and was restored in the middle of the nineteenth century.

Walking under the arch and to the end of the street, you reach the church of **La Merced**, which boasts one of the most intricate and impressive facades in the entire city, crammed with plaster moulding of interlaced patterns. The church is still in use and has been restored, but the cloisters and gardens lie ruined, exposed to the sky. In the centre of one of the courtyards is a fountain surrounded by four pools that's known as the *Fuente de Pescados*; the pools were used by the Mercedarian brothers for breeding fish. The colonial fountain in front of the church is worth a look for its superbly preserved carved decoration.

Further out to the northeast along 1 Av Norte, the badly damaged ruins of the churches of **Santa Rosa**, **Candelaria** and **Nuestra Señora de los Dolores del Cerro** are of interest to buffs only.

West of the Parque Central

The last of the ruins lie over to the west of the plaza, towards the bus station. At the junction of 4 C Poniente and 6 Av Norte stands **La Compañia de Jesús**, an educational establishment and church that was operated by the Jesuits until the King of Spain, feeling threatened by their tremendous and growing power, expelled them from the colonies in 1767. In this century the market, by now moved out of the plaza, was housed in the cloisters, at least until the 1976 earthquake: nowadays most of the ruins are closed off, though one or two rather touristy *artesania* stalls have recently moved back in.

Turning to the right in front of the bus station, and to the end of the tree-lined street Alameda Santa Lucía, you reach the spectacular remains of **San Jeronimo**, a school built in 1739. Well-kept gardens are woven between the huge blocks of fallen masonry and crumbling walls. Down behind San Jeronimo a cobbled road leads to the even more chaotic ruin **La Recolección**, where the middle of the church is piled high with the remains of the roof and walls. Recolectos friars first arrived here, asking permission to be allowed to build, in 1685, but it wasn't until 1701 that they started the church, finishing it in 1715. Months later it was brought to the ground by a huge earthquake. This second version was destroyed in 1773 and has been steadily decaying ever since.

On the other side of the bus station, to its south, is an imposing monument to **Rafael Landivar** (1731–93), a Jesuit composer who is generally considered the finest poet of the colonial era. Along with the other members of his order he was banished from the Americas in 1767. Behind the bus station at C de Recoletos 15

VOLCANO TOURS FROM ANTIGUA

A number of outfits in Antigua run guided tours to climb the **Pacaya volcano** near Guatemala City (see p.70). These trips cost $12 per person and also enable you to visit the volcano at night without having to camp out. They leave Antigua in the early afternoon to climb the volcano in the evening, coming back down in the dark and returning to Antigua at around 11pm. Some of the best tours are run by *Quetzal Volcano Expeditions* and *Juancho*, who both advertise in *Dona Luisa's*. *Gran Jaguar Tours*, 4 C Poniente 30 (☎8322712) receives consistently good reports. Avoid *Popeye* and *Yaxcha Expeditions*.

For more serious volcano climbing, Daniel Ramírez Ríos, at *Albergue Andinista*, 6 Av Norte 34, is the best and most experienced volcano guide in the country. He knows all the peaks well, speaks English, and can rent out camping equipment.

---

15 is the **K'ojom Casa de la Música** (in theory daily 3–4pm; $1), a small but delightful museum devoted to indigenous music, where you can watch a short documentary film on the history of Maya music.

Walking back to the plaza along 5 C Poniente, you'll pass the **Iglesia de San Agustín**, the remains of a vast convent complex that once occupied about half the block but has stood derelict since the earthquake of 1773, after which the Augustinians followed the government in the exodus to Guatemala City.

Eating and drinking

In Antigua the food is even more cosmopolitan than the population, and the only thing that's hard to come by is an authentic Guatemalan *comedor*. Here you can eat your way around the world in a series of sedate, sophisticated and fairly expensive **restaurants**.

If you're after a takeout, good **delis** include *La Llorona*, 4 Av Norte (Sun–Thurs 10am–10pm, Fri & Sat 10am–midnight); *Samba*, 6 Av Norte 7, and *Deliciosa*, 4 Av Norte 10. For the best **coffee** in town, if not the country, *Tostaduria Antigua*, 6 Av Sur 12 A, near the corner with 6 C is definitely the place to pick up some to take home. The tiny shop is suffused with the aroma of roasting beans and Tony will let you taste before you buy.

Restaurants and cafés

Café-Pizzeria Asjemenou, 5 C Poniente 4 . A big-time favourite for breakfast, also serving good, moderately priced meals. Try the calzone. Daily 8am–10pm.

Asados de la Calle del Arco, 5 Av Norte 7. An old Antigua favourite for its delicious barbecued meat, chicken, and Tex-Mex specialities, all at reasonable prices.

El Capuchino, 6 Av Norte 12. One of the most spectacular places in town, serving delicious Italian food, including pizza and pasta, as well as a set-course meal. Some dishes are expensive. Closed Mon.

La Casbah, 5 Av Norte 30. Not a Moroccan dish in sight, but a very pleasant roof terrace provides an excellent setting for an international menu. Closed Mon.

Restaurante y Pizzeria Catari, 6 Av Norte 52. Simple Italian cooking and decent prices have made this place a favourite for many years.

La Cenicienta, 5 Av Norte. Undoubtedly the best place for cakes and sweet snacks, though sadly the coffee is very weak.

Cevicheria Peroleto, next door to the *Jugocentro*. Popular with Guatemalans, this restaurant specializes in Peruvian pickled fish and shrimps. Very inexpensive.

Cookies etc, 3 Av Norte, just off the plaza. Mouth-watering selection of homemade cookies served with excellent coffee.

Doña Luisa's, 4 C Oriente 12. Probably the most popular place in town, frequented by foreigners – residents or tourists – and local people alike. The menu is simple, the setting relaxed, and the food tasty: chilli con carne, baked potatoes, salads, hamburgers, and superb bread and pastries baked on the premises.

La Estrella, 6 Av Norte 45. Authentic, inexpensive Chinese food.

Café Flor, 4 Av Sur 1. Formerly a Tex-Mex restaurant, now serving delicious Thai dishes, worth every centavo. Closed Sun.

La Fonda de la Calle Real, twin restaurants; the original café version at 5 Av Norte 5 and a smarter new restaurant in a beautiful colonial house at 3 C Poniente 7. Excellent food with Guatemalan specialities including *pepian* (spicy meat stew) and *chile rellenos* (stuffed peppers). A favourite with the smart set from Guatemala City, who pop by at weekends, when there is live music at the restaurant. Moderate to expensive.

Café la Fuente, in *La Fuente*, 4 C Oriente 14. Vegetarian restaurant, where you can eat in one of the nicest restored courtyards in the city to a classical music accompaniment.

Gran Muralla, 4 C Poniente 3, just off the plaza. Very Guatemalan hard-drinking bar that also serves generous portions of steaks, pasta and vaguely Chinese food at low prices.

Café Jardin, west side of the plaza. Unassuming café serving excellent breakfasts, pancakes, juices, snacks and sandwiches. Very friendly and very inexpensive.

Jugocentre Peroleto, Alameda Santa Lucía 36. The best fruit salad and granola breakfast for a healthy start to the day, as well as fantastic fruit juices and reasonable sandwiches.

La Luna Liena, 6 Av Norte 32. Elegant but not too expensive small restaurant, not far from La Merced church, serving meals from an international menu.

La Manzana Grande, 2 Av Norte 3A. A somewhat clinical atmosphere due to the spotless white decor, but don't mind that. The service is fast and the sandwiches are very good. Traditional American breakfasts are also served, cooked by the friendly Colorado proprietors. Closed Mon.

Oasis del Peregrino, 7 Av Norte 7. A little way from the centre but well worth the walk for the tranquil setting and superb, moderately priced food: salads, steak, German sausages, Hungarian goulash, *schnitzel*, pasta and a famous Sunday brunch. Mon, Tues, Thurs & Fri 5.30pm–midnight, Sat noon–midnight, Sun 10.30am–2pm.

Café Opera, 6 Av Norte 17. The Italian connection brings you superb strong coffee, ice cream and sandwiches in Italian-style surroundings, plus the occasional dose of loud opera. Closed Wed. Expensive.

Café Panchoy, 6 Av Norte and 4 C Poniente. Spotless, simple café serving good sandwiches and some traditional Guatemalan food. Closed Tues.

Panza Verde, 5 Av Sur 19. Ranked among the finest restaurants in town for its superb international food – at a price.

Peregrinos, 4 Av Norte 1. Next to *Lloyds Bank*, just off the plaza. A rather strange mixture of Italian and Tex-Mex food, but very good. Moderate prices.

Los Pollos, 7 Av and 4 C Poniente. The restaurant everyone loves to hate. The soggy fries and deep-fried chicken may not seem that tempting, but wait until you stumble out of a bar at midnight.

Quesos y Vino, 5 Av Norte 32. Stylish little Italian-owned restaurant serving good value pasta, cheese rolls and salads, washed down with European or Latin American wines.

Rainbow Reading Room, 7 Av Sur 8. Friendly, relaxed atmosphere matched by decent service, fair prices and delicious vegetarian meals; slightly better than *Café la Fuente*. Check out too the traveller's notice board, general book shop, and occasional poetry readings.

El Sereno, 4 Av Norte 16. Art exhibitions and other cultural events have made this something of an institution in Antigua, but it also serves a superb ever-changing menu of pricey international food. Closed Tues.

Las Tinajas, 6 Av Norte 13. Straightforward Guatemalan *comedor* serving all the basics, notably chicken, beef, tortillas, beans, rice and a particularly good sauce that accompanies almost everything. Very low prices.

Welten, 4 C Oriente 21. Moderate to expensive German and Austrian cuisine.

Drinking and nightlife

Evening activity is somewhat curtailed in Antigua by the new "dry law", which forbids the sale of alcohol after 1am, and by the authorities, who suspect that young foreigners are undermining the city's morals and therefore restrict licences for new bars, clubs or live music venues. The places listed below on 5 and 7 Av Norte are particularly popular with the gringo crowd and all open up around 7pm. For a more genuinely Guatemalan atmosphere, try one of the simple bars on Alameda de Santa Lucía. If you're intent on dancing as well as drinking, there's a **disco** in the *Hotel Ramada* and a single **nightclub**, the *Manhattan*, which is popular with a fairly teenage local crowd, on 5 C Poniente between 7 Av Sur and Alameda de Santa Lucía.

For more elevated pursuits, the **Proyecto Cultural el Sitio**, 5 C Poniente 15 (☎8323037) is Antigua's premier cultural venue, hosting concerts, plays in Spanish and English, exhibitions and movies. Check *The Classifieds Revue,* a free magazine available throughout town, for lists of current events.

Bars and live music

La Chimaneas, 7 Av Norte 7. The smartest of the bars, where you can play chequers and backgammon.

Gran Muralla, 4 C Poniente 3. For a drink in more Guatemalan surroundings.

Jazz Gruta, Calzada Santa Lucia 17. The most popular live music venue, not limited to jazz.

Latino's, 7 Av Norte 16. A touch rougher than *Picasso's*, this place dares to put on live music from time to time, which is when things really warm up.

Macondo's Pub, 5 Av Norte and 2 C Poniente. Happy hour from 7 to 8pm packs them in. Closed Mon.

Moscas y Miel, just off the plaza on 5 C Poniente. An old survivor – surprisingly popular, considering its absurd prices.

Picasso's, 7 Av Norte 16. Run by the irrepressible brothers Caesar and Oscar, this is generally a "happening" spot. Usually closed Sun.

Cinemas

The only functioning movie **cinema** is the *Teatro Colonial*, south of the plaza on 5 Av Sur. However, in addition to the *Proyecto Cultural el Sitio*, there are currently six **video cinemas** operating in Antigua, as listed below, which show a range of classic and art films on TV screens. Each has two or three films showing daily and the week's offerings are listed in the back of *The Classifieds Revue* (see above). If you'd rather watch **satellite TV**, then **CNN** is usually showing in the back room downstairs at *Doña Luisa's*, 4 C Oriente 12.

Cine Cafe Oscar, 3 Av Norte 2.

The Frisco Video Bar, 1 Av Sur 15.

Cinemala, 3 Av Norte 9.

Cafe Flor Cinema, 4 Av Sur 1.

Video Max, 1 C Poniente 37.

Listings

Banks and exchange *Banco G&T*, west side of the plaza (Mon–Fri 9am–8pm, Sat 10am–2pm); *Lloyds*, in the northeast corner of the plaza (Mon–Fri 9am–3pm); *Banco del Agro*, on the north side of the plaza (Mon–Fri 9am–3pm, Sat 9am–1pm); *Banco Industrial*, 5 Av Sur 4, just south of the plaza (Mon–Fri 8.30am–3pm, Sat 8.30am–12.30pm). *Banco Industrial* also gives cash payments on **Visa** cards.

Bookstores *Casa Andinista*, 4 C Oriente 5A, has a reasonable selection of English and Spanish books on Guatemala and Latin America, and a book rental service; *Casa del Conde*, on the west side of the plaza, has the widest selection of English books (Mon–Sat 9am–1pm & 2.30–6.30pm); *Poco de Todo*, on the west side of the plaza, has a wide range of English books on Guatemala and Central America, as well as some Spanish textbooks and a few secondhand books in English, Spanish and German; *Librería Pensativo*, 5 Av Norte 29, is probably the best Spanish-language bookshop in town, with an impressive selection of political books and a handful of English titles (Tues–Sun 9am–1pm & 4–7pm); *Rainbow Reading Room*, 7 Av Sur 8, has the largest selection of secondhand books, including some quality fiction – they also have a tearoom and bar so you can settle in while making a decision (daily 9am–9pm); *Librería Marquense*, 5 C Poniente 9, has a small selection of English secondhand books.

Camping equipment rent from the *Casa Andinista*, or from *Chicaq*, 6 Av Norte 34.

Car rental *Budget*, inside the *Hotel Ramada*; *Avis*, 5 Av Norte 22 (☎8320291); *Rental*, 6 Av Sur 7; *Quetzal Rentacar*, 5 Av Norte 14. All have similar prices with cars from around $60 a day, jeeps from $80.

Cultural centre *Centro Cultural La Fuente*, 4 C Oriente 14. One of the best preserved colonial buildings in Antigua, home to some of the finest of the town's businesses and a great vegetarian restaurant. If you're interested in seeing superb *huipiles* from over one hundred villages, then a visit to *Kaslan Po't* will be fascinating. Frank Mays, the owner and curator of what is in effect a museum of contemporary Maya weaving, has an extensive, almost overwhelming, collection of complete costumes, as well as books on Maya culture, and is the best person to advise how to choose a *huipil*.

Dentist Doctor De La Cruz, 3 Av Norte, between 2 and 3 calles.

Doctor Doctor Aceituno, who speaks good English, has his surgery at 2 C Oriente 17.

Horses can be rented from Rolando Perez who lives in the Colonia San Pedro El Panorama (casa no. 28), on the southern outskirts of Antigua (for reservations ☎8322809). Rolando can take you on a tour for anything from a couple of hours to a few days.

Laundry *Lavandería Central*, 5 C Poniente 7 (7.15am–7pm), offers an excellent and very friendly service; charges are by weight but a machine load usually costs less than $2. Or try *Lavandería Summer*, 7 C Poniente, 6 C Pan 15 and 5 Av (Mon–Fri 7am–7pm).

Library *CIRMA* (*Centro de Investigaciones Regionales de Mesoamerica*) is a research centre and library with facilities for students of Central America, whose work it also publishes. The library and reading room are to one side of a gorgeously peaceful courtyard at 5 C Oriente 5. The *International Library*, 5 C Poniente 15 opened in 1995 and is set to become the standard place for literature of all kinds in English.

Massage There are always a handful of alternative therapists at work in Antigua – just keep an eye on the noticeboards. *Massage Therapy of Antigua*, at *Conexion*, 4 C Oriente 14 (☎8323768), is one of the best, run by William Sutterfield, a US qualified therapist, who also organizes voluntary outreach programmes to train Guatemalan therapists. At the time of going to press *Estetica Navana*, 6 C Poniente 37, was offering massage and seaweed wraps.

Motorbikes *Natura*, 7 C Oriente 11; *Rental*, 6 Av Sur 7; and *Jopa*, 6 Av Norte 3, the most established and professional. Prices for a 200cc bike are $15 (4hr), $22 (24hr), $100 (week) and $250 (month); a touch more expensive for a 225cc bike.

Mountain bikes *Antigua Mountain Bike Hire*, El Rosario 9, rents good-quality bikes including *Trek*, *Diamond Back* and *Specialised* for $2 an hour, $20 a day, $35 a week, $75 a month, with $100 deposit. *Quetzal*, 5 Av Norte 14, offers similar bikes and prices. For accompanied bike tours check out *Mayan Mountain Cycle Tours*, 6 Av Sur 12B (☎ & fax 8322768).

Pool hall 3 C Poniente between 4 and 5 avenidas: very much a male-dominated institution although tourists of either sex are welcome, providing they can handle the stench of urine. A picture by the window embodies the seriousness with which the game is taken here. Alternatively there's *Bar Fenix*, 6 Av Norte 33.

Post office and parcels Alameda de Santa Lucía opposite the bus terminal (Mon–Fri 8am–4.30pm). *Quick Shipping*, 3 Av Norte 28 (☎8320147) operates a parcel service.

Radio The local station, *Radio Amiga*, on 1220 AM, has an English-language hour 4–5pm.

Shopping *Kaslan Po't*, in *El Fuente* (see above under "Cultural centre"), sells some of the finest *huipiles* in the country, at reasonable prices.

Swimming pool There are two beautiful but chilly spring-fed pools (daily 7am–4pm; $1) at El Pilar, on the edge of town on the road to Santa Mariá de Jesús. Past the station of the Cross you come to a large school on the left; follow the track that cuts off to the left just before it.

Travel agents *Tivoli*, 4 C Oriente 10 (☎8323041), is probably the best and most experienced all-round travel agent in town (Mon–Sat 9am–1pm & 3–5pm). Otherwise try the somewhat smarter *Turansa*, 5 Av Norte 17 (☎8322664), or the highly recommended nature and adventure specialist *Adventure Travel Center Viareal*, in *La Fuente*, 4 C Oriente 7 (☎ & fax 8323228) and 5 Av Norte 25B (☎ & fax 8320162). The latter offers superb sailing trips along the Río Dulce and economical flights to surrounding countries. *Aventureas Vaccacionales*, 1 Av Sur 11B (☎ & fax 8323352) also offer boat tours of Lake Izabal and the Río Dulce, and a very popular catamaran five-day trip to the Belizean reef. In both cases the price includes the cost of all meals, snorkel gear, fishing gear, and the use of two windsurfers.

Around Antigua: villages and volcanoes

The countryside surrounding Antigua is superbly fertile and breathtakingly beautiful. The valley is dotted with small villages, ranging from the *Ladino* coffee centre of Alotenango to the traditional Indian village of Santa María de Jesús. None is more than an hour or two away and all make interesting day trips. For the more adventurous, the **volcanic peaks** of Agua, Acatenango and Fuego offer strenuous but superb hiking. When walking anywhere around Antigua, however, keep in mind our warnings about the recent increase in **crimes against tourists** (see p.82) and take no risks with your safety.

San Felipe de Jesús

The nearest of the villages, **SAN FELIPE DE JESÚS**, is so close that you can walk there: just a kilometre or so north of Antigua following 6 Av Norte (or catch one of the minibuses from the bus terminal). San Felipe has a small Gothic-style church housing a famous image of Christ, Jesus Sepultado, said to have miraculous powers. Severely damaged in the 1976 earthquake, the church has been well restored since, and there's a fiesta here on August 30 to celebrate the anniversary of the arrival of the image in 1670. The village's other attraction is the **silver workshop**, where silver mined in the highlands of Alta Verapaz is worked and sold. To find the workshop, follow the sign to the *Platería Típica La Antigueña*.

Ciudad Vieja and Alotenango

To the south of Antigua the Panchoy valley is a broad sweep of farmland, overshadowed by three volcanic cones and covered with olive-green coffee bushes. A single road runs out this way, eventually reaching Escuintla and the Pacific coast, and passing a string of villages as it goes.

The first of these, 5km from Antigua, is **CIUDAD VIEJA**, a scruffy and unhurried village with a distinguished past: it was near here that the Spanish established their second capital, Santiago de los Caballeros, in 1527. Today, however, there's no trace of the original city, and all that remains from that time is a solitary tree, in a corner of the plaza, which bears a plaque commemorating the site of the first mass ever held in Guatemala. The plaza also boasts an eighteenth-century colonial church that has recently been restored.

The Spanish settled at first near the Cakchiquel capital of Iximché. Within a year, however, the Cakchiquel had turned against them, and the Spanish decided to base themselves elsewhere, moving their capital to the valley of Almolonga, 35km to the east between the Acatenango and Agua volcanoes. Here, on St Celia's Day 1527, in a landscape considered perfect for pasture and with plentiful supplies of building materials, the first official capital, **Santiago de los Caballeros**, was founded. The new city was built in a mood of tremendous confidence, with building plots distributed according to rank and the suburban sites given over to Alvarado's Mexican allies. Within twenty years things had really started to take shape, with a school, a cathedral, monasteries, and farms stocked with imported cattle. But while the bulk of the Spaniards were still settling in, their leader, the rapacious **Alvarado**, was off in search of action. His lust for wealth and conquest sent him to Peru, Spain and Mexico, and in 1541 he set out for the Spice Islands, travelling via Jalisco, where he met his end, crushed to death beneath a rolling horse. When news of his death reached his wife **Doña Beatriz**, at home in Santiago, she plunged the capital into an extended period of mourning, staining the entire palace with black clay, inside and out. She went on to command the officials to appoint her as her husband's replacement, and on the morning of September 9, 1541, became the first woman to govern in the Americas. On the official declaration she signed herself as *La sin ventura Doña Beatriz*, and then deleted her name to leave only *La sin ventura* (the unlucky one) – a fateful premonition.

Since the announcement of Alvarado's death the city had been swept by storms, and before the night of Beatriz's inauguration was out an earthquake added to the force of the downpour. A tremor shook the surrounding volcanoes and from the crater of the Agua volcano a great wave of mud and water slid down, accelerating as it surged towards the valley floor, and sweeping away the capital. Today the exact site of the original city is still the subject of some debate, but the general consensus puts it about 2km to the east of Ciudad Vieja, though it's probable that one of the Indian suburbs would have reached out as far as the modern village.

Further down the valley, the ragged-looking village of **ALOTENANGO** is dwarfed by the steaming, scarred cone of the Fuego volcano, which has been in a state of constant eruption since the arrival of the Spanish. A path leads from the village up the volcano, but it's extremely hard to find and follow, so unless you're with a guide it's a lot easier to climb Acatenango instead, using La Soledad as a starting point (see below).

Beyond Alotenango a rough dirt road continues down the valley to **Escuintla** (see p.202), passing through the village of El Rodeo. One, and sometimes two, buses a day connect Antigua and Escuintla, leaving Antigua at 7am and 12.30pm.

To get to Ciudad Vieja or Alotenango, there's a steady stream of **buses** leaving from outside the terminal in Antigua (opposite the post office): the last returns from Alotenango at around 7pm.

San Antonio Aguas Calientes

Further to the southwest of Antigua, beyond Ciudad Vieja, is the village of **SAN ANTONIO AGUAS CALIENTES**, set to one side of a steep-sided bowl beneath the peak of Acatenango. San Antonio is famous for its weaving, and on the stalls in the plaza you can find a complete range of the local output. This is also a good place to learn the traditional craft of back-strap weaving; if you're interested, the best way to find out about possible tuition is by simply asking the women in the plaza.

Adjoining San Antonio is the village of **SANTA CATARINA**, which has a superb ruined colonial church. Out on the edge of the village there's also a small **swimming pool** (Tues–Sun 9am–6pm) – a superb place for a chilly dip. To get to the pool, walk along San Antonio's main street until you come to the plaza in Santa Catarina and continue up the street that goes up the far side of the church. Turn left at the end and you'll come to the pool, on the right, in five minutes or so. **Minibuses** from the terminal in Antigua run a regular service to San Antonio and Santa Catarina.

Acatenango and Fuego volcanoes

To the south of Antigua, just a short way beyond Ciudad Vieja, a dusty dirt track branches off to **SAN MIGUEL DUEÑAS**, a dried-out, scrappy-looking sort of place where the roads are lined with bamboo fences and surrounded by coffee *fincas*. There's little to delay you in San Miguel itself, but you may well find yourself passing through on your way to La Soledad, the best starting point for climbing the Acatenango and Fuego volcanoes. **Buses** head out to San Miguel every half-hour or so from the terminal in Antigua, but once you progress beyond the village, traffic becomes scarce even at the best of times. If you're making for the volcanoes then you will have to either take a taxi from Antigua to La Soledad or walk for a couple of hours up the road from San Miguel Dueñas.

Climbing Acatenango

The trail for **Acatenango** starts in **LA SOLEDAD**, an impoverished village perched on an exposed ridge high above the valley. Walking up the road from San Miguel Dueñas, you come upon a cluster of bamboo huts, with a soccer field to the right. Here you'll find a small *tienda* and the last tap – so fill up on water. A short way beyond the *tienda* a track leads up to the left, heading above the village and towards the wooded lower slopes of Acatenango. It crosses another largish trail and then starts to wind up into the pine trees. Just after you enter the trees you have to turn onto a smaller path that goes away to the right; 100m or so further on take another small path that climbs to the left. This brings you onto a low ridge, where you meet a thin trail that leads to the left, away up the volcano – this path eventually finds its way to the top, somewhere between six and nine hours away. At times it's a little vague, but most of the way it's fairly easy to follow.

There are only two other important spots on the ascent, the **campsites**, which are also the easiest places to lose the trail. The first, a beautiful grassy clearing, is about ninety minutes up – the path cuts straight across, so don't be tempted by the larger track heading off to the right. Another ninety minutes above this is the second campsite, a little patch of level ground in amongst the pine trees. You're now about halfway to the top.

The trail itself is an exhausting climb, a thin line of slippery volcanic ash that rises with unrelenting steepness through the thick forest. Only for the last 50m or so does it emerge above the tree line, before reaching the top of the lower cone. Here there's a radio mast and a small yellow hut, put up by the *Guatemalan Mountaineering Club*, where you can shelter for the freezing nights – though at weekends there's the possibility that it will be full. To the south, another hour's gruelling and gasping ascent, is the main cone, a great grey bowl that rises to a height of 3975m. From here there's a magnificent view out across the valley below. On the opposite side is the Agua volcano, and to the right the fire-scarred cone of Fuego. Looking west you can see the three cones that surround Lake Atitlán, and beyond that the Santa María volcano, high above Quezaltenango.

When it comes to getting down again, the direct route towards Alotenango may look invitingly simple but is in fact very hard to follow. It's easiest to go back the same way that you came up.

Climbing Fuego

In the unlikely event that you have any remaining energy you can continue south and climb the neighbouring cone of **Fuego** (3763m). The cone is certainly impressive and when the English friar Thomas Gage saw it in 1678, he was inspired to make a comparison with the Agua volcano:

This volcano or mountain (whose height is judged full nine miles to the top) is not so pleasing to the sight, but the other which standeth on the other side of the valley opposite unto it is unpleasing and more dreadful to behold. For here are ashes for beauty, stones and flints for fruits and flowers, baldness for greenness, barrenness for fruitfulness. For water whisperings and fountain murmurs, noises of thunder and roaring of consuming metals; for running streams, flashingly of fire; for tall and mighty trees and cedars, castles of smoke rising in height to out-dare the sky and firmament; for sweet and odiferous and fragrant smells, a stink of fire and brimstone, which are still in action striving within the bowels of that ever burning and fiery volcano.

All this may seem a little exaggerated when you look across at Fuego's gently smoking cone, and from the top of Acatenango it looks comfortably close. Walking down and up the dip between the two peaks, however, does take a good few hours, and you should be wary of getting too close to Fuego's cone as it oozes overpowering sulphur fumes and occasionally spits out molten rock. Descending from Fuego is fairly problematic, too, as the trail that leads down to Alotenango is very hard to find. The bottom of the gully, though it may look tempting, is impassable – the actual trail is on the Fuego side of this dip. The only way to be really sure of a trouble-free descent is to go back over Acatenango and down the way you came up.

Fuego can also be climbed by a direct ascent from the village of Alotenango, but the climb is very hard going and the trail difficult to follow. Hire a guide if you plan to take this route.

San Juan del Obispo, Santa María de Jesús and the Agua volcano

East of Antigua the dirt road to Santa María de Jesús runs out along a narrow valley, sharing the shade with acres of coffee bushes. Before it starts to climb, the road passes the village of **SAN JUAN DEL OBISPO**, invisible from the road but marked by what must rank as the country's finest bus shelter, beautifully carved in local stone. The village is unremarkable in itself, although it does offer a good view of the valley below. What makes it worth a visit is the **Palacio de Francisco Marroquín**, who was the first Bishop of Guatemala. The place is currently home to about 25 nuns, and if you knock on the great wooden double doors one of them will come and show you around.

Marroquín arrived in Guatemala with Alvarado and is credited with having introduced Christianity to the Maya, as well as reminding the Spaniards about it from time to time. On the death of Alvarado's wife he assumed temporary responsibility for the government, and was instrumental in the construction of Antigua. He died in 1563, having spent his last days in the vast palace that he'd built for himself here in San Juan. The palace, like everything else in the region, has been badly damaged over the years, and serious reconstruction only began in 1962. The interior, arranged around two small courtyards, is spectacularly beautiful and several rooms still contain their original furniture. Attached to the palace is a fantastic church and chapel with ornate wood carvings, plaster mouldings and austere religious paintings.

There are regular **buses** to San Juan from the market in Antigua (7.30am–6pm) terminating in the church yard. Alternatively you could catch one heading for Santa María de Jesús and ask them to drop you here.

Santa María de Jesús

Up above San Juan the road arrives in **SANTA MARÍA DE JESÚS**, starting point for the ascent of the Agua volcano. Perched high on the shoulder of the volcano, the village is some 500m above Antigua, with magnificent views over the Panchoy valley and east towards the smoking cone of Pacaya. It was founded at the end of the sixteenth century for Indians transported from Quezaltenango: they were given the task of providing firewood for Antigua and the village earned the name *Aserradero*, lumber yard. Since then it has developed into a farming community where the women wear beautiful purple *huipiles*, although the men have recently abandoned traditional costume. The only place **to stay** is the *Hospedaje Oasis* (②), just off the plaza on the road into town, a clean and friendly institution that serves meals – beans, eggs and tortillas – as simple as the rooms.

Buses run from Antigua to Santa María every hour or so from 6am to 5pm, and the trip takes forty minutes. Beyond Santa María, the road continues down the east side of the volcano to the village of Palín (see p.71), on the Guatemala City–Escuintla highway. No buses cover this route, but there's a chance that you might be able to hitch a lift on a truck.

The Agua volcano

Agua is the easiest and by far the most popular of Guatemala's big cones to climb: on Saturday nights sometimes hundreds spend the night at the top. It's an exciting ascent with a fantastic view to reward you at the top. The trail starts in Santa María de Jesús (see above) – to reach it, head straight across the plaza, between the two ageing pillars, and up the street opposite the church doors. Take a right turn just before the end, and then continue past the cemetery and out of the village. From here on it's a fairly simple climb on a clear path, cutting across the road that goes some of the way up. The climb can take anything from four to six hours, and the peak, at 3766m, is always cold at night: there is shelter (though not always room) in a small chapel at the summit, however, and the views certainly make it worth the struggle.

Antigua to Chimaltenango

As an alternative to the main highway from Guatemala City, a second, smaller road connects Antigua with the Pan-American Highway, this time intersecting it at **Chimaltenango** (covered on p.106). On its way out of town the road passes through the suburb of **JOCOTENANGO**, where locally produced coffee beans are processed and which is also notorious for its brothels and gang violence. In colonial times Jocotenango was the gateway to Antigua, where official visitors would be met to be escorted into the city. There's a magnificent, crumbling church on the plaza.

Another 4km brings you to **SAN LORENZO EL TEJAR**, which has some superb hot springs. To reach the springs turn right in the village of **San Luís Las Carretas**, and then right again when the road forks: they're at the end of a narrow valley, a couple of kilometres from the main road. If you want to bathe in the steamy and sulphurous waters you can either use the cheaper communal pool or for a dollar or so rent one of your own – a little private room with a huge tiled tub set in the floor. The baths are open daily from 6am to 5pm, except Tuesday and Friday afternoons, when they are closed for cleaning.

From San Luís the main road climbs out of the Panchoy valley through Pastores and Parramos, a couple of dusty farming villages, after which a dirt track branches to **SAN ANDRÉS IZTAPA**, one of the many villages badly hit by the 1976 earthquake. San Andrés shares with the western highland villages of Zunil (see p.157) and Santiago Atitlán (see p.138) the honour of revering San Simón or Maximón, the wicked saint, who is usually housed in a chapel of his own (ask around for the *Casa de San Simón*). Once you've tracked him down you'll find that Maximón lives in a fairly strange world, his image surrounded by drunken men, cigar-smoking women and hundreds of burning candles, each symbolizing a request. The other point of interest in San Andrés is the particularly intricate weaving of the women's *huipiles*. The patterns are both delicate and bold, similar in many ways to those around Chimaltenango. The village's Tuesday market is also worth a visit.

Tragically San Andrés hit the headlines at the end of 1988, when it was the scene of the largest massacre since the return of civilian rule. On a hillside above the nearby hamlet of El Aguacate, 22 corpses were found in a shallow grave. Blame was passed back and forth between the army and the guerrillas, but nothing has been proved by either party.

After the turning for San Andrés the main road drops through pine trees into the bottom of a dip and to the **Laguna de Los Cisnes**, a small boating lake surrounded by cheap *comedores* and swimming pools, popularly known as *Los Aposeutos*. The lake is very popular with the people of Antigua and Chimaltenango, who flood out here every weekend and public holiday – it's something of a local version of Lake Amatitlán. Above the lake is the local army base, and beyond that the Pan-American Highway and **Chimaltenango**, 19km and 45 minutes from Antigua.

Buses run every twenty minutes between Antigua and Chimaltenango from around 5.30am, the last ones leaving Antigua at 7pm and Chimaltenango at 6.30pm. Buses for San Andrés Iztapa also leave hourly, between 6am and 4pm, from the market in Chimaltenango.

The Pan-American Highway

Leaving Guatemala City to the west, the **Pan-American Highway** cuts right through the central highlands as far as the border with Mexico. In its entirety this road stretches from Alaska to Chile (with a short break in southern Panamá), and here in Guatemala it forms the backbone of transport in the highlands. As you travel around, the highway and its junctions will inevitably become all too familiar, since wherever you're going it's invariably easiest to catch a local bus to the Pan-American and then flag down one of the buses heading along the highway.

There are three major junctions which you'll soon get to know well. **Chimaltenango** is the first major town on the highway and it's here that you make connections to or from Antigua (although there's also a road to Antigua that branches off the highway at San Lucas Sacatepéquez – this is used by buses travelling between Guatemala City and Antigua). Heading west, **Los Encuentros** is the next main junction, where one road heads off to the north for Chichicastenango and Santa Cruz del Quiché, another branching south to Panajachel and Lake Atitlán. Beyond this the highway climbs high over a mountainous ridge before dropping to **Cuatro Caminos** (p.160), from where side roads lead to Quezaltenango and Totonicapán. The Pan-American Highway continues on to Huehuetenango before it reaches the Mexican border at La Mesilla.

Between Guatemala City and Chimaltenango

Heading out to the west from Guatemala City along the Pan-American Highway to Chimaltenango, you travel through one of the central highland valleys, where a number of large villages are devoted to market gardening. The villages themselves are particularly scruffy, but their fields are meticulously neat and well taken care of, churning out a wide range of vegetables for both the domestic and export markets.

Leaving Guatemala City, the first place you pass is **MIXCO**, a village now absorbed into the capital's suburban sprawl. Founded in 1525 to house Pokoman refugees from Mixco Viejo, Mixco still has a large Indian population. Next along the way is **SAN LUCAS SACATEPÉQUEZ**, just before the turning for Antigua. The village dates back to before the Conquest but these days bears the scars of the 1976 earthquake and serves the weekend needs of city dwellers, with cheap *comedores* and family restaurants lining the highway. Beyond this is **SANTIAGO SACATEPÉQUEZ**, whose centre lies 1km or so to the north of the highway. The road to Santiago actually branches off the highway at San Lucas Sacatepéquez – and buses shuttle back and forth along the branch road. (Alternatively, you can walk to Santiago from a point overlooking it on the highway, a couple of kilometres west of San Lucas.) The best time to visit Santiago is on November 1, for a local fiesta to honour the **Day of the Dead**, when massive paper kites are flown in the cemetery to release the souls of the dead from their agony. The festival is immensely popular, and hundreds of Guatemalans and tourists come every year to watch the spectacle. The kites, made from paper and bamboo, are massive circular structures, measuring up to six or seven metres in diameter. Teams of young men struggle to get them aloft while the crowd looks on with bated breath, rushing for cover if a kite comes crashing to the ground.

At other times of the year, there are **markets** in Santiago on Tuesday and Sunday and the town has a small local **museum** (Mon–Fri 9am–4pm, Sat & Sun 9am–noon & 2–4pm), just below the plaza, which is crammed with tiny Maya figurines, clay fragments and pots, all donated by local people from their homes and fields. Also on display is the Guatemalan peso, dating from 1909, a traditional costume from 1901, small paper kites and a stuffed quetzal.

Beyond the entrance to Santiago the Pan-American Highway goes on past Sumpango, and through El Tejar, famous for its bricks, before reaching Chimaltenango.

Chimaltenango and around

CHIMALTENANGO was founded by Pedro de Portocarrero in 1526, on the site of the Cakchiquel centre of Bokoh, and was later considered as a possible site for the new capital. It has the misfortune, however, of being positioned on a continental divide: it suffered terribly from the earthquake in 1976, which shook and flattened much of the surrounding area. Today's town, its centre just to the north of the main road, is dominated by that fact, and like so much of the region its appearance testifies to rapid and unfinished reconstruction, with dirt streets, breeze block walls and an air of weary desperation. But it remains busy, a regional centre of transport and trade whose prosperity is boosted by the proximity of the capital.

The town's plaza is an odd mix of architectural styles, with a police station that looks like a medieval castle, a church that combines the Gothic and the Neoclassical, and a superb colonial fountain positioned exactly on the continental divide – half the water drains to the Caribbean, the other half to the Pacific. Chimaltenango's second focal point is the Pan-American Highway itself, which cuts through the southern side of the town, dominating it with an endless flow of trucks and buses. The town extracts what little business it can from this stream of traffic, and the roadside is crowded with cheap *comedores*, mechanics' workshops, and sleazy bars that become brothels by night.

The **post office** (Mon–Fri 8am–4.30pm), *Banco de Occidente* (Mon–Fri 9am–7pm, Sat 9am–1pm) and *Guatel* (7am–midnight) are all on the plaza, and if you want to stay here the *Hotel La Predilecta* (①), a block to the south on 9 C, has pleasant, simple rooms and safe parking. **Buses** passing through Chimaltenango run to all points along the Pan-American Highway: for Antigua they leave every twenty minutes between 5.30am and 6.30pm from the market in town – though you can also wait at the turn-off on the highway. To get here from Guatemala City, take any bus heading to the western highlands from the Zona 4 bus terminal.

San Martín Jilotepeque

To the north of Chimaltenango a rough dirt road runs through 19km of plunging ravines and pine forests to the village of **SAN MARTÍN JILOTEPEQUE**. The village itself remains badly scarred by the 1976 disaster, but the sprawling Sunday market is well worth a visit and the weaving here, the women's *huipiles* especially, is some of the finest you'll see – with intricate and ornate patterning, predominantly in reds and purples.

Buses to San Martín leave the market in Chimaltenango every hour or so from 4am to 2pm; the last one returns at about 3pm. The trip takes around an hour. To the north of San Martín the road continues to **Joyabaj** (see p.118). One bus a day covers this route, leaving the capital in the morning and passing through San Martín around 12.30pm; the return leaves Joyabaj early the following day.

San Juan Comalapa, Patzicía and Patzún

Heading west from Chimaltenango, a series of turns lead off the Pan-American Highway to interesting but seldom-visited villages. The first of these, 16km to the north of the road, on the far side of a deep-cut ravine, is **SAN JUAN COMALAPA**. The village was founded by the Spanish, who brought together here the populations of several Cakchiquel centres: a collection of eroded pre-Columbian sculptures is displayed in the plaza. There's also a small monument to Rafael Alvarez Ovalle, a local man who composed the Guatemalan national anthem. Like so many of the villages in this area, Comalapa's appearance still suffers from the impact of the 1976 earthquake, its plaza overshadowed by the crumbling facade of the ruined church.

In the last few decades the villagers of Comalapa have developed something of a reputation as **"primitive" artists**, and there are several galleries in the streets around the plaza where their work is exhibited and sold. The whole thing started in 1930 with Andrés Curuchich, who painted village scenes with a simplicity that soon attracted the attention of outsiders. Throughout the 1950s he became increasingly popular, exhibiting in Guatemala City, and later as far afield as Los Angeles and New York. Inspired by his example and the chance of boosting their income, forty to fifty painters are now working here, including two or three women – although success is considerably more difficult for them as painting is generally perceived as a man's task. There is a permanent exhibition devoted to the paintings of Andrés Curuchich at the Museo Ixchel in Guatemala City (see p.59). Comalapan **weaving** is also of the highest standards, using styles and colours characteristic of the Chimaltenango area. Traditionally the weavers work in silk and a natural brown cotton called *cuyuxcate*, although these days they increasingly use ordinary cotton and synthetic fibres.

As ever, the best time to visit is for the **market**, on Tuesday, which brings the people out in force. **Buses** to Comalapa run hourly from Chimaltenango (1hr) and the service is always better on a market day. There's nowhere to stay in the village and the last bus back leaves at 3 or 4pm.

Patzicía and Patzún: a route to the lake

Further to the west another branch road runs down towards Lake Atitlán, connecting the Pan-American Highway with several small villages. At the junction with the main road is **PATZICÍA**, a ramshackle sprawl still reeling from the impact of the 1976 earthquake. Despite its bedraggled appearance the village has a history of independent defiance, and in 1944 it was the scene of an Indian uprising that left some three hundred dead. Villagers were led to believe that Indians throughout Guatemala had risen up against their *Ladino* rulers, and charged through the village

The Maya Goddess Ixchel (goddess of weaving)

putting to death any they could set hands on. Armed *Ladinos*, arriving from the capital, managed to put down the uprising, killing the majority of the rebels. Ironically enough, over a hundred years earlier, in 1871, the Declaration of Patzicía was signed here, setting out the objectives of the liberal revolution.

PATZÚN, 11km from the main highway heading towards Lake Atitlán, also suffered terrible losses in 1976. A monument in the plaza remembers the 172 who died, and a new church stands beside the shell of the old one, somehow making an even more poignant memorial. Traditional costume is still worn here and the colourful Sunday market is well worth a visit. Outside the twin churches the plaza fills with traders, with the majority of the women dressed in the brilliant reds of the local costume.

Beyond Patzún it's possible to continue all the way to the small village of Godínez, high above the northern shore of Lake Atitlán, and from there along the road to Panajachel and San Lucas Tolimán. A couple of buses a day make this trip but the road is fairly rough and often closed by landslides. If you're considering this route you should also bear in mind that it has been the scene of a number of recent armed robberies, roadblocks and attacks on tourists. The situation may well have changed by the time you read this but it is advisable to proceed with caution. **Buses** to Patzún leave the Zona 4 terminal in Guatemala City every hour or so, and you can pick them up in Chimaltenango or at the turning for Patzicía.

Back at Patzicía, a second branch road leaves the Pan-American Highway to head south, past huge coffee plantations, to the villages of Acatenango and Yepocapa. It's a fairly obscure part of the country and there's no very good reason to travel this way, although there are several daily buses as far as Acatenango and one that goes all the way through to the Pacific coast, heading back to the capital via Escuintla. Buses or trucks heading for Yepocapa pass also through La Soledad, on the lower slopes of the Acatenango volcano, which is the starting point for a climb to the cone (see p.101). The **bus** that covers the round trip, Guatemala City–Chimaltenango–Acatenango–Yepocapa–Escuintla, leaves the capital daily at 5am, passing through Chimaltenango at 6am and Patzicía at around 7.30am.

Tecpán and the ruins of Iximché

The town of **TECPÁN** lies just a few hundred metres south of the Pan-American Highway, ninety minutes or so from Guatemala City. This may well have been the site chosen by Alvarado as the first Spanish capital, to which the Spanish forces retreated in August 1524, after they'd been driven out of Iximché. Today it's a place of no great interest, and you're unlikely to do more than pass through on your way to the ruins. Tecpán again suffered severely in the 1976 earthquake, and in the centre a new church stands alongside the cracked remains of the old one.

The **ruins of Iximché**, the pre-conquest capital of the Cakchiquel, are about 5km south, on an exposed hillside protected on three sides by steep slopes and surrounded by pine forests. From the early days of the Conquest the Cakchiquel allied themselves with the conquistadores, so the structures here suffered less than most at the hands of the Spanish. Since then, however, time and weather have taken their toll and the majority of the buildings, originally built of adobe, have disappeared, leaving only a few stone-built pyramids and the clearly defined plazas. Nevertheless the site is strongly atmospheric, and its grassy plazas, ringed with pine trees, are marvellously peaceful. At weekends it is a favourite local picnic spot.

The Cakchiquel were originally based further west, around the modern town of Chichicastenango, and the Cakchiquel language is still spoken throughout the central highlands and along the eastern side of Lake Atitlán. But when their villages came under the control of the Quiché, the Cakchiquel were the first to break away, moving their capital to Iximché in order to establish their independence. They founded the new city in about 1470 and from that time on were almost continuously at war with other tribes. Despite this, they managed to devote a lot of energy to the building and rebuilding of their new capital, and trenches dug into some of the structures have revealed as many as three superimposed layers. War may, in fact, have helped the process, as most of the labour was done by slaves captured in battle. When the Spanish arrived, the Cakchiquel were quick to join forces with Alvarado in order to defeat their old enemies, the Quiché. Grateful for the assistance, the Spanish established their first headquarters near here on May 7, 1524 – possibly Tecpán. The Cakchiquel referred to Alvarado as *Tonatiuh*, the son of the sun, and as a mark of respect he was given the daughter of a Cakchiquel king as a gift.

On July 25 the Spanish renamed the new settlement **Villa de Santiago**, declaring it their new capital. But in just three years the Cakchiquel had risen in rebellion, outraged by demands for tribute. Abandoning their capital, they fled into the mountains, from where they waged a guerrilla war against the Spanish until 1530, when the Spanish capital was moved to the greater safety of Ciudad Vieja, a short distance from Antigua (see p.100).

The ruins of Iximché are made up of four main plazas, a couple of ball courts and several pyramids. In most cases only the foundations and lower parts of the original structures were built of stone, while the upper walls were of adobe, with thatched roofs supported by wooden beams. You can make out the ground plan of many of the buildings, but it's only the most important all-stone structures that still stand. The most significant buildings were those clustered around courts A and C, which were probably the scene of the most revered rituals. On the sides of **Temple 2** you can make out some badly eroded murals, the style of which is very similar to that used in the codices.

It's thought that the site itself, like most of the highland centres, was a ceremonial city used for religious rituals and inhabited only by the elite. The rest of the population would have lived in the surrounding hills and come to Iximché only to attend festivals and to defend the fortified site in times of attack. Archeological digs here have unearthed a number of interesting finds, including the decapitated heads of sacrifice victims, burial sites, grinding stones, obsidian knives, a flute made from a child's femur, and large numbers of incense burners. There was surprisingly little sculpture, but most of it was similar to that found in the ruins of Zaculeu and Mixco Viejo, both of which were occupied at around the same time.

Iximché practicalities

The ruins are open daily from 9am to 4pm, and **to get there** you can take any bus travelling along the Pan-American Highway between Chimaltenango and Los Encuentros: ask to be dropped at Tecpán, from where you can walk. From Guatemala City any of the buses going to Sololá or Quiché will do: they leave the Zona 4 terminal hourly, passing through Chimaltenango. If you're coming from Los Encuentros take any bus heading for Guatemala City.

To get to the ruins simply walk through Tecpán and out the other side of the plaza, passing the *Centro de Salud*, and follow the road through the fields for about 5km, an hour or so on foot. With any luck you'll be able to hitch some of the way, particularly at weekends when the road can be fairly busy. There's nowhere to stay at the site and nothing to eat, so take a picnic; and be back on the Pan-American Highway before 6pm to be sure of a bus out.

EL QUICHÉ

At the heart of the western highlands, sandwiched between the Verapaces and Huehuetenango, is the **Department of El Quiché**. Like its neighbours, El Quiché encompasses the full range of Guatemalan scenery. In the south, only a short distance from Lake Atitlán, is a section of the sweeping central valley, a fertile and heavily populated area that forms the upper reaches of the Motagua valley. To the north the landscape becomes increasingly dramatic, rising first to the **Sierra de Chuacús**, and then to the massive, rain-soaked peaks of the **Cuchumatanes**, beyond which the land drops away into the inaccessible rainforests of the **Ixcán**.

The department takes its name from the greatest of the pre-conquest tribal groups, the **Quiché**, for whom it was the hub of an empire. From their capital **Utatlán**, which stood just west of the modern town of Santa Cruz del Quiché, they overran much of the highlands and were able to demand tribute from most of the other tribes. Although by the time the Spanish arrived their empire was in decline, they were still the dominant force in the region and challenged the conquistadors as soon as they entered the highlands, at a site near Quezaltenango. They were easily defeated, though, and the Spanish were able to negotiate alliances with former Quiché subjects, playing one tribe off against another, and eventually overcoming them all. Today these highlands remain a stronghold of Indian culture and the department of El Quiché, scattered with small villages, is the scene of some superb fiestas and markets.

For the Spanish, however, this remote mountainous terrain, with little to offer in the way of plunder, remained an unimportant backwater: only in later years, when large-scale commercial farming began on the Pacific coast, did it grow in importance as a source of cheap labour. This role has had a profound impact on the area for the last two hundred years and has forced the population to suffer horrific abuses. Perhaps not surprisingly the region became a noted centre of guerrilla activity in the late 1970s, and subsequently the scene of unrivalled repression.

For the traveller El Quiché has a lot to offer, in both the accessible south and the wilder north. **Chichicastenango**, one of the country's most popular destinations, is the scene of a vast twice-weekly market and remains a relatively undisrupted centre of Indian religion. Beyond this, at the heart of the central valley, is the departmental capital of **Santa Cruz del Quiché**, stopping-off point for trips to a string of smaller towns and to the ruins of **Utatlán**. Further to the north the paved road ends and the mountains begin. Travelling here can be hard work but the extraordinary scale of the scenery makes it all well worthwhile. Isolated villages are set in superb mountain scenery, sustaining a wealth of Indian culture and occupying a misty, mysterious world of their own. Passing over the **Sierra de Chuacús**, and down to the **Río Negro**, you reach **Sacapulas** at the

base of the **Cuchumatanes**. From here you can travel across the foothills to
Cobán or Huehuetenango, or up into the mountains to the three towns of the **Ixil
triangle – Nebaj, Chajul** and **Cotzal**.

The road for Chichicastenango and the department of El Quiché leaves the
Pan-American Highway at the **Los Encuentros** junction. From here it drops off
the southern volcanic ridge and runs into the broad central valley, a great stretch
of land suspended between the volcanoes and the mountains.

Chichicastenango

Heading north from Los Encuentros, the highway drops into the central plain.
Moving through dense pine forests, the road plunges into deep ravines and struggles out around endless switchbacks. Seventeen kilometres from the junction is
CHICHICASTENANGO, Guatemala's *"Mecca del Turismo"*. In this compact and
traditional town of cobbled streets, adobe houses and red-tiled roofs, the calm of
day-to-day life is shattered on a twice-weekly basis by the **Sunday and Thursday
market** – Sunday is the busiest. The town is conveniently placed a short hop
from the Pan-American Highway, and the market attracts tourists and commercial traders on day trips out of Antigua, Panajachel and Guatemala City, as well as

Indian weavers from throughout the central highlands. For many years the market and town managed to coexist happily, but recently the invasion of outsiders has begun to dominate and now threatens to undermine Chichicastenago's unique identity.

The market is by no means all that sets Chichicastenango apart, however, and for the local Maya population it's an important centre of culture and religion. Long before the arrival of the Spanish this area was inhabited by the Cakchiquel, whose settlements of Patzak and Chavier were under threat from the all-powerful Quiché. In a bid to assert their independence, in 1470 the Cakchiqueles abandoned the villages and moved south to Iximché (see p.108), from where they mounted repeated campaigns against their former masters. Chichicastenango itself was founded by the Spanish in order to house Quiché refugees from Utatlán, which they conquered and destroyed in 1524. The town's name is a Nahuatl word meaning "the place of the nettles", accorded it by Alvarado's Mexican allies.

Over the years Indian culture and folk Catholicism have been treated with a rare degree of respect in Chichicastenango, although inevitably this blessing has been mixed with waves of arbitrary persecution and exploitation. Today the town has an incredible collection of Maya artefacts, parallel Indian and *Ladino* governments, and a church that makes no effort to disguise its acceptance of unconventional Indian worship. Traditional weaving is also adhered to in Chichicastenango and the women wear superb, heavily embroidered *huipiles*. The men's costume of short trousers and jackets of black wool embroidered with silk is highly distinguished, although it's very expensive to make and these days most men opt for western dress. However, for fiestas and market days a handful of *cofradías* (elders of the religious hierarchy) still wear traditional clothing.

Chichicastenango's appetite for religious fervour is most evident during the **fiesta** of Santo Tomás, from December 14 to 21. While it's not the most spontaneous of fiestas it's certainly one of the most spectacular, with attractions including the *Palo Volador* (in which men dangle by ropes from a twenty-metre pole), a live band or two, a massive procession, traditional dances, clouds of incense, gallons of *chicha*, and endless deafening fireworks. On the final day, all babies born in the previous year are brought to the church for christening. Easter, too, is celebrated here with tremendous energy and seriousness.

Arrival and information

Buses heading between Santa Cruz del Quiché and Guatemala City pass through Chichicastenango every hour or so, and you can pick them up anywhere along the way. In Guatemala City they leave from the terminal in Zona 4, hourly from 4am to about 5pm. Coming from Antigua you can pick them up in Chimaltenango. From Panajachel you can either go up to Los Encuentros, or on market days there are several direct buses, supplemented by a steady flow of minibuses and a special tourist shuttle (run by *Panajachel Tourist Services*, C los Arboles) that leaves Panajachel at 8am, returning at 1pm. There is also a special shuttle service from Antigua.

If you're bitten by market fever and need to **change money** there's a *Banco del Ejercito* on 6 C, north of the plaza (Mon–Fri 9am–noon & 2–5pm, Sat 10am–1pm); *Hotel Santo Tomás* also offers exchange. The **post office** (Mon–Fri 8am–4.30pm) and **Guatel** (daily 7am–7pm) are on 6 Av, up behind the church.

Moving on

When it comes to **leaving Chichicastenango** catch any **bus** as far as Los
Encuentros and make a connection there: there are plenty of direct buses to
Guatemala City – the last leaves Chichicastenango at around 7pm. If you're heading north take a bus to Santa Cruz del Quiché, from where buses go up towards
the mountains.

Accommodation

Hotels are in fairly short supply in Chichicastenango, and if you can't find a room
you might find it easier to stay in Santa Cruz del Quiché, just half an hour away
(see p.116). Prices are often inflated on market days, though at other times you
can usually negotiate a good deal.

Hotel Chaguilá, 5 Av 5–24 (☎ & fax 7561134), half a block from the bus stop. Simple rooms
set around a large, open courtyard, with secure parking. ⑤.

Hospedaje El Salvador, down the street beside the church. Vast and business-like with
simple, cell-like rooms but the benefit of hot water. ③.

Hospedaje Giron, 6 C 4–52, just north of the corner where buses stop. Friendlier and
smaller than the *El Salvador*; no single rooms. ③.

Hotel Pascual Abaj, 5 Av Arco Gucumatz and 3 C, down the hill under the arch. Pleasant,
clean rooms with private shower and private parking. Front rooms a little noisy due to passing buses. ④.

Hotel Posada Belen, 12 C, on the edge of town beyond the *El Salvador*. New and reasonable with good views out the back. ③.

Hotel Posada Maya (*Mayan Inn*), corner of the plaza (☎7561176; fax 7561212). Chichi's
oldest tourist hotel offers good simple rooms with private showers and hot water. ⑥.

Posada Santa Marta, 5 Av – on the left down the hill under the arch. Basic but clean and
safe; no single rooms. ②.

Hotel Santo Thomas, 7 Av 5–32 (☎7561061; fax 7561306). Easily the finest upmarket establishment in town, with beautiful rooms set around two colonial-style courtyards, a restaurant,
swimming pool, sauna and jacuzzi. ⑥.

Hotel Villa Grande, on the entrance road just before you drop down into town (☎ & fax
7561053). Monstrous new concrete hotel, built into the hillside and designed to cater for tour
groups. All luxuries, including a restaurant and pool. ⑦.

The Town

Though most visitors come here to see the market, Chichicastenango also offers
an usual insight into traditional religious practices in the highlands. At the main
Santo Tomás Church, in the southeast corner of the plaza, the Indians have
been left to adopt their own style of worship, blending pre-Columbian and
Catholic rituals. The church was built in 1540 on the site of a Maya altar, and
rebuilt in the eighteenth century. It's said that local Indians became interested in
worshipping here after Francisco Ximenez, the priest from 1701 to 1703, started
reading their holy book, the Popul Vuh (see below). Seeing that he held considerable respect for their religion, they moved their altars from the hills and set them
up inside the church.

Before entering the building it's customary to make offerings in a fire at the
base of the steps or burn incense in perforated cans, a practice that leaves a cloud
of thin, sweet smoke hanging over the entrance. Inside is an astonishing scene of

avid worship. A soft hum of constant murmuring fills the air, as Indians kneel to offer candles to their ancestors and the saints. For these people the entire building is alive with the souls of the dead, each located in a specific part of the church. The place of the "first people", the ancient ancestors, is beneath the altar railing; former officials are around the middle of the aisle; common people to the west in the nave; and deceased native priests beside the door. Alongside these, and equally important, are the Catholic saints, who receive the same respect and are continuously appealed to with offerings of candles and alcohol. Last, but by no means least, certain areas within the church, and particular patterns of candles, rose petals and *chicha*, are used to invoke specific types of blessings, such as those for children, travel, marriage, harvest or illness. It's polite to enter the church by the side door and it's deeply offensive to take **photographs** inside the building – don't even contemplate it.

Beside the church is a former monastery, now used by the parish administration. It was here that the Spanish priest Francisco Ximenez became the first outsider to be shown the **Popol Vuh**, the holy book of the Quiché. His copy of the manuscript is now housed in the Newberry Library in Chicago: the original was lost some time later in the eighteenth century. The text itself was written in Santa Cruz del Quiché shortly after the arrival of the Spanish, and is a brilliant poem of over nine thousand lines that details the cosmology, mythology and traditional history of the Quiché. Broadly speaking it's split into two parts: the first is an account of the creation of man and the world, and the second describes the wanderings of ancestors of the Quiché, as they migrate south and settle in the highlands of Guatemala. The opening lines give an impression of the book's importance, and the extent to which it sets out to preserve a threatened cultural heritage:

> *This is the beginning of the Ancient World, here in this place called Quiché. Here we shall ascribe, we shall implant the ancient word, the potential and source of everything done in the citadel of Quiché.*
> *And here we shall take up the demonstration, revelation, and account of how things were put in shadow and brought to light . . .We shall write about this amid the preaching of God, in Christendom now. We shall bring it out because there is no longer a place to see it, a Council book.*

Translation by Dennis Tedlock

On the south side of the plaza the **Rossbach Museum** (Mon & Wed–Sun 8am–noon & 2–5pm) houses a broad-ranging collection of pre-Columbian artefacts, mostly small pieces of ceramics that had been kept by local people in their homes, some as much as two thousand years old. The collection is based on that of Ildefonso Rossbach, an accountant turned priest who served in Chichicastenango from 1894 until his death in 1944. Most of the pieces here were donated to him by local people.

Opposite Santo Tomás is **El Calvario**, a smaller chapel exclusively for the Indians. Inside there's a large image of Christ in a glass case that's paraded through the street during Holy Week. The steps are the scene of incense-burning rituals and the chapel is considered good for general confessions and pardons.

Beyond the plaza: the cemetery and the shrine of Pascual Abaj

The town **cemetery**, down the hill behind El Calvario, offers further evidence of the strange mix of religions that characterizes Chichicastenango. The graves are

There's been a **market** at Chichicastenango for hundreds, if not thousands, of years, and despite the twice-weekly invasions the local people continue to trade their wares. On market days Chichicastenango's streets are lined with stalls and packed with buyers, and the choice is overwhelming, ranging from superb-quality Nebaj *huipiles* to wooden dance masks, and including pottery, gourds, machetes, belts and a gaudy selection of recently invented "traditional" fabrics. You can still pick up some authentic and beautiful weaving, but you need to be prepared to wade through a lot of trash and to haggle hard – easier said than done, but your chances are better before 10am when the tourist buses arrive from the capital, or in the late afternoon once things have started to quieten down. The best of the stuff from the local villages is held in the centre of the plaza and is far more interesting than the bulk of the stalls, at least if you haven't come to buy. Even at the best of times prices here are by no means the lowest in the country, and for a real bargain you need to head further into the highlands; for non-traditional clothes the markets in Panajachel and Guatemala City are also worth a look.

marked by anything from a grand tomb to a small earth mound, and in the centre is an Indian shrine where the usual offerings of incense and alcohol are made. At the back, in a large yellow building, is entombed the body of Father Rossbach.

The churches and cemetery are certainly not the only scenes of Indian religious activity, and the hills that surround the town, like so many throughout the country, are topped with shrines. The closest of these, less than a kilometre from the plaza, is known as **Pascual Abaj**. The site is regularly visited by tourists, but it's important to remember that these ceremonies are deeply serious and you should still keep your distance and ask permission before taking any **photographs**. The shrine is laid out in a typical pattern with several small altars facing a stern pre-Columbian sculpture. Offerings are usually overseen by a *brujo*, a type of shaman, and range from flowers to sacrificed chickens, always incorporating plenty of incense, alcohol and incantations. In 1957, during a bout of religious rivalry, the shrine was raided and smashed by reforming Catholics, but the traditionalists gathered the scattered remains and patched them together with cement and a steel reinforcing rod.

To get to Pascual Abaj, walk down the hill beside the Santo Tomás church, take the first right, 9 Calle, and follow this as it winds its way out of town. You soon reach a soccer field where you're faced by two pine-clad hills – the shrine is on top of the left-hand one. If there's a ceremony in progress a thin plume of smoke will pick it out. A path goes up the right-hand side of the hill.

Eating

The eating situation is fairly poor in Chichicastenango, although all the main **hotels** do have their own restaurants – the best are the *Santo Thomas* and the *Mayan Inn*, although the food in both is very English boarding school. On the east side of the plaza are a couple of simple **snack places**, the *Mini Restaurant Gucumatz* and the *Café la Vida de los Confrias,* both of which do good breakfasts and sandwiches. Above the commercial centre, this side of the square, *Restaurant Tzijolaj* (closed Tues) has great views of the plaza from its first floor balcony. For something more substantial try the *Restaurant Gucumatz*, or the *Restaurant*

Tziguan Tinamit, or any of the many basic *comedores* in and around the market. The plaza on **market day** is a great place for lunch in one of the makeshift *comedores*, where you'll find cauldrons of stew, rice and beans.

Santa Cruz del Quiché and around

The capital of the department, **SANTA CRUZ DEL QUICHÉ**, lies half an hour north of Chichicastenango. A good paved road connects the two towns, running through pine forests and ravines, and past the **Laguna Lemoa**, a lake which, according to local legend, was originally filled with tears wept by the wives of Quiché kings after their husbands had been slaughtered by the Spanish.

Santa Cruz del Quiché itself is a pleasant sort of place where not a lot goes on. It is, however, the hub of transport for the department and really the only practical place to base yourself. There's a busy market here on the same days as in Chichicastenango – Thursday and Sunday – and palm weaving is a local speciality: Maya people can often be seen threading a band or two as they walk through town. Many of the palm hats on sale throughout the country were put together here, but if you want to buy you'll have to look hard and long to find one that fits a gringo head.

On the plaza there's a large colonial church, built by the Dominicans with stone from the ruins of Utatlán. Inside is a memorial to the priests of the department who lost their lives in the violence of the late 1970s and early 1980s. Priests were singled out during those years as they were often connected with the cooperative movement. The situation was so serious that in 1981 the Church decided to withdraw its priests from the whole department, although they've since returned to their posts. In the middle of the plaza a defiant statue of the Quiché hero Tecún Umán stands prepared for battle.

Santa Cruz practicalities

There's a good range of **hotels** in Quiché. The cheapest are right beside the bus terminal: all three are very basic, but the *Hospedajes Tropical* (①) and *Hermano Pedro* (①) are better than the *Centro America* (①). Further into town are a couple of slightly more luxurious places, both very good: the *Hotel San Pascual* (③), 7 C 0–42 (☎7551107), and the *Posada Calle Real* (②), 2 Av 7–36, which is the only one with hot showers.

Restaurants are less easy to find. The *Restaurant Maya Quiché*, on the plaza, is fairly good, though with a somewhat limited menu, or you can try the *Restaurant Lago Azul*, 2 Av 2–12, or the *Video Restaurant 2000*, a garish sort of place that does pizza and occasionally shows a film or two – there are two branches, one at 4 C and 5 Av and the other a block west of the plaza. *Restaurant Mimi Jazz* on the road from the bus terminal to the centre is reasonably priced and decent enough. The only other source of evening entertainment is the **cinema**, *Cine Astor*, at 3 Av and 6 C. If you need to change **money** there's a branch of the *Banco de Guatemala* in the northwest corner of the plaza (Mon–Thurs 8.30am–2pm, Fri 8.30am–2.30pm).

Second-class **buses** to all over the highlands run from the terminal on the edge of town. There are departures to Guatemala City hourly from 5am to 5pm; to Joyabaj hourly from 9am to 5pm; to Nebaj at 9am, 10.30am and 1pm; to Uspantán at 10am, 11am and 3pm; to Quezaltenango at 8.30am, 1pm and 2pm; and to San Marcos at 5am. If you're heading for anywhere outside the department then it's generally easiest to take any bus to Los Encuentros and change there.

The ruins of Utatlán

Early in the fifteenth century, riding on a wave of successful conquest, the Quiché king Gucumatz (Feathered Serpent) founded a new capital, Gumarcaaj. A hundred years later the Spanish arrived, renamed the city **Utatlán**, and then destroyed it. Today the ruins can be visited, about 4km to the west of Santa Cruz del Quiché.

According to the Popol Vuh, Gucumatz was a lord of great genius, assisted by powerful spirits: "The nature of this king was truly marvellous, and all the other lords were filled with terror before him . . . And this was the beginning of the grandeur of the Quiché, when Gucumatz gave these signs of his power. His sons and his grandsons never forgot him." And there's no doubt that this was once a great city, with several separate citadels spread across neighbouring hilltops. It housed the nine dynasties of the tribal elite, including the four main Quiché lords, and contained a total of 23 palaces. The splendour of the city embodied the strength of the Quiché empire, which at its height boasted a population of around a million.

By the time of the Conquest, however, the Quiché had been severely weakened and their empire fractured. They first made contact with the Spanish on the Pacific coast, suffering a heavy defeat at the hands of Alvarado's forces near Quezaltenango, with the loss of their hero Tecún Umán. The Quiché then invited the Spanish to their capital, a move that made Alvarado distinctly suspicious. On seeing the fortified city he feared a trap and captured the Quiché leaders, Oxib-Queh and Beleheb-Tzy. His next step was characteristically straightforward: "As I knew them to have such a bad disposition to service of his Majesty, and to ensure the good and peace of this land, I burnt them, and sent to burn the town and destroy it."

The site

The site is surrounded by deep ravines, with stunning views across the valley. There has been little restoration since the Spanish destroyed the city, and only a few of the main structures are still recognizable, most buried beneath grassy mounds and shaded by pine trees. The small **museum** has a scale model of what the original city may once have looked like.

The central plaza, where you'll find all the remaining buildings, is parcelled off by three **temples**, the Great Monuments of Tohil, Auilix and Hacauaitz, all of which were simple pyramids topped by thatched shelters. In the middle of the plaza there used to be a circular **tower**, the Temple of the Sovereign Plumed Serpent, but these days just its foundations can be made out. The only other feature that is still vaguely recognizable is the **ball court**, which lies beneath grassy banks to the south of the plaza.

Perhaps the most interesting thing about the site today is that *brujos*, traditional Indian priests, still come here to perform religious rituals, practices that predate the arrival of the Spanish by thousands of years. The entire area is covered in small burnt circles – the ashes of incense – and chickens are regularly sacrificed in and around the plaza. Beneath the plaza is a long constructed tunnel that runs underground for about 100m. Why it was made remains a mystery but these days it's become a favourite spot for sacrifice, the floor carpeted with chicken feathers, and candles burning in the alcoves at the end. To get to the tunnel follow the signs to *La Cueva*; it's probably best to go with one of the guards to make sure you don't disturb any secret acts.

Coming **from Santa Cruz del Quiché**, you can reach Utatlán by taxi or on foot. To walk, head south from the plaza along 2 Av, and then turn right down 10 C, which will take you all the way out to the site – with luck you might hitch a lift some of the way. You're welcome to **camp** amongst the ruins.

A rough road continues west from the ruins to San Antonio Ilotenango and from there to Totonicapan and there's a fair amount of traffic on this back route, which takes in some superb high ground.

East to Joyabaj

An astonishingly good paved road runs east from Santa Cruz del Quiché, beneath the impressive peaks of the **Sierra de Chuacús**, through a series of interesting villages set in beautiful rolling farmland. The first of the villages is **CHICHÉ**, a sister village to Chichicastenango, with which it shares costumes and traditions, though the market here is on Wednesday. Next is **CHINIQUE**, followed by the larger village of **ZACUALPA**, which has Thursday and Sunday markets in its beautiful broad plaza. The village's name means "where they make fine walls", and in the hills to the north are the remains of a pre-conquest settlement. There's a *pensión* down the street beside the church should you want to stay here.

The last place out this way is the small town of **JOYABAJ**, again with a small archeological site to its north. During the colonial period Joyabaj was an important staging post on the royal route to Mexico, but all evidence of its former splendour was lost when the earthquake in 1976 almost totally flattened the town and hundreds of people lost their lives: the crumbling facade of the colonial church that stands in front of the new prefabricated version is one of the few physical remains. In recent years the town has staged a miraculous recovery, however, and it is now once again a prosperous traditional centre: the Sunday **market**, which starts up on Saturday afternoon, is a huge affair well worth visiting, as is the **fiesta** in the second week of August – five days of unrelenting celebration that includes some fantastic traditional dancing and the spectacular *Palo Volador*, in which men spin to the ground from a huge wooden pole, a pre-conquest ritual now performed in only three places in the entire country.

While the town may have recovered economically, the remote **Maya villages** beyond are still suffering great hardship through lack of any services – from roads to hospitals. Many inhabitants are survivors of terrible massacres during the early 1980s and have had no assistance rebuilding their lives. You may, therefore, be interested in supporting a **local development project** run by fifteen indigenous community councils, under the auspices of the non-governmental, rural development organisation SCDRYS (*Sociedad Civil para el Desarollo Rural Replicable y Sostenible*), based in Quezaltenango (see p.150). A language centre has been set up, called the XOY Centre, in Joyabaj, where students can live with and learn Spanish or Quiché from locally trained teachers for $110 per week. For further information phone ☎7630409 or fax 7616873, FAO Douglas Sandoval.

It's possible to **walk** from Joyabaj, over the Sierra de Chuacús, to Cubulco in Baja Verapaz. It's a superb but exhausting hike, taking at least a day, though it's perhaps better done in reverse (as described on p.261).

Practicalities

Buses run between Guatemala City and Joyabaj, passing through Santa Cruz del Quiché, every hour or so (from 9am to 6pm from the capital and 5am to 4pm from Joyabaj). There's a good but very basic **pensión**, the *Hospedaje Mejia* (①), on the plaza in Joyabaj, and plenty of scattered **comedores** – one of the best is just off the main street beside the filling station.

For Panajachel and connections to the Pacific coast, **buses leave Joyabaj** at 8.30am and 12.30pm, heading for Cocales. It's also possible to get back to the capital along two rough and seldom-travelled routes. The first of these is **via San Martín Jilotepeque** on the daily bus that leaves Joyabaj at 2am; the second option takes you **to Pachalum**, although you'll have to rely on sporadic truck traffic as there is no longer a bus service on this route. There's nowhere to stay in Pachalum but onward buses leave for the capital at 2am, passing the ruins of Mixco Viejo – and the driver may let you sleep in the bus while you wait.

To the Cuchumatanes: Sacapulas and Uspantán

The land to the north of Santa Cruz del Quiché is sparsely inhabited and dauntingly hilly. About 10km out of town, the single rough road in this direction passes through San Pedro Jocopilas, and from there struggles on, skirting the western end of the Sierra de Chuacús and eventually dropping to the riverside town of **SACAPULAS**, two hours from Quiché in the dusty foothills of the Cuchumatanes. Sacapulas has a small colonial church, and a good market is held every Thursday and Sunday beneath a huge ceiba tree in the plaza. The women wear impressive *huipiles* and tie their hair with elaborate pom-poms, similar to those of Aguacatán.

Since long before the arrival of the Spanish, **salt** has been produced here in beds beside the Río Negro, a valuable commodity that earned the town a degree of importance. Legend has it that the people of Sacapulas originally migrated from the far north, fleeing other savage tribes. The town's original name was Tajul, meaning "hot springs", but the Spanish changed it to Sacapulas, "the grassy place", as they valued the straw baskets made locally. Along the river bank, downstream from the bridge, there are several little pools where warm water bubbles to the surface, used by local people for washing. On the opposite bank trucks and buses break for lunch at some ramshackle *comedores* and fruit stalls.

To **get to Sacapulas** you can catch any of the buses that leave Santa Cruz del Quiché throughout the morning for Uspantán or Nebaj. Getting out of Sacapulas can take a while, particularly if you arrive in the afternoon. If you want to **stay**, the *Restaurant Riv Negro* offers basic and clean rooms (②). The cook, Manuele, serves good **meals** (menus in English and Spanish) and excellent banana, pineapple and papaya milkshakes. *Panaderia Karla*, near the square, does good choco bananas and the street *comedores* serve tasty *tamales* and *enchiladas*. **Market days**, as usual, are Thursday and Sunday – the former is the larger.

The village is at the junction of two crucial backroads, with **buses** leaving for Huehuetenango in the early morning (4am & 5am), and others passing through en route between Quiché, Nebaj and Uspantán.

East to Uspantán, and on to Cobán

East of Sacapulas a dirt road rises steeply, clinging to the mountainside and quickly leaving the Río Negro far below. As it climbs, the views are superb, with tiny riverside Sacapulas dwarfed by the sheer enormity of the landscape. Eventually the road reaches a high valley and arrives in **USPANTÁN**, a small town lodged in a chilly gap in the mountains and often soaked in steady drizzle. The only reason you'll end up here is in order to get somewhere else, and with the bus for Cobán and San Pedro Carchá leaving at 3am and 3.30am the best thing to do is go to bed. (The return buses leave San Pedro Carchá for Uspantán at 10am and noon.) There are two friendly *pensiónes*, the *Casa del Viajero* (①) and the *Golinda* (①). **Buses** for Uspantán, via Sacapulas, leave Quiché at 10am, 11am and 3pm, returning at 7pm, 11.30pm and 3am – a five-hour trip.

The Ixil triangle: Nebaj, Chajul and Cotzal

High up on the spine of the Cuchumatanes, in a landscape of steep hills, bowl-shaped valleys and gushing rivers, is the **Ixil triangle**. Here the three small towns of Nebaj, Chajul and Cotzal, remote and conservative, share a language spoken nowhere else in the country. This triangle of towns forms the hub of the **Ixil-speaking region**, a massive highland area which drops away towards the Mexican border and contains at least 85,000 inhabitants. These lush and rain-drenched hills are hard to reach and notoriously difficult to control, and the relaxed atmosphere of provincial charm conceals a bitter history of protracted conflict. It's an area that embodies some of the very best and worst characteristics of the Guatemalan highlands.

On the positive side is the beauty of the landscape and the strength of indige-nous culture, both of which are overwhelming. When Church leaders moved into the area in the 1970s they found very strong communities in which the people were reluctant to accept new authority for fear that it would disrupt traditional structures, and women were included in the process of communal decision-making. Counterbalancing these strengths are the horrors of the human rights abuses that took place here over the last decade, which must rate as some of the worst anywhere in Central America.

Before the **Conquest** the town of Nebaj was a sizeable centre, producing large quantities of jade and possibly allied in some way to Zaculeu (see p.170). The Spanish Conquest was particularly brutal in these parts, however. Only on the third attempt, in 1530, did the Spaniards manage to take Nebaj, and by then they were so enraged that not only was the town burnt to the ground but the survivors

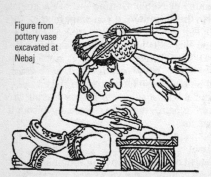

Figure from pottery vase excavated at Nebaj

were condemned to slavery as punish-ment for their resistance. In the years that followed, the land was repeatedly invaded by the Lacandon Indians from the north and swept by devastating epidemics. Things didn't improve with the coming of independence, when the Ixil were regarded as a source of cheap labour and forced to work on the coastal plantations. It is estimated that between 1894 and 1930 six thou-sand labourers migrated annually to work on the harvest, suffering not only the hardship of the actual work, but also exposure to a number of new diseases. Many never returned, and even today large numbers of local people are forced to migrate in search of work, and conditions on many of the plantations remain appalling. In the late 1970s and early 1980s, the area was hit by waves of horrific violence (see p.122–123) as it became the main theatre of operation for the **EGP** (the Guerrilla Army of the Poor). Caught up in the conflict, the people have suffered enormous losses, with the majority of the smaller villages destroyed by the army and their inhabitants herded into "protected" settlements. In the last few years the EGP have been driven back into the wilderness to the north and a degree of normality has returned to the area. New villages are springing up on the old sites and a cease-fire is sporadically maintained.

Despite all this, the fresh green hills are some of the most beautiful in the country and the three towns are friendly and accommodating, with a relaxed and distinctive atmosphere in a misty world of their own.

Nebaj

NEBAJ is the centre of Ixil country and by far the largest of the three, a beautiful old town of white adobe walls and cobbled streets. The weaving done here is unusual and intricate, its greatest feature being the women's *huipiles*, which are a mass of complex geometrical designs in superb purples, reds, yellows, greens and oranges, worn with brilliant red *cortes* (skirts). The men's ceremonial jackets, which are fast going out of use, are formal-looking and ornately decorated, modelled on those worn by Spanish officers. (The finest red cloth, often used in both the jackets and the women's sashes, originates in Germany and keeps its colour incredibly well. If you look closely at the cloth it's easy to recognize the use of "Rojo alemán"). The people of Nebaj are keen to establish a market for their weaving, but most of them can't afford to travel as far as Chichicastenango, and so as soon as you arrive in town an army of young girls, desperate to sell their cloth, will hassle you with unrelenting and disarming charm. Some people find their persistence very wearing; they never give up, chasing you every single day of your stay. You'll find an excellent shop, selling goods produced by the Ixil weaving co-op, on the main square.

There's little to do in Nebaj itself. The market is interesting, a block from the plaza in a covered building, although it's fairly quiet most days. On Thursday and Sunday the numbers swell and the action moves out into the open air. The town church is also worth a look, although it's fairly bare inside. If you're here for the second week in August you'll witness the **Nebaj fiesta**, which includes processions, dances, drinking and fireworks.

Figure from pottery vase excavated at Nebaj

Practicalities

Buses to Nebaj leave Santa Cruz del Quiché at 9am, 10.30am and 1pm, taking around five hours. The last one usually goes through to Cotzal (arriving at around 8pm) and on to the end of the road at Finca San

Francisco. You can also reach Nebaj by direct bus from Huehuetenango (6hr); see p.170.

The range of **accommodation** in Nebaj is fairly limited and you'll certainly find little in the way of luxury, although what there is does have an inimitable charm – as well as bargain rates to be found in few other areas. There are virtually no street signs in Nebaj, so you'll probably have to rely on the gang of children who act as guides and present themselves to new arrivals. The most expensive place to stay is the friendly *Hotel Ixil* (③), on the main road into town, a couple of blocks from the plaza, where all the rooms have hot water. Around the corner from each other on the northwest edge of town are the charming *Hospedaje Las Clavellinas* (formerly known as *Las Gemelitas*; ①), run by a very hospitable Ixil family, and the *Hospedaje Rinconcito* (①). Also worth checking is the *Hospedaje Kariari II*, 2 C, on the mud track towards Acul village. Wooden rooms around a light courtyard and spacious, peaceful garden (①). Finally, a

THE EGP IN THE IXIL TRIANGLE

Of the entire western highlands the Ixil triangle was one of the areas most devastated by the bitter **civil war** of the late 1970s and early 1980s. During this period the entire area became a desperate battleground and by the time the dust settled virtually all the smaller villages had been destroyed and around 15,000 people killed.

The severity of the violence is a measure of the success of the **EGP** (*Ejército Guerrillero de los Pobres* – The Guerrilla Army of the Poor), who have been fighting the army in northern Quiché for more than two decades. The EGP first entered the area in 1972, when a small group of guerrilla fighters (some of whom had been involved in the 1960s guerrilla campaign) crossed the Mexican border to the north and began building links with local people. At the time there was little military presence in the area and they were able to work swiftly, impressing the Indians with their bold plans for political and social revolution. In 1975 they opened their military campaign by assassinating Luis Arenas, the owner of Finca La Perla, to the north of Chajul, shooting him in front of hundreds of his employees. According to the EGP, "shouts of joy burst from throats accustomed for centuries only to silence and lament, and with something like an ancestral cry, with one voice they chanted with us our slogan, *Long live the poor, death to the rich.*" Other accounts, however, describe people walking for days to pay their last respects to Luis Arenas, a beloved patriarch.

These early actions prompted a huge response from the **armed forces**, who began killing, kidnapping and torturing suspected guerrillas. The organization was already well entrenched, however, and the army's brutality only served to persuade more and more people to seek protection from the guerrillas. By late 1978 the EGP were regularly occupying villages, holding open meetings and tearing down the debtors' jails. In January 1979 they briefly took control of Nebaj itself, holding a meeting in the town plaza and killing Enrique Brol, another local landowner.

The army responded with a wave of horrific attacks on the civilian population. Army units swept through the area, committing random atrocities, burning villages and massacring thousands of their inhabitants, including women and children. Nevertheless, the strength of the guerrillas continued to grow and in 1981 they again launched an attack on Nebaj, which was now a garrison town. Shortly afterwards the army chief of staff, Benedicto Lucas Garcia (the president's brother), flew into block from the plaza is the *Pensión Las Tres Hermanas* (②), Nebaj's oldest and finest hotel, consisting of damp rooms set around a large muddy courtyard. The two remaining sisters serve delicious food on request. As for **eating**, the best *comedor* in town is *Irene's*, just off the main square, and there are several others on the plaza. The *Maya-Inca*, a great new restaurant on 5 C, serves delicious Peruvian and local dishes, as well as cakes and coffee – and you can always get something to eat in the market. Nebaj has a **bank**: *Bancafe*, 2 Av 46 near the market (Mon–Fri 8.30am–4pm, Sat 8am–noon), exchanges both cash and travellers' cheques.

From Nebaj buses usually leave for Quiché at midnight and 1am, although there is sometimes one at 5am. The bus for Huehuetenango leaves daily at 1.45am. From around 10pm the buses are parked in Nebaj's plaza, so it's always worth reserving your seat and checking the intended time of departure. Note that all these times are subject to sudden change as the rough roads take a heavy toll on the buses.

Nebaj and summoned a meeting of the entire population. In a simple speech he warned them that if they didn't "clean up their act" he'd bring five thousand men "and finish off the entire population."

President Lucas Garcia was overthrown by a military coup in early 1982 and the presidency of **General Ríos Montt** saw a radical change in the army's tactics. Ríos Montt used civilian patrols to ensure the loyalty of the people and placed them in the front line of the conflict. Villagers were given ancient M1 rifles and told to protect their communities from the guerrillas. Meanwhile, the army began aggressive sweeps through the highlands, but instead of burning villages and terrorizing the population they brought people back into Nebaj to be fed and and eventually settled in new "model" villages. This new approach revealed that the people of the Ixil were in fact determined to remain neutral and had only taken sides in order to ensure their survival. Relatively quickly, whole communities adapted to the new situation and rejected contact with the guerrillas.

The guerrillas were hit extremely hard and for a brief period responded with desperate acts. On June 6, 1982, guerrillas stopped a bus near Cotzal and executed thirteen civil patrol leaders and their wives; eleven days later a guerrilla column entered the village of Chacalté, where the new civil patrol had been particularly active, and killed a hundred people, wounding another 35.

The army's offer of amnesty, twinned with a continuous crackdown on the guerrillas, soon drew refugees out of the mountains: between 1982 and 1984 some 42,000 people turned themselves in, fleeing a harsh existence under guerrilla protection. By 1985 the guerrillas had been driven back into a handful of mountain strongholds in Xeputul, Sumal and Amachel, all to the north and west of Chajul and Cotzal.

Today the EGP is thought to be on its last legs, although columns of several hundred men do still establish road blocks, hold meetings and mount attacks on the army. Meanwhile the CPR (Communities of People's Resistance) have now said that they reject both the army and the guerrillas and would rather establish some kind of independent civil society. The CPR claim to represent some 20,000 people in the contested area to the north of Nebaj and regularly protest that their villages are being bombarded by the army. For those who live in areas already controlled by the army, life is slowly returning to normal as new villages are settled every month and people return home, although there is barely enough land to go around.

Walks around Nebaj

In the hills that surround Nebaj there are several beautiful **walks**, the most inter-esting one taking you to the village of **Acul**, two hours away. Starting from the church in Nebaj, cross the plaza and turn to the left, taking the road that goes downhill between a shop and a *comedor*. At the bottom of the dip it divides, and here you take the right-hand fork and head out of town along a dirt track.

Just after you pass the last houses you'll see some pre-Columbian burial mounds to your right. These are still used for religious ceremonies, and if you take a close look you'll find burnt patches marking the site of offerings. Since the mounds are usually planted with maize they can be a bit difficult to spot, but once you get up higher above the town they're easier to make out.

Beyond this the track carries on, switchbacking up a steep hillside, and heads over a narrow pass into the next valley, where it drops down into the village. **ACUL** was one of the original so-called "model villages" into which people were herded after their homes had been destroyed by the army, and despite the spectacular setting – and the efforts of the United Nations, amongst others, to improve the standard of living – it's a sad and weary place. If you walk on through the village and out the other side you arrive at the Finca San Antonio, a bizarre Swiss-style chalet set in a neat little meadow. An Italian family have lived here for more than fifty years, making some of the country's best cheese, and visitors are welcome to have a look around – especially if they buy some produce. The man who founded the *finca* died in 1990, at the ripe old age of 99.

A second, shorter walk takes you to a beautiful little **waterfall**, La Cascada de Plata, about an hour from Nebaj. Take the road to Chajul and turn left just before it crosses the bridge, a kilometre or two outside Nebaj. Don't be fooled by the smaller version you'll come to shortly before the main set of falls.

West to Salquil Grande

A third possible excursion takes you to the village of **SALQUIL GRANDE**, 23km to the west of Nebaj. A newish road runs out this way, through the village of Tzalbal, and across two huge and breathtaking valleys. But the view is overshadowed by evidence of the scale of the recent violence. The hills beside the road are dotted with brand new villages, their tin roofs still clean and rust-free. All of these were built to replace those burnt to the ground, and are inhabited by people who have spent the last few years either starving in the mountains or shut away in the refugee camps of Nebaj. **Trucks** run out to Salquil Grande from the market in Nebaj at around 6am on most days, and certainly for the Tuesday market. There's nowhere to stay in the village but the trucks usually return a couple of hours later. Continuing west from Salquil Grande, a very rough road runs some 44km to join up with the main Huehuetenango to Barillas road, although if you are considering heading in this direction you should bear in mind that this area is still fought over.

The landscape around Salquil Grande is supremely beautiful and best enjoyed on foot. A good hike takes you to the little village of **Parramos Grande** in around two hours. Starting from the statue of a soldier on the edge of Salquil Grande, you want to take the path to the right and when this divides take a left through the *milpa*, heading downhill. Along the way you pass a couple of beautiful waterfalls, so if the sun's shining you can always pause for a chilly dip.

San Juan Cotzal and Chajul

Of the other two towns in the Ixil triangle, **SAN JUAN COTZAL** is the easier to reach. The bus that leaves Quiché at 1pm arrives in Nebaj at about 3pm, and in theory continues to Cotzal. However, the 20km from Nebaj to Cotzal can take as long as two hours to travel by bus, as the road, curving its way around the jutting green hills, is sometimes a sea of mud; and in practice this bus often doesn't show, or chooses to go no further than Nebaj. When you do get there, Cotzal itself is a huddle of steep streets, built along the shoulder of a sharp ridge and often wrapped in a damp blanket of mist. In the 1920s and 1930s this was the largest and busiest of the three Ixil towns, as it was from here that the fertile lands to the north were colonized. Once a road reached Nebaj in the 1940s, however, Cotzal was somewhat eclipsed, although there is still a high concentration of *Ladinos* here.

Intricate green *huipiles* are worn by the Indian women in Cotzal, who weave bags and rope from the fibres of the maguey plant. If you head out this way you'll almost certainly have to stay the night. The *farmacía* in the corner of the plaza rents out **rooms** (①), and the owners also run a *comedor*, so let them know if you'd like a meal.

Last but by no means least of the Ixil settlements is **CHAJUL**. Chajul, made up almost entirely of old adobe houses, with wooden beams and red-tiled roofs blackened by the smoke of cooking fires, is the friendlier of these two villages. It is also the most determinedly traditional and least bilingual of the Ixil towns. The streets are usually bustling with activity: you'll be met by an army of small children, and the local women gather to wash clothes at the stream that cuts through the middle of the village. Here boys still use blowpipes to hunt small birds, a skill that dates from the earliest of times but is now little used elsewhere. The women of Chajul dress entirely in red, filling the streets with colour, and wear earrings made of old coins strung up on lengths of wool. The traditional red jackets of the men are a rare sight these days. Make sure you visit the shop run by the local weaving co-operative, called *Va'l Vaq Quyol*, between the church and the market, where you will find some of the best quality, handmade textiles in the country at very decent prices.

The colonial church, a massive old structure, is home to the **Christ of Golgotha** and the target of a large pilgrimage on the second Friday of Lent – a particularly good time to be here. The two angels that flank the image were originally dressed as policemen, after a tailor who'd been cured through prayer donated the uniforms so that his benefactor would be well protected. Later they were changed into army uniforms, and recently they've been toned down to look more like boy scouts.

You can rent a **room** (①) from one of the men who works in the post office. Other than a steady flow of unscheduled trucks, there are regular morning buses to Chajul, especially on Tuesdays and Fridays, which are market days. The first leaves at 4am. Return buses leave at 11.30am and 12.30pm.

Beyond the triangle: the Ixcán

To the north of the Ixil triangle is a thinly populated area known as the **Ixcán**, which drops away towards the Mexican border to merge with the Lacandon rainforests. The last vestiges of the EGP are still fighting to maintain control of this region, as they are gradually driven deeper into the wilderness and threatened by the prospect of a new road cutting through from Playa Grande to Barillas.

The Ixcán has long been one of Guatemala's great untamed frontiers. In the 1960s and 1970s land-hungry migrants from Quiché and Huehuetenango began moving into the area to carve out new farms from the forest. Assisted by Maryknoll missionaries, after a few years of extreme hardship they had established thriving communities. The land yielded two crops a year and produced an abundance of fruit, coffee and cardamon. The settlers built health clinics and churches, established a system of radio communication and a transport network and began applying for collective land titles. However, in the early 1970s the EGP moved into the area and the 1980s saw it devastated by bitter fighting, in which virtually every village was burnt to the ground and thousands fled to Mexico.

Today at least 10,000 people live in the area and are subject to occasional bombardment by the Guatemalan army, who argue that the land is empty, and that consequently anyone coming under fire must in some way be connected with the guerrillas. Officially, however, this has come to a stop in the 1990s, as the government has pledged assistance to the thousands of refugees returning from Mexico, hoping that the Peace Accord with the guerrillas will finally hold. Meanwhile a new road has been cut into the jungle to the north, running parallel to the Mexican border and linking Playa Grande and Barillas.

LAKE ATITLÁN

Lake Como, it seems to me, touches the limit of the permissibly picturesque; but Atitlán is Como with the additional embellishments of several immense volcanoes. It is really too much of a good thing. After a few days of this impossible landscape one finds oneself thinking nostalgically of the English Home Counties.

Aldous Huxley, *Beyond the Mexique Bay* (1934).

Whether or not you share Huxley's refined sensibilities, there's no doubt that Lake Atitlán is astonishingly beautiful, and most people find themselves captivated by its scenic excesses. Indeed the effect is so overwhelming that a handful of devotees have been rooted to its shores since the 1960s. The lake, just three hours from Guatemala City and a few kilometres south of the Pan-American Highway, rates as the country's number-one tourist attraction. It's a source of national pride, and some Guatemalans claim that it ranks with the Seven Wonders of the World.

The water itself is an irregular shape, with three main inlets. It measures 18km by 12km at its widest point, and shifts through an astonishing range of blues, greys and greens as the sun moves across the sky. Hemmed in on all sides by steep hills and massive volcanoes, it's at least 320m deep and has no visible outlet, draining as it does through an underground passage to the Pacific coast. In the morning the surface of the lake is normally calm and clear, but by early afternoon the *Xocomil*, "the wind that carries away sin", blows from the coast, churning the surface and making travel by boat a hair-raising experience. A north wind, say the Maya, indicates that the spirit of the lake is discarding a drowned body, having claimed its soul.

San José
Chacaya
Sololá
Santa Lucía
Utatlán
Santa Cruz   San Jorge   San Andrés
La Laguna   La Laguna   Semetabaj
San Marcos   Tzununa   Panajachel
La Laguna   Santa Catarina
San Pablo La Laguna   Palopó
Santa Maria   Godínez
Visitacion
San Juan   San Pedro   San Antonio
La Laguna   La Laguna   Palopó

N

Patricia & Patzun △

Volcán
San Pedro   CERRO DE ORO
2995 m
                                          Agua Escondida
Volcán
Santa Clara   Santiago
Atitlán   San Lucas
                Tolimán
Volcán Tolimán
3158 m

*Lake
Atitlán*

Volcán Atitlán
3537 m

Pochuta

LAKE ATITLÁN

0   5 km

On the shores of the lake are thirteen villages, with many more in the hills
behind, ranging from the cosmopolitan resort-style **Panajachel** to the tiny, traditional and isolated **Tzununá**. The villages are mostly traditional farming
communities, and it's easy to travel around the lake staying in a different one
each night. Around the southwestern shores, from **Santiago** to **San Pedro**, the
Indians are **Tzutujil** speakers, the remnants of one of the smaller pre-conquest
tribes, whose capital was on the slopes of the San Pedro volcano. On the other
side of the water, from **San Marcos** to **Cerro de Oro**, **Cakchiquel** is spoken,
marking the western barrier of this tribe.

This area has been heavily populated since the earliest of times, but it's only
relatively recently that it has attracted large numbers of tourists. For the moment
things are still fairly undisturbed and the beauty remains overwhelming, but
some of the new pressures are decidedly threatening. The fishing industry, once
thriving on the abundance of small fish and crabs, has been crippled by the introduction of **black bass**, which eat the smaller fish and water birds and are, more-

over, much harder to catch. These fish stick to the deeper water and have to be speared by divers – their introduction was intended to create a sport-fishing industry. The increase in population has also had a damaging impact on the shores of the lake, as the desperate need to cultivate more land leads to deforestation and accompanying soil erosion.

Beginning in the early 1990s the shores suffered through yet another invasion: the fashionable and wealthy abandoned the blackened waters of Lake Amatitlán and moved across to Atitlán. Weekend retreats are still springing up around the shores and Saturday afternoons see the waters dotted with speedboats and skiers. In 1955 the Atitlán basin was declared a national park to preserve its wealth of cultural and natural characteristics, but this seems to have had little effect on development.

You'll probably reach the lake through **Panajachel**, a small village on the northern shore which is now dominated by tourism. It makes an ideal base for exploring the surrounding area, either heading across the lake or making day trips to **Chichicastenango**, **Nahualá**, **Sol0lá** and **Iximché**. The village has an abundance of cheap hotels and restaurants and is well served by buses. From here you can travel by boat or road to the southern shores of the lake and the more traditional villages of **Santiago** and **San Pedro**, where the landscape and the population have maintained a degree of harmony. The western shoreline is even more isolated, but it's possible to walk from **San Pedro** to **San Marcos**, a superb way to appreciate the splendours of Atitlán. Each of the surrounding villages has a distinctive character and from every angle the lake looks completely different.

Los Encuentros to Atitlán: Sololá

A couple of kilometres to the west of Los Encuentros, at the **El Cuchillo** junction, the road for Panajachel branches off the Pan-American Highway. Dropping towards the lake it arrives first at **SOLOLÁ**, the departmental capital, which is perched on a natural balcony some 600m above the water. Overlooked by the majority of travellers, Sololá is, nonetheless, a fascinating place. In common with only a few other towns it has parallel Indian and *Ladino* governments, and is probably the largest "Indian" town in the country, with the vast majority of the people still wearing traditional costume.

The town itself isn't much to look at: a wide central plaza with a recently restored clock tower on one side and a modern church on the other. However, if you stop by for the Friday **market** you'll get a real sense of its importance. Aldous Huxley described the market here as "a walking museum of fancy dress". From as early as 5am the plaza is packed, drawing traders from all over the highlands, as well as thousands of local Sololá Indians, the women covered in striped red cloth and the men in their distinctive jackets, outlandish cowboy shirts and embroidered trousers. Weaving is a powerful creative tradition in the lives of Sololá Indians and each generation develops a distinctive style based upon previous designs. You'll notice several styles of jacket, with the younger men preferring pure white, heavily embroidered cloth, and that the red and white striped cloth worn by the women is also becoming more elaborate.

Tradition dominates daily life in Sololá and the town is said to be divided into sections, each administered by an Indian clan, just as it was before the Conquest. Little is known about the details of this system, though, and its secrets are well kept. The basic design still to be seen on the back of the men's jacket is an abstraction of a bat, the symbol of the royal house of Xahil, who were the rulers of the Cakchiquel at the time of the Conquest. The pre-conquest site of **Tecpán-Atitlán**, which was abandoned in 1547 when Sololá was founded by the Spanish, is to the north of town.

Another interesting time to visit Sololá is on Sunday, when the **cofradías**, the elders of the Indian religious hierarchy, parade through the streets in ceremonial costume to attend the 10am Mass. They're easily recognizable, carrying silver-tipped canes and wearing broad-brimmed hats with particularly elaborate jackets. Inside the church the sexes are segregated, and the women wear shawls to cover their heads.

Sololá practicalities

If you'd rather not immerse yourself in Panajachel there are several simple **hotels** in Sololá itself: the *Hotel Santa Ana*, a block uphill from the plaza at 6 Av 8–35, has plain rooms around a pleasant courtyard (②); there's the similar *Hotel Paisaje*, also a block above the plaza at 9 C between 6 and 7 avenidas (②); and the *Hotel La Posada del Viajero*, on the plaza, is again basic but overpriced (②). The first two have *comedores*, and there are a few other simple **places to eat** scattered around town, although you can always eat in the market during the day.

There's a **post office** (Mon–Fri 8am–4.30pm) on the plaza and a *Banco G&T* at 9 C and 5 Av (Mon–Fri 9am–3pm, Sat 10am–2pm). For bus times refer to the Panajachel schedules, as all **buses** travelling between Panajachel and Los Encuentros pass through Sololá. There are also minibuses that run regularly between Sololá and Los Encuentros. The last bus to Panajachel passes through Sololá at around 6pm.

Nearby villages

Several other villages can be reached from Sololá, most of them within walking distance. About 8km to the east is **CONCEPCIÓN**, an exceptionally quiet farming village with a spectacularly restored colonial church. The restoration was finished in 1988 and the facade is still a shiny white. The walk out there, along a dirt track skirting the hills above Panajachel, offers superb views across the lake.

Four kilometres to the west of Sololá, along another dirt road and across a deep-cut river valley, **San José Chacayá** has a tiny colonial church with thick crumbling walls but little else. Another 8km further along the track is **Santa Lucía Utatlán**, which can also be reached along a dirt track that branches off the Pan-American Highway. From Santa Lucía the road continues around the lake, set back from the ridge of hills overlooking the water, to Santa María Visitación and **Santa Clara La Laguna**. The latter is connected by a steep trail to San Pablo on the lakeshore below: if you're planning to walk to San Pablo via Santa Clara set out early as it's a full day's hike.

On the hillside below Sololá is **SAN JORGE**, a tiny hamlet perched above the lake, whose inhabitants have been chased around the country by natural disasters. The village was founded by refugees from the 1773 earthquake in Antigua and the original lakeside version was swept into the water by a landslide, persuading the people to move up the hill.

Panajachel

Ten kilometres beyond Sololá, separated by a precipitous descent, is **PANAJACHEL**, gateway to the lake. Over the years what was once a small Indian village has become something of a resort, with a sizeable population of long-term foreign residents, whose numbers are swollen in the winter by an influx of seasonal migrants and a flood of tourists. Those same pleasures that attract the Americans have earned the town a bad reputation amongst some sections of Guatemalan society, and it's often regarded as a haven of drug-taking drop-outs. In the past the army has raided hotels in Panajachel and banished

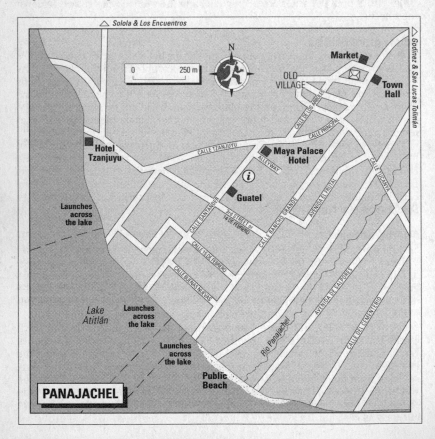

some of the occupants, but these days they're a touch more tolerant. Other locals are keen to associate themselves with the scene, and at weekends you'll see their blacked-out cars cruising the streets and riotous drinking sessions in lakeside *comedores*.

Not so long ago (although it seems an entirely different age) Panajachel was a quiet little village of **Cakchiquel** Indians, whose ancestors were settled here after the Spanish crushed a force of Tzutujil warriors on the site. In the early days of the Conquest the Franciscans established a church and monastery in the village, using it as the base for their regional conversion campaign. Today the old village has been enveloped by the new building boom, but it still retains a traditional feel, and most of the Indians continue to farm in the river delta behind the town. The Sunday market, bustling with people from all around the lake, remains oblivious to the tourist invasion.

For travellers Panajachel is one of those inevitable destinations, and although no one ever owns up to actually liking it, everyone seems to stay for a while. The old village is still attractive and although most of the new building is fairly nondescript, its lakeside setting is superb. The main **daytime activity** is hanging out, either wandering the streets, shopping, eating and drinking, or at the **public beach**, where you can swim and sunbathe, although really it's far nicer on the other side of the lake in San Pedro (see p.140). You can also pay a few dollars to use the swimming pool and private beach at *Vision Azul*, in the bay before Panajachel. **Weaving** from all over Guatemala is sold with daunting persistence in the streets here. Much of it is of the very highest standards with the weavers themselves travelling down from places like Todos Santos, Nebaj and Chajul to sell their wares. Prices can be high, so bargain hard. The main **market** day is Sunday, when the old village is alive with activity, although things are also busy on Saturday.

Panajachel also makes a comfortable base for exploring the lake and the central highlands. The markets in **Nahualá** on Sunday and **Chichicastenango** on Thursday and Saturday are both within an hour or two's travel, and the ruins at **Santa Cruz del Quiché** (Utatlán) and **Tecpán** (Iximché) can also be visited as day trips.

Arrival and information

Arriving in Panajachel the bus drops you on the main street, outside the *Maya Palace Hotel*. Over to your right, you have calles Santander and Rancho Grande, which run parallel towards the lake, and in front and to your left is the old village.

The local *Inguat* office on C Santander (Mon–Sat 8am–6.30pm, Sun noon–6pm; ☎7621392) is run by the extremely helpful Mr Hector Solis, who speaks English. Check here for boat and bus schedules and any other information you might need.

Panajachel's **post office** is in the old village, down a side street beside the church (Mon–Fri 8am–4.30pm). To make a **phone call** or send a **fax**, head to *Maya Communications* (Mon–Sat 8am–1pm & 2–6pm) a very efficient office on C Santander, which also has e-mail and computer rental; *Guatel*, halfway down C Santander (daily 7am–midnight), or the travel agent *Central America Link (CAL)* (Mon–Sat 9am–5pm; ☎ & fax 7621378) next to *Bruno's Steak House*. The oldest and most reliable **parcel service** is *Get Guated Out*, next to the *Galeria Bookstore* on C Los Arboles.

Accommodation

The streets of Panajachel are overflowing with cheap **hotels**, and there are huge numbers of **"rooms"**. The latter, as a rule, look as if they've been left over from the 1960s, their wooden walls adorned with trippy poetry and bizarre drawings, but they still offer the best deal in town, almost invariably charging a little over a dollar, with a few cents more for a hot shower. If you're in a group, and planning to stay for a while, then check the noticeboards for **houses to rent**. If you have a tent then you can either take your chances on the public beach in Panajachel, where you'll usually find a cluster of fellow campers, or pay $4 to **camp** at the *Vision Azul*, which is in the next bay in the shadow of the two concrete towers. This fee also entitles you to use the pool and private beach.

Hotels

Las Casitas, at the back of the old village, near the market (☎7621224). Very clean, friendly, safe and quiet; private bathrooms and hot water. ④.

Hotel Dos Mundos, C Santander (☎ & fax 7622078). Italian-owned new hotel, right on the main drag, which offers beautiful rooms set in a private garden, which includes a small swimming pool. The attached restaurant is also recommended for authentic Italian cuisine at moderate prices. ⑥.

TRANSPORT AROUND PANAJACHEL

BUSES
Buses arrive and leave from outside the *Maya Palace Hotel*. Throughout the day **minibuses** shuttle between Panajachel and Los Encuentros, and much of the time it's easier to catch one of these and flag down another bus on the Pan-American Highway.

To and from Guatemala City (3hr 30min). *Rebuli* run hourly buses from 5am to 3pm. *Rebuli*'s offices in Guatemala City are at 20 C and Av Bolívar in Zona 1.

To Chichicastenango (1hr 30min) at 6.45am (Thurs & Sun) 7am, 7.45am, 8.45am, 10.40am, 1pm, 3pm & 6pm. If these don't materialize or you want to travel at some other time then take any bus to Los Encuentros, where buses pass through every hour. **From Chichicastenango** at 5am, 6am, 7.30am, 11am, 1pm & 2.30pm, although again you can always change at Los Encuentros. On market days there is also a steady flow of **minibuses** between Chichicastenango and Panajachel, which are more expensive but a good deal quicker.

To Quezaltenango (2hr 30min) at 5.30am, 5.45am, 6.45am, 7.45am, 11.30am & 2.30pm.

From Quezaltenango at 5am, 6.30am, 10am, noon, 1pm & 3pm.

To San Lucas Tolimán Direct services at 6.45am & 4.30pm, or you can take a bus heading for Cocales and hitch or walk the 2km from the junction.

To Cocales (2hr 30min) at 6am, 8.30am, noon & 3.30pm.

To San Antonio Palopo at 9am & 4.30pm, returning at 5am & 10.30am.

Shuttle services
To and from Antigua Tourist shuttle operated by *Turansa* in Antigua leaves Antigua's *Hotel Ramada* on Wed, Fri & Sat at 8.30am, arriving in Panajachel at

Hotel Fonda del Sol, just off the entrance road to Panajachel (☎7621162). Very Guatemalan; 15 well-kept rooms with private shower and some cheaper ones without. ④.

Los Geranios, C Rancho Grande, down by the lake (☎7621033). Four- and six-bed bungalows, complete with kitchen and use of a pool. If it's full, there's a similar setup at *El Aguacatal*, behind the *Hotel del Lago*. ③–④ per person.

Hotel Las Jacarandas, footpath off C Rancho Grande. Simple rooms around an attractive garden, with hot water in the communal bathrooms. ③.

Hotel Maya Kanek, C Principal, near the church (☎7621104). Comfortable rooms with private showers, set around a courtyard. ③.

Hotel Monterrey, on the lakeshore; follow C Santander and turn right at the sign (☎ & fax 7621126). Very faded first-class hotel, which nevertheless has a pretty garden and the best private beach. Hot water on demand. ⑥.

Muller's Guest House, C Rancho Grande (☎7622442; Guatemala City fax 3344294). Swiss-owned, immaculate guest house with beautiful rooms and garden. ⑥.

Hotel Panajachel, opposite *Las Casitas*. Decent budget hotel with rather bare rooms. Hot showers downstairs only. ③.

Hotel Posada de Don Rodrigo, C Santander, facing the lake (☎ & fax 7622322 or 7622329). Under the same ownership as the hotel of the same name in Antigua, this brand-new building has been built in colonial style, incorporating the latest in luxury and facilities. The rooms are small and pokey, though, and the waterslide facing the lake is an eyesore. ⑦.

Hotel Primavera, near the top of C Santander (☎7622052). Clean, modern hotel; all rooms have private bathroom and hot water. ⑤.

11am; it returns at noon, arriving in Antigua at 2.40pm. Tickets from hotels and shops in Antigua and Panajachel.

To and from Guatemala City Shuttle operated by *Panajachel Tourist Services*, C Santander (next to *Hotel Regis;* ☎ & fax 7622246). In Antigua, their office is at 6 Av Sur 7 (☎ & fax 8320648). Daily except Thurs and Sun they run shuttles both ways between Panajachel to Guatemala City ($22 per person one way) and Antigua ($12 per person one way). On Thurs and Sun they run to and from Guatemala City, Antigua and Chichicastenango ($7 per person one way).

BOATS

The boat schedule has become increasingly complex in recent years as several companies run rival services. Competition has also given rise to some very sharkish behaviour on the part of those selling tickets, so make sure that the ticket you buy will enable you to leave when you want.

Tours of the lake leave from the public beach at 9.30am, visiting San Marco, San Pedro and Santiago, with plenty of time in each, returning to Panajachel at 3.30pm. $6.

Panajachel to Santiago at 8.35am, 9am, 9.30am, 10.30am, 3pm & 4pm. Returning at 6am, 7am, 11.45am, 12.30pm, 1pm, 2pm & 5pm.

Panajachel to San Pedro at 8am, 9am, 9.30am*, 11am, 11.30am*, noon, 1.15pm, 2pm, 2.45pm*, 4pm, 5.30pm, 5.30pm*, 7.30pm. Returning at 4.15am, 5am, 5.30am*, 6am, 8am, 8.30am*, 10am, 11am, noon, 12.30pm*, 2pm, 3pm & 3.30pm*.

Santiago to San Pedro at 7am, 9am, 10.30am, 11am, noon, 1pm, 2pm, 3.30pm & 4pm **San Pedro to Santiago** at 6am, 6.30am, 7am, 8.30am, 10am, 11am, noon, 2pm & 3pm.

---

* boats operated by the *Chavay* company, which leave from the beach beside the *Hotel Tzanjuyu*. All the others leave from the public beach.

Hotel Villa Martita, C Santander. Friendly, family-run guest house with a selection of parrots. ③.

Hotel Vista del Lago, right on the lakeshore (☎7621555; fax 7621562 or Guatemala City ☎3344545 ext. 4420; fax 3347518). Panajachel's modern six-storey colossus, with international standards and a guaranteed view of the lake. ⑦.

Rancho Grande Inn, C Rancho Grande (☎7622255; fax 7622247). Another longstanding Panajachel institution with warm, homely cabins, superbly kept gardens and helpful staff. ⑤.

Hotel Regis, C Santander (☎7621149; fax 7621152). Age-old establishment, rooms in individual bungalows, beautiful gardens and the added distractions of a pool, ping-pong and croquet. Ideal for travellers with children. ⑥.

Rooms and budget accommodation

Hospedaje Casa Linda, down an alley off the top of C Santander. Clean, quiet and safe, with hot water. ②.

Hospedaje Country Club, C Rancho Grande (near the old village). Rustic rooms set around a small courtyard, which is very simple but does offer secure parking. ②.

Hospedaje Garcia, beyond the *Mi Chosita* A bit more expensive but still well worth it, with the added benefit of reliable hot water. ②.

Hospedaje Londres, down a long alley off C Santander. Very basic and a touch musty, but one of the cheapest in town. ①–②.

Hospedaje Mi Chosita, on a side street off the middle of C Santander. Very bare, small and clean wooden rooms with paper-thin walls. Run by a friendly family. Laundry service. ②.

Mario's Rooms, C Santander about halfway to the beach; entrance through the side of the restaurant. Plenty of basic, clean rooms with hot water from 8am to 6pm; doors close at midnight. ②.

Hospedaje Ramos, on the public beach behind the *comedores*. Friendly, family-run establishment with hot water. Some private bathrooms. ②–③.

Hospedaje Santa Elena, off C Santander. Friendly, clean and bare rooms with hot water and lots of character; always plenty of activity, with an abundance of children and parrots. ②.

Rooms Santa Elena 1, down an alley opposite the tourist office. Pleasant and quiet; doors close at midnight. ②.

Rooms Santander, C Santander towards the beach. Clean, friendly and simple, with a nice leafy courtyard and hot water on request. ②.

Eating, drinking and entertainment

Panajachel has an abundance of **restaurants**, all catering to the cosmopolitan tastes of its floating population. For really cheap and authentically Guatemalan food there are plenty of *comedores* in the market, and several on the beach. The latter are a little more expensive, catering as they do for local day-trippers and drinking parties – but then again they also have superb views of the lake.

Cafés and restaurants

Restaurante los Amigos, C Santander. Simple, moderately priced pasta, fish, guacamole and salads.

Bombay, in the shopping arcade just past *Al Chisme*, C Los Arboles. Interesting vegetarian food which, despite the name, has nothing Indian about it. The fried tofu is good. Closed Mon.

Bruno's Steak House, C Principal at the junction with C Santander. At least five different types of steak, freshly chargrilled to your taste. Expensive.

Casablanca, next to *Bruno's*. One of Panajachel's smartest restaurants, with an international menu featuring seafood, imported pasta, Spanish dishes, and wines from Chile and Argentina. Expensive.

Al Chisme, C Los Arboles. Very popular with gringos: a smart, European-style restaurant and bar adorned with black and white photographs of former customers. Delicious food including sandwiches, crêpes, steaks, curried shrimps, and pasta, but all a little pricey.

Circus Bar, C Los Arboles. Pizza, steaks, salads, pasta or a daily set menu of three or four courses, all accompanied by a little live music. Moderate.

Hambuerguesa Gigante, C Santander. Inevitably they serve a good hamburger here, but also inexpensive breakfasts, salads, sandwiches, steaks and fish.

The Last Resort, on a side street off C Santander. One of the most popular places in Panajachel. The vast menu includes pasta, steaks, excellent cheese and vegetarian dishes; the portions are huge and the coffee is free, but don't expect to see many Guatemalans.

Mario's, C Santander. A limited range of low-cost food: huge salads, delicious yoghurt and pancakes.

La Parada, C Principal and C Santander. Bar-style café serving excellent, inexpensive breakfasts of eggs or fruit, superb juices, sandwiches and hamburgers.

El Patio, C Santander. Very good kebabs and meat dishes, moderately priced.

Pizzeria Yax Che, C Principal back in the old village. Friendly little place serving good Guatemalan pizzas that could almost be mistaken for the real thing. Moderate.

Primavera and its neighbouring kiosk *Papagayo*, C Santander. Best value breakfast in town, though lunch and dinner is expensive.

Sevananda, in the shopping arcade, just past *Al Chisme*, C Los Arboles. Popular vegetarian restaurant in the same arcade as the *Bombay*, serving wonderful Thai curries. Closed Sun.

La Unica Deli, C Principal, opposite the health centre. Refreshingly different but a little pricey. Wide range of salads, sandwiches and pastries, as well as bagels, cheeses, wines and excellent coffee, all served at tables in a peaceful garden. *Deli2* serves the same food on C Santander, just before the lake.

Nightlife

For **evening entertainment** there are three **video bars**, each showing three English-language films a day: one on C Santander, one in the *Carrot Chic* restaurant in the old part of town, and, the latest addition, *Ubu's Cosmic Cantina*, next to the *Sevananda* restaurant. There's also a local **cinema** that specializes in Mexican horror films. But the best place to head for in the evening is the *Circus Bar*, where they have **live music**. Across the road, the larger **nightclub** *La Posada del Pintor* is the best place to dance and drink the night away, with cabaret as well as music. Other nightclubs have a habit of opening and closing rapidly. Finally there's a **pool hall** in the old village, near the post office and next to *The Pink Box*. Or you can play table tennis at the *Last Resort*.

Listings

Alternative therapies A centre at the end of C Los Arboles offers Swedish acupuncture and polarity; if that's not strong enough try shamanic shape shift or eagle feather aura cleansing, which sounds as though it should cure just about anything.

Bicycle rental The outlet on the main road rents mountain bikes for $1 an hour, $6 for a day.

Boats Canoes and windsurfers can be rented on the main beach.

Books *Galeria Bookstore*, C Los Arboles, stocks a reasonable selection of secondhand books and a few new books in English.

Bank *Banco Agricola Mercantil*, at the junction of the entrance road and C Santander (Mon–Fri 9am–5pm, Sat 9am–1pm); *Banco Industrial*, C Santander (Mon–Fri 8.30am–3pm, Sat 8.30am–12.30pm) offers a worse rate, but does have a 24-hour cash till for Visa-card users.

Doctor Dr Edgar Barreno speaks good English; his surgery is down the first street that branches off to the right of C Los Arboles (☎7621008).

Language schools In general Panajachel isn't a particularly good place to study. *Academia Latinamericana Mayense*, in the heart of the old village, is the best. *Internacional*, on C Santander, is twinned with an equally poor school in Antigua.

Motorbikes *Moto Servicio Queche* at the main junction of C Santander and the entrance road rents 250cc bikes for $10 an hour, $200 for the week and 100cc bikes for $4 an hour, $100 a week. Or try *Pana Rent* next to *Circus Bar*.

Police On the plaza in the old village (☎7621120).

Taxis Usually wait outside the post office, or you can call one on ☎7621571.

Around the lake

The villages that surround the lake are all easily accessible. For an afternoon's outing, head along the shore southeast of Panajachel to **San Antonio** and **Santa Catarina Palopó**. If you want to spend a day or two exploring the area then it's well worth crossing the lake to **Santiago**, and going on to **San Pedro**. The more adventurous can walk back along the western shore – a spectacular and exhausting hike that takes a full day. These southern and western shores are by far the most beautiful and it would be a shame to visit the lake without seeing them.

The eastern shore

There are two roads around the lake's eastern shore from Panajachel: one clings to the shoreline while the other runs parallel up along the ridge of hills. Beside the lake, backed up against the slopes, are a couple of villages, the first of which, **SANTA CATARINA PALOPÓ**, is just 4km from Panajachel. The people of Santa Catarina used to live almost entirely by fishing and trapping crabs, but these days the black bass has put an end to all that and they've turned to farming and migratory work, with many of the women travelling to Panajachel to peddle their weaving. The traditional purple costume, designed in bold zigzags, is worn by both the men and the women. Much of the shoreline out this way has been developed by the wealthy, and great villas, ringed by impenetrable walls, have come to dominate the village. Very much a part of this invasion is the new hotel *Villa Santa Catarina* (☎3348023 in Guatemala City; ☎7621291 on the lake; ⑥), which has opened on the lakeshore, complete with 32 rooms, two banqueting halls, a pool and superb views of the lake.

Another 5km brings you to **SAN ANTONIO PALOPÓ**, a larger and more traditional village, squeezed in beneath the steep slope behind. The hillside above is neatly terraced and irrigated and a range of vegetables are farmed here. Again the men and women dress in beautiful traditional costumes, the men in red woven shirts and short woollen skirts similar to those in Nahualá.

The best way to visit the two villages is on foot. Catch a bus from Panajachel towards Godínez, and get off at the *mirador* about 1km before Godínez. From here you can enjoy some of the best lake views of all, and there's a path that drops through the terraces for about an hour to San Antonio. It's another hour's walk from San Antonio, through Santa Catarina, back to Panajachel. If you do plan to travel this way, check the current situation with the tourist office in Panajachel before setting out, as the area around Godínez has been the scene of a number of robberies and attacks on tourists. Alternatively, you can stick to the lower road that runs through the villages themselves. **Buses** leave Panajachel for

San Antonio at 9am and 4.30pm, returning at 5am and 10.30am, although it's usually fairly easy to hitch along this road.

If you decide **to stay** in San Antonio there are two options: the fairly upmarket *Hotel Terrazas del Lago* (⑤), down by the water, has beautiful views, although the owner, Feliks, a Polish expatriate, tends to be a little picky about when he serves meals. Otherwise you can stay in the unmarked *pensión* (①–②) near the entrance to the village, run by a delightful Peruvian woman who serves delicious food.

The higher road – to Godínez and beyond to San Lucas Tolimán

The higher of the two roads heads back into the delta behind Panajachel, before climbing up above the lake to **SAN ANDRÉS SEMETABAJ**, where there's a fantastic ruined colonial church. A path opposite the church's main entrance leads back to Panajachel, winding down through fields and coffee bushes – a nice walk of an hour or so. Beyond San Andrés the road curves around the edge of the ridge, offering an incredible sweeping view of the lake below and the irregular cone of the Tolimán volcano opposite, and arriving eventually in Godínez. A short way before is the *mirador* mentioned above, from where the path leads down to the lakeside village of San Antonio Palopó.

At **GODÍNEZ**, a ramshackle and wind-blown village, the road divides, one way running out to the Pan-American Highway (through Patzicía and Patzún – this is a very dangerous road for attack and robbery), and the other on around the lake to the village of **SAN LUCAS TOLIMÁN** in the southeast corner. Set apart from the other villages in many ways, this is probably the least attractive of the lot. The land roundabout is almost all planted with coffee, which dominates the flavour of the place. The Indians take a poor second place to the sizeable *Ladino* population, and the easy-going atmosphere of the lake is tempered by the influence of the Pacific coast. The setting, however, is as spectacular as always. The village is at the back of a small inlet of reed beds, with the Tolimán volcano rising above. There's a weekly **market** here on Friday, which is certainly the best time to drop by, although it unfortunately clashes with the market in Santiago.

The best place **to stay** is the friendly, clean and good-value *Cafeteria Santa Ana* (①); if that's full try the *Hospedaje Ordonez* (①), which is a little rougher. If you're in search of something a little more luxurious, head for the *Hotel Brisas del Lago* (④), down by the lake. San Lucas is the junction of the coast road and the road to Santiago Atitlán, and **buses** to both thunder regularly through the village. On the whole, buses head out towards Cocales and the coast in the early morning, making their way back to Santiago in the afternoon. There are also buses between here and Panajachel, running mostly in the morning. **Boats** operate between San Lucas and San Antonio Palopó on Tuesday, Thursday and Sunday, leaving San Antonio between 6 and 8am and returning around 11am.

Santiago Atitlán

On the other side of the lake, **SANTIAGO ATITLÁN** is set to one side of a sheltered horseshoe inlet, overshadowed by the cones of the San Pedro, Atitlán and Tolimán volcanoes. It's the largest and most important of the lakeside villages, and also one of the most traditional, being the main centre of the Tzutujil-speaking Indians. At the time of the conquest the Tzutujil had their fortified capital, **Chuitinamit-Atitlán**, on the slopes of San Pedro, while the bulk of the population lived spread out around the site of today's village. Alvarado and his crew, needless to say, destroyed the capital and massacred the Indians, assisted this time by a force of Cakchiquel, who arrived at the scene in some three hundred canoes.

Today Santiago is an industrious but relaxed sort of place, in a superb setting, and if you're planning a trip around the lake it's probably best to spend the first night either here or in San Pedro. During the day the town becomes fairly commercial, its **main street**, which runs from the dock to the plaza, lined with weaving shops. There's nothing like the Panajachel overkill, but the persistence of underage gangs can still be a bit much. By mid-afternoon, once the ferries have left, things revert to normal and the whole village becomes a lot more friendly. There's not a lot to do in Santiago other than stroll around soaking up the atmosphere: the old colonial church is worth a look and there's the market on Friday mornings.

As is the case in many other parts of the Guatemalan highlands, the Catholic Church in Santiago is locked in bitter rivalry with several evangelical sects, who are building churches here at an astonishing rate. Their latest construction, right beside the lake, is the largest structure in town. Folk Catholicism also plays an important role in the life of Santiago and the town is well known as one of the few places where the Indians still pay homage to **Maximón**, the drinking and smoking saint.

The traditional **costume** of Santiago, still worn a fair amount, is both striking and unusual. The men wear long shorts which, like the women's *huipiles*, are white and purple striped, intricately embroidered with birds and flowers. The women also wear a *tocayal*, a band of red cloth approximately 10m long, wrapped around their heads, which has the honour of being depicted on the 25 centavo

---

HOLY SMOKE!

Easter celebrations are particularly special in Santiago, and as Holy Week draws closer the town comes alive with expectation and excitement. **St Maximón** maintains an important role in the proceedings. On the Monday of Holy Week his image is taken to the lakeshore where it is washed, on the Tuesday he's dressed, and on the Wednesday the image is housed in a small chapel in the plaza. Here he waits until Good Friday, when the town is the scene of a huge and austere religious procession, the plaza packed out with everyone dressed in their finest traditional costume. Christ's image is paraded solemnly through the streets, arriving at the church around noon, where it's tied to a cross and raised above the altar. At around 3pm it's cut down from the cross and placed in a coffin, which is then paraded through the streets, accompanied by the Virgin Mary and Maximón.

The presence of Maximón, decked out in a felt hat and Western clothes, with a cigar in his mouth, is scorned by reforming Catholics and revered by the traditionalists. The precise **origin** of the saint is unknown, but he's also referred to as San Simón, Judas Iscariot and Pedro de Alvarado, and always seen as an enemy of the church. Some say that he represents a Franciscan friar who chased after young Indian girls, and that his legs are removed to prevent any further indulgence. "Max" in the Mam dialect means tobacco, and Maximón is always associated with *Ladino* **vices** such as smoking and drinking; more locally he's known as *Rij Laj*, the powerful man with a white beard. Throughout the year he's looked after by a *cofradía*; if you feel like dropping in to pay your respects to him ask for "*La Casa de San Simón*", and someone will show you the way. Take along a packet of cigarettes and a bottle of *Quezalteca* for the ever-thirsty saint and his minders, who will ask you to make a contribution to fiesta funds. For details on visiting San Simón in Zunil and for a warning about the gravity of the proccess, see p.157.

coin. Sadly this headcloth is going out of use and on the whole you'll probably only see it at fiestas and on market days, worn by the older women.

Around Santiago: volcanoes and the nature reserve

The land around Santiago is mostly volcanic, with only the odd patch of fertile soil mixed in with the acidic ash. Farming, fishing and the traditional industry, the manufacture of *cayucos* (canoes), are no longer enough to provide for the population, and a lot of people travel to the coast, or work on the coffee plantations that surround the volcano. The Tolimán and Atitlán **volcanoes** can both be climbed from here, but you'll need a couple of days to make it to the top of the latter. It's always best to take a guide to smooth the way, as ORPA (*Organización del Pueblo en Armas*) guerrillas may still be camped out on the slopes and there have been a number of robberies. If you're looking for a guide, ask in the hotel *Chi-Nim-Ya* (see below), or at one of the restaurants.

If you're here for the day then you can walk out of town along the track to San Lucas Tolimán, or rent a **canoe** and paddle out into the lake – just ask around at the dock. To the north of Santiago is a small island which has been designated as a **nature reserve**, originally for the protection of the *poc*, or **Atitlán grebe**, a flightless water bird. The *poc* used to thrive in the waters of the lake but two factors have now driven it into extinction: the overcutting of the reeds where it nests and the introduction of the fierce black bass, which eat the young birds – although the reserve is surrounded by an underwater fence to keep out the marauding fish. Despite the disappearance of the *poc*, the island is still a beautiful place to spend an hour or two and is an interesting destination if you're paddling around in a canoe.

Practicalities

Daily **boats** to Santiago leave from the beach in Panajachel at 8.35am, 9am, 9.30am, 10.30am, 3pm and 4pm, returning at 6am, 7am, 11.45am, 12.30am, 1pm, 2pm and 5pm – the trip takes about an hour. The village is also astonishingly well connected by **bus** with almost everywhere except Panajachel (see below).

Thanks to the steady flow of tourists, Santiago offers the full range of **accommodation**. A longstanding favourite among backpackers is the *Hotel Chi-Nim-Ya* (①–②), a two-storey, old wooden building on the left as you enter the village from the lake. Some of its comfortable rooms come with superb views and private bath. For those on a really tight budget, the *Pensión Rosita* (①), beside the church, offers simple rooms and cold water. Higher up the scale, the *Hotel Tzutuhil*, in the centre of town (☎7217174; ②–③), is a four-storey concrete building in which all rooms have private showers; the *Posada de Santiago*, on the lakeshore 1km south of the town (☎ & fax 7217167; ⑥) is an American-owned luxury hotel and restaurant with rooms in stone cabins, each with its own log fire.

There are three **restaurants** at the entrance to the village, just up from the dock. The *Buen Samaritano* is the cheapest, then comes the *Restaurant Regiemontano* and finally the slightly smarter *Restaurant El Gran Sol*. In the centre of the village you can eat at the *Hotel Tzutuhil*, or if you really want to dine in style, then head out to the restaurant in the *Posada de Santiago*.

Leaving Santiago, buses mostly depart from the central plaza and head via San Lucas Tolimán and Cocales towards Guatemala City or Quezaltenango. There are no direct services between Santiago and Panajachel, and all those that leave the village, whether for Guatemala City or Quezaltenango, go via Cocales and the coastal highway. For Guatemala City there are departures at 3am, 6am

THE EXPULSION OF THE ARMY FROM SANTIAGO ATITLÁN

Santiago Atitlán's recent history, like that of so many Guatemalan villages, is marked by trouble and violence. The village has assumed a unique role, however, as the first in the country to successfully **expel the armed forces**, and it is now seen by many as a shining example of the way forward.

Relations between the army and the village had been strained since a permanent base was established there in the early 1980s, when the ground above the village was used extensively by ORPA guerrillas. The army accused the village of supporting the insurgents and attempted to terrorize the population into subservience. Throughout the 1980s villagers were abducted, tortured and murdered – a total of around three hundred were killed over eleven years.

Under civilian rule the guerrilla threat dropped off considerably and the people of Santiago grew increasingly confident and resentful of the unnecessary army presence. Matters finally came to a head on the night of December 1, 1990, when two drunken soldiers shot a villager. The men fled to the army base on the outskirts of the village but were followed by a crowd that eventually numbered around two thousand. The six hundred soldiers inside the garrison clearly believed they were about to be overwhelmed and opened fire on the crowd, killing thirteen people, including three children, and wounding another twenty. After this incident some 20,000 villagers signed a petition calling for the expulsion of the army from Santiago and the army finally withdrew, shutting down the base.

Difficulties then arose with the police, when, on December 6, the local civil patrol discovered a group of policemen on a suspicious night-time mission. A mob soon surrounded the police station and the police were similarly forced to leave. New recruits were sent from Guatemala City to replace them, however, but for two weeks the residents refused to sell them any food and it was a month before they agreed to allow them to use the public toilet – for a monthly fee of $4.

In June 1991, Santiago's example was followed by neighbouring San Lucas Tolimán, where the killing of a community leader by a soldier led to the army's expulsion. Other villages, in more sensitive areas, have also taken steps, but have yet to succeed. In Joyabaj a mass rally in February 1992 denounced the presence of the army base as a "physical and moral danger" to the community, and early in 1993 villagers in Chajul called for the removal of the army base there.

Meanwhile the killings at Santiago were blamed on a single soldier, who was sentenced to sixteen years' imprisonment in October 1991. The Guatemalan authorities refused to accept the perspective offered by the villagers, the Minister of the Interior laying responsibility for the incident on "persons interested in destabilizing the country", while the Defence Minister argued that "the villages that request the closing of bases are being manipulated by the guerrillas."

and noon. Buses to Quezaltenango run at 3.30am and 4.30am, returning at 11am and 12.30pm. For San Pedro, boats leave Santiago at 7am, 9am, 10.30am, 11am, noon, 1pm, 2pm, 3.30pm and 4pm.

San Pedro La Laguna

Around the other side of the San Pedro volcano is the village of **SAN PEDRO LA LAGUNA**. Generally speaking fewer tourists make it here, although in recent years an offshoot of the Panajachel "scene" has established itself in San Pedro.

Nevertheless, this is still one of the most relaxed of the lakeside villages, and tourism has certainly had less impact than in Santiago and Panajachel. Tradition isn't as powerful either, and only a few elderly people, mostly men, wear the old costume, although there is a sense of permanence in the narrow cobbled streets and old stone houses. The people of San Pedro have a reputation for driving a hard bargain when trading their coffee and avocados, and have managed to buy up a lot of land from neighbouring San Juan, with whom there's endless rivalry. They're also famed for the *cayucos* (canoes) made from the great cedar trees that grow on the slopes of the San Pedro volcano.

The setting is again spectacular, with the volcano rising to the east and a ridge of steep hills running behind the village. To the left of the main beach, as you look towards the lake, a line of huge white boulders juts out into the water – an ideal spot for an afternoon of swimming and sunbathing.

The **San Pedro volcano**, which towers above the village to a height of some 3020m, is largely coated with tropical forest and can be climbed in around four hours. Any of the underage guides will be able to show you the trail (Andres Adonias Cotuc Cite, who makes a living collecting wood on the volcano, is highly recommended); get an early start in order to see the views at their best and avoid the worst of the heat. The peak itself is also ringed by forest, which blocks the view over San Pedro, although an opening on the south side gives excellent views of Santiago.

If you'd rather do something a little more relaxing, **horses** can be rented for around $5 an hour and **canoes** for a great deal less.

Accommodation

There are plenty of simple **hotels** in San Pedro, although little in the way of luxury. If you plan to stay around for a while then you might want to consider **renting a house**, which works out incredibly cheap. Ask one of the young guides to point you in the right direction, or head for the *Casa de Maria*, where there are several places for rent.

Hospedaje Balneario, in the village, facing out towards the lake. Rough little place and very much a last resort. ①.

Hospedaje Chuasinahi, on the lakeshore at the front of the village, also known as the *Hotel Villa Sol*. The finest hotel in San Pedro, its rooms clean and simple. ③.

Hospedaje La Laguna, in the centre of the village. Dark and poky. ①.

Hotel San Pedro, next door to the *Villa Sol*. A decent second choice. ③.

Hotel Ti-Kaaj, next door to the *Chuasinahi*. A little cheaper and scruffier than its neighbour. Here you can also camp or sling a hammock. ①.

Eating and drinking

The steady flow of gringo hippies has given San Pedro's **cafés** and **restaurants** a decidedly international flavour.

Comedor Alicia, in the middle of the village. Popular and authentic Guatemalan *comedor*, not entirely untouched by outsiders. It also serves granola, yoghurt and pizza.

Café Johanna, around the side of the village near the side dock. Wholemeal bread, spaghetti and yoghurt, among other things. Erratic opening hours.

El Meson, right beside the side dock. Italian-owned, serving real Italian food, accompanied by views of the lake.

Michel's, hard to find among the coffee bushes halfway around the side of the village. Named after a former French resident, this friendly and inexpensive restaurant offers pasta, pancakes, peppered steak, fruit salads and *coq au vin*.

Pizzeria Buen Gusto, just up from the front dock. As you might guess, they serve a certain Italian speciality.

Comedor Rancho, in the *Chuasinahi*. Simple eatery with an interesting menu and filling portions. If it doesn't appeal, then pop next door to the *Cafeteria El Paisaje*.

Comedor Ultima Cena, in the centre of the village. Another typical *comedor*.

Moving on

When it comes to moving on, the last **boat** to Panajachel leaves at 5pm but only if there are enough passengers. To be sure of leaving, take the 3pm boat. The last boat to Santiago is at 3pm (for a more detailed schedule see p.133). There's also a single **bus** between San Pedro and Guatemala City, struggling along the road that runs along the ridge above the western shore of the lake. The bus leaves San Pedro at 2am, arriving in Guatemala City at 7am and then returning at 2pm; while it would make an interesting trip, this is hardly the most convenient or comfortable way to travel.

The western shore: San Pedro to Sololá

The **western side** of the lake is the only part that remains largely inaccessible to cars. From San Pedro a rough dirt road runs as far as San Marcos, from where a spectacular path, a bit vague in parts, continues all the way to Sololá. Some of the boats between San Pedro and Panajachel call in at the larger villages but the best way to see the string of isolated villages along this route is on foot; it makes a fantastic day's walk. Most of the way a narrow strip of level land is wedged between the water and the steep hills behind, but where this disappears the path is cut into the slope with dizzying views of the lake below. At several of the villages along the way *tiendas* sell Coke and biscuits, so there's no need to carry water. To walk from San Pedro to Santa Cruz takes between five and six hours, so you might want to take a boat as far as San Marcos (most boats between Panajachel and San Pedro call in here), walk from there to Santa Cruz – the most interesting section – and finish the day by returning to Panajachel by boat. There are several **places to stay** this side of the lake. In **San Marcos** you'll find the *Eco-Compamento La Paz*, which offers a choice of bungalows or rooms, vegetarian meals and a sauna (①–②). *Las Piramides* is mainly a meditation centre (①–②), and there is also a simple **hospedaje** in the village (①–②). There is also accommodation in Santa Cruz (see below).

From San Pedro you follow the road to **SAN JUAN**, just 1km or so away at the back of a sweeping bay surrounded by shallow beaches – the area is known as *Aguas Cristalinas*. The village of San Juan specializes in the weaving of *petates*, mats made from lake reeds, and there's a market here on Tuesday and Saturday. Leaving the lakeside here, a trail leads high up above the village to Santa Clara La Laguna, which is connected to Sololá by a seldom-used road. The lakeside road, however, runs on through coffee plantations to **SAN PABLO LA LAGUNA**, where the traditional speciality is the manufacture of rope from the fibres of the maguey plant; you can sometimes see great lengths being stretched and twisted in the streets. Beyond this point the villages shrink significantly, starting with **SAN MARCOS**, about two hours' walk from San Pedro, which is no more than a group of houses loosely clustered around a small, ancient church. This far the road is still passable for vehicles and with a bit of luck you might get a lift in a truck; beyond San Marcos, though, it starts to deteriorate and the villages have a

greater feeling of isolation. If you continue, you'll find the people en route aston-
ished to see outsiders and eager for a glimpse of passing gringos. Nowhere is
this more true than in **TZUNUNÁ**, the next place along the way, where the
women run from oncoming strangers, sheltering behind the nearest tree in
giggling groups. They wear beautiful red *huipiles* striped with blue and yellow on
the back. The village was originally built at the lakeside, but after it was badly
damaged by a flood in 1950 the people rebuilt their homes on the higher ground.
Here the road indisputably ends, giving way to a narrow path cut out of the steep
hillside. At some points this can be a little hard to follow as it descends to cross
small streams and then climbs again around the rocky outcrops.

The next village is Jaibalito, a ragged-looking place lost amongst the coffee
bushes, and beyond here, set well back from the lake on a shelf 100m or so above
the water, is **SANTA CRUZ LA LAGUNA**, the largest of this line of villages. The
walk from San Pedro to Santa Cruz takes five to six hours in all, so by the time
you get here you'll probably be ready to take a swim and relax for the rest of the
day. On the shore, opposite a thatched jetty, you'll find the *Hotel Arco de Noe*,
which is owned by an Austrian couple. The food (which always includes vegetarian dishes), and the setting are all wonderful, with **accommodation** in beautiful
twin-bedded bungalows (⑤) or a bunk-bed budget room (③), but some guests do
report a certain excess of Austrian discipline. Directly opposite is the *Iguana
Perdida*, a simpler and more easy-going spot (④); while behind it you'll find the
Hospedaje Garcia (②) which is very basic. There is also a cheap and simple
pensión in the village.

Beyond Santa Cruz there are two ways to reach Panajachel, whether by boat
or on foot. Boats travelling between Panajachel and San Pedro stop here, or you
can rent a boat to Panajachel for $4. The path that runs directly to Panajachel is
hard to follow, and distraught walkers have been known to spend as long as
seven hours scrambling through the undergrowth. Alternatively, you could walk
up through the village to Sololá, along a spectacular and easy-to-follow path that
takes around three hours, and from there catch a bus back to Panajachel.

If you want to do this walk in the other direction – **from Sololá to San Pedro**
– you should head west out of Sololá along the dirt road towards San José
Chacayá, and as you come up out of the river valley, about 1km out of Sololá,
follow the track branching off to the left. The track can be very hard to find as
there are many leaving Sololá in this direction, so ask around before committing
yourself to any particular direction. The trail eventually brings you to Santa Cruz,
from where you simply follow the shoreline, although this is a hell of a hike for
one day and you'd be better off catching a boat from Panajachel to Santa Cruz.

The Pan-American Highway: Los Encuentros to Cuatro Caminos

Heading west from the Los Encuentros junction to Cuatro Caminos and the
Quezaltenango valley, the Pan-American Highway runs through some fantastic
high mountain scenery. The views alone are superb, and if you have a Sunday
morning to spare then it's well worth dropping into Nahualá for the market. **LOS
ENCUENTROS** itself is an all-important staging point on the Pan-American
Highway and typical of the junctions along the way, with wooden *comedores*, an

army base, and a team of enthusiastic sales people who besiege waiting buses. Here a branch road heads north to Chichicastenango, while the main highway continues west towards Quezaltenango, Huehuetenango and the Mexican border. Only a kilometre or so beyond this turning, at the **EL CUCHILLO** junction, a second road runs south to Sololá, Panajachel and the shores of Lake Atitlán.

These junctions are likely to feature heavily in your travels as it's here that you transfer from one bus to another on routes between Panajachel, Chichicastenango and the rest of the country. There are direct buses to and from all of these places, but if their schedule doesn't coincide with yours then it's easier to take any bus to the junction and intercept one going your way – all buses stop here and their destinations are yelled by the driver's assistant, touting for business. The last buses to Chichicastenango, Panajachel and Guatemala City pass through Los Encuentros at around 7pm; if you miss those you'll have to negotiate with a taxi.

Nahualá and Alaska

West of Los Encuentros and El Cuchillo the Pan-American Highway runs through some spectacular and sparsely inhabited countryside. The only place of any size before Cuatro Caminos is **NAHUALÁ**, a small and intensely traditional town 1km or so to the north of the highway, at the base of a huge, steep-sided and intensely farmed bowl. The unique atmosphere of isolation from and indifference to the outside world make Nahualá one of the most impressive and unusual Quiché towns.

The town itself is not much to look at, a sprawl of cobbled streets and adobe houses, but the Indians of Nahualá have a reputation for fiercely preserving their independence and have held out against *Ladino* incursions with exceptional tenacity. At the end of the nineteenth century the government confiscated much of their land, as they did throughout the country, and sold it to coffee planters. In protest, the entire male population of Nahualá walked the 150km to Guatemala City and demanded to see President Barrios in person, refusing his offers to admit a spokesman and insisting that they all stood as one. Eventually they were allowed into the huge reception room where they knelt with their foreheads pressed to the floor, refusing to leave until they were either given assurances of their land rights or allowed to buy the land back, which they had done twice before. The action managed to save their land that time, but since then much of it has gradually been consumed by coffee bushes all the same.

On another occasion, this time during the 1930s under President Ubico, *Ladinos* were sent to the town as nurses, telegraph operators and soldiers. Once again the Nahualáns appealed directly to the president, insisting that their own people should be trained to do these jobs, and once again their request was granted. Ubico also wanted to set up a government-run drink store, but the Indians chose instead to ban alcohol, and Nahualáns who got drunk elsewhere were expected to confess their guilt and face twenty lashes in the town's plaza.

These days the ban's been lifted, and if you're here for the fiesta on November 25 you'll see that the people are keen to make up for all those dry years. However, only a handful of *Ladinos* live in the town, and the Indians still have a reputation for hostility, with rumours circulating about the black deeds done by the local shaman. You don't have much to worry about if you drop in for the **Sunday market**, though, as this is one time that the town is full to bursting and the people seem genuinely pleased to welcome visitors.

The town's **weaving** is outstanding: the *huipiles*, designed in intricate geometrical patterns of orange on white, particularly impressed the Spanish because they featured a double-headed eagle, the emblem of the Hapsburgs who ruled Spain at the time of the Conquest. The men wear bright shirts with beautifully embroidered collars and short woollen skirts.

To **get to Nahualá** take any bus along the Pan-American Highway between Los Encuentros and Cuatro Caminos, and get off at the *Puente Nahualá*, from where it's 1km or so up the path behind the old bus shelter. There's a very basic *pensión* (①) in the centre of town, but it's easier to visit on a day trip from Chichicastenango, Panajachel or Quezaltenango.

Santa Catarina and the Alaskan heights

Beyond Nahualá the road continues west, climbing a mountainous ridge and passing the entrance road to **SANTA CATARINA IXTAHUACAN**, a sister and bitter rival of Nahualá, 8km to the other side of the highway. The costumes and traditions of the two places, which are together known as the **Pueblos Chancatales**, are fairly similar, and they're both famous as producers of *metates*, the stones used for grinding corn. These days much corn-grinding is done by machine and they've turned to making smaller toy versions and wooden furniture – both of which you'll see peddled by the roadside.

As it continues west, the road climbs above Santa Catarina, coming out on a flat plateau high up in the hills and into the most impressive section of the Pan-American Highway. Known as **Alaska**, this exposed tract of land, where the men of Nahualá farm wheat and graze sheep, shines white with frost in the early mornings. At 3000m, almost on a level with the great cones, the view is of course fantastic – this is one of the highest points on the Pan-American Highway in its entire course from Alaska to Tierra del Fuego (second only to the Cerro de la Muerte in Costa Rica, which reaches 3300m). Away to the east a string of volcanoes runs into the distance, and to the west the Totonicapán valley stretches out below you.

Further on, as the road drops over the other side of the ridge, the Quezaltenango valley opens out to the left, a broad plain reaching across to the foot of the Santa María volcano. At the base of the ridge the highway arrives at the Cuatro Caminos crossroads, the crucial junction of the extreme western highlands. Turning right here leads to Totonicapán, left to Quezaltenango, and straight on for Huehuetenango and the Mexican border.

QUEZALTENANGO AND AROUND

To the west of Lake Atitlán the highlands rise to form a steep-sided ridge topped by a string of forested peaks. On the far side of this is the **Quezaltenango basin**, a sweeping expanse of level ground that forms the natural hub of the western highlands. The Quezaltenango basin is perhaps the most hospitable area in the region, encompassing a huge area of fertile farmland that has been densely populated since the earliest of times. Originally it was part of the Mam kingdom, administered from their capital **Zaculeu** (at a site adjacent to the modern city of Huehuetenango); but sometime between 1400 and 1475 the area was overrun by the Quiché, and was still under their control when the Spanish arrived. Today the western side of the valley is Mam-speaking and the east Quiché. It was here that the conquistador Pedro de Alvarado first struggled up into the highlands, having already confronted one Quiché army on the coast and another in the pass at the entrance to the valley. Alvarado and his troops came upon the abandoned city of Xelaju (near Quezaltenango) and were able to enter it without encountering any resistance. Six days later they fought the Quiché in a decisive battle on the nearby plain, massacring the Indian warriors and killing their hero Tecún Umán. The old city was then abandoned and the new town of Quezaltenango established in its place. The name means "the place of the quetzals" in Nahuatl, the language spoken by Alvarado's Mexican allies. Quetzals may well have existed here then, but the name is more likely to have been chosen because of the brilliant green quetzal feathers worn by Quiché nobles and warriors, including, no doubt, Tecún Umán himself.

It's easy to spend a week or two exploring this part of the country; making day trips to the markets and fiestas, basking in hot springs, or hiking in the mountains. Nowadays the valley is heavily populated, with three major towns: the departmental capital of **Quezaltenango** – the obvious place to base yourself, with bus connections to all parts of the western highlands – and the textile centres of **Salcajá** and **San Francisco Totonicapán**. In the surrounding hills are numerous smaller towns and villages, mostly Indian agricultural communities and weaving centres. To the south, straddling the coast road, are **Almolonga**, **Zunil** and **Cantel**, all overshadowed by volcanic peaks, where you'll find superb natural hot springs. To the north are **Totonicapán**, capital of the department of the same name, and **San Francisco el Alto**, a small market town perched on an outcrop overlooking the valley. Beyond that, in the midst of a pine forest, lies **Momostenango**, the country's principal wool-producing centre. Throughout this network of towns and villages Indian culture remains strong, based on a simple rural economy that operates in a series of weekly markets, bringing each town to life for one day a week. Leaving Quezaltenango you can head west to the rather neglected, little visited department of **San Marcos** – a potential route to **Mexico** by the coastal crossing, and the home of the country's highest volcano. You could also follow the Pan-American Highway to **Huehuetenango**, and cross into Mexico from there.

Set in some of the finest highland scenery, the area offers excellent **hiking**. The most obvious climb is the **Santa María volcano**, towering above Quezaltenango itself. It's just possible to make this climb as a day trip, but to really enjoy it, and increase your chances of a good view from the top, you should plan to take two days, camping on the way. If you haven't the time, energy or equipment for this then try instead the hike to **Laguna Chicabal**, a small lake set in the cone of an extinct volcano. The lake is spectacularly beautiful, and can easily be reached as a day trip from Quezaltenango, setting out from the village of **San Martín Sacatepéquez**. If you yearn for a dip in the Pacific the nearest **beach** is at **El Tulate**, five to six hours' bus ride away (4hr with your own transport).

Quezaltenango

Totally unlike the capital, and only a fraction of its size, Guatemala's second city, **QUEZALTENANGO**, has the subdued provincial atmosphere that you might expect in the capital of the highlands, its edges gently giving way to corn and maize fields. Ringed by high mountains, and bitterly cold in the early mornings, the city wakes slowly, only getting going once the warmth of the sun has made its mark. The main plaza, heavily indebted to Neoclassicism, is a monument to stability, with

great slabs of grey stone that look reassuringly permanent, defying a history of turbulence and struggle. The heart of town has the calm order of a regional admin-istrative centre, while its outskirts are ruffled by the bustle of an Indian market and bus terminal. Locally, the city is usually referred to as *Xela* (pronounced "shey-la"), a shortening of the Quiché name of a nearby pre-conquest city, Xelaju. Meaning "under the ten", the name is probably a reference to the surrounding peaks.

A brief history

Under colonial rule Quezaltenango flourished as a commercial centre, benefiting from the fertility of the surrounding farmland and good connections to the port at Champerico. When the prospect of independence eventually arose, the city was set on deciding its own destiny. After the Central American Federation broke with Mexico in 1820, Quezaltenango declared itself the capital of the independent state of **Los Altos**, which incorporated the modern departments of Huehuetenango, Sololá, San Marcos and Totonicapán. But the separatist movement was soon brought to heel by President Carrera in 1840, and a later attempt at secession, in 1848, was put down by force. Despite having to accept provincial status, the town remained an important centre of commerce and culture, consistently rivalling Guatemala City. The coffee boom at the end of the last century was particularly significant, as Quezaltenango controlled some of the richest coffee land in the country. Its wealth and population grew rapidly, incorporating a large influx of

German immigrants, and by the end of the nineteenth century Quezaltenango was firmly established as an equal to Guatemala City.

All this, however, came to an abrupt end in 1902 when the city was almost totally destroyed by a massive earthquake. Rebuilding took place in a mood of high hopes; all the grand Neoclassical architecture dates from this period. A new rail line was built to connect the city with the coast, but after this was washed out in 1932–33 the town never regained its former glory, gradually falling further and further behind the capital.

Today Quezaltenango has all the trappings of wealth and self-importance: the grand imperial architecture, the great banks, and a list of famous sons. But it is completely devoid of the rampant energy that binds Guatemala City to the all-American twentieth century. Instead the city finds itself suspended in the late nineteenth century, with a calm, dignified air that borders on the pompous. *Quezaltecos* have a reputation for formality and politeness, and pride themselves on the restrained sophistication of their cultured semi-provincial existence. If the chaos of Guatemala City gets you down then Quezaltenango, relaxed and easy-going, is an ideal antidote, though there's little to detain you for more than a day or two.

Arrival and information

Quezaltenango has two bus terminals; in addition several first-class bus companies operate from offices scattered throughout the city. **Long-distance buses** stop at the **Minerva bus terminal** on the western side of town, on the northern side of the Parque Minerva, just off 6 C. It's quite a way from the centre, so you'll need to catch a local bus to and from the plaza. Local buses heading into town stop on the other side of the road, on 4 C. Separating the two is a large covered market: walk down the passage that runs through the middle of this, and on the south side cross a large patch of open ground to reach the road. Any of the small buses going to the left will take you to the plaza (local buses run Mon–Sat 6am–9pm, Sun 8am–9pm, and charge 25 centavos – you need to have some change to hand).

If you're coming from Zunil, Cuatro Caminos, Totonicapán or San Francisco el Alto, you'll pull in at the terminal for **local second-class buses**, off Calzada Independencia (7 Av) on 2 C. To get to this terminal from the plaza catch a local bus in front of the Casa de la Cultura and check that the driver is heading for Calzada Independencia.

First-class or pullman buses come and go from the office of the particular company. *Lineas Americas* (☎7621432) and *Rutas Lima* (☎7614134) are both just off Calzada Independencia (7 Av), on either side of the Esso station, on the eastern side of town. From here any local bus going west brings you to the plaza.

The official **tourist office** (Mon–Fri 8am–1pm, Sat 8am–noon; ☎7614931) is on the main plaza, to the right of the Casa de la Cultura del Occidente. Here you can pick up a map of the town and get information on trips to the surrounding villages. In addition, Thierry and Maria, owners of *El Rincon de los Antojitos*, 15 Av 5 C, are always keen to point tourists in the right direction and know the area very well. On 15 Av you'll find the **post office** at the junction with 4 C, and, for phone calls, the **Guatel** office (7am–10pm daily) just opposite. *The Shipping Center*, 15 Av 3–51, Zona 1 (Mon–Fri 9am–5.45pm, Sat 9am–noon; ☎ & fax 7632104) offer mail and parcel service, courier, phone and **fax** facilities, while *Maya Communications*, above *Tecún Bar* on the central plaza (daily 8.30am–5.30pm; ☎7612832) offers all communication services, including **e-mail**.

QUEZALTENANGO TRANSPORT CONNECTIONS

As the focus of the western highlands, Quezaltenango is served by literally hundreds of buses. **Getting to Quezaltenango** is fairly straightforward: there are direct pullmans from Guatemala City (listed below) and at any point along the Pan-American Highway you can flag down a bus to take you to Cuatro Caminos, from where buses leave for Quezaltenango every half-hour (the last at around 7pm). Coming from the coast you can catch a bus from the El Zarco junction, Mazatenango or Retalhuleu. **Leaving the city**, there are plenty of direct buses (listed below) but it's often easier to head for the Cuatro Caminos junction and go on from there.

Pullman buses
Rutas Lima run buses to Guatemala City at 8am, 2.30pm & 4.30pm; to Huehuetenango and La Mesilla at 5am & 6.30pm; and to Talisman at 5am. Their Quezaltenango office is at 2 C 6–35, just off 7 Av. Buses from Guatemala City to Quezaltenango are at 5.15am, 7.15am & 2.15pm. In Guatemala City their office is at 8 C 3–63, Zona 1.
Lineas Americas have buses to Guatemala City at 5.15am, 9.45am, 1.15pm, 3.45pm & 8pm. Their office in Quezaltenango is at 7 Av 2–3 Calles. Buses from Guatemala City to Quezaltenango run at 5.15am, 9am, 3.15pm, 4.40pm & 7.30pm. The Guatemala City office is at 2 Av 18–74, Zona 1.

Second-class buses
Buses for **Zunil** (25min), **San Francisco el Alto** (45min) and **Totonicapán** (1hr) leave every half-hour between 8am and 6pm from the small terminal just off Calzada Independencia. Or you could take any municipal bus to the *rotunda* (roundabout), which all these buses pass on their way out of the city.
From the main Minerva terminal in Zona 3 there are hourly buses to **Huehuetenango** (2hr 30min; 5.30am–5.30pm), **San Marcos** (2hr; 7am–5pm), **Mazatenango** (2hr; 5am–5.30pm), **Retalhuleu** (2hr; 4.30am–6pm), **Coatepeque** (2hr; 5am–5.45pm), and **Guatemala City** (5hr). There are also buses to **Santiago Atitlán** at 11am & 12.30pm, to **Panajachel** at 5am, 6.30am, 10am, noon, 1pm & 3pm, and to **Momostenango** (2hr; Mon–Sat 9am–5pm, 11.30am on Sun). Again, for all but the Pacific destinations and San Marcos, you can also catch these buses at the *rotunda*. The only drawback with this method is that you are unlikely to get a seat as the bus will be full by this stage.
Heading for **Santa Cruz del Quiché**, **Chichicastenango** or **Antigua** you can catch any bus going to Guatemala City and change at the relevant junction (Los Encuentros for Chichicastenango and Quiché; Chimaltenango for Antigua).
To the Mexican border at Talisman. It's possible to travel via San Marcos to the border in a day, but the quickest route is to take a bus to the coast, and intercept a pullman on the Coastal Highway (*Rutas Lima* has a daily bus to the Talisman border; 5am).
To the Mexican border at La Mesilla. The easiest way is to take a direct bus to Huehuetenango and catch another from there to the border. However, *Rutas Lima* have direct buses to La Mesilla at 5am and 6.30pm.

Orientation and city transport

Quezaltenango is laid out on a standard grid pattern, somewhat complicated by a number of steep hills. Basically, **avenidas** run north–south, and **calles** east–west. The oldest part of the city, focused around the plaza, is made up of narrow twisting streets, while in the newer part, reaching out towards the Minerva terminal and sports stadium, the blocks are larger. The city is also divided up into **zones**, although for the most part you'll only be interested in 1 and 3, which contain the plaza and the bus terminal respectively.

When it comes to **getting around** the city, most places are within easy walking distance. To get to the Minerva terminal you can take any bus that runs along 13 Av between 8 C and 4 C in Zona 1. To head for the eastern half of town, along 7 Av, catch one of the buses that stops in front of the Casa de la Cultura, at the bottom end of the plaza. You pay the driver; have some small change handy.

Accommodation

Once you've made it to the plaza you can set about looking for somewhere to stay. Quezaltenango's **hotels** are divided into two groups, one to each side of the plaza.

Pensión Altense, 9 C and 9 Av (☎7612811). Clean, friendly, central and excellent value – the best of the budget hotels. ④.

Pensión Bonifaz, northeast corner of the plaza (☎7612182; fax 7612850). Founded in 1935, this beautiful little hotel is the backbone of Quezaltenango society, very refined, with an air of faded upper-class pomposity. ⑥.

Hotel Casa Florencia, 12 Av 3–61 (☎7612326). The city's newest hotel; bright, shiny and efficient. All rooms have private bathroom. ⑤.

Casa Kaehler, 13 Av 3–33 (☎7612091). Lovely place with spotless rooms around a leafy courtyard; hot showers and some private baths. Very secure – knock on the door to get in. ④.

Santa María, 3 C 10–24, Zona 1 (☎7612660). Good budget choice, if you can get a room, with use of kitchen and hot water. ③.

STAYING WITH A MAYA FAMILY

Quezaltenango is the base for **SCDRYS** (*Sociedad Civil para al Desarrollo Rural Replicable y Sostenible*), 7 C 7–18, between 24 & 25 Av, Zona 3 (☎7630409; fax 7616873). Managed by Douglas Sandoval, this non-profit organisation is run in association with Maya community leaders in remote areas of the departments of Quiché, Huehuetenango and Quezaltenango, and provides an excellent opportunity to spend time with an indigenous family, either as a **language student** in Joyabaj (see p.118), or simply as a **guest** of a particular village. Expect to pay approximately $80–100 per person per week, less if there are several of you. The money is paid direct to the *alcalde* (mayor) of the community, who distributes 30 percent to your host family, 20 percent to the community, 25 percent to aid projects, 15 percent to *SCDRYS* and 10 percent for administration.

Hotel Modelo, 14 Av A 2–31 (☎7612529; fax 7631376). Very civilized, quiet establishment; the brand new annexe is nicer and cheaper. ④–⑤.

Pensión Quijote, 8 Av and 10 C. Cheap and a touch musty. ①–②.

Pensión Regia, 9 Av 8–26. Rough and bare rooms, but the lowest prices. ②.

Hotel Río Azul, 2 C 12–15 (☎ & fax 7630654). At the top end of the budget range: very clean and friendly and all rooms have private bathroom. ④.

Pensión Casa Suiza, 14 Av 2–36. Formerly very popular with Guatemalan business travellers, now somewhat in decline and overpriced. ④.

Casa del Viajero, 10 C and 8 Av. A little cheaper than the *Altense* but more basic. ③.

Hotel Villa Real Plaza, northwest corner of the plaza, 4 C 12–22 (☎7614045; fax 7616780). The city's second hotel and a modern rival for the *Bonifaz:* just as much in the way of luxury but short on atmosphere. ⑥.

The City

There aren't many things to do or see in Quezaltenango, but if you have an hour or two to spare then it's well worth wandering through the streets, soaking up the atmosphere and taking in the museum. The hub of the place is, obviously enough, the **central plaza**, officially known as the **Parque Centro América**. A mass of Greek columns, banks and shoeshine boys, with an atmosphere of wonderfully dignified calm, the plaza is the best place to appreciate the sense of self-importance that accompanied the city's rebuilding after the 1902 earthquake. The buildings have a look of defiant authority, although there's none of the buzz of business that you'd expect. The Greek columns were probably intended to symbolize the city's cultural importance and its role at the heart of the liberal revolution, but today many of them do nothing more than support street lights. The northern end of the plaza is dominated by the grand *Banco del Occidente*, complete with sculptured flaming torches. On the west side are the *Banco de Guatemala* and the *Pasaje Enriquez*. The latter, planned as a sparkling arcade of upmarket shops, spent many years derelict, but the project has now been revived. Inside you'll find the *Salon Tecún Bar*, a friendly place good for meeting other travellers.

At the bottom end of the plaza is the **Casa de la Cultura del Occidente**, the city's most blatant impersonation of a Greek temple, with a bold grey frontage that radiates stability and strength. The main part of the building is given over to an odd mixture of local **museums**. On the ground floor, to the left-hand side, you'll find a display of assorted documents from the liberal revolution and the State of Los Altos, sports trophies, and a museum of marimba. Upstairs there are some interesting Maya artefacts, a display about local industries and a fascinating collection of old photographs.

Along the other side of the plaza is the **Cathedral**, with the new cement version set behind the spectacular crumbling front of the original. There's another unashamed piece of Greek grandeur, the **Municipalidad** or town hall, a little further up. Take a look inside at the courtyard, which has a neat little garden set out around a single palm tree. Back in the centre of the plaza are rows and circles of redundant columns, a few flowerbeds, and a monument to President Barrios, who ruled Guatemala from 1873 to 1885.

In the bottom left-hand corner of the plaza, between the cathedral and the Casa de la Cultura, the old **Mercadito** still functions, although nowadays it's eclipsed by the larger market near the bus stations in Zona 3. Beside it, there's a three-storey shopping centre, the **Centro Comercial Municipal**.

Beyond the plaza

Away from the plaza the city spreads out, a mixture of the old and new. 14 Av is the commercial heart, a pale imitation of the capital, complete with pizza restaurants and neon signs. At the top of 14 Av, at the junction with 1 C, stands the **Teatro Municipal**, another spectacular Neoclassical edifice. The plaza in front of the theatre is dotted with busts of local artists, including Osmundo Arriola (1886–1958), Guatemala's first poet laureate, and Jesus Castillo, "the re-creator of Maya music" – another bid to assert Quezaltenango's cultural superiority.

Further afield, the city's role as a regional centre of trade is more in evidence. Out in Zona 3 is the **La Democracía Market**, a vast covered complex with stalls spilling out onto the streets. A couple of blocks beyond the market stands the modern **Church of San Nicolás**, at 4 C and 15 Av, a bizarre and ill-proportioned neo-Gothic building, sprouting sharp arches.

There's another Greek-style structure right out on the edge of town, also in Zona 3. The **Minerva Temple** makes no pretence at serving any practical purpose, but was built to honour President Barrios's enthusiasm for education. Beside the temple is the little **zoo** (free), doubling as a childrens' playground. Crammed into the tiny cages are a collection of foxes, sheep, birds, monkeys (who are, for some reason, sponsored by Toyota), wild boar and big cats, including a pair of miserable-looking lions, who have miraculously managed to raise a family. Below the temple comes the sprawling **market** and **bus terminal**, and it's here that you can really sense the city's role as the centre of the western highlands, with Indian traders from all over the area doing business, and buses heading to or from every imaginable village and town. To get to this side of the city take any of the local buses that run along 13 Av between 8 C and 4 C in Zona 1.

Eating, drinking and entertainment

There are more than enough **restaurants** to choose from in Quezaltenango, with four, fairly good pizza places on 14 Av alone. Note that almost no place opens before 8am in the morning, so forget early **breakfasts**. **Nightlife** is not as easy to come by although there are a couple of lively spots if you know where to look.

Restaurants and cafés

Artura's Restaurant, 14 Av 3–09, Zona 1. Dark and fairly cosy atmosphere, where you can combine traditional, moderately priced food food with hard drinking.

Café Baviera, corner of 13 Av and 5 C, Zona 1, just off the plaza. Excellent for snacks, such as spinach quiche, as well as the best and cheapest cappuccino in town. Daily 8am–8pm.

Café Berna, 16 Av 3–25, Zona 3, on the Parque Benito Juarez. Enduring café, which sells great cakes, milkshakes and snacks. Daily 8am–10pm.

Blue Angel Video Café, 7 C 15–22, Zona 1. Another popular gringo hang out, where you can eat great salads, fruit and vegetables. The small library offers well-thumbed paperbacks and the daily video programme is not bad at all. Daily 2–11pm.

Pensión Bonifaz, corner of the plaza, Zona 1. Always a sedate and civilized spot for a cup of tea and a cake, or a full meal, and for rubbing shoulders with the town's elite. Expensive.

Comedor Capri, 8 C 1–39, Zona 1. Straightforward, inexpensive Guatemalan eatery serving a set meal and opening early for breakfast; keep an eye on their addition when it comes to the bill.

Cardinali's, 14 Av 3–41, Zona 1. Without doubt the best Italian food outside the capital and Antigua, at reasonable prices. Make sure you are starving when you eat here because the portions are huge. They're about to open another place, *Torre di Pisa*, near the municipal theatre. Daily 11am–10pm.

Chicago Grill, 13 Av 5–38, Zona 1, in the *El Portal* commercial centre. American-run burger and sandwich restaurant, complete with *CNN* TV and a wonderfully camp waiter. Moderate prices. Mon–Sat 9am–10pm, Sun 1–9.30pm.

Deli Crepe, 14 Av, Zona 1. Good fruit juices, pancakes, and delicious sandwiches.

Establito Suizo, Diagonal 11, 7–15, Zona 1. Good low-cost burgers and tuna salads, and great Caribbean and South American music.

Helados La Americana, 14 Av 4–41, Zona 1. Best ice-cream and candy in town.

Pan y Pasteles, 4 C 26–19, Zona 3, near the Minerva bus terminal. The best bakery in town, run by Mennonites, whose fresh pastries and breads are used by all the finest restaurants. Tues and Fri only, 10am–4pm.

Pizza Ricca, 14 Av 2–52, Zona 1. Delicious, inexpensive homemade pizza and pasta.

Café Q, Diagonal 12 and 4 C, Zona 1. Popular gringo bar, which doubles up as a vegetarian restaurant. Push or knock at the door for access. Daily from 7pm.

El Rincon de los Antojitos, 15 Av and 5 C, Zona 1. Run by a French–Guatemalan couple, this friendly little restaurant offers superb – and inexpensive – Guatemalan specialities such as *pepian* (spicy chicken stew), *jocom* (traditional green sauce), and hot chocolate made with cinnamon and vanilla, as well as some vegetarian dishes. Mon–Fri 8am–1pm & 2–7pm.

Royal Paris, 2 C 14A–32, Zona 1. Simple, unpretentious restaurant set in a very pleasant, covered courtyard. The menu is international. Daily 9am–11pm.

Shanghai, 4 C 12–22, Zona 1. The best Chinese food in town, half a block from the plaza. Not too expensive.

Café Ut'z Hua, up the hill above the plaza at 12 Av 3–02, Zona 1. Simple and very Guatemalan *comedor*, if a little scruffy. Filling meals with a strong emphasis on the essentials.

Drinking and nightlife

There's not much to do in the evenings in Quezaltenango, and the streets are generally quiet by about 9pm. A couple of **bars**, though, are worth visiting. At the *Don Rodrigo*, 1 C and 14 Av, you can eat sandwiches and drink draught lager alongside the sophisticated and wealthy; while at the *Tecún*, on the west side of the plaza, you can down *Quezalteca* or sip *cuba libras* to the latest sounds imported by the gringo bar staff. The city is the home of *Cabro* beer, which has been brewed here for well over a hundred years. Not far from the local brewery, one of the city's best bars, *Aladino's*, attracts a good mix of Guatemalans and travellers, offering great music and excellent food. It's at 20 Av 0–66, Zona 3. On the edge of town you'll find a couple of **discos**: the *Music Centre*, Centro Commercial Delco, 1 C and 14 Av, and the *Garage Club*, Centro Commercial Ciani, Boulevard Minerva.

Quezaltenango is a good place to catch movies, with three **cinemas**: the *Cadore* at 7 C, 13 Av, just off the plaza, specializes in violence, horror and soft porn; the *Roma*, a beautiful old theatre at 14 Av A–34; and the *Alpino*, at 4 C and 24 Av, part of a new complex in Zona 3 near the bus terminal. Films are also sometimes shown at *La Aliansa Francesa*, 14 Av A–80, Zona 1.

Listings

Banks The *Banco de Guatemala*, *Banco Inmobiliario*, *Banco del Occidente* and *Banco del Café* (with the longest opening hours – Mon–Fri 8.30am–8pm, Sat 10am–2pm) are all in the vicinity of the plaza and will change travellers' cheques. For cash you get the best rate at the *Banquetzal*, on 14 Av, Zona 1.

Bike and car rental available at *Guatemala Unlimited* travel agency.

Camera repairs Try *Fotocolor*, 15 Av 3–25, or one of the several shops on 14 Av that sell a good range of film.

Doctors Cohen and Molina at the *Policlínica*, A C 13–15, speak some English; for real emergencies the *Hospital Privado* is at C Rudolfo Robles 23–51, Zona 1.

Language schools A booming business in Quezaltenango. As in Antigua all schools offer a package of tuition and accommodation with a family for around $120 a week. Try *Guatemalensis*, 19 Av 2–14, Zona 1; *Ulew Tinimit*, 9 C 14 Av 8–38, Zona 3 (☎7631713), or *Escuela Juan Sisay*, 15 Av 8–38, Zona 1. Other schools include *ICA*, 1 C 19–55, Zona 1 (☎7631871), where they are also happy to discuss the political and social situation; *Casa Xelaju*, 9 C 11–26, Zona 1 (☎7612628), and *The English Club* (who also offer lessons in Mam and Quiché), in the La Cuchilla neighbourhood at Diagonal 4 9–71, Zona 9 (bus #5). See the tourist office for the latest list of officially recognized language schools.

Laundry *Quick Wash n' Dry*, 7 C 13–25A, Zona 1 (Mon–Sat 8am–6pm) is the best in town. Also good value is *Lavandería El Centro*, 15 Av 3–40, Zona 1 (Mon–Sat 8am–1pm & 2–5.30pm, closed 1–2pm).

Mexican consulate 9 Av 6–19, Zona 1 (Mon–Fri 8–11am & 2.30–3.30pm). A Mexican tourist card costs $1. Hand in paperwork in the morning and collect in the afternoons.

Travel agent *SAB Tours*, 1 C 12–35, Zona 1, or *Agencia de Viajes Guatemala Unlimited*, 12 Av and C 35, Zona 1 (☎ & fax 7616043).

Olintepeque and the old road towards Huehuetenango

To the north of Quezaltenango, perched on the edge of the flat plain, is the small textile-weaving town of **OLINTEPEQUE**. According to some accounts this was the site of the huge and decisive battle between the Spanish and Quiché warriors, and legend has it that the Río Xequijel, the "river of blood", ran red during the massacre of the Quiché. These days, however, it's better known as a peaceful little village with a small colonial church and a market on Tuesdays. **Buses** for Olintepeque (20min) leave from the Minerva terminal in Quezaltenango every half-hour.

Olintepeque was a staging post on the old road to Huehuetenango, and although only local traffic heads this way nowadays you can still follow the route. Leaving Olintepeque it heads up the steep hillside onto a plateau above, arriving at the village of **SAN CARLOS SIJA**, 22km from Quezaltenango and the hub of a fertile and isolated area. There's nowhere to stay in San Carlos, but five buses a day connect it with Quezaltenango – leaving from the Minerva terminal – the last returning at about 4pm. The only real reason to come out here is for the wonderful views, or to visit the small Sunday market. Heading on from San Carlos, you can hitch a ride to the Pan-American Highway, just 10km away, where there's plenty of traffic to Quezaltenango via Cuatro Caminos or on to Huehuetenango. The old road itself continues more or less due north, rejoining the Pan-American Highway about 40km before Huehuetenango – but there's very little traffic.

The Santa María volcano

Due south of Quezaltenango, the perfect cone of the **Santa María volcano** rises to a height of 3772m. From the town only the peak is visible, but seen from the rest of the valley the entire cone seems to tower over everything around. The view from the top is, as you might expect, spectacular, and if you're prepared to sweat out the climb you certainly won't regret it. It's possible to climb the volcano as a day trip, but to really see it at its best you need to be on top at dawn, either sleeping on the freezing peak, or camping at the site below and climbing the final section in the dark by torchlight. Either way you need to bring enough food, water and stamina for the entire trip; and you should be acclimatized to the altitude before attempting it. For more **information** on climbing Santa María, or any of the volcanoes in the region, contact Natán Hardeman, who can be found at *Aladino's Bar* in Quezaltenango most nights. Otherwise e-mail him at the Inter-American School in Xela (IAS@uvg.edu.gt).

Climbing the cone

To get to the start of the climb you need to take a local bus to **Llanos del Pinal**, a twenty-minute ride: buses leave every hour or so between 7am and 5.30pm from the Minerva terminal in Quezaltenango. The village is set on a high plateau beneath the cone, and the bus driver will drop you at a crossroads from where you head straight down the road towards the right-hand side of the volcano's base. After passing a small plaque dedicated to the Guatemalan Mountaineering Club, the track bears up to the left, quickly becoming a rocky trail. At the end of a confined rocky stretch, a few hundred metres in length, the path crosses a more open grassy area and then curves further around to the left. All the way along this first section painted arrows mark the way – those signs painted with a fierce "NO" mean exactly what they say and you should backtrack until you find an alternative.

As you push on, the path continues to climb around to the left, up a rocky slope and under some trees, arriving at a flat and enclosed grassy area about the size of small football pitch. There's a grass bank to the right, a wooded area to the left, and a big boulder at the other end. This point is about ninety minutes to two hours from the start, and is an ideal place to **camp** if you want to make the final ascent in the hours before dawn. The path cuts off to the right from here, leaving from the start of this level patch of grass. (Another path heads across the grass, but this isn't the one for you.) From here on, the route is a little harder to follow, but it heads more or less straight up the side of the cone, a muddy and backbreaking climb of two or three hours: avoid the tempting alternative that skirts around to the right.

At the top the cone is a mixture of grass and volcanic cinder, usually frozen solid in the early morning. The highest point is marked by an altar where Indians burn copal and sacrifice animals, and on a clear day the **view** will take your breath away – as will the cold if you get here in time to watch the sun rise. In the early mornings the Quezaltenango valley is blanketed in a layer of cloud, and while it's still dark the lights of the city create a patch of orange glow; as the sun rises, its first rays eat into the cloud, revealing the land beneath. To the west, across a chaos of twisting hills, are the cones of Tajamulco and Tacaná, marking the Mexican border. But most impressive is the view to the east. Wrapped in the early morning haze are four more volcanic cones, two above Lake Atitlán and two more above Antigua. The right-hand cone in this second pair is Fuego, which emits a stream of smoke, rolling down the side of the cone in the early morning. If you look south, you can gaze down over the smaller cone of **Santiaguito**, which has been in constant eruption since 1902. Every now and then it spouts a great grey cloud of rock and dust hundreds of metres into the air.

South towards the coast: Almolonga to Zunil

The most direct route from Quezaltenango to the coast takes you through a narrow gash in the mountains to the village of **ALMOLONGA**, sprawled around the sides of a steep-sided, flat-bottomed valley just 5km from Quezaltenango. Almolonga is Quiché for "the place where water springs", and streams gush from the hillside, channelled to the waiting crops. This is the market garden of the western highlands, where the flat land is far too valuable to live on and is parcelled up instead into neat, irrigated sections.

In **markets** throughout the western highlands the women of Almolonga corner the vegetable trade; it's easy to recognize them, dressed in their bold, orange zigzag *huipiles* and wearing beautifully woven headbands. The village itself has markets on Wednesday and Saturday – the latter being the larger one – when the plaza is ringed by trucks and crammed with people, while piles of food and flowers are swiftly traded between the two. The Almolonga market may not be Guatemala's largest, but it has to be one of the most frenetic, and is well worth a visit.

A couple of kilometres beyond the village lie **Los Baños**, where about ten different operations offer a soak in waters heated naturally by the volcano: two good ones are *Fuentes Saludable* and *El Recreo*. For a dollar you get a private room, a sunken concrete tub, and enough hot water to drown an elephant. In a country of lukewarm showers it's paradise, and the baths echo to the sound of Indian families who queue barefoot for the pleasure of a good scrub. Below the baths is a communal pool, usually packed with local men, and a *pila* where the women wash their clothes in warm water. Below the road between the baths and the village there's a warm swimming pool known as *Los Chorros* – follow the sign to *Agua Tibia* – which you can use for a small fee.

If on the other hand you'd prefer to immerse yourself in steam, then this too emerges naturally from the hillside. To get to the **vapores**, as they're known, get off the bus halfway between Quezaltenango and Almolonga at the sign for Los Vahos, and head off up the track. Take the right turn after about a kilometre, follow this track for another twenty minutes, and you'll come to the steam baths. Here you can sweat it out for a while in one of the cubicles and then step out into the cool mountain air, or have a bracing shower to get the full sauna effect.

Buses run to Almolonga from Quezaltenango every twenty minutes, leaving from the Minerva terminal in Zona 3 and stopping to pick up passengers at the junction of 10 Av and 10 C in Zona 1. They pause in Almolonga itself before going on to the baths, which are open from 5am to 10pm, although the last bus back is at around 7pm. Beyond Los Baños the road heads through another narrow gully to join the main coast road in Zunil. Some of the buses for Zunil pass this way.

Cantel, Zunil and the Fuentes Georginas

Most buses to the coast avoid Almolonga, leaving Quezaltenango via the **Las Rosas** junction and passing through **CANTEL FABRICA**, an industrial village built up around an enormous textile factory. The factory's looms produce a range of cloths, using Indian labourers, German dyes, English machinery and a mixture of American and Guatemalan cotton. The village was originally known as Chuijullub, a Quiché word meaning "on the hill", and this original settlement (now called Cantel – Cantel Fabrica simply means "Cantel Factory") can still be seen on a height overlooking the works.

Further down the valley is **ZUNIL**, another centre for vegetable growing. As at Almolonga, the village is split in two by the need to preserve the best land. The plaza is dominated by a beautiful colonial church with an intricate silver altar protected behind bars. The women of Zunil wear vivid purple *huipiles* and carry incredibly bright shawls, and for the Monday market the plaza is awash with colour. Zunil is one of the few remaining places where **Maximón** (or San Simón), the evil saint, is still worshipped (see p.138). In the face of disapproval from the Catholic Church, the Indians are reluctant to display their Judas, who also goes by the name Alvarado, but his image is usually paraded through the streets during Holy Week, dressed in Western clothes and smoking a cigar. At other times of the year you can meet the man himself (see below).

In the hills above Zunil are the **Fuentes Georginas** (closed Mon), another set of luxurious hot springs, state-owned and named after the dictator Jorge Ubico (1931–44). A turning to the left off the main road, just beyond the entrance to the village, leads up into the hills to the baths, 8km away. You can walk it in a couple of hours, or rent a truck from the plaza in Zunil for about $5. The baths are surrounded by fresh green ferns, thick moss and lush forest, and to top it all there's a restaurant and bar beside the main pool. You can swim in the pool for $1 or rent a **bungalow** for the night (③), complete with bathtub, double bed, fireplace and barbecue. In the rainy season it can be cold and damp, but with a touch of sunshine it's a fantastic place to spend the night.

VISITING SAN SIMON IN ZUNIL

Zunil's reputation for the worship of **San Simón** is well founded, and as in Santiago Atitlán (see p.137) with a minimum of effort you can pay a visit to the man himself. Every year on November 1, at the end of the annual fiesta, San Simón is moved to a new house; discreet enquiries will locate his current home. Here his effigy sits in a darkened room, dressed in Western clothes, and guarded by several attendants, including one whose job it is to remove the ash from his lighted cigarettes – this is later sold off and used to cure insomnia, while the butts are thought to provide protection from thieves. San Simón is visited by a steady stream of villagers, who come to ask his assistance, using candles to indicate their requests: white for the health of a child, yellow for a good harvest, red for love and black for an enemy. The petitioners touch and embrace the saint, and just to make sure that he has heard their pleas they also offer cigarettes, money and rum. The latter is administered with the help of one of the attendants, who tips back San Simón's head and pours the liquid down his throat, presumably saving a little for himself. Meanwhile, outside the house a small fire burns continuously and more offerings are given over to the flames, including whole eggs – if they crack it signifies that San Simón will grant a wish.

If you **visit San Simón** you will be expected to contribute to his upkeep. While the entire process may seem chaotic and entertaining, it is in fact deeply serious and outsiders have been beaten up for making fun of San Simón. So proceed with caution.

David Dickinson

Buses to Cantel and Zunil run from Quezaltenango's Minerva bus terminal every hour or so, with the last bus back from Zunil leaving at around 5pm. All buses to and from the coast also pass through this way. Just below Zunil the road from Almolonga meets with the main coastal highway, so you can easily walk between the two villages, a trek of little more than half an hour, although some buses do use this route when heading between Quezaltenango and Zunil.

West to Ostuncalco, and towards the coast via San Martín Sacatepéquez

Heading west from Quezaltenango, a good paved road runs 15km along the valley floor, through **San Mateo**, to the prosperous village of **SAN JUAN OSTUNCALCO**, the commercial centre for this end of the valley. The large Sunday market draws people from all the surrounding villages; here you can see the furniture made locally from wood and rope, painted in garish primary colours. The village's other famous feature is the *Virgen de Rosario*, in the church, which is reputed to have miraculous powers to grant prayers. Barely 2km away, on the far side of the coast road, is the quiet, traditional village of **CONCEPCIÓN CHIQUIRICHAPA**, which hosts a very local market on Thursday, attended by only a few outsiders and conducted in hushed tones.

Buses and minibuses run every half-hour between Quezaltenango and Ostuncalco. If you find yourself enchanted by the place, there's a very relaxed **guest house** at the entrance to the village: *Cipres Inn*, 6 Av 1–29 (☎7616174; ③), a beautiful wooden house that looks like it ought to be in New England, and which boasts huge double beds, a restaurant and a garden. Beyond the village the road splits, one branch running to Coatepeque on the coast, and the other over a high pass north to San Marcos and San Pedro Sacatepéquez. The road to the coast climbs into the hills and through a gusty pass before winding down to **SAN MARTÍN SACATEPÉQUEZ**, also known as San Martín Chile Verde, an isolated Mam-speaking village set in the base of a natural bowl and hemmed in by steep, wooded hills. The village was abandoned in 1902 when the eruption of the Santa María volcano buried the land beneath a metre-thick layer of sterile pumice stone, killing thousands. These days both the people and fertility have returned to the land, and the village is once again devoted to farming. The men of San Martín wear a particularly unusual costume, a long white tunic with thin red stripes, ornately embroidered around the cuffs and tied around the middle with a red sash; the women wear beautiful red *huipiles* and blue *cortes*.

A three- to four-hour hike from San Martín brings you to **Laguna Chicabal**, a spectacular lake set in the cone of the Chicabal volcano which is the site of Indian religious rituals. To get there, head down the side of the church and turn right onto the track at the end, which takes you out of the village. Once the track has crossed a small bridge take the path that branches off to the right, and follow this as it goes up and over a range of hills, then drops down and bears around to the left – several kilometres from the village. Beyond the lip the path carries on under a ridge and then crosses a flat pass before disappearing into the trees. Just as it enters the trees, take the smaller path that branches off to the right: this goes up through the forest and curves around to the right before finally cutting up to the left and crossing over into the cone itself. All of a sudden you come into a different world, eerily still, disturbed only by the soft buzz of a hummingbird's wings or the screech of parakeets. From the rim the path drops precipitously, through thick, moist forest, to the water's edge, where charred crosses and bunches of fresh-cut flowers mark the site of ritual sacrifice. On May 3 every year *brujos* from several different tribes gather here for ceremonies to mark the fiesta of the Holy Cross: at any time, but on this date especially, you should take care not to disturb any ceremonies that might be taking place – the site is considered holy by local Indians. Note also that fog can be a problem in February, making it easy to get lost.

San Martín can be visited either as a day trip from Quezaltenango or on the way to the coast – if you want to stay, the woman who runs the *Farmacía Municipal* has a room that she rents out (①). **Buses** run along the road between Coatepeque (for the coast) and Quezaltenango every couple of hours, passing San Martín, with the last in either direction at about 5pm. From Quezaltenango buses for Coatepeque leave from the Minerva terminal in Zona 3.

Quezaltenango to Cuatro Caminos

Between the Cuatro Caminos junction and Quezaltenango, lined along the road is the small *Ladino* town of **SALCAJÁ**, one of Guatemala's main commercial weaving centres, producing much of the cloth used in the dresses worn by Indian women. The lengths of fabric are often stretched out by the roadside, either to be prepared for dyeing or laid out to dry, and on market day they're an exceptionally popular commodity.

Salcajá's other claim to fame is that (according to some historians at least) it was the site of the first Spanish settlement in the country, and its church is therefore regarded as the first Catholic foundation in Guatemala. If you're staying in Quezaltenango and travelling out to the surrounding villages then the sight of Salcajá will become familiar as you pass through heading to and from Cuatro Caminos. But the ideal time to stop off is for the market on Tuesday.

A few kilometres beyond Salcajá the main road turns sharply to the right, beside a filling station. At this point a dirt track branches off to the left, running to the edge of the valley and the village of **SAN ANDRÉS XECUL**. Bypassed by almost everything, and enclosed on three sides by steep dry hills, it is to all appearances an unremarkable farming village – but two features set it apart. The first is little more than rumour and hearsay, set in motion by the artist Carmen Petterson when she was painting here in the 1970s. She claimed to have discovered that a "university" for Indian *brujos* was operating in the village, attracting young students of shamanism from Quiché villages throughout the country. There's little sign of this in the village itself, though, except perhaps for an atmosphere that's even more hushed and secretive than usual. The second feature is the village church, a beautiful old building with incredibly thick walls. Its facade is painted an outrageous mustard yellow, with vines dripping plump, purple fruit, and podgy little angels scrambling across the surface. Less orthodox religious ceremonies are conducted at hundreds of small altars in the hills, one of which is up a hill just above the smaller painted church.

A few daily **buses** leave the Minerva terminal in Quezaltenango for San Andrés; it's easier, though, to take any bus as far as the filling station beyond Salcajá and hitch a ride from there.

Cuatro Caminos and San Cristobal Totonicapán

At **CUATRO CAMINOS** the Pan-American Highway is met by the main roads from Quezaltenango and Totonicapán. This is the most important junction in the western highlands and you'll find all the usual characteristics of Guatemalan road junctions, including the cheap motels, the hustlers and the shanty-like *comedores*. More importantly, up until about 7pm there's a stream of **buses** heading for Quezaltenango, Huehuetenango, Guatemala City and smaller villages along the way. Wherever you are, this is the place to make for in search of a connection.

One kilometre to the west, the *Ladino* town of **SAN CRISTOBAL TOTONICAPÁN** is built at the junction of the Sija and Salamá rivers. Similar in many ways to Salcajá, San Cristobal is a quiet place that holds a position of importance in the world of Indian tradition as a source of fiesta costumes, which are rented out from various outfitters. If you'd like to see one of these you can drop in at 5 C 3–20, where they rent costumes for around $50 a fortnight, depending on age and quality. The colonial church, on the other side of the river, has been restored by the local wheat-growers' association and contains some fantastic ancient altars, including ornate silverwork and images of the saints. Look out especially for the silver figure of St Michael. The market here is on Sunday. **Buses** going to San Francisco el Alto pass the village – they leave Quezaltenango from the small terminal in Zona 1, beside the cathedral.

San Francisco el Alto and Momostenango

From a magnificent hillside setting, the small market town of **SAN FRANCISCO EL ALTO** overlooks the Quezaltenango valley. It's worth a visit for the view alone, with the great plateau stretching out below and the cone of the Santa María volcano marking the opposite side of the valley. At times a layer of early-morning cloud fills the valley, and the volcanic cone, rising out of it, is the only visible feature.

An equally good reason for visiting the village is the **Friday market**, the largest weekly market in the country. Traders from every corner of Guatemala make the trip, many arriving the night before, and some starting to sell as early as 4am, by candlelight. Throughout the morning a steady stream of buses and trucks fills the town to bursting; by noon the market is at its height, buzzing with activity.

The town is set into the hillside, with steep cobbled streets connecting the different levels. Two areas in particular are monopolized by specific trades. At the very top is an open field used as an animal market, where everything from pigs to parrots changes hands. The teeth and tongues of animals are inspected by the

buyers, and at times the scene degenerates into a chaotic wrestling match, with pigs and men rolling in the dirt. Below this is the town's plaza, dominated by textiles. These days most of the stalls deal in imported denim, but under the arches and in the covered area opposite the church you'll find a superb selection of traditional cloth. (For a really good view of the market and the surrounding countryside ask the Italian monk to let you climb the bell tower.) Below this the streets are filled with vegetables, fruit, pottery, furniture, cheap *comedores*, and plenty more. By early afternoon the numbers start to thin out, and by sunset it's all over – until the following Friday.

San Francisco practicalities

There are plenty of **buses** from Quezaltenango to San Francisco, leaving every twenty minutes or so from the small bus terminal at 2 C, just off Calzada Independencia (7 Av) or just head for the *rotunda* to catch the first one passing; the first is at 6am, and last bus back leaves at about 5pm. If you'd rather stay in the town itself then there are three **hotels**. The cheapest is the *Hospedaje Central* (①) on the main street, a roughish sort of place that fills with market traders; the *Hotel Vista Hermosa* (②–③), a block or so below the plaza, is a much smarter option although it's become increasingly run-down. As its name suggests, some of the rooms (especially at the front) really do have magnificent views. Finally the newest hotel in town is the *Hotel Galaxia* (①–②), which is very neat, clean and hospitable, some of the rooms with private bathrooms and views to rival the *Vista Hermosa*. San Francisco goes to bed at around 7.30pm so if you're stuck here for an evening you might want to see what's showing at the *Cine Garcia*.

Momostenango

Above San Francisco a dirt road continues over the ridge, dropping down on the other side through lush pine forests. The road is deeply rutted, and the journey painfully slow, but within an hour you arrive in **MOMOSTENANGO**. This small, isolated town is the centre of wool production in the highlands, and *Momostecos* travel throughout the country peddling their blankets, scarves and rugs. Years of experience have made them experts in the hard sell and given them a sharp eye for tourists. The wool is also used in a range of traditional costumes, including the short skirts worn by the men of Nahualá and the jackets of Sololá. The ideal place to buy Momostenango blankets is in the Sunday market, which fills the town's two plazas.

A visit at this time will also give you a glimpse of Momostenango's other feature: its rigid adherence to tradition. Opposite the entrance to the church, people make offerings of incense and alcohol on a small fire, muttering their appeals to the gods. The town is famous for this unconventional folk-Catholicism, and it has been claimed that there are as many as three hundred Indian shamans working here. Momostenango's religious **calendar**, like that of only one or two other villages, is still based on the 260-day *Tzolkin* year – made up of thirteen twenty-day months – that has been in use since Maya times. The most celebrated ceremony is *Guaxaquib Batz*, "Eight Monkey", which marks the beginning of a new year. Originally this was a purely pagan ceremony, starting at dawn on the first day of the year, but the Church has muscled in on the action and it now begins with a Catholic service the night before. The next morning the people make for Chuitmesabal (Little Broom), a small hill about 2km to the west of the town. Here offerings of broken pottery are made before age-old altars (Momostenango means "the place of the altars"). The entire process is overseen by *brujos*, shamans responsible for communicating with the gods. At dusk the ceremony moves to Nim Mesabal (Big Broom), another hilltop, where the *brujos* pray and burn incense throughout the night.

As a visitor, however, even if you could plan to be in town at the right time, you'd be unlikely to see any of this, and it's best to visit Momostenango for the market, or for the fiesta on August 1. If you decide to stay for a day or two then you can take a walk to the *riscos*, a set of bizarre sandstone pillars, or beyond to the **hot springs** of Pala Chiquito. The springs are about 3km away to the north, and throughout the day weavers work there washing and shrinking their blankets – it's always best to go early, before most people arrive and the water is discoloured by soap.

Practicalities

There are two **hotels** in Momostenango, the *Hospedaje Roxana* on the main plaza and the *Hospedaje Paclom* (both ①–②), up the hill above the smaller plaza. There's little to choose between them: both are simple, cheap and clean. There are plenty of small *comedores* on the main plaza, and the *Hospedaje Paclom* also has a restaurant.

Buses run here from Quezaltenango, passing through San Francisco el Alto on the way. They leave the Minerva terminal in Quezaltenango every hour or so from 10am to 4pm, and from Momostenango between 6am and 3pm. On Sunday a special early-morning bus leaves Quezaltenango at 6am: you can catch this at the *rotunda*, a roundabout at the eastern edge of town – although you'll need to take a taxi as far as the *rotunda*.

Totonicapán

TOTONICAPÁN, capital of one of the smaller departments, is reached down a direct road leading east from Cuatro Caminos. Surrounded by rolling hills and pine forests, the town stands at the heart of a heavily populated and intensely farmed little region. There is only one point of access and the valley has always held out against outside influence, shut off in a world of its own. In 1820 it became the scene of one of the most famous **Indian rebellions**. The early part of the nineteenth century had been marked by a series of revolts throughout the area, particularly in Momostenango and Totonicapán; the largest of these erupted in 1820, sparked by demands for tax. The Indians expelled all of the town's *Ladinos*, crowning their leader Atanasio Tzul the "king and fiscal king", and making his assistant, Lucas Aquilar, president. His reign lasted only 29 days before it was violently suppressed.

Today, Totonicapán is a quiet place whose faded glory is ruffled only by the Tuesday market, which fills the two plazas to bursting. Until fairly recently a highly ornate traditional costume was worn here. The women's *huipiles* were some of the most elaborate and colourful in the country, and the men wore trousers embroidered with flowers, edged in lace, and decorated with silver buttons. Today, however, all this has disappeared and the town has instead become one of the chief centres of commercial weaving. Along with Salcajá it produces much of the *Jasped* cloth worn as skirts by the majority of Indian women: the machine-made *huipiles* of modern Totonicapán are used throughout the highlands as part of the universal Indian costume. On one side of the old plaza is a workshop where young men are taught to weave on treadle looms, and visitors are always welcome to stroll in and take a look around. This same plaza is home to the crumbling municipal theatre, a grand Neoclassical structure echoing that in Quezaltenango. On the second square is the modern *Banco de Guatemala*.

There are good connections between Totonicapán and Quezaltenango, with buses shuttling back and forth every half-hour or so. If you want to stay you have a choice of two **hotels**. The *Hospedaje San Miguel* (②), 8 Av 3 C, one block from the plaza, is the grander, the *Pensión Blanquita* (①) a friendly and basic place opposite the filling station at 13 Av and 4 C. **Buses** for Totonicapán leave Quezaltenango from the small terminal at 2 C, off Calzada Independencia (7 Av) and also pass by the *rotunda*. Entering the village you pass one of the country's finest *pilas* (communal washing places), ringed with Gothic columns.

The Department of San Marcos

Leaving Quezaltenango to the west, the main road heads out of the valley through San Mateo and Ostuncalco and climbs a massive range of hills, dropping down on the other side to the village of Palestina de Los Altos. Beyond this it weaves through a U-shaped valley to the twin towns of **San Marcos** and **San Pedro Sacatepéquez**. These towns form the core of the country's westernmost department, a neglected area that once served as a major trade route and includes Guatemala's highest volcano and a substantial stretch of the border with Mexico. There's little to detain you in either place, but they make useful bases for a trip into the mountainous countryside to the north.

San Pedro Sacatepéquez and San Marcos

SAN PEDRO SACATEPÉQUEZ is the larger and busier of the two towns, a bustling and unattractive commercial centre with a huge plaza that's the scene of a market on Thursday and Sunday. In days gone by this was a traditional Indian settlement, famed for its brilliant yellow weaving, in which silk was used. Over the years the town has been singled out for some highly questionable praise: in 1543 the King of Spain, Carlos V, granted the headmen special privileges as thanks for their assistance during the Conquest, and in 1876 the town was honoured by President Rufino Barrios, who with a stroke of his pen raised the status of the people from Indians to *Ladinos*.

A dual carriageway road connects San Pedro with its sister town of San Marcos, 2km west. Along the way, a long-running dispute about the precise boundary between the two towns has been solved by the construction of the departmental headquarters at **La Union**, halfway between the two. The building, known as the **Maya Palace**, is an outlandish and bizarre piece of architecture that goes some way to compensate for the otherwise unrelenting blandness of the two towns. The structure itself is relatively sober, but its facade is covered in imitation Maya carvings. Elaborate decorative friezes run around the sides, two great roaring jaguars guard the entrance, and above the main doors is a fantastic clock with Maya numerals and snake hands. The **buses** that run a continuous shuttle service between the two towns can drop you at the Maya Palace. A few kilometres away there's a spring-fed **swimming pool** where you can while away an hour or two: to get there walk from the plaza in San Pedro down 5 C in the direction of San Marcos, and turn left in front of the Templo de Candelero along 2 Av. Follow this road through one valley and down into a second, where you take the left turn to the bottom. The pool – marked simply *Agua Tibia* – is open from 6am to 6pm, and there's a small entrance fee.

SAN MARCOS, officially the capital of the department, once stood proud and important on the main route to Mexico, but these days articulated lorries roar along the coastal highway and the focus of trade has shifted to San Pedro, leaving San Marcos to sink into provincial stagnation.

Practicalities

Most of the activity and almost all the transport are based in **San Pedro**. The cheapest **place to stay** is the *Pensión Mendez* (①), a very basic place at 4 C and 6 Av. The *Hotel Samaritano* (②), 6 Av 6–44, is a clean but characterless modern building, though definitely better than the *Hotel Bagod* (②), 5 C and 4 Av. Finally, the newish *Hotel Tacana* (①–②), 3 C 3–22, is good value, and some of its rooms have private showers. In **San Marcos** the *Hotel Palacio* (①), on 7 Av opposite the police station, is an amazing old place, its rooms decaying and very musty with peeling wallpaper. There's also a relatively luxurious hotel, the *Pérez* (☎7601007; ④) at 9 C 2–25, a very dignified and long-standing establishment that's excellent value and has its own restaurant.

There are plenty of cheap **comedores** in San Pedro, fewer in San Marcos. The latter, though, makes up for it with the restaurant *Mah Kik*, an elegant, subdued and fairly expensive place behind the Chevron station. Both towns have **cinemas**: the *Cine T-manek* on the plaza in San Pedro, and the *Cine Carua*, beside the *Hotel Pérez* in San Marcos. There are **banks** on both plazas.

Second-class **buses** run hourly from San Pedro to Malacatán, Quezaltenango (both 1hr 30min) and Guatemala City, between 5am and 5pm, from a small chaotic terminal one block behind the church. *Marquensita* pullmans go direct from San Marcos to Guatemala City, passing through the plaza in San Pedro, at 2am, 2.30am, 3am, 6.30am, 9am, 11am, noon, 1.30pm and 3pm.

To Tacaná and the high country

To the northwest of San Pedro is some magnificent high country, strung up between the Tajamulco and Tacaná volcanoes and forming an extension of the Mexican Sierra Madre. A rough dirt road runs through these mountains, connecting a series of isolated villages that lie exposed in the frosty heights.

Leaving San Pedro the road climbs steeply, winding up through thick pine forests and emerging onto a high grassy plateau. Here it crosses a great boggy expanse to skirt around the edge of the **Tajamulco volcano**, whose 4220-metre peak is the highest in Guatemala. It's best climbed from the roadside hamlet of Tuchan, from where it's about four hours to the summit – not a particularly hard climb as long as you're acclimatized to the altitude.

Up here the land is sparsely inhabited, dotted with adobe houses and flocks of sheep and goats. The rocky ridges are barren and the trees twisted by the cold. At this altitude the air is thin and what little breath you have left is regularly taken away by the astonishing views which – except when consumed in the frequent mist and cloud – open up at every turn. The village of **IXCHIGUÁN**, on an exposed hillside at 3050m, is the first place of any size, surrounded by bleak rounded hills and in the shadow of the two towering volcanic cones. Buses generally stop here for lunch, giving you a chance to stretch your legs and thaw out with a steaming bowl of *caldo*.

Moving on, the road climbs to the **CUMBRE DE COTZIL**, a spectacular pass which reaches some 3400m and marks the highest point on any road in Central

America. From here on it's downhill all the way to the scruffy village of **TACANÁ**, a flourishing trading centre that signals the end of the road – 73km from San Marcos and less than 10km from the Mexican border. Cross-border ties are strong and at the end of 1988 the inhabitants threatened to incorporate themselves into Mexico if the road to San Pedro wasn't paved, claiming that this had been promised to them by the Christian Democrats in the run-up to the 1985 election. Up above the village, spanning the border, is the **Tacaná volcano** (4064m), which can be climbed from the village of Sibinal. It last erupted in 1855, so it should be safe enough. Unless you're setting out to climb one of the volcanoes there's not much to do out this way, but the bus ride alone, bruising though it is, offers some great scenery. Three **buses** a day leave the terminal in San Pedro for Tacaná, at 9am, 11am and noon, returning at 3am, 5am and 11am. The trip takes about five hours, and there is also a bus service to Sibinal and Concepción Tutuapa – at similar times. In Tacaná the best **hotel** is the *Hotel El Trebol* (①) on the entrance road, where they also do good food. Right in the village you'll also find the *Hospedaje Los Angeles* (①) and the *Pensión Celajes Tacanecos* (①).

Heading on from Tacaná, trucks occasionally provide transport to Cuilco (from where there are regular buses to Huehuetenango) and to a remote crossing point on the Mexican border called Niquimiul.

Towards the Mexican border

The main road through San Pedro continues west, through San Marcos and out of the valley. Here it starts the descent towards the Pacific plain, dropping steeply around endless hairpin bends and past acre after acre of coffee bushes. Along the way the views towards the ocean are superb. Eventually you reach the sweltering lowlands, passing through San Rafael and El Rodeo with their squalid shacks for plantation workers. About an hour and a half out of San Pedro you arrive in **MALACATÁN**, a relatively sedate place by coastal standards. If you get stuck here on your way to or from the border, try the *Pensión Lucía* (②) or the *Hotel America* (②), both on the plaza. Contrary to popular belief, there is no Mexican consul in Malacatán, but if you need to change money there is a branch of the *Banco del Cafe* (Mon–Fri 8.30am–noon & 2–5.30pm).

Buses between Malacatán and San Marcos run every hour from 5am to 5pm. There are trucks and minibuses every half-hour from Malacatán to the border at Talisman (see p.193), and plenty of pullmans pass through on their way between the border and the capital.

HUEHUETENANGO AND THE CUCHUMATANES

The **department of Huehuetenango**, slotted into the northwest corner of the highlands, is a wildly beautiful part of the country that's bypassed by the majority of visitors. The area is dominated by the mountains of the **Cuchumatanes**, but also includes a limestone plateau in the west and a strip of dense jungle to the north. The vast majority of this is inaccessible to all but the most dedicated of hikers, but there's plenty that's easy to see, too.

The **Pan-American Highway**, cutting through from Cuatro Caminos to the Mexican border, is the only paved road in the department, and if you're heading through this way you'll get a glimpse of the mountains, and perhaps a vague sense of the isolating influence of this massive landscape. With more time and energy to spare, a trip into the mountains to **Todos Santos**, or even all the way out to **San Mateo Ixtatán**, reveals an exceptional wealth of Indian culture. It's a world of jagged peaks and deep-cut valleys, where Spanish is definitely the second language and traditional costume is still rigidly adhered to. Heavily populated before the Conquest, the area has pre-Columbian ruins scattered throughout the hills, with the largest at **Zaculeu**, immediately outside **Huehuetenango**. Despite the initial devastation, the arrival of the Spanish had surprisingly little impact here, and traditional ways are still well preserved. A visit to these mountain villages, either for a market or fiesta (and there are plenty of both), offers one of the best opportunities to see Indian life at close quarters.

Heading on from Huehuetenango you can be at the **Mexican border** in a couple of hours, reach Guatemala City in five or six, or use the back roads to travel across the highlands through **Aguacatán** towards Santa Cruz del Quiché, Nebaj or Cobán.

From Cuatro Caminos to Huehuetenango

Heading northwest from Cuatro Caminos, the Pan-American Highway climbs steadily, passing the entrance to San Francisco el Alto and stepping up out of the Xela valley onto a broad plateau thick with fields of wheat and dotted with houses. The only village along the way is **POLOGUÁ**, where they have a small weekly market, a *pensión* – the *Pologuita* (①) – and a fiesta from August 21 to 27.

About a kilometre before the village, a dirt track leads north to **SAN BARTOLO**, a small agricultural centre down amongst the pine trees, some 12km from the road. The place is virtually deserted during the week, but on Sundays the farmers who live scattered in the surrounding forest gather in the village for the market. There's a small unmarked *pensión* and some thermal springs a couple of kilometres away. Another track, branching from the first a couple of kilometres before San Bartolo, connects the village with Momostenango, which is about two hours' walk. From Quezaltenango to San Bartolo there are buses at noon, 3pm, 4pm and 5pm, all going back again between 6am and 6.30am.

Beyond Pologuá the road turns towards the north and leaves the corn-covered plateau, crossing the crest of the hills and skirting around the rim of a huge sweeping valley. To the east a superb view opens out across a sea of pine forests, the last stretch of levellish land before the mountains to the north. Way out there in the middle is Santa Cruz del Quiché and closer to hand, buried in the trees, lies Momostenango. Once over the ridge the road winds its way down towards Huehuetenango. The first place inside the department is the *Ladino* village of **Malacatancito**, where Mam warriors first challenged the advancing Spanish army in 1525.

Huehuetenango

In the corner of a small agricultural plain, 5km from the main road at the foot of the mighty Cuchumatanes, **HUEHUETENANGO**, capital of the department of the same name, is the focus of trade and transport for a vast area. Nonetheless,

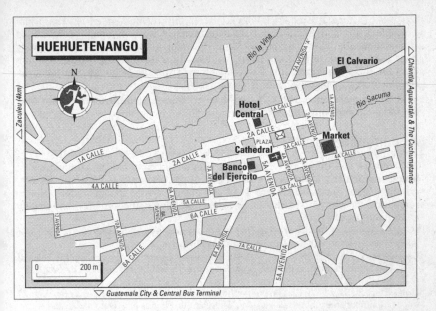

HUEHUETENANGO

N

◁ Zaculeu (4km)

Río la Vina

El Calvario

▷ Chiantla, Aguacatán & The Cuchumatanes

Río Sacuma

Hotel Central

2A CALLE
PLAZA

Market

Cathedral

Banco del Ejercito

0   200 m

▽ Guatemala City & Central Bus Terminal

its atmosphere is provincial and relaxed. The name is a Nahuatl word meaning "the place of the old people", and before the arrival of the Spanish it was the site of one of the residential suburbs that surrounded the Mam capital of Zaculeu (see p.170). Under colonial rule it was a small regional centre with little to offer other than a steady trickle of silver and a stretch or two of grazing land. The supply of silver dried up long ago, but other minerals are still mined, and coffee and sugar have been added to the area's produce.

Arrival and information

Like all Guatemalan towns, Huehuetenango is laid out on a grid pattern, with avenidas running one way and calles the other. It's fairly small so you shouldn't have any real problems finding your way around, particularly once you've located the plaza.

Arriving, you'll probably find yourself at the new purpose-built **bus terminal** halfway between the Pan-American Highway and town. Minibuses make constant trips between the town centre and the bus terminal, or you can take the larger bus, heading for **Chiantla** via the town centre.

You'll probably be coming **to Huehuetenango** from elsewhere in the highlands, in which case you might be able to pick up a direct bus somewhere along the Pan-American Highway – or you can catch any bus to Cuatro Caminos, where you'll be able to find one for Huehuetenango. There's also a regular service, with hourly departures, from the terminal in Quezaltenango.

Coming direct **from Guatemala City** the best way to travel is by pullman. *Los Halcones* run buses at 7am and 2pm from their offices in Guatemala City at 7 Av 15–27, Zona 1; *Rapidos Zaculeu* (in Guatemala City at 9 C 11–42, Zona 1) run services at 6am and 3pm; and five second-class buses a day are run by *El Condor*

(19 C 2–01, Zona 1, Guatemala City). Also highly recommended is *Transportes Velasquez*, 20 C 1–37, Zona 1 in Guatemala City; who run pullmans to Huehuetenango daily at 8.30am, 9.30am, 10.30am, 11.30am, 12.15pm and every hour from 2.30pm to 6.30pm. There are also departures every couple of hours from the main bus terminal in Zona 4. Coming from the **Mexican border** at La Mesilla there's a bus every hour from 4am to 4pm.

There's a **post office** at 2 C 3–54 (Mon–Fri 8am–4.30pm); *Guatel* is right next door at 2 C 3–56 (7am–midnight).

Accommodation

As a centre for trade and commerce Huehuetenango has an abundance of **hotels**, particularly at the very bottom end of the price range. Most are scruffy, chaotic places, clustered around 1 Av and crowded with Indian traders. Better rooms are in shorter supply, to be found mostly in the streets immediately around the plaza.

Pensión Astoria, 4 Av 1–45 (☎7641197). Run by a very friendly family, this is the finest budget hotel in town, with hot showers and a good *comedor*. ③.

Casa Blanca, 7 Av 3-41 (☎ & fax 7642586). The town's newest posh hotel, built in colonial style. The fine restaurant and spacious garden terrace is well worth a visit in its own right. ⑤.

Hotel Central, 5 Av 1–33. Classic budget hotel, with large, scruffy rooms in a creaking old wooden building and a fantastic, *comedor*. There are no singles or private baths, and with a bus company on one side and a disco on the other it can be hard to get any sleep. ②.

Hotel Centro, 6 Av 4–29. Bare and simple but clean, with tiny shower cubicles. ②.

Hotel Mary, 2 C 3–52 (☎7641618; fax 7641228). Modern and central with small but pleasant rooms, some with a private shower and loads of steaming hot water. ③.

Hotel Posada Familiar, 4 C 6–83. Friendly and clean although the covered interior does make it a little dark; some rooms have private showers. ①–②.

Hotel Roberto's, 2 C 5–49. Another reasonable and well-priced budget hotel. ②.

Todos Santos Inn, 2 C 6–74 (☎7641241). Charming new budget hotel with resident parrot. No private baths. ③.

Hotel Vasquez, 2 C 6–67 (☎7641338). Cell-sized rooms around a bare courtyard, but clean, safe, and with secure parking. ②.

Hospedaje El Viajero, 2 C 5–36. Cheap but very rough – a lot like the travellers' hotels on 1 Av. ①.

Hotel Zaculeu, 5 Av 1–14, opposite the *Hotel Central*. (☎7641086). Far and away the best hotel in town and something of an institution. Rooms in the cheaper old section surround a beautiful leafy courtyard, while in the new section they come complete with cable TV. There's also parking and a reasonable restaurant. ⑤.

The Town

Today's Huehuetenango has two quite distinct functions – and two contrasting halves – each serving a separate section of the population. The large majority of the people are *Ladinos*, and for them Huehuetenango is an unimportant regional centre far from the hub of things, a mood summed up in the unhurried atmosphere of the **plaza** at the heart of the *Ladino* half of town, where shaded walkways are surrounded by administrative offices. Overlooking it, perched above the pavements, are a shell-shaped bandstand, a clock tower and a grandiose

Neoclassical church, a solid whitewashed structure with a facade that's crammed with Doric pillars and Grecian urns. In the middle of the plaza there's a **relief map** of the department with flags marking the villages. The details are vague and the scale a bit warped, but it gives you an idea of the mass of rock that dominates the region, and the deep river valleys that slice into it.

A few blocks to the east, the town's atmosphere could hardly be more different. Here the neat little rows of arches are replaced by the pale green walls of the **market**, hub of the Indian part of town, and the streets are crowded with traders, drunks and travellers. This part of Huehuetenango, centred on 1 Av, is always alive with activity, its streets packed with people from every corner of the department and littered with rotten vegetables.

Eating, drinking and entertainment

Most of the better **restaurants** are, like the accommodation, in the central area, around the plaza. **Films** are shown two or three times a week at the cinema on 3 C, half a block west of the plaza.

Las Brasas, 4 Av 5–11. Reasonably good Chinese food but not all that cheap.

Hotel Central, 5 Av 1–33. Very tasty, inexpensive set meals, including a particularly good breakfast served from 7.30am.

Ebony and **Los Alpes**, both on 2 C, just off the plaza. Sandwiches, snacks and hamburgers.

La Fonda de Don Juan, 2 C 5–35. Good mix of local and international dishes at decent prices.

Pizza Hogareña, 6 Av 4–45, next to *Hotel Mary*. Delicious sandwiches, *churrascos*, fish, huge salads, pasta, fruit juices and pizzas.

Café Jardín, 4 C and 6 Av. Friendly place serving inexpensive but excellent breakfasts, milkshakes, pancakes and the usual chicken and beef dishes. Open 6am–11pm.

Maxi Pizza, on 2 C just off the plaza. Does just what you'd expect and does it well.

Restaurante Rincón, 6 Av A 7–21. Under the same management as the *Pizza Hogareña* and offering the same food.

Listings

Banks *Banco G&T* (Mon–Fri 9am–8pm, Sat 10am–2pm) is on the plaza, *Banco del Cafe* (Mon–Fri 8.30am–8pm, Sat 10am–2pm) a block to the south, and there's a *Banco del Ejercito* at the junction of 5 Av and 4 C. Note that you cannot exchange cash or travellers' cheques on a Saturday.

Language schools Huehuetenango is a good place to learn Spanish as you don't rub shoulders with that many gringos. As almost everywhere, schools offer a package of tuition and accommodation with a family for around $90 a week. The best is *El Portal*, 1 C 1–64 (☎ & fax 7641987), closely rivalled by *Fundacion 23*, 6 Av 6–126 (☎7641478).

Laundry Best is in the *Turismundo* Commercial Centre at 3 Av 0–15 (Mon–Sat 9.30am–6.30pm).

Mexican consulate In the *Farmacía El Cid*, on the plaza at 5 Av and 4 C. They'll charge you $1 for a tourist card that's usually free at the border.

Shopping Superb weaving is produced throughout the department and can be bought in the market here or at *Artesanias Ixquil*, a shop on 5 Av opposite the *Hotel Central*, where both the prices and quality are high. If you have time, though, you'd be better advised to travel to the villages and buy direct from the producers.

MOVING ON FROM HUEHUETENANGO

All transport, except to the village of St. Juan Atitán and the Zaculeu ruins, leaves from the **main bus terminal** outside town. To get there from the town centre, take either a minibus or the Chiantla bus from the *parada servicio urbano* just past the *Café Jardín*, or on 6 Av, between 2 and 3 C. The terminal is well laid out, each bus company with its own office, so you can easily get the latest information on timetables. Don't believe the ones painted on the walls, though. Note also that it is standard practice to buy your ticket from the office, before boarding the bus, even for second-class buses.

Buses to the **Mexican border** (2hr) leave from 6am onwards, with the last one departing at 7pm, although there tends to be more traffic in the mornings. (The same applies for all connections.) For Coatepeque on the **Pacific**, buses leave between 3am and 4.45pm. For **Quezaltenango** (3hr), the first bus leaves at 4.30am, the last at 4pm; for **Guatemala City** (6hr), there are regular departures from 2.15am to 4pm. If you want to go to **Antigua, Lake Atitlán** or **Chichicastenango**, take any bus for the capital and change at the appropriate junction (Los Encuentros for Chich and the lake, Chimaltenango for Antigua). More remote destinations are also served. Heading north, into the **Cuchumatanes mountains**, there are buses for Barillas at 10am and Soloma at 5pm, returning at 6am and 10am respectively. The **Todos Santos** bus leaves between 12.30 and 1pm, returning at 4am. Buses for **Nentón**, in the isolated northwest, leave at 5.30am and 9.30am; for Gracias a Dios, at 5am and 12.30pm, though you should always check these schedules prior to your planned day of departure.

Heading **east** and **northeast** there are regular morning buses for Aguacatán, halfway to Sacapulas; and all the way to Sacapulas at 11.30am and 12.45pm, where you can make daily connections south, for Quiché and Chichicastenango. There is also a direct bus route to Nebaj (6hr), departing daily at 11.30am, which also goes via Aguacatán and Sacapulas. The return from Nebaj to Huehuetenango leaves at 1.45pm.

For a faster and more luxurious service, **pullman buses** leave from offices in other parts of the city. *Los Halcones*, 7 Av 3–62, run pullmans to Guatemala City at 7am and 2pm; *Rapidos Zaculeu*, 3 Av 5–25, leave for the capital at 6am and 3pm.

Zaculeu

A few kilometres to the west of Huehuetenango are the ruins of **ZACULEU**, capital of the **Mam**, who were one of the principal pre-conquest highland tribes. The site (daily 8am–6pm; free) includes several large temples, plazas and a ball court, but unfortunately it has been restored with an astounding lack of subtlety (or accuracy). Its appearance – more like an ageing film set than an ancient ruin – is owed to a latter-day colonial power, the **United Fruit Company**, under whose auspices the ruins were reconstructed in 1946 and 1947; the company is, of course, notorious for its heavy-handed practices throughout Central America, and the Zaculeu reconstruction is no exception. The walls and surfaces have been levelled off with a layer of thick white plaster, leaving them stark and undecorated. There are no roof-combs, carvings or stucco mouldings, and only in a few places does the original stonework show through. Even so, the site does have a peculiar atmosphere of its own and is worth a look: surrounded by trees and neatly mown grass, with fantastic views of the mountains, it's an excellent spot for a picnic.

Not all that much is known about the early history of Zaculeu as no Mam records survived the Conquest, but the site is thought to have been a religious and administrative centre housing the elite, while the bulk of the population lived in small surrounding settlements or scattered in the hills. Zaculeu was the hub of

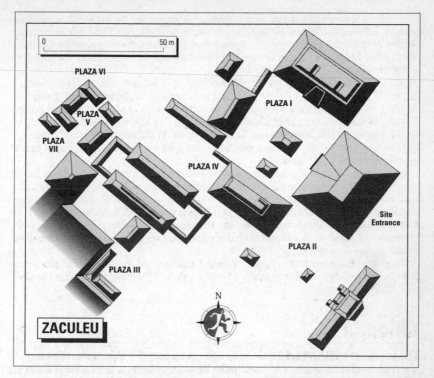

0   50 m

PLAZA VI

PLAZA I

PLAZA V

PLAZA VII

PLAZA IV

Site
Entrance

PLAZA II

PLAZA III

N

ZACULEU

a large area of Mam-speakers, its boundaries reaching into the mountains as far as Todos Santos and along the Selegua and Cuilco valleys, an area throughout which Mam remains the dominant language.

To put together a history of the site means relying on the records of the Quiché, a more powerful neighbouring tribe. According to their mythology, the Quiché conquered most of the other highland tribes, including the Mam, some time between 1400 and 1475: the Popol Vuh tells that "our grandfathers and fathers cast them out when they inserted themselves among the Mam of Zakiulew". The Quiché maintained their authority under the rule of the leader Quicab, but following his death in 1475 the subjugated tribes began to break away from the fold. As a part of this trend the Mam managed to reassert their independence, but no sooner had they escaped the clutches of one expansionist empire than the **Spanish** arrived with a yet more brutal alternative.

For the first few months the Spaniards devoted themselves to conquering the Quiché, still the dominant force in the highlands. But once they'd achieved this they turned their attention to the Mam, especially after being told by Sequechul, leader of the Quiché, that a plan to burn the Spanish army in Utatlán had been suggested to his father by **Caibal Balam**, king of the Mam. In answer to this, Pedro de Alvarado despatched an army under the command of his brother Gonzalo to mete out punishment. They were met by about five thousand Mam warriors near the village of Malacatancito, and promptly set about a massacre. Seeing that his troops were no match for the Spanish, Caibal Balam withdrew them to the safety of Zaculeu, where they were protected on three sides by deep ravines and on the other by a series of walls and ditches. The Spanish army settled outside the city, preparing themselves for a lengthy siege, while Gonzalo offered the Indians a simple choice – they either became Christians "peacefully" or faced "death and destruction".

Attracted by neither option they struggled to hold out against the invading force. At one stage a relief army of eight thousand Indians arrived from the mountains, but again they were unable to ruffle Gonzalo's well-disciplined ranks. Finally, in mid-October, after about six weeks under siege, his army starving to death, Caibal Balam surrendered to the Spanish. With the bitterest of ironies a bastardized version of his name has been adopted by one of Guatemala's crack army regiments – the "Kaibils".

Excavations at the site have unearthed hundreds of burials carried out in an unusual variety of ways; bodies were crammed into great urns, interred in vaults and even cremated. These burials, along with artefacts found at the site, including pyrite plaques and carved jade, have suggested links with the site at Nebaj. There's a small **museum** on site (daily 8am–noon & 1–6pm) with examples of some of the burial techniques used and some interesting ceramics found during excavation.

To get to Zaculeu from Huehuetenango, take one of the buses that run from 7 Av between 3 and 4 calles – make sure it's a Ruta 3 heading for Ruinas Zaculeu (not Zaculeu central).

Chiantla

The village of **CHIANTLA** is backed right up against the mountains 5km to the north of Huehuetenango. The main point of interest here is the colonial church, built by Dominican friars, which is now the object of one of the country's largest pilgrimages, annually on February 2, in honour of its image of the **Virgen del Rosario**. Legend has it that the image of the Virgin was given to the church by a Spaniard named Almengor, who owned a silver mine in the hills. Not only did the mine proceed to yield a fortune, but on his last visit to it, just after Almengor had surfaced, the entire thing caved in – thus proving the power of the Virgin. She is also thought to be capable of healing the sick, and at any time of the year you'll see people who've travelled from all over Guatemala asking for her assistance. A mural inside the church depicts a rather ill-proportioned Spaniard watching over the Indians toiling in his mines, while on the wall opposite the Indians are shown discovering God. The precise connection between the two is left somewhat vague, but presumably the gap is bridged by the Virgin. **Buses** from Huehuetenango to Chiantla travel between the main bus terminal and Chiantla every twenty minutes between 6am and 6.30pm. You can catch one as it passes through the town centre, or wait at the *calvario* (by the junction of 1 Av and 1 C), instead of heading out to the terminal.

The Cuchumatanes

The **Cuchumatanes**, rising to a frosty 3837m just to the north of Huehuetenango, are the largest non-volcanic peaks in Central America. The mountain chain rises from a limestone plateau close to the Mexican border, reaches its full height above Huehuetenango, and falls away gradually to the east, continuing through northern Quiché to form part of the highlands of Alta Verapaz. Appropriately enough the name translates as "that which was brought together by great force", from the Mam words *cucuj*, to unite, and *matan*, superior force.

The mountain scenery is magnificent, ranging from wild, exposed craggy outcrops to lush, tranquil river valleys. The upper parts of the slopes are barren, scattered with boulders and shrivelled cypress trees, while the lower levels, by contrast, are richly fertile, cultivated with corn, coffee and sugar. Between the peaks, in the deep-cut valleys, are hundreds of tiny villages, isolated by the enormity of the landscape. This area had little to entice the Spanish, and even at the best of times they only managed to exercise vague control, occasionally disrupting things with bouts of religious persecution or disease, but rarely maintaining a sustained presence. Following the initial impact of the Conquest, the people were, for the most part, left to revert to their old ways, and their traditions are still very powerful today, showing through in the fiestas, costumes and folk-Catholicism.

More recently the mountains have been the scene of bitter fighting between the army and the guerrillas. In the late 1970s and early 1980s the area was struck by a wave of violence and terror that sent thousands fleeing across the border to Mexico. These days things have calmed down, and some families have returned from exile, although many still remain in refugee camps on the other side of the border. It is, however, safe to travel into the mountains, discovering some of the country's most spectacular scenery and fascinating villages. A single rough road runs through the range, climbing the steep south face, crossing the exposed central plateau and dropping into the isolated valleys to the north. Travel here is not easy – distances are large, hotels and restaurants basic at best, buses are packed and frequent cloudbursts often make the roads impassable – but if you can summon the energy it's an immensely rewarding area, offering a rare glimpse of Indian life and some of the country's finest fiestas and markets. The mountains are also ideal for hiking, particularly if you've had enough of struggling up volcanoes.

The most accessible of the villages in the vicinity, and the only one yet to receive a steady trickle of tourists, is **Todos Santos**, which is also one of the most interesting. At any time of year the Saturday market here is well worth making a trip to visit, and the fiesta on November 1 has to be one of the most outrageous in Guatemala. Once settled, you can walk over the hills to **San Juan Atitán** and **Santiago Chimaltenango**, or head on down the valley to **San Martín** and **Jacaltenango**. Further into the mountains are the villages of **Soloma** and **San Mateo Ixtatán**, both of which have markets on Thursday and Sunday. Another good hike takes you from **San Miguel Acatán** along the edge of the hills to Jacaltenango. Beyond San Mateo Ixtatán the road comes to an end at **Barillas**, a *Ladino* town from where the jungle lowlands beyond are being colonized.

Huehuetenango to Barillas

Heading north out of Huehuetenango, the road for the mountains passes through Chiantla before starting to climb the arid hillside, and as the bus sways around the switchbacks, the view across the valley is superb. In the distance you can sometimes make out the perfect cone of the Santa María volcano, towering above Quezaltenango some 60km to the south.

At the top of the slope the road slips through a pass into the *región andina*, a desolate grassy plateau suspended between the peaks, strewn with boulders and segregated with neat earth walls. At this height the air is cool, thin and fresh, the ground often hard with frost and occasionally dusted with snow. In the middle of the plain is the *Comedor de los. Cuchumatanes*, where buses stop for a chilly lunch before pressing on through Paquix, junction for the road to Todos Santos. (Shortly before the road reaches the *comedor* a rough track branches off to the east, climbing through the mountains for 44km to Salquil Grande, from where a road runs to Nebaj – sadly this area is still fought over and the road often impassable, but if you're in search of an unpredictable adventure it does make a spectacular side trip.)

Beyond Paquix the road runs through a couple of magical valleys, where great grey boulders lie scattered among ancient-looking oak and cypress trees, their trunks gnarled by the bitter winds. A few families manage to survive the rigours of the altitude, collecting firewood and tending flocks of sheep. Sheep have been grazed here since they were introduced by the Spanish, who prized this wilderness as the best pasture in Central America.

Continuing north the road gradually winds down off the plateau, emerging on the other side at the top of an incredibly steep valley. Here the track clings to the

THE MAYAN PRIESTS OF THE CUCHUMATANES

The high peaks and rugged terrain of the Cuchumatanes guard one of the country's most traditional Indian cultures. Ethnographer Krystyna Deuss has been studying Maya rituals in these remote communities for more than ten years, focusing her attention on the prayer-makers, who occupy a position paralllel to that of local priests. Here she explains their role and some of the key rituals surrounding their office.

Some of the purest **Maya rituals** today can be found among the Kanjobal Indians of the northwestern Cuchumatanes. The office of *alcade resador* (chief prayer-maker) still exists here and the 365-day *Haab* calendar is used in conjunction with the 260-day *Tzolkin*. The former ends with the five days of *Oyeb ku*, when adult souls leave the body; the return of the souls on the fifth day brings in the new year. As this always falls on a day of *Watan, Lambat, Ben* or *Chinax*, these four day lords are referred to as the "Year Bearers" or "Chiefs". Depending on the community, the *Haab* year begins either at the end of February or the beginning of March, coinciding with the corn planting season.

The duty of the **alcade resador** is to protect his village from evil and ensure a good harvest by praying for rain at planting time and for protection against wind, pest and disease while the corn is maturing. His year of office – during which he and his wife must remain celibate – begins on January 1, the day all the voluntary municipal officials change, and in the towns of Santa Eulalia, Soloma and San Miguel Acatán where traditions are particularly strong, he lives in a house which has been especially built for him. Traditionalists regularly visit to ask for prayers and to leave gifts of corn, beans, candles and money. On the altar of the house stands the **ordenanza**, a chest that not only contains religious icons but also ancient village documents, a throwback to the time when religious and civil authorities worked as one. The chest now serves both as a symbol of authority and as a sacred object, and can only be opened by the *alcade resador*, in private, once a hillside, cut out of the sheer rock face that drops hundreds of metres to the valley floor. This northern side of the Cuchumatanes contains some of the most dramatic scenery in the entire country, and the road is certainly the most spine-chilling. A little further down, as if to confirm your worst fears, the rusting wreck of a bus lies a hundred metres or so beneath the road.

The first village reached by the road is **SAN JUAN IXCOY**, an apple-growing centre drawn out along the valley floor. There's no particular reason for breaking the journey here, but there is a small *pensión* (①), where you can get a bed and a meal. In season, around the end of August, passing buses are besieged by an army of fruit-sellers. This innocent-looking village has a past marked by violence. On the night of July 17, 1898, following a dispute about pay, the Indians of San Juan murdered the local labour contractor, and in a desperate bid to keep the crime secret they slaughtered all but one of the village's *Ladino* population. The authorities responded mercilessly, killing about ten Indians for the life of every *Ladino*. In local mythology the revolt is known as *la degollación*, the beheading.

Over another range of hills and down in the next valley is **SOLOMA**, largest, busiest and richest of the villages in the northern Cuchumatanes, with a population of around three thousand. Its flat valley floor was once the bed of a lake, and the steep hillsides still come sliding down at every earthquake or cloudburst. Soloma translates (from Kanjobal, the dominant language on this side of the mountains) as "without security", and its history is blackened by disaster; it was

year. The *resador*'s whole day is spent in prayer: at his home altar before the *ordenanza*, in church and at sacred village sites marked by crosses. Prayers for rain are often accompanied by the ritual sacrifice of turkeys whose blood is poured over the candles and incense destined to be burned at the sacred places the following day. These ceremonies are not open to the general public.

Festivals more in the public domain happen on January 1 when the incumbent *resador* hands over to his successor. In **Soloma** after an all-night vigil the *ordenanza* is carried in procession to the middle of the market square and put on a makeshift altar under a pine arch. When the incoming group arrives there are prayers and ritual drinking and they receive their wooden staffs of office, after which the outgoing *resador* (usually a man in his 60s or 70s) is free to leave for his own home. The new *resador*'s group stays in the marketplace praying, collecting alms and drinking until 3pm, when they carry the *ordenanza* back to the official residence in a somewhat erratic procession. Not withstanding a further night of vigil and ceremonial drinking, at 7am the following morning, the *resador* sets out on his first prayer-round to the sacred mountains overlooking the town.

In **San Juan Ixcoy** the year-end ceremonies differ in that the new *resador* is not appointed in advance. Here the outgoing group carries the *ordenanza* to a small chapel outside the church on the night of the 31st and leaves it in the care of a committee of traditionals. The usual all night vigil with prayers, ritual drinking and collecting alms continues throughout the following day while everyone waits anxiously for a candidate to turn up. As the office of *resador* is not only arduous, and with dwindling support from the community, also expensive, the post is not always filled on January 1. The *ordenanza* sometimes stays locked in the chapel for several days before a volunteer (usually an ex-prayer maker), takes on the office again rather than let the *ordenanza* and the tradition be abandoned.

Krystyna Deuss, The Guatemalan Indian Centre

destroyed by earthquakes in 1773 and 1902, half burnt down in 1884, and decimated by smallpox in 1885. The long white *huipiles* worn by the women of Soloma are similar to those of San Mateo Ixtatán and the Lacandones, and are probably as close as any in the country to the style worn before the Conquest. These days they are on the whole donned only for the market on Thursday and Sunday, which yet again is by far the best time to visit.

About four hours from Huehuetenango, Soloma makes a good place to break the trip. The *Río Lindo* is a good, friendly **hotel** (③) that also does food, or there's the cheaper *Hotel Central* (①), and as a last resort the *Hospedaje San Juan* (①). *Transportes Gonzalez* **buses** for Soloma leave Huehuetenango at 10am and 5pm; check also with *Transportes Barillensis* for additional departures. Buses going on to San Rafael La Independencia, San Sebastian Coatan and Barillas also pass through.

Leaving Soloma the road climbs again, on a steadily deteriorating surface, over another range of hills, to the hillside village of Santa Eulalia. Beyond, past the junction to San Rafael La Independencia, it heads through another misty, rock-strewn forest and emerges on the other side at **SAN MATEO IXTATÁN**, the most traditional, and quite possibly the most interesting, of this string of villages. Little more than a thin sprawl of wooden-tiled houses on an exposed hillside, it's strung out beneath a belt of ancient forest and craggy mountains. The people here speak Chuj and form part of a tribe of Indians who occupy the extreme northwest corner of the highlands and some of the jungle beyond; their territory borders that of the Lacandon, a jungle tribe never subjugated by the Spanish, who constantly harassed these villages in colonial times. The only industry is the manufacture of salt from some communally owned springs in the hills, and life at these heights is hard at the best of times. The only time to visit, other than for the fiesta on September 21, is on a market day, Thursday or Sunday. The rest of the week the village is virtually deserted. The women here wear unusual and striking *huipiles*, long white gowns embroidered in brilliant reds, yellows and blues, radiating out from a star-like centre. The men wear short woollen tunics called *capixay*, often embroidered with flowers around the collar and quetzals on the back. Below the village is a beautiful Maya ruin, the unrestored remains of a small pyramid and ball court, shaded by a couple of cypress trees. If you decide to **stay**, there are several extremely basic *pensiónes* – don't expect sheets – the best of which is the *El Aguila* (①), run by the very friendly family who operate the *Comedor Ixateco*. To the northwest of San Mateo a road cuts high across the mountain and is the start of a beautiful hike to Yalambojoch (see below).

Beyond San Mateo the road drops steadily east to **BARILLAS**, a *Ladino* frontier town in the relative warmth of the lowlands. Further on still, the land slopes into the Usumacinta basin through thick, uninhabited jungle. Rough tracks penetrate a short distance into this wilderness (and a local bus runs out as far as San Ramón), opening it up for farming, and eventually a road will run east across the **Ixcán** (the wilderness area that stretches between here and the jungles of Petén) to Playa Grande. For the moment, however, this land is still hotly fought over, with some of the surviving guerrillas hiding out in the forest. The cheapest place to **stay** in Barillas is the *Tienda las Tres Rosas* (①), and the best is the *Hotel Monte Cristo* (②).

Buses to Barillas, passing through all the villages en route, are operated by *Rutas Barillenses*, and leave Huehuetenango at 3am and 11.45am, taking around four hours to reach Soloma and at least eight hours to Barillas. All buses leave from the main bus terminal, and it's well worth buying your ticket in advance as they operate a vague system of seat allocation. It's a rough and tortuous trip, the buses usually filled to bursting and the road invariably appalling. Buses leaving Barillas for Huehuetenango depart at the same times, and there are also bus offices in Barillas where you can get a ticket in advance.

Hiking from San Mateo to Yalambojoch

The great forested peaks looming to the west of San Mateo Ixtatán are in fact a narrow spur of the Cuchumatanes and can easily be crossed in day. In a matter of hours you're up on top of the ridge, in a misty world of forest and high pasture, while over on the other side you soon drop onto a low-lying limestone plateau from where you can catch a bus back to Huehuetenango.

The main road from San Mateo to Barillas heads on around the side of the mountain, dipping into a narrow gulley. At the bottom of this dip – less than a kilometre east of the centre of San Mateo – another road branches off to the left, climbing into the hills. Following this you pass right over the spine of the Cuchumatanes, through high alpine pastures and beautiful pine and white oak forests, the older trees draped in mosses, ferns and bromeliads. Sadly, the trees are being cut down at a phenomenal rate to provide firewood for the nearby villages, although this does mean you may be able to catch a ride on one of the lumber lorries.

After a couple of hours' walk you emerge from the forest at the top of a huge, steep-sided valley, beside the tiny settlement of **Chizbazalum**. Sticking with the road, you want to cross the top of the valley, which drops away beneath you. Individual houses, maize fields and herds of sheep are scattered across this enormous landscape and many of the young shepherds are armed with blowpipes, a tradition probably inherited from the lowland Indians to the north. (The only other place that hunters use blowpipes is in Chajul in the Ixil triangle, where they were heavily influenced by Lacandon Indians.) The focus of this dispersed community is the village of **Patalcal**, where the road divides – you want to bear right and head up and onto the next shoulder. The road pushes out along this high ridge, but again it splits and you need to branch right. Here too the high ground is forested, but the trail soon starts to drop again, zigzagging down towards the village of Bulej – five or six hours' walk from San Mateo. If it's a clear day the views are superb, with the Mexican plateau mapped out below and the Lagunas de Montebello catching the light.

BULEJ itself is a remote farming settlement of scattered wooden buildings and fruit trees. If you happen to be here in June then the entire place will be in bloom, while in August it is awash with pears and apricots. You shouldn't have any trouble finding a place to stay here and there is a shop on the main square selling soft drinks and biscuits. If you decide to press on, then it's another couple of hours of steep descent to the village of **YALAMBOJOCH**, which is right down on the plateau and the point you finally meet up with the road from Huehuetenango. The recent history of Yalambojoch is bound up with that of Finca San Francisco, a smaller village along the road some 3km to the east. In 1982 the army massacred around three hundred people in San Francisco (see *Contexts*) and the entire population of the surrounding area fled for their lives, crossing the border into Mexico. After more than a decade people started to return, and life in Yalambojoch is beginning to return to normal. Despite all this horror you'll find the people warm and welcoming, and although they are very poor you shouldn't have any trouble finding somewhere to stay. The village of **FINCA SAN FRANCISCO** is itself also well worth a look – just follow the road to the east. Along the way you can stop off for a chilly dip in a beautiful crystal-clear stream, and in the village itself there is a small Maya temple, which is also the site of a plaque commemorating those who died in the massacre.

One or two **buses** a day connect Yalambojoch and Huehuetenango. They leave Huehuetenango at 5am and 12.30pm and take approximately eight hours, passing through Yalambojoch before spending the night at Finca Gracias a Dios, metres from the Mexican border; early the next morning they return to Huehuetenango via Yalambojoch.

San Rafael La Independencia, San Miguel Acatán and on foot to Jacaltenango

Between Santa Eulalia and San Mateo Ixtatán a branch road cuts off to the left, heading over the spine of the Cuchumatanes and curving around the other side to **SAN RAFAEL LA INDEPENDENCIA**, a small village perched on a cold outcrop. In San Rafael you'll find a couple of *comedores* and a Thursday market but nowhere to stay: however, if you ask in the office of the bus company they'll usually be able to find you a concrete floor on which you can spend the night. The next morning you can walk on down the valley, following the road or taking the path towards the larger village of **SAN MIGUEL ACATÁN**. Here there's a Sunday market and a small *pensión* in the house behind the Municipalidad. It may be possible to get a bus this far, although you'll have to confirm the schedule in Huehuetenango as they only run two or three times a week and when the road is bad often go no further than San Rafael.

From San Miguel Acatán a spectacular walk takes you along the edge of the mountains to Jacaltenango (see p.182). Setting out from San Miguel, cross the river and follow the trail that bears to the right as it climbs the hill opposite. At the fork, halfway up, take the higher path that crosses the ridge beside a small shelter. On the other side it drops down into the head of the next valley. Here you want to follow the path down the valley on the near side of the river, and through the narrow gorge to an ancient wooden bridge. Cross the river and climb up the other side of the valley, heading down towards the end of it as you go. The path that heads straight out of the valley runs to Nentón, and the other path, up and over the ridge to the left, heads towards **Jacaltenango**. Along the way there are stunning views of the rugged peaks of the southern Cuchumatanes and the great flat expanse that stretches into Mexico – on a clear day you can see the Lagunas de Montebello, a good 50km away, over the border. On the far side of the ridge the path eventually drops down to Jacaltenango through the neighbouring village of San Marcos Huista: some eight or nine tough but worthwhile hours in all from San Miguel.

Todos Santos

If you turn off at the **Paquix** junction, about 20km from Huehuetenango, you can follow a road heading west to **TODOS SANTOS**. This western road slopes down through **La Ventosa**, a narrow gulley lined with pine and cedar trees, where almost immediately you'll begin to see the traditional red costume of Todos Santos: the men in their red-and-white striped trousers, black woollen breeches and brilliantly embroidered shirt collars; the women in dark blue *cortes* and superbly intricate red *huipiles*. Further down, at the bottom of the steep-sided, deep-cut river valley, is the village itself – a single main street with a few *tiendas*, a plaza, a church, a new language school and a loose collection of houses and corn fields. Above the village flocks of sheep are grazed and below it the crops are farmed. It's a pretty typical highland village, but better known than most because of the work of writer Maud Oakes (whose *The Two Crosses of Todos Santos* was published in 1951) and photographer Hans Namuth, who has been recording the faces of the villagers for more than forty years.

As usual, most of the people the village serves don't actually live here. The immediate population is probably around twelve hundred, but there are perhaps ten times that many in the surrounding hills who are dependent on Todos Santos for trade, supplies and social life. This population is more than the land can support, and many travel to the coast in search of work. All over the country you'll see them, always dressed in *traje* – traditional costume. However, there's one event that brings them all home, the famous November 1 **fiesta** for All Saints (*todos santos*). For three days the village is taken over by unrestrained drinking, dance and marimba music. The whole event opens with an all-day horse race, which starts out as a massive stampede. The riders tear up the course, thrashing their horses with live chickens, pink capes flowing out behind them. At either end of the run they take a drink before burning back again. As the day wears on some riders retire, collapse, or tie themselves on, leaving only the toughest to ride it out. On the second day, "The Day of the Dead", the action moves to the cemetery, with marimba bands and drink stalls setting up amongst the graves for a day of intense ritual that combines grief and celebration. On the final day of the fiesta the streets are littered with bodies and the jail packed with brawlers. To view some of the community's historic costumes, tools, and traditional idols, drop in at the local **museum** ($1 donation), just off the main square.

If you can't make it for the fiesta then the Saturday **market**, although nothing like as riotous, also fills the village, and the night before you might catch some marimba. During the week the village is fairly quiet, although it's a pleasant and peaceful place to spend some time and the surrounding scenery is superb. Moreover, since the **language school** opened up in Todos Santos, a small but lively "gringo-scene" has developed, revolving around *Comedor Katy* and the school's evening events. This is either a bonus or spoils the whole place – depending on your point of view.

Todos Santos is one of the few places where people are still said to use the 260-day *Tzolkin* calendar, which dates back to Maya times. Above the village – follow the track that goes up behind the *Comedor Katy* – is the small Maya site of

---

LEARNING SPANISH IN TODOS SANTOS

Todos Santos is home to one of Guatemala's newest **language schools**, the *Projecto Linguistico de Espanol/Mam Todos Santos*. Despite the fact that Spanish is the second language here, and students get little chance to practise it with their Mam-speaking host families, if you're looking for **cultural exchange** you'll find the course highly rewarding – especially if you don't mind very basic living conditions. Courses consist of five hours' tuition a day and **accommodation with a local family**, all for $120 a week; a percentage of the profits go to local development projects. Reservations can be made through *Proyecto Linguistico Quezalteco de Español*, 5 C 2–40, Zona 1 (or Apdo Postal 114) Quezaltenango (☎7612620).

Tojcunanchén, where you'll find a couple of mounds sprouting pine trees. The site is occasionally used by *brujos* for the burning of incense and the ritual sacrifice of animals.

Practicalities

Buses leave Huehuetenango for Todos Santos from the main bus terminal around 12.30pm – get there early to mark your seat and buy a ticket. They carry on through the village, heading further down the valley, and pass through Todos Santos on the way back to Huehuetenango at 4am. There is generally also a bus later in the morning. Ask around for the latest schedule.

There are two **hotels** in Todos Santos, both very inexpensive but usually full during the fiesta – so arrive early. The *Hospedaje La Paz* (①) has one solid double bed and some smaller cots, and *Las Olguitas* (①) has plenty of tiny rooms suspended in a wooden maze above the kitchen. Most popular these days, though, is the *Hospedaje Casa Familiar* (①), run by the friendly Mrs Santiaga Mendoza Pablo. Hot showers here cost $1 a time, a service even non-residents are welcome to use. You'll find her house 30m above the main road, past *Comedor Katy*. Turning left before you reach the *Casa Familiar* brings you to an un-named orange house; this is another excellent **guest house** with a hot shower (①). The best place to **eat** is at *Comedor Katy*, just off the main plaza, heading left up the hill, though you can also find meals at *Los Olgoitas* and another *comedor* on the main square.

Three hikes from Todos Santos

The scenery around Todos Santos is some of the most spectacular in all Guatemala and there's no better place to leave the roads and set off on foot. In a day you can walk across to **San Juan Atitán**, and from there continue to the Pan-American Highway or head on to **Santiago Chimaltenango**. From the highway you'll be able to catch a bus back to Huehuetenango for the night, and if you make it to Santiago you shouldn't have any problem finding somewhere to stay. This is the more interesting walk, particularly if you set out early on a Thursday morning and arrive in San Juan before the market there has finished.

Alternatively, you can walk down the valley from Todos Santos to **San Martín** and on to **Jacaltenango**, a route which offers superb views. There's a hotel in Jacaltenango, so you can stay the night and then catch a bus back to Huehuetenango in the morning.

Walking to San Juan Atitán

The village of **SAN JUAN ATITÁN** is four or five hours from Todos Santos, across a beautiful isolated valley. The walk follows the path that bears up behind

Maya sandal taken from classic stone carving

the *Comedor Katy*, passes the ruins and climbs steeply above the village through endless muddy switchbacks, bearing gradually across to the right. You reach the top of the ridge after about an hour. From here you drop down, past some huts, to cut straight across the head of the next valley. The route takes you up and down endless exhausting ridges, through lush green forests, and over a total of five gushing streams – only the first and third of which are bridged.

Beside the first stream, about an hour and a half out of Todos Santos, is an ideal campsite, a flat patch of grass right by the water.

The valley is thinly inhabited, and mostly used by the people of San Juan to graze their sheep. Having crossed the valley the path swings up to the left and on to the top of another pass, about three hours from Todos Santos. From here you can see the village of San Juan, strung out along the steep hillside in a long thin line. To head down into the village follow one of the left-hand trails that goes out along the hillside and then drops down amongst the houses. There are several paths to choose from – all cross a series of deep ravines before emerging onto the main track that runs through the village.

Built on treacherously unstable land, San Juan is regularly hit by landslides that sweep whole houses into the valley below. The government has proposed that the entire village be moved, but the people have so far resisted this idea. It's an intensely traditional place: all the men wear long woollen coats (similar in style to the habits worn by Spanish friars), red shirts and plain white trousers. The high-backed sandals worn by both the men and the women, and also by a lot of people in Todos Santos, are a style depicted in ancient Maya carving – they are also worn in some of the villages around San Cristóbal de las Casas in Chiapas, Mexico. Like most of these mountain villages, San Juan is active only on market days, Monday and Thursday.

If you want to **stay**, the *Hospedaje San Diego*, on the hill above the plaza, makes a very basic but friendly place to rest, and the family will cook you supper on request (①). Next morning you can catch a pick-up truck to Huehuetenango at 6am (1hr), in time to make the morning bus for Todos Santos, or walk back. From Huehuetenango, the pick-ups for San Juan leave from outside the *Cafeteria Tucaná*, 2 C 2–15, around noon. Get there early for a space. In this direction the journey takes a good two hours.

On to Santiago Chimaltenango

SANTIAGO CHIMALTENANGO makes a good alternative destination. If you want to go straight here from Todos Santos, turn right when you reach the top of the pass overlooking San Juan, head along the side of the hill and over another pass into a huge bowl-like valley. The village lies on the far side. If you're coming from San Juan, follow the track straight through the village and you'll come to the same pass in just over an hour. From the top of the pass, follow the main track down into the valley as it bears around to the right, towards the village – about one and a half hours from the top. Although not as traditional as the other villages of the region, Santiago is nevertheless a beautiful old place, a compact mass of narrow cobbled streets and adobe houses.

Ask at the main terminal in Huehue for information on buses to and from Santiago Chimaltenango, otherwise you will have to walk on down the valley through coffee plantations to the village of San Pedro Necta, and beyond to the Pan-American Highway, which should take two or three hours. *Mini Trenda La Benedicion* below the market is a friendly **place to stay**.

From Todos Santos to San Martín and Jacaltenango

Heading down the valley from Todos Santos the road arrives at the one-street village of **SAN MARTÍN**, three hours away. The village is inhabited entirely by *Ladinos*, but it has a Friday market that attracts Indians from the land all around, including many from Todos Santos. A little beyond the village the road down the valley divides, with a right fork that leads 11km around the steep western edge of the Cuchumatanes. On a clear day there are spectacular views, reaching well into Mexico. At the end of the old road, on a rocky outcrop, is the poor and ragged village of **CONCEPCIÓN**, from where a new road plunges to Jacaltenango, the final destination of one of the Todos Santos buses, which returns from there to Huehuetenango at about 3am.

Perched on a plateau overlooking the limestone plain that stretches out across the Mexican border, **JACALTENANGO** is the heart of an area that was once very traditional, inhabited by a small tribe of Jacaltec speakers. However, in recent years the surrounding land has been planted with coffee and waves of *Ladinos* have swelled the population of the town. Today the place has a calm and prosperous feel to it. There are two *pensiónes* – one in the large *tienda* on the corner of the plaza and the other up the hill opposite it – and plenty of cheap *comedores* along the side of the market, which is at its busiest on Sunday.

The town can also be reached by a branch route that leaves the Pan-American Highway close to the Mexican border. **Buses** leave Huehuetenango for Jacaltenango, run by *Transportes Cuevas*, but you need to check the timetable at the terminal.

East to Aguacatán

To the east of Huehuetenango, a dirt road turns off at Chiantla to weave along the base of the Cuchumatanes, through dusty foothills, to **AGUACATÁN**. This small agricultural town is strung out along two main streets, shaped entirely by the dip in which it's built. The village was created by Dominican friars, who in the early years of the Conquest merged several smaller settlements inhabited by two distinct peoples. The remains of one of the pre-conquest settlements can still be seen a couple of kilometres to the north, and minute differences of dress and dialect linger – indeed the village remains loosely divided along pre-Columbian lines, with the Chalchitec to the east of the market and the Aguatec to the west. The language of Aguateca (used by both) is spoken only in this village and its immediate surrounds, by a population of around 15,000. During the colonial period gold and silver were mined in the nearby hills, and the Indians are said to have made bricks of solid gold for the king of Spain, to persuade him to let them keep their lands. Today the town is steeped in tradition and the people survive by growing vegetables, including huge quantities of garlic, much of it for export.

Aguacatán's huge Sunday **market** gets under way on Saturday afternoon, when traders arrive early to claim the best sites. On Sunday morning a steady stream of people pours down the main street, cramming into the market and plaza, and soon spilling out into the surrounding area. Around noon the tide turns as the crowds start to drift back to their villages, with donkeys leading their drunken drivers. Despite the scale of the market its atmosphere is subdued and the pace unhurried: for many it's as much a social event as a commercial one.

The traditional costume worn by the women of Aguacatán is unusually simple: their skirts are made of dark blue cotton and the *huipiles*, which hang loose, are decorated with bands of coloured ribbon on a plain white background. This plainness, though, is set off by the local speciality – the *cinta*, or headdress, in which they wrap their hair, an intricately embroidered piece of cloth combining blues, reds, yellows and greens.

Aguacatán's other attraction is the source of the **Río San Juan**, which emerges from beneath a nearby hill, fresh and cool. The source itself, bubbling up beneath a small bush and then channelled by concrete walls, looks a bit disappointing to the uninitiated (though as far as a caver or geologist is concerned it's a big one) but if you have an hour or two to kill it's a good place for a chilly swim – for which you have to pay a tiny fee. To get there walk east along the main street out of the village for about a kilometre, until you see a sign directing you down a track to the left. Follow this round a sharp bend to the left and then take the right turn, towards the base of the hills. From the village it takes about twenty minutes.

Regular **buses** run from Huehuetenango to Aguacatán passing by the Calvario in Huehuetenango, at the junction of 1 Av and 1 C; the first bus leaves at 10am and the last at about 4pm. The 25-kilometre journey takes around an hour. In Aguacatán the best place **to stay** is the simple *Hospedaje Aguateco* (①), with small rooms off a courtyard. If that's full try the *Hospedaje La Paz* (①). **Beyond Aguacatán** the road runs out along a ridge, with fantastic views stretching out below. Eventually it drops down into the Chixoy valley, to the riverside town of **Sacapulas** (p.119). Buses run from Huehuetenango to Sacapulas at 11.30am and 12.45pm, returning at 3am, 4.30am and 5.30am.

West to the Mexican border

From Huehuetenango the Pan-American Highway runs for 79km through the narrow Selegua valley to the Mexican border at **La Mesilla**. Travelling direct this takes about two and a half hours on one of the buses that thunder out of Huehuetenango every hour or so between 5am and 4pm. Along the way, just off the main road, are some interesting traditional villages, largely oblivious to the international highway that carves through their land. Most are best reached as day trips out of Huehuetenango.

The first of these, 20km from Huehuetenango, is **San Sebastián Huehuetenango**, a quiet little place barely 200m north of the highway. The village was the site of a pre-conquest centre, and of a settlement known as Toj-Jol, which was swept away by the Río Selegua in 1891. Further on the road runs through a particularly narrow part of the valley known as **El Tapón**, the cork, and past a turning for San Juan Atitán (12km) and another for San Rafael Petzal, 2km from the main road. Beyond this it passes roads that lead to Colotenango, Nentón and Jacaltenango.

There's just one last roadside village, La Democracia, before **LA MESILLA** and the border – if you get stuck here there's **accommodation** at *Hotel Primavera* and two cheaper *hospedajes*, *Salis* and *Benedicion*. The two sets of customs and immigration are 3km apart; there are taxis, and on the Mexican side you can pick up buses running through the border settlement of **Ciudad Cuauhtemoc** to **Comitán** or even direct to **San Cristóbal de las Casas**. Heading into Guatemala the last bus leaves La Mesilla for Huehuetenango at around 4pm, but if you get stuck there's a small hotel on the Guatemalan side. Wherever you're heading in Guatemala it's best to take the first bus to Huehuetenango and change there.

Colotenango, San Ildefonso Ixtahuacán, and Cuilco

The most important of the villages reached from the highway is **COLOTENANGO**, perched on a hillside 1km or so south from the main road. The municipality of Colotenango used to include San Rafael and San Ildefonso, until 1890 when they became villages in their own right. Ties are still strong, however, and the red *cortes* worn by the women of all three villages are almost identical. Colotenango remains the focal point for the smaller settlements, and its Saturday market is the largest in the Selegua valley. From early Saturday morning the plaza is packed, and the paths that lead into the village are filled with a steady stream of traders, Indian families, cattle, chickens, reluctant pigs and the inevitable drunks. Here you'll see people from all of the surrounding villages, most of them wearing traditional costume. The village is also worth visiting during Holy Week, when elaborate and violent re-enactments of Christ's Passion take place (the bravest of villagers takes the role of Judas, and is shown no mercy by the rest), and for its fiesta from August 12 to 15.

To get to Colotenango from Huehuetenango take any bus heading towards the Mexican border, and ask the driver to drop you at the village. They'll usually leave you on the main road just below, from where you have to cross the bridge and walk up the hill. The journey from Huehuetenango takes around 45 minutes.

On to San Ildefonso and Cuilco

Behind Colotenango a dirt road goes up over the hills and through a pass into the valley of the Río Cuilco. Here it runs high above the river along the top of a ridge, with beautiful views up the valley: below you can make out the tiny village of San Gaspar Ixchil, which consists of little more than a church and a graveyard.

Another few kilometres brings you to the larger village and mining centre of **SAN ILDEFONSO IXTAHUACÁN**. Similar in many ways to Colotenango, it has a large and traditional Indian population. In 1977 the place achieved a certain notoriety after its miners were locked out of the mine because they'd tried to form a union. In response to this they decided to walk the 260km to Guatemala City in order to put their case to the authorities. At the time this was a bold gesture of defiance and it captured the imagination of the entire nation. When they eventually arrived in the capital 100,000 people turned out to welcome them.

Beyond San Ildefonso the road slopes down towards the bottom of the valley and crosses the river before arriving at **CUILCO**, a sizeable *Ladino* town 36km from the Pan-American Highway that marks the end of the road. The Mexican border is just 15km away, and the town maintains cross-border trade links both inside and outside the law. Beyond today's village are the ruins of an earlier settlement known as **Cuilco Viejo**. Cuilco has also earned itself something of a reputation, although this time it's for producing heroin. As a result of the successful anti-drug campaigns in Mexico, poppy growers have moved across the border, and the American Drug Enforcement Agency has estimated that the area may provide enough opium to supply three times the number of heroin addicts in the US.

Three **buses** a day run between Huehuetenango and Cuilco, and if you come out this way you'll probably end up having to stay: the *Hospedaje Osorio* (①) is on the main street. If the roads are in reasonable condition trucks run south from Cuilco to the mountain village of Tacaná, from where there is a regular bus service to San Pedro.

North to Nentón and Jacaltenango

A short distance before the border, from the roadside village of **Camoja Grande**, a dirt road leads off to the north, running parallel to the border. It heads across a dusty white limestone plateau to the village of **Nentón**, and right up into the extreme northwest corner of the country, to **Gracias A Dios** and Yalambojoch. Although there are **buses** (two a day to Jacaltenango, one or two to Gracias a Dios), the only reason to venture out this way would be to walk back into the Cuchumatanes. Halfway between the Pan-American Highway and Nentón, at the junction of Cuatro Caminos, a branch road heads east towards the mountains, through lush foothills, passing the entrance to Santa Ana Huista, continuing through rich coffee country to San Antonio Huista (with the *Pensión Victoria* should you want to stay), and ending up in Jacaltenango, from where you can walk to Todos Santos (see p.178).

fiestas

The **western highlands** are the home of the traditional Guatemalan fiesta. Every village and town, however small, has its own saint's day, and based on this it has a fiesta that can last anything from a single day to two weeks. All of these involve traditional dances that mix pre-Columbian moves with more modern Spanish styles, and each fiesta has its own speciality, whether it's a horse race or a firework spectacular. Travelling in the western highlands at any time of year you'll find that a fiesta or two coincides with your trip, and it's well worth going out of your way to get to one. It's here that you'll get the best idea of the true strength of Indian culture and the vitality that lies at its heart.

JANUARY

January is a particularly active month, kicking off in **Santa María de Jésus**, near Antigua, where they have a fiesta from the 1st to 5th, with the main action on the first two days. The fiesta is as traditional as the village and includes plenty of dancing and a procession in honour of the sweet name of Jesus. In **El Tumbador**, in the department of San Marcos, there's a fiesta from the 3rd to 8th, and in **San Gaspar Ixchil**, a tiny village on the road to Cuilco in the department of Huehuetenango, they have their fiesta from the 3rd to 6th. In **Sibilia**, in the department of Quezaltenango, there's a fiesta from the 9th to 15th, with the main day on the 13th, and **Santa María Chiquimula**, near Totonicapán, has its fiesta from the 10th to 16th, in honour of the Black Christ of Esquipulas. **Nentón**, to the northwest of Huehuetenango, has a fiesta from the

13th to 16th, and **La Libertad**, to the west of Huehuetenango, from the 12th to 16th. In the central highlands **Chinique**, east of Santa Cruz del Quiché, has a very traditional fiesta from the 12th to 15th, with the final day as the main day. **Colomba**, in the department of Quezaltenango, has one from the 12th to 16th. The village of **San Antonio Ilotenango**, west of Santa Cruz del Quiché, has its fiesta from the 15th to 17th (the main day). **San Sebastián Coatan**, in the department of Huehuetenango, has a fiesta from the 18th to 20th. **El Tejar**, on the Pan-American Highway near Chimaltenango, has a fiesta from the 18th to 20th, with the final day the main day, and **Santa Lucía La Reforma**, in the department of Totonicapán, has its fiesta from the 19th to 21st. The village of **Ixtahuacán**, on the road to Cuilco in the department of Huehuetenango, has a traditional fiesta from the 19th to 24th. **San Pablo La Laguna**, on the shores of Lake Atitlán, has a fiesta from the 22nd to 26th, with the main day on the 25th. **San Pablo**, in the department of San Marcos, has its fiesta from the 23rd to 27th. The village of **Chiantla**, just north of Huehuetenango, has its fiesta from January 28 to February 2, with the final day as the main day, and finally **Jacaltenango**, to the west of Huehuetenango, also has a fiesta that starts on the 28th and goes on until February 2.

FEBRUARY

The celebratory season in February starts in **Cunén**, in the department of Quiché, with a fiesta from the 1st to 4th, with the main day on the 2nd. **Ostuncalco**, in the department of Quezaltenango, has a fiesta on the 8th. **Santa Eulalia** in Huehuetenango has its fiesta from the 8th to 13th, with the main day on the 8th, and **Patzité**, in Quiché, has a fiesta from the 6th to 10th, in which the main action is also on the 8th. **Antigua** has a fiesta to celebrate the first Friday in Lent, as does **Palestina de Los Altos**, in the department of San Marcos.

MARCH

In March fiestas are relatively scarce. Things start off in **San Jose El Rodeo**, in the department of San Marcos, where they have a fiesta from the 14th to 20th, with the main day on the 19th. **La Democracía**, between Huehuetenango and the Mexican border, has a moveable fiesta sometime during the month. **San Jose Poaquil**, near Chimaltenango, has a fiesta on the 19th. The second Friday in Lent is marked by fiestas in **Chajul** and **La Democracía**. Holy Week is celebrated throughout the country but with extreme fervour in **Antigua**: here the main processions are marched over carpets of painted sawdust and involve huge numbers of people engulfed in clouds of incense. **Santiago Atitlán** is also worth visiting during Holy Week to see Maximón paraded through the streets, usually on the Wednesday.

APRIL

San Marcos has its fiesta from the 22nd to 28th, with the main day on 25th, **San Jorge La Laguna** on the 24th, and **San Marcos La Laguna** on the 25th. **Barillas**, far to the north of Huehuetenango, has a fiesta from April 29 to May 4, and both **Zacualpa** and **Aguacatán** have moveable fiestas to mark forty days from Holy Week: **Zacualpa** also has a moveable fiesta at some stage during the month. Finally **La Esperanza**, in the department of Quezaltenango, has its fiesta from April 30 to May 4.

MAY

Cajola, a small village in the department of Quezaltenango, has its fiesta from the 1st to 3rd, with the final day as the main day. **Uspantán** has a busy and traditional fiesta from the 6th to 10th, with the main day on the 8th. **Santa Cruz La Laguna**, on the shores of Lake Atitlán, has its fiesta from the 8th to 10th, with the main day on the last day, as does **Santa Cruz Balanya**, in the department of Chimaltenango. **Patzún** has a fiesta on the 20th.

JUNE

Things start to hot up again in June, starting in **San Antonio Palopó**, to the east of Panajachel, which has a fiesta from the 12th to 14th, with the main day on the 13th. The same days are celebrated in **San Antonio Huista**, while **San Juan Ixcoy**, in the department of Huehuetenango, has its fiesta from the 21st to 25th, with the main day on the 24th. **Olintepeque**, a few kilometres from Quezaltenango, has its fiesta from the 21st to 25th. Towards the end of the month there are two very interesting fiestas high up the mountains: the first, at **San Juan Cotzal**, a very traditional village to the north of Nebaj, lasts from the 22nd to 25th, with the main day on the 24th; the second, in **San Juan Atitán** near Huehuetenango, runs from the 22nd to 26th, with the main day on the 24th. **Comalapa**, near Chimaltenango, has a fiesta on the 24th; **San Juan la Laguna**, on the shores of Lake Atitlán, from the 23rd to 26th, with the main day on the 24th; **San Pedro Sacatepéquez** from the 24th to 30th; and the isolated village of **Soloma**, to the north of Huehuetenango, from the 26th to 30th, with the main day on the 29th. At the end of the month three villages share the same dates: **Yepocapa** in the department of Chimaltenango, **San Pedro Jocopilas** to the north of Santa Cruz del Quiché, and **San Pedro La Laguna** on Lake Atitlán all have fiestas from the 27th to 30th, with the main day on the 29th. Finally in **Almolonga**, near Quezaltenango, there's a fiesta from the 28th to 30th, with the main day on the 29th, which is always a good one. Corpus Christi celebrations, held throughout Guatemala at some stage in June, are particularly spectacular in **Patzún**.

JULY

In July things start off in **Santa María Visitación**, near Sololá, where they have a fiesta from the 1st to 4th, with the main day on the 2nd. In **Huehuetenango** there's a fiesta from the 12th to 17th, and in **Momostenango** from July 21 to August 4 – a particularly traditional celebration that is well worth going out of your way for, especially on the 25th. The village of **Tejutla**, high above San Marcos, has a fiesta from the 22nd to 27th, with the main day on the 25th, as does **San Cristóbal Totonicapán**, in the department of Totonicapán. **Chimaltenango** has a fiesta from the 22nd to 27th, with the main day on the 26th; **Malacatancito**, a small *Ladino* town on the border of the department of Huehuetenango, celebrates from the 23rd to 26th, with the last day as the main day; **Santiago Atitlán** has its excellent fiesta from the 23rd to 27th, most enjoyable on the 25th; and **Antigua** has a one-day fiesta on the 25th in honour of Santiago. **Patzicía** has a fiesta from the 22nd to 27th, with the main day on the 27th, and **Santa Ana Huista**, in the department of Huehuetenango, has its fiesta from the 25th to 27th, with the main day on the 26th. Finally **Ixchiguan**, in the department of San Marcos, has a fiesta from the 29th to 31st, with the final day the main day.

AUGUST

August is a particularly good month for fiestas and if you're in the central area you can visit three or four of the very best. The action starts in **Sacapulas**, which has a fiesta from the 1st to 4th, with the last day as the main day. **Santa Clara La Laguna** has its fiesta from the 10th to 13th, with the main day on the 12th. **Joyabaj** has its fiesta from the 9th to 15th, with the last day as the main day. This is the first of August's really special fiestas and sees Joyabaj filled with Indians from throughout the valley: traditional dances here include the *Palo Volador*, in which men swing from a huge pole. The second major fiesta is in **Sololá**, from the 11th to 17th, with the main day on the 15th. This is another massive event well worth visiting for a day or two. The next is in **Nebaj**, a spectacular spot at any time of the year, where the fiesta is from the 12th to 15th, with the main day on the last day. In **Colotenango**, near Huehuetenango, they have a fiesta from the 12th to 15th, with the final day as the main day. **Cantel**, near Quezaltenango, has a fiesta from the 12th to 18th, the main day on the 15th, and **Tacaná** has a fiesta from the 12th to 15th, the main day on the 15th. In **Santa Cruz del Quiché** there's a fiesta from the 14th to 19th, with the main day on the 18th, and in **Jocotenango** the fiesta is for a single day on the 15th. **San Bartolo** has its fiesta from the 18th to 25th, climaxing on the 24th, while **Salcajá** has a fiesta from the 22nd to 28th, with the principal day the 25th. **Sipacapa**, in the department of San Marcos, has its fiesta from the 22nd to 25th, and **Sibinal**, in the same department, has its fiesta from the 27th to 30th, with the main day on the 19th.

SEPTEMBER

The fiesta in **Quezaltenango** lasts from the 12th to 18th, with the main day on the 15th. **San Mateo**, to the west of Quezaltenango, has a fiesta on the 21st, **San Mateo Ixtatán**, to the north of Huehuetenango, from the 17th to 21st, with the last day the main day, and the departmental capital of **Totonicapán** from the 24th to 30th, with the main day on the 29th. **San Miguel Acatán**, in the department of Huehuetenango, has a fiesta from the 25th to 30th, with the main day also on the 29th. Finally **Tecpán** has its fiesta from September 26 to October 5.

OCTOBER

The action in October starts up in **San Francisco el Alto**, which has its fiesta from the 1st to 6th, with its main day on the 4th. **Panajachel** has a fiesta from the 2nd to 6th, which also has its main day on the 4th. **San Lucas Tolimán**, on the shores of Lake Atitlán, has its fiesta from the 15th to 20th, with the main day on the 18th. Finally the fiesta in **Todos Santos**, one of the best in the country, starts on October 21 and continues into the first few days of November. The 29th is the main day and features a wild and alcoholic horse race, while on the 1st the action moves to the village's cemetery.

NOVEMBER

The 1st is the scene of intense action in **Todos Santos** (see above) and in **Santiago Sacatepéquez**, where they fly massive paper kites in the village cemetery. **San Martín Jilotepeque** has its fiesta from the 7th to 12th, with the main day on the 11th. **Malacatancito**, in the department of Huehuetenango, has a fiesta from the 14th to 18th, with the last day as the main day. **Nahualá** has a very good fiesta from the 23rd to 26th, with the main day on the 25th. **Santa Catarina Ixtahuacán**, in the department of Sololá, has its fiesta from the 24th to 26th, with the principal day on the 25th. **Zunil** has a fiesta from the 22nd to 26th, again with the chief action on the 25th, and **Santa Catarina Palopo** has a fiesta on that day. Finally **Cuilco**, **San Andrés Semetabaj**, **San Andrés Itzapa** and **San Andrés Xecul** all have their fiestas from November 27 to December 1. The main day in Cuilco is on the 28th, and in all the San Andréses on the 30th.

DECEMBER

Santa Barbara, in the department of Huehuetenango, has its fiesta from the 1st to 4th. **Huehuetenango** has a fiesta from the 5th to 8th, again with the last day as the main one, as does **Concepción Huista**, in the department of Huehuetenango. **Concepción**, in the department of Sololá, has its fiesta from the 7th to 9th, and **Malacatán**, in the department of San Marcos, has a fiesta from the 9th to 14th. **Santa Lucía Utatlán**, in Sololá, has its fiesta from the 11th to 15th, with the main day on the 13th.

Chichicastenango has its fiesta from the 13th to 21st, with the last day as the main day. This is another very large and impressive fiesta, with an elaborate procession and a mass of fireworks.

Chichicastenango's sister village, **Chiché**, has its fiesta from the 25th to 28th, with the last day as the main day. From the 7th December men dressed as devils chase around highland towns, particularly in those around Quezaltenango, and the night of the 7th is celebrated with bonfires throughout the country – The Burning of the Devil. Travel in the western highlands is fairly

travel details

straightforward. Along the Pan-American Highway there's an almost constant stream of buses heading in both directions: certainly between about 8am and 6pm you should never have to wait more than twenty minutes. The main towns are generally just off the highway, and it's the main connections to these that are covered below: other, more local schedules have been given in the text. The best way to explore the western highlands is to base yourself in one of these main towns and make a series of day trips into the surrounding area.

BUSES

Antigua and Chimaltenango

To Antigua direct buses from Guatemala City (45min) run every 15min from 18C and 4 Av in Zona 1 (Mon–Fri 3am–6pm); the service is less regular at weekends, when the first buses leave at around 7am. Buses **from Chimaltenango** (the junction for the rest of the highlands) leave every 20min (5.30am–7pm). One daily bus also leaves **from Escuintla** terminal (7am).

From Antigua buses **to Guatemala City** run (every 30min; Mon–Fri 3am–6pm, Sat & Sun 7am–6pm). This service is rivalled by a more exclusive and expensive tourist shuttle which connects Antigua with the city and the airport. Buses **to Chimaltenango** (1hr) leave hourly (5.30am–5.30pm). Heading between Antigua and other major places in the western highlands you need to go to Chimaltenango to catch another bus: they run every 10min or so to and from the Zona 4 terminal in Guatemala City, and heading west you can hop onto any passing bus **to Quiché, Panajachel, Quezaltenango or**

Huehuetenango. Buses to **Tecpán**, **Patzicía** and **Patzún** pass through Chimaltenango every hour or so.

Santa Cruz del Quiché and Chichicastenango

To Santa Cruz via Chichicastenango buses leave **from Guatemala City** every hour or so (5am–5pm) from the terminal in Zona 4. Along the way they can be picked up in Chimaltenango or at **Los Encuentros**, the junction for this part of the country.

From Santa Cruz del Quiché buses leave the main bus terminal **to Nebaj** at 9am, 10.30am & 1pm, returning at around midnight. Buses to **Uspantán**, which all pass through **Sacapulas**, leave Santa Cruz at 10am, 11am and 3pm, returning at 7pm, 11.30pm and 3am. **From Uspantán** there are buses for **San Pedro Carchá** at 3am and 3.30am, returning at 10am and noon. **From Sacapulas** to **Huehuetenango** there are buses at 3am, 4.30am and 5.30am. Direct buses from Santa Cruz to **Quezaltenango** leave at 8.30am, 1pm and 2pm, but it's easier to get to Los Encuentros and change there. Buses to **Joyabaj** pass through Santa Cruz (hourly; 9am–5pm). The last bus back from Joyabaj leaves at 4pm.

Lake Atitlán

Buses **to Panajachel** via **Sololá** are run by the *Rebuli* company, whose offices in Guatemala City are at 20 C 3–24, Zona 1. There are direct buses between Guatemala City and Panajachel (hourly; 5am–3pm); at other times you can travel via Los

Encuentros. **From Panajachel** there are departures to **Quezaltenango** at 5.30am, 5.45am, 6.45am, 7.45am, 11.30am and 2.30pm, and four buses a day to **Cocales**, passing **San Lucas Tolimán**, and two direct buses to San Lucas itself at 6.45am and 4.30pm. Direct buses to **Chichicastenango** leave Panajachel at 7am, 7.45am, 8.45am, 10.40am, 1pm, 3pm and 6pm.

There are also direct buses from Guatemala City **to Santiago Atitlán**, along the coastal highway, but this is a very slow route, and from Santiago to Guatemala City (3am, 6am & noon). There are also buses from Santiago Atitlán to **Quezaltenango** at 3.30am and 4.30am, returning at 11am and 12.30pm.

To get to **Nahualá** take any bus heading along the Pan-American Highway to the west of Los Encuentros.

Quezaltenango

Pullman buses between **Guatemala City and Quezaltenango** via Chimaltenango, Los Encuentros and Cuatro Caminos are run by a number of companies. *Rutas Limas*, who have offices in Guatemala City at 8 C 3–63, Zona 1, and in Quezaltenango off 7 Av (Calzada Independencia) have services from Guatemala City (5.15am, 7.15am & 2.15pm), and from Quezaltenango (8am, 2.30pm & 4.30pm). *Lineas Americas* have their offices in Guatemala City at 2 Av 18–74, Zona 1, and in Quezaltenango off 7 Av: their buses leave Guatemala City at 5.15am, 9am, 3.15pm, 4.40pm and 7.30pm, and Quezaltenango at 5.15am, 9.45am, 1.15pm, 3.45pm and 8pm.

From Quezaltenango there are hourly second-class buses from the Minerva terminal in Zona 3, for San Pedro, San Marcos, Retalhuleu, Mazatenango, Huehuetenango and Guatemala City. Details of buses to the smaller towns are given where relevant in the *Guide*. Travelling from Quezaltenango **to the Mexican border** it's quickest to take a bus for Mazatenango or Coatepeque, and then catch another from there.

From Quezaltenango to the border shouldn't take much more than 2hr.

San Marcos

Transportes Marquensita run pullman buses from **Guatemala City to San Marcos** (4.30am, 6.30am, 8.30am, 10am, 11am, noon, 1.30pm, 3.30pm & 5pm) and San Marcos to Guatemala (2am, 2.30am, 3am, 6.30am, 9am, 11am, noon, 1.30pm & 3pm). The Guatemala City office is at 21 C 12–41, Zona 1.

From San Marcos there are hourly buses to **Malacatán** and **Quezaltenango**. To get to the Mexican border you need to travel first to Malacatán, from where there are regular buses to the Talisman bridge.

Huehuetenango

Pullman buses from **Guatemala City to Huehuetenango** are run by three companies. *Los Halcones*, who have offices in Guatemala City at 7 Av 15–27, Zona 1, and in Huehuetenango at 7 Av 3–62, have two departures daily, leaving from both ends at 7am and 2pm. *Rapidos Zaculeu*, whose offices in Guatemala City are at 9 C 11–42, and in Huehuetenango at 3 Av 5–25, also run twice daily (6am & 3pm). *Transportes Velasquez*, 20 C 1–37, Zona 1 in Guatemala City run pullmans to Huehuetenango (8.30am, 9.30am, 10.30am, 11.30am, 12.15pm, 2.30pm, 3.30pm, 4.30pm, 5.30pm & 6.30pm). Second-class buses to Huehuetenango run from the Minerva terminal in **Quezaltenango** and the Zona 4 terminal in Guatemala City every hour or so.

From Huehuetenango there are buses to the border at **La Mesilla** every hour or so, with the last bus from La Mesilla to Huehuetenango at 4pm. Buses run to **Aguacatán** from 1 Av and 1 C, and there are departures to **Sacapulas** at 11.30am and 12.45pm, returning at 3am, 4.30am and 5.30am.

CHAPTER THREE

THE PACIFIC COAST

Beneath the volcanoes that mark the southern side of the highlands is a strip of sweltering, low-lying land some 300km long and on average 50km wide. Known by Guatemalans simply as **La Costa Sur**, this featureless yet supremely fertile coastal plain – once a wilderness of swamp, forest and savannah – separates the highlands from the shoreline, an unrelentingly straight stretch of black volcanic sand pounded by the Pacific surf.

Prior to the arrival of the Spanish, the Pacific coast was similar in many ways to the jungles of Petén, and certainly as rich in wildlife and archeological sites. However, while the jungles of Petén have lain undisturbed, the Pacific coast has been ravaged by development. Today its large-scale commercial agriculture – including sugar cane, palm oil, cotton and rubber plantations – accounts for a significant proportion of the country's exports. Only in some isolated sections, where mangrove swamps have been spared the plough, can you still get a sense of the way it once looked: a maze of tropical vegetation. Little, if any, of the original dry tropical forest remains, although in several areas, including the

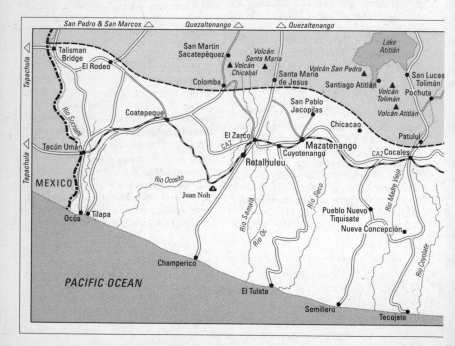

Monterrico Reserve, the unique swampy coastal environment is protected, offering a refuge to sea turtles, iguanas, crocodiles and an abundance of bird life.

As for the **archeological sites**, they too have largely disappeared, though you can glimpse the extraordinary art of the Pipil (see below) around the town of Santa Lucía Cotzumalguapa. Totally unlike the sites in the highlands and Petén – and nowhere near as spectacular – these ceremonial centres, lost beneath fields of sugar cane, reveal a hotchpotch of carvings, some of which are still used for religious rituals. However, the one site in the area that ranks with those elsewhere in the country is **Abaj Takalik**, outside Retalhuleu. For a fascinating insight into the Preclassic era of the Pacific littoral, the ruins are well worth a detour on your way to or from Mexico, or as a day trip from Xela or Retalhuleu. The site is only in the early stages of excavation, but already its significance has been clearly established.

The main attraction for travellers, however, is inevitably the **beach**, although frankly it's generally a disappointment: exposed banks of black volcanic sand, dotted with filthy palm huts and occasionally shaded by palm trees. The hotels are some of the country's worst, so if you're desperate for a dip and a fresh shrimp feast, it's far better to take a day trip from the capital or from Quezaltenango. If you are hoping to spend a few days by the sea then **Monterrico** is the spot to make for, rating as one of the country's finest beaches, with a superb stretch of clear, clean sand.

The main transport link in this region is the **coastal highway** (CA2), which covers the entire length of the coastal strip. It used to be the fastest road in the country, but spectacular corruption and mismanagement has transformed it into

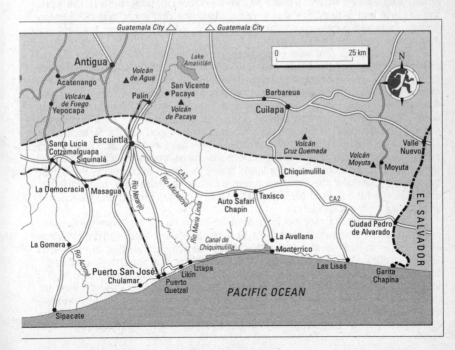

one of the slowest, with only the road into the Petén jungle in a worse state of repair. Nevertheless, it is still the busiest highway, packed with pullmans and lorries travelling to and from Mexico, so connections are easy, if not rapid.

Some history

The earliest history of the Pacific coast remains something of a mystery, with the only hints offered by the remnants of two distinct languages: **Zoquean**, still spoken by a tiny population on the Mexico–Guatemala border, and **Xincan**, which is thought to have been used throughout the eastern area. However, the extent to which these languages can be seen as evidence of independent tribes, and how the tribes might have developed the coast, remains mere speculation. It's generally held that the cultural sophistication of the peoples to the north – in what is now Mexico – spread along the Pacific coast, giving birth to the **Ocós** and **Iztapa** cultures, which thrived here some time around 1500 BC. These were small, village-based societies that had developed considerable skills in the working of stone and pottery. It's also generally believed that great cultural developments, including writing and the basis of the Maya calendar, reached the southern area via the Pacific coast.

What is certain is that some time between 400 and 900 AD the entire coastal plain was overrun by the **Pipil**, who migrated south from the Central Highlands and Veracruz area of Mexico, possibly driven out by the chaos that followed the fall of Teotihuacán. (The Pipil language is actually an antiquated form of Nahuatl, the official language of the Aztec empire.) These migrants brought with them their architectural styles and artistic skills, and the remains of their civilization show that they used a foreign calendar and worshipped the gods familiar in Mexico. The Pipil built half a dozen sites, all compact ceremonial centres with rubble-filled pyramids. Their main produce was cacao, from which they extracted the beans to make a chocolate drink and to use as a form of currency. But by the time of the Conquest the ever-expanding tribes of the highlands had started to encroach upon the coastal plain, with the Mam, Quiché, Tzutujil and Cakchiquel all claiming a slice of the action.

The first Spaniards to set foot in Guatemala did so on the Pacific coast, arriving overland from the north. Alvarado's first confrontation with Quiché warriors came here in the heat of the lowlands, before he headed up towards Quezaltenango. Once they'd established themselves, the Spanish despatched a handful of Franciscans to convert the coastal population, and were faced with a long, hard fight from the Pipil. In **colonial times** the land was mostly used for the production of indigo and cacao, and for cattle ranching, but the inhospitable climate and accompanying disease soon took their toll, and for much of that era the coast remained a miserable backwater. It was only after **independence** that commercial agriculture began to dominate this part of the country. The lower slopes of the mountains, known as the *Boca Costa*, were the first to be covered in huge coffee plantations; later, rubber, banana and sugar-cane plantations spread across the land below. By 1880 the area was important enough to justify the construction of a railway to connect Guatemala City with Puerto San José, which was subsequently extended all the way to the Mexican border.

Today the coastal strip is the country's most intensely farmed region, where entire villages are effectively owned by vast *fincas*. Much of the nation's income is generated here and the main towns are alive with commercial activity, ringed by the ostentatious homes of the wealthy and dominated by the assertive machismo of *Ladino* culture. It's the people of the highlands who are the backbone of agricultural activity, providing essential seasonal labour. In the past they were forcibly recruited, but today the shortage of land in the mountains drives them to migrate "voluntarily" for several months a year in search of work. A labourer's life, whether cutting cane or picking coffee, is harsh, dangerous and poorly paid.

Crossing the border

Approaching the coast from the Mexican border, you face some of the very worst that the region has to offer. Breathless and ugly **Coatepeque** is typical of the towns you'll find; **Retalhuleu** is somewhat more sedate. If you plan to spend any time on the coast, head east to the area around Escuintla; but if you just want to head for the beach then **El Tulate** and **Champerico** are both within easy reach of Quezaltenango and the border.

Tecún Umán and the Talismán Bridge

The coastal border with Mexico is the busiest of Guatemala's frontiers, with two points, Talismán and Tecún Umán, open 24 hours. Tourist cards for either country can be obtained at the immigration posts, but if you require a visa you'll need to get hold of one beforehand – there's a Guatemalan consulate in Tapachula on the Mexican side, and Mexican consulates in Retalhuleu, Quezaltenango, Huehuetenango and Guatemala City.

The northernmost of the two crossings is the **Talismán Bridge**, where the customs and immigration posts face each other from opposite banks of the Río Suchiate. This tends to be the more relaxed of the two as there's nothing here but a few huts and a couple of basic *pensiónes*, and it's also marginally better for first-class buses to Guatemala City. There's little difference on the Mexican side, as both crossings are thirty minutes from Tapachula and well connected by a stream of minibuses. On the Guatemalan side there's a regular flow of trucks, minibuses and buses to **Malacatán**, where there are hotels and buses for San Marcos and the western highlands. If you're heading for Guatemala City there's usually a bus waiting at the border – if not go to Malacatán and catch one from there.

The **Tecún Umán** crossing, on the edge of the dusty and bustling border town of Ciudad Tecún Umán, is favoured by most Guatemalans and all commercial traffic. The town has an authentic frontier flavour with all-night bars, lost souls, contraband and money changers, and its streets are almost permanently choked with a chaos of articulated lorries and buses, cycle rickshaws snaking through the traffic. Everything and everyone is on the move, mostly trying to get out as soon as they've arrived. If you do get stuck, there are plenty of cheap **hotels** and restaurants – the *Hotel Vanessa 2* (② for a room with a fan) is one of the best; the *Vanessa 1* is cheaper but has no fans. Otherwise you might try the *Hospedaje Marcel 2* or the *Hotel Don Jose* (both ②). Once again there's a steady stream of buses connecting the border with Guatemala City, Coatepeque and Retalhuleu.

South to the beach: Ocós and Tilapa

South of Tecún Umán a rough dirt road, running parallel to the border, bounces through clouds of thick white dust and past endless palm-oil plantations to **OCÓS** on the beach. The village is one of the most forlorn and miserable in the country, with sand streets that run past rows of filthy palm huts. Before the Conquest this was the site of a Mam settlement called Ucez, and prior to that it was part of the so-called Ocós culture, a network of small fishing and farming villages, which was one of the earliest civilizations on the Pacific coast, existing here from 1250 to 1150 BC. There is no evidence of this nowadays, however, and if you do end up in Ocós it'll probably be by mistake. The quickest way out is to take the boat across the Río Naranjo to the resort of **TILAPA**, a much better bet for spending an hour or two by the sea. If you decide **to stay** there's a single horrific *pensión* in Ocós, and a better one in Tilapa. The coastline here forms part of the **Reserva El Manchón**, which covers some 30km of prime turtle-nesting beach and extends around 10km inland to embrace a belt of swamp and mangrove, which is home to crocodiles, iguanas, kingfishers, storks, white herons, egrets and an abundance of fish. If you're interested in exploring you shouldn't have any trouble finding a boatman willing to take you on a tour of the canals and lagoons. There is a resident Peace Corps worker here, looking after the reserve, who should be a good source of local information (just ask for the "gringo").

You can also travel to and from Tilapa, without passing through Ocós, on the paved road that connects it with the coastal highway. **Buses** run between here and Coatepeque every hour or so from 5am to 6pm, and several times a day between Coatepeque and Ocós.

The coastal highway: Coatepeque and Retalhuleu

As you head east from the Mexican border, **COATEPEQUE** is the first place of any importance on the main road, a town that's in many ways typical of the coastal strip. A furiously busy, purely commercial centre, this is where most of the coffee produced locally is processed. The action is centred on the **bus terminal**, an intimidating maelstrom of sweat, mud and energetic chaos: buses run every thirty minutes from here to the two border crossings, hourly between 4am and 5pm to Quezaltenango (via Santa María and Zunil), and hourly from 2.30am to 6pm to Guatemala City. Local buses also run regularly to **Colomba**, which is in the coffee-producing foothills of the highlands, and four times a day they go on from there to Quezaltenango (via San Martín Sacatepéquez).

Coatepeque practicalities

The best place to **stay** in Coatepeque is the *Hotel Villa Real*, 6 C 6–57 (☎7751308; fax 7751939; ④), a modern hotel with clean rooms and secure parking. Significantly cheaper is the family-run *Hotel Baechli*, 6 C 5–35 (☎7751483; ④), which has plain rooms with fan and TV plus secure parking. The *Hotel Lee*, on 4 Av (③) just below the plaza is basic, but also offers secure parking. For something a little cheaper try the *Europa* (①), on 4 Av just off the plaza; still cheaper are the *Pensión Sarita* (①), the seedy *Hospedaje El Dorado* (①) and the *Pensión La Batalla* (①), just below the bus terminal on 2 C.

For **changing money** there are branches of the *Banco del Occidente* (Mon–Fri 9am–7pm, Sat 9am–1pm) and *Bamex* (Mon–Fri 8.30am–8pm, Sat 9am–1pm) on the plaza, and several more nearby. The *Guatel* office (daily 7am–10pm) for long distance and local calls, is on 5 Av, at the corner of 7 C. There's a **cinema** a short distance from the plaza, down the hill on 4 Av.

Retalhuleu

Beyond Coatepeque lies the most densely populated section of the Pacific strip, where a branch road leads to **RETALHULEU**, the largest town in this western section. The town is usually referred to as **Reu**, pronounced "Ray-oo", which is what you should look for on the front of buses. Set away from the highway, and surrounded by the walled homes of the wealthy, Retalhuleu has managed to avoid the worst excesses of the coast, protected to some extent by a combination of wealth and tradition. It was founded by the Spanish in the early years of the Conquest, when they merged the villages of Santa Catarina Sacatepéquez and San Antonio. Indian women from these two villages maintained, until recently, the tradition of wearing no blouse – though they were banned from appearing topless in public. This traditionalism marks a real division in the town between a *Ladino* population said to be proud of a lineage untainted by Indian blood, and the Indians who have repeatedly risen up against their control.

Today, however, things seem astonishingly peaceful and Retalhuleu is something of an oasis of civilization in the chaos of life on the coast. Its plaza epitomizes all this, with towering Greek columns on a shiny white *municipalidad*, a covered bandstand and an attractive colonial church. The mood is relaxed and easy-going and in the warmth of the evening young couples nestle in the bushes, birds squawk in the trees and BMWs glide through the streets. If you have time to kill, pop into the local **Museum of Archeology and Ethnology** (Tues–Sun 9am–noon & 2–6pm; small fee) in the *municipalidad*. Rooms are divided into Preclassic, Classic and Postclassic Maya periods, and display an amazing collection of anthropomorphic figurines, mostly heads. Many show a strong Mexican influence in their design, with large ear-plugs a common feature. Upstairs a fascinating collection of ancient photographs, dating back to the 1880s, provides an excellent historic record of the town's changing streetscapes and industries, deomonstrating to what extent its leading citizens tried to create a bourgeois haven among the festering plantations.

Abaj Takalik

The area around Retalhuleu was heavily populated before the arrival of the Spanish and has been the scene of a number of recent archeological digs, casting new light on the development of early Maya civilization and in particular the formative influence of other cultures from the north. Near Asintal, a small village 15km to the east of Retalhuleu, the site of **Abaj Takalik** (daily 9am–4pm; small donation), currently being excavated, has already provided firm evidence of an **Olmec** influence reaching the area in the first century AD. Excavations have unearthed enormous stela, several of them very well preserved, dating the earliest monuments to around 126AD. The only area of the nine-square-kilometre site that has been cleared so far is on the property of the Finca Margarita, and does not reveal the main plazas. But the remains of two large **temple platforms** have been cleared and what makes a visit to this obscure site really worthwhile are the carved sculptures and stela found around their base. In particular, you will find rare and unusual representations of frogs and toads – and even an alligator (monument 66). The finest carving, though, is a giant Olmec head, showing a man of obvious wealth and great hamster cheeks.

To **get to Abaj Takalik** take a local bus from Reu to Asintal, from where its a 4km walk through coffee and cacao plantations. If in your own transport, take the highway towards Mexico and turn right at the sign. Note that after the village of Asintal the unpaved track is very rough and best negotiated by four wheel drive or high clearance vehicles only.

Retalhuleu practicalities

Budget **accommodation** is in short supply in Retalhuleu. The cheapest place in town is the *Hotel Pacifico* (①), close to the market on 7 Av between 9 and 10 calles. It's fairly scruffy but your only other budget choice is the rough *Hotel Hillman* (①) on 7 Av. Otherwise rates go up steeply: *Hotel Astor*, 5 C 4–60 (☎7710475; ⑤) has rooms with fan, TV and bath, set around a pleasant courtyard, and is very good value for money. Across the road the *Hotel Modelo* (☎7710256; ④) makes an old-fashioned but decent alternative, with the same facilities for half the price. If you need a bit of luxury try the modern *Hotel Posada de Don José*, 5 C 3–67 (☎7710180; ⑤), which has good rooms, a not-bad restaurant and a pool.

The **plaza** is the hub of activity: here you'll find three **banks**, including the *Banco del Agro* (Mon–Fri 9am–3pm, Sat 8am–noon), and the **post office** (Mon–Fri 8am–4.30pm), with the *Guatel* office (daily 7am–10pm) just around the corner. The best **restaurants** are also on the plaza, as is the *Cine Moran*.

Buses running along the coastal highway almost always pull in at Retalhuleu, passing through to the bus terminal on the southern side of town. To get to the terminal you can either walk, or catch a ride with any bus going south through town along 7 Av. There's an hourly service to and from Guatemala City and the Mexican border, and there are also hourly buses to Quezaltenango, Champerico and El Tulate – last services leave at around 5pm. Retalhuleu has the only **Mexican consulate** on the Pacific coast, on the eastern edge of town at 5 C and 3 Av (Mon–Fri 4–6pm).

The El Zarco junction

Between Retalhuleu and Cuyotenango is the **El Zarco** junction, from where the main road to Quezaltenango heads up into the highlands. If that is your destination then it's generally quickest to take any bus to El Zarco and change – you shouldn't have to wait more than about twenty minutes. You can also catch a direct bus for Quezaltenango from Mazatenango, Coatepeque or Retalhuleu.

Champerico

South from Retalhuleu a paved road reaches to the beach at **CHAMPERICO**, which, though it certainly doesn't feel like it, is the country's third port. Founded in 1872, it was originally connected to Quezaltenango by rail and enjoyed a brief period of prosperity based on the export of coffee. In 1934 Aldous Huxley passed through, but was distinctly unimpressed: "Then suddenly, vast and blank, under a glaring white sky, the Pacific. One after another, with a succession of dreary bumps, the rollers broke on a flat beach." Huxley was fortunate enough to board a steamer and escape what he called "the unspeakable boredom of life at Champerico". If anything, things have got worse, as barely any trade passes through the port these days, and the rusting pier, the only feature to disturb the coastline, will doubtless soon sink beneath the waves. Champerico still supports a handful of fishermen, but spends most of its time waiting for the weekend, when hordes of weary city dwellers descend on the coast. The **beach** is much the same as anywhere else, although its sheer scale is impressive (watch out for the dangerous undertow). When you tire of testing your strength against the fury of the surf, plenty of places serve delicious **meals** of shrimp or fish, including the *Restaurant Monte Limar*, where the portions are big and the prices small.

The finest **hotel** in Champerico is the *Miramar* (③), a lovely old building with a fantastic dark wood **bar**, dark windowless rooms, hot water, a friendly atmosphere and a Spanish owner; there's no better place to take on your thirst. The *Martita* (②), just over the street, is nothing special, or you can try your luck at the *Hospedaje Buenos Aires* (①), a very seedy little boarding house.

Buses from Champerico run directly to Quezaltenango, passing through Retalhuleu, hourly from 4am to 2.30pm – coming the other way most buses leave Quezaltenango in the mornings, though there's a service from Retalhuleu throughout the day. If you're heading anywhere else, catch a bus from Champerico to Retalhuleu and then another along the coastal highway. The last bus to Retalhuleu leaves Champerico at 6pm.

Cuyotenango, El Tulate, Mazatenango and Cocales

Beyond Retalhuleu the highway runs east to **CUYOTENANGO**, one of the older towns along the way. This started life as the site of a pre-conquest Cakchiquel village and later became an important colonial town. The narrow streets and some of the older buildings bear witness to this distinguished past, but the thunder of the highway, which cuts right through the town, overwhelms all else, and its larger neighbours have long since consumed any importance that Cuyotenango once held.

Another branch road turns off for the beach here, heading 45km south to **EL TULATE**, where the village and the ocean are separated from the mainland by a narrow expanse of mangrove swamp. Though the beach itself, lined with palm trees, is another featureless strip of black sand, and the only places to stay are the shacks adjoining the open-air restaurants, where you are likely to find a sheetless reed mattress, the fried seafood is good, and its isolation is a definite boon. **Buses** to El Tulate run every hour or so from Mazatenango and Retalhuleu, with the last bus back to Mazatenango at 4pm, and the last to Retalhuleu at 5pm: small boats run a shuttle service between the end of the road and the village, meeting buses to ferry their passengers.

Back on the highway, the next stop is **MAZATENANGO**, another seething commercial town. There are two sides to "Mazate", as it's generally known. The main street, which runs down the side of the market, past the filling stations and bus terminal, is characteristic of life along the coastal highway, redolent of diesel fumes and cheap commercialization. The other half of town, centred around the plaza, is quieter, calmer and more sophisticated, with long shaded streets. There's no particular reason to linger in Mazatenango, but if you do find yourself here for the night, budget options include the *Hotel Costa Rica* (②), on the corner opposite the filling stations, and the *Hotel Sarah* (②), beside the train station, which offers good-value simple rooms with private bath. If you want somewhere decent and clean to stay, however, head for the *Hotel Alba* (☎8720264; ④) on the main highway – on the Mexican side. You get secure parking too. There are a couple of cinemas in Mazatenango and plenty of **banks**.

Buses can be caught at the small terminal above the market on the main street, or outside the filling stations – where most of the pullmans stop. They run regularly in both directions along the coastal highway, and to Quezaltenango, El Tulate, Chicacao and Pueblo Nuevo Tiquisate. Buses to most of these places run every hour or so from 8am to 4pm or 5pm.

East to Cocales

Continuing east from Mazatenango the main road passes the junction for Chicacao, a coffee centre with close links to Santiago Atitlán (see p.137), and **PUEBLO NUEVO TIQUISATE**, once the local headquarters of the all-powerful United Fruit Company, whose banana plantations stretched almost as far as its political influence. The company planted huge numbers of bananas in this area after its plantations on the Caribbean coast were hit by disease, although modern techniques have enabled many to be switched back to their original locations – the company is now owned by Del Monte. If you're intending to head south to the coast, you should ideally **stay** at the *Hotel El Viajero* (☎8847189; ③), which has simple but decent rooms with fan and TV, plus secure parking. From here you can either drive, hitch or take a local bus to Semillero or Tecojate. The better beach is at **Semillero**, and the branch road heading this way offers an interesting glimpse of sugar cane plantations and the very different houses of the workers (dormitories) and managers (great wooden houses on stilts, painted a neat New England-style green and white).

About 30km beyond Mazatenango is **COCALES**, a crossroads from where a road runs north to San Lucas Tolimán and Lake Atitlán, and south to the agricultural centre of **NUEVA CONCEPCIÓN**. Concepción is an inconspicuous little town that was recently catapulted into the headlines as the home parish of Guatemala's most radical and controversial priest, **Padre Andrés Girón**. Girón is one of the few remaining priests willing to speak out on the political left, and particularly on the touchy issue of land reform. His future remains uncertain, with the Bishop of Escuintla apparently unhappy about his stance and the death squads dogging his footsteps. Several attempts have been made to kill him, but the Padre remains undaunted and has begun to move into mainstream politics.

From Cocales **buses** run to **Santiago Atitlán**, **Panajachel** and **San Lucas Tolimán**. If you're heading this way you can wait for a connection at the junction, but don't expect to make it all the way to Panajachel unless you get here by midday. The best bet is to go to Santiago, where most of the buses will be heading, stay the night there, and take a boat across the lake in the morning. The last bus to Santiago Atitlán leaves Cocales at around 4pm.

Santa Lucía Cotzumalguapa and around

Another 23km brings you to **SANTA LUCÍA COTZUMALGUAPA**, a typically grimy Pacific town a short distance north of the highway. The main reason to visit is to explore the **archeological sites** that are scattered in the surrounding cane fields, though you should bear in mind that getting to them is never easy.

Santa Lucía Cotzumalguapa

Buses passing along the highway will drop you at the entrance road to town, while direct buses from the capital go straight into the terminal, a few blocks from the plaza. Buses to Guatemala City leave the terminal hourly from 3am to 4pm, or you can pick one up on the highway.

In the streets around the plaza you'll find several cheap and scruffy **hotels**, the best of which is the *Pensión Reforma* (②), 4 Av 4–71, which, true to its name, is owned by some friendly but fearsome Catholics – the light switches are outside the rooms and if there's any suggestion of immoral activities they'll switch your light on. Slightly smarter is the *Hospedaje Familiar* (②), opposite the *Guatel* office a couple of blocks east of the plaza. The nearest upmarket place is the *Caminotel Santiaguito* (☎8825435; ⑤), a slick motel on the main highway, which has a swimming pool and restaurant. Across the road the cheaper *El Camino* (☎8825316; ④) is expensive for what you get. Back in town there's a **bank** in the plaza, and the *Comedor Lau* on 3 Av does reasonable Chinese **meals**: the only other way to spend the evening is watching a film at the *Cine Victoria* on 3 Av.

Sites around Santa Lucía Cotzumalguapa

As for visiting the **sites**, a tour can be an exhausting and frustrating process, taking you through a sweltering maze of cane fields. Doing the whole thing on foot is certainly the cheapest way to see the sites, but also by far the hardest. Note that wandering about the cane fields alone is never a good idea, though if you must do it, do so in the mornings when, as locals would say, "the thieves are still sleeping". It's well worth investing the cash to make a round trip by taxi instead – you'll find plenty in the plaza – and if you bargain well it need not be prohibitively expensive (reckon on around $10 all in). Make sure the trip will include all the sites and fix a firm price beforehand. If you want to see just one of the sites, choose **Bilbao**, just 1km or so from the centre of town, and featuring some of the best carving. The sites are covered below, with directions, in the best order for visiting them on foot, but it's still fairly easy to get lost. If you do, just ask for *las piedras*, as they tend to be known locally.

Bilbao

Bilbao lies just north of Santa Lucía Cotzumalguapa. In 1880, more than thirty Late Classic stone monuments were removed from this site, and nine of them, probably the very finest of the Pacific coast stelae, deemed far too good to waste on Guatemala, were shipped to Germany. One was lost at sea and the others are currently on display in the Dahlem Museum in Berlin. Four sets of stones are still visible in situ, however, and two of them perfectly illustrate the magnificent precision of the carving, beautifully preserved in slabs of black volcanic rock.

To get to the site, walk uphill from the plaza, along 4 Av, and bear right at the end, where a dirt track takes you past a small red-brick house and along the side of a cane field. About 200m further on is a fairly wide path leading left into the cane for about 20m. This brings you to two large stones carved in bird-like patterns, with strange circular glyphs arranged in groups of three: the majority of the glyphs are recognizable as the names for days once used by the people of southern Mexico. Numbers are expressed only by dots and circles, without the bar that was used by the Maya to represent five. This is further evidence that the Pipil, who carved these stones some time between 400 and 900 AD, had more in common with the tribes of the far north than with those of the Guatemalan highlands or Petén.

The same cane field contains two other sets of stones, reached along similar paths further up this side of the field. The first of them is badly eroded, so that it's only possible to make out the raised border and little or nothing of the actual carving. But the second is the best of the lot, a superbly preserved set of figures and interwoven motifs. The Mexican migrants who were responsible for all this shared with the Maya a fascination for the ball game, and on this stone a player is depicted, reaching up to decidedly Mexican divinities – a fairly clear indication that the game was regarded as a form of worship. The player is wearing a heavy protective belt, which would have been made from wood and leather, and you can clearly make out several birds and animals, as well as pods of cacao beans – which were used as currency.

There's one final stone hidden in the cane, which can be reached by heading back down the side of the field and turning right at the bottom, along the other side. Here you will come across yet another entrance, opposite *Casa No. 13*, which brings you to the last carving, another well-defined set of figures. The face of this stone has been cut into, presumably in an attempt to remove it.

Finca El Baul

The second site is also out on the northern side of town, though somewhat further afield, at the **Finca El Baul**. The *finca* is about 5km from Santa Lucía Cotzumalguapa and has its own collection of artefacts, as well as a small but fascinating site out in the cane fields. To get there from the last of the Bilbao stones, walk on beyond *Casa No. 13* and onto the tarmacked road (if you're coming out of town this is a continuation of 4 Av). At the T-junction straight ahead of you turn to the right and follow the road for some 4km until it comes to a bridge. Cross this and take the right-hand fork for another kilometre or so, passing all the houses. Once out here a dirt track crosses the road, and you want to turn right along this to the base of a small hill. The site is on top of this hill, but you need to walk round to the other side to find the path up. Once there you'll see the two stones: one flat and carved in low relief, the other a massive half-buried stone head, with wrinkled brow and patterned headdress. The site has a powerful, mysterious atmosphere and is still used for religious ceremonies. In

Drawing from Stela 10 Xultun 889AD

front of the stones is a set of small altars on which local people make animal sacrifices, burn incense and leave offerings of flowers. The faces of the stone figures are smeared and stained with wax dripped from candles.

The next place of interest is the *finca* itself, a few kilometres away. This can be reached either by making your way back to the fork in the road, just after it crosses the bridge, and taking the left-hand branch, or by following the track back and continuing along it straight across the road – after a while this track emerges on the tarmacked road, and you want to turn right for the *finca*. Once you reach the *finca*, walk beyond the rows of shanty-like huts to the huge furnace, behind which the main administration building is protected by an armed guard or two. Ask in here to see the collection, which is housed in a special compound under lock and key: despite the fierce-looking security measures they're always willing to oblige. The carvings include some superb heads, a stone skull, a massive jaguar and many other interesting pieces jumbled together. Alongside all this antiquity is the *finca*'s old steam engine, a miniature machine that used to haul the cane along a system of private tracks. A visit is also interesting for the rare glimpse it offers of a working *finca*. About nine hundred people are employed on the *finca*, with their own bus service laid on from town. You may be able to get a ride on this – in Santa Lucía Cotzumalguapa buses leave from the *Tienda El Baul*, a few blocks uphill from the plaza, four or five times a day, the first at around 7am and the last either way at about 6pm.

Finca Las Ilusiones

The remaining site is on the other side of town, to the east, so if you're exploring on foot you'll probably want to leave it for another day. Here, at the **Finca Las Ilusiones**, there's another private collection of artefacts and some stone carvings. To get there walk east along the highway for about 1km, out beyond the two Esso stations and past a small football field to the north of the road. After this a track leads off to the left (north) to the *finca* itself. Outside the buildings are some copied carvings and several originals, including some fantastic stelae. The building to the left houses a small museum – ask around to unearth the man who looks after the key. Inside is a tiny room crammed with literally thousands of small stone carvings and pottery fragments. There are more carvings leant against the walls of a private courtyard, reached by crossing the bridge and turning to the left. If you manage to get a peep you'll see many figures with the flattened foreheads that are so common in Maya art, while others that look like nothing you'd expect to find in the Maya heartland.

La Democracía and the coast at Sipacate

Heading east from Santa Lucía Cotzumalguapa the coastal highway arrives next at Siquinalá, a run-down sort of place that straddles the road, from where another branch road heads to the coast. Along the way, 9km to the south, **LA DEMOCRACÍA** is of particular interest as the home of another collection of archeological relics. To the east of town lies the archeological site of **Monte Alto**, and many of the best pieces which have been found there are now spread around the town plaza under a vast ceiba tree. These so-called "fat boys" are massive stone heads with simple, almost childlike faces. Some are attached to smaller rounded bodies and rolled over on their backs clutching their swollen stomachs.

The figures resemble nothing else in the Maya world, but are strikingly similar to the far more ancient Olmec sculptures found near Villahermosa in the Gulf of Mexico. In academic circles debate still continues to rage about the precise origins of these traits, but for the moment even less is known about these relics than about the sites around Santa Lucía Cotzumalguapa. However, it seems likely that they predate almost all other archeological finds in Guatemala. The faces of the "fat boys", with their bizarre, almost Buddha-like appearance of contentment, could well be as much as four thousand years old. Also on the plaza, the town **museum** (Tues–Sun 8am–noon & 2–5pm) houses carvings, ceremonial yokes worn by ball-game players, pottery, grinding stones and a few more carved heads.

The road continues further south to **La Gomera**, a mid-sized agricultural centre where buses usually wait for a while, and beyond there to the coast at **Sipacate**. The beach at Sipacate is separated from the village by the black waters of the Chiquimulilla Canal, across which boats ferry a constant stream of passengers. In recent years the branch road heading this way has fallen into such a state of disrepair that the journey of several hours to reach Sipacate really isn't worth it. The *Hospedaje and Cafeteria Mary* (②), in the village, is the best of a poor bunch of places to **stay**, but certainly nothing special. You could also try the basic *La Costa* (③). On the beach itself, the *Rancho Carillo* is badly maintained and outrageously overpriced.

Buses to Sipacate, passing through La Democracía, leave both Guatemala City and Santa Lucía Cotzumalguapa, so if you want to head down this way the best thing to do is catch a bus to Siquinalá and wait outside the market there for one heading for La Democracia and Sipacate. Note that the trip from the main highway to Sipacate can take as long as three hours, with the last bus back to the highway leaving at 5pm. There are direct buses between Sipacate and Guatemala City, but they are extremely slow.

East from Escuintla to the border with El Salvador

The southern section of the Pacific coast is dominated by **Escuintla** and **Puerto San José**, the largest town and formerly the most important port in the region. If you're heading for the coast from Guatemala City this is probably the route you'll take, and it's a fairly easy day trip. Neither town is particularly attractive, however, and you're unlikely to stay more than a single night, if that. Further to the east is **Monterrico**, an impressive beach where you'll find the coast's most important wildlife reserve: a protected area of mangrove swamps that's home to some superb birdlife. Beyond that the coastal highway runs to the border with El Salvador, with branch roads heading off to a couple of small seashore villages.

Escuintla

At the junction of the two principal coastal roads, **ESCUINTLA** is the largest and most important of the Pacific towns. There's nothing to do here but you do get a good sense of life on the coast; its pace and energy and the frenetic commercial activity that drives it. Escuintla lies at the heart of the country's most productive region, both industrially and agriculturally, and the department's resources include cattle, sugar, cotton, light industry and even a small Texaco oil refinery. The town is also one of the oldest on the Pacific coast, built on the site of a pre-conquest Pipil settlement. Its modern name is a contraction of the Pipil word *Isquitepeque*, meaning "the hill of the dogs", a name given to the village because of the dog-like animals the Pipil kept for meat. These days there's no doubt about the commercial bustle of Escuintla's streets, but they look as though the inhabitants, swept up in all this hubbub, have completely forgotten about the town itself, leaving it to crumble around them. One side of the plaza is taken up by the mossy ruins of an old school, and the entire town is in a state of advanced decay.

Below the plaza a huge, chaotic **market** sprawls across several blocks, spilling out into 4 Av, the main commercial thoroughfare.

Practicalities

There are plenty of cheap **hotels** near 4 Av, most of them sharing in the general air of dilapidation. The *Hospedaje El Centro,* on 3 Av, a block behind the market (①) is one of the better cheap places; *Hospedaje Oriente* (①), 4 Av 11–30, is slightly more upmarket. If you feel the need to escape into a world of overhead fans and private baths try the *Hotel Izcuintla* (③), 4 Av 6–30, or the *Hotel Costa Sur* (③), 4 Av and 4 C. For real peace and quiet head for the *Hotel La Villa* (③), a very dignified hotel a few blocks from the bustle of the town centre at 3 Av 3–21.

There's a *Banco de Guatemala* at 4 Av and 7 C, *Lloyds* at 7 C 3–07, and *Banco de Occidente* and *Banco Immobiliare* on 4 Av. The latter road is lined with places where you can **eat** anything from Guatemalan seafood feasts to the inevitable *chao mein* and burgers. There are also a couple of **cinemas** in town – the *Rialto* at 5 C and 3 Av, and the *Lux* on 7 C opposite the bank.

Buses to Escuintla leave from the Treból junction in Guatemala City every thirty minutes or so from 4am to 7pm. In Escuintla they leave at the same times from 8 C and 2 Av. For other destinations there are two terminals: for places **en route to the Mexican border**, buses run through the north of town and stop by the Esso station opposite the *Banco Uno* (take a local bus up 3 Av); buses for the **coast road and inland route to El Salvador** are best caught at the main terminal on the south side of town, at the bottom of 4 Av (local bus down 4 Av). From the latter buses leave every thirty minutes for Puerto San José and Iztapa, hourly for the eastern border, and daily at 6.30am and noon for Antigua, via El Rodeo.

To the coast: Puerto San José

South from Escuintla the coast road heads through acres of cattle pasture to **PUERTO SAN JOSÉ**, another run-down and redundant port. In its prime San José, which opened as a port in 1853, was Guatemala's main shipping terminal, funnelling goods to and from the capital, but it has now been made virtually redundant by Puerto Quetzal, a container port a few kilometres to the east (and connected to Escuintla by a fast road, which is sure to accelerate the decline of San José). Today both town and port are somewhat sleazy and the main business is local tourism: what used to be rough sailors' bars pander to the needs of the day-trippers from the capital who fill the beaches at weekends.

The shoreline is again separated from the mainland, by the **Canal de Chiquimulilla**, which starts near Sipacate, west of San José, and runs as far as the border with El Salvador, cutting off all the beaches in between. For the most part it is nothing more than a narrow strip of water, but in some places it fans out into a maze of mangrove swamps, providing a home for a wide array of wildlife.

Here in San José the main resort area is on the other side of the canal, directly behind the beach. This is where all the bars, restaurants and hotels are, most of them crowded at weekends with big *Ladino* groups feasting on seafood and playing the jukebox until the small hours. The hotels are not so enjoyable, catering as they do to a largely drunken clientele. Prices are usually high and standards low: you'll be lucky if you get a sheet, and are normally expected to make do with a bare reed mat. Consider sampling the delights of San José as a day trip from the capital and making it back to civilization in time for bed. Or if you really want to spend a day or two on the coast then head along to Iztapa, or to Monterrico.

Buses between San José and Guatemala City run every hour or so all day. From Guatemala City they leave from the terminal in Zona 4, and in San José from the plaza. Most of these buses go on to Iztapa, so there's a bus every hour heading that way.

Chulamar and Likin

Leaving San José and following the coast in either direction you come upon the beach resorts of the rich. Guatemala's wealthy elite abandoned Puerto San José to the day-trippers long ago, establishing instead their own enclaves of holiday homes in pale imitation of California. The first of these is **CHULAMAR**, about 5km west of Puerto San José, reached only by private car or taxi. Here you'll find another strip of sand separated from the land by the muddy waters of the canal. On the beach there's a single upmarket **hotel**, *Hotel Santa Maria del Mar* (☎8811289; ⑤) and a string of small *cabañas*, which sleep up to six (③–④).

East of San José, past the container terminal at **Puerto Quetzal**, is the second of the resorts, **BALNEARIO LIKIN**. Here a complete residential complex has been established, based around a neat grid of canals and streets. The ranks of second homes have speedboats and swimming pools, and the entire compound comes complete with an armed guard. There are no buses to Likin itself but any of those going from San José to Iztapa will drop you at the entrance. Like all these places it's deserted during the week, when there are no boats to shuttle you to the beach, but at weekends you can drop by to watch the rich at play.

Iztapa and along the coast to Monterrico

Further east the road comes to an end at **IZTAPA**, another old port that now serves the domestic tourist industry. Of all the country's redundant ports Iztapa is the oldest, as it was here that the Spanish chose to harbour their fleets. In the early days Alvarado used the port to build the boats that took him first to Peru and then on the trip to the Spice Islands from which he never returned. In 1839 the English explorer and diplomat John Lloyd Stephens passed through on his way to Nicaragua, and found the inhabitants far from happy: "The captain of the port as he brushed them away (the swarming moschetoes), complained of the desolation and dreariness of the place, its isolation and separation from the world, its unhealthiness, and the misery of a man doomed to live there." While for some this might be a fitting description of the entire Pacific coast, there are certainly places that it fits better than Iztapa these days. If not exactly beautiful, the village is at least one of the nicer Pacific beach resorts, smaller and quieter than San José but with none of the elitism of Likin or Chulamar. The beach itself, a bank of black sand, is on the other side of the Chiquimulilla canal, and a handful of boat-men provide a regular shuttle service to and from the village.

There are also several reasonable **hotels**, another rarity in this part of the country. The *Sol y Playa Tropical* (④) is the most luxurious, a family hotel with rooms, each with private bath, set around a small pool. The *Hotel Brasilia* (②) has fewer pretensions to class, its basic second-floor rooms looking down over a huge bar and dance floor. The cheapest deal in town is the smaller, gringo-run *Río Dulce* (③), which has simple rooms with fan. **Buses** run from Guatemala City to Iztapa (every hour or so 5am–5pm) from the Zona 4 bus terminal.

Beyond Iztapa the path of the coast road is blocked by the mouth of the **Río Naranjo**. But it is possible to continue along the coast as far as Monterrico by catching a boat across the river and then a bus on the other side. You have to walk a little way east to the edge of Iztapa, and when you reach the river bank you'll have to look for a boatman to ferry you across – there are usually plenty of canoes and their owners are all too willing to earn a quetzal or two (overcharging gringos is common and often unavoidable, although it's worth attempting to bargain). On the other side is the village of **Pueblo Viejo**; it's important to make sure that this is where you're being taken, or you might end up on the beach. From Pueblo Viejo three or four buses a day go to **Monterrico** – usually at 10am, 1pm and 3pm, although the buses are old and the schedule uncertain at the best of times. Buses leave Monterrico for Pueblo Viejo at 5.30am, 11am and 2pm.

Monterrico: the beach and nature reserve

The setting of **MONTERRICO** is one of the finest on the Pacific coast, with the scenery reduced to its basic elements: a strip of dead straight sand, a line of powerful surf, a huge empty ocean and an enormous curving horizon. The village is friendly and relaxed, separated from the mainland by the waters of the Chiquimulilla canal, which in this case weaves through a fantastic network of mangrove **swamps**. Mosquitoes can be a problem during the wet season.

Beach apart, Monterrico's chief attraction is the **nature reserve**, which embraces the village, the beach – an important turtle nesting ground – and a large slice of the swamps behind, forming a total protected area of some 2800 hectares. Sadly, however, the place has declined in recent years due to lack of funding, since the reserve actually has no official status. Walking the trail you are likely to find your path blocked by heaps of domestic rubbish. The animal enclosures are falling apart and their inhabitants criminally neglected. That said, it's well worth making your way to Monterrico, if only for the fantastically beautiful ocean. This is certainly the best place on the coast to spend time by the sea.

Getting to Monterrico

There are two ways to **get to Monterrico**: either the slower route by ferry and bus from Iztapa (see opposite) or from the coastal highway at **Taxisco**, where trucks and buses run the 17km to **LA AVELLANA**. La Avellana is a couple of kilometres from Monterrico on the opposite side of the mangrove swamp, and there are boats to shuttle passengers and cars back and forth. There's a steady flow of traffic between Taxisco and La Avellana, the last bus leaving Taxisco at 4pm – if you don't want to wait for a bus it's usually easy enough to hitch a ride with a truck. There are also direct buses between La Avellana and the Zona 4 bus terminal in Guatemala City, which take around four hours, leaving La Avellana at 4am, 6am and 7.30am, and Guatemala City at 5.30am, 11am and 2pm – if these buses fail to show up just get on any bus heading for Taxisco and change there.

Accommodation

Monterrico's **accommodation**, as usual on this coast, is no great shakes, though in recent years the village has undergone a minor tourist boom, increasing the choice somewhat. Hotels often fill up at weekends, particularly during the dry season, and as there are **no phones** in Monterrico it isn't easy to book in advance; you'll do best if you try those that have reservations numbers in Guatemala City. The best budget option is the **self-catering** *Johnny's Place* (Guatemala City ☎3326973), where bungalows ($40) comfortably sleep four (though there is no restriction on numbers). It also has a pool for every two bungalows. To get there, walk through the village to the sea and turn left along the beach.

Hotel Baule Beach, a few hundred metres along the shore after turning left from the village (Guatemala City ☎4736196; fax 4713390). The most enduring gringo guest house on the entire Pacific coast, run by American Nancy Garver, a former Peace Corps volunteer, who was so enchanted by Guatemala that she decided to stay. All rooms have their own bathroom and mosquito net, and food is available – though the service is poor – including delicious plates of fresh shrimp, fish and beef. Swimming pool planned. ④.

Kaiman Inn, next door to *Baule Beach*. Italian-run inn that's overpriced considering what others offer, but has a very good Italian restaurant. ⑤.

Paradise Hotel (Guatemala City ☎4784202; fax 4784595), 2km outside the village, on the road heading for Iztapa. Best reached with your own transport. Spacious bungalows with two double beds and private bath, plus a pool and decent restaurant. ⑦.

Pez de Oro, on the beach (Guatemala City ☎3315620; fax 3316854). Another Italian-run, good value hotel with the most beautiful cottages on the beach (turn left from the village). Also an attractive, small swimming pool and very good restaurant. ⑤.

Hotel San Gregorio, on the dirt track leading to *Johnny's Place*, just before you reach the beach (Guatemala City ☎2517326). New hotel whose high walls enclose a private world of modern rooms set around a great pool. Up to four people can share a double room. ⑥.

The Biotopo Monterrico-Hawaii

Monterrico's **mangrove swamp** is a bizarre and rich environment, formed as rivers draining from the highlands find their path blocked by the black sands of the beach and spill out into this enormous watery expanse before finally finding their way to the sea through two estuaries, 30km to the east and west of the village. These dark, nutrient-rich waters are superbly fertile, and four distinct types of mangrove form a dense mat of branches, interspersed with narrow canals, open lagoons, bullrushes and water lilies. The tangle of roots acts as a kind of marine nursery, offering small fish protection from their natural predators, while above the surface the dense vegetation and ready food supply provide an ideal home for hundreds of species of bird and a handful of mammals, including racoons, iguanas, alligators and opossums.

At any time of day a trip into the swamp is an adventure, taking you through a complex network of channels and beneath a dense canopy of vegetation. The best way to go is in a small *cayuco*, and there are always plenty of children hanging around the dock in Monterrico who'll be willing to take you on a trip into the wilds, or you can rent a larger boat with an engine – but you won't see as much.

You shouldn't expect to encounter the anteaters and racoons, whichever way you travel, but you probably will see a good range of bird life, including kingfishers, white herons and several species of duck. Failing all else the trip is well worth it just to watch the local fishermen casting their nets.

The reserve is also designed to protect the beach, and in fact it was originally established for the benefit of the **sea turtles** that nest here. These are also rarely spotted, as they usually emerge from the ocean at night and lay their eggs as fast as they can before dashing back to the water. Three types of turtle nest on the beach: the Olive Ridley, the East Pacific and the monstrous Leatherback – or *baule* in Spanish, which gives the beach its name. The two smaller species nest between July and December and the Leatherbacks between mid-October and February. All use similar techniques, hauling themselves up the beach, digging a hole about 50cm deep and depositing a clutch of a hundred or so, ping-pong-ball-sized eggs. They then bury the clutch and hurry back into the ocean. The eggs of the smaller turtles take 50 days to hatch, those of the Leatherback a full 72. When their time comes, the tiny turtles, no larger than the palm of your hand, use their flippers to dig their way out and make a mad dash for the water, desperately trying to avoid the waiting seabirds. Sadly, in the wave of neglect that is hitting the reserve, more and more eggs, an important source of income for locals, are being collected from the beach and sold or eaten.

A sorry collection of iguanas, baby turtles and alligators is housed at the **headquarters** of the Monterrico reserve (daily 8am–noon & 2–5pm), beside the *Hotel Baule Beach*. A short **trail** runs along the edge of the reserve from here, taking you on a 1320-metre circuit and offering excellent birdwatching, particularly in the early morning and evening.

East to Hawaii
Further along the beach, about 5km to the east of Monterrico, is isolated **HAWAII**, accessible only by boat. This is another relaxed fishing village where the ocean life has attracted a handful of regular tourists, notably wealthy Argentinians from Guatemala City who build second homes on the beach. Locals people live by fishing and farming and there is a large turtle project, where up to eight thousand turtles are released a year. There are no hotels in Hawaii but you can visit on a day trip from Monterrico, by renting a boat from the dock.

Eating and drinking
When it comes to **eating** in Monterrico you can either dine at the the several hotels on the beach, or at one of the *comedores* in the village, the best of which is the *Divino Maestro*, where they do excellent shrimp, fish, beef, chicken and a superb shark steak with rosemary. For a **drink** and relaxed socializing with great music, head for the *Pig Pen* bar, just to your right as you reach the beach through the village. Run by friendly Canadian, Michael, this is undoubtedly the place to be of an evening. He can also point you in the right direction if you wish to rent surfboards and boats or find a guide.

From Escuintla to El Salvador

Heading east from Escuintla the coastal highway brings you to **TAXISCO**, a quiet farming centre set to the north of the main road. From here a branch road runs to **La Avellana**, from where you can catch a boat to Monterrico. If you're heading for

Monterrico then take a bus as far as Taxisco and hitch from there or ask around in the plaza. **Buses** to Taxisco leave from the Zona 4 terminal in Guatemala City, calling at Escuintla and usually going on to the El Salvador border. If you get stuck in Taxisco, make for the *Hotel Jereson* (③), on the main street.

Shortly before it reaches Taxisco the highway passes one of Guatemala's most unusual and neglected tourist sights, the **Club Auto Safari Chapin** (Tues–Sun 9.30am–5pm), Central America's one and only safari park, which is about 1km south of the highway (at Km 87.5). The land is owned by one of the great *fincero* families, whose older generation were enthusiastic big-game hunters, covering the walls of the main hacienda with the heads and skins of animals from every corner of the globe. Their children, however, developed a strong resistance to these exploits and insisted on bringing their animals home alive. The end result is a safari park that includes lions, giraffes, hippos, a pair of black rhinos, pumas, deer, antelope, coyotes and a superbly comprehensive collection of Central American animals, snakes and birds. Sadly, their elephant died after he was fed a piece of plastic and the tapir died of old age, but aside from these mishaps the animals are active and well cared for and every species, except for the black rhino, has been successfully bred here in captivity.

The park is set up and managed in a very Guatemalan style, catering almost exclusively to domestic tourists, who like to make a day of it, picnicking, feasting in the restaurant and swimming in the pools. A day ticket, which costs just under $2, entitles you to a swim and a trip through the park in a minibus, although you can drive yourself if you have a car. There is also a small walk-through zoo, laid out around a lake, which is largely devoted to Central American wildlife.

Beyond Taxisco is **CHIQUIMULILLA**, from where another branch road heads up into the eastern highlands, through acres of lush coffee plantations, to the town of Cuilapa. Chiquimulilla is another fairly nondescript town that serves as a market centre for the surrounding area, but you might easily end up here in order to change buses – if you get stuck, there are a couple of decent hotels. The town is in the heart of *Ladino* cowboy country and superb **leather goods**, including machete cases and saddles, are handcrafted in the market, so you may want to do a little shopping. From the small bus terminal, a block or so from the plaza, there's a steady flow of traffic to both the border and Guatemala City, with departures every hour or so. There are also hourly buses to Cuilapa, departing from the other side of the market.

Heading on towards the border, the highway is raised slightly above the rest of the coastal plain, giving great views towards the sea. A short distance before the border the road divides, one branch running to the seashore village of **LAS LISAS**, which is another good spot for spending time by the sea. Like all of these villages Las Lisas is separated from the mainland by the murky waters of the Chiquimulilla canal, again bridged by a shuttle of small boats. On the sandbank itself the village follows a standard pattern, with a collection of scruffy huts and palm trees behind a beautiful black sand beach. It's a great place to relax for an afternoon but accommodation is high in price and very low in quality. **Buses** run between Las Lisas and Chiquimulilla hourly from 9am to 4pm (1hr 30min).

The border with El Salvador

The coastal highway finally reaches the border with El Salvador at **CIUDAD PEDRO DE ALVARADO**, a quiet and easy-going crossing point. Most of the commercial traffic and all the pullman buses use the highland route to El

Salvador, and consequently things are fairly relaxed here. Should you get stuck for the night, *Hospedaje Yesina* (②) is right opposite the immigration post. There are second-class buses to and from the Zona 4 terminal in Guatemala City every hour or so from 1am to 4pm, all of them going via Escuintla. There's also another branch road from here to the coast, ending up at a couple of small seaside villages, Garita Chapina and Barra de La Gabina.

fiestas

Ladino culture dominates on the Pacific coast – despite the presence of a massive migrant labour force – so fiestas here tend to be more along the lines of fairs, with parades, fireworks, sporting events and heavy drinking. You'll see very little in the way of traditional costume or pre-Columbian dances, although marimba bands are popular even here and many of the fiestas are still based on local saints' days. Nevertheless, here's no doubt that the people of the coast like to have a good time and know how to enjoy themselves. Allegiances tend to be less local than those of the Indian population and national holidays are celebrated as much as local ones.

JANUARY
The year starts off in **Taxisco** from the 12th to 15th, with a fiesta in honour of the Black Christ of Esquipulas: events include bullfighting and plenty of macho bravado. In **Colomba** (a few kilometres from Coatepeque) they have a fiesta from the 12th to 16th that honours the same Black Christ and also involves bullfighting. In **Cuyotenango** there's a fiesta from the 11th to 18th, with the main day on the 15th – unlike most coastal fiestas this one includes some traditional dancing.

FEBRUARY
A moveable fiesta takes place in **Tecún Umán** some time during the month.

MARCH
Holy Week is celebrated everywhere in a combination of religious ritual and secular partying, while in **Coatepeque** they have a local fiesta from the 11th to 19th, with the main day on the 15th. In **Puerto San José** the fiesta is from the 16th to 22nd, with the principal day on the 19th, and **Ocós** has a moveable fiesta some time during the month.

APRIL
Chiquimulilla has a fiesta from April 30 to May 4.

JULY
Coatepeque has a single day of fiesta on the 25th, in honour of Santiago Apostol.

AUGUST
The port of **Champerico** has its fiesta from the 4th to 8th, with the main day on the 6th, in honour of El Salvador del Mundo.

OCTOBER
Iztapa has its fiesta from the 20th to 26th. The 24th is the main day.

NOVEMBER
1 November, All Saints' Day, is celebrated throughout the country, and people gather in cemeteries to eat and drink and to honour the dead. In **Siquinalá** they have a local fiesta from the 23rd to 26th.

DECEMBER
Retalhuleu has a fiesta from the 6th to 12th; the main day is the 8th. **Chicacao**'s fiesta, from the 18th to 21st, includes traditional dancing as the town has close links with Santiago Atitlán. **Escuintla** has a fiesta from the 6th to 15th, with the main day on the 8th, and in **Santa Lucía Cotzumalguapa** the main fiesta is held on the 25th. Finally it's the turn of **La Democracía** on the 31st.

Buses are certainly the best way to get around on the Pacific coast, and the main highway, from Guatemala City to the Mexican border, is served by a constant flow of pullmans. Heading in the other direction, to the border with El Salvador, there are no pullmans but there is a regular stream of second-class buses. On either of these main routes you can hop between buses and expect one to come along every half-hour or so, but if you plan to leave the highways then it's best to travel to the nearest large town and find a local bus from there. If you're heading up into the highlands take any bus to the relevant junction and wait for a connection there – **El Zarco** for buses to Quezaltenango and **Cocales** for Lake Atitlán – but set out early.

travel details

BUSES

The coastal highway

From Guatemala City to the Mexican border there are buses every hour or so (5hr), calling in at all the main towns along the coastal highway – including **Escuintla**, **Santa Lucía Cotzumalguapa**, **Cocales**, **Mazatenango**, **Retalhuleu** and **Coatepeque**. The bulk of these leave from the terminal at 19 C and 9 Av, in Zona 1. Two of the main companies are *Fortaleza del Sur*, who run buses to the Mexican border at **Talismán** (hourly 4.30am–7pm; 5hr), and *Rapidos del Sur*, who have buses to **Tecún Umán** (hourly 3am–4pm; 5hr). Both companies have offices on 19 C between 8 and 9 avenidas, Zona 1, Guatemala City.

From the Mexican border to Guatemala City service is also good (hourly 4am–5pm). Note, however, that the road has disintegrated between Mazatenango and Cocales, causing huge delays, and that the rest of the highway also has its fair share of massive potholes. The journey times listed below are therefore approximate.

Coatepeque to: Retalhuleu (50min); Tecún Umán (40min).

Cocales to: Escuintla (30min).

Escuintla to: Guatemala City (1hr).

Retalhuleu to: Cocales (50min); Mazatenango (30min).

From the Mexican border to Quezaltenango you have to branch off the coastal highway at one of two junctions: either travel to **Malacatán** and then up through **San Marcos**, or come along the coast road and catch a direct bus to Quezaltenango from Retalhuleu, Coatepeque or Mazatenango. If you're coming from the Talismán border it's easy enough to find a truck or bus to Malacatán, and from there there are hourly buses to San Marcos, but if you're coming from Tecún Umán it's more straightforward to travel via Retalhuleu, from where there are buses every hour to Quezaltenango.

Branching off the coastal highway

To Ocós and Tilapa buses from Coatepeque to Tilapa (hourly; 2hr), and to Ocós (3 or 4 daily; 2hr): boats connect the two.

To Champerico buses from Retalhuleu (hourly; 1hr 20min), and throughout the morning from Quezaltenango. Buses **leave Champerico** for Quezaltenango (hourly 4am–2.30pm); from Champerico to Retalhuleu buses run until 6pm.

To Escuintla from Guatemala City buses leave from El Trebol or the Zona 4 terminal in Guatemala City (hourly; 1hr). They return from 8 C and 2 Av in Escuintla and run until around 7pm. **From Escuintla** there's also a direct bus to **Antigua**, leaving the bus terminal at 7am and returning from Antigua at around 1pm. All buses to Puerto San José pass through Escuintla.

To Puerto San José there are buses from the Zona 4 terminal in Guatemala City (hourly; 2hr), and most of these go on to **Iztapa** (30min from San José), and return from there – the last bus from Iztapa to Guatemala City leaves at 5pm.

To Monterrico (2hr from Iztapa) there are buses from **Pueblo Viejo** (3 daily), across the Río Naranjo from Iztapa. They leave from Pueblo Viejo at 10am, 1pm and 3pm and from Monterrico at 5.30am, 11am and 2pm. Monterrico can also be reached from Taxisco, by taking a bus or truck to **La Avellana** and a boat from there. Buses from Taxisco run hourly 6am–4pm.

To Taxisco and Chiquimulilla there are buses every hour or so from the Zona 4 terminal in Guatemala City, many of which go on to the **border with El Salvador** at Cuidad Pedro de Alvarado.

To Las Lisas there are buses from Chiquimulilla (hourly 9am–4pm; 1hr). Most of them start out from the Zona 4 terminal in Guatemala City.

To Ciudad Pedro de Alvarado (1hr from Chiquimulilla) there are buses every hour or so from the Zona 4 terminal in Guatemala City, which come via **Escuintla** and **Taxisco**. Buses from the border to Guatemala City leave hourly from 6am to 4pm.

CHAPTER FOUR

EAST TO THE CARIBBEAN

Connecting Guatemala City with the Caribbean is the **Motagua valley**, a broad corridor of low-lying land that separates the Sierra del Espíritu Santo, marking the border with Honduras, from the Sierra de Las Minas. In fact the valley starts in the central highlands, around Santa Cruz del Quiché, cutting east through a particularly arid section of the mountains and meeting the Caribbean Highway at the El Rancho junction, where the river is surrounded by desert. From here on, the valley starts to take its true form, opening out into a massive flood plain with the parallel ridges rising on either side. The land is fantastically fertile and lush with vegetation at all times of the year, and the air is thick with humidity.

This final section, dampened by tropical heat and repeated cloudbursts, was densely populated in Maya times, when it formed the southern limit of their civilization. The valley served as an important trade route, connecting the highlands with the Caribbean coast just as it does today, and it was also one of the main sources of jade. Following the decline of Maya civilization the area lay disease-infested and virtually abandoned until the end of the nineteenth century. Its revival was part of the masterplan of the United Fruit Company, who cleared and colonized the land, planting thousands of acres with bananas and reaping massive profits. At the height of its fortune the company was powerful enough to bring down the government and effectively monopolized the country's trade and transport. Today bananas are still the main crop, though cattle are becoming increasingly important, and the Caribbean Highway, thundering through the valley, is also a vital resource, carrying the bulk of foreign trade from both Guatemala and El Salvador.

For the traveller the Motagua valley is the main route to and from Petén, and most people get no more than a fleeting glimpse of it through a bus window. But two of the greatest Maya sites are in this area: **Quiriguá**, just 5km from the main road, and **Copán**, across the border in Honduras (a side trip of a day or two). Also out towards the frontier is the holy city of **Esquipulas**, home of the famous Black Christ and the scene of Central America's largest annual pilgrimage.

Beyond the Motagua valley is Guatemala's slice of **Caribbean coastline**, where the old banana port of **Puerto Barrios** is now outdated by its squeaky-clean replacement at **Santo Tomás del Castillo**. The main point of interest in Puerto Barrios is the ferry to **Lívingston**, the country's only enclave of Caribbean culture, a laid-back seaside town set beneath beautiful lush green hills and accessible only by boat. For the best of Caribbean beach culture, however, more and more visitors hop across to the **Honduras Bay Islands**, a string of cayes with fantastic diving opportunities.

Also covered in this chapter is the **eastern highlands**, a seldom visited part of the country that shares little with the highlands of the west. Here the bulk of the population are *Ladino*, living in small towns and surviving through small-scale commercial farming. There are few sights as such, but the scenery, dominated by eroded volcanic cones, is superb. If you do see it, however, it'll probably be only in passing, as you head south towards El Salvador.

THE MOTAGUA VALLEY

The main road to the Caribbean leaves the capital in conjunction with the road for Cobán, splitting at the **El Rancho junction** beneath the parched hills of the upper Motagua, where a branch road climbs into the rain-soaked highlands of the Verapaces, and the main highway continues to the Caribbean coast. Heading on down the Motagua valley for another 20km or so the land is bleak, dry and distinctly inhospitable, with the road keeping well to the left of the river and bypassing the villages that line the railway. The first place of any note is the **Río Hondo junction**, a smaller version of El Rancho, where a waiting army of food sellers swarms around every bus that stops. Here again the road divides, with one arm heading south to Esquipulas and the three-way border with Honduras and El Salvador.

On down the valley the landscape starts to undergo a radical transformation; the flood plain opens out and the occasional cacti are gradually overwhelmed by a profusion of tropical growth. It is this supremely rich flood plain that was chosen by both the Maya and the United Fruit Company, to the great benefit of both. Here the broad expanse of the valley is overshadowed by two parallel mountain ranges; to the northwest the **Sierra de las Minas**, and over on the other side, marking out the Honduran border, the **Sierra del Espíritu Santo**.

The ruins of Quiriguá

Of one thing there is no doubt; a large city once stood there; its name is lost, its history unknown; and no account of its existence has ever before been published. For centuries it has lain as completely buried as if covered with the lava of Vesuvius. Every traveller from Yzabal to Guatimala has passed within three hours of it; we ourselves had done the same; and yet there it lay, like the rock-built city of Edom, unvisited, unsought, and utterly unknown.

John Lloyd Stephens (1841).

In 1841 John Stephens was so impressed with the ruins at **Quiriguá** that he planned to take them home, using the Río Motagua to float the stones to the Caribbean so that "the city might be transported bodily and set up in New York". Fortunately, the asking price was beyond his means and the ruins remained buried in the rainforest until 1909, when the land was bought by the United Fruit Company.

Today things are somewhat different: the ruins themselves are partially restored and reconstructed, and banana plantations stretch to the horizon in all directions. But as far as most travellers are concerned the site is still "unvisited" and "unsought". While Quiriguá certainly can't compete with the enormity of Tikal, it does have some of the finest of all Maya carving – matched only by Copán – with stelae, altars and so-called zoomorphs that are covered in well-preserved and superbly intricate glyphs and portraits.

Quiriguá name glyph

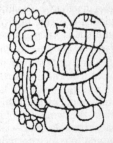

The site is surrounded by a dense stand of rainforest and the weather conditions are decidedly **tropical**; cloudbursts are the rule and the buzz of mosquitoes is almost uninterrupted – take repellent.

A brief history of Quiriguá

Quiriguá's history starts a short distance from the existing site, near the hospital, where two stelae and a temple have been unearthed, marking the site of an earlier ceremonial centre. From there it moved to a second location nearby, where another stela has been found, before finally settling at the main site you see today.

The **early history** of Quiriguá is still fairly vague, and all that is certain is that at some time during the Late Preclassic period (250 BC–300 AD) migrants from the north, possibly Putun Maya from the Yucatán peninsula, established themselves as the rulers here. Thereafter, in the Early Classic period (250–600 AD), the centre was dominated by Copán and doubtless valued for its position on the banks of the Río Motagua, an important trade route, and as a source of jade, which is found throughout the valley. At this stage the rulers themselves may well have come from Copán, just 50km away, and there certainly seem to have been close ties between the two sites: the architecture, and in particular the carving that adorns it, makes this very clear.

In the Late Classic period (600–900 AD) Quiriguá really started to come into its own. The site's own name glyph is first used in 731, just six years after its greatest leader, **Cauac Sky**, ascended to the throne. As a member of the longstanding Sky dynasty, Cauac Sky took control of a city that was already embarked upon a campaign of aggressive expansion, and in the process of asserting its independence from Copán. In 737 matters came to a head when he captured 18 Rabbit, Copán's ruler, thus making the final break. For the rest of his sixty-year reign the city experienced an unprecedented building boom: the bulk of the great stelae date from this period and are decorated with Cauac Sky's portrait. For a century Quiriguá dominated the lower Motagua valley and its highly prized resources. Cauac Sky died in 771 and was succeeded 78 days later by his son, Sky Xul, who ruled for nineteen years until being usurped by Jade Sky, who took the throne in 790. Under Jade Sky Quiriguá reached its peak, with fifty years of extensive building work, including a radical reconstruction of the acropolis. But from the end of Jade Sky's rule, in the middle of the ninth century, the historical record fades out, as does the period of prosperity and power.

The ruins

Entering the site beneath the ever-dripping trees you emerge at the northern end of the **Great Plaza**. To the left-hand side of the path is a badly ruined pyramid and directly in front of this are the **stelae** for which Quiriguá is justly famous. The nine stelae in the plaza are the tallest in the Maya world and their carving is arguably the best. The style, similar in many ways to that of Copán, always follows a basic pattern, with portraits on the main faces and glyphs covering the sides. As for the figures, they represent the city's rulers, with Cauac Sky depicted on no fewer than seven (A, C, D, E, F, H and J). Two unusual features are particularly clear: the vast headdresses, which dwarf the faces, and the beards, a fashion that caught on in Quiriguá thirty years after it became popular in Copán. Many of the figures are shown clutching a ceremonial bar, the symbol of office, which has at one end a long-nosed god – possibly Chaac, the rain god – and at the other the head of a snake. The glyphs, crammed into the remaining space, record dates and events during the reign of the relevant ruler.

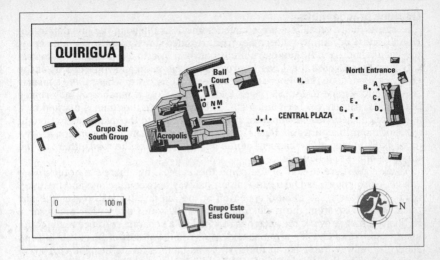

Largest of the stelae is E, which rises to a height of 8m and weighs 65 tons – it was originally sunk about 3m into the ground and set in a foundation of rough stones and red clay, but was reset in 1934 using concrete. The stelae are carved out of an ideal fine-grained sandstone, from a quarry about 5km from the site. The stones were probably rolled to the site on skids, set up, and then worked by sculptors standing on scaffolding. Fortunately for them the stone was soft once it had been cut, and fortunately for us it hardened with age.

Another feature that has earned Quiriguá its fame are the bizarre **zoomorphs**, six blocks of stone carved with interlacing animal and human figures. Some, like the turtle, frog and jaguar, can be recognized with relative ease, while others are either too faded or too elaborate to be accurately made out. The best of the lot is P, which shows a figure seated in Buddha-like pose, interwoven with a maze of others. The zoomorphs are sometimes referred to as altars and thought to be connected with the stela altar complexes at Tikal, but their size and shape make this seem unlikely.

Around the plaza are several other interesting features. Along the eastern side are some unrestored structures that may have been something to do with Quiriguá's role as a river **port** – since the city's heyday the river has moved at least 1km from its original course. At the southern end of the plaza, near the main zoomorphs, you can just make out the shape of a **ball court** hemmed in on three sides by viewing stands, although the actual playing area is still buried beneath tons of accumulated soil. The **Acropolis** itself, the only structure of any real size that still stands, is bare of decoration. Trenches dug beneath it have shown that it was built on top of several previous versions, the earliest ones constructed out of rough river stones. Apart from these central structures there are a few smaller unrestored complexes scattered in the surrounding forest, but nothing of particular interest.

Glyph from Quiriguá

Quiriguá practicalities

The **ruins** (daily; small fee) are situated some 70km beyond the junction at Río Hondo, and 4 or 5km from the main road, reached down a dirt track that serves the banana industry. All **buses** running between Puerto Barrios and Guatemala City pass by – just ask the driver to drop you at the ruins and you'll end up at the entrance road, about four hours from Guatemala City, from where there's a fairly regular bus service to the site itself (5km), as well as a number of motorbikes that shuttle passengers back and forth. The entrance to the ruins is marked by a couple of cheap *comedores* and a car park. To get back to the main road, wait until a bus or motorbike turns up. Buses, often packed with plantation workers, are the most likely to stop at the barrier – some go only as far as the road, others all the way to Morales and Bananera.

There's nowhere to stay at the ruins themselves, but there's a **hotel** in the village – also known as **Quiriguá** – about halfway between the site and the main road. To get there ask to be dropped off at the rail line (which crosses the dirt track about 1km from the main road) and walk south along the tracks for a further kilometre; by car the village is reached by a separate entrance road off the main road. Nowadays it's a ramshackle and run-down sort of place, strung out along the railway track, but in the past it was famous for its hospital of tropical diseases, run by the United Fruit Company. This imposing building still stands on the hill above the track, now a state-run workers' hospital. Up beside the hospital is the plaza, where you'll find the surprisingly good *Hotel Royal* (②). Another possible base is the friendly *La Ceiba* (③), near the village of **El Lobo** at Km 175 on the road from the capital to Flores (see p.278).

On to the coast: Puerto Barrios

Heading on towards the Caribbean, another 15km brings you to **La Trinchera**, junction for the branch road to **MARISCOS** on the shores of **Lake Izabal**. The main reason that people head this way is to catch the ferry across the lake to **El Estor**, from where early morning buses run to Cobán in Alta Verapaz. In its day Mariscos was an important stopping-off point, where travellers heading for the capital would disembark and continue overland, but nowadays it's bypassed by modern transport routes. There are a couple of cheap, scruffy **hotels** in the village, and the passenger ferry leaves at 1pm – returning at 6am. One direct bus a day runs from Guatemala City to Mariscos, departing at 6am from outside the train station at 18 C and 9 Av; and one runs from Puerto Barrios at 3pm. Both return after the arrival of the boat from El Estor at 7am. At other times take any bus along the Caribbean Highway, ask to be dropped at La Trinchera, and hitch from there to Mariscos.

Another reason to head this way is to reach *Denny's Beach* (Guatemala City ☎ & fax 3692681; VHF 09; ④), an ideal place to get away from it all. At present there is only one self-catering *cabaña* above the sandy beach or you can camp. The open-air bar and restaurant are expensive, so bring as many provisions as you can from the well-stocked supermarket at Mariscos pier. Hiring a *lancha* will set you back around $25, but if you have a reservation someone ought to come and get you if you can make radio contact.

Further down the Motagua valley the road pushes on through a blooming land-scape of cattle ranches and fruit trees, splitting again at the junction for the twin

BANANERA AND BANANAS

The unprepossessing town of Bananera has a special place in the history of Guatemala. It was here that the **United Fruit Company** made its headquarters and masterminded the growth of their massive empire. The company's land is now owned by Del Monte, who maintain a local headquarters in a neatly landscaped and well-sealed compound and continue to dominate the area. The town is still surrounded by a sea of banana plantations, with crop-dusting planes wafting overhead, a company store that supplies the faithful and a one-hole golf course (at the bottom of the airfield), testifying to the presence of foreign executives.

The United Fruit Company muscled in on the Motagua valley in the early part of this century, developing huge tracts of unused land, waging war on endemic diseases and making millions of dollars in the process. The company's fingers were in so many pies that it became known as "el pulpo", the octopus, and its political lobby was so powerful that it secured exemption from almost all taxes, controlling not only the banana industry but also the country's railways and the crucial port at Puerto Barrios. So profitable was the company that its assets multiplied fourteen times between 1900 and 1930. Its tentacles held Central America so firmly that when the socialist government of Arbenz proposed confiscating the company's unused lands in 1954, it engineered a coup and replaced the government. Del Monte, as inheritors of the empire, have kept their hands relatively clean, limiting themselves to exporting around two billion bananas a year.

towns of **MORALES** and **BANANERA**, a ramshackle collection of wooden huts and railway tracks. These squalid towns are of no interest except as the transport hub of the lower Motagua, served by all the second-class buses for Petén and a regular shuttle of minibuses to and from Río Dulce. There's also, of course, a steady flow of buses for Puerto Barrios and Guatemala City. Note that the fast *Litegua* buses (see "Puerto Barrios Travel Connections"; p.219) don't pass through Morales or Bananera. If, for whatever reason, you need to stay in Bananera, you have a choice of a couple of basic **hotels**; the *Pensión San José* (①), in the market, is probably your best bet. If it's full try the *Pensión Montavlo* (①), opposite.

A short distance beyond the turning for Morales/Bananera you pass the **Ruidosa junction**, from where the highway to Petén heads northwest, running out over the Río Dulce before being engulfed by the jungles. Another 51km brings you to the Caribbean, with the road dividing for the last time, right to the old port of Puerto Barrios and left to Puerto Santo Tomás del Castillo, the modern town and dock.

Puerto Barrios

At this last junction, unless you happen to be driving a truck, the turning for **PUERTO BARRIOS** is the one to take. Founded in the 1880s by President Rufino Barrios, the port soon fell into the hands of the United Fruit Company, who used their control of the railways to ensure that the bulk of trade passed this way. Puerto Barrios was Guatemala's main port for most of this century, and while the Fruit Company was exempt from almost all tax the users of its port were obliged to pay heavy duties. In the 1930s it cost as much to ship coffee to New Orleans from Guatemala as it did from Brazil. These days the boom is over and the town distinctly forlorn, although you'll still find all the services associated with ports, including an array of strip clubs, all-night bars and brothels. The streets are wide, but they're poorly lit and badly potholed, and the handful of fine old Caribbean houses are now outnumbered by grimy hotels and hard-drinking bars.

Across the bay is **Puerto Santo Tomás del Castillo**, the newest port facility in the country. To look at the concrete plaza, the planned housing and the fenced-off docks, you'd never guess that the place had a moment's history, but oddly enough it's been around for a while. It was originally founded by the Spanish in 1604, who inhabited it with some Black Caribs, the survivors of an expedition against pirates on Roatan Island. The pirates in turn sacked Santo Tomás, but it was revived in 1843, when a Belgian colony was established here. Today it's connected by a regular shuttle of local buses to Puerto Barrios, though other than the docks themselves there's nothing much to see.

Practicalities

Cheap **hotels** are plentiful in Puerto Barrios, designed to accommodate a typically impoverished port population, although in amongst the squalor there is also a slice of Caribbean charm. The *Hotel del Norte*, 7 C 1 Av (☎9480087; ⑤), on the seafront to the north of the banana plant and marshalling yard, is undoubtedly the finest hotel in town, an ancient wooden building reeking of faded colonial splendour. Somewhat overpriced – even accounting for the swimming pool – the rooms are small and bare and the food is poor, but the atmosphere makes up for it all (a sign at reception reads "no cats, dogs or persons of doubtful reputation"). There are two identical, modern *Europa* hotels (④–⑤), on 3 Av between 11 and 12 calles (ideally situated for catching the ferry to Lívingston), and at 8 Av and 8 C: both are good value, safe and clean, with fans and private showers. Best value for money, however, is the *Hotel Internacional*, 7 Av and 16 C (☎9480367; ④–⑤), where you have a choice of air-conditioning or fan, plus a small pool and secure parking. Another decent place is the *Hotel El Reformmados*, 16 C and 7 Av (☎ & fax 9481531; ④).

If you have the time and the money, and are hankering after some real luxury, book into the *Hotel Cayos del Diablo* (☎9482361 or 2 or 3; fax 9482364; from the US ☎1-800/528-1234; ⑦). Set on a small bay across the water from Puerto Barrios, this lovely hotel is discreetly set above a secluded beach and swimming pool, and offers all the facilities of a tropical hideaway, with spotless rooms in individual thatched *cabañas*. To get there just wait for the regular free, hotel launches which come to the main pier. Alternatively, you can pay for a private water taxi.

When it comes to **eating,** the situation is pretty much the same, with an abundance of cheap and rough places and a few better, more expensive ones. Good food is always available in the market and at the 24-hour restaurants on its edges, including *Cafesama* and *El Punto*. For something a little more refined head for the *Restaurant La Caribena*, 4 Av, between 10 and 11 calles, which does good fish and a superb *caldo de mariscos* (seafood soup). Or try the *El Canal Ingles* which is housed in an attractive old wooden house on 12 C, and offers a fine bar and restaurant, with local and international dishes. Puerto Barrios also has more than its fair share of **bars**, pool halls and nightclubs, offering the full range of late-night sleaze. None of these are hard to find. There are a couple of **cinemas** on 7 C, one of them housed in a superbly misshapen wooden building.

As for other business: the *Guatel* office is on 8 Av (daily 7am–midnight); the **post office** on 6 C (Mon–Fri 8am–4.30pm); and a branch of the *Banco G&T* at 7

PUERTO BARRIOS TRAVEL CONNECTIONS

The Caribbean Highway is served by the *Litegua* bus company, owners of the country's finest and fastest pullman **buses**. In Guatemala City these leave from the plaza in front of the train station at 9 Av and 18 C (hourly 5.30am–5pm). In Puerto Barrios they leave from 6 Av, between 9 and 10 calles (hourly 1am–4pm). The journey takes around six hours and tickets can be bought in advance, although on the whole it's not necessary. Other buses from Puerto Barrios go to Zacapa and Chiquimula: if there's no direct connection take a Guatemala City bus as far as the Río Hondo junction, from where an endless stream of pullmans heads out to Esquipulas and all points in between, for connections to Copán and the border with El Salvador. Finally there's a single bus to Mariscos, leaving from outside the market in Puerto Barrios at 3pm.

From the Muelle Municipal at the bottom of 12 C a public **ferry** leaves Puerto Barrios for Lívingston daily at 10am and 5pm, returning at 5am and 2pm. The trip takes around ninety minutes, although departure times are subject to sudden changes so it's worth checking on arrival in Puerto Barrios. This service is supplemented by a fleet of small **speedboats**, which leave when full (generally every thirty minutes or so); the business is something of a racket and there is a great deal of hustle involved in finding passengers. The speedboats are faster and more frequent than the ferries, and charge around six times more.

For Punta Gorda in **Belize** a ferry leaves on Tuesday and Friday at 7am from the dock at the end of 12 C. You have to clear immigration before you can buy a ticket; it's a good idea to do so the day before you leave. The immigration office is at the end of 9 C (7am–noon & 2–5pm); the ticket office is near the dock. Though there's an immigration office in Entre Rios, it's safer to get your Guatemalan exit stamp in Puerto Barrios if you're hiking to **Honduras**.

C and 6 Av (Mon–Fri 9am–8pm, Sat 10am–2pm). You can change money here, and at a number of other places around town.

Hiking to Honduras: Entre Rios to Corinto

If you're heading for Honduras from Puerto Barrios there are two very different options: either the long haul by bus, through Chiquimula, which takes a day or so, or the more direct, adventurous route to Corinto, which involves a five-hour journey of bus, boat and **trek** through swamp and banana plantations. The latter may seem more obvious, and indeed a longstanding treaty between Guatemala and Honduras provides for the construction of a road link along this route. The Hondurans fulfilled their part of the bargain, building a good road to the border, but Guatemala, afraid that the docks at Puerto Cortés will steal business from its own Puerto Santo Tomás del Castillo, has backed out of the deal. Nevertheless, the missing section is fairly short and if you set out early you'll certainly be in Puerto Cortés the same day. The ground is level but the heat is always tough and in the wet season you'll have to wade through rivers and mud pools.

Setting out from Puerto Barrios you want to make for **Entre Rios**, from where you should take a bus from the market (hourly from 7am), to Finca La Inca. From there take a boat across the Río Montagna to El Limitet – and from there another boat up the Río Guyamelito (around Q20 per person; though you must pay in lempiras – the boatmen will change quetzals, but at a poor rate). The trip takes 45 minutes. From the river you have to walk for about thirty minutes to the highway in Honduras, where there should be no problem finding a truck or bus heading towards Puerto Cortés. At Puerto Cortés you can get your **Honduran entrance stamp** from the immigration office (Mon–Fri 7am–5pm) on the second floor of the building in the corner of the plaza. Heading in the opposite direction you want to set out by taking a bus from Puerto Cortés to the "frontera".

LÍVINGSTON AND THE RÍO DULCE

North of Puerto Barrios the **Bay of Amatique** is ringed with a bank of lush green hills, rising straight out of the Caribbean and coated in tropical rainforest. Halfway between Puerto Barrios and the border with Belize, at the mouth of the Río Dulce, is **LÍVINGSTON**. Reached only by boat, Lívingston not only enjoys a superb setting but is also the only **Carib** town in Guatemala, a strange hybrid of Guatemalan and Caribbean culture in which marimba mixes with Marley. While certainly not unaffected by modernization, this is also the centre for a number of small and traditional villages strung out along the coast, and it has a powerful atmosphere of its own.

Information
The **immigration office**, for an exit stamp if you're heading for Belize or an entrance stamp if you've just arrived, is a block or so behind the *Hotel Río Dulce*. For **changing money**, your best bet is the *Banco del Comercio,* which is first left

CARIB CULTURE

Along with several Belizean centres, Lívingston provides the focus for a displaced people who are now strung out across the Bay of Amatique and southern Belize. Their history begins on the island of St Vincent, where their pure ancestors inter-married with shipwrecked sailors and runaway slaves. In 1795 they staged a rebel-lion against British rule, were defeated, and resettled on the island of Roatan off Honduras, from where they migrated to the mainland.

Today the **Carib culture** incorporates elements of indigenous Indian belief with African and *Ladino* constituents, and in Belize in particular they have recently attempted to revive their independent cultural identity as "Garifuna" people. To Guatemala's *Ladinos,* who've always had a problem accepting indigenous cultures, the Caribs are a mysterious and mistrusted phenomenon. They are not only subjected to the same prejudices that plague the Indian population, but also viewed with a strange awe that gives rise to a range of fanciful myths. Uninformed commentators have argued that their society is matriarchal, polygamous, and directed by a secret royal family. Accusations of voodoo and cannibalism are commonplace too, and it's often claimed that the women speak a language incom-prehensible to the men, passing it on only to their daughters. The reality is more prosaic: though the Carib culture is certainly unique, it is fast being swamped by more modern twentieth-century rhythms. Most of the beliefs that underpin Garifuna traditions, such as the notion of the spirit house and the mythical journey from Roatan, mean far less to young Caribs than Marley, dreads and weed.

from the dock, next to the *Hotel Henry Berrisford*. Out of hours you can usually change travellers' cheques, at a fairly poor rate, in one of the shops (try the *Almacen Koo Wong*). Incidentally, though the *Henry Berrisford* may not be recommended, it does have its uses as a **phone** and **fax** service (daily 8am–6pm); there's also a **Guatel** on the main street (daily 7am–midnight).

Accommodation

Houses can be rented right on the beach, a little way past the *Hotel Flamingo*, for those planning on staying a while; that said, the beach in Lívingston is not safe for **women** alone, day or night. Elsewhere, **hotels** are in plentiful supply.

Hotel Caribe, along the shore to the left of the dock (as you face the town), along a small path. Basic, budget hotel with bare rooms, some with private showers. Avoid downstairs where things get a touch smelly. ②.

Hotel Casa Rosada, about 300m left of the dock, past the *Caribe*. Cabins right on the water, with beautiful views and an intimate relaxed atmosphere, although smoking is forbidden on the premises. Excellent vegetarian meals for residents and non-residents. ④.

Hotel Flamingo, on the beach down behind *The African Place* (far side of town from the dock). Clean, pleasant German-owned hotel in a walled compound. Comfortable rooms, some with shower, and one deluxe special with balcony, and a nice hammock area to hang out in. Very safe, though the high walls mean you can hear the sea but not see it. ④–⑤.

Hotel Garifuna, follow the main street beyond its left run and branch off to the right (☎9481091). Squeaky-clean new building with spotless rooms; very safe. All rooms have fans and private shower. ③.

Hotel Río Dulce, at the top of the hill as you walk into town. Impressive colonial-style wooden building with a newish extension. Not particularly friendly and with something of a reputation for theft – go for an upstairs room if you can. The balcony is one of the best places in Lívingston for watching the world go by. ③.

Tucán Dugú, first on the right on the main street (☎9481572). Lívingston's only luxury hotel, with great views of the bay and a very pleasant bar and swimming pool (small fee for non-residents). ⑦.

Hotel El Viajero, up the hill beyond the *Río Dulce* and off to the left. Small, basic budget hotel; the rooms are safe and all have fans. ②.

The Town and around

Getting your bearings in Lívingston is fairly straightforward, as there's only one main street, which runs straight uphill from the dock for about 500m and then takes a left turn. While there's not really that much to do in town itself, other than relaxing in local style, there are a few places nearby that are worth a visit. Sadly, the local **beaches** are not of the Caribbean dream variety, and tend to be strewn with seaweed, but there are plenty of pleasant places to take a swim. Everywhere you'll find that the sand slopes into the sea very gradually. It is not safe for women to walk alone along the beaches, however, as a number of **rapes** have been reported in recent years.

The most popular trip out of town is to **Las Siete Altares**, a waterfall about 5km along the beach, but this, too, is fraught with danger. There have been **attacks on tourists** walking to and from the falls, so before you set out make sure to ask around about the current situation. If you do go, walk down onto the beach below *The African Place*, past the *Flamingo*, and follow the sand. After a couple of kilometres you come to a small river, which you have to wade across; beyond this the beach eventually peters out. Just before it does so there's a path in to the left, which you should follow inland. It soon brings you to the first of the falls, the lowest of three or four cascades. To reach the others you have to scramble up over it and follow the water: all of the falls are idyllic places to swim, but the highest one is the best of all.

Eating and drinking

There are plenty of places to **eat** in Lívingston, one of the best being *The African Place*, which serves a good range of unusual dishes and some superb seafood, including delicious fish with curry sauce. It's on the far side of town from the dock in one of Guatemala's most outlandish buildings, designed and built in a Moorish style by its Spanish owner. The hotel itself is not recommended. For **vegetarian** meals and plenty of fresh vegetables, you can't do better than the *Casa Rosada*. The *Balina Azul*, on the main street isn't bad either and you get a good view of the passing crowd. Managed by a friendly Swedish couple, *La Marina*, at the mouth of the river, serves great international food with European touches – including fresh French bread, homemade ice cream and cakes. Other than this your best bet is one of the small *comedores* on the main street, all of which do a fantastic line in simple **fried fish**. The *Comedor Coni* and the *Lívingston* are two of the best, both very simple, friendly and inexpensive. For a good **fruit juice**, or a tropical breakfast, try the *MC Tropical*, opposite the *Río Dulce* hotel.

For evening **entertainment** there are plenty of hard-drinking bars, a pool hall, and several clubs, both in town and out along the coast, where local people go to drink and dance, particularly at weekends. One of the best bars these days is the *Banana Republic*, run by American expat Jimmy. He also organizes tours to Amatique Bay, if you feel like going sailing.

The Río Dulce from Lívingston to El Relleno

> *In a few moments we entered the Río Dulce. On each side, rising perpendicularly from three to four hundred feet, was a wall of living green. Trees grew from the water's edge, with dense unbroken foliage, to the top; not a spot of barrenness was to be seen; and on both sides, from the tops of the highest trees, long tendrils descended to the water, as if to drink and carry life to the trunks that bore them. It was, as its name imports, a Río Dulce, a fairy scene of Titan land, combining exquisite beauty with colossal grandeur. As we advanced the passage turned, and in a few minutes we lost sight of the sea, and were enclosed on all sides by a forest wall; but the river, although showing us no passage, still invited us onward.*
>
> John Lloyd Stephens (1841).

Another very good reason for coming to Lívingston is to travel up the **Río Dulce**, a truly spectacular trip that takes you into the hills behind the town and eventually brings you to the main road about 30km upriver. The scenery is the main attraction, but along the way there are a couple of places where you can stop off for a while. The cheapest way to travel is on the mail boats that do the trip twice a week (leaving Lívingston on Tues and Fri at 9.30am), but if you can gather a group of five or six it's worth renting a boat and taking your time. If you really want to do it thoroughly, searching out the river's wildlife or exploring the inlets, then you'll certainly need to rent a boat – you can find them fairly easily in both Lívingston and El Relleno (see p.224), but make sure that you fix the price (around $10 per person) and schedule or the boatmen may try to hurry you.

From Lívingston the river heads into a daunting gorge, between sheer rock faces 100m or so in height. Clinging to the sides is a wall of tropical vegetation and cascading vines, and here and there you might see some white herons or flocks of squawking parakeets. A few kilometres into the gorge there's a spot, known to most boatmen, where warm sulphurous waters emerge from the base of the cliff – a great place for a swim. Afterwards, a friendly place for fried fish or a snack is the *Restaurante El Viajero*, about level with the mouth of the Río Tatin and with great views across the waters. Almost opposite is the **Ac'Tenamit Health Centre**, which caters to the needs of around forty newly established Quiché Indian villages. Driven off the land elsewhere, they have come to start again. Until the American *Guatemala Tomorrow Fund* came to work here, the people had neither schools, medical care, nor much else. Now there is a 24-hour clinic, a primary school for ninety children, as well as a self-help programme to train adults in "income generating" crafts. Volunteer doctors, nurses and dentists who can commit themselves for at least one month are very welcome. For more information contact *Ac'Tenamit/Pueblo Nuevo*, Aptdo Postal 2675, Guatemala City, Guatemala, CA (☎ & fax 2511136).

After another five or six kilometres the gorge opens out into a small lake, **El Golfete**, on whose northern shore is the **Biotopo de Chocón Machacas** (daily 7am–4pm; small donation requested), a government-sponsored nature reserve designed to protect the habitat of the manatee or sea cow, a threatened species that's seen around here from time to time. The manatee is a massive seal-shaped mammal that lives in both sea and fresh water and, according to some, gave rise to the myth of the mermaid. Female manatees breastfeed their young clutching them in their flippers, but are not as dainty as traditional mermaids, weighing up to a ton. They are exceptionally timid too, so you're unlikely to see one.

The reserve also protects the forest that still covers much of the lake's shore, and there are some specially cut trails where you might catch sight of a bird or two, or if you've plenty of time and patience a tapir or jaguar – if not, you may well encounter the tame monkey kept by one of the reserve workers. The jetty where the boats dock is great to swim from. Visitors are welcome to **camp**, but you'll need to bring your own food and some form of water purification. Alternatively, if you have river transport, you could eat your meals at the *Los Palafitos Restaurant*, just outside the reserve. In a peaceful spot, this *comedor* does great fish and shrimp and sells beers at reasonable prices.

At the western end of the Golfete is another **charity operation**, this one an orphanage for children from the capital, who are referrred here by the judicial system. *Casa Guatemala* is run entirely on donations and with the help of volunteers, who do anything from teach, nurse or instruct in carpentry, sewing or typing. There are between 80 and 150 children of all ages here at any one time and volunteers with the right background, who can stay at least one month (preferably three), are always desperately needed. The work is very stressful (starting 5am daily) and conditions basic, to say the least. But for those who can take it, it's time well spent. For more information contact *Casa Guatemala*, 14 C 10–63, Zona 1, Guatemala City (☎2325517).

Lake Izabal and the Río Dulce area

Heading on upstream, across the Golfete, the river closes in again and passes the marina and bridge at **El Relleno** (also known as **Río Dulce**), on the northern

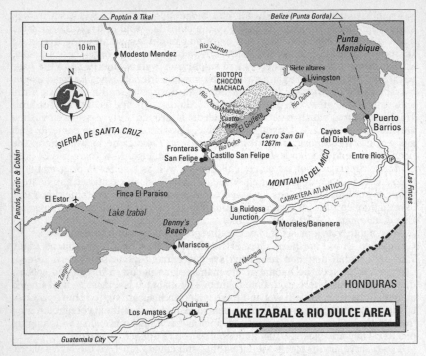

LAKE IZABAL & RIO DULCE AREA

side of the river. This part of the Río Dulce is a favourite playground for wealthy Guatemalans, with boats and hotels that would put parts of California to shame; the shores of **Lake Izabal** beyond hide increasing numbers of elite properties behind high walls and dense foliage. Here also the road for Petén crosses the river and the boat trip comes to an end, although you might try and include a stop at the *castillo*, on the other side of the bridge.

The very beautiful area along the lush banks of the Río Dulce and Lake Izabal is fast becoming a tourist destination in its own right, with plenty to keep you occupied for at least a week and a genuinely relaxed atmosphere. Staying close to El Relleno, you will be at the hub of a small but lively social scene; if you really want to get away from it all, head for **Denny's Beach** on the southern shore of Lake Izabal, or the **Finca El Paraiso** on the northern shore. The former is actually more conveniently reached from Mariscos, also on the southern shore of the lake, but you will have no trouble finding a boatman to take you to either place from El Relleno. Before you arrange anything, however, ask around about going rates and make sure you fix a price before you set out. The *Hollymar* restaurant (see p.226) is a great place for gathering information.

El Relleno/Río Dulce
The village of **EL RELLENO/RÍO DULCE** itself is little more than a truck stop, where traffic for Petén pauses before the long stretch to Flores. The road is lined with cheap *comedores* and *tiendas*, and you can pick up buses here in either direction. If you're heading towards Guatemala City or Puerto Barrios then the best

bet is to take a minibus to Morales (every 30min) and catch a bus to Guatemala City from there. If you're heading for Petén the last direct bus passes at about 3pm; after that you might be able to hitch as far as Poptún, or you can spend the night here in El Relleno, and head on in the morning. The village has plenty of basic cheap **hotels**, such as the *Hotel Marilu* (②), in the centre, and the *Hospedaje Del Río* (②). But since there are much nicer inexpensive alternatives just a short water-taxi ride away, there's little point in lingering.

Castillo de San Felipe

If you have an hour or so to spare then it's worth heading out to the **Castillo de San Felipe**, 1km upstream, which marks the entrance to Lake Izabal. The fort is a tribute to the audacity of English pirates, who used to sail up the Río Dulce and into the lake in order to steal supplies and harass mule trains. The Spanish were so infuriated by this that they built the fortress to seal off the entrance to the lake, and a chain was strung across the river. In later years the castle was used as a prison, but, since restoration and landscaping, looks exactly like a miniature medieval castle, with a maze of tiny rooms and staircases and fantastically thick walls. Alongside there's a café, swimming pool and tennis court.

About 300m away the *Hotel Humberto* (③), still one of the better budget places to **stay** around El Relleno, is looking rather dilapidated these days and is a little far from the road if you're just passing through. The quickest way to get there from the bridge is to take a water taxi to the *castillo*; returning you will have to walk 3km if you can't hitch a lift on the dirt road leading back to the highway. Also in the waterside village of **SAN FELIPE** is the *Rancho Escondido* (call VHF10 from *Tienda Reed*, on the south side of the bridge; ④), a friendly American-Guatemalan guest house and backpacker's retreat. The only problem is the inconvenient location .

Lake Izabal

Beyond the *castillo*, the broad sweep of **Lake Izabal** opens before you, with great views of the fertile highlands beyond the distant shores. Mornings are the best time for sailing or boat trips, before strong winds whip up dangerous waves later in the day. Local boatmen run trips to various places around the lake, including **Denny's Beach**, a great sandy beach, or **Finca El Paraiso**, both of which have nice bar-restaurants where it's easy to while away the time (the *finca* also has rooms; see below). If you're craving a good swim, head for Denny's; but if you're more interested in exploring the hidden treasures around the lake make for the *finca*, where you will find an amazing hot waterfall cascading into pools cooled by fresh river water (small fee). Beyond the pools, hidden in the surviving jungle, are a series of **caves** whose interiors are crowded with extraordinary shapes and colours, made even more memorable by the fact that you have to swim by torch-light to see them. Not for claustrophobes. To reach Denny's or the *finca* you can walk a good forty minutes from El Relleno in sweltering heat or take a very bumpy ride on a tractor-drawn trailer. The trailer easily takes ten people and, regardless of numbers, the return journey costs around $12.

Accommodation. eating and drinking around El Relleno

If you are travelling in a small group, a good base is the *Hacienda Tijax* on the northeastern waterfront, two minutes by water taxi from the bridge (reservations in Guatemala City: *Boutique Ceschelli*, Edificio El Portal, Av La Reforma and 14 C, opposite the *Hotel Camino Real*; ☎3335778; ②–④). You can make radio contact on VHF 09 from the *Hollymar Restaurant* (see below). This 500-acre farm is a great spot to pitch your own tent or stay in one of the rustic self-catering lodges, which comfortably sleep up to eight. Alcohol and soft drinks are sold on the farm, though provisions must be bought in El Relleno. Staying here, you not only have the opportunity to observe a working tropical farm with a large-scale rubber plantation and reforestation project underway, but also to go horseback riding in the hills beyond the river.

For something a little more upmarket, the best value for money is *Suzanna's Laguna*, on the southwestern waterfront (Guatemala City fax 3692681; ⑤), which has beautiful polished wood rooms, an open-air bar and a restaurant. If, on the other hand, you prefer a stronger Guatemalan flavour and fewer foreign boaters, go for the large hotels dotted around the river's shores. The nicest, though a little overpriced, is the *Hotel Vinas del Lago*, near the *castillo* (☎9478437; ⑥), which offers great views across the lake from its several terraces and also has its own private beach. Two others, which have both seen far better days, are the *Hotel Marimonte* (☎9478585; fax Guatemala City 3344964; ⑦); and the *Hotel Catamaran* (☎9478361; fax Guatemala City 3318450; ⑥), which is set in a more attractive location, downriver from the bridge.

For a great setting on the north of the lake, the *Finca El Paraiso* (see above) has six beautiful *cabañas* on the waterfront. Either make radio contact on VHF73, or phone Guatemala City on ☎2532397 and speak to Mrs Gabriella de la Vega Rodriguez (⑤; *cabañas* sleep up to four). Finally, a new **luxury resort** is being built near the *castillo*, due to be called *El Corozal*.

In addition to the hotel **restaurants**, the *Bar/Restaurant Hollymar*, on the northside of the El Relleno bridge, is a great place to meet other travellers, eat good food and drink the night away. You can also make radio contact to most places around the river and lake from here – if the American owner is not feeling helpful you can always radio from the *Tienda Reed*, on the south side of the bridge.

THE EASTERN HIGHLANDS

The eastern end of the highlands, connecting Guatemala City with El Salvador, has to rank as the least-visited part of the entire country. In this stronghold of right-wing politics the population is almost entirely Latinized, speaking Spanish and wearing Western clothes, although many are by blood pure Indians. Only in a couple of isolated areas do they still speak Pokoman, the region's indigenous language, which is closely related to Kekchi, the language spoken around Cobán. The *Ladinos* of the east have a reputation for behaving like cowboys, and violent demonstrations of macho pride are common.

The landscape lacks the immediate appeal of the western highlands. Not only are its peaks lower, but its features are generally less clearly defined. The volcanoes, unlike the neatly symmetrical cones of the west, are badly eroded, merging with the lower-lying hills. But the lower altitude does have a positive side: the hills are that much more fertile, and the broad valleys are lush with vegetation, similar in many ways to the highlands of El Salvador.

On the whole you're unlikely to head in this direction unless you're on your way to the border with El Salvador, in which case your best bet is to travel directly to **San Salvador** by pullman. It's a route that takes you through the southern side of the eastern highlands, and several companies can get you from one capital to the other in little over eight hours. If, however, you decide to explore this part of the country, then the best route takes you right through the central area, from **Jutiapa** to **Jalapa**, and then east to **Esquipulas**. The roads are poor but the scenery along the way is superb, taking you across vast valleys and over great ranges of hills.

Alternatively, you can head into the northern side of the eastern highlands, along a good road that branches off the Caribbean Highway and connects the towns of **Zacapa**, **Chiquimula** and **Esquipulas**. From here you can head on into Honduras and El Salvador, or make a short trip to the ruins of **Copán** in Honduras, the very best of the southern Maya sites. The landscape out this way is very different, with dry hills and dusty fields, but once again the population is very urban and Latinized.

From Guatemala City to El Salvador

Although there are several possible routes between the capital and the El Salvadorean border, it's the highland route, passing through Cuilapa, that draws the most traffic. This is not only the fastest connection between the two countries but also offers the most spectacular scenery, weaving through a series of lush valleys. The highway leaves Guatemala City through the southern suburbs of Zona 10, and climbs steeply out of the city, passing the hillside villas of the wealthy. It then reaches a high plateau from which you get a good view of the eastern side of the Pacaya volcano, its cone spraying out rocks and smoke. There are few towns out this way: the only place before **CUILAPA**, some 70km from the capital, is the small roadside settlement of Barberena. Cuilapa's claim to fame is that it is supposedly the very "centre of the Americas" – this doesn't, however, make it an interesting place to stop. There are a couple of hotels if you get stuck, and a branch road that heads south to the coastal town of **Chiquimulilla** (buses every hour or so).

Eleven kilometres beyond Cuilapa the highway splits at the **El Molino junction**. The southern fork, highway CA8, is the most direct route to the border, heading straight for the crossing at **VALLE NUEVO**, less than 50km away. This road is straight, fast and scenic, but the border crossing is little more than a customs post and there's nowhere to stay when you get there or on the way.

The northern fork, CA1, is the continuation of the **Pan-American Highway**. This road is much slower, as it passes through most of the main towns and is served only by second-class buses, but it's also considerably more interesting. If you're heading directly for El Salvador then the southern branch is the one to stick with, and if you wait at the junction a pullman for San Salvador will turn up sooner or later.

The Pan-American Highway: Jutiapa

Heading west from El Molino, the Pan-American Highway turns towards the mountains, running through an isolated valley of sugar cane, then climbing onto a high plateau. Here the landscape is more characteristic of the eastern highlands, with its open valleys and low ridges overshadowed by huge eroded volcanoes.

Bypassing the small town of Quesada, the road arrives at **JUTIAPA**. The centre of trade and transport for the entire eastern region, this is a busy and not particularly attractive place, with a steady stream of buses to and from the border and the capital, and to all other parts of the east, from Jalapa to Esquipulas. If you decide **to stay** there are plenty of places to choose from, and if you need to change money there is a branch of the *Banco del Ejercito* on 5 C.

Hourly **buses** pass through Jutiapa heading for the border and for Guatemala City, pulling in at the bus terminal right in the middle of town. Jutiapa is also the starting point for a trip across the eastern highlands to Chiquimula or Esquipulas. The quickest route takes you directly to Esquipulas, through Ipala, and buses from Jutiapa head this way. But if you'd rather take your time and see the best of this part of the country then take a bus to Jalapa, spend the night there, and then press on to Chiquimula.

Asunción Mita and the border at San Cristóbal

Heading on from Jutiapa towards the border with El Salvador the Pan-American Highway runs through El Progreso, where the roads to Jalapa and to Ipala (for the direct route to Chiquimula or Esquipulas) branch off to the north. Beyond here the road drops into yet another vast open valley, and arrives at the small town of **ASUNCIÓN MITA**, 45 minutes from Jutiapa, half an hour from the border. Despite its jaded appearance, Asunción has a considerable past: founded, according to Indian records, in 1449, and captured by the Spanish in 1550, it was an important staging post on the royal route to Panamá in colonial times. Nowadays, its only real significance is as the last town before the border; if you arrive in the evening it's easiest **to stay** the night and cross into El Salvador the next day.

Archeology enthusiasts might want to visit the **ruins** about 4km to the east of Asunción Mita along the main road – opposite the *INDECA* building. There's not much to see, but if you rummage around in the fields you should be able to find a series of small mounds, which according to legend, were built as a monument to Quetzalcoatl by an old man and a young girl who rose out of a lake.

A stream of buses and minibuses connect Asunción Mita with the **border**, 21km south. The actual crossing point is marked by the small town of **SAN CRISTÓBAL**, where there are a couple of basic *pensiónes*. The last **bus** for Guatemala City leaves the border at 3pm, and the last minibus for Asunción Mita leaves at around 5pm.

Jalapa to Ipala

Any trip through the eastern highlands should include the road **between Ipala and Jalapa**, which takes you through some truly breathtaking scenery. This is not actually on the way to anywhere, and it's a fairly long and exhausting trip, but if you've had enough of the tourist overkill of the western highlands and don't mind a bumpy ride, then it makes a refreshing change.

From Jutiapa direct buses run to Jalapa, passing over the shoulder of the Tahual volcano and through a huge bowl-shaped valley, thick with fields of sugar cane, tobacco and maize. The main towns along the way are **Monjas** and **Morazán**, two busy agricultural centres. **JALAPA** itself is a prosperous but isolated town, resting on a high plateau in the heart of the eastern highlands and surrounded by low peaks and cattle pasture. Set away from all the major roads, its busy bus terminal links all the area's smaller towns and villages. Chances are that you'll arrive here fairly late and have to **stay** the night; not a bad prospect as the *Hotel Casa del Viajero* (②), at 1 Av 0–70, has to rate as one of finest budget **hotels** in the entire country: charming, friendly and relaxed, with a good restaurant. If that's full try *Hotel Mendez* (②) at 1 C A 1–2, overlooking the bus terminal, but avoid the *Hotel Centroamerica* and the *Hospedaje Julia*, which look like classic budget hotels but offer a worse deal than the *Casa del Viajero*. There are an astonishing three branches of the *Banco G&T* (all Mon–Fri 8am–7pm, Sat 10am–2pm).

A paved road runs from Jalapa to **Sanarate**, on the main road from Guatemala City to Puerto Barrios – much the fastest route back to the capital. Alternatively, there's a very rough road to Guatemala City via Mataquesquintla and San José Pinula – only recommended to the hardy and patient as it takes a couple of days.

Buses run every hour or so from Jalapa to Guatemala City from 3am until 2.30pm via Jutiapa, and until 4pm via Sanarate. Coming from Guatemala City, direct buses to Jalapa via Sanarate leave from 22 C 1–20, Zona 1, between 4am and 6pm, a journey of just over three hours. Buses leave Jalapa for Chiquimula (6hr) via Ipala every ninety minutes from 4am to 1pm.

San Luis Jilotepéque and Ipala

Heading on from Jalapa towards Chiquimula and Esquipulas the road climbs into the hills for the most beautiful section of the entire trip, leading up onto a high ridge with superb views, and then dropping down to the isolated villages of San Pedro Pinula and **SAN LUIS JILOTEPÉQUE**, two outposts of Indian culture. The plaza of San Luis is particularly impressive, with two massive ceiba trees, a colonial church, and a couple of replica stelae from Copán – and on Sunday it's the scene of a vast Indian market. There are two fairly basic *pensiónes*.

Fourteen kilometres beyond San Luis, this back road joins the main road from Jutiapa at **IPALA**. This is an important crossroads, from where buses run to Jutiapa to the south, Jalapa in the west, Chiquimula to the north and Esquipulas in the east. The village itself is built on an open plain at the base of the Ipala volcano (1650m), which looks more like a rounded hill. The cone, inactive for hundreds of years, is now filled by a beautiful little lake ringed by dense tropical forest, and is similar in many ways to the cone of Chicabal near Quezaltenango. It is possible to climb the volcano from the village itself, a distance of around 10km, but the easiest ascent (2hr) is from the south, setting out from the village of Agua Blanca and climbing through Finca El Paxte. (A dirt road to Agua Blanca branches off the main road between Jalapa and Monjas.) The lake is said to contain a unique species of fish, the *mojarra*, which apparently has six prominent spines on its back. If you decide **to stay** in Ipala there are two grubby *pensiónes*, but you're better off pushing on to one of the larger towns.

The north: Zacapa, Chiquimula and Esquipulas

What is true of the entire eastern highlands is particularly true of the string of towns that runs along the northern side of the mountains. Here eastern machismo is at its most potent and hardly anyone lives outside the towns. The vast majority of the population are *Ladinos*, and furiously proud of it, with a reputation for quick tempers, warm hearts and violent responses. The trio of **Zacapa**,

Chiquimula and **Esquipulas** are, however, the most accessible in the eastern highlands, with a good road and fast bus service from the capital. They also offer access to two particularly interesting sites: the Maya ruins at **Copán** in Honduras, and the shrine of the **Black Christ** in Esquipulas.

The direct road branches off the Caribbean Highway at the Río Hondo junction, running through dry, dusty hills to Zacapa, and on through Chiquimula and Esquipulas to the three-way border with Honduras and El Salvador. Before Zacapa the road passes the small town of **ESTANZUELA**, which, oddly enough, has its own museum of paleontology, **El Museo de Paleontología Bryan Patterson** (daily 8am–5pm; free), dedicated to an American scientist who worked in the area for many years. The exhibits, which include the fossil of a blue whale, manatee bones, a giant armadillo shell, and the entire skeleton of a mastodon said to be some 50,000 years old, are equally unexpected. There are also some more recent pieces such as a small Maya tomb, transported here from a site 1km or so away, and in the basement some copies of Copán stelae and one or two originals. The museum has a certain amateur charm and is well worth a look if you have an hour to spare. To get here take any bus between El Rancho and ' Zacapa – including all the buses heading between Guatemala City and Esquipulas – ask the driver to drop you at the village, and simply walk straight through it, along the main street. Since it's the only museum for hundreds of kilometres, it shouldn't prove too hard to find.

Zacapa

Just 13km from the Río Hondo junction, **ZACAPA** is reached from the main road by twin bridges across the Río Grande. In the dry months this is one of the hottest towns in the country, with maximum temperatures of 35–40°C. Its atmosphere is dominated by two things: *Ladino* culture and the surrounding desert, which is irrigated to produce tobacco. There's not much to do in Zacapa, although it's pleasant enough, with a large, busy market, and the attraction of some hot springs a few kilometres to the south. The town itself is an elongated shape, strung out between the train station and the plaza – relaxed and tree-lined, with some of the finest public toilets in all of Guatemala. Here you'll find the *Banco G&T* (Mon–Fri 9am–7pm, Sat 10am–2pm), the **post office** (Mon–Fri 8am–4.30pm), and a *Guatel* office (daily 7am–midnight). There are two **hotels** of note: the very good value, Chinese-run *Hotel Wong* (②), 6 C 12–53, and, around the corner, in 6 C beside the market, the larger, basic *Hotel Central* (①). Most of the places to eat are on the main street, 4 C, which is also where you'll find the cinema, *Cine Lux*, and pool hall.

The **bus** terminal in Zacapa is 1km or so from the centre; take a local bus if you don't want to walk. From the terminal, buses leave hourly for Guatemala City, Chiquimula and Esquipulas. There are also minibuses that run between the junction at El Rancho and all of the towns out this way: in Zacapa pick them up on 13 Av between 6 and 7 calles, near the *Hotel Wong*; they don't run to any timetable but departures are regular. Coming from Guatemala City there are plenty of buses to Zacapa from the Zona 1 terminal at 19 C and 9 Av.

The hot springs of Santa Marta

The one good reason for stopping off in Zacapa is to take a trip to the luxurious **Aguas Thermales Santa Marta** (daily 8am–4pm; small fee), four or five kilometres south of town. There are no buses out this way so you'll either have to walk (you might be able to hitch some of the way) or go by taxi. To get to the hot springs on foot, walk up the street to the right of the church in Zacapa's plaza, past the *Banco G&T*. After four blocks you come to a small park where you want to take the first left, then the next right and then another left. This brings you onto a track that heads out of town across a small river – stick with this track as it continues through the fields and after about 3km it will start to drop into another small valley. Just as it does so take the left-hand fork, at the end of which you'll find the baths – if you get lost, just ask for *los baños*.

The bathing rooms are set off a small courtyard in a beautiful old building, built on a vaguely colonial model. Inside each room there's a huge tiled tub, filled with naturally heated water. It's a superbly relaxing experience, sending you to the brink of sleep – if not beyond.

Chiquimula

From Zacapa the main road continues towards the border, heading up over a low pass and into a great open valley. Set to one side of this is the town of **CHIQUIMULA**, another bustling *Ladino* stronghold. Chiquimula is the largest of these three northern towns and its dusty plaza is the main regional bus terminal, permanently congested by the coming and going of assorted traffic. Other than this it is of little note but for a massive ruined colonial church, on the edge of town beside the main road. The church was damaged in the 1765 earthquake and its ruins have gradually been left behind as the town has shifted.

There's a branch of the *Banco G&T* at 7 Av 4–75 (Mon–Fri 9am–7pm, Sat 10am–2pm); and a *Guatel* on the corner of the plaza (daily 7am–midnight). Also, the largest sombrero shop in the market changes money and travellers' cheques. As Chiquimula is the starting point for routes to Copán in Honduras and back through Ipala to Jalapa, you might well end up **staying**. If so the *Hotel Chiquimula*, 3 C 6–51 (☎9420387; ③–④) on the plaza is all right but overpriced – all rooms have private showers; the *Pensión Hernandez*, 3 C 7–41 (☎9420708; ③–④), down the hill on 3 C, is better value and has plenty of clean, simple rooms, all with fan and some with private shower, and a pool; the *Pensión España* (②) is cheaper still, but much more basic. If those are full try the *Casa del Viajero* (②), around the corner on 8 Av opposite the Shell filling station, or the more luxurious *Hotel Victoria*, 2 C 9–99 (☎9422238; ③–④), half a block west of the bus terminal, where all rooms have a private shower and cable TV.

When it comes to **eating** there are plenty of good, inexpensive *comedores* in and around the market, behind the church, as well as *Magic Burger* and *Cafe Paiz*, both on 3 C, for predictable fast food and good fruit juices. For something a little more interesting try *Bella Roma*, 7 Av 5–31, which specializes in pizza and pasta; *Lugar El Pason*, 8 Av 2–68, like a German beer garden without the noise, has good and imaginative food; while *Las Vegas*, on 7 Av off the plaza, is the town's only 24-hour restaurant, with fairly high prices and garish pink decor. Otherwise the only evening entertainment in Chiquimula is the *Cine Liv* on the plaza.

Buses to Guatemala City and Esquipulas leave every thirty minutes or so from the terminal midway between the plaza and the highway, and to Puerto Barrios until 3pm. There are buses to Jalapa (6hr), via Ipala, hourly from 5am to 6pm, and also to the border at El Florido (2hr 30min), for Copán in Honduras, hourly from 6am to 4.30pm.

Esquipulas

We returned to breakfast, and afterwards set out to visit the only object of interest, the great church of the pilgrimage, the Holy Place of Central America. Every year, on the fifteenth of January, pilgrims visit it, even from Peru and Mexico; the latter being a journey not exceeded in hardship by the pilgrimage to Mecca. As in the east, "it is not forbidden to trade during the pilgrimage", and when there are no wars to make the roads unsafe eighty thousand people have assembled among the mountains to barter and pay homage to "our Lord of Esquipulas".

John Lloyd Stephens (1841).

The final town on this eastern highway is **ESQUIPULAS**, which, now as in Stephens's day, has a single point of interest; it is almost certainly the most important Catholic shrine in Central America. Arriving from Chiquimula the bus winds through the hills, beneath craggy outcrops and forested peaks, emerging suddenly at the lip of a huge bowl-shaped valley centring on a great open plateau. On one side of this, just below the road, is Esquipulas itself. The place is entirely dominated by the four perfectly white domes of the church, brilliantly floodlit at night: beneath these the rest of the town is a messy sprawl of cheap hotels, souvenir stalls and overpriced restaurants. The pilgrimage, which continues all year, has generated numerous sidelines, creating a booming resort where people from all over Central America come to worship, eat, drink and relax, in a bizarre combination of holy devotion and indulgence.

THE ESQUIPULAS PILGRAMAGE

The history of the **Esquipulas pilgrimage** probably dates back to before the Conquest, when the valley was controlled by Chief Esquipulas. Even then it was the site of an important religious shrine, perhaps connected with the nearby Maya site of Copán. When the Spanish arrived the chief was keen to avoid the normal bloodshed and chose to surrender without a fight; the grateful Spaniards named the city they founded at the site in his honour. The famed colonial sculptor Quirio Cataño was then commissioned to carve an image of Christ for the church constructed in the middle of the new town, and in order to make it more likely to appeal to the local Indians he chose to carve it from balsam, a dark wood. (Another version has it that Cataño was hired by Indians after one of their number had seen a vision of a dark Christ on this spot.) In any event the image was installed in the church in 1595 and soon accredited with miraculous powers. But things really took off in 1737 when the bishop of Guatemala, Pardo de Figueroa, was cured of a chronic ailment on a trip to Esquipulas. The bishop ordered the construction of a new church, which was completed in 1758, and had his body buried beneath the altar.

While all this might seem fairly straightforward it doesn't explain why this figure has become the most revered in a country full of miracle-working saints. One possible explanation is that it offers the Indians, who until recently dominated the pilgrimage, a chance to combine pre-Columbian and Catholic worship. It's known that the Maya pantheon included several Black deities such as Ek Ahau, the black lord, who was served by seven retainers, and Ek-chuach, the tall black one, who protected travellers. When Aldous Huxley visited the shrine in 1934 his thoughts were along these lines: "So what draws the worshippers is probably less the saintliness of the historic Jesus than the magical sootiness of his image . . . numinosity is in inverse ratio to luminosity."

The principal day of **pilgrimage**, when the religious significance of the shrine is at its most potent, is January 15. Even the smallest villages will save enough money to send a representative or two on this occasion, their send-off and return invariably marked by religious services. These plus the thousands who can afford to come in their own right ensure that the numbers attending are still as high as in Stephens's day, filling the town to bursting and beyond. Buses chartered from all over Guatemala choke the streets, while the most devoted pilgrims arrive on foot (some dropping to their knees for the last few kilometres). There's a smaller pilgrimage annually on March 9, and faithful crowds visit year round.

Inside the **church** today there's a constant scurry of hushed devotion amid clouds of smoke and incense. In the nave pilgrims approach the image on their knees, while others light candles, mouth supplications or simply stand in silent crowds. The image itself is most closely approached by a separate, side entrance where you can join the queue to shuffle past beneath it and pause briefly in front before being shoved on by the crowds behind. Back outside you'll find yourself among swarms of souvenir and relic hawkers, and pilgrims who, duty done, are ready to head off to eat and drink away the rest of their stay. Many pilgrims also visit a set of nearby **caves** said to have miraculous powers; and there are some **hot baths** – ideal for ritual ablution.

Practicalities

When it comes to staying in Esquipulas, you'll find yourself amongst hundreds of visitors whatever the time of year. **Hotels** probably outnumber private homes and there are new ones springing up all the time. Bargains, however, are in short supply, and the bulk of the budget places are grubby and bare, with tiny monk-like cells – not designed in a spirit of religiosity, but simply to up the number of guests. **Prices** are rarely in writing and are always negotiable, depending on the flow of pilgrims. Avoid **weekends** when prices double.

Many of the least expensive places are clustered opposite the church; the best plan is to look at a few before you decide. The *Pensión Lemus* is one of the best, or try the *San Antonio*, *La Favorita* or *Paris* (all ③), all of which are simple budget hotels. For a touch more luxury head for the *Hotel Los Angeles* (④), where some rooms have private bathrooms, or the *Hotel Esquipulas* (③), a cheap annex to the *Hotel Payaqui* (⑥), where there's a pool and all rooms come with a TV and fan. There are also dozens of **restaurants** and **bars**, most of them overpriced by Guatemalan standards, a branch of the *Banco G&T* (Mon–Fri 9am–7pm, Sat 10am–2pm), and a lone cinema, the *Cine Galaxia*.

Rutas Orientales run a superb **bus** service between Guatemala City and Esquipulas, with departures every half-hour from 2am to 8.30pm. Their office in Guatemala City is at 19 C 8–18, Zona 1, and in Esquipulas it's on the main street. There are also direct buses from Esquipulas to Puerto Barrios at 6.15am, and across the highlands to Ipala and Jutiapa. If you want to get to the ruins of Copán you'll need to catch a bus to Chiquimula and change there.

On to the borders: El Salvador and Honduras

The **Honduran** border crossing at **Aguacaliente** (24hr), just 10km from Esquipulas, is served by a regular shuttle of minibuses from the main street, and taxis that will shuttle you back and forth for a dollar a time. The **El Florido** crossing, which is more convenient if you're heading for the ruins of Copán, is reached by bus from Chiquimula. There's a **Honduran consulate** (Mon–Fri 8.30am–4pm) in the *Hotel Payaqui* in Esquipulas, beside the church.

The border with El Salvador is about 24km from Esquipulas, down a branch road that splits from the main road just before you arrive at the town. Minibuses and buses serve this border too, but there's no Salvadorean consulate in Esquipulas.

Copán

Across the border in **Honduras**, less than a day's journey from Guatemala City, are the ruins of **Copán**, one of the most magnificent of all Maya sites. The architecture may not be as impressive as at Tikal or Chichén Itzá, but in other ways it is more than their equal. As at Quiriguá – and indeed all southern Maya sites – the buildings themselves are relatively low. Here the outstanding features are not the temples themselves, but the carvings that decorate them and the stelae that surround them. Maya artists at Copán and Quiriguá developed astounding skills and carved superbly rounded portraits and deep-set glyphs, many of which are still well preserved. Copán's most famous structure is the **Hieroglyphic Stairway**, the longest Maya text in existence, containing some two thousand glyphs carved onto a flight of sixty stone steps.

It's just possible to see the ruins as a day trip from Guatemala, but to make it worth your while and really take in the splendours of the site it would be a better idea to **spend a night** in Honduras. The best plan is to set out early from Guatemala so that you'll be in Copán by lunchtime, then either spend the afternoon at the ruins and return the next morning, or settle in for a day – transport from the ruins to the border is virtually nonexistent after 3pm. There's no need to get a visa as the border guards are particularly understanding and operate a special system of temporary entry so as not to invalidate your Guatemalan visa (see below).

Getting to and from the ruins

Wherever you're coming from you first need to get to **Chiquimula**, three hours from Guatemala City (buses leave every hour or so from the terminal in Zona 1, at 18 C and 9 Av; any bus going to Esquipulas will pass through Chiquimula). From the terminal in Chiquimula second-class buses, usually packed, depart for **El Florido** and the border with Honduras (hourly 6am–4.30pm; at least 2hr 30min). Twenty minutes up the road, in the direction of Esquipulas, the road for the border branches off to the left at the **Vado Hondo junction**. The journey through the Sierra del Espíritu Santo to El Florido is rough and dusty: in the few

small villages along the way the people are mostly Chorti-speaking Indians, the remnants of an isolated Indian group who've largely abandoned traditional ways.

At **EL FLORIDO** there's the most rudimentary of **border posts** (7am–6pm). Here you'll be charged around $1 for an exit fee and $3 for an entrance fee, depending on the mood of the day. Explain to the border guards that you intend to go no further than *las ruinas* (the ruins) and they'll give you a **temporary entrance stamp**, which saves a lot of hassle – they won't stamp your passport but instead give you a separate piece of paper which you simply give back to them when you return. Hence your Guatemalan visa or tourist card is not invalidated. If, on the other hand, you're heading on into Honduras, make sure you get the real thing. Money changers operate on both sides of the border, but you can also find them, or rather they'll find you, in the village: there's a bank there too, in the corner of the plaza (Mon–Fri 8–11.30am & 1.30–4pm; Sat 8–11.30am). On the Honduran side trucks, minibuses and buses provide transport to the village of **Las Ruinas de Copán**, 12km from the border and just a short walk from the site. The fare should not be more than $1.50, but you'll often be asked for more. The only answer is to bargain hard, but in the end you have no alternative source of transport and the drivers know it.

Trucks and buses head **back to El Florido** and the border throughout the morning, with the last departure at around 3pm. From El Florido to **Chiquimula** there are buses every hour or two (5.30am–3.30pm). If you want to go on **into Honduras** then you need to take a bus to **San Pedro Sula**, which often involves changing buses in **La Entrada**, about an hour away. From San Pedro Sula there are direct buses to **Tela** and **Tegucigalpa**.

By air

Getting to Copán by road can be a long and exhausting journey, so it is excellent news that *Jungle Flying*, based in Guatemala City (☎3604917; fax 3314995), have started **airborne daytrips** to the ruins. At $200 per person they're not cheap, but you do get excellent value for money. The price includes the flight (45min each way) to an airstrip on the Guatemalan side of the border, transport by minibus to the ruins (25min), a guided tour of the ruins, and an excellent lunch at the top hotel in the village of Copán Ruinas. Bring your bathing suit and towel and you can take a cooling dip in the hotel's lovely pool before heading back for Guatemala City by mid-afternoon. Though you don't pass an official border post, you will need to bring your passport. Tours leave daily from the domestic airport; check-in time is 7am.

Staying at Copán: Las Ruinas village

Once a small farming settlement, **LAS RUINAS DE COPÁN** is now largely dependent on the ruins for a livelihood, housing the site museum and providing accommodation. If you set out early enough from Guatemala you should reach the village around midday, all being well. Before heading out to the ruins you need to find somewhere to **stay** and drop off your stuff.

Accommodation

Hotels are in plentiful supply in Copán although prices are high. For some reason many places only give you a sheet, which may seem enough in the heat of the day but leaves you freezing at night – ask for a blanket.

The **price codes** we've used for accommodation in Copán are the same as those throughout the Guatemala section of the *Guide*: see p.29 for more details.

Hotel Las Brisas de Copán, on the road out of town towards the ruins (☎98/3018). A good deal at the top end of the budget range. All rooms have fans, some have showers and the water is even warm. ③.

Hotelito Copán, near the river (☎98/3411). Very decent budget hotel. All rooms with private bath. ③.

Hotel Honduras, on the exit road to the ruin. A little grubby and run-down but with inexpensive, basic rooms around a pleasant, leafy courtyard. ③.

Hotel Madrugada, right by the river (☎98/0330). Beautiful rooms with fan, and long balcony strung with hammocks to enjoy the view across the valley. ⑥.

Hotel Marina Copán, just up from the plaza (☎98/3070; fax Tegucigalpa 504/573076). The town's most upmarket establishment, decked out in colonial-style grandeur, with all the luxury you could ask for. Up to two children free, if staying in the same room as parents. ⑦.

Hotel Maya Copán, on the plaza. Simple but clean; some rooms have private showers, but always with lukewarm water. Prices negotiable. ③.

Eating, drinking and entertainment

The best **restaurant** in town is *El llama del Bosque*, with plenty of good food and fast service at reasonable prices – quetzals accepted. There are several basic *comedores*, but as always the cheapest place to eat is the market. Other than eating and sleeping there's not much to do in the evenings, although there are a couple of video cinemas. The most popular place to hang out is the *Tunkul Bar* (across the road from *El llama del Bosque*), where Rene and Mike make everyone welcome and serve excellent drinks, food and music.

A brief history of the site

In recent years great strides have been made in understanding the history of Copán, although it's important to remember that the site lies at the southern limit of Maya civilization and was largely cut off from all the other sites except Quiriguá, with which it was heavily involved. Archeologists now believe that the valley was first inhabited around 1000 BC. Graves dating from 900 BC contained a carved jade necklace from the Motagua valley in Guatemala, indicating the existence of trade in luxury goods. The next piece of evidence comes from the grave of a shaman who died in 450 AD and was buried along with a codex and some animals' teeth, perhaps the tools of his trade.

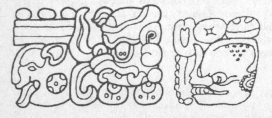
Glyph references to 18 Rabbit, God K and Copán

In the sixth century Copán emerged as a substantial city; we know that its emblem glyph was first used in 564 AD, and that the ruler depicted on Quiriguá's Monument 26 was either the fourth of fifth member of Copán's ruling dynasty. It's believed that in these early days Quiriguá, and possibly the entire southern region, was under the control of Copán. Few concrete details are known, however, until the rule of Smoke Imix (628–695 AD), when the area was developing fast. Finds from this era include grinding stones, sophisticated pottery and obsidian blades.

From then on much of our information about Copán is gleaned from the stelae at Quiriguá. In 731 AD Quiriguá's independent emblem glyph emerges for the first time, which probably indicated that the city was starting to break away from Copán. Around this time Copán's ruler was 18 Rabbit (Smoke Imix's son), and his rival at Quiriguá was Cauac Sky. Competition between the two centres came to a head in 738, a date recorded on several of Quiriguá's stelae, when 18 Rabbit was captured and decapitated by Cauac Sky, probably during a raid on Copán. This event was the start of a boom period in the fortunes of Quiriguá, but it marked a downturn for Copán. 18 Rabbit was succeeded by a short-lived ruler, Smoke Monkey (738–749), and there was little new building during these uncertain years. Political stability returned in 749 with the succession of Smoke Shell, and the city prospered until his death in 763. During his reign the famous hieroglyphic stairway, perhaps the most impressive piece of Maya architecture anywhere, was built. Smoke Shell's son, Yax Pac, took office on July 2, 763, but despite frantic attempts to maintain the building boom the city went into decline. Skeletal remains from this period indicate malnutrition and disease, and with the population somewhere around 20,000, food resources were by no means adequate. Yax Pac died in the winter of 820, ending the dynastic line of Copán.

The site came to light again soon after the Conquest, in 1576, when it was described by Don Diego de Palacios, although at the time nobody showed much interest. It wasn't until the nineteenth century that the world began to take notice, when John Lloyd Stephens published an account of it, complete with superb illustrations by Frederick Catherwood. Stephens was at the time acting as the American ambassador to Central America, but as he could find no stable government he spent most of his time in search of ancient ruins. He managed to buy the ruins of Copán, planning to chop the site up and transport it to the States:

The reader is perhaps curious to know how old cities sell in Central America. Like other articles of trade, they are regulated by the quality and by the quantity in the market, and the demand; but, not being staple articles, like cotton and indigo, they were held at fancy prices and at that time were dull of sale. I paid fifty dollars for Copán. There was never any difficulty about the price. I offered the sum for which Don Jose María thought me only a fool; if I had offered more, he would probably have considered me something worse.

John Lloyd Stephens (1834).

These days the site is in the Honduran government's hands, but US money is still very much involved. The first scientific exploration of the site was carried out between 1891 and 1894 by the Peabody Museum of Harvard, and the next major investigation by the Carnegie Institute in Washington. This second project, which began in 1935, involved the diversion of the Río Copán, which was carving into the site. Finally, the Hondurans themselves have got their hands in, and the ruins are now being studied by the *Instituto Hondureño de Antropología y Historia*.

The ruins

Before setting off for the ruins, make sure to visit the site **museum** (daily 8am–noon & 1–4pm; joint ticket for museum, ruins, and site of Las Sepulturas $6), on the village's main plaza. Here you'll see some of the miscellaneous bits and pieces unearthed from the ruins, as well as some of the larger pieces from outlying areas. There's some fantastic carving, as well as jade, obsidian, ceramics and human skulls, the main marker from the ball court and a replica of Stela B. **The ruins** themselves (daily 8am–4pm) are a few kilometres from the village, and the walk between the two takes you past some interesting stelae. If you stick to the path – on the left-hand side of the road – you'll get a better view of these, just a brief taster to whet your appetite for things to come.

At the entrance to the site there's a **visitors' centre**, where you buy your ticket, a small cafeteria, and an exhibition that includes photographs of the reconstruction work and a model of the city as it once was. Be sure, also, to visit the new **exhibition hall** containing many of the finest sculptural originals from Copán, as well as the magnificent life-size replica of the Rosalila temple, only discovered in 1989. From here you have to walk a couple of hundred metres further to the tall fence that surrounds the ruins, and a gate guarded by two superb macaws. Once inside you can either walk straight ahead and into the Great Plaza, or bear off to the right and approach it via an indirect route. This second approach is recommended, as it takes you through the East and West courts, saving the splendours of the plaza till last.

The East and West Courts

When you head to the right you'll arrive first in the **West Court**, a small, confined area that forms part of the main acropolis. The most famous feature here is **Altar Q**, at the base of Pyramid 16. The Altar was carved in 776 AD, and was originally thought to have been connected with the lunar cycle. Recent studies, however,

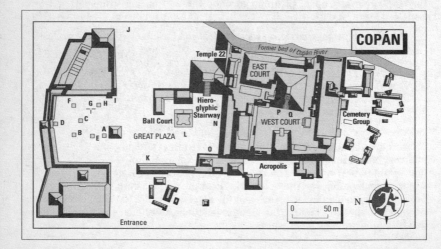

have suggested that it was dedicated to the young ruler Yax Pac (also known as New-Sun-at-Horizon), celebrating his ascension on July 2 ,763 AD. The top of the altar is carved with six hieroglyphic blocks, while its sides are decorated with sixteen cross-legged figures, all seated on cushions. For a long time the significance of all this remained a mystery, but in recent years archeologists have come up with a coherent theory. All the figures, who represent previous rulers of Copán, are pointing towards a portrait of Yax Pac, who is receiving a ceremonial staff from Mah K'ina Yax K'uk Mo, the city's first

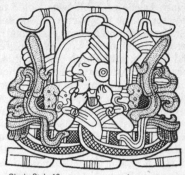

Glyph, Stela 19

ruler. The monument is therefore endorsing Yax Pac's right to rule, clear evidence of the importance of dynastic power structures. Behind this altar archeologists found a small **crypt** containing the remains of a macaw and fifteen big cats, possibly sacrificed in honour of Yax Pac and his ancestors.

In 1989, archeologists working on **Pyramid 16**, behind Altar Q, made the most exciting discovery of recent years: the uniquely undamaged facade of the **Rosalila Temple**, which appears to have been purposely buried intact within the structure you see today and has been hidden for over a thousand centuries. It was usual for the Maya to ritually deface or destroy their obsolete temples or stelae, yet with this one they took great care not to destroy the hand-modelled stucco sculptures that adorned it, making it possible to build a precise replica, which you can see at the new exhibition centre. (The original is so sensitive that it will be re-sealed from the outside world once scientific work has been completed.) Little is known so far about Rosalila, but scientists believe it was a major centre for worship during the reign of Butz'Chan, Copán's eleventh ruler (578–628AD). His rule marked the apogee of 160 years of political, social and artistic growth, which made the construction of this magnificent monument possible. No doubt it was because of its unique significance that it was carefully preserved before burial within new buildings.

On the northern side of the court is a large terraced **viewing stand**, which is in fact one side of the Central Acropolis. Its panels are decorated with worn carvings and some odd-looking figures, including two monkey gods.

Climbing the stairs on the east side of the court, behind Altar Q, brings you into the **East Court**, larger than the West but still intimate compared to the main plaza. The sides of this court are more elaborate than those of the West Court, and standing in the central dip you're surrounded by austere carvings. The best of these are the great jaguar heads, each as large as a human, with small hollows in their eyes that would once have held pieces of jade or polished obsidian. In the middle of the staircase, flanked by the jaguars, is a rectangular Venus mask, also carved in superb deep relief.

At the southern end of the East Court is **Structure 18**, a small square building with carved panels – although the process of reconstruction has revealed one or two gaps in the sequence. The floor of this structure has been dug up to reveal a magnificent tomb, probably that of one of Copán's later rulers, Sun-at-Horizon. Unfortunately, by the time archeologists unearthed it the tomb was virtually empty, having probably been looted on a number of occasions. To the south of Structure 18 is the so-called **Cemetery Group**, once thought to have been a burial site, although current thinking has it marked out as a residential complex, possibly the home of Copán's ruling elite. As yet it remains hidden in the trees and little work has been done in this part of the site. Walking back from here towards the main part of the ruins, along the eastern edge of the court, you get a superb view over the Río Copán. Between here and the river there used to be another building, Temple 20, but this was swept away long ago, and the river has now been diverted to prevent any further damage to the site.

At the northernmost end of the court, separating it from the main plaza, is **Temple 22**, one of Copán's most impressive buildings. While some of the stonework is astonishingly simple, other sections, particularly around the door frames, are superbly intricate and decorated with outlandish carving. Above the doorway is the body of a double-headed snake, its heads resting on two figures which are in turn supported by skulls. At the corners of the temple are portraits of the long-nosed rain god Chaac, a favourite Maya deity. The quality of the carving on Temple 22 has led archeologists to suggest that the East Court may have been Copán's most important plaza. Such carving is unique in the southern Maya area, and even at Quiriguá carving of this quality is confined to stelae. Only in the Yucatán, at sites such as Kabáh and Chicanna, is there anything that can compare with this.

The Great Plaza

The Great Plaza, Copán's hallmark, sums up its finest features and peculiar architectural attributes. At the southern end of the plaza the **Hieroglyphic Court** is pressed up against the Central Acropolis. On one side is the **Temple of the Inscriptions**, a great towering stairway, and at its base is **Stela N**, another classic piece of Copán carving with portraits on the two main faces and glyphs down the sides. The Great Plaza is strewn with these stelae, all of them magnificently carved and most exceptionally well preserved. The depth of the relief has protected the nooks and crannies, and in some of these you can still see flakes of paint: originally the carvings and buildings would have been painted in a whole range of colours, but only the red seems to have survived. The style of carving is similar to that of Quiriguá, and at both sites the portraits of assorted rulers dominate the decoration, with surrounding glyphs giving details of events and dates from the period of their rule. Here at Copán most of the carving has yet to be decoded: **Stela J** is perhaps the most unusual, decorated in a kind of woven pattern which is found at only one other place in the entire Maya world, Quiriguá.

On the left-hand side of the Hieroglyphic Court is the famed **Hieroglyphic Stairway**, the most astonishing work of all. The stairway is made up of some 63 stone steps, and every block is carved to form part of the glyphic sequence – a total of between 1500 and 2200 glyphs. It forms the longest known Maya hieroglyphic text, but sadly the sequence is so jumbled that a complete interpretation is still a long way off. The easiest part to understand is the dates, and these range from 544 AD to 744 AD. At the base of the stairway is **Stela M**, which records a solar eclipse in 756 AD.

To the north of the Hieroglyphic Court, Copán's **Ball Court** is one of the few Maya courts that still has a paved floor. Again the entire plaza would once have been paved like this, and probably painted too. The court dates from 775 AD, and beneath it there are two previous versions. The rooms that line the sides of the court, overlooking the playing area, would probably have been used by priests and members of the elite as they observed the ritual of the game.

As for the rest of the plaza, its main appeal lies in the various stelae, Copán's greatest feature. The vivid quality of the carving remains wonderfully clear and the portraits still have an eerie presence to them. It is these carvings, above all else, that separate Copán from all other sites, and most represent 18 Rabbit, Copán's "King of the Arts" (Stelae A, B, C, D, F, H and 4 all represent the same ruler). **Stela A**, which dates from 731 AD, has incredibly deep carving, although much is now eroded. Its sides include a total of 52 glyphs, better preserved than the main faces. **Stela B** is one of the more controversial stones, with a figure that some see as oriental, supporting theories of mass migration from the east. **Stela C** (730 AD) is one the earliest stones to have faces on both sides, and like many of the central stelae it has an altar at its base, carved in the shape of a turtle. In fact, this stela represents two rulers: the one facing the turtle is 18 Rabbit's father, who lived well into his eighties (the turtle is a symbol of longevity), while the other is the young acceder to the throne. At the northern end of the plaza, **Stela D** depicts 18 Rabbit with long hair and a beard, a fashion that he may well have taken with him when he was captured by Cauac Sky, the ruler of Quiriguá, in 738 AD. There are other stelae and altars dotted around the main plaza, all of them following the same basic pattern, ranging from the fierce-looking **Stela F** to the faceless **Stela J**, entirely covered in glyphs.

Las Sepultras

The smaller site of Las Sepultras, a couple of kilometres to the northeast of the main group, has been the scene of much archeological interest in recent years. While nothing like as impressive as Copán itself, Las Sepultras is an interesting supplement, its simpler structures reflecting domestic life in Maya times. The site is thought to have been a residential ward and is made up of some forty residential compounds containing more than two hundred rooms, which would have been inhabited by members of Copán's nobility, while smaller compounds on the edge of the site are thought to have housed the young princes, concubines and servants. Recent excavations have also yielded some rubbish heaps, which contained sea shells, old obsidian knives and scraps of carbonized food, as well as some impressive graves containing the bodies of priests and nobles dating from between 900 BC and 450 AD.

The Bay Islands (Islas de la Bahía)

Just a day or so from Copán, the **Honduras Bay Islands**, perhaps the country's greatest attraction, make an ideal extension to a brief foray onto Honduran soil. Strung along the second largest barrier reef in the world, with clear, calm waters and abundant marine life, they are ideal destinations for cheap diving, swimming, sailing and fishing. There's plenty for less active types, too, who can sling a hammock and snooze in the shade, watching the magnificent sunsets that paint the broad skies with colours as vibrant as the coral below.

A string of underwater mountain peaks extending from the mainland Omoa ridge, the three main Bay Islands, along with more than sixty smaller cayes, sweep in a 125km curve along the coastline of Honduras. **Roatan** is the largest and most developed of the group. To the north, **Guanaja** hosts some wonderful

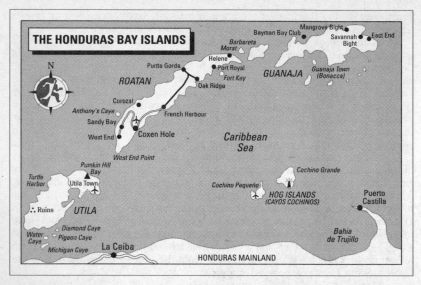

THE HONDURAS BAY ISLANDS

N

ROATAN

Punta Gorda
Port Royal
Helene
Barbareta
Morat
Bayman Bay Club
Mangrove Bight
Savannah Bight
East End

GUANAJA

Guanaja Town (Bonacca)
Fort Key
Oak Ridge
Corozal
Anthony's Caye
Sandy Bay
West End Coxen Hole
French Harbour

Caribbean Sea

West End Point
Pumkin Hill Bay
Turtle Harbor
Utila Town
∴ Ruins

UTILA

Cochino Grande
Cochino Pequeño
HOG ISLANDS
(CAYOS COCHINOS)

Puerto Castilla

Diamond Caye
Water Caye   *Pigeon Caye*
Michigan Caye La Ceiba

Bahia de Trujillo

HONDURAS MAINLAND

diving resorts, while to the south, **Utila**, the most affordable of the three, is a budget traveller's scuba diving dream.

The **Paya Indians** were the most likely first inhabitants of the Bay Islands, leaving behind ruins and fractions of ceramics. On his fourth journey to the Americas, **Columbus** landed on Guanaja on June 11, 1502, naming it "Isla de los Pinosi" (Pine Island), and the islands were half-heartedly colonized by the Spanish soon after. The swampy shores and shallow reef, impassable for big vessels, made serious settlement impossible, but in the seventeenth and eighteenth centuries provided perfect cover for **pirates** and buccaneers. The notorious pirate Captain Henry Morgan is said to be buried somewhere on Utila; his treasure from the raid on Panamá in 1671 remains undiscovered beneath Roatan.

After 1821 came an influx from the Cayman Islands, who settled on Utila, building the distinctive houses that stand on stilts, out of the range of disease-carrying insects. The islands were governed from 1852 by the British, who, much to the dismay of the locals, turned them over to Honduras because of pressure from North America, who feared British expansion. However, the islands remained culturally separate from the mainland, holding onto their language – English – and unique traditions. Even today, although Spanish is spoken in the schools and government offices, and is spreading further as growing numbers of mainlanders come in search of work, the language on the street is **English**, with a broadened and unique Creole-like accent. As in most of Central America, **religion** plays a significant role on the islands, with a large Catholic population and a considerable number of Seventh Day Adventists.

The **best time to visit**, weather-wise, is from March to May. May to November is very hot, December to February rainy, and July through October is hurricane season. The water visibility is best from February to September. Watch out for mosquitoes and **sandflies**, merciless vampires both; garlic pills and brewer's yeast are said to help prevention, while if you do get attacked, rubbing alcohol and lime juice stops the inflammation.

CHOOSE ECO-FRIENDLY

Though foreign travellers delight in the fact that they can live in bliss for $5–10 a day on the Honduras Bay Islands, life for the locals is not quite so sweet. With an **economy** in steady decline, the increasing shift towards tourism has resulted in some serious growing pains. Numbers of **lobster**, traditionally one of the best sources of income, are depleting rapidly, and an average fisherman may use up to eight tanks in one day diving deeper and deeper to find them, risking potentially fatal decompression sickness. One way for visitors to help is not to accept lobster under the legal size of 4oz in restaurants and stores. It's also a good idea to support locally owned businesses and take special care not to leave litter. It helps to bring a water purifier instead of repeatedly buying plastic jugs, and ease up on using unnecessary plastic bags. Waste facilities are hardly sophisticated, and most things go straight into the water.

Getting to the Bay Islands

You can reach all the islands from the coastal city of **La Ceiba**, 32km from Utila, which has an airport and boat dock. From **Belize**, Carlos Reyes leaves by boat from Dangriga every Saturday morning to **Puerto Cortez**, Honduras (3hr; see p.414). Once you reach Puerto Cortez, get your entrance stamp and catch a bus 57km (45min) south to San Pedro Sula. A more expensive option is to catch a **plane** from Belize City, transferring once or twice before landing in La Ceiba.

If you want to save some hassle and make it to La Ceiba or the islands in one day, catch the 4am or 5am express bus from **Copán** to San Pedro Sula and from there walk about five blocks to the *Tupsa* station on 2 Av, 5/6 C. Here you can catch the next bus to La Ceiba (hourly 5am–5pm; 3-4hr). The luxury buses usually cost the same as the public "chicken" buses, but they are few and far between, so keep your eyes open or ask around.

The bus drops you off in Central Park, where a taxi (around $2.50) can take you to the **boat dock**. The boat trip should cost around $6 to Utila or $7.50 to Roatan each way. **Flights** to Utila need to be booked in advance.

La Ceiba itself isn't a bad place to stay, especially if you want luxury at low prices. The *Hotel Tropical* (③) has air conditioned rooms, private bath and cable TV; five blocks away, the *Palace* Chinese restaurant offers huge portions and excellent vegetarian meals. There are lots of good bars and clubs on the seafront.

Utila

Utila is famed for its multitude of **scuba diving** facilities – more than ten dive schools teaching in up to eight languages – and for having some of the cheapest diving in the world. Even old-hands get excited about the waters here, where lizard fish and toadfish dart by, scarcely distinguishable from the coral; eaglerays glide through the water like huge birds flying through the air; tetchy damselfish get in your face if you invade their territory, and parrotfish chomp steadily away on the coral. Meanwhile, barracuda and nurse sharks circle the waters, checking you out from a distance.

Utila is the **cheapest** of the Bay islands, with the cost of living only slightly more than that of the mainland, and about the same as that of Guatemala. Life seems carefree, but there are some basic **laws** everyone should follow. Although there are only two police officers to enforce them, don't be fooled into complacency. Either of them can give a hefty fine or even jail you if they so feel the urge. Prohibited activities include walking the streets in a bathing suit, riding a bicycle at night without a light, and, because so many people walk around barefoot, drinking from glass bottles (especially beer bottles) on the street. Though most people on Utila are used to seeing travellers and their curious attire, as in most Central American countries, it is more polite to wear long trousers and dresses.

Arrival, orientation and getting around

Immediately upon getting off the boat or plane, you will be greeted by different dive school representatives offering free detailed **maps** of the island, which are useful to help orient yourself for the first couple of days. Competition between the schools is stiff, which can be to your advantage: many of them offer free accommodation in particular guest houses if you sign up for their courses – ask around when you arrive before heading off to look for a room.

The island's small population is concentrated on one coastal strip in the east, and there are just two **paved roads**. The **main strip**, which ribbons along the coast, has three names: **the Point** by the airport; **Sandy Bay** towards Blue Bayou, and **the Center**, by the public dock. From the crossroads here, by the bank, **Cola de Mico St** heads inland. **Bicycles** can be rented for about $3 a day at *Mermaids* restaurant, or next to the *Casino* bar.

Information

The *Green House* travel shop across from *Orma's* restaurant offers **tourist information** and a good book exchange; for an insight into local culture and goings-on, pick up a copy of the monthly *Utila Times*. The **post office** (Mon, Wed & Fri 8am–4pm, Tues & Thurs 8am–5pm, Sat 8am–noon), *Hondutel* telephone and fax service (Mon–Fri 8am–5pm, Sat 8am–noon) and the **police station** are all near each other on the left side of the road near the public dock, a short walk past *Henderson's* grocery store. To **change money**, head for the *Banchasa* in front of the public dock (Mon–Fri 8–11.30am & 1.30–4pm, Sat 8–11.30am), though note that *Henderson's* offers a better exchange rate for US money. There's an 8 percent tax in many places when you use a credit card; the nearest place for credit card encashments is La Ceiba. Many visitors to Utila come down with ear infections and mosquito bite infections; if you are afflicted, make for the **clinic** just down from the post office, heading towards the Blue Bayou on the right.

Most **stores** open at 7am, before the dive boats go out at 8am. Almost everything except for the restaurants closes by noon, and doesn't open again until 1.30 or 2pm. The one exception is the *7–11*, across the street from *Hondutel*, which is open at lunchtime, on Sunday and until 10pm.

Accommodation

Though Utila has more than 25 affordable guest houses and hotels, and a profusion of "rooms for rent", they fill up fast especially at Christmas and Easter. Luckily, everywhere is within walking distance of the public dock and airstrip. It's easy to spend longer than you've planned here: the good news is that most places give a hearty **discount** by the month, and **apartments** are available for as low as $50 a month. There are very few places to **camp** except on the cayes.

Despite interminable plans to instal 24hr **power**, the main generator for the island usually turns off at midnight and restarts at 5am, sporadically cutting out during the day. Many places have their own generators; ask before paying for a room.

FROM THE PUBLIC BOAT DOCK TO THE AIRPORT

Coopers Inn. Clean rooms with fans, 24hr power, and shared bath. The pizza restaurant has a few Danish choices. ②.

Rubi's Inn, beyond *Mermaids* restaurant (☎504/453240). Relaxing place with 24hr power, porch, and sunset views. The extremely helpful owners can do laundry, rent bicycles, and give local information. Eight rooms with fans and one clean, shared bathroom; eight more are planned, with fans, TV and private bath. Hugely popular; try to call in advance. ②–③.

Sharkey's Cabins, behind *Sharkey's Restaurant*, next to the airport. A/c rooms with table, chairs, two big beds, bath, and deck overlooking the lagoon. Good value; 24hr power. ⑤.

Trudy's Hotel, 5min from airport. Spacious rooms plus a restaurant, sun-bathing area, small alcove for swimming, and porch swings under the shade. 24hr power and fans. ③.

STRAIGHT FROM THE PUBLIC DOCK

Blueberry Hill, across from *Thompson's Bakery*, past *Las Delicias*. Owned by friendly couple Will and Norma. Very inexpensive, with basic, not particularly clean cabins. Although a couple of them have cooking facilities, there's no 24hr power, and just one shared bath. ①–②.

Countryside Inn, at the end of the road, turn left and then right at the sign. A 15 to 20min walk from town; not advisable during the wet season. Spacious, clean place in the shade of the trees with 24hr power, cooking facilities, TV, and a bit of peace and quiet. ②.

Monkey's Tail. Probably the cheapest on the island, and really rough. Absolutely no extras, just a safe place with a roof to bed down for the night. ①.

LEFT OF THE PUBLIC DOCK

Seaside Inn, past the big brown abandoned hotel on the hill and across from *Gunter's Dive School*. Good value, but a bit of a walk. Comfortable rooms with shared bath. Fans, 24hr power, and a restaurant with TV and good breakfasts. ②.

The Underground Hotel, past *Paradise Divers* on the left. Five doubles with fans and shared bathrooms; 24hr power, a comfortable living room, and a porch overlooking the town. Occasionally stuffy, this is a great place to meet people and relax; owner "Mamma" (Mrs Decker) looks out for you and cooks hearty meals in the restaurant. She's happy to cater to vegetarians, and will add garlic upon request (the locals don't much like it). ②.

Diving

Diving is the main activity on Utila, where the water temperature stays around 27°C and beautifully calm. Coral is still abundant, especially the regal pillar coral and sponges. You'll see lots of marine life, too: the parrotfish are huge, and there are a fair amount of (non-threatening) nurse sharks, sea turtles and rays. At night the water lights up with **phosphorescence**; shake your hand in the water to see tiny particles glow green. If all this inspires you to try your hand at a little **underwater photography**, Chris Phillips at *Utila Dive Center* rents underwater cameras for $25; film, classes, and developing are also available.

A standard 3–5 day **PADI course** costs roughly US$140, usually free lodging and extra dives. Most schools also offer free snorkel gear if you dive with them. When shopping around, make sure the certificate is included in the price. Anyone with **asthma** or ear problems will not be able to dive.

Utila is neither renowned for its **safety precautions** nor its experienced dive masters, and there have been several – avoidable – diving accidents in the last few years. When choosing a school, make sure that you get along with and understand your instructor. Check the equipment and boats, and ensure that every boat has working oxygen, a radio and medic first aid kit on board. *BICA* (The Bay Islands Conservation Association) next door to *Mermaids* restaurant, offer comprehensive **diving insurance** for $2 a day. Half the proceeds go towards local conservation programmes. After starting your course, make sure the instructor gives a clear rundown of the buddy check system. And lastly, if you do feel uneasy about any part of the operation, don't hesitate to say so.

It is also important that instructors insist that pupils do not touch the coral. Almost everything you see under water is alive, and it's up to each diver to protect the marine ecosystem. For more on reef etiquette, see Belize.

Swimming and snorkelling

Swimming in the water around Utila can be a bit of a hassle. Rather than jumping off any dock on the island, best head to **Blue Bayou**, a thirty-minute walk from town, where you can bathe in chest deep water and **snorkel** further out. Hammocks are slung in the shade of coconut trees and there's a food stand selling burgers and beers; snorkelling gear is also available. The views are particularly breathtaking at sunset, but watch out for the sandflies.

The best coral within swimming distance of the bay is just beyond the little **lighthouse**. The reef here hosts many schools of Blue Tang, Sergeant-Major Damselfish and Ocean Surgeon fish, along with sea cucumbers and mountainous coral. Novice swimmers, however, would do better at the shallower Blue Bayou.

Another short walk (about 25min) from the centre of the island, **Pumpkin Hill** is a beautiful display of lava rocks surrounded by a small rocky beach with waves crashing all around. The look-out tower on top of the hill gives great views of the island. There is beautiful snorkelling beyond the beach, and several **underwater caves** and cliffs. Cave diving is dangerous, however, so don't go deep inside, and don't go alone; recently a snorkeller died after getting lodged into a hole while trying to come up for air. Spiny sea urchins abound, too, so protect your feet. To get to Pumpkin Hill, walk down the street headed inland past the *Bucket of Blood* bar, and straight down the narrow sidewalk where the road splits. The trip is not advisable in the wet season, even with a bicycle.

Cayes around Utila

Most of the pretty **cayes** dotted around Utila are privately owned, and few permit camping or offer accommodation. Boats ($5 per person return trip for more than four people) can get you to **Water Caye**, a soft white sand island where coconuts crash down from the trees and the reefs are completely unharmed by tourism. There's nothing here but palm trees, sand, coconuts and you; bring all food, equipment for a camp fire and water. Someone will come by each day to collect $1 for use of the island, plus another $1 if you want to rent a hammock. There are full moon parties here every month, and best of all, no sandflies.

The fishing port for Utila, the nearby **Pigeon Caye** is crowded in comparison. You can buy groceries and wonderfully cheap fresh fish here to take to Water Caye or back to Utila. *Paradise Dive School* offers **day-trips** to Pigeon Caye every Sunday; the fee includes two dives, snorkelling, lunch and billiards. There's nowhere to stay on the island and camping is not allowed.

Eating

Honduran **cuisine** consists of bland, oily or heavy creamed starches with well-cooked meats, *tortillas* and rice and beans. Coconut is often used instead of regular oil or milk, giving it a distinctive Caribbean flavour. **Service** often takes a while, so allow plenty of time and maybe bring a deck of cards.

For **snacks**, head across the street from the bank to the "*baleada* women" who each night set up their stands and dish out steaming tasty *baleadas* (flour tortillas with beans, cheese, and onions) for less than 50¢.

Bahía del Mar, or "Captain Roy's", next to the airport. Good vegetarian dishes, whole fish dinners (including eyeballs) and pizza. Big *licuados*, and very thick hot chocolate.

The Bakery House, across from *Rubi's Inn*. Eva makes the best cinnamon rolls on the island, not to mention johnny cakes (biscuits) and special sweets.

Blue Kangaroo, or "Dorothy's", on the public dock. Local food; conch fritters are a speciality, and there's a big BBQ plate every Tuesday night. The atmosphere and conversations with Dorothy and the locals make dining here a great experience.

Island Cafe. Very tasty food, with daily specials and fast service. Portions are large; especially good seasoned fish. The eating area is outside on the deck, but you go inside to order.

Jade Seahorse, opposite the *Bucket of Blood* bar. Best and biggest *licuados* on the island, along with great snacks and breakfasts: tropical fruits with granola, honey, peanut butter, or chocolate; peanut butter pancakes; vegetarian *burritos*, and the like.

The News Cafe. Tasty European lunches including quiche, soups and pasta salads. The only place on the island for espresso and a hot pot of tea. Non-locally owned.

Seven Seas Restaurant. Casual, inexpensive, local food plus cheap beer. A good place for lunch after a dive.

Sharkey's, near the airport. A bit more expensive than the other places, but worth it for wonderful gourmet San Francisco cooking. Three nightly specials, including a vegetarian choice. Dinner only, with full bar and dance area. Closed Mon and Tues. Non-locally owned.

Thompson's Bakery. Popular place to hang out, read, drink coffee and meet other travellers; good inexpensive breakfasts, with different baked goods daily. The book exchange here is crammed with paperback romances. Open 6am–noon.

The Underground Restaurant, past *Paradise Divers* and *Henderson's*. Small restaurant serving hearty portions at good prices, with the usual Honduran cuisine, daily specials, vegetarian options, and excellent spiced ice tea. Service is usually very fast.

Drinking and nightlife

The big **party nights** on Utila are Tuesday and Saturday, starting at the *Seabreakers,* behind *Orma's* restaurant, for drinks in a bamboo bar built over the water. From there it's a short walk down the road to the *07 Salon* for free rum-lime punch (10–11pm). There's a big dance floor pounding with disco and hip-hop, or you can just hang out at the tables outside in the cool night air until 3am. On Saturday, locals rage out at the *Casino* bar to hard, synthesized reggae with a dash of salsa and merengue. It's always crowded and steaming hot, but great fun to watch, and there are several food stands next to the bar for late cheap snacks. During the **rest of the week**, a popular place for cheap beer and drinks is *Las Delicias*, opposite *Thompson's Bakery*. The *News Cafe*, next to the *Cross Creek Dive School* shows different classic cult **movies** each night on a big screen TV.

Billiards is a national sport in Honduras, and the Bay Islands are no exception. On Utila, the biggest pool hall, *YiYo*, is alongside the *Bucket of Blood* bar, down a narrow path behind a house. There's another, the *Sandy Bay* pool hall, across from the *Bayview* hotel. Both places tend to be filled with hard-playing locals who can usually run the table within two turns. Gambling is not advisable.

Leaving Utila
Leaving Utila, The *MC Starfish* and *Tonia C II* leave for La Ceiba every Monday at 4am and 5am, returning on Tuesday. Ask at the *Green Ribbon* grocery store at the point, or locals around the public dock for more information on unscheduled boats. If you've stayed longer than planned and need to **extend your passport stamp,** simply give your passport to Archie at *Henderson's* grocery store on Sunday; he'll take it into La Ceiba and get you stamped for another month for a total cost of $3.50.

The Hog Islands (Cayos Cochinos)

The **Hog Islands**, set in emerald waters 17km northeast of La Ceiba, comprise two small islands – **Cochino Grande** and **Cochino Pequeño** – and thirteen palm-fringed **cayes**. All are privately owned and see few tourists, but it's well worth making the effort to get out here. With a vast expanse of unexplored reef, the entire area is a **marine reserve**, maintaining the coral and fish in its natural state. On land the hills are studded with hardwood forests, palms and cactus.

Cochino Grande can be explored by foot; there's a Garifuna village and school on the east side, and a lighthouse where you can search for giant iguanas and watch incredible sunsets. There is an abundance of fish and turtles on the north side of the island, and shallow reefs close to shore. **Staying** in Paradise doesn't come cheap, however: the one resort, *Plantation Beach Resort* costs more than US$800 per week, including three buffet meals, three boat dives and unlimited shore diving daily (☎1-800/628-3723 in the US; ☎420974 in Honduras).

The most easily accessible **caye** is Chachahuate. Garifuna fishermen have been living here for centuries and for a small charge they allow a few travellers to sling hammocks, camp, or rent huts. Life is extremely basic: there's no electricity, and the diet consists of fried fish, rice and beans, along with warm sodas and beers (ice is imported almost daily); try to bring supplies with you.

There is nowhere to rent snorkel equipment on the Hog Islands.

Getting to the Hog Islands
The easiest way to **get to the Hog Islands** is to take a direct **bus** from **La Ceiba** to Nueva Armenia (daily except Sun, 9am & noon). You could also hop on any bus to Trujillo, Tocoa, Sonaguera, or Olanchito, alighting at Jutiapa and hitching to Nueva Armenia. It takes nearly three hours to walk. There are no hotels in Nueva Armenia, but you may be able to sling a hammock before hitching a ride the next morning on one of the many **boats** that set off for the cayes (around $1.50). Charter boats cost almost $12, and prices go up on Sunday.

Roatan

Some 50km from La Ceiba, **Roatan** is the largest of the Bay Islands, more than 40km long, and about 3km wide. Accommodation is geared towards wealthy vacationers looking for a week of island bliss, doing anything from scuba diving to nature hiking in the hardwood forests. **Coxen Hole** is the commercial centre, while **West End** is the place to head for absolute relaxation. The sandflies are worse here than on Utila, but not quite as bad as on Guanaja.

Roatan is another splendid **diving** destination, and though rates are higher than at Utila, they seem much more safety conscious and professional here; there is a recompression chamber at *Anthony's* in Sandy Bay. The four dive schools in West End offer fun dives for $25 a tank; a PADI course costs between $150 and $200. The *Cornerstone Emergency Medical Service* (☎ and fax 451515; radio channel #26) treat dive emergencies 24 hours a day.

Getting to and around Roatan

Roatan is easily accessible: **cargo boats** from Utila, Guanaja or La Ceiba include the *Utila Express*, *Tonia C II*, and *Utila Tom*. Roatan's new airport greets frequent international **flights** and services from La Ceiba.

There is a **paved road** from West End to just past French Harbour, where the road continues, unpaved, to Oak Ridge and Punta Gorda. **Taxis** and **minibuses** round the island set off from the front of *HB Warren* grocery store in Coxen Hole, but if you really want to explore, you'll need to **rent a car or motorbike**. There's a rental place at the airport, and you can rent jeeps for $45 per day in Sandy Bay.

Coxen Hole

The capital of the Bay Islands, **Coxen Hole** (aka Roatan Town) is where the boats dock and the planes land; it's also the site of immigration, customs, the law courts for all the islands, and most of Roatan's hotels. The two main roads are **Back St**, which runs along the water, and **Ticket St**, which goes to West End.

There are **banks** on almost every corner, plus branches in Oak Ridge and French Harbour, and a *Hondutel* (Mon–Sat 7am–9pm) at the end of the path behind *Banchasa*. The island **hospital** (24hr) is on Ticket St.

ACCOMMODATION

Although Coxen Hole has a good choice of **places to stay**, some of the cheapest hotels have occasional water shortages and filthy bathrooms; ask to see your room before you decide on where to stay.

Airportview Hotel. Large rooms, some with air-conditioning; very convenient if you have to catch an early flight. ③–④.

Hotel Cayview, Back St (☎451202). Extremely stylish, with air-conditioning, private bath, hot water, cable TV, sun deck, restaurant and laundry. Special fishing trips available. ④–⑤.

Hotel Coral. Double rooms with fans, and one communal bath. Popular among Peace Corps volunteers. ②.

RESTAURANTS AND NIGHTLIFE

There are plenty of cheap **places to eat** in Coxen Hole, and a number of stores selling provisions. As for **nightlife**, people from all over the island hit Coxen Hole at the weekend to drink and dance. *Paragua's* and *Harborview* are both informal and rarely charge a cover. After midnight they're sweat holes, so dress light.

HB Warren grocery store, centre of Coxen Hole. Eat burgers, salads, and chicken on stools at the cafe counter; not that cheap, but quick.

K & J Restaurant, across the street from the boat dock. Good, hearty and cheap home cooking: stewed chicken and red beans and rice, or fish, of course.

The **Roatan Express Mart**, a few paces from the boat dock. A clone of a US gas station, with hot dogs on the roaster, popcorn in the machine, and marshmallow pies on the counter. Junk food heaven with a spark of nostalgia.

Sandy Bay

Midway between Coxen Hole and West End, the **Sandy Bay Marine Reserve** aids in the conservation of the reef ecosystem. Across from *Anthony's Key Resort*, nature trails weave through the jungle to the **Cambola Botanical Gardens** (daily 8am–4pm), a riot of beautiful flowers, lush ferns and tropical trees. A twenty-minute walk from the gardens to the top of Monte Carambola brings you to a nursery for iguanas and parrots. The **Institute for Marine Sciences** next to *Anthony's* offers seven dolphin shows (daily except Wed 8.30am–6pm; $2) and a museum with educational displays on the dolphins and coral and a few Paya artefacts.

ACCOMMODATION AND EATING

There are few **places to stay** in Sandy Bay unless you want to rent a house or possibly trade your first born to stay in the resorts. The best place to **eat** is *Kent's*, opposite the *Sunrise Resort.* .

Anthony's Key Resort (☎451003; fax 451140). Extremely luxurious resort, where you get treated like royalty and can snorkel with dolphins for $65 a pop. Diving packages $675 per week. ⑥.

The Bamboo Inn. Friendly place, with seven average rooms with fans. ④.

Beth's Hostel, on a footpath heading towards the beach. Two singles and two doubles with shared bath and a common sitting and kitchen area. Snorkel gear available, and discounts for volunteer organizations. Strictly no smoking. ③.

The Sandy Bay Seafood Restaurant and Mini Hotel, northeast of *Anthony's*. Three rooms with private bath, and good, fairly inexpensive food at the restaurant. ③.

West End

With its calm waters and incredible soft white beaches, **West End** makes the most of its ideal setting, gearing itself mainly towards travellers who can afford to pay that bit more for their own little slice of heaven. *Librería Casi Todo,* on the main street close to the paved road, has a great **book exchange**, along with details of boat **excursions** and local **information**. On weekends, they offer **sailing Spanish lessons** for $25 per day, which includes snorkel gear and drinks. There's an **Intertel** office (Mon–Sat 7am–7pm) inside the *Supertienda Chris* toward the east side of town. Just thirty minutes from the village by foot ($1.50 return trip on a skiff boat) brings you to a completely preserved and uninhabited **beach** and coral area, ideal for bathing, snorkelling, or simply lazing. The *West Point Restaurant* here serves great food.

ACCOMMODATION

Coconut Tree Hotel, where the paved road ends. Private, clean cabins with three double beds, hot water, fans and a refrigerator. Nice restaurant and mini-mart next door. ⑤–⑥.

Jimmy's Big Room, at the end of the road on the water. One room on high stilts filled with mattresses and mosquito nets; no privacy or luxury, but ideal for backpackers. There's a shower and bathroom outside, and a table and chairs beneath the room; its site, right on the sand in front of the water, affords wonderful sunset views. Jimmy offers free homemade repellent to deter the sandflies, and rents out horses and snorkel gear. ②.

Sam's, across the bridge after the wide road ends; turn left three houses down. Odd-shaped house with ten rooms, some with three beds. Stuffy and small, but with a working bathroom, and friendly owners. The cheapest option after *Jimmy's*. ②.

Seaview Hotel, on the east side of the main street. Basic, everyday rooms, with a good restaurant. Rates increase if you want a fan and little table. ③.

EATING

Cindy's Place. Picnic-like dining with healthy portions of inexpensive daily specials; the Saturday lunchtime barbecue costs $3.50.

The Coffee Stop. Breakfast on banana pancakes, omelettes and fresh-baked cookies. It's a bit pricey, but there's a relaxing atmosphere and comfortable chairs in the shade.

New York Pizza, *next to Jimmy's*. Good, reasonably priced pizzas plus burgers, fries and fish dinners. Best of all, however, is the volleyball net out front. There are ten high school volleyball teams on the island, so it isn't hard to spark up a game.

Salt and Pepper, signed, up the hill. Four or five courses of a different gourmet cuisine each night; the bill usually runs to about $9.

Stanley's Restaurant and bakery, up the hill from *Salt and Pepper*. Homemade local food, including excellent coconut bread with each meal.

Yoly's Pizza, on the main street. Tasty pizza topped with garlic and herbs. The patio at the front is a popular hangout at night. Not open every day.

DRINKING AND NIGHTLIFE

Drinking can drain your pocket fast in West End. Best seek out the half-price **happy hours** at many of the restaurants and bars; starting at around 4.30pm, many of them last until 10pm. A popular circuit starts at *Yoly's*, heading on to *Posada del Sol*, then ending at *New York Pizza*. Keep your eyes open, however, because hours do change. *Fosters and Vivians* bar, over the water, is a popular hangout at night, as is *Chino's* restaurant. There are also **movies** each evening at the *Bamboo Hut*. On Saturday nights there's a mass exodus to Coxen Hole.

Around the island

About 10km northeast of Coxen Hole, **French Harbour** is the second largest town in Roatan. This is where most of the island's money comes and goes – not from tourism, but from shrimp and lobster packaging. It's unlikely that you'll need to **stay** here, but if you're stuck, try the rock-bottom *Hotelito Brooks* (②).

Oak Ridge, another 10km or so north, is a quaint town of old wooden houses strung along the mainland and a caye. You can get to the caye by dory for 25¢. It's a little-touristed spot, with few places to **stay**; locals often rent out their spare rooms, and there's the *Hotel San Jose* (③), which has a good pizzeria and supermarket next door. North of Oak Ridge along an unpaved road, the Garifuna coastal village of **Punta Gorda** is the oldest established community on Roatan. To this day, the locals retain their own language, music, crafts, religion and food.

A three-hour walk from Oak Ridge, **Port Royal** is best known for the **Port Royal Park and Wildlife Reserve**, the largest refuge on the island, which protects the water supply and birds and mammals such as the opossum and agouti. Pirates loved the sheltered coast here, and you may well stumble across the forlorn remains of forts and shipwrecks on the beautiful beaches. There are no roads or public transport to Port Royal.

Guanaja

The easternmost Bay Island, **Guanaja** is the most beautiful, undeveloped and expensive of all the islands, designated a Marine National Park. There are actually two islands; the largest one boasts the highest point of the entire group

(428m), covered with Caribbean pine forest and hardwoods. More than 50km long, and about 6km wide, it's a stunning, untouched place, with lovely waterfalls and incredible views of sea and jungle; unfortunately, there are more sandflies here than on any of the other islands.

Six hundred metres away the tiny island of **Guanaja Town**, or "Bonacca", is the commercial centre and main residential area, with the bulk of the reasonably priced accommodation. All the houses here are built on stilts above the water – vestiges of early settlement by the Cayman islanders – and the only way to get around is by water taxi, which adds both to the atmosphere and to the cost of living.

Arrival and information

Guanaja airstrip, which is in the heart of the big island, next to the canal, is served by daily **flights** from the mainland. There are also several unscheduled **boat trips** a week from French Harbour on Roatan and La Ceiba, plus a few from Trujillo and rarely Utila. From the big island it is easy to catch a **water taxi** to the town; and there are collective boats from the pier at Savannah Bight, at the east end of the big island (daily 7am, 11am & 6pm; 60¢). You could also try hitching a free ride in the mornings from the big island to Guanaja Town, joining locals as they make their way to work. The *Capitania de Puerto*, on pier one across the street from the *Islena* office offers more information on unscheduled boat arrivals and departures.

You'll find most of the things you need on **Main St** in Guanaja Town, including *Banchasa* and *Banco Atlantida* (Mon–Fri 8.30am–4.30pm, with a ninety-minute break for lunch), and *Hondutel* (daily 7am–9pm). There's a **clinic** across the street from the Seventh Day Adventist church, but they don't treat minor illnesses at the weekend.

Accommodation

Budget travellers have little choice when it comes to staying on Guanaja; most people come here on pricey, all inclusive **packages** that include unlimited diving. Almost all the budget rooms are in the small, congested **Guanaja Town**, though the big island is developing fast. In Guanaja Town, just follow the street from the pier until it ends; the road going left to right is where you'll find most of the places to stay.

Airport Hilton, next to the airport on the big island. Three rooms with fans along the waterside; convenient if you have to catch a flight the next day. ③–④.

Hotel Alexander, Hog Caye. Twelve seafront rooms with private bath and satellite TV. If you want to spend a bit more, you can have air-conditioning; for a bit less you get a non-seafront room. You can go snorkelling right off the dock. ⑤.

Carter Hotel, left turn from the pier above the *Banco Atlantida*. Reasonable rooms with fans and private bath. ③.

George's Inn. The cheapest around, with three fairly hot and stuffy double rooms. ③.

Hotel Miller. Twenty clean rooms with ceiling fans and shared bath. Good, if quite pricey, restaurant on site, and snorkelling and BBQ trips to Southwest Caye. ④.

Hotel El Rosario. Five large modern rooms with ceiling fans and private bathroom; some have air-conditioning and cable TV. ④.

PACKAGES ON THE BIG ISLAND

Bayman Bay Club (☎454191 or 454179), on the northwest side of Guanaja. Sixteen cottages with balconies and ceiling fans, set in jungle overlooking the beach. The dock reaches all the way to the reef which makes for excellent shore diving. About $125 a day, including two boat dives, buffet meals, nature hikes, billiards, libraries and much more. The price decreases a bit the longer you stay.

Posada Del Sol (☎454311), on the south side of the island at the foot of the hills overlooking the sea. Twenty-three a/c rooms with high ceilings. Good dive sites all around, underwater photography, water skiing, deep sea fishing, tennis courts, exercise room and swimming pool; all included in the rate of $145 per day.

Around the big island

Marble Hill, on the northern side of the big island has great caves and beautiful beaches in almost complete seclusion; volcano and black rock **underwater caves** also abound. **Diving** is excellent on the southern shore, with clear water and intriguing natural formations such as caves, walls, and tunnels – there's even a cave entrance said to have been the hideout for nineteenth-century filibusterer William Walker during his ill-fated attempt to take over Honduras. You can get down to the *Jado Trader*, a huge ship wrecked in 1987, and lodged 28m below the surface. Diving can be difficult if you don't go through a resort package; if you want to do it independently, ask at the *Cafe Coral* in Guanaja Town, or the *Dive Freedom Dive Shop* (☎454180). You could also approach the resort dive boats to see if they can fit you in for a special price (usually around $25 per tank).

Fishing and **snorkelling** can be fixed with local fishermen and boatmen who charge around $10 to take you out on the water. In many areas, however, the reef is close enough to swim to if you have your own snorkel gear.

Eating, drinking and nightlife

There are several restaurants in **Guanaja Town**, although the truly gourmet experiences are reserved for the package resorts on the big island. Most places close around 9pm and are also closed on Saturday due to the large percentage of Seventh Day Adventists who don't work on the Sabbath. *Glenda's* has good food for around $3 a plate; locals gather here to listen to country music, drink beer, and watch sports on the TV. Nearby, *Cafe Coral* is the hangout for dive masters, some locals and foreign employees. *Cafe Fifi* across the street offers traditional cuisine for around $2.25 a plate, along with *Restaurant TKO* which is right of the main street from the pier.

The island's one **disco**, the *Mountain View*, has a huge dance floor surrounded by water and mountains. It really gets going on the weekends and there is no cover charge. Ignore the sign out front that says it is a private club; it's open to all (Tues–Thurs until midnight; Sat & Sun until 2am or 3am).

fiestas

JANUARY
El Progreso (near Jutiapa) kicks off the fiesta year in the eastern highlands. The action lasts from the 12th to 15th; the final day is the most important. **Cabañas** (near Zacapa) has a fiesta from the 19th to 21st, in honour of San Sebastian; the 19th is the main day. **Ipala**'s fiesta, which includes some traditional dances and bullfighting, is from the 20th to 26th: the 23rd is the main day. There's also the great pilgrimage to **Esquipulas** on the 15th.

FEBRUARY
San Pedro Pinula, one of the most traditional places in the east, has a fiesta from the 1st to 4th, in which the final day is the main one. **Monjas** has a fiesta from the 5th to 10th, with the 7th as the main day. **Río Hondo** (on the main road near

Zacapa) has its fiesta from the 24th to 28th; the 26th is the principal day. Both **Pasaco** (in the department of Jutiapa) and **Huite** (near Zacapa) have moveable fiestas around carnival time.

MARCH
Jerez (in the department of Jutiapa) has a fiesta in honour of San Nicolas Tolentino from the 3rd to 5th, with the last day as the main one. There's a smaller day of pilgrimage to the Black Christ of Esquipulas on the 9th. **Moyuta** (near Jutiapa) and **Olapa** (near Chiquimula) both have fiestas from the 12th to 15th. **Morales**, a town with little to celebrate but its lust for life, has a fiesta from the 15th to 21st, with the main day on the 19th. **Jocotán** (halfway between Chiquimula and El Florido) has a moveable fiesta in March.

APRIL
April is a quiet month in the east but **La Unión** (near Zacapa) has a fiesta from the 22nd to 25th.

MAY
Jalapa has its fiesta from the 2nd to 5th, with the 3rd the main day. **Gualán** (which is near Zacapa) has a fiesta from the 5th to 9th.

JUNE
The only June fiesta out this way is in **Usumatlán**, from the 23rd to 26th.

JULY
Puerto Barrios has its fiesta from the 16th to 22nd, with the main day on the 19th: this has

something of a reputation for its (enjoyably) wild celebrations. **Jocotán** (near Chiquimula) has its fiesta from the 22nd to 26th. **Esquipulas** has a fiesta in honour of Santiago Apostol from the 23rd to 27th.

AUGUST
Chiquimula has its fiesta from the 11th to 18th, with the main day on the 15th: sure to be a good one, this also includes bullfighting. Over on the other side of the highlands, **Asunción Mita** has a fiesta from the 12th to 15th. **San Luis Jilotepéque** has its one-day fiesta on the 25th.

SEPTEMBER
Sansare (between Jalapa and Sanarate) has its fiesta from the 22nd to 25th, with the 24th as the main day.

NOVEMBER
Sanarate celebrates from the 7th to 14th and **Jutiapa** from the 10th to 16th, with the middle day as the main day. **Quesada** (near Jutiapa) has a fiesta from the 26th to 30th.

DECEMBER
Zacapa has its fiesta from the 4th to 9th, with the main day on the 8th, and **San Luis Jilotepéque** from the 13th to 16th. **Cuilapa** goes wild from the 22nd to 27th, and **Lívingston** has a Caribbean carnival from the 24th to 31st: one of the best places in the country to spend Christmas.

travel details

Bus is the best way to get around the eastern highlands. For the northeastern area simply take a bus to either Puerto Barrios or Esquipulas, as these pass through all the main towns in between. To travel into the central highlands you need to catch a bus heading for Jutiapa, and change buses there.

BUSES
The Motagua valley
Buses for **Puerto Barrios** leave Guatemala City hourly from the terminal at 9 Av and 18 C in Zona 1. The very best of these, luxury pullmans, are run by

Litegua (5.30am–5pm), whose office is at 15 C 10–40. **From Puerto Barrios** there are buses to Guatemala City (1am–4pm) from their office on 6 Av, between 9 and 10 calles. The trip takes about 6hr and tickets can be bought in advance. All buses run past the entrance road for **Quiriguá**, about 4hr from Guatemala City, and virtually everywhere else along the way except **Morales** and **Bananera**: for these you can change at the **Ruidosa junction** where the road to Petén turns off.

From Puerto Barrios there are also buses to **Morales and Bananera** every hour or so; to **Esquipulas** during the morning, and to **Mariscos** at 3pm daily.

From Morales and Bananera there are regular buses and minibuses to **Río Dulce**, where you can pick up buses to Petén.

To Mariscos there's a direct bus from 18 C and 9 Av in Guatemala City at 6am, and one from Puerto Barrios at 3pm – you can also hitch to Mariscos from the **La Trinchera** junction on the main Caribbean Highway.

The eastern highlands

To Esquipulas regular pullman buses, run by *Rutas Orientales*, leave from 19 C and 9 Av in Zona 1, Guatemala City (every 30min; 4am–6pm). **Buses from Esquipulas** to Guatemala City (every 30min; 2am–8.30pm) call in at **Zacapa** and **Chiquimula**. If you're coming from Puerto Barrios or Petén and want to head out this way then you can pick up one of these at the **Río Hondo junction** on the Caribbean highway.

From Esquipulas there is also a regular flow of minibuses and buses to the borders with El Salvador and Honduras. There are also buses to **Jutiapa** and **Jalapa**, and during the morning to **Puerto Barrios**.

From Chiquimula there are buses (3/4 daily; 9am–3pm) to the **El Florido** border crossing, from where trucks and buses run to **Copán** in Honduras. There's also a regular service to **Ipala**, and on to **Jalapa** (6hr).

To Jutiapa there are buses every hour or so from the Zona 4 bus terminal in Guatemala City; most of them go on to **Asunción Mita** and **San Cristóbal Frontera** – the border with El Salvador. The last bus from the border to Guatemala City is at 2.30pm. All buses between Guatemala City and Jutiapa pass through **Cuilapa**, from where there are hourly buses to **Chiquimulilla**.

From Jutiapa there are buses to all parts of the eastern highlands, including **Esquipulas**, **Ipala** and **Jalapa**.

To San Salvador several companies run a direct service from Guatemala City via the **Valle Nuevo** border crossing (hourly; 8hr). Companies serving this route include *Mermex*, *Taca* and *Trascomer*. Their offices in the capital are all at the junction of 1 C and 5 Av in Zona 4. Or you can go by *Tica Bus*, whose office is at 11 C 2–38, Zona 9.

BOATS

From Puerto Barrios to Lívingston there's a daily ferry service at 10am and 5pm, returning at 5am and 2pm. A steady shuttle of speedboats opertate between Puerto Barrios and Lívingston, leaving when they are full.

From Puerto Barrios to Punta Gorda in **Belize** a boat leaves at 7am on Tues and Fri .

From Lívingston up the Río Dulce there's a mail boat on Tues and Fri.

From Mariscos to El Estor a ferry leaves daily at 1pm, returning at 6am.

CHAPTER FIVE

COBÁN AND THE VERAPACES

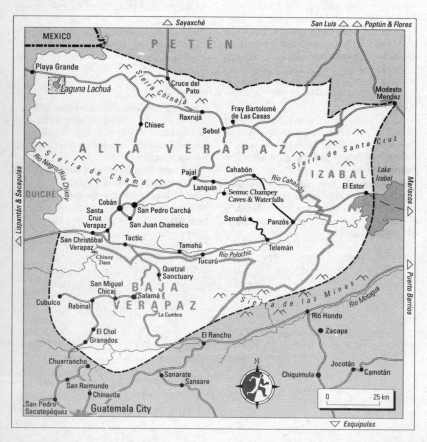

W hile essentially a continuation of Guatemala's western highlands, the mountains of Alta and Baja Verapaz have always been set apart in a number of ways: certainly, the flat-bottomed Salamá valley and the mist-soaked hills of Cobán are physically unlike any of the other mountainous areas. **Baja Verapaz**, the more southerly of these two departments, is sparsely populated, a mixture of deep river valleys, dry hills and lush tropical forest. A single road runs through the department, connecting the towns of **Salamá**, **Rabinal** and **Cubulco**, while the rest of the land is dotted with tiny hamlets. **Alta Verapaz**, the wettest and greenest of Guatemala's highlands, occupies the higher land to the north. Local people say it rains for thirteen months a year here, alternating between straightforward downpour and the drizzle of the *chipi-chipi*, a misty rain that hangs interminably on the hills, although the mountains are now being deforested at such a rate that weather patterns may soon be disrupted. For the moment, however, the area's tight, twisting hills remain almost permanently moist, coated in resplendent vegetation and vivid with greenery. The capital of Alta Verapaz is **Cobán**, from where roads head north into Petén, west to El Quiché, and east to Lake Izabal.

The **history** of the Verapaces is also quite distinct. Long before the Conquest local Achi Indians had earned themselves a unique reputation as the most bloodthirsty of all the tribes, said to sacrifice every prisoner that they took. Their greatest enemies were the Quiché, with whom they were at war for a century. So ferocious were the Achi that not even the Spanish could contain them by force. Alvarado's army was unable to make any headway against them, and eventually he gave up trying to control the area, naming it *tierra de guerra*, the "land of war".

The church, however, couldn't allow so many heathen souls to go to waste, and under the leadership of **Fray Bartolomé de Las Casas**, the so-called apostle of the Indians, they made a deal with the conquistadors. If Alvarado would agree to keep all armed men out of the area for five years, the priests would bring it under control. In 1537 Las Casas himself, accompanied by three other Dominican friars, set out into the highlands. Here they befriended the Achi chiefs, and learning the local dialects they translated devotional hymns and taught them to the bemused Indians. By 1538 they had made considerable progress, converting large numbers of Indians and persuading them to move from their scattered hillside homes to the new Spanish-style villages. At the end of the five years the famous and invincible Achi were transformed into Spanish subjects, and the king of Spain renamed the province *Verapaz*, "True Peace".

Since the colonial era the Verapaces have remained isolated and in many ways independent: all their trade bypassed the capital by taking a direct route to the Caribbean, along the Río Polochic and out through Lake Izabal. The area really started to develop with the **coffee boom** at the turn of the century, when German immigrants flooded into the country to buy and run *fincas*, particularly in Alta Verapaz. By 1914 about half of all Guatemalan coffee was grown on German-owned lands and Germany bought half of the exported produce. Around Cobán the new immigrants intermarried with local families and established an island of European sophistication. A railway was built along the Polochic valley and Alta Verapaz

MARKET DAYS IN THE VERAPACES	
Monday	**Saturday**
Senahú; Tucurú.	Senahú.
Tuesday	**Sunday**
Chisec; El Chol; Cubulco; Lanquín;	Chisec; Cubulco; Purulhá;
Purulhá; Rabinal; San Cristóbal	Rabinal; Salamá; San Jerónimo; Santa
Verapaz; San Jerónimo; Tres Cruces.	Cruz; Tactic.

became almost totally independent. This situation was brought to an end by World War II, when the Americans insisted that Guatemala do something about the enemy presence, and the government was forced to expel the landowners, many of whom were unashamed in their support for Hitler.

Although the Verapaces are now well connected to the capital and their economy integrated with the rest of the country, the area is still dependent on the production of coffee, and Cobán is still dominated by the huge coffee *fincas* and the wealthy families that own them. Here and there, too, hints of the Germanic influence survive. Taken as a whole, however, the Verapaces remain very much Indian country: Baja Verapaz has a small Quiché outpost around Rabinal, and in Alta Verapaz the Indian population, largely **Pokomchí** and **Kekchí** speakers, the two languages of the Pokoman group, is predominant. The production of coffee has cut deep into their land and their way of life, the *fincas* driving many people off prime territory to marginal plots. Traditional costume is worn less here than in the western highlands, and in its place many Indians have adopted a more universal Kekchí costume, using the loose hanging *huipile* and locally made *cortes*.

The northern section of Alta Verapaz includes a slice of Petén rainforest, and in recent years Kekchí Indians have fanned out into this empty expanse, reaching the Río Salinas in the west and making their way across the border into Belize. Here they carve out sections of the forest and attempt to farm, a process that threatens the future of the rainforest and offers little long-term security for the migrants.

Where to go

For visitors the Verapaces are less inviting than the western highlands, and far fewer tourists make it out this way. But if you've time and energy to spare then you'll find these highlands are astonishingly beautiful, with their unique limestone structure, moist, misty atmosphere and boundless fertility. The hub of the area is **Cobán**, nowadays subdued and somewhat miserable once the rain really settles in, but still the place from which to set out to explore and the starting point for several adventurous trips. In August it hosts the **National Folklore Festival**; in Baja Verapaz, the towns of **Salamá**, **Rabinal** and **Cubulco** also have famous fiestas. From Cubulco you can continue on foot, over the Sierra de Chuacús, to Joyabaj, a spectacular and exhausting hike.

Heading between the two departments, beside the main road, is the **quetzal sanctuary**, where you can occasionally see one of Central America's rarest birds, prized since the earliest of times. Heading out to the north of Cobán you can reach the beautiful **Semuc Champey**, a natural set of bathing pools surrounded by lush tropical forest. Cobán is also the starting point for three seldom-travelled back routes: east down the Río Polochic to **Lake Izabal**, north through Pajal to **Fray Bartolomé de Las Casas** and Sayaxché, or west to **Uspantán** for Santa Cruz del Quiché and Nebaj (or all the way across to Huehuetenango).

ACCOMMODATION PRICE CODES

All accommodation reviewed in the Guatemala section of this guide has been graded according to the following **price scales**. These refer to the cost of a double room in US$. For more details see p.28.

① Under $2	③ $5–10	⑥ $35–55
② $2–5	④ $10–20	⑦ Over $55
	⑤ $20–35	

Baja Verapaz

A strange but dramatic mix of dry hills and fertile valleys, Baja Verapaz is crossed by a skeletal road network, with only the towns of **Salamá**, **Rabinal** and **Cubulco** served by buses. All of these have interesting markets and are famed for their fiestas, where you'll see some unique traditional dances. The other big attraction is the **quetzal sanctuary**, set to one side of the main road to Cobán.

The main approach to both departments is from the Caribbean Highway, where the road to the highlands branches off at the **El Rancho** junction. As this road climbs steadily into the hills, the dusty browns and dry yellows of the Motagua valley soon give way to an explosion of greens, in dense pine forests that offer superb views. All too often, though, the mountains are shrouded in a blanket of cloud. Some 48km beyond the junction is **La Cumbre de Santa Elena**, where the road for the main towns of Baja Verapaz turns off to the west, immediately starting to drop towards the floor of the Salamá valley. Surrounded by steep hillsides, with a level flood plain at its base, the valley appears entirely cut off from the outside world.

Here at its eastern end is the village of **SAN JERÓNIMO**, which is bypassed by the road for Salamá. In the early days of the Conquest Dominican priests built a church and convent here and planted vineyards, eventually producing a wine that earned the village something of a reputation. In 1845, after the religious orders were abolished, an Englishman replaced the vines with sugar cane and began brewing an *aguardiente* that became equally famous. These days the area still produces cane, and a fair amount of alcohol, although the English connection is long gone. Minibuses connect Salamá and San Jerónimo, but there's no particular reason to visit the village unless you're exceptionally keen on *aguardiente*.

Salamá, Rabinal and Cubulco

At the western end of the valley is **SALAMÁ**, capital of the department of Baja Verapaz. The town has a relaxed and prosperous air, and like many of the places out this way its population is largely Latinized. There's not much to do, other than browse in the Sunday market, though a couple of things are worth a look. On the edge of town is a crumbling colonial bridge, now used only by pedestrians, and the old church is also interesting, with huge altars, darkened by age, running down either side. The **fiesta** in Salamá runs from September 17 to 21. If you decide **to stay**, the pick of the hotels is the *Hotel Tezulutlan* (④), a gorgeous old building with rooms set around a leafy courtyard that's also home to a pair of macaws. *Pensión Juarez* (②), a basic budget hotel up the end of 5 C, past the police station, is cheaper. Also in Salamá are a branch of the *Banco del Cafe* (Mon–Fri 9am–5pm, Sat 10am– 2pm) and a post office (Mon–Fri 8am–4.30pm).

Buses from Guatemala City to Salamá, Rabinal and Cubulco (hourly 5.30am–4pm) are operated by *Rutas Verapacenses,* departing from outside the train station in Zona 1, at 19 C and 9 Av. They return

Detail from Chixoy Valley vase

from Cubulco between 1am and 1.30pm. If you're only going as far as Salamá
there is a steady shuttle of minibuses to and from La Cumbre for connections
with pullman buses running between Cobán and Guatemala City.

To the west of Salamá the tarmac ends and a dirt track pushes on, climbing out
of the valley over a low pass and through a gap in the hills, to San Miguel Chicaj,
a small, traditional village clustered around a colonial church. Beyond here the
road climbs again, this time to a greater height, reaching a pass with magnificent
views across the surrounding hills, which step away into the distance.

An hour or so from Salamá you arrive in **RABINAL**, another isolated farming
town that's also dominated by a large colonial church. Here the proportion of
Indian inhabitants is considerably higher, making both the Sunday market and
the fiesta well worth a visit. Founded in 1537 by Bartolomé de Las Casas himself,
Rabinal was the first of the settlements in his peaceful conquest of the Achi
nation: about 3km northwest are the ruins of one of their fortified cities, known
locally as Cerro Cayup. Nowadays the place is best known for its oranges,
claimed to be the best in the country – and they certainly taste like it.

Rabinal's **fiesta**, January 19 to 25, is famous above all for its dances. The most
notorious of these, an extended dance drama known as the *Rabinal Achi*, was last
performed in 1856, but many other unique routines are still performed. The
patzca, for example, is a ceremony calling for good harvests, using masks that
portray a swelling below the jaw, and wooden sticks engraved with serpents, birds
and human heads. If you can't make it for the fiesta, the Sunday market is a good
second best. Rabinal has a reputation for producing high-quality *artesania*, including carvings made from the *arbol del morro*, the Calabash tree, and traditional
pottery. There are several fairly basic **hotels** in Rabinal, the best of which is the
Posada San Pablo (②), a superb budget hotel with spotless rooms. If you can't get
in there, try the *Hospedaje Caballeros* (②), or, as a last resort, the *Pensión
Montagua* (①), which is part of a rough *cantina*.

Leaving Rabinal the road heads on to the west, climbing yet another high ridge
with fantastic views to the left, into the uninhabited mountain ranges. To the
north, in one of the deep river valleys, is the Chixoy hydroelectric plant, where
over three-quarters of Guatemala's electricity is generated.

Another hour of rough road brings you down into the next valley and to
CUBULCO, an isolated, Latinized town, surrounded on all sides by steep,
forested mountains. Cubulco is again best visited for its fiesta, this being one of
the few places where you can still see the *Palo Volador*, a pre-conquest ritual in
which men throw themselves from a thirty-metre pole with a rope tied around
their legs, spinning down towards the ground as the rope unravels, and hopefully
landing on their feet. It's as dangerous as it looks, particularly when you bear in
mind that most of the dancers are blind drunk: in 1988 an inebriated dancer fell
from the top of the pole, killing himself. The fiesta still goes on, though, as
riotous as ever, with the main action taking place on January 23. The best place to
stay is in the large *Farmacía* (①) in the centre of town, and there are several
good *comedores* in the market.

On from Cubulco: the back routes

If you'd rather not leave the valley the same way that you arrived, there are two
other options. One bus a day, leaving Cubulco at 9am, heads back to Rabinal and
then, instead of heading for La Cumbre and the main road, turns to the south,

crossing the spine of the Sierra de Chuacús and dropping directly down towards Guatemala City. The trip takes you over rough roads for around nine hours, through El Chol, Granados and San Juan Sacatepéquez, but the mountain views and the sense of leaving the beaten track help to take the pain out of it all.

Hiking from Cubulco to Joyabaj

If you'd rather leave the roads altogether, an even less travelled route takes you out of the valley on foot, also over the Sierra de Chuacús, to Joyabaj. The hike takes between eight and ten hours, but if you have a tent it's probably best to break the trip halfway at the village of **TRES CRUCES** (if you don't have one you'll probably be able to find a floor to sleep on). The views, as you tramp over a huge ridge and through a mixture of pine forest and farmland, are spectacular.

The hills around Cubulco are covered in a complex network of paths so it's worth getting someone to point you in the right direction, and asking plenty of people along the way – for the first half of the walk it's better to ask for Tres Cruces rather than Joyabaj. Broadly speaking the path bears up to the right as it climbs the hillside to the south of Cubulco, crossing the mountain range after about three hours. On the other side is an open, bowl-shaped valley, where to reach Tres Cruces you walk along the top of the ridge that marks the right-hand side of the valley – heading south from the pass. Don't drop down into the valley until you reach Tres Cruces. The village itself is the smallest of rural hamlets, perched high on the spine of the ridge, and far from the reach of the nearest road. On Thursday mornings the tiny plaza is crammed with traders who assemble for the market, but otherwise there's nothing but a couple of simple *tiendas*. Beyond Tres Cruces you drop down into the valley that cuts in to the right (west) of the ridge, and then follow the dirt road out of the valley, onto the larger Joyabaj to Pachalum road – turn right for Joyabaj (p.118).

Towards Alta Verapaz: the quetzal sanctuary

Heading for Cobán, and deeper into the highlands, the main road sweeps straight past the turning for Salamá and on around endless tight curves below forested hillsides. Just before the village of Purulhá is the **biotopo del quetzal** (daily 6am–4pm), a 1153-hectare nature reserve designed to protect the habitat of the endangered quetzal. The reserve is a steep and dense rainforest, through which the Río Colorado cascades towards the valley floor.

Visiting the reserve

Paths through the undergrowth from the road complete a circuit that takes you up into the woods and around above the reserve headquarters. There are fairly large numbers of quetzals hidden in the forest but they're extremely elusive. The **best time of year to visit** is just before and just after nesting season (April/May), and the best time of day is **sunrise**; in general they tend to spend the nights up in the high forest and float across the road as dawn breaks, to spend the days in the forest below. Whether or not you see a quetzal, the forest itself, usually damp with mist, is well worth a visit: a profusion of lichens, ferns, mosses, bromeliads and orchids, spread out beneath the towering canopy.

There are **camping** and hammock spaces at the reserve, and a stream-fed pool for bathing. A kilometre or so past the entrance is the *Pensión El Ranchito del*

THE RESPLENDENT QUETZAL

The **quetzal**, Guatemala's national symbol – and with the honour of lending its name to the currency – has a distinguished past but an uncertain future. The feathers of the quetzal were sacred from the earliest of times, and in the strange cult of Quetzalcoatl, whose influence spread throughout Mesoamerica, the quetzal was incorporated into the plumed serpent, a supremely powerful deity. To the Maya the quetzal was so sacred that killing one was a capital offence, and the bird is also thought to have been the *nahual*, or spiritual protector, of the Indian chiefs. When Tecún Umán faced Alvarado in hand-to-hand combat his headdress sprouted the long green feathers of the quetzal; when the conquistadors founded a city adjacent to the battleground they named it **Quezaltenango**, the place of the quetzals.

In modern Guatemala the quetzal's image saturates the entire country, appearing in every imaginable context. Citizens honoured by the president are awarded the Order of the Quetzal, and the bird is also considered a symbol of freedom, since caged quetzals die from the rigours of confinement. Despite all this the sweeping tide of deforestation threatens the very existence of the bird, and the sanctuary is about the only concrete step that has been taken to save it.

The more resplendent of the birds, and the source of the famed feathers, is the male. Their heads are crowned with a plume of brilliant green, the chest and lower belly is a rich crimson, and stretching out behind are the unmistakeable long, golden-green tail feathers. The females, on the other hand, are an unremarkable brownish colour. The birds nest in holes drilled into dead trees, laying one or two eggs at the start of the rainy season, usually in April or May.

Quetzal, where you can either **stay** in one of the two shared wooden huts (②) or have a more luxurious room to yourself, complete with a private bathroom (④). There's no electricity and the *comedor*'s menu is usually limited to eggs and beans, although the one major compensation is that quetzals are often seen here; hotel staff sometimes insist on charging an entrance fee even if you just want to come in and look around. If you're after more luxurious accommodation try the *Hotel Posada Montaña del Quetzal* (☎3351805; ⑤), 4.5km before the reserve on the way from Guatemala City, which offers pleasant rooms with warm water and private showers and has its own restaurant.

Buses from Cobán pass the entrance hourly, but make sure they know you want to be dropped at the *biotopo* as it's easy to miss.

Alta Verapaz

Beyond the quetzal sanctuary the main road crosses into the department of Alta Verapaz, and another 13km takes you beyond the forests and into a luxuriant alpine valley of cattle pastures hemmed in by steep, perpetually green hillsides.

The first place of any size is **TACTIC**, a small town adjacent to the main road, which is passed straight through by most buses. Tactic has earned its share of fame as the site of the **pozo vivo**, the living well. A sign points the way to this decidedly odd attraction, opposite the northern entrance road. The well itself is a small pool that appears motionless at first, until your eye catches the odd swirl in the mud – legend has it that the water only comes to life when approached. The colonial church in the village is also worth a look, as is the Chi-ixim chapel, high above the town. If you fancy a cool swim, then head for the *Balneario Cham-che*, a crystal-clear spring-fed pool, on the other side of the main road, opposite the centre of town. The simple *Pensión Central* (②), on the main street north of the plaza, has a pair of beautiful resident macaws; if it's full, try *Pensión Sulmy* (②).

Further towards Cobán, the turning for **SAN CRISTÓBAL VERAPAZ** peels off to the left. A pretty town surrounded by fields of sugar cane and coffee, it's set on the banks of **Lake Cristóbal**, a favourite spot for swimming and fishing, although a shoe factory on the shore has now badly polluted the water. Legend has it that the lake was formed in 1590 as a result of a dispute between a priest and local Indians over the celebration of pagan rites. According to one version the earth split and swallowed the Indians, sealing their graves with the water, while another has it that the priest fled, hurling maledictions so heavy that they created a depression which then filled with water. The Pokomchí-speaking Indians of San Cristóbal are among the last vestiges of one of the smallest and oldest highland tribes. If you're thinking of visiting the village, though, make enquiries at the tourist office in Cobán first. It was here, in 1994, that an American tourist was beaten up so viciously (she has since died), that the US State Department issued a travel **warning** against Guatemala, which is still in force.

West from San Cristóbal the rough road continues to **Uspantán** (in the western highlands) from where buses run to Santa Cruz del Quiché, via Sacapulas, for connections to Nebaj and Huehuetenango. To head out this way you can either hitch from San Cristóbal or catch one of the buses that leaves San Pedro Carchá at 10am and noon, passing just above the terminal in Cobán ten minutes later, and reaching San Cristóbal after about another half-hour.

Cobán

The heart of these rain-soaked hills and the capital of the department is **COBÁN**, where the paved highway comes to an end. If you're heading up this way you're likely to be here for a night or two, which on first impressions can be a gloomy prospect. When the rain settles in, Cobán can have something of a dull atmosphere, weary and inactive, and in the evenings the air is usually damp and often cold. That said, the sun does put in an appearance most days, and the town makes a useful base to recharge your batteries, eat well, sleep well and make day trips into the mountains.

Arrival and information

Transportes Escobar Monja Blanca, one of Guatemala's best bus services (their latest *especials* have onboard TV and video), have regular departures between **Guatemala City** and Cobán (both hourly 2.30am–4pm; 4–5hr). In the capital the office is at 8 Av 15–16, Zona 1; in Cobán you'll find them on the corner of 2 C and 4 Av, Zona 4. Buses to **local destinations** such as Senahú, El Estor, Lanquín and Cahabón leave from the terminal, down the hill behind the town hall. There are also regular departures from **San Pedro Carchá** (see p.266), a couple of kilometres away from Cobán.

Cobán's plaza boasts the country's newest and most efficient **tourist office** (privately run), open for enquiries about anything from accommodation and bus schedules to tours (Mon–Sat 9am–noon & 2.30–6pm). To **change money** choose from *Banco G&T,* 1 C and 2 Av (Mon–Fri 9am–7pm, Sat 10am–2pm), *Banco del Cafe* 1 Av 2–68 (Mon–Thurs 8.30am–8pm, Fri 8am–8pm, Sat 10am–2pm), and

Banco del Agro, 1 C and 3 Av (Mon–Fri 9am–8pm, Sat 9am–1pm). *Guatel* has its main office in the plaza (daily 7am–midnight), and the **post office** is at 2 C and 2 Av (Mon–Fri 8am–4.30pm).

For **car rental**, there's a *Tabarini* office in the same building as the *Café Tirol* on 1 C, across from the *Posada* (Mon–Fri 7am–7pm, Sat & Sun 7am–noon & 2–7pm; ☎9522059) and a local outfit, *Inque Rentautos* (☎9522994). In the *Centro Commercial Cabrera*, at the sharp end of the plaza, you can wash and dry a machine-load of **laundry** for around a dollar (Mon–Sat 8am–noon & 2–5pm).

Accommodation

Unless you're here for one of the August fiestas you'll probably only pause for a day or two before heading off into the hills, out to the villages, or on to some other part of the country. There are, however, plenty of **hotels** in town.

Hostal de Acuña, 4 C 3–17 (☎9521547). Undoubtedly the most popular budget choice, offering spotless rooms for 2–6 people, with comfortable bunks. Dorms are built in the garden of a colonial house, on whose verandah guests and visitors can enjoy excellent home cooking, including pizza and blueberry pie. Highly recommended. ③.

Hotel Central, 1 C 1–74, down the side of the cathedral (☎9521442). At the upper end of the budget range, a clean, comfortable and friendly hotel with Germanic decor. Rooms, all with shower and hot water, are set around a pleasant courtyard and there is a good *comedor*. ③.

Pensión Familiar, at the sharp end of the plaza. One of the rougher hotels, used by travelling salespeople and prostitutes. Simple and bare, with two lovely toucans and warm water. ①–②.

Hotel la Fe, 4 Av 2–21, around the corner from the bus company *Escobar Monja Blanca*. Friendly, clean and quiet. ③.

Hotel Marie Andre, 6 Av 1–16. Pleasant modern hotel whose small, neat rooms each have a TV and private bathroom. ③.

Hospedaje Maya, 1 C, opposite the *Cine Norte*. Large, basic hotel used by local travellers and traders. Warm showers and friendly staff. ②.

Hotel la Paz, 6 Av 2–19 (☎9521358). Safe, pleasant budget hotel run by a very vigilant *señora*. Some rooms have private bathroom. ③.

Hotel la Posada, 1 C 4–12, at the sharp end of the plaza (☎9521495). By far the city's finest hotel, a superb colonial-style building, said to be the oldest in the city, with a beautiful, antique-furnished interior. The rooms are set around two gorgeous courtyards and manage to offer all the obvious luxuries without compromising the sedate and civilized atmosphere. Its excellent restaurant and café mark it out as a stronghold of Cobán's refined elite. ⑤.

Posada de Carlos V, 1 Av 3–44 (☎ & fax 9513502). Beautiful, colonial style hotel with modern luxuries on the road to San Pedro Carchá, a little outside town. ⑥.

The Town

Cobán's imperial heyday, when it stood at the centre of its own isolated world, is long gone, and the glory well faded. The **plaza**, however, remains an impressive triangle, dominated by the cathedral, from which the town drops away on all sides. A block behind, the **market** bustles with trade during the day and is surrounded by food stalls at night. Life in Cobán revolves around **coffee**: the sedate restaurants, tearooms, trendy nightclubs and overflowing supermarket are a tribute to the town's affluent elite, while the crowds that sleep in the market and plaza, assembling in the bus terminal to search for work, are migrant labourers heading for the plantations. Since the fast road linked Cobán with the capital, the *finqueros*, wealthy owners of the coffee plantations, have mostly moved to Guatemala City, but a small residue still base themselves in Cobán. Hints of the days of German control can also be found here and there, whether in the architecture, incorporating the occasional suggestion of Bavarian grandeur, or the posters of the "Fatherland" that are peeling from the walls of the cinema.

The one "sight" in Cobán lies just outside town: the **Vivero Verapaz**, a former coffee *finca* now dedicated to the growing of orchids, which flourish in these sodden mountains. The export of the blooms is illegal in Guatemala but the farm produces some seven hundred indigenous varieties, as well as a handful of hybrids which they've put together themselves, all of which are sold within Guatemala. The plants are nurtured in a wonderfully shaded environment, and a farm worker will show you around and point out the most spectacular buds, which are at their best between November and January. The farm is on the old road to Guatemala City, which you reach by leaving the plaza on 3 C, the road that runs past the *Pensión Familiar*, and at the bottom of the hill you turn left, go across the bridge and follow the road for 3–4km. Any taxi driver will be able to take you.

The *Epiphyte Adventures* company, who aim to promote "low impact tourism as a vehicle for rural development and biological conservation" offer some highly informative **tours** around Alta Verapaz, including to the Semuc Champey pools (see p.267), the Laguna Lachuá National Park (see p.272), and a French-owned eco-lodge near the remote Candelaria caves (see p.271). This last is most closely tied to the company's ideals; roughly twenty indigenous families contribute their services and in return receive almost 62 percent of the tour price. Prices are comparitively high, but you can be sure your money is well spent. Contact them in Cobán on ☎9522213 or at their head office in Flores on ☎9260775.

Finally, if you enjoy Coban's slightly subdued atmosphere you could spend some time **studying Spanish** at the *Instituto Cobán International* (*INCO Int*) on 2 C 1–23 (☎ & fax 9521497). Prices are around $120 per week, which includes twenty hours of teaching, two excursions and full board.

Eating, drinking and entertainment

When it comes to **eating** in Cobán you have a choice between fancy European-style restaurants and very basic, cheap *comedores*. For really cheap food, your best bet, as always, is the **market**, but remember that it's closed by dusk, after which street stalls set up in the plaza selling barbecued meat and warm tortillas.

Hostal Acuña, 4 C 3–17. The most relaxed place to eat in town, and a good place to meet other travellers. Three course meals cost around $5, and there are plenty of cheaper options, wth a good selection of fruit and vegetables.

Kam Mun, on the entrance road to Cobán, coming from the capital. Excellent and very clean Chinese restaurant. Daily noon–9.30pm.

Pastelería Mus Mus Hab, 1 C. Everything from steaks to pancakes.

Hotel La Posada, 1 C 4–12, at the sharp end of the plaza. The smartest restaurant in town, offering traditional Guatemalan specialities as well as standard international cuisine. The café, on the verandah outside, serves superb breakfasts, coffee, tea and snacks. It's an excellent place to watch life go by, as well as being slightly cheaper.

Cafe Central, 1 C, down an alley beside the cathedral. Good snacks, sandwiches and french fries; stays open until 11pm.

Cafe Santa Rita, 1 C, on the plaza down the side of the cathedral. Cheap Guatemalan food.

Cafe Tirol, on the north side of the plaza. Relatively upmarket by Guatemalan standards, though cheaper than the *Posada*. Serves 22 different types of coffee, superb breakfasts, hot chocolates, pancakes and sandwiches. Tues–Sun 7am–8.30pm.

Nightlife
Generally speaking Cobán is a quiet place, particularly so in the evenings, although behind closed doors people do indulge in some very metropolitan pleasures. There are two **cinemas**, the *Cine Centro* in the plaza, and the *Cine Norte*, on 1 C. Strange though it may seem the town also has several **nightclubs**, the best of which is the *Oasis*, on 6 Av, just off 1 C. While not recommended for women on their own, the club is fun if you're in a group; it's busiest on Friday and Saturday nights, when the town's young, rich and trendy come out to enjoy themselves.

San Pedro Carchá

Only a few kilometres away, connected by a regular shuttle of buses, **SAN PEDRO CARCHÁ** is a smaller and poorer version of Cobán, with none of the coffee money and a greater percentage of Indians. These days the two towns are merging into a single urban sprawl, and many of the buses that go on towards Petén, or even over to Uspantán, leave from Carchá. Some of the *Escobar* buses from Guatemala City continue to Carchá; others stop at Cobán, in which case you'll have to catch a local bus between the two. These leave from outside the cinema on 1 Av in Cobán and from the plaza in Carchá.

In San Pedro Carchá itself the **regional museum** (Sat & Sun 9am–noon & 2–5pm; open at other times except Tues if there is someone to unlock the door), in the street beside the church, is worth a visit. It houses a collection of Maya artefacts, dolls dressed in local costumes, and a mouldy collection of stuffed birds and animals, including the inevitable moulting quetzal. Another excursion takes you a couple of kilometres from the centre of town to the **Balneario Les Islas**, a stretch of cool water that's a popular spot for swimming. To get there walk along the main street beside the church and take the third turning on the right. Follow this street for about 1km and take the right-hand fork at the end.

If you're planning a speedy departure then you might prefer **to stay** here in the *Pensión Central*, just off the plaza, or the *Hotel La Reforma* (both ②), 4 C 8-45. For **changing money**, here's a branch of the *Banco del Ejercito* on the plaza (Mon–Fri 9am–1pm & 2.30–5.30pm, Sat 10am–2pm). **Moving on**, buses to local destinations such as Senahú, El Estor, Lanquín and Cahabón leave from the plaza. Two buses a day leave from beside the *bomberos* at 10am and noon **to Uspantán** (pausing just above the terminal in Cobán), for connections to Sacapulas, Nebaj and Quiché. They return from Uspantán at 3am and 3.30am.

San Juan Chamelco

A few kilometres southeast of Cobán, easily reached by regular local buses from the terminal, **SAN JUAN CHAMELCO** is the most important Kekchí settlement in the area. Most of your fellow bus passengers are likely to be women dressed in traditional costume, wearing beautiful cascades of old coins for earrings, and speaking Kekchí rather than Spanish. Chamelco's focal point is a large colonial church, whose facade is rather unexpectedly decorated with an Indianized version of the Habsburg double eagle – undoubtedly a result of the historic German presence in the region. Inside, you will find the usual hushed devotional tones and flickering candles around the altars. The most significant treasure, the church bell, is hidden in the belfry; it was a gift to the Indian leader Juan Matalbatz from no less than the Holy Roman Emperor Charles V.

The large market around the church sells anything from local farm produce to blue jeans, but very little in the way of crafts, and the best time to visit the village is for its annual **fiesta**, on June 16. A special feature of the festival is the procession, during which participants dress up in a variety of outfits from pre-conquest Maya costumes to representations of local wildlife, in celebration of the local Kekchí culture and environment.

If you enjoy Chamelco's peaceful atmosphere, and would like to explore the beautiful countryside, a great **place to stay** is *Don Jeronimo's* (⑤ full board), a vegetarian guest house/retreat run by an eccentric American, who has been living off the land for a good twenty years, and is the only grower of blueberries in Guatemala. You'll find him either by walking 5km from Chamelco to the Aldea Chajaneb, or by catching a bus from outside the *Tienda Maranatha*, on the street running behind the church. Ask to be dropped off at the appropriate footpath.

East to Lanquín, Semuc Champey and beyond

Northeast of Cobán and San Pedro Carchá a rough, badly maintained road heads off into the hills, connecting a string of coffee *fincas*. For the first few kilometres the hills are closed in around the road, but as it drops down into the richer land to the north the valleys open out. Their precipitous sides are patched with cornfields and the level central land is saved for the all-important coffee bushes. As the bus lurches along, clinging to the sides of the ridges, there are fantastic views of the valleys below.

The road divides at the **Pajal** junction (43km from Cobán), where one branch turns north to Sebol and Fray Bartolomé de Las Casas and the other cuts down into the valley to **LANQUÍN** (another 12km). Here you'll find a fairly nondescript village, surrounded by the usual acres of coffee, with two fairly simple places to stay: best is the *Divina Providencia* (①), which serves good meals and has hot showers. *Tienda Mary* (①) is more basic. For a touch more luxury, try the hotel *El Recreo* (☎9522160; ④), on the entrance road; prices rise at weekends.

The Lanquín caves

Just a couple of kilometres from the village, the **Lanquín caves** are a maze of dripping, bat-infested chambers, stretching for at the very least 3km underground. To find them simply walk along the road heading back to Cobán and turn right, where a dirt road turns off towards the river, just before you reach the *Recreo* hotel. A walkway, complete with ladders and chains, has been cut through the first few hundred metres and electric lights have been installed, which makes it all substantially easier, though it remains dauntingly slippery. Before you set out from the village ask in the *municipalidad* if they can turn on the lights, but fix the fee before you set off. It's also well worth dropping by at dusk, when thousands of bats emerge from the mouth of the cave and flutter off into the night. A small car park near the entrance to the caves has a covered shelter where you're welcome to camp or sling your hammock.

Semuc Champey

The other attraction around Lanquín, the extraordinary pools at **Semuc Champey** are harder to reach than the caves, but a great deal more spectacular. A regular pick-up service shuttles tourists back and forth, leaving Lanquín at 8am and coming back around noon, but if the pick-up doesn't turn up, or you decide you'd rather walk, then it should take two or three hours to get there. This can be extremely tough going if the sun is shining – take plenty of water – but if the walk is hell the pools are close to paradise. To get there, set out from the village along the gravel road that heads to the south, away from the river. Once beyond the houses this starts to climb back and forth, out of the valley and down into another, then wanders through thick tropical vegetation where bananas and coffee grow beside scruffy thatched huts. Just as you start to lose hope, the river appears below the road, but there's a little way to go yet. The road heads upstream for 1km or so before crossing on a suspension bridge. On the other side of this you want to turn to the right and head on upstream, first on the road and then along a muddy track that brings you, at long last, to the pools.

The pools themselves are a staircase of turquoise waters suspended on a natural limestone bridge, with a series of idyllic pools in which you can swim – watch out for sharp edges. The bulk of the river runs underground beneath this natural bridge and if you walk a few hundred metres up the valley you can see the water plunging furiously into a cavern, cutting under the pools to emerge below. If you have a tent or a hammock it makes sense to stay the night – there's a thatched shelter, and the altitude is sufficiently low to keep the air warm in the evenings. Be warned, though, it is not safe to leave your belongings unattended.

Beyond Lanquín

Beyond Lanquín the road continues to **Cahabón** (which has a basic *pensión*), another 24km to the east, and from there an even rougher road heads south to Panzós (see below), cutting high over the mountains through superb scenery. In the unlikely event of the road being in a good enough state of repair, there's an occasional bus between these two places, but normally transport is by pick-ups that carry people and property between the two – although even these are increasingly rare.

Buses to Cahabón, passing through Lanquín, leave Cobán daily at 6am, 12.30pm, 2pm & 3pm (3hr). Buses from Lanquín to Cobán depart at 5am, 7am, 2pm and 3pm. Buses coming back from Cahabón to Cobán pass through Lanquín at around 5am, 7am and 3pm. Buses pass Pajal for **Fray Bartolomé de Las Casas** and **Raxruja** (see p.271) twice each morning.

Down the Polochic valley to Lake Izabal

If you're planning to head out towards the Caribbean from Cobán, or simply interested in taking a short trip along backroads, then the **Polochic valley** is an ideal place to spend the day being bounced around inside a bus. Travelling the length of the valley you witness an immense transformation as you drop down through the coffee-coated mountains and emerge in the lush, tropical lowlands. To reach the head of the valley you have to travel south from Cobán along the main road to Guatemala City; shortly after Tactic you leave the luxury of tarmac and head off into the valley. The scenery is pure Alta Verapaz: V-shaped valleys where coffee commands the best land and fields of maize cling to the upper slopes wherever they can. The villages are untidy-looking places where the Kekchí Indians are largely *ladinized* and seldom wear the brilliant red *huipiles* that are traditional here.

The first village in the upper end of the valley is Tamahú, and below it is Tucurú, beyond which the valley starts to open out and the river loses its frantic energy, wandering gently across the flood plain. High above Tucurú, in the mountains to the north, is the **Chelemá Quetzal Reserve**, a large protected area of pristine cloud forest which contains one of the highest concentrations of quetzals anywhere in the world, not to mention an array of other birds and beasts, including some very vocal howler monkeys. The reserve is extremely difficult to reach and you really need a four-wheel drive to get you up there – if you'd like to drop by for a couple of days, contact the reserve's office in Cobán at 6 Av, Zone 1 (☎9513238), opposite the *Hotel La Paz*.

Beyond Tucurú cattle pastures start to take the place of the coffee bushes, and both the villages and the people have a more tropical look about them. Next comes La Tinta, and then Telemán, the largest of the squalid trading centres in this lower section of the valley.

A side trip to Senahú

From Telemán a side road branches off to the north and climbs high into the lush hills, past row upon row of neatly ranked coffee bushes. As it winds upwards a superb view opens out across the level valley floor below, exposing the river's swirling meanders as it runs through a series of oxbows and cut-offs.

Set back behind the first ridge of hills, the small coffee centre of **SENAHÚ** sits in a steep-sided bowl. The village itself is a fairly unremarkable farming settlement, but the setting is spectacular to say the least, and it is the ideal starting point for a short wander in the Alta Verapaz hills. A daily **bus** connects Senahú and Cobán, leaving Cobán at 6.30am, 11.30am and 2.30pm from the terminal; the first bus returns from Senahú at 4pm (always ask the drivers for the latest timetable); or you could easily hitch a ride on a truck from Telemán. There are a couple of simple *pensiones* in the village.

Two kilometres to the east of Senahú a gravel road, occasionally served by buses, runs to the *Finca El Volcán*, and beyond there you can continue towards Semuc Champey (see above), passing the *Finca Arenal* en route. The walk takes at least three days, and with the uncertainty of local weather conditions you can expect to be regularly soaked, but the dauntingly hilly countryside and the superb fertility of the vegetation make it all worthwhile. The best way to find the route is to hire a guide in Senahú, but you do pass several substantial *fincas* where you can ask directions.

Panzós

Heading on down the Polochic valley you reach **PANZÓS**, the largest of the valley villages. Its name means "place of the green waters", a reference to the swamps that surround the river, infested with alligators and bird life. It was here in Panzós that the old Verapaz railway from the Caribbean coast ended, and goods were transferred to boats for the journey across Lake Izabal. These days you have to go all the way to the lakeshore at El Estor to find the ferry. In 1978 Panzós made a brief appearance in international headlines when a group of *campesinos* attending a meeting to settle land disputes were gunned down by the army and local police. About a hundred men, women and children were killed, and the event is generally regarded as a landmark in the history of political violence in Guatemala, after which the situation deteriorated rapidly.

Beyond Panzós the road pushes on towards Lake Izabal, and just before El Estor it passes a huge and deserted **nickel plant**, yet another monument to disastrous foreign investment. In the mid-1960s, prompted by a chance discovery of high-grade nickel deposits, the International Nickel Company of Canada formed *Exmibal* (*Exploraciones y Explotaciones Mineras de Izabal*), which then built and developed the mine and processing plant. After thirteen years of study and delay the plant opened in 1977, functioned for a couple of years at reduced capacity, and was then shut down as a result of technical problems and the plummeting price of nickel. Today the great, ghost-like structure stands deserted, surrounded by the prefabricated huts that would have housed its workforce. There is, however, some prospect of a revival as the owners of the plant are considering reopening it to mine cobalt from the surrounding hills. For the moment the plan is in an early, tentative, stage.

El Estor

EL ESTOR itself, 1km or so further on, settled back into provincial stupor after the nickel boom but is now undergoing a revival, at the centre of a regional development boom. Fresh farmlands are being opened up all the time, a new road is planned along the north shore of the lake and oil companies have discovered a large oil field beneath the lake itself. The prospect of oil wells in the lake has prompted a mixed reaction among locals as eager entrepreneurs squabble with environmentalists. Shell, meanwhile, who will operate the rigs, have promised huge compensation should they blacken the water or wipe out a species or two. Shell are by no means the first foreign presence here: the town's name is said to have derived from a local mispronunciation of the name given to it by English pirates, who came up the Río Dulce to buy supplies ("The Store"). These days the only boat that drops by is the **ferry for Mariscos**, which leaves daily at 6am, returning at 1pm. On the other side it's met by two buses, one to Guatemala City and the other for Puerto Barrios.

The best **hotel** in El Estor is the *Hotel Vista del Lago* (☎9497205; ③), a beautiful colonial-style wooden building beside the dock, which the owner claims was the original "store" that gave the village its name. All rooms have private bathrooms, and second-floor rooms have superb views of the lake. A little cheaper is the *Hotel Villela* (③), a block up from the *Vista del Lago*, which is surrounded by a beautiful garden and has private showers. Simpler still, the *Hospedaje Santa Clara* (③) has basic, clean rooms, some with their own shower. For a delicious French **meal**, not too expensive, check out *Restaurante El Dios del Sol*, on the eastern side of town.

There's not a lot to do in El Estor, although it does have a friendly, relaxed atmosphere, particularly in the warmth of the evening when the streets are full of activity – and don't miss the pool in the plaza, which harbours fish, turtles and alligators. However, you could spend a few days exploring the surrounding area, much of which remains undisturbed. If you find yourself with an afternoon to spare there's a **canyon**, El Boqueron, in the hills to the east, which is an excellent place for a swim; to get there follow the road to the east of town for 8km, or arrange to have someone take you there by boat. The delta of the **Río Polochic** is particularly beautiful, a maze of swamp, marsh and forest which is home to alligators, monkeys, tapirs and an abundance of bird life, while the lake itself abounds with fish, including tarpon and snook.

The best place to enquire about **tours** around El Estor is *Hugo's Restaurant* on the main plaza. In addition, the irrepressible Oscar Paz, who runs the *Hotel Vista del Lago*, is an enthusiastic promoter of the area and will arrange a boat and guide to explore any of the surrounding countryside, go fishing in the lake or visit the hot springs at *Finca Paraiso*.

Buses for El Estor leave the terminal in Cobán at 4am, 5am, 6.30am, 8am, 8.30am, 10.30am, 11.30am, 12.30pm, 1pm, 2pm & 3pm (8hr); it's a bumpy but beautiful ride. They return to Cobán early in the morning.

North towards Petén

In the far northern section of the Alta Verapaz, the lush hills drop away steeply onto the limestone plain that marks the frontier with the department of Petén. The road network here is rough and ready, to say the least, and each year roads return to jungle while others are cut and repaired. Understandably, then, all existing maps of the area are riddled with errors. At present, two roads head north: the first from Cobán via Chisec, the second from San Pedro Carchá, via Pajal. Both meet up with a dirt road running along the northern edge of the mountains from Modesto Mendez in the far west to Playa Grande and beyond in the east. If you're heading for Sayaxché you'll want to make for the small settlement of **Raxrúja** (about 20km west of **Fray Bartolemé de las Casas** and **Playa Grande**), from where trucks and buses head north. Otherwise there are a number of interesting towns and villages in this ever-changing frontier world.

Raxrúja and the Candelaria caves

RAXRÚJA, 26km southeast of Cruce del Pato, is the best place to pick up a truck (or the occasional bus) north to Sayaxché and Flores or west to Playa Grande and the Ixcán. Little more than a few streets and an army base straggling round the bridge over the Río Escondido, a tributary of the Pasión, it has the only **accommodation** for miles around and you may end up staying at one of the basic *pensiones* in order to get an early start the next day. The unnamed *pension* opposite the football field is the best.

The limestone mountains to the west of Raxrúja are full of caves. Some of the best are the **Candelaria caves**, 10km west. The most impressive cave mouths are on private property, a short walk from the road, jealously guarded by Daniel Dreux who has built the **Complex Cultural de Candelaria** conservation area. Though he also offers wonderful **accommodation** in wooden dorms and a bungalow, the complex is often block booked by French tour groups, and there's little, if any, chance of getting a place by turning up on spec. Contact *STP* travel agency in Guatemala City, 2 Av 7–78 Zona 10 (☎3346235) or *Epiphyte Adventures* in Cobán (see p.265). Up the hill behind the cabins are some huge cave entrances, though you'll only be allowed to see them as part of a tour. It's also possible to raft or kayak through the caves on the beautiful jade green river but, again, you'll need to organize this with a specialist travel agency in Guatemala City or through *Epiphyte Adventures*.

The area beyond Raxrúja, where the rolling foothills of the highlands give way to the flat expanse of southern Petén, is known as the **Northern Transversal Strip** and is the source of much contentious political debate in Guatemala. In the 1970s it was earmarked for development as a possible solution to the need for new farmland and pressures for agrarian reform, but widespread corruption ensured that huge parcels of land, complete with their valuable mineral resources, were dispersed no further than the generals: the land was dubbed "Generals' Strip". Since then oil reserves have been developed around Playa Grande, in the west of the strip, and the area has seen heavy fighting between the army and guerrillas.

From Raxrúja you can travel east to **FRAY BARTOLOMÉ DE LAS CASAS** a couple of hours away. There are three **hotels** here – the best is *Pensión Ralios* (①) – and buses to San Pedro Carchá (8hr) and Cobán. For some reason the village has been left off most maps, though **Sebol**, a beautiful spot on the Río Pasión where tributary waterfalls cascade into the main channel, is marked.

Playa Grande (Cantabál, Ixcán)

Continuing west from Raxrúja, trucks regularly make the 90km journey over rough roads to **Playa Grande** (6hr plus) the bridging point of the Río Negro. There's nothing here but the bridge, a huge army base and a couple of *comedores*, but it's a loading point for grain travelling downriver, so you might get a boat.

The town formerly known as **PLAYA GRANDE** (also referred to as **CANTABÁL** or **IXCÁN**), 7km west of the river crossing, is an authentic frontier settlement with cheap hotels, rough bars and brothels. It's also the administrative and transport centre of the region. The best **place to stay** is the *Hospedaje Reyna* (①) – basic but clean with at least some semblance of a courtyard.

One point of interest in this area is the **Laguna Lachuá National Park**, a beautiful little lake a four-kilometre walk from the main road (30min by truck) east of Playa Grande (any truck driver will point you in the right direction – the entrance is signposted right by the road). One of the least visited national parks in Central America, this is a beautiful, tranquil spot, the clear, almost circular lake completely surrounded by dense tropical forest. Though it smells slightly sulphurous, the water is good for swimming, with curious horseshoe-shaped limestone formations by the edge that make perfect individual bathing pools. You'll see otters and an abundance of birdlife, but watch out for mosquitoes. There's a large thatched *rancho* by the shore, ideal for camping or slinging a hammock (available for rent). Though fireplaces and wood are provided, you'll need to bring food and drinking water.

You can get to Playa Grande **from Cobán** on one of the endless stream of trucks setting out from the corner of the bus terminal – a journey of at least eight hours. There are also regular flights from the airstrip in Cobán.

Into the Ixcán

The Río Negro marks the boundary between the deptartments of Alta Verapaz and Quiché; the land to the west is known as the **Ixcán**. This huge swampy forest, some of which was settled in the 1960s and 1970s by peasants migrating from the highlands, became a bloody battleground in the 1980s and parts of it are still occasionally fought over today. In the last couple of years the Ixcán has become a focal **repatriado** settlement as refugees who fled to Mexico in the 1980s are resettled in a string of "temporary" camps west of the the river. Travelling further west, across the Ixcán and into northern Huehuetenango, though no longer hazardous, is still fairly ardous, taking at least two or three days to get from Playa Grande to Barillas (see p.176). **Veracruz**, 20km (1hr 30min) from Playa Grande, is the first place of note, a *repatriado* settlement at the cross-roads beyond the Río Xalbal. Some buses continue to Mayalan, 12km away, across the presently unbridged Río Piedras Blancas. Here the road ends and you'll have to walk the next 15km to **Altamira** on the far bank of the Río Ixcán. If you're in good shape it'll take about four or five hours, passing several tiny villages; the path is easy to follow. At the last village, **Ranch Palmeras**, ask for directions to the crossing point on the Ixcán, where boys will pole you across the flowing river. Once across, Altamira is still a few kilometres away up the hill. From here a regular flow of trucks make the 30km journey to Barillas, taking at least four hours over some of the worst roads in the country. It's a spectacular journey, though, especially as you watch the growing bulk of the Cuchumatanes rising ever higher on the horizon. You can also get trucks over the border in **Mexico**, taking you to Chajul on the Río Lacantún in Chiapas, but you need a Guatemalan exit stamp first, probably best obtained in Cobán or Flores.

fiestas

The Verapaces are famous for their fiestas, and in Baja Verapaz especially you'll see an unusual range of traditional dances. In addition, Cobán hosts the **National Fiesta of Folklore**, at the start of August, which is attended by indigenous groups from throughout the country.

JANUARY
Rabinal's fiesta, famed for its traditional dances, runs from the 19th to 25th, with the most important events saved for the 21st. **Tamahú** has a fiesta from the 22nd to 25th; again, the 25th is the main day.

MAY
Santa Cruz Verapaz has a fiesta from the 1st to 4th, including the dances of *Los Chuntos*, *Vendos* and *Mamah-Num*. **Tucurú** celebrates from the 4th to 9th, with the main day on the 8th.

JUNE
Senahú has its fiesta from the 9th to 13th, with the main day on the 13th. In **Purulhá** the action is from the 10th to 13th, which is the principal day. **San Juan Chamelco** has a fiesta from the 21st to 24th, in honour of San Juan Bautista. In **San Pedro Carchá** the fiesta is from the 24th to 29th, with the main day on the 29th: here you may witness the dances of *Moros y Cristianos* and *Los Diablos*. **Chisec** has a fiesta from the 25th to 30th; the main day is the 29th.

JULY
Cubulco has a very large fiesta from the 20th to 25th, in honour of Santiago Apostol. Dances include the *Palo Volador*, *Toritos*, *Los 5 Toros* and *El Chico Mudo*, among others. **San Cristóbal Verapaz** has a fiesta from the 21st to 26th, also in honour of Santiago.

AUGUST
The fiesta in **Cobán** lasts from July 31 to August 6, and is immediately followed by the **National Fiesta of Folklore**. **Tactic** has a fiesta from the 11th to 16th, with the main day on the 15th. In **Lanquín** the fiesta runs from the 22nd to 28th, with the last day as the main day. In **Chajal** the fiesta takes place from the 23rd to 28th, and in **Panzós** it lasts from the 23rd to 30th.

SEPTEMBER
Cahabón has a fiesta from the 4th to 8th, with the main day on the 6th. **Salamá** has its fiesta from the 17th to 21st, with the principal day on the 17th. In **San Miguel Chicaj** the fiesta runs from the 25th to 29th, and in **San Jerónimo** it lasts from the 27th right through until October 10.

DECEMBER
Santa Cruz El Chol has a fiesta from the 6th to 8th, with the main day on the 8th.

travel details

BUSES
Baja Verapaz
Rutas Verapacenses, with offices in Guatemala City at 19 C 9 Av, Zona 1, run buses **from Guatemala City** to Salamá, Rabinal and Cubulco (hourly 5.30am–4pm), returning regularly from Cubulco to the capital (hourly 1.30am–1pm).

A daily bus from Guatemala City **to Cubulco via El Chol** leaves the Zona 4 terminal at about 4am, and from Cubulco on the return journey at 9am.

Heading for Baja Verapaz **from Cobán** or from Guatemala City you can also take any bus between Cobán and the capital and get off at **La Cumbre de Santa Elena**, from where minibuses run to Salamá.

Alta Verapaz

Guatemala City to Cobán services (hourly 4am–5pm; 4–5hr), calling at all points in between including the Biotopo and Tactic, are run by *Transportes Escobar Monja Blanca*. In Guatemala City their office is at 8 Av 15–16, Zona 1, and in Cobán (back to the capital hourly 2.30am–4pm) at 3 Av and 0 C.

Cobán to Tactic and San Cristóbal Verapaz. Every hour or so from the terminal down the hill behind the *municipalidad*.

Cobán to Senahú (around 7hr). Departures from main terminal at 6.30am, 11.30am & 2.30pm. From Senahú to Cobán the bus leaves at 4am, but you should check this the night before.

Cobán to El Estor (around 7hr). From the terminal in Cobán at 4am, 5am, 6.30am, 8am, 8.30am, 10.30am, 11.30am, 12.30pm, 1pm, 2pm & 3pm. Ask the drivers for return schedule from El Estor; most buses leave early.

San Pedro Carchá to Uspantán (5hr). Two daily, 10am and noon. From Uspantán there's a connecting bus to Santa Cruz del Quiché, which passes through Sacapulas for connections to Nebaj. Buses for San Pedro Carchá leave Uspantán at 3am and 3.30am.

San Pedro Carchá to Fray Bartolomé de Las Casas. Daily at 6am, and sometimes a second bus mid-morning and a third at midday. One 6am departure also goes to Raxrúja, from where there are pick-ups to **Sayaxché**. If this doesn't materialize take the first bus to Las Casas and then a pick-up to Sayaxché. Coming the other way a bus leaves Las Casas for Carchá at 6am.

San Pedro Carchá to Cahabón (4hr). Four buses daily, at 6am, 12.30pm, 2pm & 3pm, passing through **Lanquín** (3hr). Check for return schedule with the bus drivers.

CHAPTER SIX

PETÉN

The vast northern department of **Petén** occupies about a third of Guatemala but contains less than 2 percent of its population. This huge expanse of swamps, dry savannahs and tropical rainforest forms part of an untamed wilderness that stretches into the Lacandon forest of southern Mexico and across the Maya Mountains to Belize. Totally unlike any other part of the country, much of it is all but untouched, with ancient ceiba and mahogany trees that tower 50m above the forest floor. Undisturbed for so long, the area is also extraordinarily rich in **wildlife**. Some 285 species of bird have been sighted at Tikal alone, including a great range of hummingbirds, toucans, blue and white herons, hawks, buzzards, wild turkeys, motmot (a bird of paradise) and even the elusive quetzal, revered since Maya times. Many of these can be seen quite easily in the early morning and evening, when their cries fill the air. Beneath the forest canopy are many other species that are far harder to locate. Among the mammals are the massive tapir or mountain cow, ocelots, deer, coatis, jaguars, monkeys, plus crocodiles and thousands of species of plants, snakes, insects and butterflies.

Recently, however, this position of privileged isolation has been threatened by moves to colonize the country's final frontier. Waves of **settlers**, lured by offers of free land, have cleared enormous tracts of jungle, while oil exploration and commercial logging have brought with them mountains of money and machinery, cutting new roads deep into the forest. The population of Petén, in 1950 just 15,000, is today estimated at 350,000, a number which puts enormous pressure on the remaining forest. Various attempts have been made to halt the tide of destruction and in 1990 the government declared that 40 percent of Petén would be protected by the **Maya Biosphere Reserve** although little is done to enforce this.

The jungle of Petén also provides shelter for some of Guatemala's guerrilla armies, in particular the FAR (Rebel Armed Forces), who occasionally emerge to confront the army. In part this explains why the government is so keen to develop the region, but in practice the conflict has led to many of the settlers becoming refugees, driven across the border into Mexico; the oil industry, too, has had to withdraw from some of the worst-hit areas. In the last few years, however, the situation has improved considerably, and fighting is now confined to a few of the most remote border areas, with many refugees being resettled in Petén.

The new interest in the region is in fact something of a reawakening, as Petén was once the heartland of the **Maya civilization**, which reached here from the highlands some 2500 years ago. More than 200 Maya sites have been reported in the Petén area: many of them completely buried in the jungle, and some known only to locals. Here Maya culture reached the height of its architectural, scientific and artistic achievement during the Classic period, roughly 300–900 AD. Great

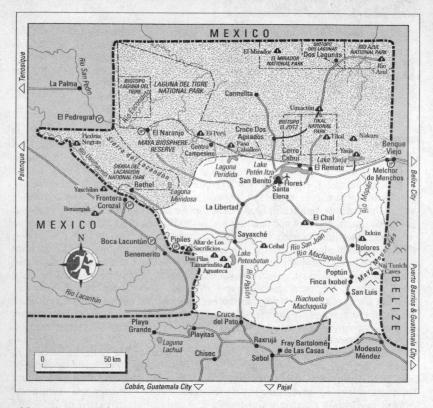

cities rose out of the forest, surrounded by smaller satellite centres and acres of raised and irrigated fields. Tikal and El Mirador are among the largest and most spectacular of all **Maya ruins** – Tikal alone has some 3000 buildings – but they represent only a fraction of what was once here. At the close of the tenth century the cities were mysteriously abandoned, and many of the people moved north to the Yucatán where Maya civilization continued to flourish until the twelfth century.

By the time the Spanish arrived the area had been partially recolonized by the Itzá, a group of Toltec-Maya (originally from the Yucatán) who inhabited the land around Lake Petén Itzá. The forest proved so impenetrable that it wasn't brought under Spanish control until 1697, more than 150 years after they had conquered the rest of the country. Although the Itzá resisted persistent attempts to Christianize them, their lakeside capital was eventually conquered and destroyed by Martín de Ursúa and his army, thus bringing about the defeat of the last independent Maya tribe. The Spanish had little enthusiasm for Petén, though, and under their rule it remained a backwater, with nothing to offer but a steady trickle of chicle – the basic ingredient of chewing gum, which is bled from sapodilla trees. Independence saw no great change, and it wasn't until 1970 that Petén became genuinely accessible by car. Even today the network of roads is skeletal, and many routes are impassable in the wet season.

The hub of the department is **Lake Petén Itzá** where the three adjacent towns of **Flores**, **Santa Elena** and **San Benito** together form the only settlement of any size. You'll probably arrive here, if only to head straight out to the ruins of **Tikal**, Petén's prime attraction. But the town is also the starting point for buses to the **Belize border** and for **routes to Mexico** along the Río San Pedro and the Río Usumacinta from Bethel. Arriving from Belize it's probably better to base yourself at the small lakeside village of **El Remate**, halfway between Flores and Tikal. If you plan to reach any of the more distant ruins – **El Mirador**, **Yaxjá**, **Nakúm** or **Río Azul** – then Flores is again the place to be based. To the south is **Sayaxché**, surrounded by yet more Maya sites including **Ceibal**, which boasts some of the best-preserved carving in Petén. From Sayaxché you can also set off down the Río Pasión to **Mexico** and the ruins of **Yaxchilán**, or take an alternative route back to Guatemala City – via Cobán in Alta Verapaz.

GETTING TO PETÉN FROM THE CAPITAL

Most visitors arrive in Petén by bus or plane directly from the capital: **by air** it's a short fifty-minute hop; **by bus** it can take anywhere between ten and twenty hours and is a gruelling experience. If you travel overland be warned that the roads are poor and that Petén jungles are still host to some of the country's guerrillas, who very occasionally stop buses to re-educate the passengers. There's no need to worry, however, as they're only interested in lecturing you, and possibly extracting a dollar or five as war tax. More threatening are the **robbers**, often armed, who regularly stop the tourist minibuses along the road from Tikal/Puente Ixlú and Puente Ixlú/Melchor. These characters are not usually violent but they are determined – be especially careful when changing buses. That said, they tend to leave the "chicken buses" alone, and the risk overall, while real, is small.

Air tickets can be bought from any travel agent in Guatemala City, Antigua, Panajachel or Quezaltenango. You could also get them direct from the airline but this is a great deal more expensive. Five domestic airlines – *Aerovivas*, *Avcom*, *TAPSA*, *Tikal Jets* and *SAISA* – and *Aviateca*, the national airline, fly daily to Petén. The domestic airlines depart from their offices inside the airport perimeter (entrance on Av Hincapie). *Aviateca* departs from the **international side** – make sure your taxi driver knows which flight you're on. All airlines have flights departing at 7am and *Aviateca* also has an afternoon flight at 5pm. A return ticket costs around $110 (more on *Aviateca*) but there are often special offers available at travel agents. Many flights are heavily in demand and overbooking is common. Of the domestic carriers *Tikal Jets* offer the best service and have the largest craft; they also have a connection in Flores with *Tropic Air* of Belize. *Aviateca* and *Aerocaribe* have connections with Cancún; the latter via Chetumal. For airline telephone numbers, see p.66.

Buses from Guatemala City **to Santa Elena** are run by six companies, all operating from a sleazy and dangerous part of Zona 1 between 16 and 17 calles and 8 and 10 avenidas. Between them they operate around 20 buses per day; all of which pass Río Dulce (for **Livingston**) bridge about 5hr later, on a fast paved road. If you want a reasonably comfortable ride, you need only concern yourself with *Fuente del Norte* (☎2513817) and *Maxima* (☎2324684), the only two companies that run the new, extremely comfortable Mercedes *pullman* services (sometimes known as *lujo*). Fares are about 40 percent more than the standard *corriente* services, but still reasonable at about $12 one way, and the journey takes 10–12hr (as opposed to 14–20hr). Both companies are on the corner of 9 Av and 17 C.

Guatemala City to Flores

If you don't want to do the 554-kilometre trip from the capital to Flores in one go, it's easy enough to do it in stages. Just past the village of **El Lobo**, at Km 175, 100m east of the Río Lobo bridge, *La Ceiba* (③) is a friendly, relaxing place to break the journey, run by an English–Guatemalan couple. Offering good food, budget rooms and camping on the banks of the river, it's ideal if you're visiting the Quiriguá ruins (see p.213). Most buses make a stop in **Morales** on the Caribbean Highway (see p.217). Shortly afterwards, the road to Petén turns north at the **Ruidosa junction**, soon crossing the Río Dulce, stopping-off place for the boat to or from Lívingston. From here it continues through Modesto Méndez – where the tarmac ends – and on through San Luís to **Poptún**, about 100km short of Flores and the best place to break the trip. Work is underway to pave the stretch between Río Dulce and Poptún; you can also fly there with *Koppsa* (☎3606354) from Guatemala City.

Finca Ixobel

A couple of kilometres south of Poptún is the *Finca Ixobel* (☎9277363) a working farm that provides **accommodation** to passing tourists. The farm was originally operated by Americans Mike and Carole DeVine, but on June 8 1990, Mike was murdered by the army. This prompted the American government to suspend military aid to Guatemala, and after a drawn-out investigation, which cast little light on their motives, five soldiers were convicted of the murder in September 1992. Two others have managed to evade capture and their commanding officer, Captain Hugo Contreras, escaped from jail shortly after his arrest.

Carole remains in Guatemala, and continues to pursue the case of Mike's murder with the assistance of a Guatemalan Special Prosecutor. Recent revelations indicate that the CIA heard/knew in advance of a plot to kill her husband. The *finca* remains as popular as ever – record occupancy is now well over a hundred, with latecomers bedding down in hammocks in *champas*, large circular thatched huts.

In the cool foothills of the Maya Mountains, surrounded by lush pine forests, *Finca Ixobel* is a superbly beautiful and relaxing place, where you can swim in the pond, walk in the forest, and stuff yourself with delicious home-grown food. They arrange four-day hikes into the jungle, plus horse-riding day trips and short excursions to nearby caves. There's a guesthouse with private rooms (③), dorms, camping (both ②), hammock space and tree houses The latter are very popular, although only one is actually in a tree: the rest are on high stilts among the pines (both ①). You run up a tab for accommodation and food, paying when you leave – which can be a rude awakening. To get to the *finca* ask the bus driver to drop you at the gate (marked by a large sign), from where it's a walk of about 1km.

Poptún and around

POPTÚN makes a very useful stopoff on the way to Flores, with a *Guatel* office and a bank, and several *pensiónes*. Nowadays the best is the *Izalco* (②): clean and friendly with shared bathrooms. *Pensión Isabelita* (②), with basic rooms along one side of a courtyard, is also good.

The limestone hills surrounding Poptún are riddled with **caves** and coated in lush tropical forest. The largest cave contains an underground river and waterfall that you can swim through, leaping into the cascade, but the most impressive is **Naj Tunich** (Stone House), which was discovered in 1980. Unfortunately, you can't see the wonders within, as it has been closed to visitors since it was severely vandalized in 1989. Its walls are decorated with extensive hieroglyphic texts (400 glyphs in total) and **Maya murals,** which, in addition to depictions of religious ceremonies and ball games, include several graphic and well-preserved drawings of erotic scenes, a feature found nowhere else in Maya art. Caves were sacred to the ancient Maya, who believed them to be entrances to Xibalba, the dreaded underworld. The glyphs and pottery found here all date to a relatively short period from 733 to 762 AD.

Four kilometres north of Poptún, just past the village of **Machaquilá**, you can **camp** at *Cocay Camping* (②) on the banks of the river. It's run by Christina and Paco, who used to work at *Finca Ixobel*, and they offer much the same kind of service. Get off the bus at the south side of the river bridge and follow the signs west for fifteen minutes. Over the bridge to the right, the new *cabañas* of the *Villa de los Castellanos* (☎9277222; fax 9277365; ⑤), offer a comfortable base for adventurous visitors to explore the forests, rivers and caves of central Petén. One amazing five-day horseback trip heads west through an area seldom seen by outsiders; across the Machaquilá Forest Reserve, camping at San Miguel caverns and the ruins of Machaquilá, before descending the Río Pasión to Ceibal (see p.304).

Most buses call in at the village of **Dolores**, set back from the road another 20km north of Poptún. Founded in 1708 as an outpost for missionaries working out of Cobán, these days it's a growing town and the area around is becoming settled by returning refugees. An hour's walk to the north are the unrestored Maya ruins of **Ixkún**, a mid-sized site made up of eight plazas. Fifteen kilometres north of Dolores a road branches northeast, making a short cut to the **Belize border**. Some buses from Guatemala to Melchor use this route, though it's liable to flooding and often in bad condition.

A further 30km brings you to the village and ruins of **El Chal**, signed on the west side of the village and less than 500m from the road. Call in at the small hut by the entrance for a free tour with the guard. There are several plazas and a ball court; the palace complex, built on a ridge gives a view of the surrounding countryside. Although some bush has been cleared, the buildings are largely unrestored – the most remarkable features are a couple of stelae and nearby altars with clearly visible glyphs and carved features. If you need to **stay,** there are a couple of basic hotels, the *Medina* and the *Bienestar* (both ①). From here the road continues unpaved but level and in reasonable condition to Santa Elena.

Other routes to Petén

Coming from the Guatemalan highlands, you can also reach Petén along the backroads **from Cobán** in Alta Verapaz, a long, exhausting and adventurous route covered in more detail on p.271. **From Belize or Mexico**, you can enter the country through Petén. The most obvious route is from Belize, through the border at Melchor de Mencos, but there are also two river routes that bring you through from Palenque or Tenosique in Mexico. All of these are covered later in this chapter.

Flores, Santa Elena and San Benito

Officially, **FLORES** is still the capital of Petén, but in practice its position of importance belongs to quieter times that are now long past. A cluster of cobbled streets and ageing houses built around a twin-domed church, the town fills an island in Lake Petén Itzá. Connected to the mainland by a causeway, its sedate, old-world atmosphere is rarely disturbed by the changes that are transforming the rest of Petén. The modern emphasis lies across the water in **SANTA ELENA** and **SAN BENITO**: chaotic, sprawling towns both, dusty in the dry season, mud-bound during the rains. Santa Elena, opposite Flores at the other end of the causeway, is strung out between the airport and the market, and takes in several hotels, the offices of the bus companies, and a well-established residential area. San Benito, further west, is at the forefront of the new frontier, complete with rough bars, villains, prostitutes, sleazy hotels and mud-lined streets. The three once distinct towns are now often lumped together under the single name of Flores.

The **lake** is a natural choice for settlement, and its shores were heavily populated in Maya times. The city of **Tayasal**, capital of the Itzá, lay on the island that was to become modern Flores. Cortes passed through here in 1525, on his way south to Honduras, and left behind a sick horse which he promised to send for. In 1618 two Franciscan friars arrived to find the people worshipping a large white idol in the shape of a horse called "Tzimin Chac", the thunder horse. Unable to persuade the Indians to renounce their religion they smashed the idol and left the city. Subsequent visitors were less well received; in 1622 a military expedition of twenty men was invited into the city by Canek, chief of the Itzá, where they were set upon and sacrificed to the idols. The town was eventually destroyed by Martín de Ursúa and an army of 235 in 1697. The following year the island was fortified in order to be used as an outpost of the Spanish Empire on the Camino Real (Royal Road) to Campeche. For the entire colonial period (and indeed up to the 1960s) Flores languished in virtual isolation, having more contact with neighbouring Belize than the capital.

Today, despite the steady flow of tourists passing through for Tikal, the town retains a genteel air, with residents greeting one another courteously as they meet in the streets. Though it has little to detain you in itself – a leisurely thirty-minute stroll around the cobbled streets and alleyways is enough to become entirely familiar with the place – Flores does offer the most pleasant surroundings in which to stay, eat and drink.

Arrival

Arriving by bus from Guatemala City you'll be on or near C Principal in Santa Elena, just a few blocks from the causeway to Flores. Coming from the Belize border on *Pinita* you'll probably be dropped at the *Hotel San Juan*, round the corner from the causeway. The **airport** is 3km east of the causeway; a $2 taxi-ride into town per person. **Local buses**, known here as *urbanos,* cover the route for Q0.50 but this entails a time-consuming change half way. They run across the causeway about every ten minutes. Getting **back** to the airport, local buses leave from the Flores end of the causeway about every twenty minutes.

Information

The knowledgeable staff at the **INGUAT** desk in the arrivals hall at the **airport** (Mon–Sat 7.30–9am & 3–5.30pm – sometimes also on Sun) can give you reason-

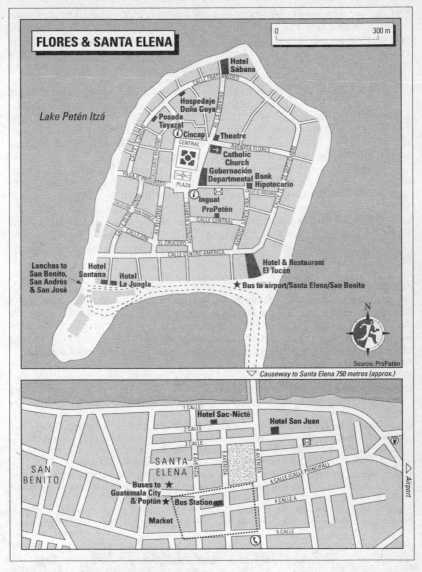

FLORES & SANTA ELENA

0   300 m

Lake Petén Itzá

CALLE FRATERNIDAD

Hotel
Sábana

Hospedaje
Doña Goya

Posada
Tayazal

Cincap

CENTRAL

Theatre

AVENIDA FLORES

Catholic
Church

Gobernación
Departmental

Bank
Hipotecario

PASAJE PROGRESO

PLAZA

Inguat
ProPetén

CALLE EL ROSARIO

CALLE CENTRAL

EL CHUCERO

CALLE CENTRO AMERICA

Lanchas to
San Benito,
San Andrés
& San José

Hotel
Santana

Hotel
La Jungla

Hotel & Restaurant
El Tucán

★ Bus to airport/Santa Elena/San Benito

N

Source: ProPetén

▽ Causeway to Santa Elena 750 metres (approx.)

1 CALLE

Hotel Sac-Nicté

2 CALLE

Hotel San Juan

3 CALLE

SANTA
ELENA

SAN
BENITO

Buses to ★
Guatemala City
& Poptún ★ Bus Station

4 CALLE (CALLE PRINCIPAL)

4 CALLE

4 CALLE A

Market

5 CALLE

▷ Airport

able maps and information, as well as the useful free listings magazine, *Petén*. There's another *Inguat* office on the plaza in Flores (Mon–Fri 8am–4pm; ☎9260533); staff are helpful but will probably direct you across the plaza to **CINCAP** (*Centro de Información sobre la Naturaleza, Cultura y Artesanías de Petén*, Tues–Sat 9am–1pm & 2–8pm, Sun 2–6pm) to examine their more detailed maps, books and leaflets about northern Petén. Here in the *Castillo de Arismendi* you can see exhibits on historical and contemporary Petén and buy medicinal herbs, collected as part of the effort to promote forest sustainability. The **café** upstairs has superb views over the lake. If you're planning to go on a trip to remote parts of the **Maya Biosphere Reserve** (see p.288), check with *ProPetén* on C Central (Mon–Fri 8am–5pm; ☎9261370; fax 9260495) for current information on route conditions, accommodation and guides.

The **post office** in Flores is two doors away from the *Inguat* office; in Santa Elena it's on 2 C, 7 Av, two blocks east of the *Hotel San Juan* (Mon–Fri 8am–4.30pm). The **Guatel** office is in Santa Elena on 5 C, but you're better off using one of the private **telephone** and **fax** services; try *Hotel Alonzo* in Santa Elena or, in Flores, *Cahui*, 30 de Junio (daily 7am–7pm; ☎ & fax 9260494), which is also a good place to leave messages and pick up information.

There's a *Banco de Guatemala* in Flores and a branch of the *Banco G&T* on the main road between Santa Elena and San Benito (Mon–Fri 9am–8pm, Sat 10am–2pm). Note that the **banks** in Flores only change travellers' cheques; the best place for **cash** is *Banoro Bank* near *Banco G&T* (Mon–Sat 8.30am–8pm). For straightforward, swift **credit card cash advances** use *Banco Industrial* in Santa Elena for *Visa* (they also have a working ATM) and *Banco G&T* for *Mastercard*. Otherwise Flores and Santa Elena are full of sharks offering to change money, often at poor rates.

Accommodation

Accommodation in Flores/Santa Elena has undergone a boom in recent years and the sheer number of new **hotels** keeps prices very competitive. There are several good budget places in Flores itself, making it unnecessary to stay in noisier and dirtier Santa Elena unless you have a really early bus to catch – even then you can arrange a taxi. All the top-range hotels listed below take **credit cards**.

FLORES

Hotel la Casona de la Isla, on the west side of Flores, overlooking the lake (☎9260532; fax 9260163). Modern rooms with private bath and a swimming pool with fountains on the terrace. ⑤.

Hospedaje Doña Goya (no phone). Excellent budget guest house, with clean light rooms with fan; the best prices on the island. Some private baths, and rooms at the front have balconies. The family are very friendly, and can organize trips to nearby caves; Chile, who used to work at *Finca Ixobel* (see p.278), speaks good English, some Dutch and German. ③.

Hotel Jungla, a couple of blocks left of the causeway (☎9260634). The best value in this price range, with gleaming tiled floors and private baths with hot water. A rooftop *mirador* allows views over the town and lake. Good restaurant. ④.

Hotel la Mesa de Los Mayas, in the midst of old Flores, down a side street branching off the road around the west side, just past *Hotel Petén* (☎ & fax 9261240). The hotel is a new addition to the restaurant, which is a long-standing Flores institution. It's a pleasant place with good prices, though a little dark. ④.

Hotel Petén, on the west side of Flores (☎9261692). Friendly, small, modern hotel, run by the ever-helpful Pedro Castellanos, with a terrace overlooking the lake. Rooms are set off a leafy courtyard with hot water, fans, private bath and views of the lake. ⑤.

Hotel Sábana, north side of Flores (☎ & fax 9261248; fax 9260163). Large, modern place with nice lake views, especially from the restaurant. Some rooms a/c; all good value. ⑤.

Hotel Santana, by the dock for boats to San Benito and San Andrés (☎9260491; fax 9260662). Recently modernized three-storey building with a small pool and patio overlooking the lake. Comfortable, clean, small rooms with fan and private bath; first floor rooms have private lakeside terraces and air-conditioning. ⑥.

Posada Tayasal, C Union, on the far side of the island from the causeway (☎9260568). Well-run budget hotel, with very clean, comfortable rooms, plus some private baths; shared bathrooms have hot water. Roof terrace, information service, and tours to Tikal. ③–④.

Hotel Tucán, a few metres east of the causeway, on the waterfront (☎9260577). Small, friendly guest house; its restaurant, the best on the island, is far better than the accomodation. Four rooms with fan. ③.

Villa del Lago, next to the *Toucan* (☎ & fax 9260508). Modern two storey building with good value rooms; same management as the *Toucan*. The small breakfast terrace at the rear is a good place to enjoy the sunrise. ④.

SANTA ELENA

Hotel Alonzo, 6 Av, the street leading up from the causeway (☎9260105). New budget hotel determined to keep prices low. Rooms are clean, some with balcony, and a few have private bathrooms; the *baño general* is a little grubby. Public telephone and reasonable restaurant. On the *Fuente del Norte* bus route. ②–③.

Hotel Jade, approaching the causeway to Flores. A backpackers' stronghold: excellent value, simple rooms with good views of the lake. ②.

Hotel Leo Fu Lo, on the other side of the *Jade*. Newish establishment, run by the same people as the *Jade*. Good restauarant attached. ②.

Hotel Sac-Nicte, 1 C 4–45 (☎ & fax 9260092). Smart, clean rooms with fans and private shower; second-floor rooms have good views of the lake. ③.

Hotel San Juan, 8 C, a block from the causeway (☎ & fax 9260042). Conveniently doubles as the *Pinita* bus terminal and travel agent, organizing trips to Tikal, but not particularly good value, and distinctly unfriendly. Most guests are captives straight off the *Pinita* bus; choose elsewhere if you can, as it's very noisy with buses in the early morning. Some a/c rooms, and some with bath. ②–⑤.

Eating and drinking

Good, cheap places **to eat** are in short supply in Santa Elena and few enough in Flores, although a couple of good restaurants cater specifically to tourists. Flores boasts a handful of **comedores**, and a number of **cafés** on the main square and in the surrounding streets – the most popular is the *Café-Bar Gran Jaguar* on the square itself.

FLORES

La Canoa, C Centro America. Popular, good-value place, serving pasta, great soups, and some vegetarian and Guatemalan food, as well as excellent breakfasts.

The Chaltunhá, opposite *Hotel Santana*, right on the water. Great spot for lunch, snacks and sandwiches, and not too expensive.

Restaurant Gran Jaguar, Av Barrios. Guatemalan restaurant geared up for tourists. Good value complete meals include soup, salad, tea, coffee and a pastry.

Jungla, a couple of blocks left of the causeway. The *Mesa*'s chief rival: a little cheaper but a lot less interesting.

El Kóbena, across the street from the *Toucan*. Small restaurant for everything from breakfast to *enchilidas*.

Restaurant Leo Fu Lo, on the other side of the *Jade*. Delicious, expensive Chinese food.

Mesa de los Mayas, in old Flores, down a side street branching off the road around the west side, just past *Hotel Petén*. International and Guatemalan food, with local specialities such as armadillo, *tepesquintle*, wild turkey, deer and local river fish.

Pizzeria Picasso, across the street from the *Tucán*, next door to *El Kóbena*. Run by the same family as the *Tucán*, serving great pizza under cooling breezes from the ceiling fans.

Las Puertas, signed on C Santa Ana. Slightly upmarket, very good pasta, worth it for the atmosphere and occasional live music.

Hotel Santana, by the dock for boats to San Benito and San Andrés. The usual mix of meat, pasta and fish dishes.

El Tucán, a few metres east of the causeway, on the waterfront. Excellent fish, enormous chef's salads, good value meals with fries, and the best waterside terrace in Flores. The nicest restaurant in town.

Vegetarianos, further along the street from *El Kóbena*. Uninspired veggie food in a *comedor*-style setting.

SANTA ELENA

Restaurant Petenchel, on the same street as *Hotel San Juan*, past the park. Simple, good food: the nicest place to eat within two blocks of the main street. You can leave your luggage here while checking on buses or looking for a room.

Restaurant los Amigos, up from the causeway, past *Hotel Alonzo* and across from *Guatel*. Santa Elena's best restaurant, with a fairly extensive menu that caters for vegetarians.

Listings

Bike rental *Cahuí*, 30 de Junio (daily 7am–7pm; ☎ & fax 9260494). Bikes for Q5 per hour.

Car rental Several firms, including *Budget*, *Hertz*, *San Juan* and *Koka*, operate from the airport. *Hertz* also have an office in the *Hotel Tziquinaha*, on the airport road, and *San Juan* in the *Hotel San Juan* in Santa Elena. All offer cars, minibuses and jeeps, with prices starting at around $70 a day for a jeep.

Doctor *Centro Medico Maya*, 2 Av and 4 C, by *Hotel Diplomatico* in Santa Elena (☎9260180) are helpful and professional, though no English is spoken.

Language school The *Eco-Escuela* in San Andrés offers individual tuition in a classroom overlooking the lake; see p.286.

Laundry *Lavandería Amelia*, behind *CINCAP* in Flores, Petenchel, on the street that encircles Flores (both $3 to wash and dry), and a couple on C Centro America.

Travel agents The most helpful is *Arco Iris* (☎9260786). They sell flights, and have the best prices for tours to the ruins and around the lake. For tailor-made tours to the ruins throughout Petén, use *Expedicion Panamundo*, 2 C 4-90 in Santa Elena (☎ & fax 9260501). The manager, Julio Alvarado, provides guides with archeological expertise. You pay more here, but you are guaranteed good value. *EXPLORE*, in Flores on C Central America (☎9260665; fax 9260550) have specialist knowledge of the Petexbatún area; *Agencia de Viajes Tikal* (☎9260758), a small friendly agency in Santa Elena on the same street as the *Hotel San Juan* a block from the causeway, only books tickets and tours but will let you leave luggage while you look for a room.

Voluntary work *ARCAS* (*Asociación de Rescate y Conservación de Vida Silestre*; or Wildlife Conservation and Rescue Association; ☎9260077), runs a rescue service for animals taken illegally as pets from the forests, and always needs volunteers. The work, while rewarding, can be very demanding and you'll need to commit for at least three weeks. Information from the office in Santa Elena, two blocks south of *Guatel*.

MOVING ON FROM FLORES

All the Guatemala City **bus companies** have offices on C Principal in Santa Elena, and there are more than 20 departures daily to the capital. Though it's impossible to list them all, as a rule the more comfortable buses leave in the evening. For travel **around Péten** *Rosita, Pinita*, and *Del Rosio* have only basic buses, and are always crowded. The latter two hike their rates for tourists, so before buying a ticket be sure to pick up the list of regulated fares at *Inguat* or *CINCAP*; it also details departure times. It's best to get on *Pinita* buses in the market, as they are often full by the time they pass the *San Juan* hotel.

Travelling on **to Belize**, *Pinita* buses leave for the border at Melchor de Mencos at 5am, 8am and 10am. *Rosita*, departing from the market in Santa Elena, run buses at 11.30am, 2.30pm and 5.30pm. The *Hotel San Juan* also operates a special express service leaving daily at 5am, which gets to Belize City at 11am and continues to the **Mexican border** at Chetumal, arriving at 1pm – this service is about four times more expensive than the public bus but very much faster and more comfortable. For **Naranjo** (and **boats** to La Palma, Mexico) *Pinita* leave at 5am, 9.30am, 11.30am, and 2pm, and *Del Rosio* at 5am. Along with the regular minibuses to **Tikal**, there's a daily service run by *Pinita*, leaving at 1pm and continuing on to Uaxactún. *Pinita* also runs to **Bethel**, on the Río Usumacinta (5am); **San Andrés** (7am, 8am, noon & 1pm) and **Sayaxché** (6am, 10am, 1pm; plus *Del Rosio* at 12.30pm). If you're heading for **Copán**, *Maria Elena* has a 6am departure from Santa Elena to Chiquimula and Esquipulas. It returns to Santa Elena at 6am.

Tickets for **flights** to Guatemala City can be bought at the airport or the hotels *San Juan* and *Petén* and at any of the travel agents in Santa Elena and Flores. Other flights include the *Aviateca* service to Cancún (5pm); *Tropic Air* to Belize City (Mon–Fri 9.30am & 4.30pm), and *Aerocaribe* to Cancún via Chetumal (Mon–Fri 5.30pm).

For the route to **Mexico** along the Río San Pedro, see p.306.

Around Flores

For most people Flores is no more than an overnight stop, but if you have a few hours to spare, the lake and surrounding hills offer a couple of interesting diversions. The most obvious excursion is a **trip on the lake**. Boatmen can take you around a circuit that takes in a *mirador* and small ruin on the peninsula opposite and the **Peténcito zoo** (daily 8am–5pm; $1) with its small collection of sluggish local wildlife, pausing for a swim along the way. (Note that the concrete waterslide by the zoo can be dangerous and has caused at least one death.) The fee is negotiable but it's obviously cheaper if you can get together a group of four or five people. You'll find the boatmen in Flores behind the *Hotel Yum Kax*, in the southwestern corner of town, and at weekends and holidays at the start of the causeway. If you'd rather paddle around under your own steam you can rent a canoe for around $2 an hour.

Of the numerous **caves** in the hills behind Santa Elena, the most accessible is **Aktun Kan** – simply follow the Flores causeway through Santa Elena, turn left when it forks in front of a small hill, and then take the first right. Otherwise known as *La Cueva de la Serpiente*, the cave is the legendary home of a huge snake: there's a small entrance fee ($1), for which the guard will turn on the lights and explain to you some of the bizarre names given to the various shapes inside.

San Andrés and San José

Though accessible by bus and boat, the traditional villages of **San Andrés** and **San José**, across the lake from Flores, have until recently received few visitors. The pace of life is slower here even than in Flores and the people even more courteous and friendly. The streets, sloping steeply up from the shore, are lined with one-storey buildings: some of *palmetto* sticks and thatch, some coated with plaster, and others hewn in brightly painted concrete. Pigs and chickens wander freely.

In the past the mainstay of the economy was the arduous and poorly paid collection of chicle, the sap of the sapodilla tree, for use in the manufacture of chewing gum. This involves setting up camps in the forest, working for months at a time in the rainy season when the sap is flowing. Today, natural chicle has largely been superseded by artificial substitutes, but there is increasing demand for the original product. Other forest products are also collected, including *xate*, (pronounced *shatay*), leaves used in floral arrangements and exported to North America and Europe, and pimiento, known as allspice. Since the creation of the Maya Biosphere Reserve (see p.288), however, efforts have been made to provide villagers with alternative sources of income.

Getting to the villages is no problem during daylight. *Lanchas* leave from the beach next to the *Hotel Santana* in Flores (6.15am & 5.15pm; Q2), or you can go by boat across to San Benito and pick up *lanchas* there. Once off the boat head left 45° and look for the *Coca-Cola* stand; *lanchas* leave when full, and you'll usually catch one around midday. If you're desperate to get across from Flores or San Benito a chartered *expreso* will cost Q40. **Buses** leave for San Andrés from the market in Santa Elena at 7am, 8am, noon and 1pm; if they don't continue to San José it's an easy downhill walk. **Returning** is simple in the mornings, with *lanchas* at 6am, 7am and noon, and there are regular buses throughout the day.

San Andrés

Most outsiders in **SAN ANDRÉS** are students at the only **language school** in Petén, the *Eco-Escuela*. Since nobody in the village speaks English a course here is an excellent opportunity to immerse yourself in Spanish, without the distractions of Antigua, though it may be daunting for absolute beginners. For more information, check at *ProPetén* in Flores. In the USA you can contact *Conservation International Eco-Escuela* (☎202/973-2264; fax 887-5188).

The best of San Andrés' few simple **comedores** is the *Angelita*, at the top of the hill next to the road junction. Nearby, the only **hotel** in the village, the *Hospedaje El Reposo* (②) offers simple, clean budget rooms, a few with private bath; all have electricity but power cuts are common, so bring a flashlight or candles. Far more luxurious is the *Hotel Nitún* (☎ 9288132; fax 9288113; ⑦ including transport from Flores; discounts for *Rough Guide* readers), 3km west. Thatched stone *cabañas* with hardwood floors have large bedrooms and private bathrooms, and the restaurant serves superb food. This is also the base for *Monkey Eco Tours*, organizing well-equipped expeditions to remote archeological sites. Contact Flores ☎ & fax 9260494 or José Antonio Gonzalez of *Mesoamerica Explorers*, 7 Av 13-01, Edificio La Cúpula, Zona 9, Guatemala City (☎ & fax 3325045).

San José

Just 2km east along the shore from San Andrés, above a lovely bay, **SAN JOSÉ** is even more relaxed than its neighbour. The village is undergoing something of a cultural revival: Itzá, the pre-conquest Maya tongue is being taught in the school, and you'll see signs in that language dotted all around. Over the hill beyond the village is a secluded rocky beach where there's a shelter to sling a hammock and a couple of cabins to rent. A kilometre inland from here, at Nueva San José, the *Posada Yaxni'k* (☎ & fax 9265229; ④) boasts simple, clean rooms with home-made furniture and private bath (no hot water) in a restored *finca* that's now part of a **women's co-operative**; guests can also learn about the use of traditional medicinal plants. Beyond San José a signed track on the left leads 4km to the Classic period **ruins of Motúl**. The site is fairly spread out and little visited (though there should be a caretaker about), with four plazas. In plaza B a large stela in front of a looted temple depicts dancing Maya lords. Plaza C is the biggest, with several mounds and courtyards, while plaza D has the tallest pyramid. It's a secluded spot, ideal for bird-watching, and probably best visited by bicycle from either of the villages. With your own vehicle or bike you could follow the dirt road round the north shore to meet the Tikal road at El Remate.

El Remate, Puente Ixlú and Cerro Cahuí

On the eastern shore of Lake Petén Itzá, 30km from Santa Elena on the road to Tikal, **EL REMATE** offers a pleasant alternative to staying in Flores. Just 2km north of the junction with the road to Belize/Melchor, it's a quiet, friendly village, growing in popularity as a convenient place to base for visits to Tikal, and with several worthwhile places to visit nearby. At the road junction itself, formerly known simply as El Cruce, is the even smaller village of **PUENTE IXLÚ**, where you'll find a thatched information hut with toilets. Inside, a large map of the area shows the little restored **ruins of Ixlú**, 200m down a signed track from the road, on the shore of **Lake Salpetén**. The *Zac Petén* restaurant, on the Melchor side of the junction, is the best place to eat; they'll also let you store your bags. A new *campamento* has been built on the lake shore and you can rent canoes.

Getting to El Remate is easy: every minibus to Tikal passes through the village, while local buses from the market in Santa Elena run to **Jobompiche**, a village on the lake near the Biotopo Cerro Cahuí (see below) and to **Socotzal** on the way to Tikal (every couple of hours 8am–5pm). Coming from the **Belize border**, get off at Puente Ixlú – from here you can walk or hitch the 2km to El Remate.

On the north shore of the lake, 2km from the main road, the **Biotopo Cerro Cahuí** (daily; free) is a 650-hectare wildlife conservation area comprising lakeshore, ponds and some of the best examples of undisturbed tropical forest in Petén. The smallest and most accessible of Petén's *biotopos*, it contains a rich diversity of plants and animals, and is especially recommended for bird-watchers. There are hiking trails, a couple of small ruins and two thatched *miradores* on the hill above the lake; pick up maps and information at the gate where you sign in.

Accommodation from El Remate to Cerro Cahuí

The range of accommodation at El Remate has expanded in recent years, yet each place listed below (in the order you approach it from the village) has a distinctive charm. They're well spaced, with no sense of overcrowding.

Beyond *La Casa Roja*, the route follows the road to Jobompiche, along the north shore of the lake. None is more than 5km from the junction with the Tikal road. There are no private **phone numbers**: to contact any of the places below leave a message on the community telephone (☎9260269).

El Mirador del Duende, El Remate, reached by a stairway cut into the cliff, right opposite the lakeside information kiosk. Hammocks and beds in open-sided, whitewashed stucco *cabañas*, decorated with glyphs. The owner was born nearby, and is an expert on jungle lore, leading hikes to all Petén's archeological sites. The restaurant, high above the lake, serves vegetarian food. ①–③.

La Mansión del Pajaro Serpiente, just beyond *Mirador del Duende* (☎ & fax 9260065 in Flores). Stone built thatched two storey *cabañas* in a tropical garden; the most comfortable accommodation on the road to Tikal. Each suite has a living room, bedroom and immaculate bathroom plus superb lake views. When available, the smaller *cabañas*, usually used by tour guides or drivers, are just as comfortable and about a third of the price. ⑤–⑦.

THE MAYA BIOSPHERE RESERVE

The idea of Biosphere Reserves, conceived in 1974 by UNESCO, is an ambitious attempt to combine the protection of natural areas and the conservation of their genetic diversity with scientific research and sustainable development. The **Maya Biosphere Reserve**, created in 1990, covers 16,000 square kilometres of northern Petén: in theory it is the largest tropical forest reserve in Central America.

On the premise that conservation and development can be compatible, land use in the reserve has three designations: **core areas** include the national parks, major archeological sites and the *biotopos*, areas of scientific investigation. The primary role of core areas is to preserve biodiversity; human settlements are prohibited though tourism is permitted. Surrounding the core areas are **multiple use areas** where inhabitants, aided and encouraged by the government and NGOs, are able to engage in sustainable use of the forest resources and small scale agriculture. The **buffer zone**, a 15km wide belt along the southern edge of the reserve, is intended to prevent further human intrusion while containing many existing villages.

Fine in theory, particularly when you consider that much of the northern reserve skirts the Calakmul Biosphere Reserve in Mexico and that protected land in Belize forms much of the reserve's eastern boundary. In practise, however, the destruction of Petén's **rainforest** proceeds virtually unchecked. Less than 50 percent of the original cover remains and illicit logging, often conducted from Mexico with the complicity of Guatemalan officials, is reducing it further. Although the soil is thin, poor migrant families from Guatemala's agriculturally impoverished southeastern departments arrive daily to carve out *milpa* – slash and burn – holdings in the sparsely settled buffer and multiple use zones. Oil extraction takes place in core areas in the northwest and new roads are being built. Some areas of the reserve are being allocated for *repatriado* – returning refugee – settlement, causing acrimony between those arms of the government tasked to assist the refugees and those whose job it is to protect the reserve.

Although alarming and very real, the threats to the integrity of the reserve are being tackled by a number of government agencies and NGOs, both Guatemalan and international. Foreign funding, from aid programmes and conservation organizations, provides much of the finance for protection and people living in remote villages realize that their future depends on sustainable use of forest resources. Tourism is an accepted part of the plan and, though most visitors see little outside Tikal and Flores, a trip to the more remote *biotopos* and national parks is possible as guides and basic infrasructure become more organized.

La Casa de Don David, 300m beyond *La Mansión* on the oppsoite side of the road. Great value bungalows – one with kitchen – and B&B rooms in gardens down to the lakeshore. Owner David Kuhn built *Gringo Perdido* twenty years ago and is a mine of information about Petén. It's worth stopping by for breakfast even if you're not staying; the food's great and you'll pick up valuable tips. David will pick up from Puente Ixlú if you let him know. ④.

Hospedaje de los Mayas, at the junction of the road to Cerro Cahuí and Jobompiche. Four beds, with mosquito nets, in a simple stick and thatch room. Meals are with the family. ②.

La Casa Roja, 500m down the road to Cerro Cahuí. The best budget hotel by the lake: simple, well-constructed stick and thatch *cabañas* with lake views, plus camping. Swimming, canoe rental, and a good, inexpensive restaurant. ④.

El Gringo Perdido, 3km from the road in the Cerro Cahuí *biotopo* (contact *Viajes Mundial* in Guatemala City: ☎2320605; fax 2538761). Long-established place offering rooms with bath; a mosquito netted bunk in a wooden *cabaña* ; camping, and a fine restaurant. The setting, in forest leading to the lake, is supremely tranquil, and they offer guided canoe tours. ②–⑤.

Hotel Camino Real, beyond Cerro Cahuí, 4km from the highway (☎9260209; in Guatemala City ☎3334633; fax 3374313). Luxury option in extensive lakeside grounds. Lovely rose pink *cabaña*-style rooms rise in tiers from the private beach and guests have free use of kayaks and rowing boats. Superb pool and restaurant, car rental and travel agency. ⑦.

Tikal

Just 65km from Flores, towering above the rainforest, are the ruins of **Tikal**, possibly the most magnificent of all Maya sites. The ruins are dominated by five enormous temples: steep-sided granite pyramids that rise some 40m from the forest floor. Around them are literally thousands of other structures, many still hidden beneath mounds of earth.

The site itself is surrounded by the **Tikal National Park**, a protected area of some 370 square kilometres, and is on the edge of the even larger Maya Biosphere Reserve. The trees around the ruins are home to hundreds of species including spider monkeys, toucans and parakeets. The sheer scale of the place is overwhelming, and its atmosphere spellbinding. Whether you can spare as little as an hour or as long as a week, it's always worth the trip.

Getting there

The best way to reach the ruins is in one of the **tourist minibuses** – VW combis known as *colectivos* – that meet flights from the capital and are operated by just about every hotel in Flores and Santa Elena, including the *Hotel Petén. Hotel San Juan* is the largest operator, with departures at 6am, 8am and 10am, returning at 2pm, 4pm and 5pm (1hr; $6 return). In addition a **local bus** (*Pinita*) leaves the market at 1pm, passing the *Hotel San Juan* and arriving at Tikal about two hours later; it then continues to Uaxactún (see p.298), returning at 6am. There is also a tourist minubus departure at 4am – useful if you want to see the ruins at dawn but would rather not stay at the site. It's usually billed as the **"sunrise at Tikal"** trip, though the appearance of the sun is generally delayed by mist rising from the humid forest – in effect adding to rather than detracting from the experience.

If you're travelling from Belize to Tikal, there are usually no need to go all the way to Flores: instead get off at **Puente Ixlú** (see p.287) – the three-way junction at the eastern end of Lake Petén Itzá – to change buses. The local bus from Santa Elena to Tikal and Uaxactún passes at about 2pm, and there are plenty of passing minibuses all day long.

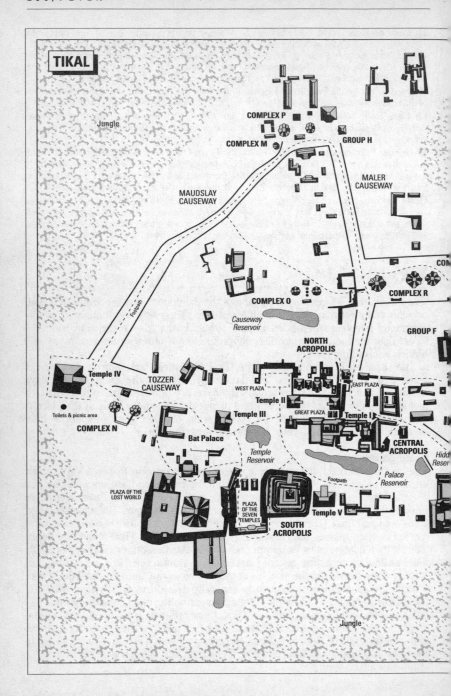

TIKAL

Jungle

COMPLEX P

COMPLEX M

GROUP H

MALER
CAUSEWAY

MAUDSLAY
CAUSEWAY

Footpath

COMPLEX O

COM

COMPLEX R

*Causeway
Reservoir*

GROUP F

NORTH
ACROPOLIS

Temple IV

TOZZER
CAUSEWAY

WEST PLAZA

EAST PLAZA

Temple II

Toilets & picnic area

COMPLEX N

Temple III

GREAT PLAZA

Temple I

CENTRAL
ACROPOLIS

Bat Palace

*Temple
Reservoir*

*Hidd
Reser*

PLAZA OF THE
LOST WORLD

Footpath

*Palace
Reservoir*

PLAZA
OF THE
SEVEN
TEMPLES

Temple V

SOUTH
ACROPOLIS

Jungle

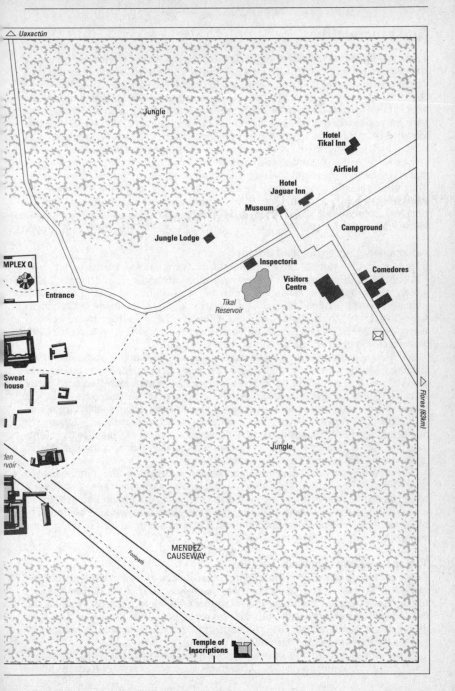

Site practicalities

Plane and local bus schedules are designed to make it easy to visit the ruins as a day trip from Flores or Guatemala City, but if you can spare the time it's well worth staying overnight. Partly because you'll need the extra time to do justice to the ruins themselves, but more importantly, to spend dawn and dusk at the site, when the forest canopy bursts into a frenzy of sound and activity. The air fills with the screech of toucans and the roar of howler monkeys, while flocks of parakeets wheel around the temples, and bats launch themselves into the night. With a bit of luck you might even see a fox sneak across one of the plazas.

Entrance to the national park costs $8.50 a day and you're expected to pay again if you stay overnight, although this is not strictly enforced. If you arrive after dusk you will automatically be issued with a ticket for the next day. The ruins themselves are open from 6am to 5pm, and extensions to 8pm can be obtained from the *inspectoría* (7am–noon & 2–5pm), a small white hut on the left at the entrance to the ruins.

Accommodation, eating and drinking

There are three **hotels** at the ruins, all of them fairly expensive, but with discounts out of season. The largest and most luxurious is the *Jungle Lodge*, which offers bungalow accommodation (⑤) and some "budget" rooms (④), although these are often full, and a pool; reservations can be made in Guatemala City (29 C 18–01, Zona 12; ☎4768775; fax 4760294.) Next door are the reasonably priced *Jaguar Inn* (☎9260002; ⑥ full board) and the *Tikal Inn* (☎ & fax 9260065; ⑤), where you get a private shower and use of a pool.

Alternatively, for a $6 fee you can **camp** or sling a **hammock** under one of the thatched shelters in a cleared space used as a campsite. Hammocks and mosquito nets (essential in the wet season) can be rented either on the spot or from the *Comedor Imperio Maya*. At the entrance to the campsite there's a shower block, although water is sporadic and electricity only available from 6pm to 9.30pm. The *Jaguar Inn* also has a couple of tents, complete with mattresses and drinking water (③); during the dry season you'll need a blanket as the nights can be cold. It is also possible to **camp within the ruins**, although this is, strictly speaking, against the regulations.

The three simple **comedores** at the entrance to the ruins offer a limited menu of traditional Guatemalan specialities – eggs, beans and chicken. For longer, more expensive menus, there's a restaurant in the *Jaguar Inn* and an overpriced café in the new visitors' centre. During the day cold drinks are sold at a number of different sites within the ruins, although it is always a good idea to bring some water.

The site museum and other facilities

Between the *Jungle Lodge* and *Jaguar Inn* hotels is the one-room **Morely Museum** (Mon–Fri 9am–5pm, Sat & Sun 9am–4pm; $2), which houses some of the artefacts found in the ruins, including tools, jewellery, pottery, obsidian and jade. There's a reconstructed tomb and the remains of Stela 29, one of the oldest pieces of carving found at Tikal, dating from 292 AD. A series of photographs reveals the extent to which they've been restored.

At the entrance to the ruins there's a **post office**, a handful of shops, and a visitors' centre containing a selection of the finest stelae and carvings from the site, a scale model of Tikal and a café. Two **books** of note are usually available. The best guide to the site is *Tikal, A Handbook to the Ancient Maya Ruins,* while *The Birds of Tikal,* although by no means comprehensive, is useful for identifying some of the hundreds of species. There are **toilets** in the visitors' centre, behind the central plaza, and near Temple IV (bring your own toilet paper).

The rise and fall of Tikal

According to archeological evidence, the first occupants of Tikal arrived around 700 BC, probably attracted by its position raised above surrounding seasonal swamps and by the availability of flint for making tools and weapons. There's nothing to suggest that it was a particularly large settlement at this time, only simple burials and a few pieces of ceramics found beneath the North Acropolis. The first definite evidence of buildings dates from 500 BC, and by about 200 BC the first ceremonial structures had emerged, including the first version of the **North Acropolis**.

Two hundred years later, at around the time of Christ, the **Great Plaza** had begun to take shape and Tikal was already established as a major site with a large permanent population. For the next two centuries art and architecture became increasingly ornate and sophisticated. The styles that were to dominate throughout the Classic period were perfected in these early years, and by 250 AD all the major architectural traits were established. Despite this, Tikal remained very much a secondary centre, dominated, along with the rest of the area, by **El Mirador**, a massive city about 65km to the north.

The closing years of the **Preclassic** era were marked by the eruption of the Ilopango volcano in El Salvador, which smothered a huge area of the highlands, including much of Guatemala and Honduras, in a thick layer of volcanic ash. Trade routes were disrupted and alliance patterns altered. The ensuing years saw the decline and abandonment of El Mirador, creating a power vacuum and opening the way for the expansion of several smaller sites. To the south of El Mirador the two sites of Tikal and Uaxactún emerged as substantial centres of trade, science and religion. Less than a day's walk apart and growing rapidly, the cities engaged in a heated competition which could have only one winner. Matters finally came to a head on January 16, 378 AD, when, under the inspired leadership of Great Jaguar Paw, Tikal's warriors overran Uaxactún. The secret of Tikal's success appears to have been its alliance with the powerful highland centre of **Kaminaljuyú** – on the site of modern Guatemala City – which was itself allied with **Teotihuacán**, the city that dominated what is now central Mexico.

The victory over Uaxactún enabled Tikal's rulers to dominate central Petén for the next three centuries, during which time it became one of the most elaborate and magnificent of all Maya city states monopolizing the crucial lowland trade routes, its influence reaching as far as Copán in Honduras and Yaxchilán on the Usumacinta. The elite immediately launched an extensive rebuilding programme, including a radical remodelling of the North Acropolis and the renovation of most of the city's finest temples.

Tikal emblem glyph

It is clear that Tikal's alliance with Kaminaljuyú and Teotihuacán remained an important part of its continuing power: stelae and paintings from the period show that Tikal's elite adopted Teotihuacán styles of clothing, pottery and weaponry. The paintings on some vases are even thought to show the arrival of traders and emissaries from Teotihuacán in Tikal. This extended period of prosperity saw the city's population grow to somewhere between 50,000 and 100,000, expanding to cover an area of around thirty square kilometres. Debate still rages about the exact function of Tikal, but it's now widely accepted that it was a real city, surrounded by farmland rather than forest. The elite lived in the centre, possibly housed in the area around the Central Acropolis, and the ordinary people in small residential compounds dotted around the core of the site and out in the fields.

In the middle of the sixth century, however, Tikal suffered a major setback. Already weakened by upheavals in Mexico, where Teotihuacán was in decline, the city now faced a major challenge from the east, where the city of **Caracol** (in the Maya Mountains of Belize) was emerging as a major regional power. Caracol's ambitious leader, Lord Water, launched his first attack on Tikal in April 556 AD, but failed to take the city; a year later he was back, this time managing to assume control and subdue Tikal's powerful elite. Between September 17, 557, and March 18, 692, no new monuments were erected at Tikal, and most of the previous stelae were deliberately erased. During this period of subjugation Tikal was probably not occupied by an invading army but it was almost certainly over-shadowed by the new power of Caracol.

The effect of Caracol's assault was to free many smaller centres throughout Petén from Tikal's influence, creating fresh and disruptive rivalry. By the middle of the seventh century, however, Caracol's stranglehold had begun to relax and Tikal embarked upon a dramatic renaissance under the formidable leadership of **Ah Cacaw**, Lord Chocolate. Just 1.67m tall, this dynamic leader was a giant among the Maya people, who on average stood at just 1.57m. During his reign the main ceremonial areas, the East Plaza and the North Acropolis, were completely remodelled, reclaimed from the desecration suffered at the hands of Caracol. Tikal regained its position among the most important of Petén cities under Ah Cacaw and, as a tribute, his son Caan Chac (who ascended the throne on December 12, 734 AD, and is known as Ruler B), had the leader's body entombed in the magnificent Temple 1. Ah Cacaw's strident approach gave birth to a revitalized and powerful ruling dynasty: the site's five main temples were built in the hundred years following his death, and magnificent temples were still under construction at Tikal as late as 889 AD.

What brought about Tikal's final **downfall** remains a mystery, but what is certain is that around 900 AD almost the entire lowland Maya civilization collapsed. Possible causes range from earthquake to popular uprising, but the evidence points in no particular direction. We do know that Tikal was abandoned by the end of the tenth century. Afterwards, the site was used from time to time by other groups, who worshipped here and repositioned many of the stelae, but it was never occupied again.

Rediscovery

After its mysterious decline little is known of Tikal until 1695 when Father Avendano, lost in the maze of swamps, stumbled upon a "variety of old buildings". The colonial powers were distinctly unimpressed by Petén and for the next 150 years the ruins were left to the jungle. In 1848 they were rediscovered by a government expedition led by Modesto Méndez. Later in the nineteenth century a Swiss scientist visited the site and removed the beautifully carved wooden lintels from the tops of Temples 1 and 4 – they are currently in a museum in Basel – and in 1881 the English archeologist Maudslay took the first photographs of the ruins, showing the main temples cloaked in tropical vegetation.

Until 1951 the site could only be reached – with considerable difficulty – on horseback, and although there was a steady trickle of visitors the ruins remained mostly uncleared. Then the Guatemalan army built an airstrip, paving the way for an invasion of archeologists and tourists. In 1956 the Tikal project was started in order to mount one of the most comprehensive investigations ever carried out at a Maya site. By the time it was completed in 1970 the report stretched to 28 volumes and included the work of 113 archeologists. Despite this, astonishingly little is known for certain about the ruins or their history.

The ruins

The sheer scale of the ruins at Tikal can at first seem daunting. But even if you make it only to the main plaza, and spend a hour relaxing on top of a temple, you won't be disappointed. The **central area**, with its five main temples, forms by far the most impressive section; if you start to explore beyond this you can wander seemingly forever into the maze of smaller structures and outlying complexes.

From the entrance to the Great Plaza

Walking into the ruins the first structures that you come to are the evocatively named **Complex Q** and **Complex R**, two of the seven sets of twin pyramids that were built to mark the passing of each *katun*, a period of twenty 360-day years. This is an architectural feature found only at Tikal and Nakúm, a site to the east. Only one of the pyramids is restored, with the stelae and altars re-erected in front of it. The stelae at the base of the pyramid are blank, as a result of erosion, but there's a superbly carved example – Stela 22* – in the small enclosure set to one side, recording the ascension to the throne of **Chitam**, Tikal's last known ruler, in the month of the parrot, 768 AD. He is portrayed in full regalia, complete with an enormous sweeping headdress and the staff of authority. Q and R were Chitam's main contribution to Tikal's architectural heritage and the last great structures to be built at the site.

Following the path as it bears around to the left, you approach the back of Temple 1 through the **East Plaza**. On the left side, behind a small ball court, is a broad platform supporting a series of small buildings known as the **Marketplace**, and in the southeast corner of the plaza stands an imposing temple, beneath which were found the remains of several severed heads, the victims of human sacrifice. Behind the marketplace is the **Sweat House**, which may have been a kind of sauna similar to those used by highland Indians today. It's thought that Maya priests would take a sweat bath in order to cleanse themselves before conducting religious rituals.

From here a few short steps bring you to the **Great Plaza**, the heart of the ancient city. Surrounded by four massive structures, this was the focus of ceremonial and religious activity at Tikal for around a thousand years, and was still in

---

*This is a copy of Stela 22, the original of which can be seen in the visitors' centre at the entrance to the site, although you probably won't be able to tell the difference.

use long after the rest of the city had been abandoned. The earliest part is the North Acropolis; the two great temples, which disrupted its original north–south axis, weren't built until the eighth century. The plaza covers an area of one and a half acres, and beneath today's grass lie four layers of paving, the oldest of which dates from about 150 BC and the most recent from 700 AD. Temple 2 can be climbed, and although the ascent can be a hair-raising experience, it's well worth it for the views from the top. At present the steeper stairway on Temple 1 is roped off, though it may be reopened in the future.

Temple 1, towering 44m above the plaza, is the hallmark of Tikal – it's also known as the Jaguar Temple because of the jaguar carved in its door lintel (which is now in a museum in Basel). The temple was built as a burial monument to contain the magnificent **tomb of Ah Cacaw** (Lord Chocolate), one of Tikal's most impressive rulers, who ascended the throne in 682 AD (see p.294). It was constructed shortly after his death in 721 AD, under the direction of Ah Cacaw's son and successor Caan Chac. Within the tomb at the temple's core, the skeleton was found facing north, surrounded by an assortment of jade, pearls, seashells and stingray spines, which were a traditional symbol of human sacrifice. There was also some magnificent pottery, depicting a journey to the underworld made in a canoe rowed by mythical animal figures. A reconstruction of the tomb is on show at the site museum. Hundreds of tons of flint and rubble were poured on top of the completed tomb and the temple was built around this, with a staircase of thick plastered blocks running up the front. The staircase, currently being restored, was a skeleton structure, over which the final surface would have been built. The whole thing is topped by a three-room building and a hollow roof comb that was originally painted in cream, red and possibly green. On the front of the comb it's just possible to make out a seated figure and a stylized serpent. The view from the top of the temple, raised just above the forest canopy, is incredible; the great plaza spread out below you, with the complex structures of the North Acropolis to the right and the Central Acropolis to the left. Standing opposite, like a squat version of Temple 1, is **Temple 2**, known as the Temple of the Masks for the two grotesque masks, now heavily eroded, that flank the central stairway. As yet no tomb has been found beneath this temple, which now stands 38m high, although with its roof comb intact it would have equalled Temple 1. The echo from the top of either temple is fantastically clear and crisp as the sound bounces between them.

The **North Acropolis**, which fills the whole north side of the plaza, is one of the most complex structures in the entire Maya world. In traditional Maya style it was built and rebuilt on top of itself, and beneath the twelve temples that can be seen today are the remains of about a hundred other structures. As early as 100 BC the Maya had constructed elaborate platforms supporting temples and tombs here; in about 250 AD the entire thing was torn down and rebuilt as a platform and four vaulted temples, each of which was rebuilt twice during early Classic times. Archeologists have removed some of the surface to reveal these earlier structures, including two four-metre-high masks. In 1959 a trench was dug deep beneath the platform, unearthing a bizarre burial chamber in which the body of a ruler lay surrounded by nine retainers killed for the occasion, along with turtles, a crocodile, and a mass of pottery.

In front of the North Acropolis are two lines of **stelae** with circular altars at their bases, all of which were originally painted a brilliant red. These were once thought to show images of the gods, but archeologists now believe the carvings are of members of Tikal's ruling elite. This elite was certainly obsessive in its recording of the city's dynastic sequence, linking it with great historical moments and reaching as far back into the past as possible. Many of the stelae, throughout the site, bear the marks of ritual defacement, which was carried out when one ruler replaced another to erase any latent powers that the image may have retained. Many of the stelae now in the main plaza were set up in their current positions long after the decline of the city by people who still worshipped here.

The Central Acropolis and Temple 5

On the other side of the plaza is the **Central Acropolis**, a maze of tiny interconnecting rooms and stairways built around six smallish courtyards. The buildings here are usually referred to as palaces rather than temples, although their precise use remains a mystery. Possibilities include law courts, temporary retreats, administrative centres, and homes for Tikal's elite. What we do know is that they were constantly altered and adapted, with rooms, walls and doorways added and repositioned on a regular basis. The large two-storey building in Court 2 is known as **Maler's Palace**, named after the archeologist Teobert Maler who made it his home during expeditions in 1895 and 1904.

Behind the acropolis is the palace reservoir, one of at least twelve clay-lined pools that were fed by a series of channels with rainwater from all over the city. Further behind the Central Acropolis is **Temple 5** (58m) which supports a single tiny room and is thought to be a mortuary shrine to an unknown ruler. Climbing the temple isn't easy, as you have to scramble over rocks and roots, but the view from the top is superb, with a great profile of Temple 1 and a side view of the central plaza. Sadly, it's impossible to climb onto the roof comb and you have to settle for a view through the trees, which is still very impressive.

From the West Plaza to Temple 4

Maya prisoner incised on a bone from Temple 1 tomb, Tikal

Behind Temple 2 is the **West Plaza**, dominated by a large Late Classic temple on the north side, and scattered with various altars and stelae, which, like those in the Great Plaza, owe their present position to Postclassic people, who rearranged many of the smaller monuments. From here the **Tozzer Causeway** – one of the raised routes that connected the main parts of the city – leads west to **Temple 3** (55m), covered in jungle vegetation. A fragment of Stela 24, found at the base of the temple, dates it at 810 AD. Around the back of the temple is a huge palace complex, of which only the **Bat Palace** has been restored. Further down the causeway, on the left-hand side, is **Complex N**, another set of twin pyramids. In the northern enclosure of the complex, the superbly carved **Stela 16** shows the ruler Ah Cacaw, who was buried beneath Temple 1. The altar at its base bears a sculpted scene and a text that possibly refers to the death of his wife.

At the end of the Tozzer Causeway is **Temple 4**, the tallest of all the Tikal structures at a massive 64m. Built in 741 AD, it is thought by some archeologists to be the resting place of the ruler Coon Chac, whose image was depicted on wooden lintels built into the top of the temple. At the top are three rooms, separated by walls 12m thick: to reach them you have to scramble over more roots and rocks, and finally up a metal ladder around the side of the pyramid. Slow and exhausting as this is, it's always worth it, offering one of the finest views of the whole site. All around you the green carpet of the canopy stretches out to the horizon, interrupted only by the great roof combs of the other temples. At any time this view is enthralling – at sunset or sunrise it's unbeatable.

From Temple 4 the **Maudslay Causeway** leads to **Group H**, which includes two more twin-pyramid structures, and from here the **Maler Causeway** takes you back down to the East Plaza, past yet another set.

The Mundo Perdido, the Plaza of the Seven Temples and the Temple of the Inscriptions

The other main buildings in the centre of Tikal are to the south of the Central Acropolis. Here, reached by a trail from Temple 3, you'll find the **Plaza of the Seven Temples**, which forms part of a complex dating back to before Christ. There's an unusual triple ball court on the north side of the plaza, and to the east is the unexcavated South Acropolis. To the west of here is the **Mundo Perdido**, or Lost World, another magical and very distinct section of the site with its own atmosphere and architecture. The main feature is the great pyramid, a 32-metre-high structure whose surface hides four earlier versions, the first dating from 700 BC. Little is known about the ruins in this part of the site, but archeologists hope that further research will help to explain the early history of Tikal. Finally there's the **Temple of the Inscriptions**, reached along the Méndez Causeway from the East Plaza behind Temple 1. The temple (only discovered in 1951) is about 1km from the plaza. It's famous for its 12-metre roof comb, the back of which is a huge hieroglyphic text, only just visible these days.

Outside the main area are countless smaller **unrestored structures**. Compared to the scale and magnificence of what you've seen already they're not that impressive, but armed with a good map (the best is in Coe's guide to the ruins), it can be exciting to explore some of the rarely visited outlying sections. Tikal is certain to exhaust you before you exhaust it.

Uaxactún and around

Twenty-four kilometres north of Tikal, strung out by the side of an airstrip, are the village and ruins of **UAXACTÚN**. With a couple of places to stay, several *comedores* and a daily bus to Santa Elena, the village is an ideal jumping-off point for the remote northern ruins of El Zotz, Río Azul and El Mirador. Substantially smaller than Tikal, the site is thought to date from the same period, although there's also evidence of much earlier occupation and the main group of structures is known to have been rebuilt over a period of 500 years. During the Preclassic period Uaxactún and Tikal coexisted in relative harmony, all hopes of expansion overshadowed by the presence of El Mirador to the north. By the first century AD, however, El Mirador was in decline and rivalry between Tikal and Uaxactún took off as both cities began to expand, embarking on grand building programmes. The two finally clashed on January 16, 378 AD, when Tikal's warriors conquered Uaxactún, forcing it to accept subordinate status.

Detail from Uaxactún vase

The overall impact of Uaxactún may be a little disappointing after the grandeur of Tikal, but if you're planning a stroll through the forest then this is an excellent spot to make for. You'll probably have the site to yourself, giving you the chance to soak up the atmosphere. The most interesting buildings are in **Group E**, east of the airstrip, where three reconstructed temples, built side by side, are arranged to function as an observatory. Viewed from the top of a fourth temple, the sun rises behind the north temple on the longest day of the year and behind the southern one on the shortest day. It's an architectural pattern that was first discovered here but has since been found at a number of other sites. Beneath one of these temples the famous **E-VII** was unearthed, the oldest building ever found in Petén. Its three phases of construction probably date back to 2000 BC, but still seem connected with much later Maya architecture. The original pyramid had a simple staircase up the front, flanked by two stucco masks, and post holes in the top suggest that it may have been covered by a thatched shelter. Over on the other side of the airstrip is **Group A**, a series of larger temples and residential compounds, some of them reconstructed, spread out across the high ground. In amongst the structures are some impressive stelae, each sheltered by a small thatched roof.

Practicalities

Several tour companies in Flores run **day trips** to Uaxactún, and it's easy enough to get there independently. A dirt road, recently improved, links Tikal with Uaxactún, passing the entrance to the ruins at Tikal and skirting around the side of the site before heading north.

Staying overnight you have three options. The *EcoCampamento*, run jointly by *ARCAS* and Uaxactún's guide association (☎9260077 in Flores), has tents and hammocks, protected by mosquito nets, under a thatched shelter (Q20 per person; Q15 if you bring your own gear), while the welcoming *Hotel y Campamento El Chiclero* (④), where the bus stops and parks overnight, offers clean rooms without bath. Owner Antonio Baldizón organizes 4-wheel drive trips to Río Azul, and his wife Neria prepares excellent home cooked food. You can camp or sling a hammock for Q15. Manuel Soto, who built *Mirador del Duende* in El Remate (see p.287), operates *Tecomate* (②), a similar camping, *cabaña* and hammock place at the entrance to the village. He can guide walking trips to any of the more remote Maya sites.

Drawing from polychrome Uaxactún plate

Uaxactún's **guide association** has a small **information office** at the end of the airstrip and will organize **camping trips** to any of the remote northern sites, into the jungle, east to Nakum, and to Yaxha, towards Belize. Equipment is carried on horseback; price ($25 per person per day for a group of three or more) includes guide, horses, camping gear and food. Check in *CINCAP* or *ARCAS* in Flores.

El Zotz, Río Azul and El Mirador

Away to the north of Tikal, lost in a sea of jungle, are several other substantial **ruins** – unrestored and for the most part uncleared, but with their own unique atmosphere. The bulk of the temples lie beneath mounds of earth, their sides coated in vegetation, and only the tallest roof combs are still visible. Doubtless in a year or two they'll be reached by road – today dirt tracks go as far as Río Azul and El Zotz – but for the moment they remain well beyond the reach of the average visitor. Perfect if you're in search of an adventure and want to see a virtually untouched Maya site.

El Zotz

Thirty kilometres west of Uaxactún, along a rough jeep track, sometimes passable in the dry season (with four-wheel drive), is **El Zotz**, a large Maya site in the *biotopo* of El Zotz/San Miguel. To **get there** you can rent vehicles in Uaxactún, or rent a pack horse, guide, food and camping equipment (around $25 all in) from Uaxactún's guide association. After about four hours – almost half way – you come to **Santa Cruz**, now almost abandoned, where Pablo Perez makes a living from selling honey and crocodile skins. He'll direct you to the *aguada* for water (you'll need a filter) and will let you camp if you decide to split the journey. At the site itself you'll be welcomed by the guards who look after the *biotopo* headquarters. You can camp here, and, with permission, use the kitchen and drinking water. Remember to bring some food to share with the guides.

Totally unrestored, El Zotz has been systematically looted, although there are guards on duty all year. The three main temples are smothered in soil and vegetation, but using the workers' scaffold you can climb to the top of the tallest structure, spectacular in itself. Zotz means "bat" in Mayan and each evening at dusk you'll see tens, perhaps hundreds of thousands of **bats** of several species emerge from a cave near the campsite. It's especially impressive in the moonlight, the beating wings sounding like a river flowing over rapids – one of the most remarkable natural sights in Petén.

Walking on, it takes about four and a half hours to get to **Cruce Dos Aguadas**, a crossroads village on a bus route to Santa Elena (bus leaves at 7am). There are a couple of basic *tiendas* and *comedores* here, the best of which is the *Comedor Patojas* where they'll let you sling a hammock or camp. Northwards the road goes to Carmelita (see p.302) for El Mirador and west to Pasos Caballos for El Perú (see p.312; not possible in the rainy season). You could do this trip in reverse by taking the noon bus from Santa Elena to Dos Aguadas, heading to El Zotz the next morning. While this route is shorter, entailing less walking, there's also less forest cover than on the route from Uaxactún, and less chance of seeing wildlife.

Río Azul

Río Azul, a remote site in the northeast corner of Petén, 177km from Flores, was discovered in 1962. The city and its suburbs are thought to have had a population of around 5000, scattered over 750 acres. Although totally unrestored, the core of the site is similar in many ways to Tikal, only smaller. The tallest temple (AIII) stands some 47m above the forest floor, poking its head out above the treetops and giving magnificent views across the jungle. Investigations suggest that the site peaked in the late Preclassic era but remained an important centre well into the Classic period.

Several incredible **tombs** have been unearthed, lined with white plaster and painted with vivid red glyphs. Tomb 19 is thought to have contained the remains of one of the sons of Stormy Sky, Tikal's great expansionist ruler (who ruled Tikal shortly after it conquered Uaxactún), suggesting that the city may have been founded by Tikal to consolidate the border of its empire. Nearby tombs contained bodies of warriors dressed in clothing typical of the ancient city of Teotihuacán in central Mexico, further supporting the theory that Tikal may have derived much of its power from an alliance with this mighty city.

Extensive **looting** occurred after the site's discovery, with a gang of up to eighty men plundering the tombs once the archeological teams had retreated to Flores in the rainy season. During the late 1960s and early 1970s the looting business reached its height, Río Azul supplying the international market with unique treasures. The gangs stripped the tombs bare, hacking away their elaborately decorated walls and removing some of the finest murals in the Maya world. Working with simple tools, several of their number are thought to have died when tombs caved in on them, and in due course, the bodies, buried alongside their Maya ancestors, will probably be unearthed by archeologists. More recently, several new tombs have been discovered, although there's nothing to compare with the murals that have been removed. Today there are two resident guards.

The **road** that connects Tikal and Uaxactún continues for another 95km north to reach Río Azul (a total of 115km from Tikal). This route is only passable in the dry season, and even then it's by no means easy. The three-day round trip by **jeep** (a day each way and a day at the site) involves frequent stops to clear the road. **Walking** or on **horseback** it's four days each way – three at a push. Trips (around $300 per person) can be arranged through a number of agents: check with the *Inguat* representative at Flores airport, at *CINCAP* or *ProPetén* in Flores; *Avinsa*, 4 C 8–15, Santa Elena; *Hotel el Chiclero* in Uaxactún, or *Aventuras Sin Limites*, with offices in the *Hotel Frontera Palace* (☎9265196) at the Belize border (see p.313). Once you arrive at Río Azul you'll be welcome to **stay** at the guard's camp and may even encounter a lonely group of archeologists. The campsite at Ixcán Rio, on the far bank of the Río Azul, is 6km from the main ruins, and during rainy periods vehicles many not be able to ford the river; fortunately, a dugout canoe is provided to carry you and the supplies. For much of the year the river is reduced to a series of pools, and the road continues another 12km to **Tres Banderas**, where the borders of Guatemala, Mexico and Belize meet. Eventually, you'll be able to get your exit stamp in Uaxactún and continue to Mexico using this route: check in Flores or El Remate.

El Mirador

El Mirador is perhaps the most exotic and mysterious of all Petén's Maya sites. Still buried in the forest, this massive city matches Tikal's scale, and may even surpass it, although little is known about its history. Discovered in 1926, it dates from an earlier period than Tikal, flourishing between 150 BC and 150 AD, when it was the dominant city in Petén. Little archeological work has been done here but it's clear that the site represents the peak of Preclassic Maya culture, which was perhaps far more sophisticated than was once believed.

The core of the site covers some sixteen square kilometres, stretching between two massive pyramids that face each other across the forest on an east–west axis. The site's western side is marked by the massive **Tigre Complex**, made up of a huge single pyramid flanked by two smaller structures, a triadic design that's characteristic of El Mirador's architecture. The base of this complex alone would cover around three football fields, while the height of the main pyramid is 43m, equivalent to a twelve-storey building. In front of the Tigre Complex is El Mirador's sacred hub: a long narrow plaza, the **Central Acropolis**, and a row of smaller buildings. Burial chambers unearthed in this central section had been painted with ferric oxide to prevent corrosion and contained the bodies of priests and noblemen, surrounded by the obsidian lancets and stingray spines used to pierce the penis, ears and tongue in ritual bloodletting ceremonies. The spilling of blood was seen by the Maya as a method of summoning and sustaining the gods, and was clearly common at all the great ceremonial centres.

To the south of the Tigre Complex is the **Monos Complex**, another triadic structure and plaza, named after the local howler monkeys that roar long into the night and after heavy rainfall. To the north, the **Leon Pyramid** and the **Casabel Complex** mark the boundary of the site. Heading away to the east, on the other side of the main plaza and the Central Acropolis, the **Paleston Causeway** runs some 500m to the smaller East Group, the largest of which (about 1km from the Tigre Complex) is the **Danta Complex**, another triadic structure, rising in three stages to a height of 70m, which makes it the tallest Maya structure known.

The area **around El Mirador** is riddled with smaller Maya sites, and as you look out across the forest from the top of either of the main temples you can see others rising above the horizon on all sides – including the largest (as opposed to the tallest) Maya pyramid, Calakmul in Mexico. Raised causeways connect many of these smaller sites to El Mirador and some are currently being investigated by visiting archeologists. Among the most accessible are **Nakbé**, 10km south, where a huge Maya mask (5m by 8m), was found in September 1992, and **El Tintal**, around 21km southwest, which you'll pass on your way in from Carmelita.

GETTING TO EL MIRADOR

Any journey to El Mirador is a substantial undertaking, involving an arduous 60km truck ride north from San Andrés to **Carmelita**, a *chicle* and xate gathering centre at the end of the road, followed by two days of hard jungle hiking, during which you'll need a horse to carry your food and equipment. If you don't mind basic living conditions the trip offers an exceptional chance to see virtually untouched forest, and perhaps some of the creatures inhabiting it. The first night after leaving Carmelita is spent – in a simple thatched shelter if you've no tent – by an *aguada* (a waterhole of dubious quality) near the ruins of **Tintal**, a large site which you'll be able to explore on the way back. Another day's walking brings you to the guards' huts at **El Mirador**, where you'll be welcome to stay, using their hearth to cook on. You should bring along food or drink for the guards, who spend forty days at a time in the forest, subsisting on beans and tortillas. The journey, impossibly muddy in the rainy season, is best attempted from mid-January to August; February to April is the driest period. The only other serious hazards are the *garraptas* (ticks), for which you'll need a pair of tweezers and a trusty companion. Whether you take a tour or go independently you're advised to examine the information and maps in *ProPetén* and in *CINCAP* first.

ProPetén organize a five-day **tour** ($85 each for two people) from Carmelita to El Mirador, which includes guide, packhorse, and a night at the *Campamento Nakbe* in Carmelita – you need to bring your own food and water purification system. Other tour companies in Flores offer trips, almost certainly more expensive. It's also perfectly feasible to travel **independently**, arranging a guide and horse in Carmelita (about $25 a day), and bringing your own food and camping gear. To get to Carmelita, take a bus from Santa Elena to San Andrés (see p.286); the noon service continues to Cruce Dos Aguadas (see p.300) a third of the way to Carmelita. From either place trucks will take you the rest of the way, although the road is appalling, making progress unpredictable – expect to pay around $4-5 for the ride. Check with *ProPetén* in Flores before setting out – they often have vehicles going to Carmelita and will know the road conditions. When you arrive at Carmelita ask for Luis Morales, president of the Tourism Committee; he'll arrange guides for the trip and accommodation at the *campamento*. One of the best guides is Carlos Catalan; you can also contact him at the *Restaurant Petenchel* in Santa Elena.

Sayaxché and around

Southwest of Flores, on a lazy bend in the Río Pasión, is **SAYAXCHÉ**, an easy-going settlement that's an ideal base for exploring the forest and its huge collection of archeological remains. A frontier town at the junction of road and river, Sayaxché is an important point of storage for grain and cattle and the source of supplies for a vast surrounding area which is being steadily cleared and colonized. The complex network of rivers and swamps that cuts through the forested wilderness here has been an important trade route since Maya times, and there are several interesting ruins in the area. Upstream is **Ceibal**, a small but beautiful site in a wonderful jungle setting; to the south is **Lake Petexbatún**, on the shores of which are the small ruins of **Dos Pilas**, **Aguateca** and **Tamarindito**. A visit to these offers great opportunities to wander in the forest and watch the wildlife.

Sayaxché practicalities

Getting to Sayaxché from Flores is fairly straightforward, with three *Pinita* **buses** (6am, 10am & 1pm; 2hr) and one *Del Rosio* service (12.30pm) plying the 62km of rough road. The bus brings you as far as the north bank of the Río Pasión, directly opposite Sayaxché. *Del Rosio* cross the river on the ferry; *Pinita* stop on the north bank, from where passengers are ferried across by motorized canoes or a large, flat-bottomed barge.

The best **hotel** in Sayaxché is the *Guayacan* (②, ③ with private bath), a modern building right beside the river, whose basement floods in the wet season. The owner, Julio Godoy, is one of the great patriarchs of Sayaxché. He used to guide big-game hunters until hunting was outlawed, and knows the area extremely well. For a cheaper room, head left down the street above the *Hotel Guayacan* to the *Hospedaje Mayapan* (②). If that's full then try the *Hospedaje Sayaxché* (①) or the *Hospedaje Margot* (①), both very much last resorts. There are plenty of reasonable places to **eat**, the best being the *Restaurant Yaxkin* (closes 8pm); *La Montaña* is almost as good, owned by the knowledgable and helpful Julián Mariona, who arranges **trips** for groups of six or more to all the places mentioned above (around $40 a day) – or to anywhere else you might care to visit. If he can't help you, he'll direct you to someone who can, whether you want to rent a fishing rod or a jeep. There are also always plenty of **boatmen** eager to take you up- or downriver, although they tend to drive a hard bargain. Finally, Pedro Mendez Requena, of *Viajes Don Pedro* (☎ & fax 9286109) offers **tours** of the area from his office on the riverfront. Prices are again high, although it can be fun to shoot the breeze and subtly negotiate a deal. Don Pedro knows the captains of all the *tiendas aquaticas* (trading boats) heading downstream to Benemérito (see p.307), and is a good man to discuss your plans with. Though generally you'll need a horse or a boat to get to the remote sites of **Aguateca** and **Dos Pilas**, during the dry season a four-wheel drive truck runs from Sayaxché to both, leaving at 4am and taking around three hours to reach Dos Pilas.

Changing dollars is relatively easy in Sayaxché and you can change travellers cheques at a good rate in the *Banco Corporativo*, on the corner of the park. They may also have facilities for cash advances.

The ruins of Ceibal

The most accessible and impressive of the sites near Sayaxché is **Ceibal**, which you can reach by land or river. By boat it's easy enough to make it there and back in an afternoon. Not much commercial river traffic heads upstream, however, so you'll probably have to **rent a boat** – ask around at the waterfront and be prepared to haggle: boats take up to six people and generally charge around $40. The two-hour ride is followed by a short walk through towering rainforest. **By road** Ceibal is just 17km from Sayaxché. Trucks that leave Sayaxché in the mornings for El Paraiso, or anywhere to the south, pass the entrance road to the ruins, from where it's an eight-kilometre walk to the site. It should be a day trip, but you may end up stranded at the entrance road waiting for a truck back. If you have a tent or hammock (with mosquito net) you might as well stay – bring food to share with the guards and you'll always be welcome.

Surrounded by untouched forest and shaded by huge ceiba trees, **the ruins** of Ceibal are partially cleared and restored, and beautifully landscaped into a mixture of open plazas and untamed jungle. Although it can't match the enormity of Tikal, and many of the largest temples lie buried under mounds, Ceibal does have some outstanding carving, superbly preserved by the use of hard stone. The two main plazas are dotted with lovely stelae, centred around two low platforms. Fragments of stucco found on these platforms suggest that they were originally decorated with ornate friezes and painted in brilliant shades of red, blue, green, pink, black and beige. During the Classic period Ceibal was a relatively minor site, but it grew rapidly between 830 and 930 AD, apparently after falling under the control of colonists from what is now Mexico. In this period it was the largest southern lowland site, with an estimated population of around 10,000. Outside influence is clearly visible in the carving here: speech scrolls, straight noses, waist-length hair and serpent motifs are all decidedly non-Maya. The architecture is also very different from that of the Classic Maya sites, including the round platforms that are usually associated with the Quetzalcoatl cult, which spread from the north at the start of the Postclassic period, around 1000 AD.

Lake Petexbatún

A similar distance to the south of Sayaxché is **Lake Petexbatún**, a spectacular expanse of water ringed by dense forest and containing plentiful supplies of snook, bass, alligator and freshwater turtle. The shores of the lake abound with wildlife and Maya remains and though the ruins themselves are small and unrestored, they do make interesting goals as part of a trip into the forest. Their sheer number suggests that the lake was an important trading centre for the Maya.

If you can get together a group of three or four it's well worth arranging a boat and guide to take you on a **two- or three-day trip** around the lake. The simplest way to do this is to ask Julián at the *Montaña* in Sayaxché. There are plenty of options – touring the lake on foot, by boat or on horseback, wandering in the jungle, fishing, or bathing in the natural warm springs on the lakeshore – but whichever you opt for you'll need a guide. It's cheapest to **stay** at the sites themselves, camping or sleeping in a hammock, although if you do feel the need for a little luxury there are three **hotels** around the lake. Owned by Julián, the *Posada Caribe* (☎ & fax 9286114; ⑦), on the river before it enters the lake, offers clean, screened cabins and reasonable food. A budget dorm and daily boat service from Sayaxché are planned, and there are boat trips to Aguateca; negotiate rates in advance. The two other hotels are on the lake, both being upgraded. *Mahogany Lodge* (☎3317646; ⑦), has wooden *cabaña*s set in forest on a peninsula jutting into the lake, and camping in comfortable beds under a thatched roof with screens ($20). *Posada San Mateo* nearby caters for upmarket tours and is of little use to passing independent travellers – its bar, however, is a great place to stop off for an ice-cold beer.

Aguateca

Of the two main sites on Lake Petexbatún, **Aguateca**, perched on a high outcrop at the southern tip of the lake, is the more accessible. Discovered in 1957, the site remains completely unrestored, although in recent years it has been the subject of intense archeological investigation. Throughout the Classic period Aguateca was dominated by the nearby city of Dos Pilas, and reached its peak at the beginning of the eighth century, when the latter was developing an aggressive policy of expansion, mounting military campaigns against nearby centres. Stela 2, dated 741 AD, records an attack on Tikal that was mounted in alliance with Ceibal and Dos Pilas, while Stela 1 records the capture of a ruler from Piedras Negras in the same year. After 761 AD Dos Pilas began to lose control of its empire and members of the elite moved their headquarters to Aguateca, attracted by its strong defensive position. Their enemies, however, soon caught up with them, and sometime after 790 Aguateca itself was overrun.

Surrounded by dense tropical forest and with superb views of the lake, Aguateca has a magical atmosphere. You can clearly make out the temples and plazas, dotted with well-preserved stelae. The carving is superbly executed, the images including rulers, captives, hummingbirds, pineapples and pelicans. If you ask the two guards who live here, they'll give you an enthusiastic and well-informed tour, explaining the meaning of the various images and showing you the stelae shattered by looters who hoped to sell the fragments. Aguateca is also the site of the only known **bridge** in the Maya world, which crosses a narrow gash in the hillside, but it's not actually that impressive in itself.

The guards always welcome company and if you want to **stay** they'll find some space for you to sling a hammock or pitch a tent, but you'll need to bring a mosquito net and food. To reach the site from Sayaxché takes a couple of hours and boatmen will usually charge around $150 for the round trip (not unreasonable if you can muster a group). You can also get there by truck in the dry season (see p.304).

Dos Pilas and around

A slightly closer (and therefore cheaper) option is **Dos Pilas**, another unreconstructed site, buried in the jungle a little way west of the lake. This was the centre of a formidable empire in the early part of the eighth century and again boasts some superb carving. From Sayaxché a 45-minute speedboat trip takes you to *Rancho El Caribe*, at the northern tip of the lake, from where it's a further 12km on foot to the ruins. Again, it may be possible to get there by truck during the dry months (see p.304). Two guards live at the site and it's certainly possible to stay here – as always, you should bring a tent or hammock and mosquito net, and enough food to share with the guards. Otherwise you can make a day trip of it and return to Sayaxché in the evening, or stay at the nearby *Posada Caribe*.

Using either Dos Pilas or the hotel as a base, you can fish in the lake, or ask the guards to guide you to the nearby sites of **Tamarindito** (which was responsible for the rebellion against Dos Pilas in 761 AD) and **Arroyo de Piedras**, both of which can be reached on foot. Some days, particularly Sundays, you may be able to get a lift as far as *Rancho El Caribe* (where you can camp), but if not you'll have to rent a boat. Local boats take villagers to Sayaxché; this ends up much cheaper.

Routes to Mexico

River trade between Guatemala and Mexico is increasing rapidly, as are the number of tourists making several obscure border crossings. The most common routes use the cargo boats that make the trip **from Sayaxché** to Benemérito, on the Mexican bank of the Río Usumacinta, several times a week, or **from Flores** via El Naranjo and along the Río San Pedro to La Palma in Mexico. Increasing numbers are travelling the backroads and using the **Bethel–Frontera Corozal** route, the best way to visit the ruins of Yaxchilán (see p.309) and Bonampak. All are reasonably well organized and the people along the way are now used to seeing foreign faces. **Border formalities** are relatively straightforward on the San Pedro route, where there's a Guatemalan immigration office in El Naranjo and a Mexican one along the river at El Pedregal. On the Río Usumacinta there is a Guatemalan immigration post at the riverside army base in Pipiles and a new one at Bethel. On the Mexican side there are immigration posts at a number of places along the Usumacinta, including Boca Lacantún, just outside Benemérito, and Frontera Corozal. Though it's easy enough to cross the border without getting your passport stamped, if you are caught you'll almost certainly live to regret it and could well end up in a Mexican police station for hours, while they leaf through FBI photographs and try to identify you. The Mexican army is usually the first official organization to greet you and anywhere in this part of Chiapas you can expect to have your papers examined by patrols; that said, officials are always very polite and never give tourists any cause for concern.

From Sayaxché to Benemérito and into Mexico

Downriver from Sayaxché the **Río Pasión** snakes its way through an area of forest and swamp that is gradually being occupied by a mixture of well-organized farming cooperatives and impoverished migrants. Along the way tiny river turtles bask on exposed rocks, white herons fish in the shallows and snakes occasionally slither across the surface of the river. There are two main landmarks: a slick American mission on the left-hand bank and the army post at **Pipiles** on the right, which marks the point where the rivers Salinas and Pasión merge to form the Usumacinta. All boats have to stop at Pipiles, where passengers present their papers at the immigration post and luggage may be searched.

On the south bank of the river not far from Pipiles is the small Maya site of **Altar de los Sacrificios**, discovered by Teobert Maler in 1895. Commanding an important river junction, this is one of the oldest sites in Petén, but these days there's not much to see beyond a solitary stela. The beach below, which is exposed in the dry season, is often scattered with tiny fragments of Maya pottery, uncovered as the river eats into the base of the site, carving into ancient burials.

From Pipiles it's possible to head **up the Río Salinas**, south along the Mexican border, through an isolated area visited only by traders buying maize and selling soft drinks and aspirin. Between trips these entrepreneurial geniuses can be found in Sayaxché, loading and unloading their boats, and for a small fee they might take a passenger or two. Most boats only go part of the way up the Salinas, but if you're really determined you can travel all the way to Playitas or Playa Grande (see p.272), and there join the road east to Raxrúja and Fray Bartolomé de Las Casas, or head west across the Ixcán (p.272). This is a rough trip for which you'll need a hammock, a mosquito net, a week or two, and a great deal of patience.

Following the **Usumacinta** downstream from Pipiles you arrive at **BENEMÉRITO** in Mexico, a sprawling frontier town at the end of a new dirt road from Palenque. Passengers from Sayaxché are charged a few dollars for what is usually an eight-hour trip, although boats with business along the way can take a couple of days to get this far. Benemérito is the destination of most of the cargo traffic, but if you're in a hurry, or want to go further down the Usumacinta to Yaxchilán, you can rent a fast boat – expect to pay around $150 from Sayaxché to Benemérito (3–4hr), or double that to Yaxchilán (8hr). **From Benemérito** you can head on to Yaxchilán by boat or, much cheaper, by bus to Frontera Corozal and then by boat. Benemérito has a few basic hotels and *comedores*. The best restaurant in town is the *A y D* on the main road, parallel to the river and about 1km from it; the owner speaks some English, changes dollars, and can give bus information.

Buses leave Benemérito for Palenque (9hr) at least five times a day. The first **immigration post** that you'll pass is a couple of kilometres outside Benemérito at Boca Lacantún, where the road for Palenque crosses the Río Lacantún – ask the bus driver to stop for you while you go in and pick up a tourist card.

By road from Benemérito to Frontera Corozal

Between Benemérito and Palenque there's a 20km branch road off the main route to the riverside village of **FRONTERA COROZAL**, the nearest settlement to Yaxchilán. A daily bus from Palenque leaves at 9am and passes the junction for Corozal at 4pm – otherwise, hitching is possible, though traffic is scarce. The bus returns to Palenque at 4am. In Frontera Corozal itself there's nowhere official to

stay, although this may change as the whole area opens up. Certainly, if you ask around you'll be able to find somewhere to sling a hammock, and you should be able to **camp** on the football pitch once the evening game has drawn to a close. The village does have a couple of simple *comedores* and an **immigration post** – so if you arrive directly by boat from Sayaxché, or across the river from Bethel (see below), you can get a tourist card here. If you want to visit Yaxchilán you *must* register at the immigration post. For details of the river trip from Benemérito to Frontera Corozal, see below.

From Bethel to Frontera Corozal

Very few commercial boats do the trip between Sayaxché and Frontera Corozal, but if you're in a group of five or more you could always rent a boat to take you there, which should take about six or seven hours. The cheapest and best way to get there from the Guatemala side, however, is along the rough road to **BETHEL** on the Río Usumacinta, where there is a new Guatemalan immigration post. Two buses a day leave Flores for Bethel (5am & 1pm), passing the junction just north of Sayaxché a couple of hours later. It's a tough and exhausting bus ride (at least 5hr from Flores), but at Bethel it's relatively easy to find a *lancha* heading downstream, or you can rent one (Q150 for three people to Frontera Corozal; $100 to Yaxchilán).

Bethel itself is a pleasant village with wide grassy streets and plenty of trees to provide shade. You can **camp** above the riverbank and there are several **comedores** and *tiendas*. Though clearly the remains of an important Maya city, today the **Bethel ruins**, 1.5km from the village, are little more than tree-covered mounds, their existence unknown to archeologists until 1995. There's an **eco-campamento** set among them – the *Posada Maya* – with thatched shelters for tents and hammocks on top of a wooded cliff high above the river. Prices are relatively high for camping (Q30 per person) but this includes comfortable beds (with sheets) in mosquito-proof tents. *Cabañas* are under construction. Ask for Don Prospero in the village. The men of the village can guide you through the jungle to a cenote and can arrange trips to other ruins.

By river to Yaxchilán and Piedras Negras

As you head downriver from Benemérito, the **Río Usumacinta** marks the border between Guatemala and Mexico, passing through dense tropical rainforest, occasionally cleared to make way for pioneer villages and cattle ranches, particularly along the Mexican bank. In the past this border area has been the scene of fighting between the Guatemalan army and guerrilla forces, but these days you're unlikely to meet either. Seven-day **trips down the Usumacinta**, from Bethel to Tenosique are run by *Maya Expeditions* at 15 C 1-91, Zona 10, Guatemala City (☎3634955; fax 3634164).

Below Benemérito the first place of any interest on the river is the **Planchon de Figuras**, at the mouth of the Lacantún, a river that feeds into the Usumacinta from the Mexican side. One of the least-known and most unusual of all Maya sites (though hardly a site in the conventional sense), this consists of a superb collection of graffiti carved into a great slab of limestone that slopes into the river. Its origin is completely unknown, but the designs, including birds, animals, temples and eroded glyphs, are certainly Maya. A little further downriver is the Chorro waterfall, a series of beautiful cascades some 30km before Frontera Corozal.

Yaxchilán

Boats to the Maya **ruins of Yaxchilán**, 15km beyond Frontera Corozal, can be rented in Sayaxché, Benemérito and Frontera Corozal. Rates are high: if you're on your own or in a small group, it's cheaper to get on a boat that's being used by a tour group, or to get a lift with one of the local boats that can sometimes be persuaded to go on to the ruins. If you're coming from Guatemala and plan to travel all the way to Yaxchilán by boat then it's cheaper to rent one for the whole trip – speak to Julian in Sayaxché.

The ruins are undeniably the most spectacular on the Usumacinta, superbly positioned on the Mexican bank, spread out over several steep hills within a great loop in the river. This is an important location, and carvings at Yaxchilán, like those at the neighbouring sites of Bonampak and Piedras Negras, tell of repeated conflict with the surrounding Maya centres. By 514 AD, when its emblem glyph was used for the first time, Yaxchilán was already a place of some size, but its era of greatness was launched by the ruler Shield Jaguar, who came to power in 682 and extended the city's sphere of influence through a campaign of conquest. At this stage it was sufficiently powerful to form a military alliance that included not only the Usumacinta centres but also Tikal and Palenque. Shield Jaguar was succeeded by Bird Jaguar III, possibly his son, who seems to have continued the campaign of military expansion. Less is known about the later years in Yaxchilán, although building continued well into the Late Classic period so the site was probably occupied until at least 900 AD.

What you see today is a collection of plazas, temples and ball courts strung out along the raised banks of the river, while the low hills in the centre of the site are topped with impressive palaces. The structures are all fairly low, but each of the main temples supports a massive honeycombed roof, decorated with stucco carvings. The quality of this carving is yet again exceptional, though many of the best pieces have been removed to museums around the world: one set of particularly fine lintels is displayed in the British Museum in London.

More recent finds, however, including some incredibly well-preserved carving, remain on site. When the layers of vegetation are peeled back the original stonework appears unaffected by the last thousand years, with flecks of red paint still clinging to the surface. Yaxchilán's architecture focuses heavily on the river, and the remains of a built-up bank suggest that it might have been the site of a bridge or toll gate. At low water you can see a pyramid, about 8m square at the base, 6m high, with a carved altar on top. Built on the river bed and completely submerged at high water, it is believed by archeologists to be a bridge abutment.

Until fairly recently the site was still used by Lacandon Indians, who came here to burn incense, worship, and leave offerings to their gods. The whole place still has a bewitching atmosphere, with the energy of the forest, overwhelming in its fertility, threatening to consume the ruins. The forest here is relatively undisturbed and buzzes with life; toucans and spider monkeys loiter in the trees, while bats are now the main inhabitants of the palaces and temples.

Arriving at the site by boat you'll be met by one of the guards who live here to ward off the ever-present threat of looting. They are happy to show you round the site, though they generally ask a small fee for their labours. You're welcome to camp too, though mosquitoes can be a problem – whether you're staying or not – particularly in the rainy season.

Piedras Negras

Downstream from Yaxchilán, the ruins of **Piedras Negras** stand on the Guatemalan side of the river. Despite being possibly as extensive as Tikal, this is one of the least accessible and least visited of Maya sites. Though many of the very best carvings are on display in the National Museum of Archeology in Guatemala City, where they're a great deal easier to see, there's still plenty to experience on site. Piedras Negras, whose name refers to the stones lining the river bank here, was closely allied with Yaxchilán and probably under its rule at various times. Maps of this area often show an airstrip alongside the site, but this has long been lost to the jungle, so don't count on landing here.

Piedras Negras emblem glyph

Upon arrival, the most immediately impressive monument is a large rock jutting over the riverbank with a carving of a male seated figure presenting a bundle to a female figure. This was once surrounded by glyphs, now badly eroded and best seen at night with a torch held at a low angle. Continuing up the hill, across plazas and over the ruins of buildings you get some idea of the city's size. Several buildings are comparatively well-preserved, particularly the **sweat baths**, used for ritual purification; the most imposing of all is the **Acropolis**, a huge complex of rooms, passages and courtyards towering 100m above the riverbank. A **megalithic stairway** at one time led down to the river, doubtless a humbling sight to visitors (and captives) before the forest invaded the city. Another intriguing sight is a huge double-headed turtle glyph carved on a rock overhanging a small valley. This is a reference to the end of a *katun*; inside the main glyph is a giant representation of the day sign Ahau (also signifies Lord), recalling the myth of the birth of the maize god. During research carried out at Piedras Negras in the 1930s the artist and epigrapher Tatiana Proskouriakoff noticed that dates carved on monuments corresponded approximately to a human life span, indicating that the glyphs might refer to events in one person's lifetime, possibly the rulers of the city. Refuted for decades by the archeological establishment, the theory was later proved correct.

Traditionally, the presence of FAR guerrillas in the region protected the ruins from systematic looting – neither looters nor the army dared enter. Now the guerrillas are just a memory and access from the Mexican bank is becoming easier, it remains to be seen how long Piedras Negras can maintain its relatively untouched state.

Below Piedras Negras the current quickens and the river drops through two massive canyons. The first of these, **Cañon de San José**, is a narrow corridor of rock sealed in by cliffs 300m high; the second, the **Cañon de las Iguanas**, is less dramatic. Travel on this part of the river is treacherous and really only possible on white-water rafts: smaller craft have to be

Human sacrifice depicted on Stela II, Piedras Negras

carried around the two canyons, and under no circumstances is it possible to travel upriver.

El Naranjo and the San Pedro river route into Mexico

The most direct and popular route **from Flores to Mexico** takes you along the Río San Pedro, through a remote, deforested area. The river trip starts in **EL NARANJO**, a small settlement in the northwest of Petén. *Pinita* buses from Flores run to El Naranjo at 5am, 9.30am, 11.30am and 2pm; there's also a *Del Rosio* service at 5am. They return at the same times; the trip, over rough roads, takes between four and five hours. El Naranjo is a rough spot, consisting of little more than an army base, an immigration post and a main street leading to the ferry, with a few shops, *comedores* and basic hotels. Once you arrive you'll need to confirm the **boat schedule**; there's usually a service ($20 per person) for Mexico at around 1pm, returning from La Palma at 8am. The Guatemalan immigration post is next to the dock, and you'll be charged a fee to leave; generally $5 for Americans and Q5 for Europeans, with "regulations" often depending on the whim of the official. You can change money with the boatmen or at the *tienda*, but rates are poor. If you miss the boat, there's little to do here, though you could wander around the ruins near the dock; the army has machine-gun posts on top of the pyramids but the soldiers are friendly enough.

The *Hotel Quetzal* (②) by the boat dock is the most convenient **place to stay**, but it's basic and uncomfortable with dark cramped rooms and filthy toilets, and the restaurant serves poor, overpriced meals. Across the river, a few minutes by boat upstream from the ferry, the friendly, family-run *Posada San Pedro* has much better accommodation in *cabañas* with private bath and mosquito-netted beds (☎9261276 in Flores; Guatemala City ☎3341823; ④). It is mostly used by tour groups but if you're in a small group it may be worthwhile to see if they have space. You could also try the *CECON* headquarters, across from the ferry 150m downstream – a boy in a canoe will take you for a couple of quetzals. This is the administrative centre for the *biotopo* Laguna del Tigre, and if not in use by students and scientists there may be dorm space. They'll also let you use the kitchen.

Heading downriver, the next port of call is the Mexican immigration post, about an hour away. Beyond that another three hours brings you to **LA PALMA** in Mexico, a small riverside village with bus connections to Tenosique, a good transport hub. There's nothing much in La Palma, but at a hut beside the river you can buy cold beer and food, and sling your hammock if you miss the bus. This same hut, owned by Nicolás Valenzuela, is the place to wait if you're heading into Guatemala on the afternoon boat. Entrepreneur Nicolás changes money – at a bad rate, but if you're in need of pesos or quetzals it's the best you'll get. If you miss the last (5pm) bus to Tenosique (and coming from Guatemala most people do), it's best to refuse Nicolás' offer of a taxi, as the last bus out of there is at 7pm and you're likely to miss that too. Resign yourself to staying the night and making an early start – the first bus out is at 6am. You can **camp** in the shelter at restaurant *Parador Turistico* by the river bank, which has the best **food** in town; they also have a couple of basic **rooms to rent**.

If you're entering Guatemala from La Palma you'll be able to catch a bus to Flores (4–5hr) from the immigration post in El Naranjo at about 2pm.

The Ruta Guacamaya and the ruins of El Perú

To the east of El Naranjo, in the upper reaches of the Río San Pedro, is **El Perú**, a seldom-visited and unreconstructed archeological site buried in some of the wildest rainforest in Petén. The temple mounds are still coated in vegetation but the site is perhaps most famous for its many well-preserved **stelae**. The two guards welcome visitors, particularly if you bring along a little spare food. You can get there by boat from El Naranjo, travelling upriver for a day, spending a day at the site and then heading back the next day, but a more practical route is being developed by *ProPetén* in Flores. Known as **La Ruta Guacamaya**, this is an exciting five-day trip by truck, horse and boat along rivers and through primary forest, taking in remote ruins and the largest concentrations of scarlet macaws in northern Cental America. Contact *ProPetén* for full details.

From Flores to Belize

The hundred kilometres from Flores to the border with Belize takes you through another sparsely inhabited section of Petén, a journey of around three hours by bus. **Buses** leave from the *Hotel San Juan* in Santa Elena at 5am, 8am and 10am, and *Rosita* buses from the market at 11.30am, 2.30pm and 5.30pm. You'll need to set out early in order to get to San Ignacio or Belize City the same day: if you catch the 5am service you can make it straight through to Chetumal, in Mexico. Along the way the bus passes through Puente Ixlú (p.287), halfway between **Tikal** and Flores, so if you're coming directly from the site you can pick it up there. Once again you should set off as early as you can to avoid getting stranded.

Hotel San Juan also operates an **express service** to Belize City (5hr; $20) and Chetumal (8hr; $36), leaving the hotel at 5am. More than twice as expensive as the public bus, this service is quicker and smoother and takes you right through.

Lake Yaxhá and the ruins of Yaxhá and Nakúm

About halfway to the border, **Lake Yaxhá** is a shallow limestone depression similar to Lake Petén Itzá, ringed by dense rainforest. The lake is home to two Maya sites and offers access to a third, **Nakúm**, to the north. The first two can be visited by car in a day, but Nakúm is more remote, demanding a couple of days or more, for which you'll need a hammock and food at the very least.

The Yaxhá ruins

The main Flores–Belize road passes about 8km to the south of the lake – ask the driver to drop you at the turning, from where it's a sweltering two-hour walk along the branch road to the lake. Here the road heads around to the right towards a *finca*, but to make it to **the ruins of Yaxhá** you want to bear off to the left, along a smaller track. At the ruins you'll find a couple of guards, who are permanently stationed here to ward off potential looters. Stuck out in the wilderness they're always pleased to see strangers and will be glad to show you around.

The ruins, rediscovered in 1904, are spread out across nine plazas. Though clearing and restoration work has recently begun, don't expect any of the manicured splendour of Tikal, but do count on real atmosphere as you attempt to discover the many features still half hidden by the forest. The most unusual aspect of Yaxhá is that the town appears to have been laid out on a grid pattern, more typical of Teotihuacán than of the less systematic growth of a Maya centre.

There is another small site, known as **Topoxte**, on the lakeshore, reached by dirt road from the eco-camp. It's not particularly impressive, but again there's one very unusual feature: everything is built on a miniature scale, including tiny temples and stelae. Inevitably an American archeologist has suggested that the site is evidence of a race of pygmy Maya.

If you want to **stay**, the wonderful *El Sombrero Eco-Campamento* (☎9265299; fax 9265198; in Guatemala City ☎4482428; in San Ignacio, Belize ☎092/3508; ②–⑤), on the south side of the lake just off the road, has no-smoking rooms with solar power in wooden jungle lodges and space for camping. Meals – somewhat pricey – are served in the open-air restaurant, and there's a library of books on wildlife and the Maya. They can also organize boat trips and horseback tours to ruins as distant as Tikal. There's another *eco-campamento*, run by *Inguat*, on the far side of the lake, below the ruins, where you can pitch a tent or sling a hammock beneath a thatched shelter for free.

The ruins of Nakúm

About 20km north of Lake Yaxhá are the unrestored **ruins of Nakúm**, a somewhat larger site. The road between Yaxhá and Nakúm is rarely passable so if you plan to visit both sites you'll probably have to walk to Nakúm. The most impressive structure is the residential-style palace, which has forty rooms and is similar to the North Acropolis at Tikal. It's thought that Nakúm was a trading post in the Tikal empire, funnelling goods to and from the Caribbean coast, a role for which it is ideally situated at the headwaters of the Río Holmul. Once again there are a couple of guards permanently posted at the site and they'll be more than willing to show you around and find a spot for you to sling a hammock or pitch a tent.

If you'd rather not walk back to the road from Nakúm then it's also possible to **walk to Tikal** in a day, a distance of around 25km. To do this you'll need to persuade one of the guards to act as a **guide** as there's nothing marking the route. Alternatively, you could bring a guide with you for the entire trip, which is certainly the best course of action if you're in a group. To arrange a guide, speak to *Inguat* or see *CINCAP* in Flores; expect to pay around $40 per day for a guided trip from Flores to Yaxhá, Nakúm and Tikal. *El Sombrero* offer a horse-riding adventure along this route, which can include a day's fishing in the lake. It's also possible to make the trip the other way around, from Tikal to Yaxhá, if you ask around amongst the guards at the site. Approached from this direction, however, the circuit is somewhat anti-climactic, as the sites get smaller and smaller.

Melchor de Mencos and the border

MELCHOR DE MENCOS marks the Guatemalan side of the Belize–Guatemala border. There are several cheap hotels and *comedores*, though only one place worth staying: just before you leave Guatemala there's one last tourist shop, useful if you wish you'd bought more in the highlands or have a few quetzals to get rid of. If you get stuck overnight, head for the *Hotel Frontera Palace* (☎ & fax 9265196; ④), just over the bridge on the riverbank, where rooms in pleasant thatched cabins have the luxury of hot water. There's also a restaurant. The owner, Marco Gross, who runs a small gift shop and travel agency, knows Petén extremely well and can organize trips to any of the Maya sites. The next best place to stay is the *Hilton* (②), overlooking a rather smelly creek at the far end of the street.

The Guatemalan and Belizean **border posts** are on the eastern bank of the river. Despite the countries' differences, border formalities are fairly straightforward; you have to pay a small departure tax on leaving Guatemala. **Money changers** will pester you on either side of the border and will give a fair rate, once you've bargained with a couple. There's also a **bank** (Mon–Fri 8.30am– 2pm) just beyond the immigration building next to the *Frontera Palace*.

Buses leave **for Belize City** every hour or so, right from the border. Indeed, most actually begin their journey from the market in Melchor; for others you may have to take a shared taxi to Benque Viejo or to San Ignacio (Bz$4 per person; 20min). The journey takes a little over three hours along a good, fast, paved road.

If you can muster a small group and are in a real hurry to get to Belize City, or beyond into Mexico, then you might consider renting a minibus, which will enable you to make it right through to Mexico in a day: contact the *Hotel Petén* in Flores. Heading in the other direction, there are buses from Melchor **to Flores** at 3am, 5am, 8am, 11am, 1pm and 3pm (possibly also 5pm). As usual it's well worth setting out early, when the bus service is at its best.

fiestas

Petén may not offer Guatemala's finest fiestas, but those that there are abound with typical *Ladino* energy and feature fireworks and heavy drinking. In some of the smaller villages you'll also see traditional dances and hear the sounds of the marimba – transported here from the highlands along with many of the inhabitants of Petén.

JANUARY
Flores has its fiesta from the 12th to 15th; the final day is the most dramatic.

MARCH
San José has a small fiesta from the 10th to 19th.

APRIL
Poptún's fiesta, from April 27 to May 1, is held in honour of San Pedro Martír de Merona.

MAY
San Benito has a fiesta from the 1st to 9th, which is sure to be wild and very drunken. The border town of **Melchor de Mencos** has its fiesta from the 15th to 22nd, with the last day as

the main day. **Dolores** has a fiesta from the 23rd to 31st, with the principal day on the 28th.

JUNE
Sayaxché has a funfair on the 16th, in honour of San Antonio de Padua.

JULY
Santa Ana's action runs from the 18th to 26th.

AUGUST
San Luís has a fiesta from the 16th to 25th, with the main day on the last day.

OCTOBER
San Francisco's fiesta runs from the 1st to 4th.

NOVEMBER
San Andrés, across the lake from Flores, has a fiesta from the 21st to 30th, with the last day the main day.

DECEMBER
Finally **La Libertad** has its fiesta from the 9th to 12th.

travel details

Buses

This is a rundown of the **scheduled bus services** available: for details of other options, see the relevant accounts in the text.

From Guatemala City to Flores (12–15hr), *Fuente del Norte* (17 C 8–46, Zona 1, Guatemala City; ☎2513817) leave at 7.30am, 3pm, 5pm, 7pm and 9pm. *Maya Express* (17 C 9–36, Zona 1, Guatemala City; ☎2321914), run buses at 4pm, 6pm and 8pm. All pass through Poptún and Río Dulce bridge for **Lívingston**.

From Flores to Guatemala City there are at least 20 departures per day, including *Fuente del Norte* at 8am, 11am, 3.45pm, 7pm and 9pm; *Maya Express* at 4pm, 6pm and 8pm. All pass Poptún and Río Dulce.

From Flores to Tikal minibuses (less than 2hr) leave from the *Hotel Petén* and *Hotel San Juan* at 4am, 6am, 8am and 10am, returning at 2pm, 4pm and 5pm; and also from the airport, connecting with planes from Guatemala City. The *Pinita* bus at 1pm (2hr) calls at Uaxactún; it returns at 6am.

From Flores to Sayaxché *Pinita* (at the *Hotel San Juan*) have buses at 6am, 10am and 1pm (2hr); in addition, *Del Rosio* buses to **Cruce del Pato** pass Sayaxché. Buses return **from Sayaxché to Flores** four times daily. There are no scheduled services from Sayaxché to Benemérito, Mexico (by boat), but buses run twice a day from Flores to Cruce del Pato (for Raxrúja in the Verapaces).

From Flores to Melchor de Mencos (3hr), *Pinita* run buses at 5am, 8am, 10am; *Rosita* at 11.30am, 2.30pm and 5.30pm, returning at 3am, 5am, 6am, 8am, 11am, 1pm and 3pm.

From Flores to Belize there is a minibus to Belize City at 5am; the early bus from Flores to Melchor de Mencos can get you to Chetumal the same day.

Flores to El Naranjo (5hr). *Pinita* buses run at 5am (to connect with the boat), 9.30am, 11.30am and 2pm, returning at the same times.

Melchor de Menchos to Flores has a minibus as required; there are also 6 local buses daily (3hr).

Boats

From Flores/San Benito to San Andrés, boats (25min) leave when full, in daylight hours only.

From Flores to San Andrés there are *directo* services at 6.15am and 5.15pm.

From San Andrés to Flores boats leave at 6am, 7am and noon.

From El Naranjo the boat to **La Palma** in Mexico leaves at 1pm.

From Sayaxché to Benemérito, Mexico, a trading boat leaves most days (at least 12hr); rented speedboats take 2hr 30min–3hr.

From Sayaxché to Rancho el Caribe on the Río Petexbatun there's a daily *lancha* (2hr).

Planes

Guatemala City to Flores (50min). *Aerovias, Aviateca, Tikal Jets* and *Tapsa* fly once daily, with outward flights in the early morning, around 7am, returning at around 4pm. *Aviateca* fly twice daily at 7am and 4pm in both directions.

From Flores there are also flights **to Belize City** with *Tropic Air* (Mon–Fri 9am & 4pm).

From Flores to Cancún there are flights with *Aviateca* (Tues, Wed, Fri, Sat & Sun) and with *Aerocaribe* (Mon, Wed & Fri). You can also charter flights to Uaxactún, Dos Lagunas, El Naranjo, Sayaxché, Poptún, Río Dulce, Lívingston and to the Honduras border.

PART THREE

BELIZE

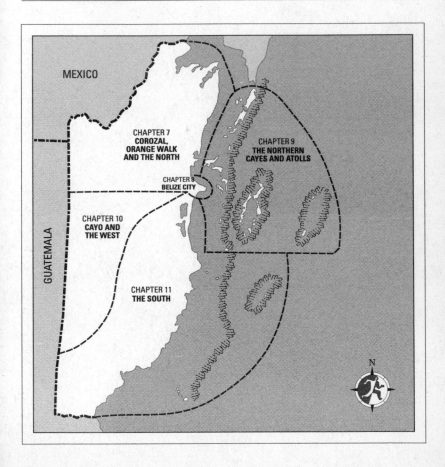

MEXICO

CHAPTER 7
**COROZAL,
ORANGE WALK
AND THE NORTH**

CHAPTER 9
**THE NORTHERN
CAYES AND ATOLLS**

CHAPTER 8
BELIZE CITY

CHAPTER 10
**CAYO AND
THE WEST**

GUATEMALA

CHAPTER 11
THE SOUTH

N

Introduction

Belize is an anomaly. Peaceful, democratic and English-speaking, it seems in many ways not to belong in Central America at all. And indeed, to an extent, it is more a Caribbean nation than a Latin one, looking out from the coast rather than inland for its trade and alliances. On the other hand it has plenty of distinctively Central American features too, above all a blend of cultures and races that includes, in a tiny population, Maya, Mestizo, African and European. Spanish runs a close second as a spoken language to the rich local Creole.

The peaceful atmosphere, together with the spectacular natural beauty of the landscape and coast, has started to draw increasing numbers of tourists every year. Well over half of them are from North America, but a growing number come from Europe, mostly from Britain. Belize is by no means crowded, however; although it's barely bigger than Wales it has the lowest population density in Central America, and its land area is balanced by an almost equivalent amount of territorial waters, giving visitors plenty of scope to explore little-visited islands as well as the heartland of the ancient Maya culture.

Several operators now run tours from the UK to Belize – and quite a number from the US – but it's still an ideal place to travel independently. There are numerous small hotels (starting at about the price of a youth hostel), inexpensive restaurants and plenty of public transport. Belizeans are extremely friendly and are genuinely pleased when visitors enjoy their country.

Physically the land increases in elevation as you head south and west and the population decreases correspondingly. The highest land in Belize is the rugged hilly area in the south-central region, where the granite peaks of the Maya Mountains rise to over 1000m. The main rivers rise in the west and flow north or east to the Caribbean. In the Cretaceous limestone of the western mountains, rivers have formed some of the largest cave systems in the world, few of which have been fully explored.

Offshore, the Barrier Reef, cayes and coral atolls shelter a vast number of marine species and protect the mainland from the ocean swell. The coastal waters are shallow and very productive, brilliant for divers and fishermen alike. Beneath the sand the coastal shelf is a continuation of the limestone on the mainland, with more caves and sinkholes.

■ Where to go

Northern Belize is relatively flat and often swampy, with a large proportion of agricultural land. As everywhere in Belize there are Maya ruins and nature reserves here. **Cuello**, near Orange Walk, is the oldest known Maya site, and there are nature reserves at **Shipstern** and **Crooked Tree**. Adjacent to the Guatemalan border is the potentially vast **Rio Bravo Conservation Area**.

The largest of the cayes, **Ambergris Caye**, is about the size of Barbados and becoming extremely popular. More than half of all tourists to Belize have the resorts of **San Pedro**, the only town on the island, as their destination. **Caye Caulker**, to the south, is also being developed, though without the same urgency as Ambergris Caye; this is the most popular of the islands with independent travellers. Many of the other cayes are becoming easier to reach, and organized trips are available to the atolls of **Lighthouse Reef** and **Glover's Reef**. Dedicated divers and naturalists will find these very rewarding. Even on the cayes, however, there are relatively few **beaches** suitable for swimming, and the mainland coast is almost entirely low-lying, swampy and covered in mangroves. The lagoons inland offer superb wildlife habitats, and a visit to **Lamanai**, on the shores of New River Lagoon, combines a nature safari with an ancient Maya centre.

Almost every visitor will have to spend at least some time in **Belize City**, even if only passing through, as it's the hub of the country's transport system, for both inland and the cayes. First-time visitors may be shocked initially by the decaying buildings and the pollution of the river but it's possible to spend several pleasant hours in this former outpost of the British Empire, now the bustling commercial heart of the country. The capital, **Belmopan**, is primarily an administrative centre.

For those interested in seeing the abundant tropical flora and fauna, anywhere in Belize is wonderful; an astonishing array of birds are readily visible, making **nature tourism** increasingly popular. In the west **San Ignacio** has everything for the ecotourist: Maya ruins and rainforest, rivers and caves, and accommodation in every price range. The magnificent ruin of **Xunantunich** is at the road and riverside on the

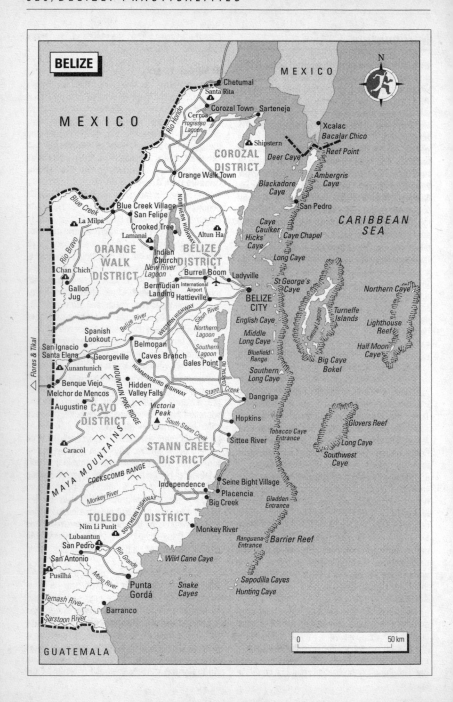

way to the Guatemalan border, and **Caracol**, the largest Maya site in Belize, can be visited from here.

The main town of the south-central region, **Dangriga**, is very small and acts mainly as a market for the citrus-growing area of the Stann Creek valley. Local people are now realizing the potential of Dangriga as a base for tourism on the central cayes (little developed at present) and for visiting the **Maya Mountains** and the **Cockscomb Basin Jaguar Preserve**. Further south, the road that follows the narrow coastal plain is unpaved. The few villages are located on the coast, with the delightful **Placencia** at the tip of a long, curving peninsula. **Punta Gorda**, the main town of Toledo District, is very small indeed and most tourists are here on their way to or from the ferry to **Puerto Barrios** in Guatemala. However, if you venture inland you'll find the villages of the **Mopan** and **Kekchi Maya**, set in some of the most stunning countryside in Belize. **San Antonio** is the largest and serves as a focus, having the only hotel, but others are equally interesting and now have simple guest houses. Surrounding these villages is the only true rainforest in Belize, with caves, rivers and the Maya ruins of **Lubaantun**, **Uxbenka** and **Pusilha** within reach.

Getting around

With just four main roads, and only two that are truly all-weather – the Northern and Western highways – Belize doesn't offer a great range of options when it comes to getting around. But, as always, it makes the most of what it's got, with boats, planes, buses and trucks making it possible to get just about anywhere – eventually. The main areas are well served by public transport, but it can take a while to get to some of the more distant corners of the country, where rough roads and heavy rainfall often conspire to disrupt the best-laid plans.

■ Buses

Buses are by far the most popular mode of transport. The service on the Northern and Western highways, to the borders with Mexico and Guatemala, is particularly good, with departures every hour or so. Heading north the buses cross the border and go into the Mexican town of Chetumal, while going west most buses terminate in San Ignacio or Benque, with some continuing to the border town of Melchor de Mencos in Guatemala. The two main companies on the **northern route** are *Batty* (15 Mosul St, Belize City; ☎02/72025) and *Venus* (Magazine Rd, Belize City; ☎02/73354). The **western route** too is served by *Batty*, and by *Novelos* (W Collet Canal, Belize City; ☎02/77372). On both these routes *Batty* operates the morning schedule, with the rival company taking over in the afternoon. The Hummingbird and Southern highways, to Dangriga and Punta Gorda, are not so well provided for. However, *Z-Line* (Magazine Rd, Belize City; ☎02/73937) run several daily buses to Dangriga and three daily to Punta Gorda – which is a good eight to nine hours from Belize City – and *James* runs a bus twice weekly to Punta Gorda. On all of these routes except *James*, tickets can be bought in advance from the offices in Belize City; if you get on the bus somewhere along its route then you can pay the driver, which is what most people do. The vast majority of buses are second-class, although a couple of luxury express buses do run to Chetumal. *Batty* is particularly recommended for this route; they even serve continental breakfast.

Heading away from the main highways you'll be relying on the **local bus services** operated by smaller local companies. In most cases these own just one bus, so a breakdown can bring the whole service to a halt. Local buses run to many of the smaller villages, operating alongside a fleet of **trucks** that also form part of the informal transport network, serving small and out of the way places. The service tends to be very slow indeed, catering to everyone's needs – providing they're in no hurry.

The details for both types of bus service are given in the text, but be warned that services are reduced on Sunday. If you stick to the buses you'll find that travel is cheap: the journey from Belize City to Chetumal, for example, costs around US$4.50.

■ Driving

Driving in Belize is subject to the same limitations as bus travel. The Northern and Western highways offer easy motoring and smooth roads, and over half of the Hummingbird Highway is now paved, but in the south the roads are rough and distances are long. If you're heading into Guatemala, the only way to go is west, as the ferry to Guatemala from Punta Gorda doesn't take cars. Any car will be able to take you through the north with ease, but if you want to head off the beaten track or make your way down south then you'll need high clearance and four-wheel drive. The best guide to Belize's roads is Emory King's *Driver's Guide to Beautiful Belize*, which is sold at hotels and filling stations throughout the country and offers a characteristically Belizean account of the network. If you're driving your own car then bear in mind that though unleaded petrol is easily available, it can be difficult to get hold of spare parts. Bring an assortment from home in case things should go wrong. **Insurance** is available from an agent just inside the border or in Belize City – it will cover you against damage to third parties, but fully comprehensive cover is not available. Under Belize's new seatbelt law, you'll be fined Bz$25 for not belting up.

As in Guatemala, **car rental** is very expensive, but cars, Jeeps, four-wheel-drive trucks and Land Rovers are available from several companies in Belize City – their addresses are listed in the *Guide*.

■ Hitching

In the more remote parts of Belize the bus service will probably only operate once a day, if at all, and unless you have your own transport, **hitching** is the only other option. The main drawback is the shortage of traffic, but if cars do pass they'll usually offer you a lift. Bear in mind that many local trucks also operate as buses and you're expected to offer the driver some money.

■ Cycling

Seeing Belize from a **bike** is fairly straightforward, particularly in the north and west where there's not that much traffic and the roads are well surfaced. Cycling is popular and you'll find repair shops in all the towns. There's a sponsored "Hike and Bike for the Rainforest" in Cayo every October: visitors are welcome to take part.

You'll need to think twice before you head south, where a mountain bike is virtually a necessity; that said, getting around this way is increasingly popular, and in Placencia many resorts have bikes available for guests.

Bikes can sometimes be carried on top of buses, though few Belizean buses have the roof racks that are such a familiar sight in Guatemala. If you're really lucky – and there is room – the driver might even let you take the bike *onto* the bus.

■ Boats and ferries

There are several daily scheduled **boats** from Belize City to Caye Caulker and San Pedro on Ambergris Caye, as well as a dozen or so waiting by the dock to fill up with passengers. There's also a fairly regular shuttle of boats between these two islands. The only coastal boat services are a twice-weekly ferry from Punta Gorda to Puerto Barrios in Guatemala and a weekly canoe between Dangriga and Puerto Cortes, Honduras.

Boats can also be **chartered** for travel along the rivers and out amongst the islands. If you're planning to explore the country's river network then San Ignacio is the ideal base, with canoes readily available to rent for an hour or a week. Sea kayaks can also be rented in Placencia for trips on the Monkey River, which is ideal for birdwatching, and from Shipyard for trips to the ruins of Lamanai. Out on the islands you can charter a boat to spend a few hours on the reef, snorkelling and fishing. Some boatmen will also take tourists on a sailing tour of the cayes for a week or so, camping along the way. If you've come to Belize to go diving then you might want to consider a live-aboard **dive boat**. Several of these operate out of Belize City (see *Belize City* and *The Northern Cayes and Atolls* for addresses).

■ Planes

Within Belize *Maya Airways* (☎02/72312) and *Tropic Air* (☎02/45671) offer a scheduled service to all of the main towns and out to San Pedro, also served by *Island Air* (☎02/31140), and there are several charter airlines in operation too. This adds up to two or three daily **flights** on each of the main routes – from Belize City to Punta Gorda, Independence, Dangriga, Corozal and Placencia – and literally dozens to San Pedro and Caye Caulker. A flight from Belize City to San Pedro costs around US$23; you can fly from the Municipal Airport, about 1km north of the centre of Belize City, or from Belize International Airport. Again the service is more limited on Sunday.

If you can afford it, flying is a good way to travel – especially to the south, where buses take a while, or out to San Pedro, when you get superb views of the hills and the clear blue sea, skimming along at low altitude in a small plane.

Flights to Guatemala City and to Flores are increasingly popular with those who can't face the rigours of the road.

Accommodation

Hotels in Belize fall into two categories: the first catering for big-spending American tourists, and the second for local people and budget travellers. All Belizean accommodation is expensive by Central American standards, though, and certainly in comparison with Guatemala.

A simple room in Belize usually costs at least Bz$15 (US$7.50), for facilities no better than a cheap Guatemalan hotel. On a budget, you're most likely to end up in a basic room with a shared bathroom at the end of the corridor. If you want the luxury of a private bathroom you should expect to pay at least Bz$25. Price fluctuations are fairly unpredictable and oddly enough Belize City, San Ignacio and Placencia offer some of the best budget accommodation in the whole country, while in Orange Walk there's very little available. Out on Caye Caulker prices are reasonable but in San Pedro almost everything is overpriced. Elsewhere you won't have any problem finding a decent and inexpensive room. The exception to every rule is Belmopan, where there are only three hotels, the cheapest of which charges Bz$36 for a single: if you have things to do in Belmopan it's better to stay in San Ignacio, which is far more pleasant anyway.

Finding a room is no problem, as all the towns are so small that you can see what's on offer in no time, and walk between all the hotels. Even in Belize City most options are within 1km of the Swing Bridge. On the whole there's always accommodation available, but during the peak season, from December to April and especially at

Christmas and Easter, you may have to look a little longer. Checking-in is typically informal, though in most establishments you'll be expected to sign a register, and even go so far as listing your passport number. In some cases you simply pay your money and take your room. It's a good idea, however, to take a look at the room before parting with your cash: check that the fan works and that it's reasonably insect-proof – a good fan will keep most beasts at bay. Insects are only really a problem on the islands where, when the wind drops, the sandflies will get at you however well you're protected.

■ Camping

With Belizean prices way outstripping those in the rest of Central America you might consider **camping** as a way of keeping within a tight budget. You'll easily be able to find somewhere to pitch a tent or sling a hammock in coastal villages like Placencia and Hopkins, but out on Caye Caulker or in San Pedro restrictions tend to be a little tougher. You can also camp out in the area around San Ignacio, where local ranches offer campsites for passing travellers, surrounded by lush tropical forest. Sadly, there are only two places where you can pitch a tent in the Mountain Pine Ridge Forest Reserve – at the entrance and at Augustine – which would otherwise be ideal for camping. In the north you should also be able to camp out at the Crooked Tree Wildlife Reserve and the Bermudian Landing Baboon Sanctuary. Down south a tent will enable you to spend some time wandering inland, around the Maya villages and ancient ruins, and there's a superb campsite beside the Blue Creek.

Communications – mail, phones and media

Thanks to its recent colonial entanglement with Britain, Belize is blessed with excellent telecommunications and postal networks, and is particularly well connected to Europe.

■ Mail

Belizean postal services are perhaps the most efficient in Central America, although they're also probably the most expensive. **Incoming mail** is kept at the main post office in Belize City, on the northern side of the Swing Bridge (8am–noon &

ACCOMMODATION PRICE CODES

All Belizean accommodation reviewed in this guide has been graded according to the following **price scales**. These refer to the cost of a double room in high season (generally Dec–Easter) in Belize dollars (Bz$), but do not include the government hotel tax of 7 percent. To work out the price in US$, simply divide the Belizean figures by two.

① under Bz$20	⑥ Bz$100–140
② Bz$20–30	⑦ Bz$140–190
③ Bz$30–40	⑧ Bz$190–250
④ Bz$40–70	⑨ over Bz$250
⑤ Bz$70–100	

1–5pm), for a couple of months, and if it's not collected they return it to sender. If you want to collect your mail from the post office have it sent to *General Delivery, The Main Post Office, Belize City* (or any of the District Town post offices); you'll need some kind of ID, preferably a passport, to pick it up. Although this is fairly reliable, *American Express* are safer still – their office is at *Belize Global Travel*, 41 Albert St, Belize City, and you'll need to show an *Amex* credit card or travellers' cheque to pick anything up.

Sending letters and cards home is easy enough and the stamps, decorated with coral formations and tropical fish, are a considerable added bonus. A normal air-mail letter takes around eight days to reach Europe (Bz$.75), three days to the US (Bz$.60). If you're sending a **parcel** you have to go to the special parcel office, next door to the main post office in Belize City. Parcels leaving the country have to be wrapped in a cardboard box, possibly inspected by customs, and tied with string. A parcel sent to Europe by sea, which is a lot cheaper than air mail, might take as long as two months to arrive but it will usually get there eventually.

■ Phones

Belize has a surprisingly modern phone system. The first phone reached here in 1902 and today the country has some of the latest satellite communications hardware. Payphones are an increasingly common sight throughout the country, and you'll find them all over Belize City. Phonecards are sold at *BTL* offices (see below) in units of Bz$10, Bz$20, Bz$30 and Bz$50.

Domestic call charges from payphones are steep: between Bz$2.25 to Bz$3.50 for the first three minutes, a three-minute minimum and no off-peak discounts.

It's easy enough to dial direct into and out of Belize: a call to Europe costs Bz$18 per minute, and to the States Bz$10 for the first three minutes, about a third more for person to person. If you use a phonecard you only pay per minute. None of these prices includes VAT at 15 percent.

Calling collect is easy using *Home Country Direct*, available at the International Airport, main *BTL* office and larger hotels. Simply dial the access code (on every phone) to connect with an operator in your home country. To **call Belize collect** from North America use *Belize Direct*: contact AT&T, MCI or Sprint for the access number.

The main office of *Belize Telecommunications Limited* (*BTL*) is at 1 Church St, Belize City (daily 8am–6pm), but you can make a call from the *BTL* office in any town in the country. Many smaller villages have a shared "community telephone", which may have just one public phone in the exchange or a few extensions in homes and elsewhere. Often this is supplemented by a cellular phone number – note that not all public phones can connect to cellular phones.

Most hotels and businesses now have **fax machines** and any *BTL* office will have a public fax you can use. Numbers are listed separately in the telephone directory. *BTL* also control access to e-mail and the internet in Belize; call toll free ☎144.

■ Media

Although Belize, with its English-language media, can make a welcome break in a world of Spanish, this doesn't necessarily mean that it's very easy to keep in touch with what's happening in the rest of the world. In Belize City you should be able to get hold of copies of *Time* and *Newsweek*, and perhaps even *The Economist*. **Foreign newspapers** are rarely available for sale, but copies of British newspapers – usually *The Times* and *The Telegraph* – are sometimes available at the Bliss Institute in Belize City: they get there about a week after publication. The British High Commission in Belmopan has a wider selection. *Mom's Inn* in Belize City gets the *Miami Herald*. The *Book Centre*, on Church St in Belize City, has the largest selection of magazines – and some newspapers – in the country.

The five national **newspapers**: *The People's Pulse*, *The Reporter*, *The Belize Times*, *The Amandala* and *The Observer*, are all published weekly (on Friday) and most of them, excepting *The Amandala* and *The Observer*, stick religiously to a party line. Local news, normally reported in a very nationalistic manner, takes pride of place and international stories receive very little attention indeed. *The Belize Review*, subtitled "News, Views and Ecotourism", a monthly magazine published in Belize, can be more interesting. You might also want to look at *Belize Magazine*, a bi-monthly magazine published in the US and readily available in Belize: expensive and aimed mainly at would-be property buyers, it nevertheless has some excellent colour photography and occasional interesting articles on Maya sites or Belizean wildlife.

There are two national **television** stations, channels 7 and 11, which show an almost uninterrupted stream of imported American shows, mixed in with a few news programmes – their best features are the locally produced home-made adverts and short fillers. Channel 7 has local news at 6.30 and 7pm and some educational programming; Channel 11, billed the "Family Channel", shows mainly PG-rated movies with some religious slots. In Belize City, there's a good local news programme at 6.30pm on Channel 5. Some towns and villages also have **cable TV**, giving them access to American soaps and a steady diet of films. Many of the cable showings are pirated from satellite – CNN and The Sports Channel are favourites.

There are also three **radio** stations. *Radio Belize*, which broadcasts on 830, 910, 930 and 940 kHz, and on 91.1 and 3.28 MHz, and *Friends FM*, which broadcasts on 88.9 MHz, are operated by the Broadcasting Corporation of Belize and partly sponsored by the government. *Radio Belize* is talk-based, with plays and cultural and educational programmes, while *Friends* is primarily a music station. From time to time they run plays from the BBC and *Radio Belize* transmits the World Service daily from midnight to 6am. The other station, *KREM*, is privately owned and plays mostly music. You can also pick up other Caribbean stations, which come wafting in across the sea and blast out pure reggae. If you have a short-wave receiver you will be able to pick up the BBC World Service between 6am and midnight. There's also a British Forces radio station, BFBS on FM.

Eating and drinking

Belizean food is a distinctive mix of Latin America and the Caribbean, with Creole cuisine dominating the scene but plenty of other influences playing an important part. Mexican *empanadas* are as common as chow mein and hamburgers. In a few places Belizean food is a real treat, and the seafood is particularly good, but in all too many it's a neglected art, conforming to a single simple recipe – beans and rice.

■ Where to eat

The quality of the food rarely bears much relation to the appearance of the restaurant, and a full range of **bars**, **cafés** and smooth-looking **restaurants** are on offer. Out on the islands and in small seashore villages some restaurants are little more than thatched shelters, with open sides and sand floors, while you'll just as often find upmarket hotels with polished floors, tablecloths and napkins. Only in Belize City, though, do you have much choice, with fast food and snack bars sprouting on street corners but a few surprisingly elegant restaurants as well. Even here most places are somewhere between the two, serving up good food but not too concerned about presentation.

In very small villages, where there is no restaurant, you should be able to find someone who, on a regular basis, cooks for passing travellers. Local people should be able to point you in the right direction. This is often a great opportunity to sample the delights of traditional Creole food.

Travelling, you'll find that food often comes to you as street traders offer up tacos, *empanadas*, fish burgers and fruit to waiting bus passengers. The practice isn't quite as common as elsewhere in Central America but it still makes a pleasant diversion on most journeys.

Most Belizeans eat their main meal in the evenings, but in a country noted for its informality anything goes, and if you want to eat steak for breakfast and scrambled eggs for dinner nobody will be at all bothered. For **vegetarians** the pickings are slim as Belizeans have never had much enthusiasm for the land. The fruit here is good and there are some locally produced vegetables, largely thanks to the Mennonites, but they can be hard to come by. Your best hope, apart from cooking for yourself, is within the **Chinese** community, who run restaurants in all of the main towns.

■ What to eat

The basis of any **Creole** meal is **beans** and **rice**, and in small restaurants and cafés this type of food features heavily. In many cases it means exactly that, and nothing more, but usually it's served with **chicken**, **fish** or **beef**, and backed up by some kind of sauce, often cooked with the beans. Vegetables are scarce in Creole food but there's often a side dish of fried **bananas** or **plantains**. At its best Creole food is delicious, taking the best from the sea and mixing it with the smooth taste of coconut, another favourite ingredient, and a range of herbs and spices. But all too often what you get is a stodgy mass, with little in the way of flavour. Often, too, you'll find an Anglicized version of Creole cooking, still based on seafood, rice and beans, but including **steaks**, **chips** (fries) and deep-fried **chicken**.

Seafood is almost always excellent. **Red snapper** is invariably fantastic, and you might also try a **shark steak**, **conch fritters** or a plate of **fresh shrimps**; avoid **turtle** steaks, however – they're still on the menu in many places, but they're a protected species, threatened with extinction. Out on Caye Caulker the food is often exceptional, and the only worry is that you might get bored with **lobster**. Anticipating that possibility they serve it up in an amazing range of dishes: pasta with lobster sauce, lobster and scrambled eggs, lobster chow mein, or even lobster curry.

From time to time you might also come across local **game**. The **gibnut** (paca) is a local favourite – when it was served up to the Queen of England it was described by the British tabloids as a type of rat; in fact it's a herbivorous rodent, about the size of a badger, that looks like a giant guinea pig. **Brocket deer**, **warrie** (a type of wild pig) and **armadillo** are also eaten by local people, but they rarely make their way into restaurants.

Chinese food will probably turn out to be an important part of your trip, and when there's little else on offer Belize's many Chinese restaurants are always a safe bet. In Belize City some of them are very good indeed, but elsewhere they tend to look a little run-down and serve bland food. Other Belizean ethnic minorities are now starting to break into the restaurant trade; there's an excellent **Sri Lankan** restaurant in San Ignacio, for example, serving superb curries.

Travelling around you'll also be confronted by an array of snacks. On the whole these tend to be Mexican and Guatemalan delicacies such as *empanadas*, *tamales*, tacos and *chiles rellenos*, but you'll also come across local specialities like **fish burgers** and **coconut bread**.

■ Drinks

The most basic **drinks** to accompany food are water, beer and Coke. All three are available at every restaurant and bar. Belizean **beer**, *Belikin*, is extremely popular, though overpriced at more than US$1.50 a bottle (more out on the cayes). The lighter *Crown Beer* is cheaper. Both come in regular lager-type beer and dark beer (stout) varieties. *Belikin* is often available on draught as well as in bottles, which works out slightly cheaper. *Premium Belikin* is more expensive than the other two but often all you'll be able to get in upmarket hotels and restaurants. Imported European and American beers cost roughly double. Tap **water**, in the cities at least, is not to be recommended: though safe, it's highly chlorinated. Mineral water is available in bottles, as is a predictable range of fairly cheap soft drinks including **Sprite**, **Fanta** and **Pepsi**.

Some locally produced **wines** are sold in shops and restaurants, mostly made from fruit and cashew nuts. Cashew nut wine, made in many villages, particularly in the Belize River valley, is very rich and full-bodied – a good vintage tastes almost like brandy. You can also get hold of imported wine, which is far from cheap. Local **rum** is the best deal in Belizean alcohol, however. Both dark and clear varieties are made in Belize, brewed in true Caribbean style and tasting delicious. Many Belizeans like to mix rum with condensed milk – known as *rumpopo*. The locally produced gin, brandy and vodka are poor imitations – cheap and fairly nasty.

One last drink that deserves a mention is **seaweed**, a strange blend of actual seaweed, milk, cinnamon, sugar and cream. If you see someone selling this on a street corner, give it a try.

Opening hours and holidays

It's very difficult to be specific about **opening hours** in Belize, as people tend to take each day as it comes and open up when the mood takes them, but in general most places are open 8am–noon and 3–8pm. The lunch hour – noon to 1pm – is almost universally observed and it's hopeless to try and get anything done then. Some shops and businesses work a half-day on Wednesday and Saturday, and everything is liable to close early on Friday, with the weekend coming up. Banks and government offices are only open Monday to Friday. Watch out for **Sundays**, when everybody takes it easy; shops, and sometimes restaurants, are closed, the bus service is limited, and few internal flights operate. Archeological sites, however, are open every day.

The main **public holidays**, when virtually everything will be closed, are shown above.

Fiestas and entertainment

In Belize it's only in the outlying areas, such as around San Ignacio and in the Maya villages of the south, that you'll find traditional village fiestas. Elsewhere, national celebrations are the main excuse for a day-long party, and the rhythms of the Caribbean dominate the proceedings. But here you'll feel less of an outsider and always be welcome to dance and drink with the locals. The main celebrations are National Day, Independence Day, Columbus Day and Garifuna Settlement Day, all of which are celebrated across the country.

You will, however, find plenty of entertainment at any time, as Belizeans are great party people and music is a crucial part of the country's culture.

▣ Dance

Traditional dance is still practised by two ethnic groups in Belize: the Maya and the Garifuna. The best time to see Garifuna dances is November 19, Garifuna Settlement Day, and the best place to see them is either Dangriga or Hopkins. Maya dances are still performed at fiestas in the south and west. The village of San José Succotz, to the west of San Ignacio, has fiestas on March 19 (St Joseph) and May 3 (Holy Cross), while down south you'll find traditional fiestas in San Antonio around January 17, and in San Pedro towards the end of June. In many ways these fiestas resemble their counterparts in Guatemala.

Elsewhere, modern music and **modern dance** is the mood of the day. Dance is very much a part of Creole culture and all national celebrations are marked by open-air dances. Almost all villages, particularly those along the coast, have their own discos, with dancing going on into the small hours. Dancers take their lead from the Caribbean, merging styles from Jamaica and Cuba.

▣ Music

Belizean **music** is a lively mixture of Caribbean and Latin American rhythms with haunting melodies played on Maya instruments. Creole music combines all of the elements, but many individual styles are thriving too – see p.501 in *Contexts*, "Music in Belize". Modern Latin American music is also popular; merengue, salsa and even Mexican mariachi are all heard throughout Belize, though perhaps more in the north and west, where the Spanish-speaking population is that much larger.

It has to be said, though, that 90 percent of what you'll actually hear will be **reggae** or **punta**, and the sounds of Bob Marley dominate the airwaves. But everywhere you go you'll hear music, either played or performed: look out especially for anything advertised as a *jumpup*, an apt Belizean term for a dance. The term covers a multitude of sins: one great one had posters inviting people to a "Big massive jumpup", scheduled to end when "food gone, rum gone and people gone".

▣ Sport

Sport in Belize is a reflection of the local environment, and most of what's on offer is connected to the water in some way. Sport **fishing** is popular, particularly out on the atolls, where wealthy tourists spend their time and money in pursuit of a whole range of fish. **Sailing**, **diving** and **snorkelling** are also extremely popular. Diving courses, for experts or beginners, are run in San Pedro, Caye Caulker, Placencia and some of the other cayes. If you want to book a course in advance then look at the listings for these places in the text, or write to or fax one of the travel agents mentioned: if you're planning a fishing trip they should also be able to give you information on fishing trips. Away from the coast, **canoeing, rafting and "tubing"** – floating down rivers in a giant inner tube – are extremely popular, particularly in the Cayo district, where there are plenty of people keen to arrange this for you. **Sea kayaking**, too, is becoming more popular and a number of outfits organize trips.

Back on land, Belize's amazing subterranean landscape is becoming ever more accessible, with several qualified **caving** guides leading tours. *Caribbean Cowboy* in Belize City (☎02/33303; fax 35833) organize specialist cave rafting and diving expeditions. Two caving instructors, Ian Anderson of Cayes Branch and Pete Zubrzycki in San Ignacio are founder members of the Belize Cave Rescue Team. You should have no problems going **horse-riding**, either, and there are some superb rides to be had through forested hills and Maya ruins.

The main spectator sport is **football**, although there aren't many level stretches of ground on which to play. Nevertheless, this is probably the national game, closely followed by basketball. Athletics is also popular, as are softball, baseball and American football, at least on TV. As in the rest of Central America, **cycling** is closely followed and there are sometimes races in Belize, though scope for these is limited given the state of the roads. Finally, there are a number of **horse-racing** meets around New Year.

■ Film and TV

A couple of well-known **films** have been shot in Belize – *The Mosquito Coast* and *The Dogs of War* – but there's no local film industry as such. Nevertheless, going to the movies is popular and there are two cinemas in Belize City and one in San Ignacio. In other towns they show films from time to time, usually on a Saturday night, in the town hall. Most of what's on offer is imported directly from the US and new films get this far south with amazing speed. Some are released in Belize before they reach Europe.

On **TV** you can watch American soaps and local news programmes. Most towns also have cable, serving up a steady diet of American films. A good series of locally produced **videos**, "The Best of Belize All Over", shows slices of local life to the accompaniment of great Belizean music – they're only suitable for playing on US equipment, however. For more information contact *Great Belize Productions*, 17 Regent St, Belize City (☎02/77781). They also produce a daily news programme and an annual video anthology of news relevant to Belize.

Crafts, markets and shops

Compared to its neighbours, Belize has less to offer in terms of traditional **crafts** or neighbourhood **markets**. The latter are purely food markets, but here and there you might come across some impressive local crafts. Some of these are dependent on the destruction of the reef, so think twice before you buy. They include black coral, often made into jewellery, and turtle shells, which look far better on their rightful owners. The turtle fishing season in Belize is now very much restricted and it is against the law to take turtle products out of the country. You will certainly have them confiscated on entering the USA, Canada or Europe, and may face a fine as well.

The excellent **National Handicrafts Center** in Belize City (see p.356), run by the Belize Chamber of Commerce, is the best place to buy souvenirs, including baskets, carvings in wood, slate and stone, paintings, prints and music recordings. There are often exhibitions by Belizean artists here too. The producers are paid fair prices for their work and no longer have to hawk it on the streets.

For **everyday shopping** you'll find some kind of shop in every village in Belize, however small, and if you have the time to hunt around, most things you'd find in Europe are also available in Belize. Luxury items, such as electrical goods and cameras, tend to be very expensive, as do other imported goods, including tinned food. Film is a little more expensive than at home, but easy to get hold of.

Trouble and harassment

Belize has earned itself a reputation for criminal activities, and while it's true that the capital has a high crime rate, it certainly doesn't live up to some of the stories. The atmosphere on the streets is much less intimidating since the introduction of the tourist police (see p.348), violence is rare, and on the whole petty crime is the only common pest. Nevertheless, it pays to be aware of the dangers.

■ Crime

There are two centres of crime in Belize: Belize City and Orange Walk, which is the centre of the Belizean drugs industry. The capital is perhaps the greatest worry as theft is now fairly common. The majority of cases involve **break-ins** at hotels. When you're searching for a room bear this in mind and avoid places that seem overexposed. Out and about there's always a slight danger of **pickpockets** and **petty theft**, but this is certainly no greater here than in the surrounding countries, and with a bit of common sense you've nothing to fear. There's also a chance of something more serious happening, such as a **mugging**. During the daytime there's little to worry about. However, at night you should stick to the main streets and it's never a good idea to go out alone, particularly for women. If you arrive in Belize City at night take a taxi to a hotel, as the bus stations are in a particularly derelict part of town – though not bad enough to worry about daylight arrivals.

Having said all this, muggings are really not that common, and your greatest fear is the mood of intimidation on the streets, which makes Belize City feel far more dangerous than it actually is.

■ Harassment

Verbal abuse is certainly the most threatening aspect of life on the streets in Belize. Again the only real problem is Belize City, where there are always plenty of people hanging out on the streets, commenting on all that passes by. For anyone with a white face, the inevitable "Hey, white boy/white chick – what's happening?" will soon become a familiar sound. At first it can all seem very threatening, as you struggle through the city, your mind full of terrifying tales. But if you take the time to stop and talk, you'll find the vast majority of these people simply want to know where you're from, and where you're heading – and perhaps to offer you a deal on boat trips, money exchange, or even bum a dollar or two. Once you realize that they mean no harm the whole experience of Belize City will be infinitely more enjoyable. Obviously, the situation is a little more serious for women, and the abuse tends to be more offensive. But once again, annoying though it is, it's unlikely that anything will come of it and you can usually talk your way out of a dodgy situation without anyone losing face.

■ Drugs

Belize has long been an important transshipment link in the chain of supply between the producers in South and Central America and the users in North America, with minor players often being paid in kind, creating a deluge of illegal drugs. **Marijuana**, **cocaine** and **crack** are all readily available in Belize, particularly in Belize City, Orange Walk, San Pedro, Caye Caulker and Dangriga. Whether you like it or not you'll receive regular offers. All such substances are illegal, and despite the fact that dope is smoked openly in the streets, the police do arrest people for possession of marijuana and they particularly enjoy catching tourists. So if you want to indulge in this local pastime be discreet. If you're caught you'll probably end up spending a couple of days in jail and paying a fine of several hundred US dollars: expect no sympathy from your embassy.

Directory

AIRPORT TAX Leaving Belize by air you'll have to pay an airport tax of Bz$20 and a Bz$2.50 security tax: transit passengers who've been in the country for less than 24 hours don't have to pay. The new *PACT* (see *Contexts*), which costs Bz$7.50, is payable at *all* exit points. An entry tax of around US$20 is likely to be introduced in the future.

ARCHEOLOGY Belize's Maya sites, in addition to being tourist attractions in their own right, are often the subject of systematic archeological research. At any one time several sites will be undergoing excavation and investigation, and there are frequent open-days or seminars to which visitors are welcome. The *Belize River Archeological Survey* (BRASS) at UC Santa Barbara (☎805/893-8191) and the UCLA team (☎310/206-8934) are particularly open to such projects; for more details, contact the Belize Archeology Department on ☎08/22106.

BEGGARS Rare in Belize and those that there are don't fit the Latin American mould. Most operate in Belize City and aim exclusively at tourists, bumming a bottle of beer or a dollar or two. They tend to be persistent but harmless.

CONTRACEPTION Condoms are available from chemists in Belize City, as are some brands of the Pill, but it's better to bring enough to last the trip. If you're using the Pill – or any other orally administered drug – bear in mind that severe diarrhoea can reduce its efficacy.

ELECTRICITY The mains supply is 110 volts AC with American-style three-pin sockets. Electrical equipment made for the US and Canada should be OK – anything from Britain will need a transformer and a plug adaptor – but ask in your hotel before you do anything. Electricity supply is pretty dependable, but if you're bringing any delicate equipment (like a laptop), you'll need a good surge protector. Some hotels and small villages have their electricity supplied by local generators, and the voltage is then much lower.

EMBASSIES AND CONSULATES The vast majority of embassies and consulates are still in Belize City, but UK, Panamá, Venezuela, Chile, El Salvador and India are all represented in Belmopan. Addresses are listed in the relevant sections.

GAY BELIZE There's no open gay community in Belize and the cities are too small to support any exclusively gay bars. Things here are easy-going so you needn't expect any great hassle, but it's probably still a good idea to be discreet in order to avoid verbal abuse.

IMMIGRATION On entering Belize, most visitors will be granted a stay of thirty days. This can be extended in increments of thirty days for up to six months at any immigration office for Bz$25. It's often cheaper and easier, however, to cross a border and re-enter: you probably won't even need to stay overnight.

INFORMATION The country's only real source of tourist information is the tourist board in Belize City, but there's also an information booth open at the airport for incoming flights, and numerous offices of the *Belize Tourist Industry Association* (BTIA) around the country. Although this is really an industry organization, they do try to help with information and especially complaints about hotel standards or service. For in-depth information on social, cultural, political and economic matters concerning Belize, the place to look is the *Society for the Promotion of Education and Research* (SPEAR). Their centre at the corner of Pickstock St and New Rd, Belize City (☎02/31668; fax 32367) also has an excellent library and video collection.

LAUNDRY The only towns that have any kind of laundry service are Belize City, Placencia, San Ignacio and San Pedro – addresses are listed in the *Guide*. Elsewhere you can usually get away with doing your laundry in your hotel room.

ODD ESSENTIALS Insect repellent and sun protection lotion are a good idea, and both are available in Belize. Also recommended are a flashlight, pocket compass and alarm clock.

STUDENT CARDS won't do any harm, but aren't likely to do you much good either.

TIME ZONES Belize is on Central Standard Time, six hours behind GMT and the same as Guatemala.

TIPS Tipping is by no means standard practice in Belize but then again it is often done, so it's really up to you.

TOILETS Public toilets are very rare indeed, though there is an excellent one in the new Belize City market. The best in the country is in the *Z-Line* bus terminal in Dangriga. In hotels and restaurants standards are extremely variable, but toilets are never considered a high priority. On the whole toilet paper is provided, but it's always a good idea to travel with your own roll, just in case.

WEIGHTS AND MEASURES The imperial system is still used in Belize. This book is metric throughout, except when we refer to addresses on main roads outside towns that are commonly referred to in terms of their Mile number. See box on p.21.

THE WOMEN'S MOVEMENT Women in Belize are a good deal more liberated than many of their sisters in Latin America: male emigration has traditionally left women as the head of many Belizean households, and they play an important part in some industries, especially in the service sector. The Government of Belize has a Policy Statement on Women outlining the efforts taken to implement equal rights and advance the status of women. The Department of Women's Affairs, under the Ministry of Human Resources, acts as an umbrella organization for all women's groups in the country and assists with income-generating projects. The department produces a quarterly newsletter, *Equality*, and has offices in all the district towns, in Belmopan at the Ministry of Social Development, West Block (☎08/22637) and in Belize City at 26 Albert St, PO Box 846 (☎02/77379). The *Women Against Violence Against Women* movement is based at 10 Zericote St.

WORK There's virtually no chance of finding paid temporary work in Belize as at least half of the population is underemployed. Work permits are only on offer to those who can prove their ability to support themselves without endangering the job of a Belizean. There are opportunities for voluntary work , however; see p.6.

CHAPTER SEVEN

COROZAL, ORANGE WALK AND THE NORTH

Northern Belize is an expanse of relatively level land, where swamps, savannahs and lagoons are mixed with rainforest and farmland. For many years this part of the country was largely inaccessible and had closer ties with Mexico – where most of the original settlers came from – than Belize City. The Indian and Mestizo farming communities were connected by a skeletal network of dirt tracks, while boats plied the route between Belize City and

Corozal. In 1930, however, the Northern Highway brought the region into contact with the rest of the country, opening up the area to further waves of settlers.

Today, the largest settlement in the north is **Orange Walk**, the main centre for sugar production. Further to the north is **Corozal**, a small and peaceful Caribbean town with a strong Mexican element – scarcely surprising as it lies just fifteen minutes from the border. Throughout the north Spanish is as common as Creole, and there's a mild Latin flavour to both of these places.

Most visitors to northern Belize are here to see the **Maya ruins** and wildlife reserves. The largest of the ruins is **Altun Ha**, near the old Northern Highway to the north of Belize City, while **Lamanai**, on the shores of the New River Lagoon, features some of the most impressive pyramids in the country. Although many of the sites are difficult to reach, Lamanai is served by regular boat tours along the **New River** and a good road to the nearby village of **Indian Church**. The smaller sites include **Cuello**, west of Orange Walk, and **Santa Rita** and **Cerros**, both near Corozal.

The four **wildlife reserves** each offer a different approach to conservation and an insight into different environments. The most northerly is the **Shipstern Nature Reserve**, reached from the village of Sarteneja, where a section of tropical forest is preserved with the help of the income from a butterfly farm. At the **Crooked Tree Wildlife Sanctuary** a network of rivers and lagoons offers protection to a range of migratory birds, and at the **Bermudian Landing Community Baboon Sanctuary** a group of farmers have combined agriculture with conservation, much to the benefit of the black howler monkey. By far the largest and most ambitious conservation project, however, is the **Rio Bravo Conservation Area**, comprising 229,000 acres of tropical forest and river systems in the west of Orange Walk district. This vast, practically unspoilt area, containing several Maya sites, adjoins the border with Guatemala and stretches to Mexico in the north, opening the door to the exciting possibility of a three-nation natural reserve.

Travelling around the north is fairly straightforward if you stick to the main highway. *Venus* and *Batty* between them operate bus services every hour from 4am to 7pm between Belize City and Chetumal on the Mexican border, calling at Orange Walk and Corozal. Smaller roads and centres are served by a fairly regular flow of trucks and buses, and several companies now operate **tours** to the Maya sites and nature reserves, though these can be expensive.

The border with Mexico

Heading **into Belize** from Mexico you can pick up a bus for Belize City (4hr; Bz$10) near the new terminal in **Chetumal**. This will take you to the **Santa Elena** border crossing on the River Hondo. The Mexican immigration and customs posts are on the northern bank; when you're finished there, simply walk across the bridge to their Belizean counterparts – the bus waits to pick you up again at Belizean immigration; border formalities take just a matter of minutes. Most travellers will be allowed a thirty-day stay, which can be extended in Belize City or Belmopan. Don't try to bring in cheaper cigarettes or liquor from Mexico – imports are prohibited. **Money changers** on the Belize side won't rip you off, and if you're carrying US dollars in cash it's possible to negotiate a slightly better rate than the standard two Belize dollars for one American dollar. For details of the bus service to Belize City, see "Travel Details" at the end of the chapter.

At present both *Venus* and *Batty* buses to and from Belize use the market in Chetumal as their depot, rather than the official bus station, due to an ongoing dispute with the Mexican authorities. The market is only a few blocks from the Mexican bus station, a ten-minute walk or a short taxi ride.

Corozal and around

Continuing south 14km from the border, the road meets the sea at **COROZAL**, Belize's most northerly town, just thirty minutes from Chetumal. The original settlement was founded here in 1849 by refugees from the massacre in Bacalar, Mexico, who were hounded south by the Caste Wars. Today's grid-pattern town is a neat mix of Mexican and Caribbean, its appearance largely due to reconstruction in the wake of Hurricane Janet in 1955. This is a fertile area – the town's name derives from the cohune tree, which the Maya recognized as an indicator of fecundity – and in the recent past much of the land was planted with sugar cane. Tumbling sugar prices have now forced farmers to try a range of alternative crops, often with great success.

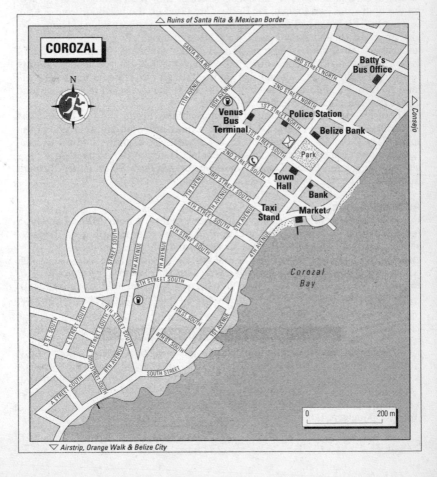

There's little to do in Corozal, but it's an agreeable place to spend the day on the way to or from the border, and is hassle-free, even at night. There's a breezy shoreline park shaded by palm trees, while on the tree-shaded main **plaza**, the town hall is worth a look inside for the vivid depiction of local history in a mural by Manuel Villamar Reyes. In two of the plaza's corners you can see the remains of a small fort, built to ward off Indian attacks. On October 12, Columbus Day – or PanAmerica Day, as it is now known – celebrations in Corozal are particularly lively; Mexican fiesta merging with Caribbean carnival.

The **telephone area code** for Corozal is ☎04.

Arrival and information

All **buses** between Belize City and Chetumal pass through Corozal, roughly hourly in each direction. For the border (20min) they pass through more or less on the hour from 7am to 9pm; for Belize City (3hr) on the half-hour from 5.30am to 7.30pm. The *Venus* bus depot (☎22132) is near the northern edge of town opposite the Shell station; *Batty* buses (☎23034) stop on 4th Ave, north of the park, and have a small office selling maps and books on Belize. *Island Air* (☎22874 local agent; ☎026/2345 main office) and *Tropic* (☎026/2012) operate daily **flights** to Corozal from Belize City and San Pedro, though other domestic carriers will land if arranged. *Jal's* travel agency (☎22163) at the the south of town, beyond *Tony's Inn*, can organize international flights.

There are two **banks** in Corozal – *Bank of Nova Scotia* and the *Belize Bank* (Mon–Fri 8am–1pm, Fri also 3–6pm), and a **post office** on the west side of the main plaza (Mon–Fri 8.30am–noon & 1–4.30pm). For **organized tours** to local nature reserves and archeological sites, contact Henry at *Caribbean Village* (he's also the agent for *Belize Transfer Service*), or *Ma-Ian's Tours* either through *Tony's Inn* or on ☎22744.

Accommodation

Corozal has plenty of hotel rooms in all price ranges. At **Four Miles Lagoon**, a few kilometres from the border, a couple of places offer **camping** on the lakeshore; *Lagoon Camping* has RV sites for Bz$20 and tent sites forBz$10.

Capri, on the seafront at the southern end of 4th Ave (☎22042). Basic rooms, some with private bath. The large, dingy bar is usually quiet, except when there's a dance on. ①.

Caribbean Village Resort, south end of town, across from the sea (☎22045; fax 23414). Whitewashed, thatched cabins, with hot water, among the palms. Plus an inexpensive restaurant, trailer park (Bz$24) and camping (Bz$10). The owner, Henry Menzies, an expert on local attractions, arranges tours and airport pick-ups. Good value; accepts *Visa/MC*. ③.

Hok'ol K'in Guest House, facing the sea a block south of the market (☎23369; fax 23329). New hotel in centre. Large rooms with private bath; ground floor is wheelchair-friendly. ⑤.

Hotel Maya, south end of town, facing the sea (☎22082; fax 22857). A bit pricey for what you get, but clean and well-run with private bathrooms; new rooms have a/c. The owner, Rosita May, is the local agent for *Island Air*. Accepts *Visa/MC*. ④.

Nestor's, 5th Ave South, between 4th and 5th streets (☎22354). Budget hotel, with private showers, though some rooms smell musty. Popular sports bar and restaurant. ②.

Papa Don's, 5th Ave South, next to *Nestor's*. Very cheap, basic, and friendly. ①.

Tony's Inn and Beach Resort, on the beach, about 1km south of the plaza (☎22055; fax 22829; in USA ☎1-800/447-2931). A touch of well-run luxury in a superb location with secure parking. The spacious, a/c rooms with king-size beds overlook landscaped gardens and a pristine beach bar. There's also an excellent new restaurant. Accepts *Visa/MC/AmEx*. ⑤–⑥.

Eating

The best cheap **meals** in Corozal are at ᵤₑ tiny, two-table *Loncheria Barrera*, in the southwest corner of the main square, where they serve great Mexican-style dishes. There's a mix of Belizean and Chinese cuisine at the *Bumper Chinese Restaurant*, on the main road opposite the *Hotel Capri*, and the popular bar at *Nestor's* serves American and Belizean food. Otherwise, you might want to eat where you're staying: *Hotel Maya* serves very good Mexican food, there's a wonderful restaurant at *Tony's*, and *Haley's* in *Caribbean Village* is renowned locally for its fine, inexpensive food.

Around Corozal: Santa Rita and Cerros

Two small Maya sites can be visited from Corozal. The closest is **Santa Rita** (daily; Bz$5), on the northern side of the town. To get there follow the main road in the direction of the border and when it divides take the left-hand fork, which soon brings you to the hospital, the power plant, and the raised Maya site; about fifteen minutes' walk in total. Founded around 1500 BC, Santa Rita was in all probability the powerful Maya city known as Chetumal, which dominated the trade of the area. It was still a thriving settlement in 1531 AD, when the conquistador Alonso Davila entered the town, which had been tactically abandoned by the Maya; he was driven out almost immediately by Na Chan Kan, the Maya chief, and his Spanish adviser Gonzalo Guerrero. Pottery found here has connected Santa Rita with other sites in the Yucatán, and there were once some superb Mixtec-style murals similar to those found at Tulum. You won't be spellbound by the enormity of the place, though, as only a fraction of it has been unearthed, and it's thought that much of the ancient city is covered by present-day Corozal. The main remaining building is a small pyramid; burials excavated here include that of an elaborately jewelled elderly woman, dated to the Early Classic period, and the tomb of a Classic Period warlord, buried with the symbols of his elite status.

Cerros, a late Preclassic centre on the southern shore of Corozal Bay, grew from a small fishing village to a major city in only two generations; its strategic position at the mouth of the New River enabling it to dominate the regional water-borne trade. This was was one of the earliest places in the Maya world to adopt the rule of kings. Despite initial success, however, Cerros was abandoned by the Classic Period, eclipsed by shifting trade routes. The site includes three large acropolis structures, ball courts and plazas flanked by pyramids. The largest building is a 22-metre high temple – its intricate stucco masks, representing the rising and setting sun, and Venus as Morningstar and Eveningstar, are presently covered to prevent erosion. Restoration schemes are afoot, along with plans to charge an entrance fee of Bz$10. Cerros is best reached by **boat**, easy enough to organize at the market in Corozal, though if you want a guide you're better off arranging a **tour** (see p.334). In the dry season it's possible to **drive** to the site through the villages of Progresso and Copper Bank – call the Copper Bank community telephone (☎22950) to check road conditions. Any time of the year mosquitoes can be a problem, so bring **repellent**.

Sarteneja and the Shipstern Reserve

Until recently, the largely uninhabited **Sarteneja peninsula**, jutting out towards the Yucatán in the northeast of Belize, could only be reached by boat. The only village is **Sarteneja**, a lobster-fishing centre populated by Spanish-speaking Mestizos; the rest of the peninsula is covered with dense forests that support an amazing array of wildlife. Since the region's closest links have always been with Mexico, the idea of Belize nationality is still fairly novel here.

Shipstern Nature Reserve

The **Shipstern Nature Reserve** (daily; Bz$10 including guided walk), established in 1981, covers an area of 31 square miles. The bulk of the reserve is made up of what's technically known as "tropical moist forest", although it contains only a few mature trees as the area was wiped clean by Hurricane Janet in 1955. It also includes some wide belts of savannah – covered in coarse grasses, palms and broad-leaved trees – and a section of the shallow Shipstern Lagoon, dotted with mangrove islands. Taking the superb guided walk along the Chiclero Trail you'll encounter more named plant species in one hour than on any other trail in Belize.

Shipstern, managed by the Belize Audubon Society, is a bird-watcher's paradise. The lagoon system supports blue-winged teal, American coot, thirteen species of egret and huge flocks of lesser scaup, while the forest is home to flycatchers, warblers, keel-billed toucans, collared aracari and at least five species of parrot. In addition there are crocodiles, manatees, coatis, jaguars, peccaries, deer, racoons, pumas and an abundance of weird and wonderful insects and butterflies. Though the reserve's butterfly farm didn't prove as lucrative as hoped, manager Donald Tillet and the wardens still tend the butterflies carefully, releasing them into the forest when mature. Visitors can walk around, observing the insect life cycle from egg to brilliant butterfly – an amazingly peaceful experience.

All **buses** to Sarteneja pass the entrance to the reserve. You can **stay** at the headquarters near the visitors centre; there are two neat four-bed dorms (Bz$20 per person) with cooking facilities, and a two-roomed house for rent. For **information** call *BAS* on ☎02/35004. Ask, too, about the Wood Stork Project, a new area of the reserve 18km south, with fully equipped **camping platforms** in a real jungle setting among freshwater creeks and lagoons.

Sarteneja

Five kilometres beyond the reserve, the quiet village of **SARTENEJA** is only just beginning to experience tourism. You can easily arrange excursions into the surrounding area: ask along the seafront or in the thatched *Mira Mar* bar. Akil

Gongora, who lives near the *Mira Mar*, can take you to the many nearby ruins or to seek out wildlife in the lagoons both in the reserve and beyond. You may also be able to get a ride in a sailboat or skiff leaving for Consejo or Chetumal or even across the bay to Ambergris Caye. The only **hotel**, *Diani's* (☎04/32084; ②), is right in the centre of town, facing the shore. It has an inexpensive restaurant. For a lovely room in a **private house** call ☎04/32158 (⑤ including breakfast).

Recent road improvements have made it easier to **get to Sarteneja**; from Belize City the *Perez* bus leaves the *Texaco* station on North Front St at 11.30am and 1pm, and *Venus* at 12.30pm. They all pass hrough Orange Walk, stopping at *Zeta's* store on Main St ninety minutes later. The whole journey takes less than four hours. *Venus* also run a daily service from Chetumal to Sarteneja via Orange Walk, at 1.30pm. Buses return from Sarteneja at 4am, 5am, 6am and 8am.

Orange Walk

ORANGE WALK, with a population of just under 12,000, is the largest town in the north of Belize and the centre of a busy agricultural region. Like Corozal, it was founded by Mestizo refugees fleeing from the Caste Wars in Yucatán in 1849, who chose as their site an area that had long been used for logging camps and was already occupied by the local Icaiché (Chichanha) Maya. Throughout the 1850s and 60s the Icaiché Maya were in conflict with both the Cruzob Maya, who were themselves rebelling against Mestizo rule in Yucatán (and supplied with arms by British traders in Belize), and the British settlers and colonial authorities in Belize. The leader of the Icaiché, Marcos Canul, organized successful raids against British mahogany camps, forcing the logging firms to pay "rent" for lands they used and even briefly occupying Corozal in 1870. In 1872 Canul launched an attack on the barracks in Orange Walk. The West India Regiment, which had earlier retreated in disarray after a skirmish with Canul's troops, this time forced the Icaiché to flee across the Rio Hondo, taking the fatally wounded Canul with them. This defeat didn't end the raids, but the Maya ceased to be a threat to British rule in northern Belize; a small monument opposite the park in Orange Walk commemorates the last (officially the only) battle fought on Belizean soil.

MENNONITES IN BELIZE

The **Mennonites** arose from the radical Anabaptist movement of the sixteenth century and are named after the Dutch priest Menno Simons, leader of the community in its formative years. Recurring government restrictions on their lifestyle, especially regarding their pacifist objection to military service, forced them to move repeatedly. Having removed to Switzerland they travelled on to Prussia, and in 1663 a group emigrated to North America. After World War I they migrated from Canada to Mexico, eventually to arrive in Belize in 1958. Perseverance and hard work made them successful farmers, and in recent years prosperity has caused drastic changes in their lives. The Mennonite Church in Belize is increasingly split between a modernist section – who use electricity and power tools, and drive trucks, tractors and even cars – and the traditionalists, who prefer a stricter interpretation of their beliefs. Members of the community, easily recognizable in their denim dungarees, can be seen trading their produce and buying supplies every day in Orange Walk and Belize City.

Nowadays, the few remaining Icaiché Maya live in the village of Botes, on the Mexican border near the Rio Hondo.

Orange Walk has traditionally thrived, first with the growth of the sugar and citrus industries, and after the fall in sugar prices, with the profits made from marijuana. Recently, however, pressure from the US government has forced Belizean authorities to destroy many of the marijuana fields, and today the town has less of a Wild West atmosphere than just a couple of years ago. The land around Blue Creek and Shipyard has been developed by **Mennonite** settlers, members of a Protestant religious group who choose to farm without the assistance of modern technology. The town itself, while not unattractive, boasts few tourist attractions, and Corozal, less than an hour away, is a better place to spend the night. It is, however, the starting point for visiting the ruins of Cuello or Lamanai, and several local operators now offer tours (see p.340).

The **telephone area code** for Orange Walk is ☎03.

Practicalities

Buses pull up on the main road in the centre of town, offically Queen Victoria Avenue but always referred to as the Belize–Corozal road. It's lined with hotels, restaurants and filling stations, so there's no need to walk far. Though budget **accommodation** is fairly limited, the cheapest options can be found along this road: the Chinese-run *Tai-San* (☎22752; ②–③), above the restaurant, and, less expensive still, *Jane's Guest House* (☎22473; ①) on the corner of Baker and Riverside streets. Slightly more expensive is the a/c *Mi Amor* (☎22031; ④), but the best hotel is the *Victoria* (☎22518; fax 22847; ④), at the southern end of town, where most of the rooms have balconies, some are a/c, and there's a pool.

Of the two **banks** just east of the park, the *Bank of Nova Scotia* gives the best rates for travellers' cheques; getting a cash advance at the *Belize Bank* is time-consuming and expensive. The **post office** and **police station** are near each other at the north end of town.

The majority of **restaurants** in Orange Walk are Chinese, though there are a few Belizean-style places serving simple "Mexican" food or rice and beans. *Lover's Restaurant*, tucked away in the far corner of the park at 20 Lover's Lane, offers the best Belizean food (and is the meeting place for the *Novelo's* Jungle River Tours), while *Juanita's*, on the side street by the *Shell* station has the best Mexican dishes. For Mexican *pan dulces* and bread, try the *Panificadora la Popular*, on Beytias Lane, off the northeast side of the square. The *Lamanai Inn*, on Riverside St, is a pleasant waterside **bar** and restaurant, where you can also rent boats for river trips. Nightlife boils down to the *Mi Amor* disco, or the *Tropicala* **disco** in the *Victoria Hotel* every Friday and Saturday. There are a number of bars and clubs dotted around town, some of them serving as brothels.

There's at least one **bus** an hour in either direction along the main road, heading north on the hour and south on the half-hour. *Batty* have a small office on the main road opposite the *Tai-San* hotel (☎22858). For **Sarteneja**, there are four buses between 1.30pm and 3.30pm from *Zeta's Store* on Main St, two blocks east of the Belize–Corozal road. **Local buses** to the surrounding villages leave from near the crossroads in the centre of town. *Caribbean Holidays*, on Beytias Lane (☎22803), is able to book international flights.

Maya sites around Orange Walk

Although the **Maya sites** in northern Belize have been the source of a number of the most important archeological finds anywhere in the Maya world, they are not (with the exception of Lamanai) as monumentally spectacular as some in the Yucatán. The area around Orange Walk is some of the most productive arable farmland in Belize, and this was also the case in Maya times – aerial surveys in the late 1970s revealed evidence of raised fields and a network of irrigation canals, showing that the Maya practised skilful intensive agriculture. In the Postclassic era this region became part of the powerful Maya state of Chactemal, controlling the trade in cacao beans (which were used as currency) grown in the valleys of the Hondo and New rivers. For a while the Maya here were even able to resist the conquistadors, and long after nominal Spanish rule had been established in 1544 there were frequent Maya rebellions: in 1638 they drove the Spanish out and burned the church at Lamanai.

Cuello and Nohmul

Cuello lies about 5km west of Orange Walk. Discovered in 1973 by Norman Hammond, until recently the site was thought to be one of the earliest in the Maya empire, originating in 1500 BC. However, new ideas suggest that it in fact dates back to 1000 BC, a theory that even Hammond himself has had to agree with. The site itself isn't very impressive, and there's not much to look at except a single small pyramid and several earth-covered mounds.

The ruins are behind a factory where *Cuello* rum is made; the site is on their land, so you should ask permission to visit by phoning ☎22141. Cuello can be reached by simply walking west from the plaza in Orange Walk for a little under an hour; or you can take the San Felipe **bus** from the side of the fire station at the junction of the Belize–Corozal road and San Antonio road, at around 10am. A taxi to the site costs around Bz$10.

Situated on the Orange Walk–Corozal boundary, just west of the village of San Pablo, **Nohmul** (Great Mound) is a major ceremonial centre with origins in the Late Formative period. During the Classic period it was abandoned, to be reoccupied by a Yucatecan elite during the Early Postclassic. The ruins cover a large area, comprising two groups connected by a causeway, with several plazas around them. The main structure is an acropolis platform surmounted by a later pyramid which, owing to the site's position on a limestone ridge, is the highest point in the area. As at so many of Belize's Maya sites, looters have plundered the ruins and, tragically, at least one structure has been demolished for road fill – that said, as one of the sites earmarked for tourism, some structural restoration has taken place.

Nohmul lies amid sugar-cane fields, 2km west of the village of **San Pablo**, which is 12km north of Orange Walk on the Northern Highway. Any bus between Corozal and Orange Walk goes through the village. To visit the site, contact Estevan Itzab, who lives in the house across from the village water tower.

Lamanai

Though they can't match the scale of the great sites in Mexico and Guatemala, the **ruins of Lamanai** (daily 8am–4pm; Bz$10) are the most impressive in Belize, and their setting on the New River Lagoon – in the 950-acre Archeological

Reserve, now the only jungle for miles around – gives them a special quality that is long gone from sites served by a torrent of tourist buses.

Lamanai is one of only a few sites whose original Maya name is known – it translates as "Submerged Crocodile", hence the numerous representations of crocodiles. *Lamanai*, however, is the seventeenth-century mistranslation of *Lamanyan*, and actually means "Drowned Insect". The site was occupied up until the sixteenth century, when Spanish missionaries built a church alongside to lure the Indians from their heathen ways. More than seven hundred structures have been mapped by teams led by David Pendergast of the Royal Ontario Museum, the majority of them still buried beneath mounds of earth. Seven troops of black howler monkeys make Lamanai their home and you'll certainly see a couple of them peering down through the branches as you wander the trails.

The most impressive feature is the prosaically named N10-43, a massive **Late Preclassic temple**, the largest Preclassic structure in the entire Maya region, though one which was extensively modified later. The view across the surrounding forest from the top of the temple is magnificent. Structure P9-56 is a sixth-century pyramid with a four-metre-high mask carved in the side; it overlies several smaller, older buildings, the earliest being a superbly preserved temple from around 100 BC. There are a number of other well-preserved and clearly defined glyphs. Traces of later settlers can be seen around the nearby village of **Indian Church**: to the south of the village are the ruins of two churches built by Spanish missionaries, and to the west are the remains of a nineteenth-century sugar mill, built by Confederate refugees from the American Civil War.

The small **archeological museum** at the site, so far the only such museum in Belize, houses an amazing collection of artefacts, mostly figurines depicting gods and animals. The most unusual item is a drum the size and shape of a pair of binoculars. Nazario Ku, one of the guards at the site, is very knowledgeable about Maya culture and will happily act as a guide.

PRACTICALITIES

Getting to Lamanai is relatively easy nowadays, with a good road used by a twice-weekly bus, but the most pleasant way to get there is by river. A number of operators organize **day trips** for US$30–50 per person. The most informative is *Jungle River Tours*, run by the knowledgable Antonio and Herminio Novelo and based in Orange Walk at the *Lover's Restaurant* (☎22293; fax 23749). The *Lamanai Lady* departs daily from the toll bridge 9km south of Orange Walk; book through *Discovery Expeditions* in Belize City (☎02/31063; fax 30750). This is an expensive tour but costs can be reduced if you book ahead and make your own way to the toll bridge: the *Batty* buses that leave Belize City at 6 and 7am for Chetumal meet the *Lamanai Lady* at the departure point in time for the 9am start. Mario, guide on the *Lamanai Lady*, is a wildlife expert and will point out the lurking crocodiles and dozens of species of bird, including snail kites, you might otherwise miss. The best **bargain** for independent travellers wanting to experience the river route is *Lamanai Maya Tours* (☎23839), right by the toll bridge. Barbara or John not only organize the trip but can also rent you a two bedroom house near the site for around Bz$50.

To get to Lamanai **by road**, head south from Orange Walk and turn right by *Dave's Store*, where a signpost gives the distance to Lamanai as 35 miles.

Continue along the Yo Creek road as far as **San Felipe**, where you should bear left for the village of Indian Church, 2km from the ruins. By **bus**, pick up the 10am service to San Felipe (Mon–Sat) from the crossroads by the Fire Station in Orange Walk. On Tuesday and Thursday it continues to Indian Church (call the community phone in Indian Church on ☎03/23369 to check bus times). If you're thinking of **hitching** to Lamanai bear in mind that traffic is scarce on the 20km stretch from San Felipe; you're better off taking the bus and staying two nights. A couple of places offer **rooms**, or speak to Nazario at the site and he'll let you camp at his house or rent you a hammock very cheaply. You can eat with the family. More comfortable accommodation nearby is available in the thatched *cabañas* at *Lamanai Outpost Lodge* (☎ & fax 02/33578; *Visa/MC/AmEx* accepted; ⑦), set in extensive gardens sweeping down to the lagoon. Guests can use canoes or take a "moonlight safari" to spot nocturnal wildlife, or even take part in Maya research under the supervision of archeologist Herman Smith.

The Rio Bravo Conservation Area and Gallon Jug

In the far northwest of Orange Walk district is **The Rio Bravo Conservation Area**, a 229,000-acre tract designated for tropical forest conservation, research and sustained-yield forest harvests. Immediately to the south, privately owned **Gallon Jug**, managed under similar conservation principles, adds a further 100,000 acres; together they comprise by far the largest area of protected land in northern Belize. This astonishing conservation success story actually began with a disastrous plan in the mid-1980s to clear the forest, initially to fuel a wood-fired power station and later to provide Coca-Cola with frost-free land to grow citrus. Environmentalists were alarmed, and their strenuous objections forced Coca-Cola to drop the plan, though the forest remained threatened by agriculture.

An imaginative project to save the threatened forest by purchasing it, **The Programme for Belize** was initiated by The Massachusetts Audubon Society and launched in 1988. Funds were raised from corporate donors and conservation organizations but the most widespread support was generated through an ambitious "adopt-an-acre" scheme, enthusiastically taken up by schools and individuals in the UK and North America. Coca-Cola itself, anxious to distance itself from the charge of rainforest destruction, has donated more than 90,000 acres. Today rangers with powers of arrest patrol the area to prevent illegal logging and to stop farmers encroaching onto the reserve with *milpas* (slash and burn cornfields).

The forest teems with **wildlife**: including all five of Belize's cat species, tapirs, monkeys and crocodiles, plus more than 300 species of birds. The strict ban on hunting, enforced for almost ten years, makes the Rio Bravo and Gallon Jug area the best place in Belize to actually see these beasts; even pumas and jaguars are frequently spotted. The guarded boundaries also protect at least a hundred **Maya sites**, most of them unexcavated and unrestored, though many have been looted.

There's no **public transport** to Rio Bravo, but if you're staying at the field station you can get a bus to San Felipe and arrange to be picked up there. Heading to Rio Bravo or Gallon Jug in your own vehicle, take the road west from Orange Walk via Yo Creek and San Felipe to the Mennonite village of Blue Creek, on the Rio Hondo (you can cross the river to the Mexican village of **La**

Unión, though officially you can't travel further into Mexico). Beyond Blue Creek the road (paved here and in good condition all the way to Gallon Jug) climbs steeply up the Rio Bravo escarpment, then turns south to the field station and Gallon Jug. Charter **flights** use the airstrips at Blue Creek and Gallon Jug.

The Rio Bravo field station

At present the only place to stay in the Rio Bravo Conservation Area is the wonderful **Rio Bravo field station** (another lodge is planned at Hill Bank, at the south end of New River Lagoon), near the northern boundary of the reserve, 75km southwest of Orange Walk. Set in a former *milpa* clearing in the forest, the comfortable dorms (US$65) and *cabañas* (US$80 per person; sleep 6) have a tranquil, studious atmosphere. Deer and ocellated turkeys feed contentedly around the cabins, adding a Disney-like element. Camping is not allowed. Adjacent to the station, the huge Classic Maya city of **La Milpa**, the third largest in Belize – with probably the biggest plaza in the Maya world – is being investigated as part of a long term archeological survey by Boston University.

Prices, though high (discounts for student groups), include three good meals and two excursions or lectures per day; guests can use the library and spotting scopes. A day visit, which includes a guided tour of La Milpa or one of the trails is US$20. Contact the manager, Bart Romero, through the PFB office, 2 South Park St, Belize City (☎02/75616; fax 75635) or write to *PFB*, Box 749, Belize City.

Gallon Jug and Chan Chich

Forty kilometres south of the field station, the former logging town of **Gallon Jug**, set in neat fenced pastures, is the home of Barry Bowen, reportedly the richest man in Belize. In the 1980s, his speculative land deals led to an international outcry against threatened rainforest clearance. The experience apparently proved cathartic; Bowen is now an ardent conservationist and most of the 125,000 acres here are strictly protected. The focal point is the luxurious **Chan Chich Lodge** (☎02/75634; fax 76961; in USA ☎1-800/343-8009; ⑤), with twelve large thatched *cabañas* set in the plaza of the Classic Maya site of Chan Chich, surrounded by superb forest. The construction of the lodge on this spot (all Maya sites are technically under government control) was controversial at the time, but received Archeology Department approval as it was designed to cause minimal disturbance. Certainly the year-round presence of visitors and staff does prevent looting – a real problem in the past. It is a truly awe-inspiring setting; grass-covered temple walls crowned with jungle tower up from the lodge and the forest explodes with a cacophany of bird calls at dawn. You can drive here, but most guests fly in to the **airstrip** at Gallon Jug; *Javier's Flying Service* (☎02/45332) has three scheduled flights a week.

Crooked Tree and south to Belize City

Heading south from Orange Walk along the Northern Highway you pass the branch road for the **Crooked Tree Wildlife Sanctuary**, a reserve that takes in a vast area of inland waterways, logwood swamps and lagoons. Founded in 1984 by the Belize Audubon Society and covering four separate lagoons and 16,000 acres, it provides an ideal resting place for thousands of **migrating birds**, such as snail kites, tiger herons, snowy egrets, ospreys and black-collared hawks. The reserve's most famous visitor is the **jabiru stork**, the largest flying bird in the New World, with a wingspan of 2.5m. Belize has the biggest nesting population of jabiru storks at one site: they arrive in November, the young hatch in April or May, and they leave just before the rainy season gets under way. If you set off to explore the lagoons you might also catch a glimpse of howler monkeys, crocodiles, coatis, turtles or iguanas. The **best time to visit** for bird-watchers is from late February to June, when the lagoons shrink to a string of pools, forcing wildlife to congregate for food and water.

In the middle of the reserve, straggling around the shores of a lagoon, 5km from the main road, is the village of **CROOKED TREE**. One of the oldest inland villages in the country, its existence is based on fishing and farming – some of the mango and cashew trees are reckoned to be more than a hundred years old, and during January and February the air is heavy with the scent of cashew blossom. Immediately over the causeway, across the lagoon, is the **Sanctuary Visitor Centre**, where you pay the Bz$8 visitor fee to Steve Tillet and the other wardens, who provide a wealth of information on the area's flora and fauna. They also sell trail maps, and give information on accommodation and camping and canoe trips.

Arrival

There are four daily **buses** to Crooked Tree from Belize City. The *Jex* bus leaves from the Pound Yard bridge at 10.30am, 4.30pm and 5.30pm; the *Batty* bus leaves at 4pm Monday to Friday, noon on Saturday and 9am Sunday. Returning buses leave at 6am, 6.30am and 7am, with an extra service on Friday afternoon. As always it's a good idea to check the times by calling the community phone on ☎02/44101 or 44333. For an **organized tour** contact Homer Leslie at *Native Guide Systems*, 2 Water Lane, Belize City (☎02/78247). In Crooked Tree, you can use the **telephone** at the *Jex* store – the best stocked in the village – just past the visitor centre.

Accommodation

Most of the accommodation at Crooked Tree is in resort-type lodgings. If this is not your scene, there is reasonably priced **bed and breakfast** accommodation available through the Belize Audubon Society (☎02/35004; ③). Otherwise, several of the resort lodges have space for **camping** but the cheapest site is likely to be someone's farm.

The best of the **package lodges** is the remote *Chau Hiix Lodge* (☎02/73787; in USA ☎407/322-6361; fax 322-6389), where five well-appointed cabins are set in 4000 acres of forest and wetlands on the southern edge of the sanctuary at Sapodilla lagoon. Just getting here is an adventure, as the boat (no road access) navigates broad lagoons and tiny creeks, with the reward of comfortable isolation. Chau Hiix ("small cat") is a nearby Maya site that hasn't been looted, offering potentially revolutionary discoveries to the University of Indiana team excavating here. Packages include transport from the airport, all meals, guided trips and use of boats and canoes; two people each pay US$525 for three nights; US$935 for a week.

Bird's Eye View Lodge (☎02/32040; fax 24869). Comfortable, if incongruous-looking concrete building, right on the lakeshore. All rooms have private bath and there's an inexpensive dorm (Bz$20) and camping (Bz$10). Room rates include breakfast. ⑥.

Crooked Tree Resort (☎02/75819; fax 74007). Neat wood-and-thatch cabins on the lakeshore. ⑤.

Paradise Inn (☎02/44101 or 44333). Beautiful thatched cabins, at the north end of the village just paces from the lake, built by the owner Rudy Crawford. His son, Glen, is one of the best guides in the village, and there are boats available for bird-watching trips. Great home-cooked meals. ⑤.

Sam Tillet's Hotel (☎02/12026). Sam, known locally as the "king of birds" for his expertise, used to manage *Crooked Tree Resort*. Though not on the lake, the three rooms here (with more planned) are the best value in the village. The garden attracts a wide variety of birds. Camping available, and boats and vehicles for tours. ④.

The ruins of Altun Ha

Fifty-five kilometres north of Belize City and just 9km from the sea is the impressive Maya site of **Altun Ha** (Bz$10), which was occupied from around 1000 BC until abandoned in 900 AD. Its population probably peaked at 3000 inhabitants. Its position close to the Caribbean coast suggests that it was sustained as much by trade as agriculture – a theory upheld by the discovery of trade objects such as obsidian and jade, neither of which occur naturally in Belize and both very important in Maya ceremony. The jade would have come from the Motagua valley in Guatemala and much of it would probably have been shipped onwards to the north.

The core of Altun Ha is clustered around two Classic period plazas, both dotted with palm trees. Entering from the road, you come first to Plaza A. Large temples

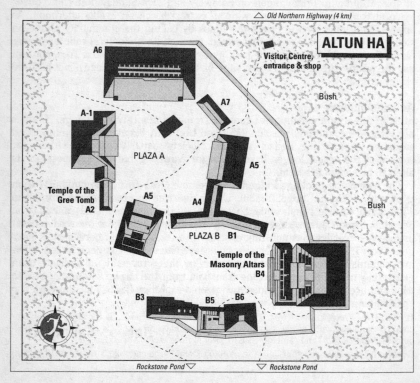

enclose it on all four sides, and a magnificent tomb has been discovered beneath Temple A-1, **The Temple of the Green Tomb**. Dating from 550 AD, this yielded a total of three hundred pieces, including jade, jewellery, stingray spines, skin, flints and the remains of a Maya book. Temple A-6, which has been particularly badly damaged, contains two parallel rooms, each about 48m long and with thirteen doorways along an exterior wall.

The adjacent Plaza B is dominated by the site's largest temple, **The Temple of the Masonry Altars**, the last in a sequence of buildings raised on this spot. This was probably the main focus of religious ceremonies, with a single stairway running up the front to an altar at the top. Several priestly tombs have been uncovered within the main structure, but most of them had already been desecrated, possibly during the political turmoil that preceded the abandonment of the site. Only two of the tombs were found intact; in one of them archeologists discovered a carved jade head of **Kinich Ahau**, the Maya sun god. Standing just under 15cm high, it was the largest carved jade to be found anywhere in the Maya world at the time of its discovery in 1968; today it's kept hidden away in the vaults of the Belize Bank, there being no national museum to display it.

Outside these two main plazas are several other areas of interest, though little else has yet been restored. A short trail leads south to **Rockstone Pond**, which was dammed in Maya times, at the eastern edge of which stands another mid-sized temple. Built in the second century AD, this contained offerings that came from the great city of Teotihuacán in the Valley of Mexico.

Practicalities

Altun Ha is fairly difficult to reach, but there is a daily **bus** from Cinderella Plaza in Belize City (call ☎03/22041 to check times) along the Old Northern Highway to the village of **MASKALL**, passing the turn-off to the site at **LUCKY STRIKE** (community phone ☎02/44249), just 3km from Altun Ha. Any travel agent in Belize City will arrange a **tour** and increasing numbers make the visit as part of a day trip from San Pedro (p.365). There's no **accommodation** at the site but you can ask the caretaker for permission to camp nearby, or press on 15km to Maskall. Near Maskall at Mile 39, Old Northern Highway, *Pretty See Jungle Ranch* (☎03/12005; in US: ☎1-800/936-1111; ⑨) has cool thatched cabins – with CD players and fridges – in a forest setting, plus an excellent restaurant on site. Room rates include breakfast, horseriding, and use of bicycles.

If money's no object, you can submit to the hedonistic (and undoubtedly therapeutic) pleasures of the outrageously Californian-style *Maruba Resort and Jungle Spa*, Mile 40, Old Northern Highway (☎03/22199; in USA: ☎713/799-2031; fax 795-8573; ⑨). Each room and cabin is luxurious, verging on the opulent, with hand-built wooden furniture and feather beds (there are alternatives if you're allergic). All are decorated individually; one does boast larger-than-life carved wooden penises for door handles, but they're not obtrusive. The food is excellent, and you'd need to stay a week to take advantage of all the body treatments. If the African honey bee pat or seaweed body wrap sound just too decadent then perhaps a jungle sand scrub would be more to your liking.

The Bermudian Landing Community Baboon Sanctuary

The **Community Baboon Sanctuary** is one of the most interesting conservation projects in Belize, and almost certainly the most cost-effective. It was established in 1985 by Dr Rob Horwich and a group of local farmers (with help from the Worldwide Fund for Nature), who adopted a voluntary code of practice to harmonize their own needs with those of the wildlife. A mixture of farmland and broad-leaved forest along the banks of the Belize River, the sanctuary coordinates eight villages and more than a hundred landowners in a project combining conservation, education and tourism.

The main focus of attention is the **black howler monkey** (locally known as a baboon), an endangered subspecies of howler that exists only in Belize, Guatemala and Mexico. They generally live in groups of between four and eight, and spend the day wandering through the leaf canopy feasting on leaves, flowers and fruits. At dawn and dusk they let rip with the infamous howl, a deep and rasping roar that carries for miles. Results of the breeding programme were so successful that by 1992 eighteen black howler monkeys had been successfully relocated to the Cockscomb Basin, since when numbers have grown.

The sanctuary is also home to around two hundred bird species, plus iguanas, anteaters, deer, peccaries and coatis. Special **trails** are cut through the forest so that visitors can see it at its best, and you can wander these alone or with a guide. The interpretative **visitors centre** (Bz$10; includes a short guided walk), which is home to Belize's first natural history museum, sells an excellent guidebook telling you everything about the reserve and its inhabitants.

Practicalities: Bermudian Landing

The village of **BERMUDIAN LANDING** is at the heart of the area, an old logging centre that dates back to the seventeenth century. It's a small place, so you should let them know that you're coming, particularly if you plan to stay the night. Get in touch with Fallet Young, the sanctuary manager, by calling the community telephone on ☎021/2001. You can **camp** at the visitors centre for a small fee (①), and a number of local families offer **bed and breakfast** (③) and meals. The newest place to stay in the village is the very friendly *Jungle Drift Lodge* (☎01/49578; fax 02/78160; ③–④) – ideal for independent travellers, as the bus stops just 75m from the entrance. They offer neat, clean *cabañas*, some with deck and private bath, and shared bathrooms have hot water. Right above the riverbank, shaded by trees with a profusion of tropical plants in the gardens, you're practically guaranteed close-up views of the baboons. They also have canoes to rent, and organize a trip downriver to the village of Isabella Bank (22km). Camping is also available (Bz$10).

There are several **shops** in the village, plus a bar called *Enda's Cool Spot*, which serves simple meals of beans and rice. The Sanctuary comprises eight villages along the Belize River, from Flowers Bank to Big Falls. All of them welcome visitors and you'll find plenty of places where you can rent canoes or horses.

Buses run from Belize City to the sanctuary: Mr Oswald McFadzean's bus that leaves from the corner of Orange St and Mosul St, near the *Batty* bus depot, and Mr Sydney Russell's from Cairo St, near the corner of Orange St and Euphrates Ave (Mon–Fri 12.15pm & 4.30pm, Sat noon, 12.15pm, 1pm & 4.30pm; buses return at 5.30am & 6.30am). On the way to Bermudian Landing you'll pass a turning to **Burrell Boom**, on the Belize River. Here you'll find *Baboon River Canoe Rentals* (☎028/2101), where you can rent a canoe to float and paddle the 28km down the Belize River to Belize City. If you have your own vehicle and are heading directly west you can save time and considerable distance by cutting down through Burrell Boom to **Hattieville**, on the Western Highway, thus avoiding Belize City altogether.

The approach to Belize City

Back on the Northern Highway, there's not much else to stop for before Belize City. At **Ladyville** you pass the **International Airport**; there's a branch road to Airport Camp, the main base of the British Forces in Belize. Units regularly undertake jungle training in Belize. The side road to the airport is the next one south of the hotel, a two-kilometre walk.

From here it's just 15km to Belize City and, with the road very close to the river, heavy rain sometimes causes flooding on this stretch. If you notice a large, brightly painted concrete building on the left-hand side of the road called *Raul's Rose Garden* you may care to know that it's not a nursery in the horticultural sense but a brothel. The Haulover Bridge takes the road over the mouth of the Belize River, past the *Rio Haul Motel* (☎ 02/44859; ⑤); next door, on the coast, is the attractive *Privateer* bar and restaurant, often with live music at weekends. Beyond this point you begin to enter the spreading suburbs of Belize City, where expensive houses are constructed on reclaimed mangrove swamps.

travel details

Buses

From Chetumal to Belize City (15 daily; 4hr, express services 3hr) via **Corozal** (1hr 30min) and **Orange Walk** (2hr 30min). *Venus* buses run hourly from 3.30am to 11am, then *Batty* takes over until 6.30pm. **To Sarteneja** *Venus* leave at 1.30pm, passing Orange Walk at about 1.30pm.

From Belize City to Chetumal (15 daily; 4hr, express services 3hr) there are hourly departures from *Batty's* terminal, 15 Mosul St (☎02/72025), from 4am to 11am. The express service leaves at 6am. *Venus* (☎02/77390) runs hourly from noon to 7pm, leaving from Magazine Rd. From around the *Batty* depot and over the nearby canal bridge several companies operate buses to Orange Walk, Ladyville and villages en route. Most leave in the late morning and early afternoon.

To Sarteneja (3hr 30min) the *Perez* bus leaves the Texaco station on N Front St (Mon–Sat 11.30am & 1pm). *Venus leaves* at 12.30pm. All buses pass Orange Walk. Buses return from **Sarteneja to Belize** at 4am, 5am, 6am & 8am. There is one daily bus back to **Chetumal**.

To the Bermudian Landing Baboon Sanctuary (1hr 15min) there are 3 buses daily (except Sun) from Belize City, one leaving at noon. One departs from the corner of Orange St and Mosul St, the other from the corner of Orange St and Euphrates Ave.

To Crooked Tree there are 4 daily buses (1hr 30min).

To Burrell Boom there's a bus Mon–Sat at 11am from Vernon St, half a block from *Batty's* depot (55min).

To Maskall (for Altun Ha) there's a daily bus at 12.30pm (1hr 30min).

From Orange Walk to Indian Church (for Lamanai) buses leave on Tuesday and Thursday at 10am (2hr).

Planes

Island Air (☎026/2345) and *Tropic Air* (☎026/2012) operate daily flights **from San Pedro to Corozal and Belize City**.

CHAPTER EIGHT

BELIZE CITY

The narrow, crowded streets of **Belize City** can initially be daunting to anyone who has been prepared by the usual tales of crime-ridden urban decay. Admittedly, at first glance the city is unprepossessing. Its buildings – many of them dilapidated wooden structures – stand right at the edge of the road, and few sidewalks offer refuge to pedestrians from the ever-increasing numbers of cars and trucks. Narrow bridges force the traffic to cross in single file over almost stagnant canals, which are still used for much of the city's drainage. Vultures circle overhead or sit with drooping wings on rotting riverside jetties. The overall impression is that the place has never recovered from some great calamity – an explanation that is at least partly true. Belize has suffered several devastating hurricanes, the latest in October 1961, when Hurricane Hattie tore the city apart with winds of 240kmph, leaving a layer of thick black mud as the storm receded. The hazards of Belize City, however, are often reported by those who have never been here. If you approach the city with an open mind and take some precautions with your belongings, you may well be pleasantly surprised.

HASSLE

Walking in Belize City **in daylight** is perfectly safe if you observe common-sense rules. The introduction of specially trained **tourist police** in 1995 made an immediate impact on the level of hassle and this, coupled with the legal requirement for all tour guides to be licenced, drove away the hustlers and really reduced street crime. That said, it's still sensible to proceed with caution: most people are friendly and chatty, but quite a few may want to sell you drugs or bum a dollar or two. The best advice is to stay cool. Be civil, don't provoke trouble by arguing too forcefully, and never show large sums of money on the street, especially American dollars – some money changers will give you better than the usual fixed rate of two dollars Belize for one US, but tourists are scammed every day changing money on the street. Be discreet if you smoke dope. Marijuana might be readily available, but it is illegal, and busting tourists can help a policeman get promoted. Buying drugs on the street can also mark you out as an easy target. Women wearing short shorts or skirts will attract verbal abuse from local studs.

The virtual absence of nightlife (most bars and restaurants are closed by 9.30pm) means there's little reason to walk the streets **after dark**; if you do venture out, bear in mind that anyone alone is in danger of being mugged. Even in what appears to be a quiet area you shouldn't carry more cash than you need. It's certainly safer to take a taxi at night, especially if you're arriving by bus in the dark. You'll soon learn to spot dangerous situations and in the city centre you can always ask the **tourist police** (they look like ordinary policemen, with a prominent identification badge) for advice or directions; they'll even walk you back to your hotel if it's near their patrol route.

Most visitors hurry through on their way to catch their next bus or a boat out to the cayes, but the city has a distinguished history, a handful of sights, and an astonishing energy. The 60,000 people of Belize City represent every ethnic group in the country, with the **Creole** descendants of former slaves and Baymen forming the dominant element, generating an easy-going Caribbean atmosphere.

A brief history
Exactly how Belize came by its name is something of a mystery, but there are plenty of possibilities. It could be a corruption of "Willis", the name of a famous English pirate who may have landed here in 1638; a similar claim is made of Peter Wallace, a Scotsman who founded a colony here in 1620. Those preferring a more ancient origin believe the name to be derived from *beliz*, a Maya word meaning "muddy", or from the Maya term *belekin*, meaning "towards the east". Another possibility is that it is a corruption of the French word *balise* – "beacon" – as there may have been a light marking the estuary of the Belize River.

What is known is that by the late seventeenth century, buccaneers were cutting logwood in this region, using a settlement at the mouth of the river during the rainy season, the mangrove swamp being consolidated with wood chips, loose coral and rum bottles. By the 1700s Belize Town was well established as a centre for logwood cutters, their families and their slaves; after the rains had floated the logs downriver the men returned here to drink and brawl, with huge Christmas celebrations going on for weeks. The sea front contained the houses of the **Baymen**, as the settlers called themselves; the slaves lived in cabins on the south side of Haulover Creek, with various tribal groups occupying separate areas.

The core of the settlement was on St George's Caye until a Spanish raid in 1779, when many of the inhabitants were captured and several of the Baymen fled. They returned in 1783, when Spain agreed to recognize the rights of the British settlers, and their new mainland capital soon grew into the main centre of the logwood and mahogany trade on the Bay of Honduras. Spanish raids continued, however, until the Battle of St George's Caye in 1798, when the settlers achieved victory with British naval help – a success that reinforced the bond with the British government.

The nineteenth century saw the increasing influence of **British expatriates**, colonial-style wooden housing dominating the shoreline as the "Scots clique" began to clean up the town's image and take control of its administration. Belize also became a base for Anglican missionaries: in 1812 the Anglican cathedral of St John was built to serve a diocese that stretched from Belize to Panamá.

Fires in 1804, 1806 and 1856 necessitated extensive rebuilding, and there were epidemics of cholera, yellow fever and smallpox in this period too. Despite these reversals, the town grew with immigration from the West Indies and refugees from the Caste Wars in the Yucatán. In 1862 Belize became the colony of **British Honduras**, with Belize City as the administrative centre, and in 1871 Belize was officially declared a Crown Colony, with a resident governor appointed by Britain.

For the people of Belize the twentieth century has been dominated by uncertainty over their relationship with the "mother country". In 1914 thousands of Belizeans volunteered to assist the war effort, but when they arrived in the Middle East they were confronted by a wall of prejudice and racism, and consigned to labour battalions. In 1919 the returning soldiers rioted in Belize City, an event that marked the onset of Black consciousness and the beginning of the **independence movement**.

On September 10, 1931, the city was celebrating the anniversary of the Battle of St George's Caye when it was hit by a massive **hurricane** that uprooted houses, flooded the entire city and killed about a thousand people – 10 percent of the population. Disaster relief was slow to arrive and many parts of the city were left in a state of squalid poverty. This neglect, together with the effects of the Depression, gave added momentum to the campaign for independence, and the city saw numerous rallies and marches in an upsurge of defiance against the British colonial authorities. In 1961 the city was again ravaged by a hurricane: 262 people died, and the damage was so serious that plans were made to relocate the capital inland to Belmopan. (Hattieville, on the Western Highway, began life as a refuge for those fleeing the hurricane.) The official attitude was that Belize City would soon become a redundant backwater as Belmopan grew, but in fact few people chose to leave for the sterile "new town" atmosphere of Belmopan, and Belize City remains by far the most populous place in the country.

Belize gained internal self-government in 1964, and the goal of **full independence** was reached in 1981, with Belize joining the Commonwealth as a sovereign state. Loyalty to the monarchy remains strong, though – as shown by the tumultuous welcome given to Queen Elizabeth on her visits in 1985 and 1994. Since independence the rise of foreign investment and tourism has made an impact, and Belize City is now experiencing a major construction boom.

Orientation and city transport

Belize City is divided neatly into north and south halves by the **Haulover Creek**, a delta branch of the Belize River. The pivotal point of the city centre is the **Swing Bridge**, always busy with traffic and opened twice a day to allow larger vessels up and down the river. **North** of the Swing Bridge things tend to be slightly more upmarket; here you'll find the most expensive hotels, most of the embassies and consulates, and – in the King's Park area – some very luxurious houses. **South** of the Swing Bridge is the market and commercial zone, with banks, offices and supermarkets; the foreshore is the prestige area, home to an expensive hotel and the colonial Governor's residence. The area west of the main thoroughfares, Regent and Albert streets, is unsafe after dark.

The city is small enough to make **walking** the easiest way to get around; all hotels are within reach of Swing Bridge. If you arrive at night, take a **taxi**: they run from the bus terminals and the rank on Albert St, by Battlefield Park. Fares within the city are fixed (Bz$5 for one person plus Bz$2 for each extra person; Bz$10 to the municipal airport). For other journeys agree the fare in advance.

Transport terminals

The four main **bus companies** in Belize have their terminals in the same western area of the city, around the Collet Canal and Magazine Rd, a particularly derelict part of town known as Mesopotamia. It's only 1km from the centre and you can easily walk – or, especially at night, take a taxi – to any of the hotels listed below. Boats returning **from the cayes** pull in at Courthouse Wharf (Ambergis Caye) or the *Texaco* station on N Front St, just beyond the Swing Bridge, from where it's a short walk to any of the hotels or bus depots. Taxis are usually waiting to take passengers to the international airport (Bz$30).

Belize City has two **airports**. International flights land at the **Phillip Goldson International Airport**, 17km northwest of the city at Ladyville, just off the

Northern Highway. Arriving here can be chaotic, with a crush of people waiting anxiously for trolleys to trundle in with their luggage. Not infrequently, baggage is left on board, to return from San Salvador or Tegucigalpa in a couple of days. The new terminal, opened in 1990, initially alleviated some of the overcrowding but even this is sometimes swamped by the huge increase in visitor numbers. If you land here, the only way into the city is by taxi (Bz$30), or walk to the Northern Highway (25min) and try to flag down a bus or truck there.

Domestic flights come and go from the **municipal airport**, a few kilometres north of the town centre. Taxis are always available, or it's a twenty-minute walk.

Information

The Belize **tourist board** main office is at 83 N Front St (Mon–Fri 8am–noon & 1–5pm; ☎77213; fax 77490). The friendly, knowledgeable staff give out free bus timetables, a hotel guide and a city map. Superb topographical **maps** of Belize are sold at the *Survey Department*, above the post office (entrance on N Front St). A two-sheet map covering the whole country (1:250,000) costs Bz$10 per sheet, and there is a series of 44 sheets covering the whole country (1:50,000), for Bz$3 each. They also have geological maps and a land-use map.

The main branches of the *Atlantic, Nova Scotia, Belize* and *Barclays* **banks** are on Albert St (Mon–Thurs 8am–1pm, Fri 8am–1pm & 3–6pm). *Barclays* has no surcharge for *Visa* and *MC* cash advances (*Belize Bank* charge Bz$15), and UK customers can use their *Connect* card and cash personal cheques. Cash in US$ is sometimes available, though you may need to produce an air ticket – or even get a permit from *Central Bank* on Bishop St, though this is rare. Many shops, hotels and restaurants change travellers' cheques and cash, and money can sometimes be changed on the streets at a slightly better rate, but take care.

The main **post office** is in the Paslow Building, on the corner of Queen St, immediately north of the Swing Bridge (Mon–Thurs 8am–noon & 1–3pm, Fri 8am–noon & 1–4.30pm). The parcel office is next door on N Front St. There are several **payphones** and **cardphones** dotted around the city, and it's easy to make international calls from the main *BTL* office, 1 Church St (Mon–Sat 8am–6pm); they also offer a cheap and efficient fax service.

> The **telephone area code** for Belize City is ☎02.

Accommodation

Accommodation in Belize is far more expensive than in Guatemala and prices for even the most basic places can come as quite a shock to budget travellers. There are about fifty **hotels** in Belize City, around a third of which cost between Bz$25–45 double, with at least another half-dozen in the range of Bz$45–75. The selection below covers all price ranges. For a more comprehensive list, pick up a copy of *Where to Stay in Belize* from the **tourist board**.

The north side
Most of the budget hotels north of the river are clustered on or near **N Front St**, with more upmarket hotels generally located in the historic **Fort George area** or along the **seafront**, where the residents can benefit from the sea breezes.

BUDGET HOTELS AND GUEST HOUSES

Bon Aventure, 122 N Front St (☎44248). Next door to the *North Front Street Guest House* and equally good value. ②.

Dim's Mira Rio, across the road from the *North Front Street Guest House* (☎34147). Reasonable rooms with washbasin and toilet. The bar is good for information, as boat owners often call in for a beer – there's also simple but tasty Creole and Garifuna food. ②.

Downtown Guest House, 5 Eve St, near the end of Queen St (☎30951; fax 32057). Best value budget place in the city. Small, very friendly, clean and secure; even the shared bathrooms have reliable hot water. You can receive a fax, get laundry done and the owner, Kenny, will cook a bargain breakfast. ②–③.

Marin's Travelodge, 6 Craig St, towards the hospital (☎45166). Comfortable, clean and really quiet. The rooms are well furnished and the showers excellent. ②.

North Front Street Guest House, 124 N Front St (☎77595). A favourite with European and North American visitors: friendly, helpful and just a block from the boats to Caye Caulker. New management has improved the whole place; you may need to book. ②.

MODERATE TO EXPENSIVE

Bakadeer Inn, 74 Cleghorn St (☎31400; fax 31963). Smart, comfortable and safe, all rooms have a/c, cable TV and a refrigerator. Delicious breakfast buffet. Accepts *Visa/MC*. ⑥.

Chateau Caribbean, 6 Marine Parade (☎30800; fax 30900). Luxurious, a/c, colonial-style hotel with cable TV and some sea views. Often used as a movie set. Accepts *Visa/MC*. ⑦.

Colton House, 9 Cork St (☎44666; fax 30451). Beautifully kept colonial house, dating from the 1920s; the best guest house in Belize. Rooms are individually decorated in English country house style, each with an immaculate bathroom, and the downstairs garden room has a/c and TV. No meals are served but you can enjoy tea on the verandah. Owners Alan and Ondina Colton keep an extensive book and video library on Belize. ⑤.

Four Fort Street (☎30116; fax 78808). Large rooms with ceiling fans in an expertly restored colonial house. Beds are comfortable four-posters, draped with mosquito nets, and the upstairs sitting room is furnished with wicker couches. Also a very popular restaurant. Breakfast included. Accepts *Visa/MC*. ⑥.

Freddie's Guest House, 86 Eve St, on the city edge near the waterfront, past the Center for Environmental Studies (☎33851). Three secure and peaceful rooms with gleaming bathrooms. The best value in this price range. ④.

Glenthore Manor, 27 Barrack Rd, off Queen St (☎44212). Lovely rooms with balconies in a large, very comfortable colonial-style house. Breakfast included. ④–⑤.

Radisson Fort George, 2 Marine Parade, north side of the harbour mouth (☎33333; fax 73820). Flagship of the city's hotels, with its own dock. The grounds (including pool) are an oasis of calm on the edge of the sea. All rooms with huge cable TV, fridge and minibar. The Club Wing, reached by the only glass elevator in Belize, has unbeatable sea views. ⑧–⑨.

Ramada, on the seafront 1km north of the centre (☎32670; fax 32660). The latest of Belize City's luxury hotels, with 118 rooms, a pool, beauty salon, theme bars and a marina. ⑧.

South side

Belcove Hotel, 9 Regent St West (☎73054). You pay for the luxury of a balcony over the river with a view of the Swing Bridge. There's a certain thrill of being on the edge of the dangerous part of town, though the hotel itself is quite secure. The friendly, knowledgeable owner, Danny Weir, organizes day trips to the reef at Gallows Point. ③.

Bellevue Hotel, 5 Southern Foreshore (☎77051; fax 72353). The top hotel on the south side of the Swing Bridge. A/c, colonial-style rooms, and a relaxing courtyard with palms and pool. The Harbour Room bar is good – they serve tea in the afternoon – and the disco a focal point of the city's nightlife, with live music at weekends. Accepts *Visa/MC*. ⑥.

Isabel Guest House, across Swing Bridge, above and behind *Central Drug Store* (☎73139). Small, friendly, Spanish-speaking guest house, with large rooms with private shower. ③.

Mopan Hotel, 55 Regent St (☎77351; fax 75383). Large wooden building run by avid conservationist Jean Shaw – a mine of information on Belize – and popular with naturalists, writers and scientists. Very good value breakfasts, and you can order dinner. Jean is an agent for *Aerovias* and will arrange flights to Guatemala. Accepts *Visa/MC/AmEx*. ⑤.

Sea Side Guest House, 3 Prince St (☎78339), half a block from the southern foreshore. A clean, well-run hotel that's become a bustling meeting place for European travellers – and you really can see the sea. Meals can be ordered, and there's a beer and wine licence. Some rooms have hostel-style dorm beds (Bz$16). ③.

The City

Richard Davies, a British traveller in the mid-nineteenth century, wrote of the city: "There is much to be said for Belize, for in its way it was one of the prettiest ports at which we touched, and its cleanliness and order ... were in great contrast to the ports we visited later as to make them most remarkable." Most of the features that elicited this praise have now gone. In some other cities, **wooden colonial buildings** would be preserved as heritage showpieces, but here their only chance of escaping decrepitude is to be turned into a hotel or restaurant. Yet even in cases where the decay is too advanced for the paintwork, balconies and carved railings to be restored, the old wooden structures remain more pleasing than the concrete blocks that have replaced so many of them.

Before the construction of the first wooden bridge in the early 1800s, cattle were winched over the waterway that divides the city – hence the name Haulover Creek. The present **Swing Bridge**, made in Liverpool and opened in 1923, is the only manually operated swing bridge left in the Americas. Every day at 5.30am and 5.30pm the endless parade of vehicles and people is halted by policemen, and the process of turning begins. Using long poles inserted into a capstan, four men gradually lever the bridge around until it's pointing in the direction of the harbour mouth. During the few minutes that the bridge is open, the river traffic is busier than that on the roads, and traffic is snarled up across the whole city. There's a possibility, however, that the bridge may soon be demolished, since a new drawbridge has been built a few blocks upriver, relieving some of the congestion. A vocal preservation campaign has been mobilized.

The north side

Immediately on the **north side** of the Swing Bridge is the **Paslow Building**, a vast, run-down structure built entirely of wood, which has the post office on the ground floor and other government offices above. Along to the right, beyond the shops and offices, the "temporary" market still operates, boasting a greater range of produce than the official new market over the Swing Bridge.

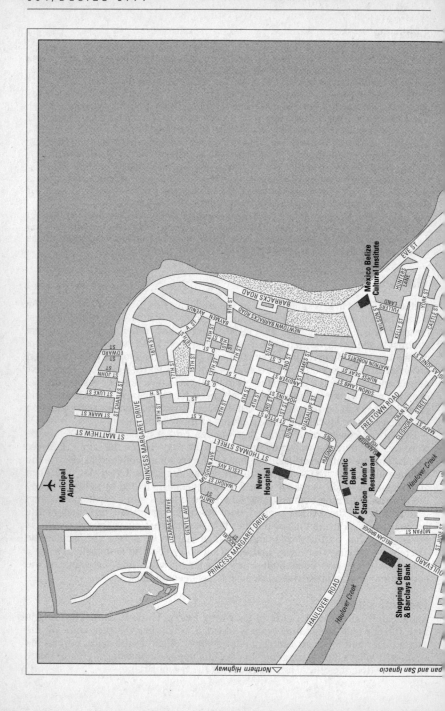

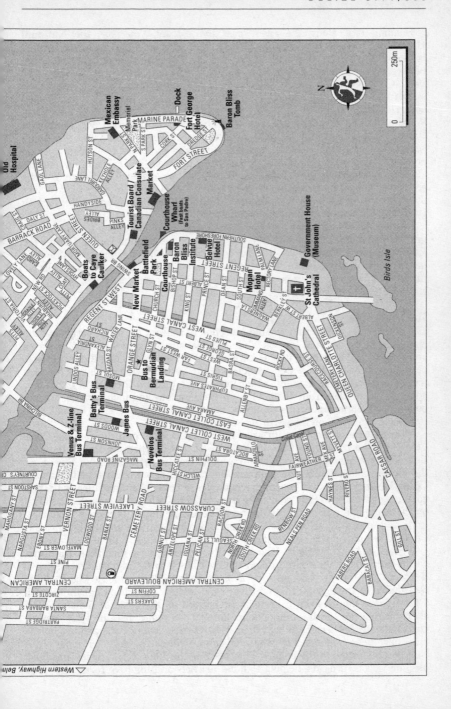

250m

N

Old
Hospital

Mexican
Embassy

Memorial
Park

MARINE PARADE

Dock

Fort George
Hotel

Baron Bliss
Tomb

FORT STREET

Tourist Board /
Canadian Consulate

Market

Courthouse
Wharf
(Fast boats
to San Pedro)

Government House
(Museum)

SOUTHERN FORESHORE

Birds Isle

Boats
to Caye
Caulker

BARRACK ROAD

HANDYSIDE

DALY ST

QUEEN STREET

New Market

Battlefield
Park

Baron
Bliss
Institute

Belvue
Hotel

REGENT STREET

Mopan
Hotel

St John's
Cathedral

QUEEN CHARLOTTE STREET

REGENT ST WEST

WEST CANAL STREET

ORANGE STREET

Bus to
Bermudian
Landing

Batty's Bus
Terminal

James Bus

EAST COLLET CANAL STREET

WEST COLLET CANAL STREET

Venus & Z-line
Bus Terminal

Novelos
Bus Terminal

MAGAZINE ROAD

CAESAR ROAD

COURTNEY'S CI

MAHOGANY ST

VERNON STREET

LAKEVIEW STREET

CEMETERY ROAD

BANAK ST

MAYFLOWER ST

CURASSOW STREET

FAIRWEATHER

FABERS ROAD

CENTRAL AMERICAN BOULEVARD

CENTRAL AMERICAN

COFFIN ST

DAKERS ST

▽ Western Highway, Belm

Heading east along the river, past the market, you pass the **National Handicraft Center** and **Custom House**, with adjacent wharves, beyond which is the lighthouse and the tomb of Baron Bliss, Belize's greatest benefactor (see below). Naturalists will gain from a visit to the **Belize Audubon Society** at 12 Fort St (☎34985). The society sells books, maps and posters, and organizes slide shows and talks on all aspects of wildlife and conservation. It has established several wildlife reserves in Belize and participates in conservation education. Walking around the shoreline you pass the *Fort George* hotel and **Memorial Park**, which honours the Belizean dead of World War I. In this area you'll find several well-preserved colonial mansions, many of the finest now taken over by embassies and upmarket hotels. A superb example is the US Embassy, further along, constructed in New England, dismantled and shipped to Belize. Nearby are the offices of the **Programme for Belize**, founded in May 1989 to save over 250,000 acres of the country's rainforest. Call in at the headquarters, 2 S Park St (☎75616), for news from the enthusiastic staff.

Beyond the US Embassy and the Peace Corps headquarters is the city jail, as grim as you might expect, and then comes Eve Street and the **Belize Center for Environmental Studies** worth a visit for anyone seriously interested in Belize's natural and cultural history. It's also the home of the Association for Belizean Archeology, formed to preserve archeological sites and artefacts, which has started a fund to establish a museum in Belize.

The south side

The **south side** is generally the older section of Belize City: in the early days the elite lived in the seafront houses while the backstreets were inhabited by slaves and labourers. These days it's the commercial centre, containing the main shopping streets, banks and travel agencies. Right by the Swing Bridge is the new three-storey **covered market**, which opened in 1993 on the site of the rather decrepit old market from 1820. Though the new one is much cleaner, it's not popular with either traders or shoppers, most of whom have carried on using the "temporary" market, on the north side of the river.

Albert Street, running south from the Swing Bridge, past the rotating Coca-Cola clock – a reminder of the importance of that company in the economy of Belize – is the main commercial thoroughfare. On the parallel **Regent Street** are the former colonial administration and court buildings, known together as the **Court House**. These well-preserved examples of colonial architecture, with their columns and fine wrought iron, were completed in 1926 after an earlier building on the same site was destroyed by fire. The Court House overlooks a patch of grass and trees with an ornamental fountain in the centre, ambitiously known as Central Park until it was renamed Battlefield Park in the early 1990s.

A block behind the Court House, on the waterfront, is the **Bliss Institute**, which looks like a squat airport control tower but is in fact the cultural centre of Belize City (Mon–Fri 8.30am–noon & 2–8pm, Sat 8.30am–noon). The Institute was funded by the legacy of Baron Bliss, a moderately eccentric Englishman with a Portuguese title. A keen fisherman, he arrived off the coast of Belize in 1926 after hearing about the tremendous amount of game fish in local waters. Unfortunately, he became ill and died without ever having been ashore, but he must have been impressed by whatever fish he did catch, as he left most of his considerable estate to the colony. This became the Bliss Trust, which has been used on various projects, helping to build markets and improve roads and water supplies. In gratitude, the authorities declared March 9, the date of his death, Baron Bliss Day. The Bliss building is the home of the **National Arts Council** and hosts exhibitions, concerts and plays. Just inside the entrance are stelae and altars from Caracol, priceless examples of Maya art that seem to have been dumped in a corner while somewhere is found to display them; a small plaque gives an account of the scenes depicted on the stones. Upstairs you'll find the national library and copies of the Belizean newspapers.

At the end of Albert St is **St John's Cathedral**, the oldest Anglican cathedral in Central America and one of the oldest buildings in Belize. Looking like a large English parish church, it was begun in 1812, its red bricks brought over as ballast in British ships. The main structure, roof and mahogany beams have survived more than 150 years of tropical heat and hurricanes. Here, in great pomp, the kings of the Mosquito Coast were crowned between 1815 and 1845, taking the title to a British Protectorate extending along the coast of Honduras and Nicaragua. The Miskito Indians were keen to keep their links with Britain to avoid Spanish colonial rule, and so kings were crowned and their children baptized in Belize's cathedral.

West of the cathedral is **Yarborough Cemetery**, which was used until the end of the nineteenth century, when it reached full capacity. The graves have fallen into disrepair but a browse among the stones will turn up fascinating snippets of history. Most of the occupants were members of the elite: the cemetery is named after the magistrate who owned the land and allowed the burial of prominent people here from 1781 – commoners were admitted only after 1870.

On the way to the seafront from the cathedral, the well-preserved white-painted, green-lawned **Government House**, built in 1814, was the residence of the governor when Belize was a British colony. A plush red carpet leads down the hall to the great mahogany staircase, the walls lined with prints and photos of

---

SHOPPING FOR SOUVENIRS

As you walk around the city, you may well be approached by street peddlers selling **wood carvings**, often exquisitely executed, of dolphins, jaguars, ships and other subjects. These are made from zericote wood, said to grow only in Belize, and make quite unusual gifts. If you're interested, it's sensible to make a deal on the spot – though be careful about showing money on the street – as there's a terrific mark-up in the hotel shops. Gifts like these can also be bought safely and reliably at the *National Handicrafts Center* on Fort St (Mon–Fri 8am–5pm; ☎33636). Another gift option is a set of wildly colourful Belize **stamps**, often depicting the animals and plants of the country; relatively cheap and easy to post home, they are available from the *Belize Philatelic Society* on Queen St, around the corner from the post office. **T-shirts**, some with Rasta or Creole slogans, also make distinctive Belizean presents: some of the best bargains are to be found at the Chinese and Indian stores along Albert St and Queen St; *Sings*, 35 Albert St, has the best selection at reasonable prices.

Souvenirs **you should not buy** are **shells, coral** or **turtle products** – indeed **marine curios** of any kind. By resisting the temptation to buy reef souvenirs you will be helping to keep them alive. Many animal and plant souvenirs you may be offered in Belize are listed in Appendix I to CITES (Convention on International Trade in Endangered Species) and their trade is prohibited, so you wouldn't be allowed to bring them into the US, Canada or Europe anyway. Protected species include the cats of Belize, monkeys, many birds of prey and parrots, marine turtles, other reptiles and nearly all orchids.

sombre past governors. Plans are afoot to open the place as a museum; check progress with Jean Shaw at the *Mopan Hotel* or with the tourist board. At the very end of this strip of land, connected to the mainland by a narrow wooden causeway, is the island known as **Bird's Isle**, a venue for reggae concerts and parties.

Eating, drinking and nightlife

The multitude of **restaurants** in Belize City don't offer much in the way of variety. There's the tasty but monotonous **Creole** fare of rice and beans, plenty of seafood and steaks, and a preponderance of **Chinese** restaurants, usually the best bet for **vegetarians**. Vegetables other than cabbage, carrots, onions and peppers are rarely served in restaurants and these are likely to be the main components of any salad. As always, the **market**, and the "temporary" market on the north bank of the river, are the best places to eat cheaply, with basic dishes of rice and beans, beef, fish and chicken. Greasy fried chicken is available as takeaway from small restaurants all over the city: a Belizean favourite known as **"dollar chicken"**, whatever the price. If you're really in a hurry, *HL's Burger*, Belize City's answer to *McDonald's*, has a growing number of outlets, serving standard but safe-fast food fare. The big **hotels** have their own restaurants, naturally quite expensive but with much more varied menus.

If you're **shopping for food**, the main **supermarkets** – *Brodie's* and *Romac's* – are worth a look; they're on Albert St, just past the park, and their selection of food is good if expensive, reflecting the fact that much is imported. Milk and dairy products, produced locally by Mennonite farmers (see p.337), are delicious and good quality. As for other staples, wholewheat and French bread is sold at *Kee's Bakery*, 53 Queen St, and naturally enough, local **fruit** is cheap and plentiful, though highly seasonal – Belizean citrus fruits are among the best in the world.

In the listings below we have quoted a phone number in places where it is recommended you should **reserve a table**.

Restaurants and cafés north of the river

Chateau Caribbean, 6 Marine Parade. For undisturbed views of blue sea and offshore islands, head up the steps to this cool first-floor restaurant, where prices are more reasonable than you'd guess from the gleaming white linen and cutlery. Order something inexpensive and forget for a while the heat and noise of the city.

Fort Street Restaurant, 4 Fort St (☎30116). Superb Creole and American food in relaxing surroundings in restored colonial house. Popularity has led to an increase in prices.

The Grill, 164 Newtown Barracks Rd (☎34021). Away from the centre, near the *Ramada*, this is one of the best restaurants in the city. Well-prepared steak, seafood and pasta, with a good salad bar and a vegetarian option.

Mom's, 7145 Slaughterhouse Rd (☎45523). A move to more spacious surroundings (including room for the only moose head in Belize) has given this long-established restaurant a chance to expand and improve the menu. A good selection of tasty Mexican dishes complements traditional Creole food, vegetarian dishes and a great salad bar. Packed lunches prepared. Happy hour Wed–Fri 5–7pm. Closed Sat.

New Chon Saan, N Front St, opposite the *Texaco* station. Large portions of Chinese food, unfortunately accompanied by violent Chinese Kung-fu fighting videos.

Pepper's Pizza, 2215 Baymen Ave. Decent pizza restaurant that delivers. Open 5–11pm, until midnight Fri & Sat.

Sea Rock, 35 Queen St. Good Indian food in a quiet, clean restaurant; don't be put off by the unprepossessing surroundings.

Restaurants and cafés south of the river

Dit's, 50 King St. Great pastries and inexpensive Creole food such as cowfoot soup.

GG's Café and Patio, 2B King St. Delicious, reasonably priced Creole-style meals. Tables in the palm-filled patio are often busy with expats, travellers and Belizean businesspeople.

Macy's, 18 Bishop St (☎73419). Long-established, reasonably priced Creole restaurant that's popular with locals and extremely busy at lunchtimes. They also serve traditional game: armadillo, deer and gibnut (a type of large rodent), but thankfully no longer turtle.

The Marlin, 11 Regent St West, next to the *Belcove Hotel*. Good, inexpensive, local food in large portions – and you can eat on the verandah overlooking the river.

Mexican Corner, King St, near the canal bridge. Great Mexican food.

Pop'n'Taco, corner of King St and Regent St. Chinese-run restaurant, serving cheap Chinese food, despite the name.

River Side Patio, at the rear of the market. Good place to relax with a drink as you watch the bridge swing. Mexican-style food, and entertainment on Fri and Sat evenings.

Drinking, nightlife and entertainment

Belize City's more sophisticated, air-conditioned **bars** are found in the most expensive establishments, and there aren't many of those. At the lowest end of the scale are dimly lit dives, effectively men-only, where, though there's the possibility that you'll be offered drugs or be robbed, it's more likely that you'll have a thoroughly enjoyable time meeting easy-going, hard-drinking locals. There are several places between the two extremes, most of them in restaurants and hotels – for example, *The Marlin* restaurant (see above) and *Dim's Mira Rio* hotel (see "Accommodation"). One of the best is *Lindbergh Landing*, past the *Ramada* at 164 Newtown Rd, next to *The Grill* restaurant. A quiet, open-air bar with sea views, it's located at the spot where Charles Lindbergh landed in Belize in 1928. The *Calypso Bar* at the *Ramada* frequently hosts top local bands.

Nightlife, though not as wild as it used to be, is becoming more reliable and the quality of live bands is improving all the time. The *Radisson Fort George* and the *Bellevue* hold regular dances, and if you're after **live music**, there's reggae at the *Lumba Yaad Bar*, on the riverbank just out of town on the Northern Highway. It can get out of hand – best go at lunchtime on Saturdays.

Listings

American Express *Belize Global Travel*, 41 Albert St (☎77363) is the safest place to receive mail, and has a fax service.

Books The *Belize Book Shop*, Regent St opposite the *Mopan Hotel*, has the largest selection; *Book Centre*, 2 Church St also sells magazines. Many of the larger hotels sell books, magazines and papers and some operate book exchanges. A few, along with *Mom's Restaurant*, sell *Time*, *Newsweek* and *The Miami Herald*. For reading on Belize and surrounds check out the SPEAR library on Pickstock St and New Rd (☎31668).

Embassies and consulates Though the official capital is at Belmopan, some embassies remain in Belize City and are normally open weekday mornings. *British High Commission*, based in Belmopan operates a consular clinic at 11 St Marks St, Kings Park, near the municipal airport (Mon 9–11am); *Canada* (cannot issue passports), 83 N Front St (☎31060); *Honduras*, 91 N Front St (☎45889); *Mexico* (tourist cards), 20 Park St (☎31388); *USA*, 29 Gabourel Lane and Hutson St (☎77161).

Film developing For prints, slides and fast passport photos, try *Spooners*, 89 N Front St .

Immigration The Belize Immigration Office is in the Government Complex on Mahogany St, near the junction of Central American Blvd and the Western Highway (Mon–Thurs 8.30–11.30am & 1–4pm, Fri 8.30–11.30am & 1–3.30pm; ☎24620). Visa extensions cost Bz$25.

Laundry *Central America Coin Laundry,* 114 Barrack Rd (Mon–Sat 8.30am–9pm; reduced hours Sun); *Drop-Off Laundromat,* 6 Water Lane (daily 6am–9pm), and many hotels.
Medical emergencies Hospital ☎77725; Dr Gamero, Myo-On Clinic, 40 Eve St (☎45616).
Police ☎72210.
Travel agents The largest, and the best for booking international flights, is *Belize Global Travel,* 41 Albert St (☎77363; fax 75213). *Belize Air Travel,* 31 Regent St (☎73174; fax 75922);

TRAVEL DETAILS: MOVING ON FROM BELIZE CITY

BY BUS

Moving on from Belize City by **bus** couldn't be simpler. Most of the bus **companies** are in the same area, along the Collet Canal and Magazine Rd, a short walk from the centre of town. The main companies are: *Batty,* 15 Mosul St (☎72025); *Novelo,* 19 W Collet Canal (☎77372); *Venus* (☎73354), and *Z-Line,* Magazine Rd (☎73937).

NORTHBOUND BUSES

Batty is the main operator on the route to the north and **Chetumal** in Mexico – they can make reservations on Mexican buses – and also serve the route to San Ignacio. *Batty* leave hourly from 4am to 11am for **Chetumal** (4hr) via **Orange Walk** (2hr) and **Corozal** (3hr), with an express service at 6am. *Venus,* who also cover the north, operate every hour from noon to 7pm. For **Sarteneja** (3hr 30min), the *Perez* bus leaves the *Texaco* station on N Front St at 11.30am and 1pm, and there's a *Venus* service at 12.30pm. To the **Bermudian Landing Baboon Sanctuary** (1hr 30min) there are two buses daily except Sunday; one leaves at noon from the corner of Orange St and Mosul St, the other at 1pm from the corner of Orange St and George St, near the *Batty* terminal. To **Crooked Tree** (1hr 30min), the *Jex* bus leaves Pound Yard Bridge by Collet Canal at 10.30am, 4.30pm and 5.30pm; the *Batty* bus goes from its terminal (Mon–Fri 4pm, Sat noon, Sun 9am). For **Maskall,** buses leave from Cinderella Plaza (Mon–Sat 12.30pm; 2hr).

BUSES WEST AND SOUTH

Heading **west from Belize City,** *Batty* run a frequent service (at least hourly 5.30am–10.15am) to **San Ignacio** (3hr) **via Belmopan** (1hr); there's an express at 7am. Most buses cross the Guatemalan border into **Melchor,** where you can continue to Flores. *Novelo* cover the same route, going on to **Benque Viejo** (3hr 30min) and **Melchor** (hourly 11am–8pm, less frequent on Sun).

The **Southern Highway** doesn't see anything like the number of buses as do the Northern and Western highways, and trips into the south can take all day, travelling via Belmopan and Dangriga. Most buses still pass through Belmopan, but some use the short cut called the Coastal Road. To **Dangriga** (3hr 30min), *Z-Line* depart at 8am, 9am, & 10am, then hourly from noon to 5pm; the 8am, noon and 3pm services make the connection to **Punta Gorda** (8hr). There is reduced service on Sunday. You can also get to Punta Gorda on the *James* bus, which leaves the Pound Yard Bridge at 7am Wed & Sun. There are also at least two daily buses to **Gales Point** for the manatee sanctuary (1hr 30min).

BY AIR

There are **international flights** from Belize international airport to Miami, New York, New Orleans, Houston and LA, and to San Salvador, San Pedro Sula and Tegucigalpa, Honduras. *Aerovias* flies four times a week to **Flores** (35min) and **Guatemala City** (1hr 30min) while *Tropic Air* has two daily flights, morning and afternoon, to Flores. There are currently no flights between Belize and Mexico. Of

Caribbean Holidays, 81 Albert St (☎72593; fax 78007); *Universal Travel*, Handyside St (☎30963), and *Jal's*, 148 N Front St (☎45407; fax 30792), can book domestic and international flights. For **tours** within Belize try *S&L Travel*, 91 N Front St (☎77593; fax 77594); *Native Guide Tours*, 2 Water Lane (☎75819; fax 74007); *Discovery Expeditions*, 126 Freetown Rd (☎30748; fax 30750), or *Melmish Maya Tours*, 1840 Chancelor St (☎35399; fax 31531).

Western Union Belize Chamber of Commerce, 63 Regent St (☎75924; fax 74984).

the **airlines** *TACA* (at the airport: ☎025/2163) are represented by *Global Travel*, 41 Albert St (☎77185), where you can confirm return flights. *Continental* are at 32 Albert St (☎78309; airport ☎025/2488); *American* (☎32522) in the Valencia Building, on the corner of New Rd and Queen St, and *Aerovias* based at the *Mopan Hotel* (☎75445). For *Tropic* call ☎45671 or ☎026/2012; for *Island Air* ☎31140 or ☎026/2345. If you're **leaving** from the international airport, arrive early, and don't forget the Bz$20 departure tax plus Bz$2.50 "security tax" and Bz$7.50 exit tax (the last helps finance **PACT**, Belize's Protected Areas Conservation Trust; see p.500).

On **domestic routes**, *Maya* (6 Fort St; ☎44234; international airport ☎025/2336), *Tropic* and *Island Air* between them operate flights from both airports to **Caye Caulker** (15–20min) and **San Pedro** (10min from Caye Caulker) at least hourly from 7am to 5pm; only *Tropic* and *Island Air* have regular flights to **Corozal** (20min). *Maya* offer six daily flights to **Dangriga** (25min); all but the last continue to **Placencia** (a further 30min) and **Punta Gorda** (35min beyond Placencia), both of which are served by *Tropic* (3 daily). There is no shortage of extremely good value **charters** to any airstrip in Belize; the best airline, *Javier's Flying Service* (☎45332) fly from the municipal airport regularly to Gallon Jug and Lighthouse Reef.

BY BOAT

If you're planning to go straight **to the cayes** you should be able to get a **boat** to Caye Caulker from *A&R's Texaco Station* on N Front St, by the Swing Bridge (Bz$15; 10am–4pm; 45min). For **Ambergris Caye** (for **San Pedro**; Bz$20; 1hr 15min; all call at Caye Caulker) most boats depart from Courthouse Wharf south of the river. The *Triple J* leaves at 9am and others at 3pm and 4pm. Only the *Thunderbolt* leaves from the Swing Bridge, at 1pm.

BY CAR

Renting a car can be a good idea for couples or groups. Visiting the main tourist sites you're unlikely to get lost, though not having a trained guide can be a disadvantage. All the main car rental **companies** offer cars, Jeeps and four-wheel drives for between Bz$150 and Bz$200 a day, plus US$15 per day for insurance. You'll usually have to be over 25 and will need to leave either a credit card, travellers' cheques or a large cash deposit. Many outfits do not offer comprehensive insurance, so the renter is likely to be held liable for any damage, however caused, to the vehicle. Note that some companies consider driving a car on minor dirt roads (especially in the south) to be taking the vehicle "off-road", which may invalidate your insurance. Check carefully before signing anything. Companies include *Avis*, 50 Vernon St (☎70730) and at the airport (☎025/2385); *National*, 126 Freetown Rd (☎31587) and at the airport (☎025/2117); *Crystal* at Mile 1 1/2 on the Northern Highway (☎31600), which also rents motor-homes; and *Sutherland*, 127 Neal Pen Rd (☎76471). *Budget*, 771 Bella Vista, 5km out of town (☎32435) is the only operator to honour insurance provisions that may be applicable if you pay by credit card. *Safari*, next to the *Radisson* (☎35395) rent only *Isuzu Troopers* (US$110 per day, including comprehensive insurance – higher at peak times).

CHAPTER NINE

THE NORTHERN CAYES AND ATOLLS

Belize's spectacular **Barrier Reef**, with its dazzling variety of underwater life and string of exquisite islands – known as cayes – is the main attraction for most first-time visitors to the country. The longest barrier reef in the western hemisphere, it runs the entire length of the coastline at a distance of 15km to 40km from the mainland. One of the richest marine ecosystems on earth, it's a paradise for scuba divers and snorkellers, the incredible coral formations teeming with hundreds of species of brilliantly coloured fish. The entire area of reef, islands and coastline has been proposed as a **World Heritage Site** – in other words, a place of such significance that its "deterioration or disappearance" would constitute "a harmful impoverishment of the heritage of all nations of the world", to quote the World Heritage Convention. Official classification would enable funds from UNESCO to be used for protection of the reef, which is essential as Belize itself lacks the necessary resources. Unfortunately, Belize is not yet a party to the World Heritage Convention. At present protected areas include the **Hol Chan Marine Reserve** off San Pedro and **Half Moon Caye Natural Monument**, part of Lighthouse Reef, and more and larger marine reserves are planned.

Most of the **cayes** (pronounced "keys") lie in shallow water behind the shelter of the reef, with a limestone ridge forming larger, low-lying islands to the north, while smaller, less frequently visited outcrops are clustered toward the southern end of the chain – often merely a stand of palms and a strip of sand. Though the cayes themselves form only a tiny proportion of the country's total land area, Belize has as much territorial water as it does land, and the islands' tourism and lobster fishing accounts for a substantial amount of foreign currency earnings. In recent years the town of **San Pedro**, on **Ambergris Caye**, has undergone a transition from a predominantly fishing economy to one geared to commercial tourism. To counter this development the **Bacalar Chico National Park and Marine Reserve** is planned for the northern end of the island. **Caye Caulker**, to the south, is less – but increasingly – developed, and remains popular with budget-minded travellers. **St George's Caye**, Belize's first capital, occupies a celebrated niche in the nation's history and still has some fine colonial houses and a couple of resorts. But in all, only about 30 out of a total of more than 450 cayes have any tourist development, and in some instances this amounts to just a single, exclusive lodge. Many of the other cayes are populated only by fishing communities, whose settlements fluctuate with the season.

Beyond the chain of islands and the coral reef are two of Belize's three **atolls**: the **Turneffe Islands** and **Lighthouse Reef**. Here the coral reaches the surface,

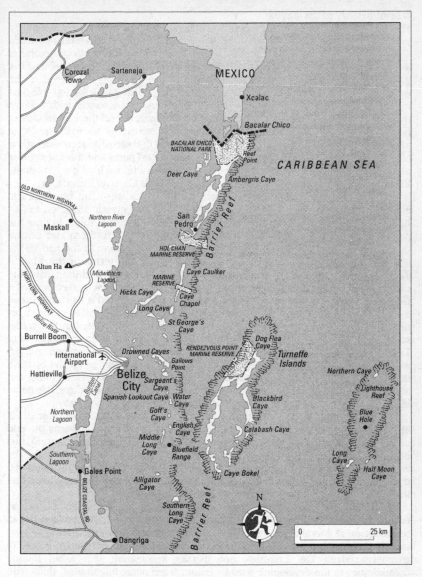

enclosing a shallow lagoon, with some cayes lying right on top of the encircling reef. These tropical idylls now have small, expensive hotels offering sport fishing and diving to big-spending visitors; the Turneffe Islands have a marine research station – and a planned marine reserve – on **Calabash Caye**, while Lighthouse Reef's **Great Blue Hole** attracts divers from all over the world.

A brief history of the cayes

The earliest inhabitants of the cayes were **Maya** peoples or their ancestors. By the Classic period (300–900 AD) the Maya had developed an extensive trade network stretching from the Yucatán to Honduras, with settlements on several of the islands. At least some cities in Belize survived the Maya "collapse" and the trade network existed throughout the Postclassic era – until the arrival of the conquistadors. **Columbus** may have sighted the coast of Belize on his last voyage to the "Indies" in 1502; his journal mentions an encounter with a Maya trading party in an immense dugout canoe off Guanaja, one of the Bay Islands of Honduras (see p.241). Traces of Maya civilization remain on some of the cayes today, especially on Ambergris Caye, which boasts the site of **Marco Gonzalez**, near the southern tip, and the remains of a number of ports and trading centres on the north and west shores. Evidence of coastal trade, such as shell mounds, have also been found on other islands, including Moho Caye off Belize City.

Probably the most infamous residents of the cayes were the **buccaneers**, usually British, who lived here in the sixteenth and seventeeth centuries, taking refuge in the shallow waters after plundering Spanish treasure ships. In time the pirates settled more or less permanently on some of the northern and central cayes. But life under the Jolly Roger became too hot for them in the late 1600s, after Britain agreed to stamp out privateering under the terms of the Madrid Treaties, and a number of them turned instead to logwood cutting. But the cutters (the Baymen) still kept their dwellings on the cayes – specifically **St George's Caye** – as the cool breezes and fresh water offered a welcome break from the steaming swamps where the logwood grew. The population of the cayes remained low during the seventeenth and eighteenth centuries, but the settlement on St George's Caye was regarded by the Baymen as their capital until 1779, when a Spanish force destroyed it, imprisoning 140 of the Baymen and 250 of their slaves. The Baymen returned in 1783 and took revenge on the Spanish fleet in 1798 in the celebrated Battle of St George's Caye. From then on, however, although the elite of the Baymen still kept homes on St George's Caye, the population of the islands began to decline as Belize Town (later City) grew.

Fishermen and turtlers continued to use the cayes as a base for their operations, and refugees fleeing the Caste Wars in the Yucatán towards the end of the last century also settled on the islands in small numbers. During this century the island population has increased steadily, booming with the establishment of the fishing cooperatives in the 1960s, which brought improved traps, ice plants, and access to the export market. There's now the possibility that the lobster-fishing industry will destroy itself by overfishing.

At around the same time came another boom, as the cayes of Belize, particularly Caye Caulker, became a hang-out on the hippy trail, and then began to attract more lucrative custom. The islanders generally welcomed these new visitors: rooms were rented and hotels built, and a new prosperity began to transform island life. Luxuries not usually associated with small fishing communities in the developing world – colour televisions, telephones, skiffs with large outboard motors – are all evidence of the effects of tourism.

Visiting the cayes

The increasing popularity of Belize as a holiday destination has led to an escalation in land prices, and real estate offices proliferate on San Pedro's main streets, tempting wealthy visitors to invest in a Caribbean island. Luckily, most of the islands are too small and remote to entice the developers. Indeed, getting to many of the cayes and atolls can be a problem, especially if you're limited by time and finances. Several organizations have conservation projects on the cayes, requiring self-funded **volunteers**, or you could see if a visiting yacht owner needs a crew (they're not all millionaires); alternatively, if you can get together a group of three or four, you might rent a boat for a week or so – easily done on Caye Caulker – and let a local boatman show you the lesser-known parts of the reef.

Life on the cayes is supremely relaxing, tempting you to take it easy in a hammock, feast on seafood, and sip rum as the sun sets. The most accessible and cheapest of the islands is **Caye Caulker**, and if you feel the urge to see what's beneath the waves it's easily done from here or **Ambergris Caye**. **Divers** can visit sites of almost unbelievable beauty and isolation, either joining a group day trip or staying at a lodge on the edge of the reef; instruction is readily available. This kind of fun can be expensive, though. **Snorkelling** is far cheaper, and often just as rewarding. Again, day trips are on offer on both of the main cayes, visiting three of four different reef sites in a day, each revealing a new coral landscape and array of tropical fish.

Bird-watching, as anywhere in Belize, is fascinating. Around two hundred species live in or visit the coastal areas and cayes, from ospreys to sandpipers and flamingoes to finches. Many otherwise rare birds are relatively common here; for instance, the preservation of the red-footed booby on Half Moon Caye was the main reason for establishing a National Monument there in 1982. Catch-and-release **fly-fishing** for bonefish is popular, too, particularly at the Turneffe Island flats; but this is expensive, and you'll probably want to bring your own equipment. Fishing trips for species such as snapper, barracuda and grouper are easily arranged, and a local guide can take you to the best spots. Most snorkelling trips can include a chance of fishing using a handline.

Ambergris Caye

The most northerly and by far the largest of the cayes is **Ambergris Caye**, separated from Mexico by a narrow, deep channel dug by the Maya. The island's main attraction is the former fishing village of **SAN PEDRO**, facing the reef just a few kilometres from the southern tip, 58km northeast of Belize City. If you fly into San Pedro, which is the way most visitors arrive, the views are breathtaking: the sea appears so clear and shallow as to barely cover the sandy bed, and the mainland and other islands stand out clearly. Probably the best view is of the reef's white crest, dramatically separating the vivid blue of the open sea from the turquoise water on its leeward side. The aircraft fly at so low an altitude, around 100m, that photographs taken from inside the cabin generally turn out well.

As you land at the tiny airstrip, with the sea on each side, a glimpse at San Pedro shows it taking up the whole width of the island. It's not a large town, but its population of two thousand is the highest on any of the cayes. Although you're never more than a stone's throw from the Caribbean, in the built-up area most of the palms have been cut down, and traffic has increased considerably in recent years, creating deep ruts (which become mud holes after rain) in the sandy streets. San Pedro is the main destination for over half the visitors to Belize, and the tourist industry here caters mainly for North American package tours – almost all prices are quoted in US dollars. Some of the most exclusive hotels,

GETTING TO AND FROM AMBERGRIS CAYE

Flying to San Pedro is the easiest and most popular approach: from Belize City *Maya Airways* (☎44234), *Island Air* (☎31140; 2345 in San Pedro) and *Tropic* (☎45671;2012 in San Pedro) between them have flights at least hourly from 7am to 5pm (25min).

Though **boats** from Belize City to San Pedro (1hr 15min) are less frequent than those to Caye Caulker (see p.374), there are a few regular fast services.The *Triple J* (☎02/44375) is the best boat on the run and the first to leave, at 9am from Courthouse Wharf, returning at 3pm. The *Andrea* (☎2578) leaves the wharf at 3pm, returning at 7am, and the *Banana Boat* leaves at 4pm, returning at 8am.The *Thunderbolt* leaves the Swing Bridge at 1pm, returning at 7am (Mon–Sat only).

Travelling **from San Pedro to other cayes**, any of the above scheduled boats also stop at Caye Caulker, and will call at St George's Caye or Caye Chapel if you ask. Any boat with the letters CC on its side is from **Caye Caulker**; these generally arrive in San Pedro in the early afternoon, at the dock beside the *Tackle Box*, and you'll probably be able to get a ride back with one.

Tropic and *Island Air* fly from **San Pedro to Corozal**, so you could head into Mexico without returning to Belize City.

restaurants and bars in the whole country are here; most of the cheaper places are in the original village of San Pedro, which is also where most of the action takes place, particularly in the evenings.

Arrival and information

Arriving boats usually dock at the main pier on the front (reef) side of the island, almost in the centre of the town, though the *Thunderbolt* docks at *Cesario's* at the back of the island; head down Black Coral St to *Rock's* supermarket. Arriving at either **dock**, you're pretty much in the centre of town; if you land at the **airport**, there are golf buggies and taxis to take you to your hotel. Formerly called Front, Middle and Back streets, the town's three **main streets**, running parallel to the beach, have been given names in keeping with the new upmarket image – Barrier Reef Drive, Pescador Drive and Angel Coral Drive. Most locals stick to the old names; in any case it's impossible to get lost.

The **telephone area code** for San Pedro is ☎026.

Despite being Belize's premier tourist destination, San Pedro has no official tourist office. There are, however, a couple of places you should head for **information**. A few blocks south of the town centre along Pescador St, you'll find the independently run *Belize Visitor & Tours* (daily 8am–8pm; ☎2728; fax 2402), whose staff provide an unbiased information and booking service for hotels (in all price ranges), tours and restaurants in San Pedro and throughout Belize. They also sell guidebooks and maps of San Pedro as well as the excellent *Traveller's Reference Map* of Belize. Most gift shops also sell the cartoon-style (but accurate) *Savanna's Bohemian Guide*, a map of Ambergis Caye, and it's always worth picking up a copy of the *San Pedro Sun*, the island's weekly paper. If you want a guide to the history, biology and geology of the caye, *The Field Guide to Ambergris*

Caye, by R L Woods and others, is available in San Pedro and in some hotels and bookshops in Belize City. Richie Woods himself, a Belizean marine biologist, can often be found around San Pedro.

You needn't worry about **changing money**, as travellers' cheques and US dollars are accepted – even preferred – everywhere. San Pedro's **post office** (Mon–Thurs 8am–noon & 1–5pm, Fri 1–4.30pm) is in the Alijua building opposite the *Atlantic Bank*. There are two **laundries** in Pescador Drive; washing costs US$3, drying another US$3.

If you arrive by boat at the main dock or the nearby *Texaco* dock, walk up the street opposite, turn first right and you'll see *Eva's Gift Shop* (☎2627). Here, as well as gaining information on hotels, you can arrange **snorkelling, diving** or **sailing** trips, often for much less than it would cost to book the same trip through your hotel. There are a couple of **travel agencies** on Barrier Reef Drive: *Amigo Travel* (☎2180; fax 2192) and *Travel and Tour Belize* (☎2031; fax 2185) have great expertise in arranging trips throughout Belize and Central America. Both provide all the usual services, including local and international flights.

Finally, in a resort destination like San Pedro you're never far from a souvenir shop, but if you're in the mood to do some selective **gift shopping**, try *Rainforest Rescue*, on Barrier Reef Drive. They sell beautifully designed, high quality T-shirts and speciality foods produced in Belize, and a percentage of the profits goes to the Belize Audubon Society. At *Iguana Jack's*, opposite the primary school on Barrier Reef Drive, John Wetserhold creates unique, life-like ceramic iguanas and lizards, often featured climbing around his hand-sculpted vases.

Accommodation

There are more than fifty **hotels** on Ambergris Caye, most of which are in San Pedro or just a short walk or taxi ride from the airstrip. A number of places send out their own golf carts to pick you up. All but a couple are ouside the reach of budget travellers, who should stroll down **Pescador Drive** to find the bargains. As you walk around the island you may see "room for rent" signs; these are generally for locals but worth a try if you plan to stay for a while. There's nowhere that you can **camp** legally, and sleeping rough is not recommended.

Don't even consider turning up at Christmas or Easter unless you've **booked** a room; at other times in the high season (Dec–Easter), you should be OK. If you've arrived on spec, you're welcome to use the free phone in the airport to call hotels. It's worth asking if **discounts** (of as much as 10 or 15 percent) are available, during the summer and autumn especially, and even in the high season.

ACCOMMODATION PRICE CODES

All Belizean accommodation reviewed in this guide has been graded according to the following **price scales**. These refer to the cost of a double room in high season (generally Dec–Easter) in Belize dollars (Bz$), but do not include the government hotel tax of 7 percent. To work out the price in US$, simply divide the Belizean figures by two. For more details see p.323.

① under Bz$20	④ Bz$40–70	⑦ Bz$140–190
② Bz$20–30	⑤ Bz$70–100	⑧ Bz$190–250
③ Bz$30–40	⑥ Bz$100–140	⑨ over Bz$250

Budget and mid-range accommodation

Barrier Reef Hotel, near the waterfront in the centre of town, opposite the park (☎2075; fax 2719). Distinctive, colonial style building with a pool. Most rooms have a/c. Good restaurant. Accepts *Visa/MC/AmEx*. ⑥.

Conch Shell Hotel, on the beach north of the centre (☎2062). Simple, comfortable rooms with fans and hot showers; some have cooking facilities. Good low-season discounts. ⑤.

Del Rio Cabañas, 10-minutes walk north of the centre (☎ & fax 2286; in US: ☎318/984-9655). Very comfortable wood-and-thatch cabins, facing the sea and surrounded by plants: one sleeps 3 (US$80), the other, with kitchen, sleeps 5 (US$120). Also new budget rooms with shared bath. The owners, the Badillos, are very hospitable; Fido offers good-value fishing trips and visits to Altun Ha (see p.344). Best book in advance. ④.

Hideaway Sports Lodge, south of the town, just past the *Texaco* station (☎2141; fax 2269). Large rooms with fan or a/c, especially good value for groups. Relaxing pool area and on-site restaurant serving tasty fish and chips. Guests can rent bicycles. Accepts *Visa/MC*. ⑤–⑥.

Laidy's Apartments, along the beach north of the town centre (☎2682). Well-furnished rooms, all with private bath and hot water; good value if you're sharing. ⑤.

Lily's, in the town centre, south of the main dock (☎2059). Two-storey beachfront hotel; good value considering its sea views. Recently renovated a/c rooms, plus a good restaurant below the hotel. No single rates. Accepts *Visa/MC*. ⑤.

Martha's, Pescador Drive across from *Elvie's Kitchen* (☎2053). Clean, comfortable rooms with fan, bedside lights, and private bathrooms with hot and cold water. ④.

Milo's, at the end of Barrier Reef Drive, on the left just before the *Paradise Hotel* (☎2033; fax 2198). The best-value budget hotel on the island; basic but clean rooms, some with private bath. Shared bathrooms have hot water. Singles available; quoted prices include tax. ②–④.

Ruby's, Barrier Reef Drive, a short walk from the airstrip (☎2063; fax 2434). Clean, comfortable, family-run hotel that's often booked up. Rooms get better views and increased rates the higher up you go; all are good value. ②–④.

Pricier hotels

Caribbean Villas Hotel, just over 1km south of town (☎2715; fax 2885; in US: ☎913/776-3738). Spacious, very comfortable rooms and well-equipped suites, all with ocean views, set in a garden of native plants on the beachfront. Plenty of peace and quiet; especially relaxing if you're immersed in the hot tub. The best value smaller hotel in this range. Free bikes mean you can cycle into town in ten minutes. Accepts *Visa/MC/AmEx*. ⑦–⑨.

Changes in Latitudes, south of town, near the *Belize Yacht Club* (☎ & fax 2986). Very friendly small B&B half a block from the beach. Immaculately clean rooms, some a/c. The Canadian owners, Sue and Lori, help organize the annual *Sea and Air Festival* and are mines of information. Accepts *Visa/MC/AmEx*. ⑥.

Mata Rocks Resort, 1.5km south of town on the beachfront (☎2336; in US: ☎1-800/288-8646). Nine comfortable rooms, some of them studios with cooker, fridge and microwave. Rates include breakfast; the *Squirrel's Nest* beach bar serves tasty BBQ. No credit cards. ⑥.

Paradise Resort Hotel, at the north end of town (☎2083). Long-established resort hotel with a range of accommodation from thatched doubles and *cabañas*, some a/c, to modern villas with kitchenettes and pool, sleeping up to 6. The shady gardens lead to a beach and private dock, and there's *La Playa Deli* for snacks. ⑦–⑧.

Ramon's Village, on the beach in front of the airstrip (☎2071; fax 2214). The largest resort, with every facility; pricey if you're not on a package. Lovely two-storey wood-and-thatch *cabañas* with balcony, most a/c, set among palms on a beautiful white beach. Accepts all credit cards, unsurprisingly. ⑧–⑨.

San Pedro Holiday Hotel, on the sea front, just south of the town centre (☎2014; fax 2295). San Pedro's oldest hotel, with all modern facilities. Rooms at the front have refrigerators and *Celi's Deli* serves good-value snacks. Accepts *Visa/MC/AmEx*. ⑦.

Victoria House, 3km south of town (☎2067; fax 2429; in US: ☎1-800/247-5159). Luxury *cabañas* or hotel rooms in spacious grounds on the beachfront. Excellent service; you get the best value on an all-in package. Accepts *Visa/MC/AmEx*. ⑨.

Exploring the caye and the reef

The **water** is the focus of daytime entertainment on Ambergris Caye, from sunbathing on the docks to windsurfing, sailing, fishing, diving and snorkelling, and even taking trips on glass-bottomed boats. Many hotels will rent equipment and there are several specialist **dive shops** offering instruction. Before going snorkelling or diving, whet your appetite with a visit to the excellent **Hol Chan Marine Reserve office** (☎2247), Caribeña St, near the *Texaco* station on the lagoon side. They have photographs, maps and other displays on the reserve (see p.370), and the staff will be pleased to answer your questions. They can also tell you if the USAID **conch hatchery**, just north of the main part of town beyond the *Paradise Hotel* and the school, is open to visitors. If it is, the manager will let you look at the tiny conches in various stages of growth prior to being released onto the sea bed, where they replenish the vast numbers taken by fishermen.

A **warning**: there have been a number of accidents in San Pedro where speeding boats have hit people **swimming** off the piers. A line of buoys, clearly visible, indicates the "safe area", but speedboat drivers can be a bit macho and may have been drinking; be careful when choosing where to swim.

Diving

For anyone who has never dived in the tropics before, the **reefs near San Pedro** are fine, but experienced divers looking for high-voltage will be sorely disappointed. This is a heavily used area which has long been subjected to intensive fishing, and much of the reef has been plundered by souvenir hunters. To experience the best diving in Belize you need to take a trip out to one of the atolls.

Local dives are best done with independent operators rather than the bigger dive shops; you get instruction and guiding more suited to your needs. Among

OFFSHORE AND LIVE-ABOARD DIVE BOATS IN SAN PEDRO

Several **live-aboard dive boats** are based in San Pedro, most of them sleeping five or six; you should book well in advance. The *Offshore Express* (☎2013; US$125 per day, including equipment) runs trips of two to seven days and is the only offshore boat to take both divers and snorkellers. The *Blue Hole Express* (☎2982; US$165 for a day trip; about US$15 extra for dive gear) specializes in day trips to the Blue Hole and the atolls, using a fast, twin diesel boat. The *Flying Manta*, a 10m Crusader, also does a one day Blue Hole trip, taking in three dive stops for US$165; the *Manta IV*, a 22m single diesel, offers great two-day Blue Hole trips with five dives, good food and hot showers for US$250. To book the last two contact Gary Cooper at the *Belize Dive Center*, on the dock at the *Belize Yacht Club* (☎2797; fax 2892; in US: ☎1-800/938-0860). Gary offers *Rough Guide* readers a 20 percent discount and free equipment if you book directly with him at San Pedro.

Trips include all food and you can usually be picked up at Caye Caulker on request; the boats are crewed by professionals and carry safety equipment.

the best local **operators** are Dave McGaughey, a PADI master instructor, owner of *Dive Dreams* (☎3223). Larry and Suzanne Parker run the highly professional *Reef Divers* (☎2943); Larry is the senior NAUI instructor in Belize. Both of these carry full safety gear including oxygen and first aid kit. In general, an **open water certification**, which takes novices up to the standard of a fully qualified sport diver, costs around US$350, and a more basic, introductory course at one of the resorts around US$125. For qualified divers a two-tank dive costs around US$45, including tanks, weights, air and boat; shop around for the best prices. To **book** the operators above or the dive boats recommended in the box above, contact Chris Allnatt at the *Blue Hole Dive Center,* on Barrier Reef Drive (☎ & fax 2982).

Snorkelling, sailing and other trips

Just about every hotel in San Pedro offers **snorkelling** trips, costing around US$15 for three hours, plus about US$4 to rent mask, fins and snorkel. If you've never put this equipment on before, practise from a dock first, and get used to seeing shoals of colourful fish. Generally, the options available mean you can either head north to the spectacular Mexico Rocks or Rocky Point or, more commonly, south to the **Hol Chan Marine Reserve** (see below). **Night snorkelling**, a truly amazing experience, is also available.

Several boats take snorkellers out for an utterly relaxing day trip to **Caye Caulker**, employing a mix of motor and sail, allowing you to enjoy two leisurely snorkelling stops, an open bar and lunch on Caye Caulker, returning to San Pedro at sunset. Trips range from US$35 for the sailboat *Rum Punch* to US$65 for the *Ambergrita*, a 10m sailboat, which sleeps four comfortably. The popular, safe *Winnie Estelle* is probably the best overall value.

Other activities include **windsurfing** (US$15–60); **para-sailing** (US$40 a flight) and **water skiing** (US$50 per hour). Many of the larger hotels and resorts rent **hobie-cats** or **kayaks**, or you could check out the equipment and prices at *Island Adventures*, at *Fido's* dock (☎2697). If you want to capture the **underwater wildlife** on film but don't have a suitable camera you can rent one from *Joe Miller Photography* on Pescador (☎2577). Joe is a renowned photographer and offers advanced **instruction**, E-6 **slide processing** and can even undertake emergency repairs. *Blue Hole Dive Center* (☎2982) rents excellent cameras at similar prices.

Day trips to the runs of **Altun Ha** (see p.344) are increasingly popular from San Pedro. Rounding the southern tip of the island in a fast skiff, you head for the mainland at the mouth of the Northern River, cross the lagoon and travel up the river to the tiny village of **Bomba**. With a good guide this is an excellent way to spot wildlife, including **crocodiles** and **manatees**, and the riverbank trees are often adorned with **orchids**. If you like the wood carvings for sale in the gift shops on the island then stop and examine those offered by the people of Bomba; prices here are lower, and the money goes directly to the carver's family. Two of the best **guides** are Daniel Nuñez (☎2314) and Fido Badillo (☎2286).

The Hol Chan Marine Reserve

The **Hol Chan Reserve** takes its name from the Maya for "little channel", and it is this eponymous break in the reef that forms the focus of the reserve. Established in 1987, its three zones – covering a total of around thirteen square kilometres – preserve a comprehensive cross-section of the marine environment, from coral reef through seagrass beds to mangroves. All three habitats are closely linked: many reef fish feed on the seagrass beds, and the mangroves are a

SAFEGUARDING THE BELIZE BARRIER REEF

Coral reefs are among the most complex and fragile ecosystems on earth. Colonies have been growing at a rate of less than 5cm a year for thousands of years; once damaged, the coral is far more susceptible to bacteria, which can quickly lead to large-scale irreversible damage. Remember to follow these **simple rules** while snorkelling, diving or in a boat:

- Never anchor boats on the reef – use the permanently secured buoys.
- Never touch or stand on corals – protective cells are easily stripped away from the living polyps on their surface, destroying them and thereby allowing algae to enter.
- Don't remove shells, sponges or other creatures from the reef, or buy reef products from souvenir shops.
- Avoid disturbing the seabed around corals – quite apart from spoiling visibility, clouds of sand settle over corals, smothering them.
- If you're either a beginner or an out-of-practice diver, practise away from the reef first.
- Don't use suntan lotion in reef areas – the oils remain on the water's surface.
- Check you're not in one of the new marine reserves before fishing.
- Don't feed or interfere with fish or marine life – this can harm not only sea creatures and the food chain, but snorkellers too – large fish may attack, trying to get their share!

nursery area for juvenile fish. As your boat approaches, you'll be met by a warden who explains the rules and collects the entry fee (Bz$3).

At fish-feeding time, tourists congregate both on the water and in it. It's more peaceful to head for another part of the reef, where you might see more fish and less trampled corals. A great deal of damage has already been caused by snorkellers standing on the coral or holding onto outcrops for a better look – on all the easily accessible areas of the reef you will clearly see the white, dead patches, especially on the large brain coral heads. **Never touch** the coral – not only does it damage the delicate ecosystem (see above), it can also sting and cause agonizing burns, and even brushing against the razor-sharp ridges on the reef top can cause cuts that are slow to heal.

Around the caye

Bikes, mopeds and very expensive golf carts can be rented from the travel agencies to follow the rough track running north and south from the town. Heading south, you could ride at least part of the way to **Marco Gonzalez**, a Maya ruin near the southernmost tip of the island. The site is hard to find and there's not a lot to see today (though plenty of mosquitoes), but studies have shown it was an important trade centre, with close links to Lamanai. North, you'll come up against the Boca Del Rio, the river about ten minutes' walk from town.

You might also take a day trip with Daniel Nuñez to some of the previously inaccessible **Maya sites** on the northwest coast of the island. In a day you can visit three or four of the ten or more sites. **Santa Cruz** is a very large site, known to have been used for the shipment of trade goods in the Postclassic era, though the true function of most of the stone mounds here remains uncertain. On **San Juan** beach you'll be crunching over literally thousands of pieces of Maya pottery. Perhaps the most spectacular site is **Chac Balam**, a ceremonial and administrative centre; getting there entails a walk through mangroves to view deep burial chambers, scattered with thousands more pottery shards. There's a real air of adventure and discovery as you explore these ancient sites, now covered with thick bush. On the way back, you navigate **Bacalar Chico**, the channel separating Belize from Mexico, and recently proposed as a new national park and marine reserve. It's so narrow you can practically touch the mangroves on either side as you sit in the boat. At the mouth of the channel the reef is close to the shore; the boat has to cross into the open sea, re-entering the lagoon as you approach San Pedro and so completing a circumnavigation of the island.

Despite all the development, there is a surprising amount of **wildlife** on the caye, including deer, peccary and even a few of the cats of Belize in the thick forests of the north. Turtles nest on some northern beaches, and volunteers are needed to patrol the nest sites when the eggs are being laid: contact the Belize Audubon Society (see p.356) or the Hol Chan Reserve office (see p.369).

Eating and drinking

There are plenty of places to eat in San Pedro, and **prices** are generally higher than elsewhere in Belize. **Seafood** is prominent at most restaurants, which tend to reflect the tastes of the town's predominantly North American guests – often with service to match, a rarity in most parts of Belize. You can rely on plenty of steak, shrimp, chicken, pizza and salads. Many **hotels** have their own dining room, and do **beach barbecues**; there are several **Chinese** restaurants, too, the cheaper ones representing the best value on the island.

Buying your own food isn't particularly cheap here: there's no market and the grocery stores are stocked with imported canned goods. *Rock's* on Pescador and *Milo's* at the north end of Barrier Reef Drive offer the best value. Cooking might also be a problem, as it's not as easy in San Pedro to improvise your own beach barbecue as it is on other islands. For the staples, though, the *Señor Paz* bakery, next door to *Manelly's Ice Cream Parlour* in the town centre, has a wide selection of **breads**, including Mexican-style *pan dulces*.

Restaurants

Ambergris Delight, next to the *Casablanca* hotel. A truly Belizean restaurant, lethargically serving rice and beans, fish and burgers at bargain prices.

Bon Apettite Cafe, Coconut Drive, by the airstrip. Tiny, spotless place, serving the best value breakfasts and lunches on the island. Stop by to pick up a freshly baked bun or see what the special is. Open 7am– 6pm.

Celi's Restaurant, in the *Holiday Hotel*. Good seafood and evening barbecues. Closed Wed. *Celi's Deli* does delicious breakfasts and snacks, including the best *tamales* in town.

Duke's, Coconut Drive, across from *Ramon's*. Excellent, family-run restaurant serving great fish, steaks and Mexican food (dinner includes a drink and dessert), surrounded by John Wayne memorabilia. Breakfast and dinner only. Accepts *Visa/AmEx*.

Elvie's Kitchen, across the road from *Martha's* hotel. The place for burgers and fries, accompanied by delicious, Mexican *licuado*-like fruit drinks. A huge tree, the biggest in the town, dominates the centre of the room. Slick service and reasonable prices.

Jade Garden, Coconut Drive, south of town. The best Chinese restaurant – good value, too.

Leny's Place, near the airstrip. Small, Chinese-run, Mexican restaurant serving the best omelettes in Belize. Extremely good value.

Little Italy, next to the *Spindrift Hotel* (☎2866). The finest Italian restaurant in San Pedro; excellent food and service, and a good wine list. Some tables on a patio overlooking the sea;

you may have to book for dinner in high season. Their great-value Mexican-style lunch buffet (11.30am–2pm) has lots of choice.

Ruby's Cafe, Barrier Reef Drive, next to *Ruby's Hotel*. Delicious home-made cakes, pies and sandwiches, and freshly brewed coffee. Open at 6am, so it's a good place to order a packed lunch if you're going on a trip.

Bars and nightlife

Sandals Pub (next to *Milo's*), whose name is spelled out in flip-flops nailed to the wall, is a friendly **bar** where the prices are not quite as outrageous as most, and the cool sand floor is a treat for your feet. It's worth checking to see if Mike's doing a barbecue. Some of the hotels have fancy bars, several of which offer happy hours, while back from the main street are a couple of small **cantinas** where you can buy a beer or a bottle of rum and drink with the locals. *Traveller's Cantina*, on Pescador, complete with bat-wing doors, caters to locals and tourists.

Entertainment in San Pedro becomes more sophisticated every year. *Big Daddy's* **disco**, in and around a beach bar near the main dock, has early evening piano, and a lively reggae band later on. Happy hour runs from 5 to 9pm and there's a daily beach barbecue. The extremely popular *Tarzan's Disco and Nite Club*, opposite the park, has a very lively dance floor. *The Tackle Box* bar, at the end of the *Coral Beach Hotel* pier is a good spot to catch a local band.

Caye Caulker

South of Ambergris Caye and 35km northeast of Belize City, **Caye Caulker** is the most accessible island for the independent traveller, and long a favourite spot for backpackers on the "gringo trail". Until recently, tourism existed almost as a sideline to the island's main source of income, **lobster fishing**, which has kept the place going for more than twenty years.

Although the lobster catch increased for many years after the setting up of fishing cooperatives, the deployment of more traps over an ever wider area led to the rapid depletion of the **spiny lobster**, once so common they could be scooped onto the beaches with palm fronds. Today their numbers are dangerously low, and specimens smaller than the legal 4oz are frequently taken and sold to local restaurants. Recent catches were so low that the fishermen were taking the traps in by mid-January, a month earlier than the end of the legal season. As fishing has declined, islanders have had to diversify. Fishermen have become barmen, and fishing boats now offer snorkelling trips; new hotels and bars are being built, older ones improved, and prices – low for years – have begun to rise.

For the moment, however, Caye Caulker remains relaxed and easy-going, managing to avoid most of the commercialism of Ambergris Caye's San Pedro, though with the building of the airstrip and an ever-growing number of hotels and vehicles, it too is beginning to resemble one of the Florida Keys. Recently, the decision was made to allow construction on the large, previously uninhabited northern part of the island, and houses have been built on the south point.

As yet there is little air conditioning on the island, which is fine most of the time, when a cooling breeze blows in from the sea, but can mean some very sticky moments if the breeze dies. **Sandflies and mosquitoes** can cause almost unbearable irritation on calm days. Sandflies are the worst: inactive in breezy

Flights on the San Pedro run stop at the airstrip (call the airlines on p.366 for information); some also stop at **Caye Chapel** on request. *Skybird* is Caye Caulker's own airline, operating both scheduled and charter flights (☎2124 or 02/32596 in Belize City). However, most visitors to Caye Caulker still arrive by **boat**. Passenger boats, known locally as "skiffs" (as opposed to a canoe-shaped "dory"), tie up behind *A&R's Texaco Station* on N Front St in Belize City. The establishment of the **Caye Caulker Water Taxi Association** means you no longer have to run the gauntlet of hustlers offering to take you to "the islands". Simply get to the dock and you'll be told which is the next boat and when it leaves. The first departure is around 10am; they run until about 4pm, and the trip takes around 45 minutes. You can safely leave your luggage with any of the Caye Caulker boat owners if you want a look round the city before you leave. All scheduled boats to San Pedro (see p.366) call at Caye Caulker; the first is the *Triple J*, which leaves Courthouse Wharf at 9am. You'll be dropped off at one of the piers at the front of the island, usually at the longest one, known as the "front bridge". **From Caye Caulker to the other cayes**, ask around among the boatmen, or call in at the water taxi office in the early morning. If you're heading for one of the small or uninhabited islands you may have to hire someone to take you there.

Leaving for Belize City, it's best to check in at the water taxi office by the telephone office and book a place in a boat returning the next day, especially if you want an early (7am) boat; the staff will also know the times that the boats on the San Pedro–Belize City run call at Caye Caulker.

conditions, at other times they make a good **insect repellent** essential (though even that does not seem to last very long). Some swear by Avon's *Skin-So-Soft*.

Arrival and information

If you arrive at either the "front" dock or the "back" dock (easily recognizable, as they are longer than the others), simply follow your nose to the **water taxi office**, effectively the centre of the village. They can give **information** and will hold your luggage while you look for a place to stay.

The *Atlantic Bank* (Mon–Fri 8am–noon & 1–2pm) gives *Visa* **cash advances**, and an increasing number of businesses accept plastic for payment. The **post office** is south of the village centre and the *BTL* office is on the corner leading to the main dock. Ilna Axillou, who runs Caye Caulker's **travel agency**, *Dolphin Bay Travel* (☎ & fax 2214), has outstanding local knowledge, and can arrange flights.

Accommodation

Most of the year it's easy enough to find an inexpensive room in one of the small clapboard hotels, but to arrive at Christmas or New Year without a **reservation** could leave you stranded. Even the furthest **hotels** are no more than ten minutes' walk from the "front" dock. There are no street names on the island, but places are pretty easy to find: the following listings are given roughly in the order you'd come to them walking from the dock.

The **telephone area code** for Caye Caulker is ☎022.

M&M Apartments (☎2229) have **houses for rent** near the football field, or try *Heredia's Apartments* (☎2132). You'll come across other places as you walk around. Prices start at about Bz$300 per week.

North from the "front" dock

Castaways, a few hundred metres north of the dock, past the park and police station (☎2294). Basic, clean guest house; all rooms have fans. The balcony gives a great view of the passing traffic (mostly pedestrian) and palm fronds dipping in the breeze – and the restaurant below is good value. ②.

Míra Mar, next door to *Castaways* (☎2157). Clean, simple rooms, some with private bath. ②.

Sandy Lane Hotel, behind *Mira Mar* (☎2217). Another small, quiet, inexpensive place. ②.

Martinez Caribbean Inn, half a block past *Míra Mar*, on the seafront (☎2133). Secure and well run; all rooms with private bath and hot water. The best rooms are at the front, the less expensive ones to the rear. Popular with groups. ③.

Rainbow (☎2123). Two-storey concrete building with little ambience or privacy: the rooms open onto the path. Clean and safe, though, with bath and hot water. Accepts *MC/Visa*. ④.

Barbara's Rooms, towards the north end near the split (☎2025). Friendly, Canadian-run place, with simple, clean rooms, away from the bars and secure for women. No single rates. Guests can use the phone to make collect calls. ②.

South from the "front" dock

Morgan's Inn, opposite *Galería Hicaco* (where you enquire; ☎2178; fax 2239). Two quiet, private houses set back from the beach; good for long stays but no cooking facilities. ④.

Lena's (☎2106). Basic accommodation on the water. Some rooms with private bath. ②–③.

Daisy's (☎2150). Simple, budget rooms run by a friendly family. ②.

Edith's, on the corner past *Lena's* (☎2161). Charging slightly higher prices than it used to, but there's hot water, and rooms are better furnished than at most budget places. Some private baths. Bz$2 discount if you book a boat back to Belize City here. ③.

Tropical Paradise Hotel, overlooking the cemetery (☎2124; fax 2225). Standard rooms and smart-looking a/c huts and suites with bathrooms with hot water. Accepts *Visa/MC*. ④–⑥.

Tree Tops Hotel, across from the post office, just before *Tom's* (☎2008; fax 2115). Easily the best hotel on the island (indeed the country) at this price, just 50m from the water. Five comfortable rooms, with fridge, cable TV and powerful ceiling fan; booking ahead is advised. Although only one room has private bath, the shared baths (no hot water) are immaculate. Owners Terry and Doris Creasey are extremely helpful and German is spoken. ④.

Tom's Hotel (☎2102). A large hotel for Caye Caulker, with twenty bargain rooms, though with cabins in the grounds, it's getting quite cramped. Snorkelling equipment for rent, and the owner runs excellent trips to the reef. ②–④.

Monique's Resort, across from the post office (☎2140). A pair of small cabins with hot and cold water in a peaceful location – good value for a couple, though not that near the shore. ④.

Jiminez Cabañas (☎2175). Clean, comfortable wood-and-thatch cabins – the best value on the island – surrounded by a delightful garden shaded by coconut trees. Secondhand English-language books for sale. ④.

The Anchorage, right on the beach. Whitewashed, Maya-style oval huts with thatched roofs. Fantastic location, but becoming rather run-down, so you might get a bargain. ③–④.

Ignacio's Beach Huts, just past *The Anchorage* (☎2212). Overbuilt site, with the newer cabins overshadowing the older ones, but still a bargain. ②.

Shirley's Guest House, a little way beyond *Ignacio's*, the last hotel on the south end of the island (☎2145). Worth the walk if you want peace and quiet and comfortable, clean rooms. Slightly more expensive than average, but still good value. ⑤–⑥.

Exploring the reef and the caye

The reef is certainly an experience not to be missed: swimming along coral canyons surrounded by an astonishing range of fish, with perhaps even the odd shark or two (these will almost certainly be harmless nurse sharks). Here as everywhere, snorkellers should be aware of the fragility of the reef and be careful not to touch any coral – even sand stirred up by fins can cause damage (see p.371). Most reef trips last several hours and take in a number of sites, often including the protected Hol Chan Marine Reserve (see p.370); some allow fishing along the way. Dolphins often accompany boats on the way to the reef.

Trips to the reef from Caye Caulker are easily arranged, provided four or five people want to go (Bz$15–20 per person). The best place to check is at the water taxi office – ask, too, about manatee-spotting trips. You can also book reef trips from several hotels, *Edith's* and *Daisy's* for example, and the *Tropical Paradise* has a glass-bottomed boat. One of the best day outings is offered by Ras Creek, in his tiny cabin cruiser *Reggae Muffin* (Bz$25). Ras shows you nurse sharks and eagle rays in their element as you float above them, with your feet hooked over a pole. Rum punch is provided, and guests help prepare lunch.

An extended sailing trip to the uninhabited reefs and islands is not cheap, but better value here than in Belize City – try *Seaing is Belizing* (☎2189), where James Beveridge offers, for example, five-day trips for around US$300 for two people. Of the several outlets on the island renting **snorkelling equipment**, *Island Sun*, at the north end (☎2215), and *Belize Diving Services*, by the football field (☎2143), are two of the best in terms of price and quality (some of the stuff offered by hotels tends to be old and leaky). Gamusa, a friendly giant, offers similar trips in his own easy-going, rasta-crewed boat. **Kayaks** are available too: try *Daisy's* hotel or ask Ellen MacRae at the *Galería Hicaco* (☎2178).

For a really well-informed tour of the reef, contact marine biologist Ellen at the *Galería Hicaco*: she can explain exactly what it is you're seeing in this amazing underwater world. She also does slide shows and conducts **Audubon bird walks**, an introduction to the dozens of bird species of the caye – waders from herons to sandpipers, with pelicans, spoonbills and the ever-present frigate birds swooping with pinpoint accuracy on morsels of fish. Ellen is also the driving force behind the attempt to establish the **Siwa-Ban Nature Reserve** on Caye Caulker, to protect the endangered black catbird; it is hoped this reserve will eventually be similar in size and importance to the Hol Chan Reserve.

If you'd like to learn **underwater photography** then get in touch, again, with James at *Seaing is Belizing*. The office is next to *Dolphin Bay Travel*, and he and his wife Dorothy run a gift shop that sells photos, slides and film, and develops film. They do slide shows and operate a book exchange service, too.

Sub-aqua diving is available from *Belize Diving Services* (☎2143; fax 2217), by the football field, expertly run by American Frank Bounting, who offers some of the best-value diving in Belize. He will take you night-diving or cave-diving – one of the world's largest single-chamber underwater caves runs right beneath Caye Caulker. Two-tank dives for qualified divers cost US$45 including equipment, and a four-day course should cost around US$300, which is cheap by Caribbean standards. *Frenchie's* (☎2234; fax 2074) offers enthusiastic, knowledgeable trips, with some great reef diving and coral gardens, and day trips to the Blue Hole. However, to experience the best that Belize has to offer you should take a live-aboard dive trip to the outer atolls – see p.369.

You'll see signs for **fishing trips** as you walk around. Some of the best are operated by Porfilio Guzman (☎2152) and Roly Rosado; ask for them by name – any of the locals will direct you. Otherwise, Neno and Ramon Rosado, both experienced boat skippers, run fishing, diving and river trips in the *Red Scorpion* and the *Pegasus* (☎2122 or 02/31138).

Around the caye and trips to other islands

Swimming isn't really possible from the shore as the water's too shallow. You have to leap off the end of piers or go to "the cut", a deep channel at the north end of the village created in 1961 when Hurricane Hattie sliced Caye Caulker in two. Here you can see the damage done when mangroves are cut down – the cut was narrower before this area was developed and there's now a desperate attempt to build shore defences. The northern part of the island is long and narrow, covered in mangroves and thick vegetation that comes right down to the shore. These mangrove shallows swarm with small fish called "sardines" by the fishermen, who use them as bait to catch snapper. **Salt-water crocodiles** are sometimes seen here, but you're more likely to find them on the Turneffe Islands or in the more remote coastal areas. This area is now threatened with development, though, and has already been divided up into lots.

Caye Caulker is a good base for **day trips** to the other cayes, especially Goff's and English cayes and even the atolls of the Turneffe Islands and Lighthouse Reef. The best is Jim and Cindy Novelo's expedition to the exquisite **Half Moon Caye** (see p.380), the most easterly of Belize's islands, on the *Sunrise*. This all-day trip takes snorkellers to places previously only accessible to divers on live-aboard boats, to explore reefs on the Turneffe Islands and Lighthouse Reef. After meeting the red-footed booby (and the huge hermit crabs) face to face, it's back in the boat for the unique splendour of the Blue Hole. Rates include lunch but not snorkel gear (Dec–April Tues 6am; US$65; ☎2195).

For islands and the reef to the **south**, such as Goff's, Sergeants and English cayes, visit the water taxi office or book through *Dolphin Bay Travel* ☎2214.

Eating, drinking and entertainment

You can buy food at several **shops and supermarkets** on the island, which receive regular supplies of bread, milk and vegetables. Also, many houses advertise banana bread, coconut cakes and other home-baked goodies, and there's a good **bakery** on the street leading to the football field. On the front street, call in at *Cindy's* for superb fresh fruit, yoghurt and carrot cake. Cindy is also an expert on **Belizean music**, and can make tapes of your favourite tracks. As you walk around you might see children selling bread or pastries from bowls balanced on their heads; it's always worth seeing what snacks are on offer.

Good home cooking, large portions and very reasonable prices are features of all the island's **restaurants**, half of which you'll pass while looking for a room.

Lobster (in season) is served in every imaginable dish, from curry to chow mein; **seafood** generally is good value, accompanied by rice or potatoes.

Restaurants, cafés and bars

Along the **main street**, one block back from the shore, are *Marin's Restaurant*, with a shady outdoor dining area and the best water on the island, and the particularly good *Rodriguez Home Restaurant*; a few metres further on, *Syd's Bar* serves great food. Just past here is *Glenda's*, where you can buy fresh orange juice and delicious cinnamon rolls and whose small restaurant is a favourite breakfast meeting place. Walking north along the waterfront, you'll come to a proliferation of new **beach bars and restaurants**: *Martinez*, and the *Rainbow Restaurant*, on a deck over the water, are the best. The restaurant at the *Tropical Paradise* serves Belizean and American-style food at reasonable prices and is usually quite busy. Up the street from here, the *I&I's* is a popular three-storey bar and restaurant – be careful negotiating the stairs on the way down. Serving Italian/American food, the *Sand Box*, in its new central location by the main dock, is still the best restaurant on the island, and often packed.

Caye Caulker's **social scene** oscillates around the various bars. Most people are friendly enough, but as the evening wears on and drink takes its toll it can get rowdy. The island is a favourite weekend R & R destination for British soldiers, who are often very young and get drunk quickly, when the macho tendency takes over. Be careful with your money – Caye Caulker has a criminal element and a drug problem, but only three policemen. **Television** is a feature of most bars, with baseball, game shows and soaps as the programming staples. Home-made commercials and brief fillers of Belizean scenes and wildlife provide a touch of local interest. Otherwise, evening entertainment mostly consists of relaxing in a restaurant over dinner or a drink, or gazing at the tropical night sky.

The rest of the reef

Although Caye Caulker and San Pedro are the only villages anywhere on the reef, there are several other islands that can be visited, some of them supporting fishing camps or upmarket resorts, others completely uninhabited. Caye Caulker is within day-trip distance of some of these (see pp.376–7), and there are also a couple of isolated islands where budget travellers can find reasonably priced accommodation. Tourism in Belize is developing each year, so there are likely to be more hotels and resorts on offer than are listed here.

In addition to the places we cover below, there are superbly isolated hotels – called **lodges** – on a few reefs and cayes. **Prices**, not low, include transport from Belize City or the international airport, accommodation, all meals, and usually diving or fishing. The attraction of these lodges is the "simple life" scenario. Buildings are low-key, wooden and sometimes thatched, and the group you're with will probably be the only people staying there. There are no phones (most are in radio contact with Belize City), electricity comes from a generator, and views of palm trees curving over turquoise water reinforce the sense of isolation.

Caye Chapel

As a diversion during a snorkelling trip you could visit **Caye Chapel**, immediately south of Caye Caulker. Quite different from Caye Caulker, privately owned

Caye Chapel has an airstrip, golf course, marina and (usually deserted) hotel, the *Pyramid Island Resort* (☎02/44409; ⑥). The beaches are cleaned daily and the bar is open all day – perfect for a cold beer after a hard day's snorkelling. It was on Caye Chapel that the defeated Spanish fleet paused for a few days after the **Battle of St George's Caye** in 1798, and, according to legend, some of their dead are buried here. Belize City–San Pedro flights pick up passengers on Caye Chapel.

English and Goff's cayes, Gallows Point and Spanish Lookout Caye

The tiny islands of **English Caye** and **Goff's Caye** are popular as day trips from Belize City and Caye Caulker. **Gallows Point**, the site of hangings in earlier days is larger, with thick mangroves harbouring manatees and salt-water crocodiles. *Gallows Point Reef Resort*, about 15km from Belize City, offers a house, hotel rooms (some with bath) and camping on a prepared site (☎02/75819; ②–⑧).

The *Spanish Bay Resort* (☎02/77288; fax 72797), has five comfortable *cabañas* built over the water at **Spanish Lookout Caye**, south of Gallows Point. Packages include transport from the airport to the caye, meals and diving; typically around US$485 for three nights.

St George's Caye

Tiny **St George's Caye**, around 15km from Belize City, was capital for the Baymen of the eighteenth century, but doesn't offer much for the casual visitor. Anyone interested in Belizean history, however, could head for the small grave-yard of the early settlers on the southern tip of the island. The island, home today to a few fishermen, also boasts a couple of hotels and luxury holiday villas and acts as an adventure training centre for the British forces in Belize. While you're here you may meet Karl and Angelika Bishof, an Austrian couple who run *Bela Carib* (☎02/77600), a company that carefully collects and exports tropical fish. The tanks contain a fascinating display of reef creatures and, just to show you're not idly poking around, take a look at the great T-shirts in the gift shop.

Accommodation on the caye is luxurious and expensive, generally sold as a package. *Cottage Colony* (☎02/77051; fax 73253; ⑦) is a collection of extremely comfortable colonial-style wooden houses with modern facilities and a dining room overlooking the Caribbean. The price of US$1250 for a week's diving includes pick-up from the airport, two dives per day and all meals; it's a little more for fishing and less for simple relaxation. Write to the *Bellevue Hotel*, PO Box 428, Belize City. *Saint George's Lodge* (☎02/44190; fax 31460; ⑨) is an all-inclusive diving resort comprising a main lodge and six luxury wood-and-thatch cottages with private verandahs. The price (more than US$250 per day for the cottages) includes airport transfer, diving and meals. There's no drinks licence but guests can bring their own. Write to *Saint George's Lodge*, PO Box 625, Belize City.

The Bluefield Range

In the **Bluefield Range** cayes, 35km southeast of Belize City, you can stay on a remote fishing camp. *Ricardo's Beach Huts* (☎02/31609; 3 days/2 nights US$150 per person) offer simple, comfortable accommodation (min 2 nights) right on the water, in huts built on stilts. All meals – including fresh fish and lobster – are included, as is transport from Belize City. Ricardo Castillo is a reliable, expert fishing guide, scrupulously practising conservation of the reef. For more information ask at *Dim's Mira Rio* bar, 59 N Front St, Belize City (☎02/44970), where the trips start, or contact *S&L Travel* in Belize City (☎02/77593).

The Turneffe Islands

Though shown on many maps as one large island, the virtually uninhabited **Turneffe Islands** are an oval archipelago 60km long, enclosed by a beautiful coral reef. Situated 40km from Belize City, they consist of low-lying mangrove islands and sandbanks – some quite large – around a shallow lagoon. A few places offer all-inclusive accommodation, at a price. *Turneffe Flats* (PO Box 1676, Belize City), a fishing and diving lodge on the windward, eastern side, charge US$1700 per person for a week's fishing, including the airfare from Miami, New Orleans or Houston. *Turneffe Island Lodge* (PO Box 480, Belize City; ☎02/30236; fax 31711; in US: ☎1-800/338-8149), at the southern tip of the islands on Caye Bokel, charges US$1300 per person for a week of diving, more for fishing. Halfway down the eastern side, *Blackbird Caye Resort* (☎02/33504; fax 30268), is a self-styled "ecotourism development" charging from US$1400 for a week of diving or fishing. Accommodation is in ten wood-and-thatch *cabañas*; there's no bar, so you'll have to bring your own drinks. Research on bottlenose dolphins, sponsored by Oceanic Society Expeditions, is being carried out here by volunteers on the *Belize Dolphin Project*. Contact Betty Taylor, 1415 Louisiana, Houston, Texas 77002 (☎713/658-1142; fax 658-0739).

The construction of resorts on this remote, fragile island has meant cutting down mangroves, the cause of much controversy among conservationists. South of Blackbird Caye, **Calabash Caye** is the base for *Coral Cay Conservation*, where volunteers take part in a research project to complete a systematic investigation of the entire atoll. Participants stay at the University College of Belize marine research centre, sleeping in purpose-built cabins.

The islands can also be visited on day trips from San Pedro or Caye Caulker.

Lighthouse Reef and Half Moon Caye

About 80km east of Belize City is Belize's outer atoll, **Lighthouse Reef**, made famous by Jacques Cousteau, who visited in the 1970s. The two main attractions are the Blue Hole, which attracted Cousteau's attention, and the Half Moon Caye Natural Monument. The **Blue Hole**, technically a "karst-eroded sinkhole", is a shaft about 90m in diameter and 145m deep, which drops through the bottom of the lagoon and opens out into a complex network of caves and crevices. Its depth gives it a peculiar deep blue colour, and according to local legend it's home to an enormous sea monster. Cousteau's investigations have shown that caves underlie the entire reef, and that the sea has simply punctured their roof at the site of the Blue Hole. Unsurprisingly, the Blue Hole and Lighthouse Reef are major attractions for **divers**, offering incredible walls and drop-offs. Several **shipwrecks** form artificial reefs; the most prominent is the *Ermlund*, which ran aground in 1971, looming over the reef just north of Half Moon Caye. You can visit the atoll as either a day or overnight trip from San Pedro (p.367) or Caye Caulker (p.377) and *Lighthouse Reef Resort*, on privately owned Northern Caye has luxurious villas and *cabañas* in splendid isolation. Guests fly in on a fishing or diving package costing around US$1500 a week (☎ & fax 02/31205; in US: ☎1-800/423-3114).

The **Half Moon Caye Natural Monument**, the first marine conservation area in Belize, was declared a national park in 1982. Its lighthouse was first built in 1820 and has not always been effective: several wrecks testify to the dangers of the reef. The 45-acre caye is divided into two distinct ecosystems: in the west, guano from thousands of seabirds fertilizes the soil, allowing the growth of dense vegetation, while the eastern half has mostly coconut palms growing in the sand.

A total of 98 bird species has been recorded here, including frigate birds, ospreys, mangrove warblers, white-crowned pigeons and – most important of all – a resident population of 4000 **red-footed boobies**, one of only two nesting colonies in the Caribbean. The boobies came by their name because they displayed no fear of humans, enabling sailors to kill them in their thousands, and they still move only reluctantly when visitors stroll through them. Their nesting area is accessible from a platform built by the Belize Audubon Society and recently rebuilt by *Raleigh Expeditions* volunteers. Apart from the birds, the island supports iguanas and lizards, and both loggerhead and hawksbill turtles nest on the beaches, which also attract the biggest land crabs in Belize.

There's no accommodation on the caye, but **camping** is allowed with the permission of the Belize Audubon Society (see p.356). Bring food and water and register with the park warden when you arrive.

TRAVEL DETAILS

For a rundown of **flights** and **boats** to the cayes from Belize City and between the cayes themselves, see p.366 and p.374.

CHAPTER TEN

CAYO AND THE WEST

Heading west from Belize City to the Guatemalan border, you travel
through a wide range of landscapes, from open grassland to rolling hills
and dense tropical forest. It's a journey that takes you from the heat and
humidity of the coast to the lush foothills of the Maya Mountains, and
into an area increasingly influenced by Spanish-speaking Mestizos, including
large numbers of refugees from other Central American countries.

A single road connects Belize City with the Guatemalan border. This is the
Western Highway, a fast, paved route that leaves Belize City through mangrove

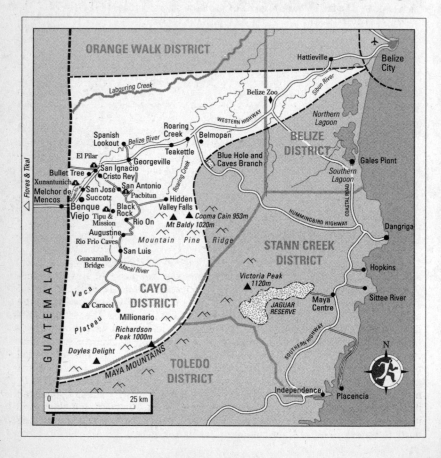

<table>
<tr><td colspan="3" align="center">**ACCOMMODATION PRICE CODES**</td></tr>
</table>

All Belizean accommodation reviewed in this guide has been graded according to the following **price scales**. These refer to the cost of a double room in high season (generally Dec–Easter) in Belize dollars (Bz$), but do not include the government hotel tax of 7 percent. To work out the price in US$, simply divide the Belizean figures by two. For more details see p.323.

① under Bz$20	④ Bz$40–70	⑦ Bz$140–190
② Bz$20–30	⑤ Bz$70–100	⑧ Bz$190–250
③ Bz$30–40	⑥ Bz$100–140	⑨ over Bz$250

swamps and heads inland across open savannah scattered with pine trees. Before reaching Belmopan the road passes several places of interest: the **Belize Zoo**, well worth a visit if you're interested in the country's natural history, the **Monkey Bay Wildlife Sanctuary**, and **Guanacaste Park**, a smallish reserve designed to protect a section of the original forest. Beyond this is the capital, **Belmopan**, established in 1970 and surely one of the smallest capital cities in the world.

Heading further west, following the Belize River valley, you start to climb into the foothills of the Maya Mountains, a beautiful area where the air is clear and the land astonishingly fertile. South of the road, **Mountain Pine Ridge** is a pleasantly cool region of hills and pine woods traversed by good dirt roads. The chief town is **San Ignacio** on the Macal River, the ideal base for exploring the forests, rivers and ruins of western Belize. San Ignacio, the main town of Cayo District, is becoming known as a centre for Belize's growing "ecotourism" industry. The ruins of **Caracol**, the largest Maya site in Belize and a focus for current archeological research, lie deep in the jungle of the Vaca plateau, south of San Ignacio.

Between San Ignacio and the Guatemalan border, the road climbs past the hilltop ruins of **Cahal Pech** then descends, following the valley of the Mopan River 15km to the frontier bridge. At the village of **San Jose Succotz** an ancient ferry crosses the river, allowing access to the Maya site of **Xunantunich**, from the top of which you can view the Guatemalan department of **Petén**.

Belize City to Belmopan

Leaving Belize City through the cemetery, the Western Highway skirts the shoreline, running behind a tangle of mangrove swamps and past **Cucumber Beach Wharf**, a graveyard for the rusting hulks of beached ships. At Mile 5 the road passes the entrance to **Buffer Hole Beach** – no more than a clearing in the mangroves with a pleasant thatched bar overlooking the shore. The water is shallow and silty but clean enough to bathe in. A few kilometres further, you cross the **Sir John Burden Canal**, an inland waterway, now a nature reserve, that connects the Belize River with the Sibun River. This is the route taken by small boats travelling down to Dangriga and Gales Point (see p.409) via the **Northern and Southern lagoons**. The next place along the highway is **HATTIEVILLE**, named after the 1961 hurricane that created the refugees who initially populated it. The village started life as a temporary shelter for the homeless, but since then it has become rather more permanent. Just before Hattieville, there's a turning north to Burrell Boom, a short cut to the Northern Highway.

The curious steep hills to the left on this part of the road are limestone outcrops, quarried for road-building. The highest is **Gracie Rock**, near the Sibun River, the set of fictional "Geronimo" in the film *The Mosquito Coast*. Along with the Northern and Southern lagoons, the **Sibun River area** supports numerous bird species and jaguars, tapir, howler monkeys and some large crocodiles, and a conservation project has been proposed to protect the river from its mouth up, where there are nesting beaches of the endangered hawksbill turtle. If you want to **stay** in this area and **cruise the lagoons**, take a left turn in Hattieville, down the road to Freetown Sibun. Here *River Haven* (☎02/70529; fax 70530), run by Canadians Ray Parker and Beth McBride, offers the only **houseboats** for rent in Belize. As well as the houseboats, which sleep four (US$790 per weekend, US$1580 per week), there are cabins (US$130) and *cabañas* (*D*).

About 25km beyond Hattieville, the junction of the Manatee Road, a short cut heading southeast to Gales Point and **Dangriga**, is marked by a sign and a couple of bars; the *Midway Resting Place* and the *Roadway Inn*. This dirt road is in good condition and served by **buses** taking the coastal road south.

The Belize Zoo

The first point of interest out this way is the **Belize Zoo**, at Mile 29 (daily 9.30am–4pm; Bz$10 for non-Belizeans, Bz$5 for Peace Corps, VSO and military). Set up in 1983 by Sharon Matola, after an ambitious wildlife film (*Path of the Raingods*) left her with a collection of semi-tame animals, the zoo is organized around the theme of "a walk through Belize", with a trail that takes you into the pinelands, the forest edge, the rainforest and the river forest, introducing a selection of animals from each environment. The residents, all native to Belize, include a Baird's tapir (locally known as a mountain cow) called April who is well known to the schoolchildren of Belize; it is hoped that April and her mate Danta will breed. All the Belizean cats are represented and some, including the jaguars, have bred successfully. There's also a wide range of birds (including toucans, macaws, a spectacled owl and several vultures); other inhabitants include monkeys (spider and howler), crocodiles and various snakes.

The zoo is actively involved in conservation and captive breeding, and runs a series of touring outreach programmes. Importantly, it also aims to encourage the support of local people. Opposite, *The Tropical Education Center*, as the name suggests, focuses on school and college groups but is well worth a look.

To **get to the zoo** take any bus between Belize City and Belmopan and ask the driver to drop you; there's a sign on the highway. A 200m walk brings you to the entrance and the Gerald Durrell Visitor Centre. It's feasible to visit on a day trip from Belize City: the staff know the times of buses back. If you're interested in supporting the work of the zoo, write to PO Box 1787, Belize City.

The Monkey Bay Wildlife Sanctuary and onward

On the left of the highway, 2km past the zoo, is the **Monkey Bay Wildlife Sanctuary**, a 1070-acre protected area extending to the Sibun River, which encompasses five distinct vegetation and habitat types. The bay takes its name from the historical presence of both howler and spider monkeys, which are only now beginning to return after a thirty-year absence. Adjoining the sanctuary across the Sibun River is the 2250-acre Monkey Bay Nature Reserve, which extends the wildlife corridor south through karst limestone hills to connect with the Manatee Forest Reserve. The **entrance** to the sanctuary is about 400m in from the highway at Mile 31 1/2, easily reached by any bus along the highway. Facilities include a field research station which serves as library, museum and classroom, and there's a **bunkhouse** (Bz$15) and **camping** (Bz$10) on raised platforms. The director, Matt Miller also organizes canoe trips on the Sibun River.

Beyond the zoo and Monkey Bay is the branch road to the village of Churchyard, on the Sibun River. Next comes *Cheers*, a friendly **bar** run by an English couple, where you can get good food (including chip butties) at reasonable prices. They have reliable **information** and operate a book exchange. Just beyond here *JB's Bar* is an old favourite with the British Army, whose mementoes deck the walls alongside a word of thanks from Harrison Ford and the crew of *The Mosquito Coast*. The food is better than ever, thanks to a French manager and there's a small **house for rent** (Bz$50 per night). *JB's* marks the boundary between the Belize and Cayo Districts, and here the open expanse of pine and savannah gives way to rich pastures and citrus groves. The road continues, well-surfaced and fast, to the junction with the Southern Highway.

Two kilometres before the turning for Belmopan, opposite the airstrip, another track leads off to the right, this time to the *Banana Bank Lodge* (PO Box 48 Belmopan; ☎08/23180; fax 23505; ⑤–⑧) on the north bank of the Belize River, crossed by foot-passenger boat. This 4000-acre ranch is owned by an American couple, John and Carolyn Carr, who offer horse-riding, canoeing, swimming and natural history trips. There are dozens of Maya mounds, some quite large, and huge tropical trees nearby. Six wood-and-thatch *cabañas* have views sweeping down to the Belize River, and there are five rooms (one with water bed) in the house – all beautifully furnished but without electricity. Rates include breakfast; the food, mostly home-produced, is superb. There's also a small collection of animals at the ranch, including a tame jaguar. To get there by car, follow the sign to the right at Mile 47, just before Belmopan, and drive to the riverbank – someone will come down to ferry you across – or take the marked turn-off to the right just beyond **Roaring Creek** village, crossing the Belize River on an old hand-cranked ferry. Without your own vehicle, call to arrange a pick-up in Belmopan.

Guanacaste Park

At the junction for Belmopan is **Guanacaste Park** (Bz$5), a small (and mosquito-ridden) wildlife reserve where you can wander through a superb area of lush tropical forest. Founded in 1973 and officially dedicated as a National Reserve in 1988, the park covers a total area of 52 acres, bordered by the highway, Roaring Creek and the Belize River. The main attraction is a huge **guanacaste** or tubroos tree, a 40-metre-high, spreading hardwood that supports some 35 species. Hanging from its limbs are a huge range of bromeliads, orchids, ferns, cacti and strangler figs, which blossom spectacularly at the end of the rainy season. The bark is particularly hard and partially water-resistant, and it's traditionally favoured for use as feeding troughs, dugout canoes, and mortars for hulling rice. A good-sized guanacaste can produce two or three canoes; this specimen escaped being felled because its trunk split into three near the base. In season the guanacaste produces ear-shaped fruit, used as cattle feed.

Other botanical attractions include young mahogany trees, cohune palms, a cotton tree and quamwood, while the forest floor is a mass of ferns, mosses and vines. As the park is so close to the road your chances of seeing any four-footed **wildlife** are fairly slim, but armadillos, white-tailed deer, jaguarundi, opossums and agouti have nevertheless all been seen, and recently a small number of howler monkeys have used the park as a feeding ground. Birds also abound, with around fifty species, among them blue-crowned motmots, black-faced ant-thrushes, black-headed trogons, red-lored parrots and squirrel cuckoos.

There's a visitor centre near the entrance, with an orchid display, as well as four or five short **trails** to take you on tours through the park and along the banks of the Belize River. Sadly, there's only the single mature guanacaste tree, but the rest of the park is just as fascinating and offers a very accessible glimpse of the Belizean forest, as well as some inviting pools for a swim. To reach the park take any bus heading between Belmopan and either San Ignacio or Belize City, and get off at the junction of the Western Highway and the road leading to Belmopan, just a couple of kilometres from Belmopan itself.

Belmopan

From Guanacaste Park the main road splits in two: one branch (the Western Highway) pushes on towards San Ignacio and the Guatemalan border, while the other turns to the south towards the unlikely capital of **BELMOPAN**, where it becomes the Hummingbird Highway, heading all the way to Dangriga.

Belmopan was founded in 1970 after Hurricane Hattie swept much of Belize City into the sea. The government decided to use the disaster as a chance to move to higher ground and, in a Brasília-style bid to focus development on the interior, chose a site in the geographical heart of the country. The name of the city combines the words Belize and Mopan, the language spoken by the Maya of Cayo. The layout of the main government buildings, designed in the 1960s, is modelled on a Maya city, grouped around a central plaza, with a number of constructions incorporating a version of the traditional roof comb. These long, grey concrete administrative buildings, set away from the road, surrounded by grass, won their British architect an award. Now, as with so much of the architecture of that generation, they present a dismal, shoddy prospect, unsuited to their function. In classic new-town terms Belmopan was meant to symbolize the dawn of a new era, with tree-lined avenues, banks, a couple of embassies and telecommunications worthy of a world centre. Today it has all the essential ingredients bar one – people. Arriving in the market square or bus station, the first thing that strikes you is a sense of space. Very few Belizeans other than government officials (who had no option) have moved here. The population of this new capital was planned at 5000 for the first few years, eventually rising to 30,000. Today, however, it stands rooted at around 6000, as the majority of Belizeans still prefer the congestion of Belize City to the boredom of Belmopan.

Virtually the only reason (apart from changing buses) for any tourist to visit Belmopan was its Archeological Vault. Recent government spending cuts have forced its closure, leaving no permanent venue to display the outstanding range of archeological artefacts found in Belize, though the theatre opposite the market square sometimes has temporary displays. To find out what's available call the Archeology Department on ☎22106. The **Archives Department** (Mon–Fri 8am–noon & 1–4.30pm; ☎22247), 26–28 Unity Blvd, also welcomes visitors, with photographs and documents providing a fascinating glimpse of old Belize.

BELMOPAN

0   300 m

Practicalities

Buses from Belize City to San Ignacio, Benque Viejo and Dangriga all pass through Belmopan, and *Shaws* run a frequent service between Belmopan and San Ignacio, so there's at least one bus an hour in either direction from 4.30am to 6.30pm; the last bus from Belmopan to San Ignacio leaves at 9pm. It's a good idea to pick up some food or a cold drink here, especially if you're heading south – all the buses south originate in Belize City but take a break in Belmopan, ninety minutes down the road. Unless you've come to visit a government department, there's no particular reason to stay any longer than it takes your bus to leave.

The nearest **restaurant** is the *Caladium*, beside the *Novelos* bus terminal (where you can leave luggage), though *Yoli's*, next to the filling station, has more attractive surroundings. Nearby you'll also find *The International Cafe*, **banks** (including *Barclay's*, for cash advances), a bakery and a small **market**. At the top of the market square is the Ministry of Natural Resources, where you can buy **maps**; the **post office** is just behind here. The **British High Commission**

(☎22146) is situated on the North Ring, behind the National Assembly building, and the **US Embassy** has an office here (☎22617). The office of the **phone** company is beside the large satellite dish, and the **immigration** office is in the main administrative building. *Elisa's Travel* (☎22855; fax 23744), in the shopping centre near the *Bull Frog Inn* (see below) sell international **air tickets**.

Hotels in Belmopan cater for the needs and expense accounts of diplomats and aid officials; San Ignacio, less than an hour away, is far more interesting and less expensive. If you do have to stay here, the *El Rey Inn*, 23 Moho St (☎23438; ④), is the cheapest option. The best place in town is *Bull Frog Inn*, 23 Half Moon Ave (☎22111; fax 23155; ⑤–⑥), with comfortable rooms and a very pleasant restaurant and bar. The *Belmopan Hotel* (☎22340; fax 23066; ⑤), near the bus terminal, is rather run down, but has a pool.

Belmopan to San Ignacio

Beyond Belmopan the scenery becomes more rugged, with thickly forested ridges always in view to the south. The road stays close to the valley of the Belize River, passing through a series of villages: Roaring Creek, Teakettle, Ontario, Unitedville and Esperanza. There's been something of an accommodation boom, along this route, with a couple of long-established cottage-style lodges now joined by several newer enterprises.

Ten kilometres south of the highway, between Roaring and Barton creeks, **Tapir Mountain Nature Reserve** protects 2728 hectares of the northern foothills of the Maya Mountains, a rich, well-watered habitat covered in tropical moist forest and home to Belize's national symbols; Baird's tapir, the keel-billed toucan, the black orchid and the mahogany tree. The reserve, managed by the Belize Audubon Society, is accorded Belize's highest category of protected land. As one criterion of this is to "maintain natural processes in an undisturbed state", Tapir Mountain is not readily accessible to the public – call *BAS* (☎02/35004) for information. You can, however, **stay** nearby at *Pook's Hill Jungle Lodge* (☎081/2017; fax 08/22948; ⑦ including breakfast). The nine-kilometre track to the lodge is bumpy but in good condition, clearly signposted from **Teakettle** village at Mile 52 1/2; if you're travelling by bus call ahead and someone will pick you up. There's no electricity but hot water is provided by burning *cohune* nuts. The seven *cabañas*, in a small clearing above a terraced hillside overlooking the thickly forested Roaring River valley, have breathtaking views across the reserve to Mountain Pine Ridge. The location also held attractions for the ancient Maya – there's a plaza and some small structures behind the *cabañas*. There are more substantial ruins nearby that you can visit on horseback.

At Mile 56, just across Warrie Head Creek, is the entrance to *Warrie Head Ranch and Lodge* (☎02/75317; fax 75213; ⑥), formerly a logging camp but now a working farm, offering comfortable cabins and rooms, and canoe trips on Iguana Creek. On Barton Creek, at Mile 62, is *Caesar's Place*, Caesar and Antonieta Sherrard's cafe and guest house, with comfortable, attractive rooms, trailer hookups, space for camping, and delicious home cooking (☎092/2341; fax 3449; ⑤). Caesar makes jewellery and wood carvings and the gift shop is one of the best in Belize; it's a great place to pick up information about Guatemala and

Mexico, too. You can find out here about *Black Rock River Lodge*, Caesar's *other* place on the Macal River in the hills south of San Ignacio (see p.398).

At **Georgeville** a track leads south to **Mountain Pine Ridge** (see p.398). This is the Chiquibul Road, which reaches deep into the forest, crossing the Macal River at the Guacamallo Bridge, and it's here that you should get off if you're hitching to **Augustine/Douglas Silva**, headquarters of the Mountain Pine Ridge Forest Reserve. The road is well used by villagers, foresters and tourists, but you're only allowed to camp at the entrance to the reserve or in Augustine. You really need four-wheel-drive, or a mountain bike, to properly explore this fascinating and exciting area of hills and jungle. Eleven kilometres along the road is *Mountain Equestrian Trails* (☎092/3310; fax 23361; in US: ☎1-800/838-3918; ⑨ including breakfast), where you'll find expensive but very comfortable accommodation in a tropical forest setting, on the edge of the Pine Ridge; the four thatched *cabañas*, with hot water and lit by oil lamps, are some of the best in Belize. If you want to get even closer to nature *MET* also has an idyllic **tented camp**, *The Divide Limited*, which is the base for low-impact wildlife safaris, taking you deep into the Chiquibul forest. The basic price is US$55 per person, including three good meals and service charge (and there are excellent packages available) but to get the most out of the experience you should consider a horse-back or rafting trip with *The Divide's* expert guides – Jim Bevis, owner of *MET*, led the first commercial crossing of the Maya Mountain divide. As the name implies, *MET* is primarily oriented towards **horse-riding** vacations and is unquestionably Belize's premier riding centre, with superb riding on nearly 100km of forest trails encompassing various ecosystems.

Jim and Marguerite Bevis, who own *MET*, are also founder members of the **Slate Creek Preserve**, a privately owned tract of over 3000 acres of limestone karst forest, bordering the Mountain Pine Ridge Forest Reserve. Local landowners, recognizing the importance of conservation and sustainable development, have cooperated voluntarily to establish the preserve, following the guidelines in UNESCO's Man and the Biosphere Programme. This project, though ambitious, is just one example of how concern for the environment in Belize is being translated into practical projects benefiting local people.

Central Farm, Santa Elena and Maya Mountain Lodge

At **Central Farm**, Belize's agricultural research centre, there are often vacancies for VSO volunteers (see p.6 in *Basics*). Past here, on the right, is the road to Spanish Lookout, a successful Mennonite farming community. At the side of the highway is the **Holdfast Camp**, formerly a British Army base and now location of Cayo's *Matthew Spain* charter airstrip (also served by a *Maya* flight).

SANTA ELENA is San Ignacio's sister town, on the eastern bank of the Macal River, which is crossed by the Hawksworth Bridge, built in 1949 and still the only road suspension bridge in Belize. Though quite a large town, Santa Elena has none of the attractions of San Ignacio, but it is the site of the turn-off to the **Cristo Rey road** towards Augustine/Douglas Silva and the Mountain Pine Ridge. Two kilometres along this road is the excellent *Maya Mountain Lodge* (☎092/2164; fax 2029; ⑨–⑦), run by Bart and Suzi Mickler. Set in rich tropical forest, it provides a fascinating introduction to the wildlife of Belize. Accommodation is in colourfully decorated individual *cabañas*, each with a private bath, electricity and hot water; the larger and slightly cheaper *Parrot's Perch* cabin is ideal for groups. Delicious meals are served in an open-sided dining room, which provides another opportunity for bird-watching; motmots, aracaris and trogons fly just metres away from the table. The lodge hosts student groups and has a library and lecture area; they especially welcome families, with plenty of activities for kids, including the best illustrated trail guide in Belize. You can safely let your children use it to explore the forest and hilltop ruin above the cabins. There are great packages available, and if there's space, independent travellers (unless part of a group or in a rented car) can receive a 50 percent discount if carrying this guide. For more information, write to PO Box 46, San Ignacio, Cayo District, Belize.

Though most visitors choose to stay in San Ignacio itself, there are a few **hotels** in Santa Elena. By far the best of these is the *Snooty Fox Guest House* (☎092/2150; fax 3556; ④–⑤), high above the Macal River at 64 George Price Ave, where the spotless rooms are very good value. There's secure car parking, a restaurant, good swimming and the best value canoe rental in the area – just Bz$40 per day, including life jacket and ice chest.

San Ignacio and Cayo District

About 35km west of Belmopan, at the heart of Cayo District on the west bank of the Macal River, stands **SAN IGNACIO**, a friendly, relaxed town that draws together much of the best in inland Belize. The focus of tourism in west-central Belize, it's surrounded by fast-flowing rivers that tumble towards the coast, and the forested hills that begin here roll all the way across Guatemala and south to the Maya Mountains. It's an ideal base from which to explore inland Belize, offering good food, inexpensive hotels and restaurants, and frequent bus connections. The population is typically varied: Mestizos dominate and Spanish is the main language, but you'll also hear plenty of English and see Creoles, Mopan Maya, Mennonites, Lebanese, Chinese and even Sri Lankans. The evenings are cool and the days fresh – a welcome break from the sweltering heat of the coast – and there's a virtual absence of mosquitoes and other biting insects.

Until the Western Highway was built in the 1930s (the western part of the road wasn't paved until the 1980s), local transport was by mule or water. It could take ten days of paddling to reach San Ignacio from Belize City, though later small steamers made the trip. Nowadays, river traffic, which had almost died out, is enjoying something of a revival as increasing numbers of tourists take river trips.

Some history

Like many places in Belize, San Ignacio probably started life as a logging camp. A map drawn up in 1787 simply states that the Indians of this general area were "in friendship with the Baymen". Later it was a centre for the shipment of chicle, the sap of the sapodilla tree and basis of chewing gum. The self-reliant *chicleros*, as the collectors of chicle were called, knew the forest intimately, including the location of most, if not all, Maya ruins. When the demand for Maya artefacts sent black-market prices rocketing later this century, many of them turned to looting.

The name originally given to this central area was **El Cayo**, the same word that the Spanish used to describe the offshore islands. (San Ignacio town is usually referred to as **Cayo** by locals, and this is the name you'll often see indicated on buses.) It's an apt description of the area, in a peninsula between two converging rivers, and also a measure of how isolated the early settlers felt, surrounded by the forest. It wasn't just the jungle they had to fear; the forest was also home to a

Maya group who valued their independence. **Tipu**, a Maya city that probably stood at Negroman on the Macal River, was the capital of the province of Dzuluinicob, where for years the Indians resisted attempts to Christianize them. The early wave of conquest, in 1544, made only a little impact here, and the area was a centre of rebellion in the following decades. Two Spanish friars arrived in 1618, but a year later one of them found that the entire population was still practising idolatry. The idols were smashed and the native priests flogged, but by the end of the year the Maya had again driven out the Spaniards. Four years later, Maya from Tipu worked as guides in an expedition against the Itzá and in 1641 the friars returned, determined to Christianize the inhabitants. To express their defiance the pagan priests conducted a mock mass, using tortillas, and then threw out the friars. From then on little is known about Tipu, although it must have remained an outpost of Maya civilization, providing refuge to other Maya fleeing Spanish rule. It retained a measure of independence until 1707 when the population was forcibly removed to Lake Petén Itzá. There are many other Maya ruins, including Cahal Pech and Pilar, in the area.

Arrival and information

Buses stop in the marketplace, behind the *Hotel Belmoral*. *Batty* (☎2508) and *Novelos* run regular express services to Belize City stopping only in Belmopan (3hr), and some to the border (30min), more or less hourly throughout the day (the first to the border at 7.30am). *Shaws* also run a good service to and from Belmopan, with at least five buses a day. If you're heading for the ruins of Xunantunich or the border, a shared **taxi** only costs Bz$4 (pick-up by the *Hotel Belmoral*) and hitching is easy. **Car rental** is offered by *Western Auto Rental* (☎3134). San Ignacio's **airstrip**, generally used by charter planes, is also served by a daily *Maya* flight to Belize (☎02/44234). For international **air tickets** make for *Universal Travel*, 8 Mossiah St (☎3884; fax 3885).

The **telephone area code** for San Ignacio is ☎092.

Most facilities are on Burns Ave; notably the *Belize Bank* (Mon–Thurs 8am–1pm, Fri 8am–1pm & 3–6pm), and the *Atlantic Bank*. If you need Guatemalan quetzals you can save time at the border by using the services of the **moneychangers** who'll approach you; they are honest and reliable but it's better to do the transaction inside a restaurant. The *Arts and Crafts of Central America*, two doors from *Eva's*, sells reasonably priced Guatemalan **gifts**, books and **maps**. Past here, under the *Tropicool Bar*, *Caesar's Gift Shop* sells the same jewellery and wood carvings as at his place on the Western Highway; you can also find out about *Black Rock River Lodge*, in the Macal River Valley (see p.398). The *BTL* office is above the *St Martin's Credit Union* on Far West St (Mon–Fri 8am–noon & 1–4pm, Sat 8am–noon); you'll find the **post office** above the police station, on the San Ignacio side of the bridge, and a public **phone** at the taxi rank nearby.

Accommodation

There are more than a dozen **hotels** in San Ignacio, most of which offer very good value. Before you do anything here, though, step into *Eva's* bar and restaurant at 22 Burns Ave (☎2267), and have a word with owner Bob Jones, who knows all there is to know about San Ignacio and the surrounding area. Whether

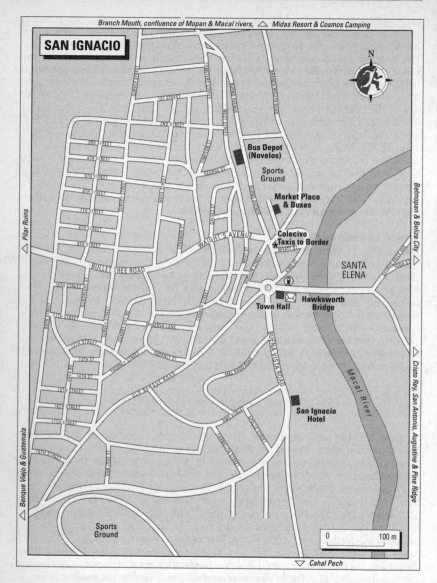

Branch Mouth, confluence of Mopan & Macal rivers, △ Midas Resort & Cosmos Camping

SAN IGNACIO

1ST STREET
2ND STREET
3RD STREET
4TH STREET
5TH STREET
6TH STREET
7TH STREET
8TH STREET
9TH STREET
11TH STREET
BULLET TREE ROAD
WAIGHT'S AVENUE
WYATT ST.
KING ST.
10TH STREET
12TH STREET
MINERVA LANE
JOHNNY ST.
13TH ST.
14TH ST.
15TH STREET
MEL HAN ROAD
OLD BENQUE ROAD
AMA STREET
16TH STREET
17TH STREET
18TH STREET
SAN JOSE ST.

HUDSON STREET
BURNS AVENUE
HENRY ST.
BURNS SOUTH ROAD

Bus Depot (Novelos)

Sports Ground

Market Place & Buses

Colecivo Taxis to Border

△ Pilar Ruins

SANTA ELENA

🅿
✉ Hawksworth Bridge
Town Hall

BUENA VISTA ROAD

San Ignacio Hotel

Macal River

◁ Benque Viejo & Guatemala

▷ Belmopan & Belize City

▷ Cristo Rey, San Antonio, Augustine & Pine Ridge

WESTERN HIGHWAY

Sports Ground

0 _____ 100 m

▽ Cahal Pech

N

you're in search of a cheap overnight stop or a country cottage for a week of luxury, Bob will be able to point you in the right direction.

ACCOMMODATION IN TOWN

Central Hotel, 24 Burns Ave (☎2253). Reasonable hotel with hot water and shared baths. Good local information and the balcony is great for observing activity in the street below. ②.

Hi-Et Hotel, West St, behind *Eva's* (☎2828). Family-run hotel with one downstairs room and four basic rooms upstairs, each with a tiny balcony, all sharing a cold water bathroom. The best of the really rockbottom places; it also has a laundry service. ②.

Martha's Guest House, West St, behind *Eva's* (☎3647). Three comfortable rooms in Martha and John August's home. Guests can use the small kitchen with permission – you can rent the entire house for a very reasonable rate. The homely atmosphere means rooms are much in demand. Trips to the Pine Ridge or Caracol are cheaper than most, and they have a range of good books on Belize. Also a good drop-off laundry. ③.

Midas Resort, Branch Mouth Rd (☎3172; fax 3845). The only resort actually in town, and the best value in Cayo. Very comfortable Maya-style thatched *cabañas* with private bathroom, set on the riverbank; camping also available. Within walking distance of the town but with the peace and quiet of the countryside. Accepts *Visa/MC*. ④.

PACZ Hotel, 4 Far West St, two blocks behind *Eva's* (☎2110). Great bargain, especially for three sharing (no single rates). Pete, the owner, runs adventurous caving and rafting tours, and rents bikes. Just five rooms, with hot water, so call ahead if you can. ③.

Princesa Hotel, 3 Burns Ave (☎2256; fax 2760). The first hotel you see as you come in to town. Excellent budget rooms, the best deal in town for private hot shower. Shared bathrooms are planned downstairs. ③.

Tropicool Hotel, Burns Ave, 75m past *Eva's* (☎3052). Beneath the bar of the same name (but no noise from above). Four bright, clean budget rooms with ceiling fan and shared hot water bathrooms, a sitting room with TV, and a laundry area. Discounts on rum drinks from the bar for guests. ②.

Venus Hotel, 29 Burns Ave (☎3203; fax 2225). Three-storey hotel with good rates, and the best deal in town if you want to stay a week. Some rooms have a private bath and a few have a/c and TV. The rear balcony has views over the market down to the river. Ask here about *Cahal Pech Village* (see below). Accepts *Visa/MC*. ④.

ACCOMMODATION AROUND CAHAL PECH

The hotels below are all within 3km of San Ignacio, and are listed in the order you approach them on the road to Cahal Pech Maya site (see p.396).

San Ignacio Hotel, 18 Buena Vista St (☎2034; fax 2134). In a superb location, just ten-minutes' walk uphill from the town centre, with views over the Macal River valley. San Ignacio's premier hotel, renowned locally for hosting Queen Elizabeth on her last visit. Spacious, comfortable rooms (some with balcony and a/c), and a dining room terrace overlooking the pool (Bz$5 non-guests) and gardens. Guided trails down to the river and up to a forested hilltop are ideal for early morning bird-watching. Accepts *Visa/MC/AmEx*. ⑥–⑦.

Piache Hotel, across the road from the *San Ignacio Hotel*, higher up the hill (☎2032; fax 2685). Very friendly place with great views, run by Ethel and Godsman Ellis, whose daughter Zoila wrote *On Heroes, Lizards and Passion* (see "Books" in *Contexts*) – they're experts on Garifuna history and will organize trips for guests. The hotel has a flower-filled garden, complete with a bar. Unfortunately, a little overpriced compared to others in the area. ⑤.

Cahal Pech Village, Cahal Pech Hill, below the site (☎3740; fax 2225). Well designed "village" of comfortable wood-and-thatch *cabañas* on a hillside overlooking San Ignacio. Each *cabaña* – named after a Belizean Maya site – has a wooden deck and hammock; interiors are decorated with Guatemalan textiles. All have electricity and private bath with hot water. The 16-room hotel is equally comfortable. To book, ask at *Venus* in town. Accepts *Visa/MC*. ⑤.

Rose's Guest House, by the entrance to the site (☎ & fax 2282). Friendly bed and breakfast in a good location. Clean, simple rooms (shared bath) are a little bare to justify the price. ⑤.

The Log Cabins, just past Cahal Pech, on the road to Benque (☎2289; fax 2823). Solid log-built double cabins with hot water. Very roomy and comfortable. Guests can order good home-cooked breakfasts and packed lunches. ⑤.

Windy Hill Cottages, just beyond and across from the *Log Cabins*, 3km from town (☎2017; fax 3080). The first of the "out-of-town" resorts (others are covered on p.397) with 25 very comfortable cabins. Many tours on offer, and nature trails through the grounds. There's also a small pool and a recreation room with cable TV. Accepts *Visa/MC*. ⑦.

Eating

Along with its budget hotels, San Ignacio has several good, inexpensive **restuarants**. If your hotel lets you cook, then the Saturday **market** is worth a visit; it's the best in Belize, with local farmers bringing in fresh-picked produce. For general groceries *Celina's Store*, two blocks from the *Tropicool Bar* down Burns Ave, has the widest selection and the best prices. In the centre of town are plenty of **fruit stands** laden with bananas, oranges and papayas. You can pick up good fresh **bread** and baked goods oppposite *Eva's* on Burns Ave, and most afternoons small boys will be around selling freshly cooked *empanadas* and *tamales*.

Eva's Bar, 22 Burns Ave. Good, reasonably priced, filling meals, including chilli, chicken, tasty Creole dishes, and some veggie options. Usually busy, it's a great place to meet travellers and local tour operators. There's a public phone and a gift shop.

Martha's Kitchen, West St, behind *Eva's*. Under the guest house of the same name and just as well-run. Great breakfasts with strong, locally-grown coffee, pizza and traditional food, and delicious cakes for dessert. The patio tables are a popular place to meet for breakfast.

Maxim's, Far West St behind *Martha's*. One of the best of San Ignacio's numerous Chinese restaurants, serving large portions.

Sandcastle Bar, on the riverbank, behind the market square. Slightly more expensive than other places, but worth it for good steak and seafood. It's also an American-style sports bar, so you can get good *nachos* and other such bar snacks.

Serendib Restaurant, 27 Burns Ave. Excellent Sri Lankan curries and seafood at very reasonable prices. Good service too.

The Running W Restaurant, *San Ignacio Hotel* , 18 Buena Vista St Excellent food in tranquil surroundings, and not at all expensive. Breakfasts are especially good value.

Drinking and nightlife

As well as the restaurants listed above, most of which double as **bars**, there's the British influenced *Tropicool Bar*, with a dartboard, pool table and an evening happy hour; the *Western Bar*, overlooking the market, is a typically Belizean **club**: dark and extremely noisy. The *Blue Angel Disco*, on Hudson St, now thankfully soundproofed, often has bands at weekends, but has lost its pre-eminent position in the local music scene to the *Cahal Pech Tavern*, a huge thatched structure dominating the hilltop next to *Cahal Pech Village*. It's a regular venue for some of the best bands in Belize – and soundproofed for the benefit of *Village* guests.

Around San Ignacio

San Ignacio's best feature is its location. The river and the surrounding countryside, with hills, farms, streams and forest, are equally inviting, and there are many ways to enjoy them – on foot, by boat or even on horseback. You can easily use the town as a base for day trips, but if you'd like to stay in the countryside, numerous guest houses and ranches in the area offer **cottage-style accommodation** and organized trips. On the whole standards are very high and most of them cater mainly to North Americans on packages who come here after a week on the reef, a phenomenon known as a "surf and turf holiday". Prices are around US$100 a day, but if you can afford it then your every need will be looked after. They're often booked up in the peak season (Christmas to Easter) but, if open, can offer reduced prices in low season. Most offer horse-riding, bird-watching, canoeing, good home cooking and various trips into the surrounding area. All are well signposted from San Ignacio.

The countryside around Cayo is ideal for exploring on **horseback** which, as with canoeing, can be arranged by the big resorts at a price. If you're on a tight budget one of the best deals is offered by Charlie Collins, who runs *Easy Rider*. Charlie knows the area well, her horses are cared for and she carefully matches riders to the right horse. Contact her by cellular phone (☎014/8276) or through *Eva's* bar. Fred Prost, who runs the *Parrot Nest* cabins in Bullet Tree Falls, also has horses for rent, and he knows who's reliable among the local guides. Again ask at *Eva's*, who also rent good-quality **mountain bikes** (Bz$5 per hour). For the **Maya sites** around San Ignacio, the most reliable and recommended operators are *International Archaeological Tours*, 23 Burns Ave (☎3991; fax 2760).

Barton Creek Cave

Of the many **cave trips** available in Cayo the most fascinating is to **Barton Creek Cave**, accessible only by river, and only on a tour (around 4–5hr; Bz$45 per person; minimum three; contact *Martha's Guest House*). Your guide is David, a multi-lingual Belizean who'll carefully and responsibly show you the astonishing Maya artefacts in the cave. First you drive through the traditional Mennonite settlement of **Upper Barton Creek** to the cave entrance, framed by jungle at the far side of a jade-green pool, where you board the canoe. The river is navigable for about 1600m, and in a couple of places the roof comes so low you have to crouch right down in the canoe, before ending in a gallery blocked by a huge rockfall. The clear, slow-moving river fills most of the cave width, though the roof soars in places 100m above your head, the way ahead illuminated by a 1,000,000 candlepower lamp. Several **Maya burials** line the banks; the most awe-inspiring indicated by a skull set in a natural rock bridge used by the Maya to reach the sacred site. You can climb up to view the remains, some of which are surrounded by pottery vessels, but only from the opposite bank as, like all caves in Belize, Barton Creek Cave is a registered archeological site, and nothing must be touched or removed. If it's been raining a **subterranean waterfall** cascades over the rocks – a truly unforgettable sight. Beyond lie many more miles of passage-ways, only accessible on a fully equipped expedition.

Branch Mouth

Perhaps the easiest introduction to this region is to take the twenty-minute walk to **Branch Mouth**, where the Macal and Mopan rivers merge to form the Belize River. The track leads north from the football field, past rich farmland, with thick vegetation, tropical flowers and butterflies on either side. At the confluence of the rivers is a huge tree, with branches arching over the jade water. A rusting iron mooring ring in the trunk is a reminder of the past importance of river transport; now there are swallows skimming the surface, parrots flying overhead and scores of tiny fish in the water. The scar of raw earth on the opposite bank is evidence of severe flooding in recent years, when the river has risen within metres of the suspension bridge and has even inundated the streets of San Ignacio.

If you're looking for somewhere to **camp**, it's only a fifteen-minute walk from town along Branch Mouth Road to the *Cosmos Campground* (☎092/2116; ①), where you'll find decent showers, flush toilets and a kitchen area. As well as tent space (Bz$6), there are eight clean, simple cabins, some with private bath (①–②). The site extends right down to the river, and you can rent canoes, bicycles and horses at affordable prices. Ask at the manager's house (signed) on the way; he himself offers budget rooms (①) and sells delicious fruit juices.

If you walk all the way along to the end of Branch Mouth Road you're within hailing distance of *Las Casitas Resort*, just across the river – they'll send a canoe to pick you up . There's a range of accommodation here, from camping (①) to private *cabañas* (④) overlooking the river, together with a pagoda-style thatched bar and restaurant. Don't be afraid to ask for a discount. The owners, the Obando family, have lived in the area for generations and really enjoy imparting their extensive knowledge of local history, archeology and wildlife.

Cahal Pech

Twenty minutes out of town to the southwest, along the Benque road, lie the ruins of **Cahal Pech**. The name means "place of ticks" in Mopan Maya, and is certainly not how the elite families who ruled here in Classic times would have known it. Entering the site through the forest, surrounded by temple platforms and the remains of dwellings, your gaze is drawn to **Structure 1**, the Audiencia. If you're used to seeing finely executed, exposed stonework at reconstructed Maya sites then the thick overcoat of lime-mortar on buildings here may come as a bit of a shock. The Classic Maya, however, viewed bare stone facings as ugly and unfinished; they covered all surfaces with a thick coat of mortar or stucco.

Cahal Pech was the royal acropolis-palace of an elite Maya family during the Classic period, and there's evidence of monumental construction from at least as early as the Middle Preclassic, 400 BC. Most of what you see dates from the late ninth century AD. There's a **visitors centre** and small museum (daily 8am–4pm; Bz$10). For a cultural experience of an entirely different nature you can stroll across to the adjacent hilltop for a drink at the *Cahal Pech Tavern* (see p.394).

The Mopan River: El Pilar and Buenavista del Cayo ruins

To the west, the village of **Bullet Tree Falls** on the Mopan River is a five-kilometre walk or short ride away from San Ignacio. From here you can visit the ruins of **El Pilar**, the largest Maya site in the Belize River valley, covering 40 hectares and including 70 major structures grouped around 33 plazas. El Pilar's long sequence of construction began in the Preclassic era and continued right through to the Terminal Classic, when some of the largest existing temples were completely rebuilt. A causeway runs west into Guatemala, and it's easy to stray over the border. Excavation and investigation have taken place, and over the long term parts of the site will be restored and an entry fee charged. For the moment you can reach the ruins by a rough (motorable) road climbing the escarpment, 15km from Bullet Tree; ask the caretaker to show you around.

The Cahal Pech site is known to have been a satellite of a wider political region, whose centre was **Buenavista del Cayo**, on the east bank of the Mopan. These ruins are on private land and to visit you need permission from the owner, Pablo Guerra, a shopkeeper in Benque. The site was excavated between 1984 and 1989 by Jennifer Taschek and Joseph Ball, who discovered a palace, ball courts, carved stelae, plazas and courtyards. A number of important burial items were also found here, including the famous Jauncy vase, now in Belmopan. There's also evidence that the Maya established workshops to mass-produce pottery on the site. Since excavation most of the structures have been covered over but there is a charming palace and courtyard in a glade. You can easily visit the site on horseback; *Easy Rider* (see p.395) runs tours.

Rushing down from the Guatemalan border, the Mopan offers excellent possibilities for **white-water rafting**. *Clarissa Falls* (see below) rents rafts and can arrange trips, or see Pete Zubrzycki at *PACZ Hotel*, San Ignacio (☎092/2210).

ACCOMMODATION

There is less accommodation along the Mopan branch of the Belize River than there is along the Macal (see below), but what's available is more within the reach of the budget traveller and no less special for that. The resorts below are listed in order according to distance from San Ignacio.

Parrot Nest, just past Bullet Tree Falls, 5km from San Ignacio (☎092/3702). Fantastic thatched cabins built, very securely, up a tree. Shared bathroom with hot shower. You can rent horses and ride through the forest across the river to visit the ruins of Pilar; you'll need a guide. Trucks and cars leave for Bullet Tree from San Ignacio, and it's easy to hitch. ④.

Clarissa Falls, along a signed track to the right off the Benque road, just before the *Chaa Creek* turn (☎092/3916). Restful place, popular with Europeans. Simple, clean, stick-and-thatch cabins, camping, and a cabin with hammock ($8); shared hot water showers. Excellent value if you're on a budget. The restaurant serves fantastic home cooking, and there's a bar. Horse-riding, canoeing, rafting and tubing at reasonable rates. ①–④.

Nabitunich, down a track just beyond the *Clarissa Falls* turn, off the Benque road (☎093/2309; fax 3096). Mayan for "Stone House", this is the best of the resorts on the Mopan River. Camping or simple, beautiful cabins set in gardens with spectacular views of the Castillo at Xunantunich. Run by friendly Rudy and Margaret Juan, *Nabitunich* is deservedly popular with bird-watchers and archeologists: the team from UCLA currently excavating Xunantunich stay in their own cabins here. ①–⑥.

The Macal River

If the idea of a day or more on the river appeals, then any of the resorts can **rent canoes**, but by far the best-value guided trip is offered by *Toni's River Adventures*; contact Toni at *Eva's* bar. For Bz$25 per person you will be expertly paddled upriver for a whole day and you'll see far more wildlife under Toni or Clifford's guidance than you could alone. You can also make the trip all the way to Belize City: a week of hard paddling, camping on the riverbank each night.

This trip is the best way to visit the **Rainforest Medicine Trail** (☎092/3870), a botanical version of the Belize Zoo, taking you through the forest along the Macal riverbank to seek out many of the plants and explain their medicinal properties. The trail is dedicated to Don Eligio Panti, a Maya bush doctor (*curandero*) who passed on his skills to Dr Rosita Arvigo at *Ix Chel Tropical Research Station*, where the trail now begins, taking in a wide range of traditional healing plants, some of them now used in modern medicine. The medical knowledge of the Maya was extensive, and the trail is fascinating: there are vines that provide fresh water like a tap; poisonwood, with oozing black sap, its antidote always growing nearby; and the bark of the negrito tree, once sold for its weight in gold in Europe as a cure for dysentery. You'll also see specimens of the tropical hardwoods of the jungle that have been exploited for economic reasons. Today, several plants from the Belize rainforest are being investigated as potential treatment for AIDS; Rosita and the staff at *Ix Chel*, in collaboration with the New York Botanical Garden, are at the forefront of this research. The more mundane products of the forest range from herbal teas to blood tonic. *Traveller's Tonic*, a preventative for diarrhoea, really works, as does *Jungle Salve* for insect bites.

A visit to the marvellous **Chaa Creek Natural History Centre** (daily 8am–5pm; Bz$10), in the grounds of *Chaa Creek*, is the best introduction to Cayo's history, geography and wildlife. If you're spending more than a couple of days in the area try to see this first. With fascinating and accurate displays of the region's flora and fauna, vivid archeological and geological maps, and a scale model of the Macal Valley, it also has the **Butterfly Breeding Centre** where you can admire the magnificent Blue Morpho. Call (☎092/2037) to check on current events.

ACCOMMODATION

Crystal Paradise Resort, in the village of Cristo Rey, on the east bank of the river (☎092/2823; fax 2772). Owned by the Belizean Tut family, who built the *cabañas* and lovely thatch-roofed dining room. Two delicious meals a day included. Electricity and hot water, and some cabins have private baths. Victor will pick you up in San Ignacio in his motorized canoe if you call before 4.30pm, or you can hitch along the Cristo Rey road; a taxi costs about Bz$25. ⑦.

Chaa Creek Cottages, on an unpaved turnoff 10km along the road to Benque (☎092/2037; fax 2501). Whitewashed wood and stucco *cabañas* in beautiful grounds high above the Macal River, with a justly deserved reputation for luxury and ambience. There's a fine restaurant and bar with spacious outdoor deck. One of the first cottage resorts in Cayo, it's often featured in TV travel shows, and owners Mick and Lucy Fleming are likeable, modest celebrities. Cookery course in Belizean specialities available. June–Nov 40 percent discount. ⑧.

Macal River Campsite, on the east bank, near *Chaa Creek* (☎092/2037; fax 2501). The brainchild of Mick of *Chaa Creek*, with roomy tents under tarps on raised wooden bases. It's camping in comfort, with hot water in clean, tiled bathrooms, and oil lamps in the evening. Big meals are included – though you have to do your own washing up. US$45 per person. ⑦.

duPlooy's, further along the *Chaa Creek* track (☎092/3101; fax 3301). First-rate accommodation, beautifully located in farmland and forest on the banks of the Macal. Spacious private bungalows with deck, king-size bed and sofa bed, fridge and coffee-maker; Jungle Lodge rooms, each with private porch (2 rooms connect for more space); and the Pink House (which can be rented by groups), with 6 rooms, each with a double and single bed. Also a kitchen and a large, screened porch. The deck extending from the bar, overlooking the river cliffs, is a superb bird-watching site. Activities include canoeing, horse-riding and bird-watching in addition to organized trips to Cayo's attractions. ⑤–⑨.

Ek Tun (☎091/2002; in US: ☎303/442-6150; PO Box 18748, Boulder, Colorado 80308-8748), in a remote location on the east bank of the Macal, not directly accessible by road. The most luxurious stick-and-thatch *cabañas* in the country; only two, to preserve the sublime isolation. Each cottage has two bedrooms, one in the loft, hot water shower and deck overlooking the garden. Trails lead through the forest and along the river cliffs, where you can observe the rare orange-breasted falcon; gourmet dinner is served under the thatch overlooking the river. This is the highest easily navigable point on the Macal River, and you can canoe down to San Ignacio. The 200-acre tract of forest borders the Mountain Pine Ridge Reserve, and there is much evidence of Maya occupation in the area. ⑦.

Black Rock River Lodge, west bank of the Macal River (☎092/2341; fax 3449). Not directly accessible by road, but a twenty-minute hike (the bags go on horseback) from the end of the dirt road from San Ignacio. Set high above the river with stunning views of the jungle-clad limestone cliffs of the upper Macal valley, deluxe *cabañas*, have private hot shower and floors made of smooth stones from the river. Shared bath *cabañas* and a bunkhouse (Bz$20) also available. Call at *Caesar's Place* on the Western Highway (see p.388) or the gift shop in San Ignacio (see p.391) to make transport arrangements. It's a fairly easy hike from here to Vaca Falls, or Vaca Cave, which contains some Maya pottery. ⑤–⑥.

The Mountain Pine Ridge

South of San Ignacio the **Mountain Pine Ridge Forest Reserve** is a spectacular range of rolling hills and jagged peaks that runs parallel to the border with Guatemala. The peaks are some of the oldest rocks in Central America, granite intrusions that have thrust up from below and are part of the bedrock that underlies the entire isthmus. In amongst this there are also some sections of limestone, riddled with superb caves, the most accessible of which are the **Rio Frio Caves** in Augustine/Douglas Silva. For the most part the landscape is semi-open, a mixture of grassland and pine forest growing in nutrient-poor, sandy soil, although in the warmth of the river valleys the vegetation is thicker gallery forest, giving way to rainforest south of the Guacamallo Bridge. Here fertility is ensured by plentiful rainfall, which also renders the smooth, sandy roads in the Pine Ridge difficult to use in the wet season. The rains feed a number of small streams, most of which run off into the Macal and Belize rivers. One of the most scenic is the **Rio On**, rushing over cataracts and forming a gorge – a sight of tremendous natural beauty within view of the picnic shelter. On the northern side of the ridge are the **Thousand-Foot Falls**: actually over 1600ft (488m) and the highest in Central America. The long, slender plume of water becomes lost in the valley below, giving rise to their other, more poetic name – **Hidden Valley Falls**.

The Pine Ridge is virtually uninhabited but for three or four tourist lodges and one small settlement, **Augustine/Douglas Silva**, site of the reserve headquarters. The whole area is perfect for **hiking** and **mountain biking**, but **camping** is allowed only at Augustine/Douglas Silva and at the Mai Gate, beyond San Antonio, and officially you need permission from the forestry department in Belmopan (in practice you'll almost certainly be allowed to if you ask nicely when you arrive). It's fairly hard – though rewarding – to explore this part of the country on your own, and unless you have a car or come here on an organized tour, you may have to rely on hitching. If you set off early you should be able to make it from Augustine/Douglas Silva to the Thousand-Foot Falls and back in a day, hitching some of the way and then walking the last few kilometres. To explore the many forestry roads branching off the main reserve road, you need the 1:50,000 topographic maps from the Ministry of Natural Resources in Belmopan.

Getting there

Though the cheapest way to explore the Mountain Pine Ridge is by **hitching** in from Georgeville or along the Cristo Rey road from Santa Elena, you'll need to set off early and won't get any further than Thousand-Foot Falls. Keen to encourage responsible tourism, forestry officers are allowing visitors to travel to Augustine/Douglas Silva in the forestry vehicles that generally leave San Ignacio in the early morning; contact the conservation officer in Belmopan (☎08/22079) or San Ignacio (☎092/3280). In Augustine/Douglas Silva you can camp or stay in the **bunkhouse**, and it's an easy walk from here to the Rio Frio Caves.

The best way to get around is to rent a **mountain bike** in San Ignacio; the bus to San Antonio (see below) takes bikes, or you could put them in the back of a passing pick-up truck. It's also possible to **hike** in, of course, and **organized tours** can be arranged: if you're staying at any of the Cayo resorts a full day's tour of the Pine Ridge costs around US$40–50 per person for a group of four; more if you want to go to Caracol. Tommy (contact through *Eva's* bar) can take you on a superb tour for about half the price. *Batty* buses (☎02/74924) sometimes organize trips to the Pine Ridge at weekends and holidays.

Recent road improvements in the Pine Ridge, particularly on the road to Caracol, make a trip in a **rental car** perfectly feasible – most of the year. Always check road conditions and heed the advice of the Forestry officials.

San Antonio and Pacbitún

There are two **entrance roads** to the reserve, one from the village of **Georgeville**, on the Western Highway, and the other from Santa Elena, along the Cristo Rey road and through the village of **SAN ANTONIO**. The villagers here are descendents of Maya (Uxcawal is their name, in their own language) refugees, who fled the Caste Wars in Yucatán in 1847; many people still speak Yucatec. Their story is told in a fascinating book *After 100 Years*, a written account of San Antonio's oral history, by Alfonso Antonio Tzul. Nestled in the Macal River valley, surrounded by scattered *milpa* farms, with the forested Maya Mountains in the background, the village is poised to become a base for hiking and horseback tours along old *chiclero* trails. The home of the late Don Eligio Panti, the famous *curandero* who died recently at the age of 108, it's a superb place to learn about traditional Maya healing methods, not least by going to see the Garcia sisters, who grew up in the village determined not to let Maya culture be swamped by outside influence. They run the *Chichan Ka Guest House* at the approach to the village (☎092/3310; fax 08/23361; ③); simple but comfortable **rooms** (some with private bath) and panoramic views of the Maya Mountains. It's a very relaxing place to stay; meals are prepared in the traditional way, always accompanied with corn *tortillas*, often using organic produce from the garden – and courses are offered in the gathering and use of medicinal plants. The sisters are also renowned for their slate carvings, and their **gift shop** has become a favourite tour group stop. Next door is the small **Tanah Museum** (Bz$6), proceeds from which go towards the establishment of a 500-acre Botanical Garden and Maya Reserve. The *Mesh* **bus to San Antonio** (Mon–Sat 10.30am & 2.30pm; 1hr) departs from the market in San Ignacio, returning at 6am and 7am.

Three kilometres east of San Antonio, on the road to the Pine Ridge, are the ruins of **Pacbitún**, a major ceremonial centre. One of the oldest known Preclassic sites in Belize (1000 BC), it continued to flourish throughout the Classic period, and Maya farming terraces and farmhouse mounds can be seen in the hills all around. Pacbitún, meaning "stones set in the earth", has at least 24 temple pyramids, a ball court and several raised causeways. The tombs of two elite women yielded the largest haul of musical instruments ever found in one place; drums, flutes, ocarinas (wind instruments) and the first discovery of Maya maracas. Though the site is not open to casual visitors, José Tzul, who lives on the right just before the entrance, runs *Blue Ridge Mountain Rider* (☎092/2322) and can arrange horseback tours of the area, taking in Pacbitún (US$50 per day).

The forest reserve

Not far beyond San Antonio, the roads meet and begin a steady climb towards the **entrance to the reserve** proper. One kilometre beyond the junction is a new **campsite** (①) run by Fidencio and Petronila Bol, a delightful couple, and owners of *Bol's Nature Tours*. Fidencio used to work as a caretaker at several Maya sites, including Pacbitún and Caracol, and Petronila has compiled *A Book of Maya Herbs*. It's a good base, on a ridge with views over to Xunantunich. Fidencio can guide you to several nearby caves – the aptly named Museum Cave holds dozens of artefacts, including intact bowls.

About 5km uphill from the campsite is the **Mai Gate**, a forestry checkpoint with reserve information as well as toilets and drinking water. Though there are plans to levy an **entrance fee**, for the moment all you have to do is list your name in the visitors' book (to ensure there's no illegal camping). Once you've entered the reserve, the dense, leafy forest is quickly replaced by pine trees. After 3km a branch road heads off to the left, running for 7km (about an hour and a half's walk) to a point which overlooks the **Thousand-Foot Falls**.

There's a shelter with toilets at the falls, and since the site is privately owned you'll be approached by Pedro, the caretaker, for the entrance fee (Bz$3). The setting is spectacular, with rugged, thickly forested slopes across the steep valley – almost a gorge. The waterfall itself is about 1km from the viewpoint, but try to resist the temptation to climb around for a closer look: the slope is a lot steeper than it first appears and, if you do get down, the ascent is very difficult indeed. The small gift shop sells cold drinks but no food. The beautiful wooden cabins here belong to the *Hidden Valley Institute for Environmental Studies*, a research establishment affiliated to the nearby *Hidden Valley Inn*, which you'll have seen on the way in (see "Accommodation" below).

One of the reserve's main attractions has to be the **Rio On Pools**, a gorgeous spot for a swim, 11km further on. Here the river forms pools between huge granite boulders before plunging into a gorge, right beside the main road. Another 8km from here and you reach the reserve headquarters at **AUGUSTINE**. This small settlement, housing forestry workers, has recently been renamed **DOUGLAS SILVA** (after a local politician); some of the signs have already been changed. If you're heading for **Caracol**, this is where the Forestry Department check your permit and give advice on road conditions. You can **stay** at the campsite or the **bunkhouse** (①), for which you need camping gear. The building with the thatched tables sells basic supplies and cold beer, but there are no phones.

The **Rio Frio Caves** are a twenty-minute walk from Augustine, following the signposted track from the parking area through the forest to the main cave, beneath a small hill. The Rio Frio flows right through and out of the other side of the hill here and if you enter the foliage-framed cave mouth, you can scramble over limestone terraces the entire way along into the open again. Sandy beaches and rocky cliffs line the river on both sides.

ACCOMMODATION IN THE MOUNTAIN PINE RIDGE

Blancaneaux Lodge, off the main road to Augustine, by the airstrip (☎092/3878; fax 3919). Sumptuous lodge overlooking Privassion Creek. Owned by Francis Ford Coppola, it features a few Hollywood excesses, not least the prices. Villas with two spacious rooms decorated with Guatemalan and Mexican textiles and an enormous screened porch can cost up to US$500. *Cabañas* (US$145, including breakfast) and lodge rooms (US$90 with shared bath) are more affordable. Meals feature pizza and fine Italian wines. Guests can be flown in. ⑨.

Five Sisters Lodge, at the end of the road past *Blancaneaux* (☎ & fax 092/2985). The best location in the Pine Ridge. Set on the hillside among the pines, comfortable palmetto-and-thatch *cabañas* with hot showers give views of the eponymous waterfalls cascading over the granite rocks of Privassion Creek. Less expensive rooms are in the main building. Manager Cesar Bedran is a landscape gardener, and his skill is evident in the profusion of flowers. Electricity is provided by a small, unobtrusive hydro but the oil lamps are wonderfully romantic. Rates include breakfast; other meals are good value if you're on a day trip. ⑤–⑦.

Hidden Valley Inn, on the Cooma Cairn road to Thousand-Foot Falls (☎08/23320; fax 23334; in US: ☎1-800/334-7982). Twelve roomy, well-designed cottages at the highest elevation of any accommodation in Belize. Each has a fireplace stacked with logs to ward off the evening chill. Even the vegetation, pines and tree ferns, appears distinctly untropical, and hiking trails take you to secret waterfalls. Meals are in the spacious main house, with the ambience of a mountain lodge; wood-panelled walls, a crackling log fire and a well-stocked library. Phillip Mai, the guide here, is a bird expert with an impressive list of sightings and can unfailingly take you to see the orange-breasted falcon. Rates include breakfast. ⑧.

Pine Ridge Lodge, on the road to Augustine, just past junction to Thousand-Foot Falls
(☎092/3310; fax 2267; in US: ☎216/781-6888). Small resort on the banks of Little Vaqueros
Creek, with a choice of Maya-style thatched cabins or more modern ones with red tiled
roofs. The grounds and trees are full of orchids and trails lead to pristine waterfalls. The
restaurant is a favourite refreshment stop on tours of the Pine Ridge. ⑤.

The ruins of Caracol

Beyond Augustine the main ridges of the Maya Mountains rise up to the south,
while to the west is the Vaca plateau, a fantastically isolated wilderness. Here the
ruins of **Caracol**, the largest known Maya site in Belize, were lost in the rainforest for several centuries until their rediscovery by *chicleros* in 1936. They were
first systematically explored by A H Anderson in 1938: he named the site Caracol
– Spanish for "snail" – because of the large numbers of snail shells found there.
Other archeologists visited and made excavations in the 1950s, but early reports
took a long time to reach the public domain as many documents were destroyed
by Hurricane Hattie in 1961. In 1985 the first detailed, full-scale excavation of the
site, the "Caracol Project", began under the auspices of Drs Arlen and Diane
Chase of the University of Central Florida. Initially expected to take at least ten
years, research continues to unearth a tremendous amount of material on the
everyday life of all levels of Maya society.

Caracol covers more than three square kilometres, with at least thirty-two
large structures and twelve smaller ones around five main plazas. The largest
pyramid, **Canaa**, is the tallest in Belize at 42m, and several others are over 20m
high. The dates on stelae and tombs suggest an extremely long occupation, with
the population peaking at the height of the Classic period, around 700 AD. Glyphs
carved on altars tell of war between Caracol and Tikal (see p.294), with power
over a huge area alternating between the two great cities. One altar dates
Caracol's victory over Tikal at 562 AD – a victory that set the seal on the city's
rise to power. Archeological research has revealed some superb tombs, with
lintels of iron-hard sapodilla wood supporting the entrances and painted texts
decorating the walls. The site is so isolated that archeologists can only work in
the spring and summer, and in the past it was badly looted while they were away.
Today, a permanent team of caretakers are on guard all year, and the British
Army and Belize Defense Force make frequent patrolling visits.

It is an amazing experience to be virtually alone in this great abandoned city,
the horizon bounded by jungle-covered peaks, through which it's only three
hours on foot to Guatemala. Ask one of the caretakers, Benjamin Panti, to be your
guide; he spends a great deal of time at the site and is truly an expert on Caracol
and the surrounding forest. He may show you the altars and stelae deliberately
broken by logging tractors in the 1930s. Beneath Canaa a series of looted tombs
still have traces of the original painted glyphs on the walls. At the top of this
freshly restored structure is a small plaza; an altar here has revealed signs of a
female ruler. Ask Benjamin to point out the intact altar he discovered as he was
planting corn. This clearly depicts two bound captives with a row of glyphs above
and between them and has been dated at 810 AD. One of the most awe-inspiring
sights in this fantastic city is an immense, 700-year old ceiba tree – sacred to the
Maya – with enormous buttress roots twice as high as a human being. The Maya-
built reservoir is still used when the archeologists are in residence. Caracol is a
Natural Monument Reserve, a haven for wildlife as well as archeologists, and
you may catch sight of ocellated turkeys feeding in the plazas and tapirs dining at
night on the succulent shoots growing on cleared areas.

Fifteen kilometres beyond Caracol is the vast **Chiquibul Cave System**, the longest cave system in Central America, containing what is reputed to be the largest cave chamber in the western hemisphere. The entire area is dotted with caves and sinkholes, which were certainly known to the ancient Maya and probably used for ceremonies; as yet there has been no cave found in Belize which does not contain Maya artefacts. You need to come on a properly organized expedition if you want to explore.

Succotz and the ruins of Xunantunich

Back on the Western Highway, the village of **SAN JOSE SUCCOTZ** lies about 10km west of San Ignacio, right beside the Mopan River, just before Benque Viejo. It's a very traditional village in many ways, inhabited largely by Maya Indians, who celebrate fiestas here on March 19 and May 3. Under colonial administration the Maya of Succotz sided with the British, a stance that angered other groups, such as the Icaiché, who burnt it to the ground in 1867. Today it's a quiet village, and the main reason most people visit outside fiesta times is to see the ruins of **Xunantunich** (pronounced Shun-an-tun-ich), "the Stone Maiden", a Classic-period centre.

The site was explored in the 1890s by Dr Thomas Gann, a British medical officer, and in 1904 Teobalt Maler of the Peabody Museum took photographs and made a plan of the largest structure, A–6, commonly known as **El Castillo**. Gann returned in 1924 and excavated large numbers of burial goods and removed the carved glyphs of Altar 1, the whereabouts of which are now unknown. British archeologist J Eric S Thompson excavated a residential group in 1938, unearthing pottery, obsidian, jade, a spindle, seashells, stingray spines and hammers. Later excavations revealed signs of an earthquake in about 900 AD, but this was

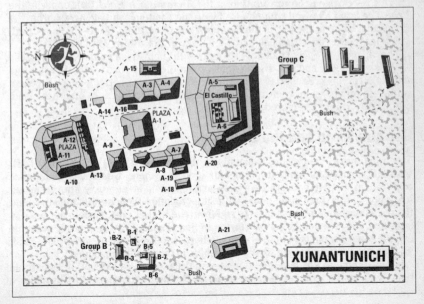

recently discovered to have been merely a settling of the massive building. The UCLA team excavating here have found evidence of Xunantunich's role in the power politics of the Classic period; probably allied as a subordinate partner, along with Caracol, to the regional superpower Calakmul, against Tikal. By the Terminal Classic, Xunantunich was already in decline, though still apparently populated until around 1000 AD, after the so-called Classic Maya "collapse".

To **get to the site** from Succotz you have to cross the river on the old chain ferry (8am–5pm, lunch break around noon; Mon–Sat free, Sun Bz$3). From the riverbank a track leads through the forest for a couple of kilometres to the ruins, where an **entrance fee** is charged (Bz$10). The **visitor centre** has several fairly well preserved stelae from the site. For an interpretation of their glyphs ask Eduardo Alfaro, one of the caretakers; if he's not busy he'll also be your guide.

The site itself is built on top of an artificially flattened hill and includes five plazas, although the remaining structures are grouped around just three of them. The track brings you out into plaza A–2, with large structures on three sides. Plaza A–3, to the right, is almost completely enclosed by a low, acropolis-like building, and plaza A–1, to the left, is dominated by El Castillo, the city's largest structure at more than 40m. As is so often the case, the building is layered, with later versions built on top of earlier ones. It was once ringed by a decorative stucco frieze carved with abstract designs, human faces and jaguar heads, depicting a king performing rituals associated with assuming authority: this has been extensively restored. The climb up El Castillo can be terrifying, but the views from the top are superb, with the forest stretching out all around and the rest of the ancient city mapped out beneath you.

The Preclassic ruins of **Actuncan** are a couple of kilometres north.

Succotz practicalities

There's very basic **accommodation** at the *Xunantunich Hotel* (①), opposite the ferry. The large blue and white house flying the Guatemalan flag, across from the ferry and a block to the left, is the **Guatemalan Consulate** (Mon–Fri 9am–1pm), which may save you a trip back to the embassy in Belize City for a visa.

The villagers of Succotz identify strongly with their Maya culture. The Magaña family's art gallery and **gift shop** (signed from the main road) sells superb wood and slate carvings. Zacharias Cano, the weekend ferry operator, is an excellent guide and organizes inexpensive horseback trips to nearby caves on private land, camping overnight if required.

Benque Viejo and the border

The final town before the Guatemalan border is **BENQUE VIEJO DEL CARMEN**, just half an hour from San Ignacio, where Guatemala and Belize combine in almost equal proportions and Spanish is certainly the dominant language. It's a quiet little place with little to offer the passing traveller, and there's a constant stream of taxis to and from the border post. **Hotels** are basic at best, and you're much better off staying in San Ignacio. The best bet here is just outside town, on the way to the border, where the *Woodlands Resort* (☎093/2553; ④), has ten comfortable, if rather plain cabins in flower-filled grounds.

If you've time to kill, and are interested in the cultural aspects of Mestizo traditions, you might want to visit the small *El Ba'lum Art Gallery*, 43 Churchill St

(Mon & Tues 1–4pm, Wed–Sat 9am–noon & 2–4.30pm; Bz$2). There are displays of old photographs and documents, logging and chicle-gathering equipment, paintings and musical instruments. *Cubola*, Belize's foremost book and music publishers, have an interesting gift shop at 35 Elizabeth St (☎093/2241), selling unusual crafts, including brightly painted models of Belize's colonial-style houses, as well as recordings of the country's top bands.

Buses leave for Belize City from the *Novelos* **bus terminal**, on George St, hourly between 3am and 11am.

Crossing the border

The border itself is a little under 2km beyond Benque Viejo. Some **buses** continue all the way to the Belizean immigration post or even to the market in Melchor, but if yours doesn't there are plenty of taxis providing a shuttle service for a few dollars. The border is open from 6am to midnight; there is an exit charge of Bz$7.50. Guatemala charges a Q5 entry (and exit) tax, even if you already have a visa. Guatemalan **tourist cards** (which should be free but rarely are) and even visas (US$10) can be issued here. However, you'd be very unwise to leave getting a visa this late: although the immigration staff will generally give you a permit to travel to Tikal or to visit the market in Melchor de Mencos, just over the bridge, there's no guarantee. If you get refused, try the **Guatemalan consulate** by the ferry in Succotz (see p.404). It's always best to cross the border in daylight – Guatemalan immigration closes at around 8pm. There are a couple of restaurants and cantinas at the border; they're not up to much but then nor are the ones in Melchor itself. However, just over the border, *Hotel Frontera* (see p.313), right on the riverbank, has comfortable cabins with hot water.

Buses on to **Flores** (see p.380) will call at the immigration post to pick up passengers, and you'll certainly be approached by drivers of the minibuses which shuttle between the border and **Tikal** (US$10) and Flores. Otherwise, a shared taxi from the border to the marketplace **bus station** costs 50¢ per person.

travel details

Buses

Belize City to Belmopan (1hr 15min), **San Ignacio** (3hr) **and the Guatemalan border** (3hr 30min) services operated by *Batty*, 15 Mosul St, Belize City (☎02/72025): at least hourly 5.30–10.30am. Most continue to Melchor in Guatemala. *Novelos*, 19 W Collet Canal, Belize City (☎02/77372), operate an hourly service to **Benque Viejo** (3hr 30min), calling at Belmopan and San Ignacio, from 11am to 8pm, with an extra service on Friday at 9pm, calling at Belmopan only. Any bus heading to or from Dangriga in the south (7 daily; 2hr) also stops at Belmopan.

From the border to Belize City *Novelos* buses leave **Benque Viejo** hourly from 3am to noon.

Batty run from **San Ignacio** from noon to 5pm, calling at Belmopan; many services depart from **Melchor**. *Shaws* run between Belmopan and Melchor about hourly, 7.30am–4pm. There are more frequent buses on this route on Sunday for the Melchor market.

Between **San Ignacio and the border**, *colectivo* taxis leave when full, during daylight. From San Ignacio **to San Antonio** buses leave at 10.30am and 2.30pm (1hr), returning at 6am and 7am.

Planes

There is one daily scheduled *Maya* flight, usually in high season, between **Belize** and **Central Farm** (50min).

CHAPTER ELEVEN

THE SOUTH

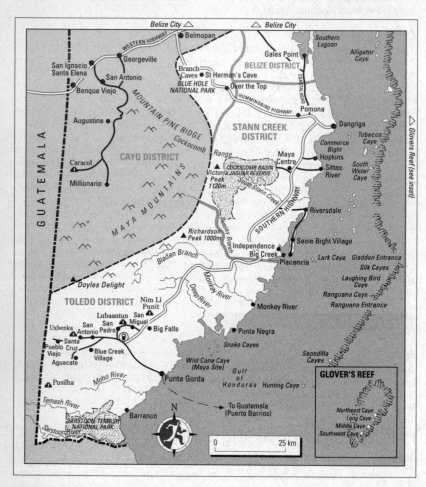

To the south of Belmopan Belize is at its wildest. Here the central area is dominated by the Maya Mountains, which slope down towards the coast through a series of forested ridges and valleys carved by sparkling rivers. As you head further south, the climate becomes more humid, promoting the growth of dense **rainforest**, rich in wildlife. The forests here have evolved to cope with periodic hurricanes sweeping in from the Caribbean and have in the past been selectively logged for mahogany. Among the broadleaf forests there are also large stands of Caribbean pine, looking strangely out of place in the tropics. The **coastal strip** south of Belize City is a band of savannah, swamp and lagoon, while beyond Dangriga the shoreline is composed of sandy bays, peninsulas and mangroves. In the far south the estuaries of several slow-moving tidal rivers, lined with the tallest **mangrove forest** in Belize, form the country's most recent nature reserves.

Population density in this part of Belize is low, with most of the towns and villages located on the coast. **Dangriga**, the largest settlement, is home of the **Garifuna** people – descended from Carib Indians and shipwrecked, enslaved Africans (see pp.412–13) – and allows access to a number of idyllic cayes, some of which sit right on top of the **Barrier Reef**. The villages of **Gales Point**, on Southern Lagoon, north of Dangriga, and **Hopkins**, on the coast to the south, are worth visiting to experience their tranquil way of life; further south, **Placencia** has become established as the focus of coastal tourism in southern Belize.

Inland, the Maya Mountains remain unpenetrated by roads, forming a solid barrier to land travel except on foot or horseback. The Belize government, showing supreme foresight, has placed practically all of the mountain massif under some form of legal protection, whether as national park, nature reserve, wildlife sanctuary or forest reserve. The most accessible area of this rainforest, though still little-visited by tourists, is the **Cockscomb Basin Wildlife Sanctuary**, a reserve designed to protect the sizeable jaguar population and a good base for exploring the forest. You'll come across plenty of tracks – but don't count on seeing a jaguar. The Southern Highway comes to an end in **Punta Gorda**, a final outpost, from where you can head south to Guatemala or visit Maya villages and ruins in the southern foothills of the Maya Mountains.

The Hummingbird Highway

The **Hummingbird Highway**, heading southeast from Belmopan to Dangriga, is one of the best roads in Belize, though the first, potholed section is a more accurate introduction to the rigours of travel in southern Belize. The scenery is magnificent, as the road heads steadily over the hills through lush forest, with the eastern slopes of the **Maya Mountains**, coated in greenery, rising to the right. Until recently, much of this forest was untouched, but here and there Salvadorean or Guatemalan refugees have hacked down a swathe of jungle to plant maize and beans, and you're rarely out of sight of citrus plantations.

The hills form part of a ridge of limestone mountains, riddled with underground rivers and caves, several of which are accessible. About 19km out of Belmopan the road crosses the **Caves Branch River**, a tributary of the Sibun River. The upper reaches of this and other nearby valleys hold some of Belize's finest **caves**.

St Herman's Cave, the Blue Hole and Caves Branch Jungle Camp

Just beyond the Caves Branch River, **St Herman's Cave** is one of the most accessible in Belize. You pay the entrance fee (Bz$8; valid also for the Blue Hole) at the new visitor centre, then follow the marked trail for ten minutes to the cave entrance, squashed beneath a dripping rock face. To enter, down steps that were originally cut by the Maya, you'll need a flashlight. Inside, you clamber over the rocks and splash through the river for about thirty minutes, admiring the stunning formations, before the cave appears to end. To continue beyond, and emerge from one of the other entrances, you need to go on an tour – one of the best is organized by Pete Zubrzycki of *PACZ Hotel* in San Ignacio (see p.393).

A signed trail leads 3km from the cave, over the ridge, to the **Blue Hole National Park** (Bz$8), which you can also reach by continuing along the highway. The Blue Hole is actually a short but deep stretch of underground river, whose course is revealed by the collapse of a karst cavern, flowing on the surface for about 50m before disappearing beneath another rock face. Its cool, fresh turquoise waters, surrounded by dense forest and overhung with vines, mosses and ferns are perfect for a refreshing dip.

Any bus between Belmopan and Dangriga will drop you at the cave or the Blue Hole, making an easy day trip (the wardens know the times of onward buses), but to really appreciate the mysteries of caving in Belize you should **stay** nearby at *Caves Branch Jungle Camp* (☎ & fax 08/22800); signed from the highway, halfway between St Herman's Cave and the Blue Hole and about 1km from the road. Owned by Ian Anderson, who for several years has led tours through some of the area's most spectacular caves, the camp offers a range of comfortable accommodation on the banks of the river: spacious, screened *cabañas* (⑤), a bunkhouse (Bz$30 per person) and camping (Bz$10). Delicious, filling meals are also served. The **guided cave trips** are not cheap (on average about US$60 per person) but well worth it. All the caves contain Maya artefacts – ceramics, carvings and the like – with abundant evidence of Classic period ceremonies. Some caves are dry, and you must take great care not to touch the glittering crystal formations as you climb over rocks and around stalagmites. You can also float on **inner tubes** 8km along a subterranean river, your headlamps piercing the intense darkness. Jacinto and Glyss, the guides, are also experts in natural history, and lead **wildlife treks** in the frorest, including a four-day "Jungle Quest" survivial course.

Over the Top and Five Blues Lake National Park

Beyond the Blue Hole the Hummingbird Highway is well paved, undulating smoothly through the increasingly hilly landscape, eventually crossing a low pass. This is the highest point on the road, and the downhill slope is appropriately, if unimaginatively, called **Over the Top**. On the way down the road passes through St Margaret's Village, where a women's cooperative arranges bed and breakfast **accommodation** in private houses (☎081/2005; ②).

Past the village, the *Over the Top Restaurant* stands on a hill at Mile 32, overlooking the junction of the track to **Five Blues Lake National Park**, 4200 acres of luxuriantly forested karst scenery, centered around a lake. Named for its constantly changing colours, the lake is another cenote or "blue hole", caused by a cavern's collapse. Register at the office by the road junction, where you can arrange a guide; if this is closed ask at *Over the Top*, who will also let you leave luggage. It's about an hour's walk to the lake and the road is passable in a good vehicle. Trails enable you to explore the practically deserted park and boats can be rented on the lake.

Two kilometres along the track to Five Blues Lake, a branch to the right fords a river and continues another 3km through orange groves and forest to *Tamandua* (☎ & fax 08/22458), an organic fruit farm in a small valley surrounded by towering, jungle-draped limestone cliffs. Run by English expats Janet and Bernard Dempsey, it's an amazingly peaceful **place to stay** – bounded on three sides by the park, with plenty of opportunity to encounter wildlife. The thatched, A-frame cabins (④), perched above a creek (used for bathing), are great value; there's also a bunk-house (②) with a kitchen, and you can camp (①). Meals are taken with the family.

Continuing south for 3km on the Hummingbird Highway from Over the Top there's more accommodation at *Palacio's Mountain Retreat*. Retired policeman Augustus Palacio has has built ten *cabañas* (④; ⑤ including breakfast), overlooking a river; it's great for swimming and there's a ten-metre waterfall just upstream. There are also three bed and breakfast rooms in the main house. The bus stops right outside.

On towards Dangriga

Palacio's Mountain Retreat marks the start of the **Stann Creek valley**, the centre of the Belizean citrus fruit industry. Bananas were the first crop to be grown here, and by 1891 half a million stems were being exported through Stann Creek (now Dangriga) every year. However, this banana boom came to an abrupt end in 1906, when disease destroyed the crop, and afterwards the government set out to foster the growth of **citrus fruits**. Between 1908 and 1937 the valley was even served by a small railway, and by 1945 the citrus industry was well established.

Today it accounts for about 13 percent of the country's exports and, despite widely fluctuating prices, is heralded as one of the nation's great success stories – although for the largely Guatemalan labour force, housed in rows of scruffy huts, conditions are little better than on the oppressive coffee *fincas* at home. The presence of tropical parasites, such as the leaf-eating ant, has forced the planters to resort to powerful insecticides, including DDT. Two giant pulping plants beside the road produce concentrate for export. The Hummingbird Highway comes to an end at Middlesex and continues as the Stann Creek Valley Road.

Gales Point and the Belize Coastal Road

At Melinda, 14km from Dangriga, an improved dirt road heads north to the small Creole village of **GALES POINT**, which straggles along a narrow peninsula jutting into the Southern Lagoon. The lagoons are such an essential breeding ground for rare wildlife, including jabiru storks, turtles, manatee and crocodiles, that the government has established the **Manatee Special Development Area** to encourage sensitive conservation-oriented development. The area is bounded on the west by the limestone Peccary hills, riddled with caves, and the shores of the lagoons are cloaked with mangroves. Scenery and wildlife are the big attractions here and renting a dory (traditionally a dugout canoe) for about Bz$10 per day allows you to explore the waterways, or you can take a trip with Moses Andrewin, an expert local guide.

The villagers have formed the Gales Post Progressive Cooperative to administer the Manatee Sanctuary, and several houses offer simple bed and breakfast **accommodation** (②). Camping is available for Bz$5 per day. For more information and bookings call Alice or Josephine on the Gales Point community telephone (☎05/22087). *Gentle's Cool Spot*, the bar-restaurant where the bus stops, also has a few simple, clean rooms (②). At the tip of the peninsula, *Manatee Lodge* (☎08/23320; fax 23334; in US: ☎1-800/334-7942; ⑧) offers comfortable, non-smoking, accommodation in a spacious, two-storey, colonial-style building; meals are superb. On the upper floor a wooden deck offers great views at sunrise and sunset. If you have a car, this is an ideal place to break the journey – driving down the peninsula at night is not advisable.

Gales Point is served by at least two daily **buses** on the Belize City/Danriga route, using the Manatee (Coastal) Road, heading south at La Democracia on the Western Highway and thus avoiding Belmopan. Some tour companies use the old water route along the Burdon Canal and into the lagoons; take this trip if you can, for glimpses of the wildlife.

Dangriga

The last stretch of the Hummingbird Highway is flat and relatively uninteresting. Ten kilometres before Dangriga, the filling station is a useful place to refuel without going into town; beyond is the junction with the Southern Highway to Punta Gorda. **DANGRIGA**, formerly called Stann Creek, is the district capital and the largest town in southern Belize.

Though Dangriga is the cultural centre of the **Garifuna**, a people of mixed indigenous Caribbean and African descent, who overall form about 11 percent of the country's population, it is not the most exciting of places unless you're here during a festival – and even then the inflated hotel prices are something of a turn-off. Although the atmosphere is enjoyably laid-back there's little to do during the day. It's a useful base, however, for visiting south-central Belize, the cayes offshore and the mountains and jaguar reserve inland.

Arrival and information

Z-Line **buses** (☎02/79907) for Dangriga leave from the same terminal as *Venus* in Belize City, on Magazine Rd, at 8am, 9am, 10am and hourly from noon to 5pm. The 9am and 1pm departures use the Coastal Road (via Gales Point). Arriving at the Dangriga terminal you're at the south end of town; you can leave luggage here. It's 1km or so to the centre, though many buses continue to the bridge and a shuttle bus plies the main street. The centre of town is marked by the **road bridge** over the South Stann Creek, with the main thoroughfare leading north as Commerce St and south as St Vincent St. Almost everything you're likely to need is on or near these roads. For reliable **tourist information**, call in at the *River Cafe* by the bridge on the south bank of the river.

There are three **banks** in Dangriga, the *Belize Bank, Barclays* and *The Bank of Nova Scotia,* all on the main street. **The post office** is on Caney St, in the southern half of town, a block back from the sea.

The **telephone area code** for Dangriga is ☎05.

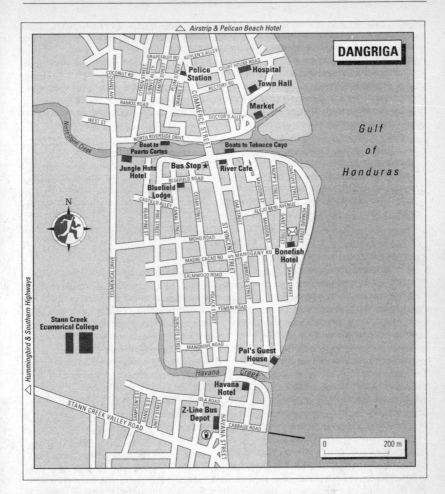

Accommodation

Walking down Commerce St, you'll pass several **cheap hotels**, such as the *Chameleon*, *Tropical* and *Catalina*. Though convenient, they're very basic, and it's worth looking further afield. Dangriga has experienced something of a hotel-building boom in the last few years, resulting in an ample choice of places to stay.

Bluefield Lodge, 6 Bluefield Rd (☎227420). Very good value rooms, some with private bath, on the south side of town. ③.

Bonefish, 15 Mahogany Rd (☎22165; fax 22296). Upmarket hotel with cable TV, hot water, carpets and a/c. Can arrange fishing tours and inland trips. ⑥.

Chaleanor Hotel, 35 Magoon St (☎22587; fax 23038). New hotel with very clean, spacious rooms, all with private bath, plus a rooftop restaurant. The best value at this price. ④.

Jungle Huts, on the riverbank to the south of town (☎23166). Thatched *cabañas* and hotel rooms with private bath and hot and cold water. ④–⑤.

Pal's Guest House, 868 Magoon St, by the bridge over Havana Creek (☎22095). Good value accommodation in two buildings: budget rooms (some shared bath) are in the older part; beachfront rooms all have private baths and TV. ③–④.

Pelican Beach Hotel, on the shore north of the town, next to the airstrip (☎22024; fax 22570). The most expensive hotel in town; only worth it if you get a beachfront room. ⑥–⑦.

Rio Mar Hotel, 1 Waight St (☎22201). Right by the sea at the river mouth. The rooms aren't great, though some come with bath, and the balcony does have sea views. ③–④.

Riverside Hotel, right beside the bridge (☎22168). Clean rooms (some with bath) in a good location with a vantage point over the river. Prices are per person; good deal for singles. ②.

A BRIEF HISTORY OF THE GARIFUNA

The Garifuna trace their history back to the island of **St Vincent**, one of the Windward Islands in the eastern Caribbean. At the time of Columbus' landing in the Americas the islands of the Lesser Antibes had recently been settled by Indians from the South American mainland, who had subdued the previous inhabitants, the Arawaks. These new people called themselves *Kalipuna*, from which the name *Garifuna*, meaning cassava-eating people, probably evolved, but the Spanish named them *Caribs*, their word for cannibal. The natives the Europeans encountered were descendants of Carib men and Arawak women.

In the early seventeenth century Britain and France vied for control of the islands, fighting each other and the Caribs. The admixture of African blood came in 1635 when two Spanish ships, carrying slaves from Nigeria to their colonies in America, were wrecked off St Vincent and the survivors took refuge on the island. At first there was conflict between the Indians and the Africans, but the Caribs had been weakened by wars and disease and eventually the predominant race was Black, with some Indian blood. They were known as the **Black Caribs**.

For most of the seventeenth and eighteenth centuries St Vincent was nominally under British control but in practice it belonged to the Caribs. Britain attempted to gain full control of the island in 1763 but was driven off by the Caribs, with French assistance. Another attempt twenty years later was more successful, and in 1783 the British imposed a treaty on the Caribs, allowing them over half of the island: the treaty was never accepted, however, and the Caribs continued to defy British rule, resulting in frequent battles, in which the French consistently lent the Caribs support. The last serious attempt by the Caribs to establish their independence took place in 1795, when both sides suffered horrendous casualties. The Caribs lost their leader, Chief Joseph Chatoyer, and on June 10, 1796, after a year of bitter fighting, the French and Caribs surrendered to the British.

The colonial authorities could not allow a free Black society to survive amongst slave-owning European settlers, so it was decided to deport the Carib population. They were hunted down, their homes (and in the process their culture) destroyed, and hundreds died of starvation and disease. The survivors, 4300 Black Caribs and 100 Yellow Caribs, were transported to the nearby island of Balliceaux and within six months over half of them had died, many of yellow fever. On March 3, 1797, the remaining survivors were loaded aboard ships and sent to **Roatan**, one of the Bay Islands, off the coast of Honduras (see p.248). One of the ships was captured by the Spanish and taken to Trujillo, on the mainland, and barely 2000 Caribs lived to make the landing on Roatan, where the British abandoned them.

Perhaps in response to pleas for help from the Caribs, who continued to die on Roatan, the Spanish Commandante of Trujillo arrived and took possession of the island, shipping the 1700 survivors to Trujillo where they were in demand as labourers. The Spanish had never made a success of agriculture here and the arrival of the

Soffie's, Chatuye St, on the south bank of the river, heading towards the sea (☎22789). Run by an exuberantly friendly Belizean returned from the US. Rooms with bath, a balcony with fine sea and river views, and a restaurant serving good Creole and Garifuna food. ④.

Eating and drinking

On the south bank of the river, just over the bridge, the *River Cafe* (☎39908) is a new restaurant catering to visitors waiting for boats to Tobacco Caye. Run by an English couple, Katherine and Jim Noakes, and serving good meals (including vegetarian), it's *the* place to pick up information on the surrounding area and has a payphone. At

Caribs, who were proficient at growing crops, benefited the colony considerably. The boys were conscripted and the Carib men gained a reputation as soldiers and mercenaries. Soon they began to move to other areas along the coast, and in 1802, 150 of them were brought as wood-cutting labourers to work in Stann Creek and Punta Gorda. Their intimate knowledge of the rivers and coast also made them expert smugglers, evading the Spanish laws that forbade trade with the British in Belize. Their military skills were even more useful and by 1819 a Carib colonel was commander of the garrison at San Felipe in Guatemala, while in 1820 two Carib soldiers received (posthumous) awards from the king of Spain for their bravery in the defence of Trujillo.

In the early **nineteenth century** small numbers of Caribs moved up the coast to Belize, and although in 1811 Superintendent Barrow of Belize ordered their expulsion, it had little effect. When European settlers arrived in Stann Creek in 1823 Caribs were already there and were hired to clear land. The largest single migration to Belize took place in 1832 when vast numbers fled from Honduras, by then part of the Central American Republic, after they had supported the wrong side in a failed revolution to overthrow the Republican government. It is this arrival which is today celebrated as Garifuna Settlement Day, though it seems likely many arrived both before and after.

In 1825 the first Methodist missionaries arrived in Belize, and by 1828 they had begun to visit Stann Creek, or "Carib Town" as the setters knew it. They were outraged to discover a bizarre mix of Catholicism, ancestor worship and polygamy, in which the main form of worship was "devil dancing", but they had little success in their struggle to Christianize the Caribs beyond the adoption of various new rituals such as baptism.

By the start of this century, the Caribs – or Garifuna, the name which they call themselves – were well established in the Stann Creek area, with the women employed in bagging and stacking cohune nuts and the men working in agriculture. Throughout the nineteenth and twentieth centuries the Garifuna travelled widely in search of work. To start with they confined themselves to Central America (where they can still be found all along the Caribbean coast from Belize to Nicaragua), but in World War II Caribs supplied crews for both British and US merchant ships. Since then trips to the US have become an important part of the local economy, and there are small Garifuna communities in New York, New Orleans, Los Angeles and even in London.

Since the early 1980s Garifuna culture has undergone something of a revival, and as a part of this movement the town was renamed Dangriga, a Garifuna word meaning "standing waters". The most important day in the Garifuna calendar is November 19, **Garifuna Settlement Day**, in Dangriga a time of wild celebration, when the town erupts with music, dance, drink and dope. A group of local people re-enact the arrival from Roatan, landing on the beach in dugout canoes. Christmas and New Year are also celebrated in unique Garifuna style, and the town is home to some of the country's most popular artists, including painters, drum makers, the Waribagabaga Dancers and the Turtle Shell Band.

the south end of town, *Pola's Kitchen*, 25 Tubroose St serves good value Garifuna specialities and has a no smoking policy that is probably unique in Belize.

If you're in search of a reasonably priced meal try *Burger King* – not what you might think, it serves good rice, chicken, fruit juices, fish and conch soup, a Belizean delicacy. Of the several good Chinese restaurants on the main street, the *Starlight* is the best value. Also worth trying are *Le Elegante*, 8 Ramos Rd, and the *Sea Flame*, right in the centre on Commerce St.

For picnic supplies you could try the **market** on the north bank of the river, by the sea, but it's very small – for other groceries best head for the *Southern Pride* supermarket, by *Barclays Bank*.

There's no shortage of **bars** in Dangriga, though some, particularly those calling themselves clubs, like *The Kennedy Club*, *The Culture Club* and the *Harlem Club*, are particularly dubious-looking, both inside and out. In the centre of town, near the bridge, the *Riviera Nite Club* is Dangriga's newest and most sophisicated nightspot. Along the beach to the north of the centre, the *Round House Reggae Club* is a good place to meet the locals and dance on the sand.

MOVING ON FROM DANGRIGIA

Returning **to Belize City**, *Z-Line* (☎22732) leave at 5am, 6am, 8am, 9am, 10am, 10.15am, 1.30pm and 4pm. If you're continuing south bear in mind that buses to **Punta Gorda** don't originate here. *Z-Line* dominate the route: on the Belize City–Punta Gorda run they leave Dangriga at noon, 4pm and 7pm; the journey takes five hours over dirt roads. You should buy a ticket in advance. All buses to Punta Gorda stop at **Independence** – also known as **Mango Creek** – where you can pick up boats to Placencia, and there's also a *Z-Line* bus daily at 2.30pm. Buses from Dangriga to **Placencia** and **Hopkins** depart daily at noon and 1pm, calling at Hopkins and Sittee River. Other bus companies occasionally attempt to run services to the south, but never seem to survive long, as *Z-Line* muscles them out of the way. The *James* service between Belize and Punta Gorda (see "Moving on from Belize City"; p.360), which runs at least three days a week, is pretty reliable.

Maya Airways (☎02/44234) operate regular **flights** between Dangriga and Belize Municipal airport. The airstrip is on the shore just north of the *Pelican Beach Hotel*, with departures every two hours from 6.30am to 4.30pm – check schedules at *Treasured Travels*, 64 Commerce St (☎22578; fax 23481), or at the *Pelican*.

For Puerto Cortes in Honduras a fast **skiff** leaves each Saturday at 9am (around 3hr) from the north bank of the river, two blocks up from the bridge; be there an hour before departure with your passport so that the skipper, Carlos Reyes (☎05/23227), can take care of the formalities.

Offshore from Dangriga: Columbus Reef

About 20km off Dangriga is the **Columbus Reef**, a superb section of the Barrier Reef with some small cayes scattered along its length. These cayes were originally visited by turtle fishermen for catching hawksbill turtles; **Tobacco Caye** was later farmed by the first Puritan settlers, taking its name from the main crop.

Tobacco Caye
Tobacco Caye, ideally situated right in the middle of the reef, is the easiest to reach and has the most accommodation options. You're bound to have been

approached in Dangriga by hustlers but you should ignore them; the residents of this privately owned island, whose boats provide the transport, are unlikely to hassle you. **Boats** leave every day from near the bridge, but there are no regular departures; check details at the *River Cafe*. The most prompt and reliable service is operated by Captain Buck, though any of the hotel owners will probably take you. It's a forty-minute trip and the one-way fare is Bz$30.

The island is tiny, just five acres in area. If you stand in the centre you're only a couple of minutes from the shore in any direction, with the unbroken reef stretching north for miles. Sunsets can be breathtakingly beautiful, outlining the distant Maya Mountains with a purple and orange aura

ACCOMMODATION

Island Camps (☎ & fax 05/23433). Seven small double cabins and three larger cabins, one with private bath. Simple living quarters but the food is excellent and a solar panel provides light in the evening. *Earthwatch* volunteers are based here for part of the year, studying reef ecology. Meals Bz$30 per day. ④.

Gaviota Coral Reef Resort (☎05/22294; fax 23477). Cabins on the sand and rooms in the main building (upstairs rooms are more expensive), all with shared bath. Good snorkel equipment for rent, and the owner can arrange transport. Meals included. ⑤–⑥.

Reef's End Lodge (☎05/22419; fax 22828). Stay right on the shore in a cabin room or in one of a pair of private *cabañas*. The restaurant (room rates include meals) is built over the sea on the tip of the reef, and the bar is a fantastic place to enjoy the sunset. Scuba diving, fishing and snorkelling can be arranged. ⑥–⑦.

South Water Caye

Eight kilometres south and slightly larger, **South Water Caye** is arguably one of the most beautiful – and exclusive – islands in Belize. Like Tobacco Caye it sits right on the reef and offers fantastic snorkelling and scuba diving in crystal clear water. The island's **accommodation** is upmarket and expensive and has to be booked in advance; rates given are either for groups or for an all-inclusive package. Overnight rates are available, but this entails paying at least US$125 one way for a skiff from Dangriga.The tiny island off the south end of the caye is **Carrie Bow Caye**, where the *Smithsonian Institute* has a research station; there is no tourist accommodation.

PACKAGE ACCOMMODATION

Blue Marlin Lodge (☎05/22243; fax 22296; in US: ☎1-800/798-1558). Six luxury a/c cabins and comfortable doubles. The thatched dining room, which extends over the sea, serves delicious meals. Specializes in diving holidays: instruction leading to PADI certification is available and there's a veritable fleet of dive boats. US$1400 for a week's package.

Leslie Cottages (☎05/22119; in US: *International Zoological Expeditions,* 210 Washington St, Sherborn, MA 01770; ☎508/655-1461; fax 655-4445). Run by *IZE*, these are often used for tropical field research but are ideal for a quiet holiday. A week in a one-bedroom cottage for four costs US$555, a two-bedroom cottage for five US$655. Complete packages for four including transportation, accommodation, meals and maid service cost US$600 per person.

Osprey's Nest and Frangipani House, at the south end of the island (book through the *Pelican Beach Hotel*, PO Box 14, Dangriga, Belize; ☎05/22044; fax 22570). Idyllic Belizean-style wooden houses built on stilts over the white sand and shaded by palms. There is ice but no electricity; lighting is provided by kerosene lamps. US$170 with meals.

Pelican Inn (aka *Pelican University*; book through the *Pelican Beach Hotel*), on the west side of the island. Two-storey hotel with five rooms, a large kitchen and recreation area. US$60 per person per day for groups of 10 to 22, including meals.

The Southern Highway

To the south of Dangriga the country becomes more mountainous, with development restricted to the coastal lowlands. The road deteriorates and the towns and villages are increasingly isolated. Setting off in this direction is the Southern Highway, 160km of potholed and deeply rutted road. Unlike the Hummingbird Highway, this stretch has not yet had the honour of tarmac, though there are plans to pave it near Punta Gorda. In any case, the road surface is frequently graded and in the last few years a number of bridges have been built, high above the river levels, so it should be passable except during the very worst rainstorms. For the entire distance the road is set back from the coast, running beneath the peaks of the Maya Mountains, often passing through pine forest and vast citrus and banana plantations. Several branch roads lead off to idyllic coastal villages, the best of which are **Hopkins** and **Placencia**. From the village of Maya Centre another road leads west, into the Cockscomb Basin and to the Jaguar Preserve.

Just before the highway comes to an end in **Punta Gorda** another road leads west into the southern foothills of the Maya Mountains, where there are some delightful Maya villages with ruins scattered in the surrounding hills. Punta Gorda is the southernmost town in Belize, from where onward transport is a daily skiff and a twice-weekly ferry service to **Puerto Barrios** in Guatemala.

Hopkins

HOPKINS, a twenty-minute boat ride south of Dangriga, has to be one of the most relaxing destinations in Belize. Stretching for more than 1km along a shallow, gently curving bay, the village is home to around a thousand Garifuna people, who make their living from small-scale farming and fishing, often paddling dugout canoes to pull up fish traps, or using baited handlines. Their houses, built closely together, are traditionally small wooden structures, thickly shaded by palm trees and usually raised on stilts to allow air to circulate, though there are still some built on the simple Maya design of poles and a thatched roof. Since the devastation brought by Hurricane Hattie in 1961, however, most building has been in less appealing but more secure concrete block. Named after a Roman Catholic bishop who drowned in 1923, the village was first settled in 1942, after a hurricane had levelled the Garifuna community of Newtown, a few kilometres to the north.

The view back towards the village from the sea, with the high ridges of the Maya Mountains in the background, is breathtaking. You'll be made to feel welcome by the exuberant friendliness of the villagers, particularly the children. They're also proud of their traditions, and Garifuna Settlement Day, November 19, is celebrated enthusiastically with singing, dancing and above all the beating of drums, an integral part of the Garifuna culture. Only recently having become part of the tourist circuit, Hopkins still sees few visitors, and if you come here you enter what feels like almost a different age. Though the village has piped water, electricity and telephones, light is still provided by candles or kerosene lamps in many houses, and a flashlight comes in useful. The main hindrances to the peace of Hopkins are the crowing of the roosters and the howling of the dogs, both of which conspire to keep the nights short.

Arrival and orientation

The **bus** to Hopkins leaves the *Z-Line* terminal in Dangriga daily at 1pm, continuing to Sittee River (for the boat to Glover's Reef) and passing through on the return from Placencia at about 7am. There are also plenty of **trucks** between Dangriga and Hopkins, making hitching a possibility. The best and quickest way to get here, though, is by **boat**. Ask around where the boats tie up by the bridge in Dangriga if anyone from Hopkins is in town – they may be willing to give you a lift and might even be able to arrange accommodation.

As there are no street names, the best way to locate anything in Hopkins is to describe its position in relation to the point where the road from the Southern Highway enters the village; this divides the place into roughly northern and southern halves. At the time of writing there are no private phones, but you can make calls on the two **community telephones**; ☎05/22033 in the *Nuñez* store at the roadside in the south of the village, and ☎05/22803 in the *BTL* office.

Accommodation

Caribbean View Hotel, just north of the centre. Basic, inexpensive, cramped rooms; only two actually view the sea. ②.

Jaguar Reef Lodge, on the beach, 1km beyond the south end of the village (☎ & fax 021/ 2041; in USA: ☎1-800/289-5756). New, luxury resort with large, thatched *cabañas* in a superb location. Often used by top nature tour companies. Kayaks for guests, a dive shop with instruction, and even non-divers can descend to 8m with the new C-Breathe system, where you're supplied with air from the surface. Reduced rates in summer. ⑧.

Lebeha Camp, at the north end of the village. Run by American Donna Showme, offering inexpensive hammocks and camping, good vegetarian food and fresh bread. She also has a large (4 person) aluminium canoe for rent at Bz$10 per hour. ①.

Ransome's Seaside Garden (☎05/22889 in Dangriga). Wonderful two-bedroom fully-furnished cabin, set in a tropical garden south of the centre. Owner Barry Swan has kayaks and bicycles for rent. The cabin has a kitchen and you can order meals. ④.

Sandy Beach Lodge, on the beach at the south end (☎05/22560). Simple, spacious rooms in wood-and-thatch cabins, most with private bath, run by Belize's only women's cooperative. Meals are served at set times only. There's also a house for rent at Bz$80 per day. ③–④.

Swinging Armadillos, on the beach 150m north of the centre. Two small and comfortable rooms perched over the sea at the side of a small bar and restaurant. The owner, Mike Flores, has a boat and a truck for trips and rents bikes. ③.

Eating and drinking

A few simple **restaurants** and **bars** have opened up in Hopkins in recent years. *Over the Waves*, on the beach in the village centre is recommended; if you ask you'll be allowed to leave luggage here while you look for a room. *Swinging Armadillos*, 120m north, is a great little restaurant, billed as a "hammock lounge", where you can swing in the shade and enjoy the sea breeze while sipping a cold drink. Finally you can get good food at the *Lebeha Camp* if you book in advance. For **live music**, look out for the Hopkins Ayumahani Band, who play at the *Laru Beya* bar, on the beach where the road from the highway enters the village.

Sittee River and Glover's Reef

A few kilometres south of the Hopkins turn-off is the junction of the road east to **SITTEE RIVER**, a pleasant place in its own right, but most useful as a jumping-off point for Glover's Reef. The dirt road from the highway roughly follows the north bank of the river, as does the village itself; the road from Hopkins has been improved. Most visitors are kayakers on their way to *Glover's Atoll Resort* (see below), and there are just a couple of places to **stay**. On the way in from Hopkins the good-value *Toucan Sittee* is by far the best option, set in a beautiful riverbank location graced by toucans every morning. Some of the rooms (③) and apartments (⑤) have fridges, there's a dorm and you can camp (Bz$7). The food is really good, with lots of fresh fruit and vegetables, and they rent a range of equipment including canoes, double kayaks, bikes and a boat. In the village itself there's the basic *Glover's Guest House* (☎05/23048; ①). Sandflies in Sittee River can be atrocious and the mosquito nets provided are essential. A few kilometres further down the river at Possum Point there's a **campsite** that's part of an ecological field station with an offshore reef ecology centre on Wee Wee Caye (②). Inexpensive **meals** can be had in the village at *Hill Top Farm* and *Isolene's*, and there are a couple of shops for basic supplies, including beer, rum and even cashew wine. The Sittee River community phone is near *Hill Top Farm* (☎05/22006 or 22888)

The 1pm *Z-Line* bus from Dangriga to Placencia calls at Sittee River, and any bus travelling the Southern Highway can drop you at the road junction with the village. Hitching is another option.

Glover's Reef

The southernmost of Belize's three coral atolls, **Glover's Reef** lies between 40 and 50km off Dangriga. Named after a British pirate, the reef is roughly oval in shape, about 35km north to south, and its only cayes are in the southeastern section. What makes Glover's Reef so unusual among the remote atolls is that it offers accommodation within the reach of budget travellers, at the *Glover's Atoll Resort* (☎05/23048). There are nine simple **beach cabins** (U$95 per person per week, including transport from Sittee River) and space for **camping** (U$60 per week), overlooking the reef on Northeast Caye, but these are only available when not booked by groups of sea kayakers – it's essential to call first. You need to bring your own food, unless you're in a group, in which case you can organize to be catered for. Activities include sea kayaking, fishing, snorkelling and scuba diving, which is spectacular, thanks to a huge underwater cliff and some tremendous wall diving. The resort's boat drops off visitors at Sittee River on Saturday afternoon and collects the new load on Sunday morning. The trip takes up to three hours in a skiff, longer if under sail.

You can also stay – much more expensively – on **Southwest Caye**, 10km from Long Caye, at the *Manta Reef Resort* (☎02/331895; in the US: ☎1-800/342-0053). Diving and fishing packages cost around U$1400 per week.

The Cockscomb Basin Jaguar Reserve

The jagged peaks of the **Maya Mountains** rise to the west of the Southern Highway, their lower slopes covered in dense rainforest. The tallest summits are those of the Cockscomb range, which includes Victoria Peak, at 1120m the highest mountain in Belize. Beneath the ridges is a sweeping bowl, part of which was declared a jaguar preserve in 1986; it has since been expanded to cover an area of more than forty thousand hectares, and is today the **Cockscomb Basin Jaguar Reserve**. A rough track connects the sanctuary with the main highway, branching off at the village of **MAYA CENTRE**. Heading towards the reserve, it runs through towering forest, fording a couple of fresh, clear streams before it crosses the Cabbage Hall Gap and reaches the Cockscomb Basin. Buses between Dangriga and Punta Gorda, Placencia or Independence pass Maya Centre.

The reserve itself was the result of a mid-1980s study, sponsored by the New York Zoological Society, into whether a reserve could be viably established in Belize to protect its large jaguar population. The area was inhabited in Maya times, and the ruins of **Chucil Balam**, a small Classic period ceremonial centre, still lie hidden in the forest. It was also exploited by the mahogany loggers, and the names of their abandoned camps, such as Leave If You Can and Go to Hell, illustrate how they felt about life in the forest. Technically, this is a tropical moist forest, with an annual rainfall of 400cm that feeds a complex network of streams and rivers, most of which eventually run into the Swasey River and the South Stann Creek.

The forest is home to a sizeable percentage of **Belize's plant and animal species**. Among the mammals are tapir, otter, coati, deer, anteater, armadillo and, of course, jaguar. Over 290 species of bird have also been recorded, including the endangered scarlet macaw, the great curassow, the keel-billed toucan and the king vulture. And there's an abundance of reptiles and amphibians, including the red-eyed tree frog, the boa constrictor and the deadly fer-de-lance (known as tommy-goff in Belize). The forest itself is made up of a fantastic range of plant species, including orchids, giant tree ferns, airplants and trees such as banak, cohune, mahogany and ceiba. It's an ideal environment for plant-spotting, serious bird-watching or for seeking out the ever-evasive wildlife, and special trails have been cut to give visitors a taste of the forest's diversity. These take you along the river banks, through the forest or even, if you're suitably prepared, on a two-day hike to Victoria Peak. The **Ben's Bluff Trail**, for example, is a strenuous but worthwhile hike from the riverside to the top of a forested ridge – where there's a great view of the entire Cockscomb Basin – with a chance to cool off in a delightful rocky pool on the way back. Inner tubes are available from the warden's office; walk upstream and float down for an amazing view of the forest. Although the basin could be home to as many as fifty of Belize's six-hundred-strong jaguar population, your chances of seeing one are very slim.

Practicalities

You need to sign in and pay the entrance fee (Bz$10) at **the craft centre** in Maya Centre on the Southern Highway before entering the reserve. A small shop (with attached bar run by Julio Saqui) sells basic supplies and cold drinks; this is a good place to find out about guides if you're thinking of attempting the hike to Victoria Peak. If you need somewhere to **stay**, Aurora Saqui, one of the Garcia sisters, runs *Nuuk Che'il* (Mayan for "in the middle of the forest") *Cottages* (④): simple but delightful thatched *cabañas*, with shared bathroom and hot water. Saqui has developed a medicinal trail and makes traditional herbal medicines, for sale in the H'men Herbal Centre. The community telephone (☎05/22666) is next to the *Mejentz'il Restaurant*.

From Maya Centre it's a ten-kilometre walk or drive to the reserve headquarters: walking takes a couple of hours, up a gentle slope. At the headquarters, in a cleared grassy area surrounded by beautiful tropical foliage, there's an excellent **visitor centre** and some simple but comfortable hut **accommodation** (②); the **campground** (Bz$5) is a little further on. You'll have to bring your own food, but the huts do have a gas stove. You need a **permit** to stay overnight in the reserve: they're obtainable from the *Belize Audubon Society* in Belize City, the *Pelican Beach Hotel* in Dangriga, or from the site headquarters. At the time of writing, new upmarket accommodation and a campsite were under construction.

There is an opportunity for a limited amount of **voluntary work** in the reserve, maintaining trails, working in the visitor centre or even tracking howler monkeys. Write to Ernesto Saqui, Director CBWS, PO Box 90, Dangriga, Belize.

Sapodilla Lagoon Wildlife Refuge and Black Cat Lodge

Continuing on the Southern Highway for 3km past Maya Centre you'll reach the turn off for the privately owned **Sapodilla Lagoon Wildlife Refuge** (signed on the left-hand side of the road; buses will stop here), where you have a better chance of actually spotting a jaguar or a nesting jabiru stork than anywhere else in the country. The refuge, owned by American Larry Staley, stretches along both sides of the highway, from the eastern foothills of the Maya Mountains to the coast at Sapodilla Lagoon, bounded in part by the Sittee River, and includes a range of habitats. Larry has built trails and observation platforms and converted the main house into *Black Cat Lodge*, which his girlfriend Anna runs like a very relaxed youth **hostel**. It's a 25-minute walk from the road, and accommodation is in bunk beds and hammocks, with shared bathroom. The price (Bz$40 per person) includes three meals (which you cook yourself; bring your own drinks), horse riding and use of the canoe. **Camping** is free, and you pay only for food. There's no need to book; just show up, even at night, though you can write to Larry, c/o Sittee River Village.

The Placencia peninsula

PLACENCIA, an especially welcome stop after the bus ride from Belize City or Belmopan, is a small, laid-back fishing village, catering to an increasing number of tourists. Shaded by palm trees, cooled by the sea breeze, and perched on the tip of a long, narrow, sandy peninsula, 75km south of Dangriga, it's light years from the hassle of Belize City. A good dirt road connects the village with the Southern Highway, turning east to Riversdale, then south through **Maya Beach** and the Garifuna village of **Seine Bight**. Travelling along the sand road south down the peninsula you'll pass half a dozen or so upscale resorts, most of them owned and operated by expatriate North Americans. Accommodation is usually in cabins with private bathrooms and electricity. Meals, if not included in the tariff, come to around US$30 per day, and hotel tax and a 10 percent service charge may be added to bills. In addition to the pleasures of a Caribbean beach just a few steps away, most of the hotels also have access to Placencia Lagoon.

> The **telephone area code** for Placencia and the peninsula is ☎06.

Maya Beach and Seine Bight to Placencia

The first of the peninsula's resorts, on the beautiful stretch of coast called **Maya Beach**, are the *Green Parrot Beach Houses* (☎ & fax 224880; ⑦), owned by Canadians Ray Twanow and Colleen Fleury, whose rates are a pleasant change from the generally overpriced peninsula. Raised on stilts, the beach houses sleep up to five people: each has a spacious deck, superb kitchen and a loft bedroom with a queen and a single bed. There's also an excellent restaurant.

Just south of the *Green Parrot* are the six wood-and-thatch cabins of *Singing Sands Inn* (☎ & fax 22243; in US: ☎1-800/617-2637; ⑦), owned by Australians Bruce Larkin and Sally Steeds. The coral outcrops here are great for snokelling and you can learn to dive. Some 3km further, the small, previously little-visited Garifuna vilage of **SEINE BIGHT** now has several (mostly overpriced) resorts and hotels. One of the best, run by English couple Mike and Pamela Hazeltine, is the *Hotel Seine Bight* (☎22491; ④–⑥), which has just three rooms, including a spacious upstairs suite with deck. The popular, intimate restaurant has a full-service international menu; you may have to book for dinner in high season. The daily lunch buffet is always good value. The only other reasonably priced accommodation is *Aunt Chigi's Place* (③), a distinctive collection of brightly painted green and yellow buildings set back from the road near the school.

Seine Bight, reputed to have been founded by privateers in 1629, was possibly given its present name by French fishermen deported from Newfoundland after Britain gained control of Canada. The village is certainly worth a visit even if you're not staying; you can play pool in the *Sunshine Bar*, listen to Garifuna music in the *Kulcha Shak* (which also has basic but overpriced rooms), on the beach to the south, and visit *Lola's Art Gallery and Cafe*, where Lola Delgado displays her superb (and affordable) oil and acrylic paintings of village life. Her work is in great demand to decorate the rooms of the resorts and she's also a fine cook.

Seine Bight to Placencia

Beyond Seine Bight another series of resorts offers upscale **accommodation;** they're listed in the order you approach them from the north.

Serenity Resort, 1km south of Seine Bight (☎23232; fax 23231). Twelve comfortable, sky-blue cabins with patio, and a 10-bedroom hotel with a conference centre, often used by church and study groups. It's an alcohol-free resort, but there's an excellent restaurant. ⑦.

Rum Point Inn, just north of the airstrip (☎23239; fax 23240; in US: ☎1-800/747-7888). Expert naturalists the Beviers offer the most sumptuous rooms on the peninsula; the giant mushroom-shaped whitewashed cabins are spacious, cool and very comfortable. With emphasis on archeology, science and natural history, the library is the best of any hotel in the country, and there's a first-class restaurant (non-residents must book). US$224 double, including meals, high season. Accepts *Visa/Mastercard/AmEx*. ⑨.

Kitty's Place, just south of the airstrip (☎23227; fax 23226). Conveniently near the village, with a variety of accommodation including apartments, beach *cabañas*, garden rooms, a studio and budget rooms, *Kitty's* is one of the nicest options in this area. The restaurant serves delicious Belizean and international food, and the long-established dive shop (PADI certification US$350) also caters ably to snorkellers. ⑤–⑧.

Turtle Inn, 1km north of the village (☎23244; fax 23245). Seven wood-and-thatch *cabañas* on a gorgeous, palm-lined beach. Skip White, the American owner, has built a superb, relaxed, resort for diving, fishing and jungle tours, and boasts that there's no added service charge; tips are optional. Guests can use sea kayaks and bicycles. Rates include breakfast. ⑧.

Village Inn, at the north end of the village, just before the water tower (☎23217). Simple, relatively good value rooms and houses, best for longer stays. Kayaks for rent. ④–⑥.

Placencia village

The easiest way to reach Placencia village is on one of the regular *Maya Airways* or *Tropic Air* flights from the international or municipal airports (about 45min). Cheaper is the direct **bus from Dangriga**, which leaves at noon and 1pm (via Hopkins and Sittee River). You can also hop over easily from **Independence/ Mango Creek**, the small town just across the lagoon, where residents come to buy supplies and the older children go to school. (Incidentally, though some maps show Mango Creek and Independence as two places, Mango Creek is the creek that lends its name to one end of town; Independence begins at the road junction.) Buses to Independence leave Dangriga daily at about 2.30pm (2hr) or you can take any service to or from Punta Gorda.

From Independence a new service, the *Hokey Pokey* (☎22376; 50min; Bz$12), leaves for Placencia at 8.30am and 2.30pm; the boatman usually meets the arriving buses. Boats return at 10am and 4pm. Otherwise, if you wait around for a while, you may be able to get a lift on a boat with a Placencia local. The fare depends on what you're willing to pay – reckon on around Bz$15. A charter costs about Bz$30.

Though of little intrinsic interest, Independence is a useful transport hub. For details, see p.425.

Arrival and information

The two daily **buses** from Dangriga end up at the beachfront filling station (and return at 5 and 6am), right at the end of the peninsula, but if you're looking for budget rooms you should get off when you see the *Kingfisher Sports* office, on the right hand side of thre road, about halfway through the village. Head left for **the sidewalk**, a concrete walkway that winds through the palms like an elongated garden path, and you'll be at the centre of a cluster of hotels and restaurants.

There's no **tourist office**, but locals are glad to answer questions and the *Orange Peel Gift Shop* supplies hand-drawn maps. The nearest **bank** is in Independence/Mango Creek (Friday mornings only) and, while travellers' cheques are readily accepted, you may find it difficult to cash one. The **post office**, without a permanent home (currently based in *Sonny's Resort*), is rather disorganized; the public telephone, in the office next to the filling station, is a little more reliable. The **filling station** itself keeps irregular hours; if you're driving fill up when you can. If your hotel doesn't do **laundry**, try *Willie's Laundry*, at the north end of the village.

Finally, if you're heading **to Honduras**, *Kingfisher Sports* (☎23175; fax 23204) run a skiff service, leaving every Saturday at 9am, to Puerto Cortes (US$50; 3hr; book by 3pm Fri at the latest), from where there are easy connections to San Pedro Sula and La Ceiba and from there to the Bay Islands (p.241).

Accommodation

In Placencia village proper there's a wide choice of **accommodation**, and you should have no problem finding a room provided you don't arrive at Christmas, New Year or Easter without a booking. Possibilities begin at the sidewalk, and as you wend your way down it seems as though every family is offering **rooms**.

BUDGET ACCOMMODATION

Clive's, at the northern end of the sidewalk. The cheapest option, with simple cabins and plenty of space for camping. ①.

Conrad and Lydia's Rooms, near the north end of the sidewalk (☎23117). Very good value, clean, secure rooms run by a friendly family, who'll cook breakfast on request. ②–③.

Deb & Dave's Last Resort, on the road, 50m past *Kingfisher Sports* (☎23207). The nicest budget place in the village; lovely wooden rooms with shared hot water bathroom. Dave is a superb tour guide. ③.

Gail's, to the right of the sidewalk, near the centre; look for the sign. Two simple but roomy cabins; each can sleep three. ②.

Julia's Rooms, in the centre of the village, just south of the *Seaspray* (☎23185). Small hotel, with basic rooms on the beach, between the sidewalk and the sea. There's a porch, though not much sea view. ②.

Jo-Jo's Rooms, by the sidewalk, north of the centre (☎23168). A couple of bargain cabins, run by a friendly Canadian expatriate. ②.

Paradise Vacation Resort, follow the path to the right from the end of the sidewalk, at the main dock(☎23179; fax 23256). Two-storey hotel where most of the rooms have private bath and hot water. Large deck upstairs where you can enjoy the breeze. Very good value. ③.

Seaspray Hotel, on the beach in the centre of the village (☎23148). Popular hotel, with a range of accommodation, all with hot water bath. Though mostly good value, some rooms are overpriced, so check what you're getting. ④–⑤.

Traveller's Inn, signed from the sidewalk, just south of the centre (☎23190) Five basic rooms – cheapest in the village – with shared bath, and some in a separate building with private bath. ②.

MID-RANGE AND ABOVE

Barracuda and Jaguar Inn, signed just past the market, towards the south end of the village (☎23330; fax 23250). Two varnished wooden cabins with two double beds and coffee-maker, and a large deck with lounge chairs and a hammock, set in tropical gardens; the best value in this range. Run by Canadian Wende Bryan and Englishman Anton Holmes, the bar is a great place to exchange information and arrange trips. Rates (discounts if you show the *Rough Guide*) include breakfast. ⑤.

Coconut Cottage, on the beach, just south of the centre (☎ & fax 23234). Two gorgeous, well-decorated cabins in a quiet location, equipped with fridge, coffee-maker and hot water shower. Run by Kay and Joel Westby; Joel is one of the best fishing guides in the village. ⑥.

Marlene's Apartment, west from the south dock, past *Brenda's* (☎23264). The best studio apartment in the village, with a double and a single bed and a kitchen with a huge fridge and stove. A balcony runs along the front and you can watch the sunrise over Placencia Caye. The restaurant serves the best home cooking in Placencia; rates include breakfast. ⑥.

Ranguana Lodge, on the beach in the centre of the village (☎ & fax 23112). Very friendly and well run, with beautiful white *cabañas* with hardwood interiors. All have hot water, fridge and coffee maker, plus balcony and hammocks. Three are on the beach; the two others have sea views.This is the place to book for Ranguana Caye (see p.425). Accepts *Visa/MC*. ⑥.

Trade Winds, on the south point (☎23122; fax 23201). Five cabins with fridge, coffee-maker, hot water and deck on a spacious plot, facing sea breezes. Run by Janice Leslie, Placencia's former postmistress and a mine of local knowledge. You can book *Maya* tickets here. ⑥.

Eating and drinking

There are plenty of good **restaurants** in Placencia, though even more than else-where in Belize, places change management fast, so it's always worth asking a resident's advice first. Most places close early; you'll certainly have a better choice if you're at the table by 8pm. .

Fresh **bread** is available from John *The Bakerman*, just north of the market, and from a number of local women who bake Creole bread and buns. The large shop known as the **market** is the main place for produce or any other shopping: get there early, as fresh goods are soon sold out. A new store, *Dis' n' Dat*, in the centre of the village, sells a wide range of non-perishable foods and there are several small grocery stores.

Brenda's Caribbean Cafe, on the south beach. Some of the best Creole food in Placencia, though prices and quality are variable.

BJ's, near the north end of the village. Another good, Creole, family-run restaurant.

Chili's, at the south point, near the main dock. A bargain food counter in what Bill, the owner calls, a "chicken shed"; try the enormous vegetarian burrito. Best at lunchtime.

Cove Restaurant, north along the beach at the Cove resort (☎23233). Worth the walk along the beach to try the best international dishes in the village. Small menu with fresh, gourmet food; desserts a speciality. Closed Thursday.

Daisy's Ice Cream Parlour, set back from the sidewalk, just south of the *Seaspray*. Long-established and deservedly popular place for ice cream, cakes and snacks, now serving complete meals.

Kingfisher, on the beach in the centre of the village. Good seafood in a fine location.

Marlene's Restaunt, just past *Brenda's* (☎23264). Great for breakfast (usually the first to open), serving good coffee and fantastic home made bread and cakes. Lunch and dinner are equally good, especially for fish, but it's tiny so you may have to book.

Omar's Fast Foods, on the sidewalk, just south of the centre. Really inexpensive, and sometimes even fast. Great, filling burritos.

Pickled Parrot Bar & Grill, at the *Barracuda and Jaguar Inn*. Consistently the best restaurant in the village, serving fresh seafood and international dishes.

Tentacles, built over the water at the south end. Superb location to enjoy the sunset. Steaks, pasta and seafood, but variable service and quality.

Nightlife

The **evenings** in Placencia are as relaxed as the days and there are plenty of **bars**, ideal for drinking rum and watching the sun set. A pleasant walk or cycle ride north takes you along the beach to *Kitty's*, which has great bar snacks. There's also satellite TV, which attracts American football fans at weekends, and a library with a wide selection of books, especially on Belize and Latin America. *Mike's Caribbean Club* and the *Dockside Bar* are favourite meeting places at the south end of the village. If you feel the urge to **dance**, try the *Cozy Corner Disco*, on the beach, which is open every night except Monday; it also has a very good beachside snack bar, open late.

Around Placencia, offshore and inland

Placencia **lagoon** is ideal exploring in a kayak. You may even spot manatee, though it's more likely to be a series of ripples as the shy giant swims powerfully for cover. Further out, the main **reef** lies about 30km offshore. Here are the **Silk Cayes**, where the Barrier Reef begins to break into several smaller reefs and cayes, and also many smaller islands and coral heads closer to the shore, including the **Bugle Cayes** and **Lark Caye**. Some hotels run trips to Laughing Bird Caye, a recently expanded National Park, but this can be expensive unless you go in a group.

In general, trips from Placencia can be tailor-made to your preference and your pocket, and you can arrange anything from an afternoon on the water to a week of camping, fishing, snorkelling and sailing. The best **fishing** guides in the village are Joel Westby at *Coconut Cottage* (see p.423) and Bernard Leslie (☎23162), who has a small office near the southern end of the sidewalk. For **scuba diving**, *Deep End Divers* (☎23294; fax 23295), on the lagoon across from *BJ's Restaurant* offer friendly, safety-conscious service, excellent guides and good dockside facilities. Also in Placencia is the long-established *Placencia Dive Shop* (☎23313; fax 23226) at the south end of the sidewalk by the main dock. They offer full service diving and equipment rental. Both dive shops offer full certification courses for around US$350.

It's also worth heading inland from Placencia; up the thickly forested banks of the **Monkey River** or to the Jaguar Preserve (see p.418).

French Louis Caye

Kitty Fox and her partner Ran (from *Kitty's Place*; see p.421) offer a great sea kayaking trip to **French Louis Caye**, a tiny island fringed with mangroves 10km offshore. You paddle the kayak, camp on the caye overnight (using your own equipment, or sleeping in a hammock in the two-storey wooden house if no one else is using it) and food is provided; all for US$50 per person, including snorkelling gear. If you want exclusive use of the caye it costs US$150 for two people, including transport and snorkelling equipment; you can cook at the wooden house or Kitty can organize someone. Mosquitoes are not a problem as there's no open fresh water. All around is great snorkelling, with numerous hard and soft corals, sea anemones and huge schools of tiny fish among the mangrove roots. There's even a resident pair of ospreys, nesting in a mature white mangrove, successfully rearing chicks every year.

Ranguana Caye

Thirty-five kilometres southeast of Placencia is **Ranguana Caye**, a jewel of an island just 120m long by 20m wide. The sand is softer here, the palm trees taller and more stately than in Placencia, and the sunsets glorious, silhouetting mountain ranges in Honduras and the Maya Mountains in Belize. The *Ranguana Reef Resort* (contact *Ranguana Lodge* in Placencia; ☎ & fax 23112) offers camping (②) and accommodation in beautiful wooden cabins (⑥), which face into the almost constant breeze. The showers and toilets are immaculate and there's even hot water and electricity. Ranguana Caye is surrounded by patch reefs; for divers the shelf and drop-off down to 800m begin 750m offshore. Transport to the caye is not included in the price; a boat for up to four people costs US$75 each way.

The Monkey River

One of the best day trips from Placencia takes you by boat 20km southwest to the almost pristine **Monkey River**, which teems with fish, bird life and, naturally enough, howler monkeys. Dave Dial, of *Monkey River Magic* (☎23209; fax 23291), runs the best tours, his wildlife expertise complemented by the experienced local guides from Monkey River village. Tours set off by 7am and cost US$40. A thirty-minute dash through the waves is followed by a leisurely glide up the river and a walk along forest trails. Lunch is usually taken on a sandbank on the river or you can get a meal in *Alice's Restaurant* in the village, where there's also time to enjoy a drink in the *Driftwood Bar*, at the river mouth, on the widest beach in Belize.

INDEPENDENCE TRAVEL CONNECTIONS

Just across the lagoon from Placencia (see p.422 for details of boats), Independence is a useful travel hub. Heading north, *Z-Line* buses leave for **Dangriga** (2hr) at 8am, noon and 3pm, and south to **Punta Gorda** at 2pm, 6pm and 9pm. The *James* bus also passes through (heading north Sun, Tues & Fri; heading south Mon, Wed & Sat). *Z-Line* buses take a rest/meal stop at the *Cafe Hello* in Independence; the *James* bus stops at *Marita's*, on Hercules Ave. The **food** at these places is fine, but try not to get stuck **overnight** here. If you do, the *Hello Hotel* (☎06/22428; ④–⑤), mainly used by business people, has some a/c rooms; you could also try the clean, simple *Ursula's Guest House* (②) on Gran Main St. The *Barclays Bank* in Independence, open Friday mornings, gives cash advances.

If you want to **stay**, try the budget *Enna's Hotel* (③); call Monkey River community telephone on ☎06/22014. At the time of writing, Dave was also building cabins and a campsite upriver.

The far south

Beyond the Placencia and Independence junctions, the Southern Highway leaves the banana plants and the small, grim settlements squashed beside the plantation roads, twisting at first through pine forests, and crossing numerous creeks and rivers. There are few villages along the way, and new citrus plantations are always in view, the neat ranks of trees marching over the hills.

About 35km north of Punta Gorda, **Nim Li Punit** was a Late Classic Maya site possibly allied to nearby Lubaantun. The site was discovered in 1976 and a total of 25 stelae were found, eight of them carved, including one that measured 9m in height, the tallest yet found in Belize. Unfortunately, the site was badly looted soon after its discovery; archeological work did not begin until 1983 and in 1986 another stela and a royal tomb were unearthed. The site is signposted about 1km west of the Southern Highway, surrounded by the fields of the nearby Maya village of **Indian Creek**. Just below the turn-off for the ruins is *Whitney's* store and filling station, which is better stocked than many shops in Punta Gorda and has fresh bread every day.

A little further south, the road to **Silver Creek** branches off to the right and with your own transport you can use this route to visit the Maya villages and the ruins of Lubaantun (see p.432). Near the village of **BIG FALLS** is the only **hot spring** in Belize, a luxurious spot for a warm bath. The spring is on a farm belonging to Peter Alaman, who also runs a small shop and guest house (②). Ask permission if you want to camp; it'll cost a few dollars. Don't expect to have it all to yourself at weekends, however, as the pools are a popular picnic spot.

To get to either of the above you may have to try your luck hitching along the Southern Highway, though in the early afternoon there are buses to the nearby villages, leaving from the Civic Center in **Punta Gorda**.

Punta Gorda

The Southern Highway eventually comes to an end in **PUNTA GORDA**, the last town in Belize and the heart of the isolated Toledo District, an area that has always been hard to reach and remains largely overlooked by planners and developers. However, work has begun paving the first section of the highway north from Punta Gorda, and the few visitors who make it out here are rewarded by spending a few days at the Maya villages inland.

To the north of Punta Gorda are the remains of the Toledo settlement, which was founded in 1867 by emigrants from the US. Many of the original settlers soon drifted home, discouraged by the torrential downpours and the rigours of frontier life, but their numbers were boosted by Methodists from Mississippi. The Methodists were deeply committed to the settlement and, despite a cholera epidemic in 1868, managed to clear 160 acres. By 1870 sugar was the main product, with twelve separate estates running their own mills. The settlement reached its peak in 1890, after which it was threatened by falling sugar prices. Most farmers moved into alcohol production, but for the Methodists this was out of the

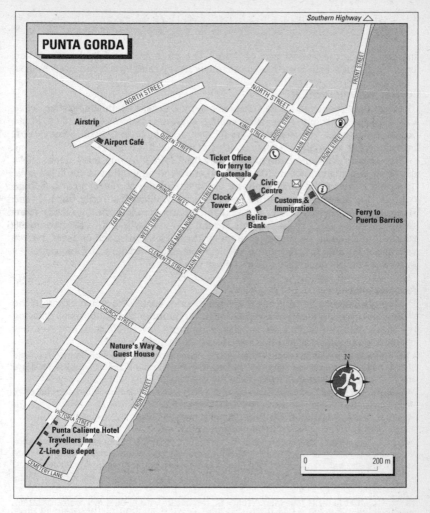

PUNTA GORDA

Southern Highway

FRONT STREET

NORTH STREET

NORTH STREET

KING STREET

MIDDLE STREET

MAIN STREET

Airstrip

QUEEN STREET

Airport Café

Ticket Office
for ferry to
Guatemala

PRINCE STREET

FAR WEST STREET

WEST STREET

JOSE MARIA NUNEZ STREET

BACK STREET

Clock
Tower

Civic
Centre

Customs &
Immigration

Belize
Bank

Ferry to
Puerto Barrios

CLEMENTS STREET

MAIN STREET

CHURCH STREET

Nature's Way
Guest House

FRONT STREET

N

VICTORIA STREET

Punta Caliente Hotel
Travellers Inn
Z-Line Bus depot

CEMETERY LANE

0   200 m

question, and they preferred to feed their molasses to their cattle or simply throw it in the rivers. By 1910 their community was destitute, although it was largely as a result of their struggle that Toledo was permanently settled.

Today's town is populated by a mixture of Mestizos, Garifuna, Maya – who make up more than half the population of the district – Lebanese, Chinese and Creoles, and is the focal point for a large number of villages and farming settlements. The busiest day is Saturday, when people from the surrounding villages come in to trade.

Despite the recent minor building boom, Punta Gorda remains a small, unhurried, friendly town and you won't encounter any hassle. Its position on low sea cliffs allows cooling breezes to reduce the worst of the heat but there's no deny-

> The **telephone area code** for Punta Gorda is ☎07.

ing that this is the wettest part of Belize. The trees are heavy with mosses and bromeliads, their lush growth encouraged by heavy rains which can last for days.

Arrival and information

The best **bus** service to Punta Gorda is run by *Z-Line,* with buses leaving Belize City at 8am, noon and 3pm daily, calling at Dangriga four hours later. Punta Gorda consists of five streets – Front Street, Main Street, Back Street, West Street and Far West Street – all of which run parallel to the shore.

The **Toledo Visitors Information Center** (*TVIC*), by the ferry dock, offers excellent information about Punta Gorda, and accommodation in the local area. The **post office** and a **public phone** are in the group of government buildings opposite the **immigration office**, near the ferry dock. The only **bank** is the *Belize Bank,* at the top corner of the main square, across from the Civic Center (Mon–Fri 8am–1pm, Fri also 3–4pm). It's not always easy to get Guatemalan quetzals in Punta Gorda; there may be a moneychanger by the dock on ferry days or you might be able to get some from the Guatemalan traders at their stalls. It's best to get rid of your Belize dollars before you leave.

Accommodation

During the last couple of years there has been a spate of **hotel** building in the village, in the expectation of a rapid rise in the number of "ecotourists" enjoying the area's many attractions. While visitor numbers have increased, however, few people spend long here, and there are plenty of bargains.

Charlton's Inn, 9 Main St (☎22197; fax 22471). Two-storey concrete building, with private bath and hot water, some a/c and safe parking. Owner Duwane Wagner, an agent for *Maya* and *Tropic,* is welcoming and there's cold water to drink. ②–④.

Mahung's, corner of North and Main streets (☎22044). Cheap and basic but does have hot water and some private baths. Bicycle rental available. ②–③.

Miramar, Front St (☎22033). The largest hotel in town and, amazingly, winner of an international award for tourism. All rooms have private bath. ④–⑤.

Nature's Way Guest House, 65 Front St (☎22119). The best budget place in Punta Gorda; renowned as a meeting place and information point. Dorm accommodation (Bz\$16), overlooking the sea, and a couple of private rooms. Good meals in the wholefood restaurant. ②.

St Charles Inn, 23 King St (☎22149). Clean and quiet, with carpeted rooms with TV. At the top end of the scale for Punta Gorda, and recommended. ③–④.

Tate's Guest House, 34 José María Nuñez St, two blocks west of the town centre (☎22196). A quiet, family-run hotel with some a/c rooms. ③–④.

Wahima, 11 Front St. Inexpensive, basic and friendly; some rooms have a/c, fridge and TV. A small restaurant/bar next door provides local colour. ②–③.

Eating and drinking

Most **restaurants** tend to be rather basic in Punta Gorda, but there are a couple of newer places where the quality is somewhat higher, and certainly it's easy to get a filling meal at a reasonable price. Some of the best food is served in tiny family restaurants. Of the several Chinese restaurants on Front St, the best is the *Mira Mar.* Further along, the *Morning Glory Cafe* (closed Mon) serves seafood, burgers and snacks in clean, bright surroundings, while at *Bobby's Restaurant,*

Main St, you can eat the good old Creole staples of rice and beans. Finally, the *Airport Cafe* (at the airstrip) is surprisingly good. There's a bakery on Front St, past the Texaco station. Bars and clubs like the *Starlight* on Main St provide Punta Gorda's **nightlife**, and if you're desperate for loud **music** there's the sleazy *Southside Disco* in the town centre, or the *Massive Rock Disco* opposite the bus depot.

Staying around Punta Gorda: Toledo's ecotourism project

Ecotourism is a buzzword throughout Belize, and several projects in Toledo are poised to reap the benefits. Their aim is to achieve a balance between the need for economic development and the need to preserve the rich natural and cultural heritage of the area. It is hoped that small numbers of "low impact" visitors will provide additional income to villages without destroying the communities' traditional way of life.

At the Punta Gorda ferry dock, the *TVIC* promotes the "host family network", which involves visitors staying in a village with a Mopan or Kekchí Maya family, participating in village work – grinding corn, chopping firewood, cooking tortillas and the like – and sleeping in a hammock. The *Toledo Ecotourism Association,* operating from an office at *Nature's Way,* runs a **Guest House and Eco Trail Program**, involving eleven villages in the southern Toledo District. Each village has an eight-bed guest house, and meals are taken at different houses to allow distribution of the income. Each village has its own attraction, be it a cave, waterfall, river or ruin. Guided walks or horse rides cost around Bz$7 per hour (4hr minimum) and there may also be canoes to rent. The villagers have an extensive cultural knowledge of the medicinal uses of plants and their ancient Maya myths. This can be an excellent way to experience village life without feeling like an intruder. The association is also the driving force behind the **Habiabara Garinagu Cerro** project, designed to preserve traditional Garifuna culture as well as enabling farmers to earn a living from commercial agriculture. For information contact the *Toledo Ecotourism Association,* 65 Front St, Punta Gorda (☎22119 or 22203).

MOVING ON FROM PUNTA GORDA

The *Z-Line* depot in Punta Gorda is at the south end of José María Nuñez St (☎22165); **buses** leave for Belize City at 5am, 9am and noon (9hr). The *James* bus meets the ferry on its arrival in Punta Gorda and continues to Belize City at 11am on Tuesday and Friday, at 6am on Sunday, leaving from the small yard on Front St, opposite the ferry dock.

Buses for the **Maya villages** leave from the streets next to the Civic Center. Most bus companies are literally one-man operations and Sunday is their day off. To **San Antonio** two buses, *Chun's* and *Prim's,* leave at 1pm Monday, Wednesday, Friday and Saturday, returning at 5am. These last buses also operate a service to **Blue Creek** and **Aguacate** – check at the *TVIC.*

It's possible to **fly** to and from Punta Gorda: tickets can be bought at the *Belize Tourism Centre* on Front St and Bob Pennell's hardware store on Main St. If you want to continue south, tickets for **ferries** are sold on the day only, from 8.30am at the office of *Agencia de Lineas Maritimas Puerto Santo Tomas de Castillo Izabal Guatemala,* at 24 Middle St.

Out to sea: the cayes and the coast

The cayes and reefs off Punta Gorda mark the southern end of Belize's Barrier Reef. The main reef has already started to break up here, leaving several clusters of islands, each surrounded by a small independent reef. The closest to Punta Gorda are the **Snake Cayes**, hundreds of tiny islands in the mouth of a large bay, where the shoreline is a complex maze of mangrove swamps. On Wild Cane Caye archeologists, with the assistance of *Earthwatch* volunteers, have found evidence of a Maya coastal trade centre. Further out, in the Gulf of Honduras, are the **Sapodilla Cayes**, the largest of which, **Hunting Caye**, has an immigration post and is frequented by Guatemalan as well as Belizean day-trippers. There is a proposal to designate Hunting Caye a national park.

Though visited by specialist sea-kayaking tours, the whole area receives relatively little attention from international tourism and is very interesting to explore. If you'd like to spend a day or two out on the reef talk to someone with a boat in Punta Gorda, such as Bobby of *Bobby's Bar,* or Memo, who usually meets arriving buses and can take you on reasonably priced fishing or snorkelling trips.

From Punta Gorda you can see range upon range of mountains in Guatemala and Honduras, but the Belizean **coastline south** of here is flat and sparsely populated. Rivers meander across a coastal plain covered with thick tropical rainforest; the Temash River is lined with the tallest mangrove forest in the country. In the far south the Sarstoon River, navigable by small boats, forms the border with Guatemala. The only village here is **BARRANCO**, a small, traditional Garifuna settlement of two hundred people, which you can visit through the village guest house programme (see p.429).

Towards the mountains: Maya villages and ruins

Heading inland from Punta Gorda towards the foothills of the Maya Mountains, you meet yet another uniquely Belizean culture. Here **Mopan Maya** are mixed with **Kekchí** speakers from the Verapaz highlands of Guatemala. For the most part each group keeps to its own villages, language and traditions, although both are partially integrated into modern Belizean life and many speak English. Guatemalan families have been arriving here for the last hundred years or so escaping repression and a shortage of land at home, and founding new villages deep in the forest. It's estimated that about twelve families a year still cross the border to settle in land-rich Belize, along routes that have been used for generations. The villages are connected by road and there's a basic bus service from Punta Gorda, although moving around isn't that easy and in many places you'll have to rely on hitching, despite the fact that there isn't much traffic. Another option is to rent a bike from *Mahung's* (see p.428).

San Antonio and Uxbenka

The Mopan Maya village of **SAN ANTONIO**, perched on a small hilltop, is the easiest settlement to reach, as it's served by regular buses from Punta Gorda *(Chun's* and *Cho's,* from the Civic Center). It also has the benefit of *Bol's Hill Top Hotel* (community phone ☎07/22124; ②), which has simple **rooms** and superb views, and is a good place for **information** on local natural history and archeology. There are a couple of shops in the village, and you can get **meals** at Theodora's or Clara's houses, next to *Bol's.* The area is rich in wildlife, surrounded by jungle-clad hills and swift-flowing rivers. Further south and west are the villages of the Kekchí Maya, fairly recent immigrants who still retain strong cultural links with Guatemala.

The founders of San Antonio were from the Guatemalan village of San Luis just across the border, and they maintain many age-old traditions. Among other things the Indians of San Luis brought with them their patron saint – opposite *Bol's Hotel is* the church of San Luis Rey, currently looked after by American nuns. The church is the third to stand on the site (two previous versions were destroyed by fire) and its most remarkable feature is a set of superb stained-glass windows, donated by the people of St Louis, Missouri. The Indians also adhere to their own pre-Columbian traditions and fiestas – the main one takes place on June 13, and features marimba music, masked dances and much heavy drinking.

Seven kilometres west from San Antonio towards the village of **Santa Cruz** are the ruins of **Uxbenka**, a fairly small Maya site, superbly positioned on an exposed hilltop, with great views towards the coast. Uxbenka's existence only became known to archeologists in 1984 after reports of looting in the area: there's now a site caretaker, who lives in Santa Cruz. As you climb the hill before the village you'll be able to make out the shape of two tree-covered mounds to your left. Though the site has not been fully excavated, you can still make out a couple of pyramids and a plaza, and there are several badly eroded stelae, protected by thatched shelters.

Blue Creek and Pusilha

About 4km before the village of San Antonio, at *Ray's Cool Spot*, where you can get a meal and a drink, a branch road heads off south and west to the village of **BLUE CREEK**, where the main attraction is the village's namesake – a beautiful stretch of water that runs through magnificent rainforest. Whether you're walking or driving you won't miss the river, as the road crosses it just before it enters the village.

To get to the best swimming spot, walk upriver along the right-hand bank (facing upstream), and in about ten minutes you'll come to a lovely turquoise pool and the wooden cabins of *Slattery Biological Station*, used by North American student groups. The source, where the water gushes from beneath a mossy rock face, is about another fifteen minutes' walk upriver. Alongside this is the entrance to the **Hokeb Ha** cave, which is fairly easy to explore. The entire area is made up of limestone bedrock honeycombed with caves, many of which were sacred to the Maya, and doubtless there are still plenty of others waiting to be rediscovered. If you want to experience the cave in solitude don't come on a Sunday: it's starting to get crowded.

Further to the west of Blue Creek is the Kekchí village of **Aguacate**, beyond where the road climbs a ridge leading to the valley of the Moho River, near the border with Guatemala. Further up the valley are the ruins of **Pusilha**, a large Maya ceremonial centre. The city is built alongside the river on a small hilltop and although many of the buildings are quite extensive, none is very tall, reaching a maximum height of just 5 or 6m. The site has yielded an astonishing number of carved monuments and stelae, including zoomorphs in a style similar to those at Quiriguá in Guatemala (see p.213), leading archeologists to suggest that at some stage Pusilha may have been under Quiriguá's control. The site's most unusual feature is the remains of a stone bridge.

The ruins are accessible by boat, on foot or on horseback, which could make the whole business rather expensive. Sylvano is the best guide in Blue Creek and can take you to Maya altars deep in the Blue Creek cave, accessible only by boat.

San Pedro and the ruins of Lubaantun

To visit the ruins of Lubaantun from San Antonio, get a lift along the road to the Southern Highway and turn left at the track leading **to SAN PEDRO COLUMBIA**, a Kekchí village. The bus to San Antonio drops you at the entrance road, about 3km from the village – there's sometimes a truck waiting to ferry passengers over the final section of the journey. Head through the village and cross the Columbia River, just beyond which you'll see the track to the ruins, a few hundred metres on the left. If you ask around in the village one of the older boys will gladly show you the way; the ruins are twenty minutes' walk away.

Lubaantun, which means "Place of the Fallen Stones" in modern Mayan – not its original name – is a major Late Classic ceremonial centre which at one time covered a large area. The site is on a high ridge and from the top of the tallest building you can (just) see the Caribbean, over 30km away. Maya architects shaped and filled the hillside, with retaining walls as much as 10m high. Some restoration has now begun and the pyramids are quite impressive, as is the surrounding forest.

It now seems that the site was only occupied briefly, from 700 to 890 AD, very near the end of the Classic period. There are five main plazas with eleven major structures and three ball courts. The architecture is unusual in a number of ways: there are no stelae or sculpted monuments other than ball court markers, and the whole site is essentially a single acropolis, constructed on a series of low ridges. Another unusual feature is the absence of mortar. In this case the stone blocks are carved with particular precision and fitted together, Inca style, with nothing to bind them. The plainness and monumentality of Lubaantun's architecture is again similar to the later buildings at Quiriguá in Guatemala, and there may have been some connection between the two sites.

Lubaantun was brought to the attention of the colonial authorities in 1903 and the governor sent Thomas Gann to investigate. A survey in 1915 revealed many structures, and three ball-court markers were removed and taken to the Peabody Museum. The British Museum expedition of 1926 was joined in 1927 by J Eric S Thompson, who was to become the most renowned Maya expert of his time. No further excavations took place for over forty years until Norman Hammond mapped the site in 1970, producing a reconstruction of life in Lubaantun which showed the inhabitants' links with communities on the coast and inland. Lubaantun's wealth was created by the production of cacao beans, used as money by the civilizations of Mesoamerica.

Late Classic figurine found at Lubaantun

Bed and breakfast **accommodation** is offered by Alredo and Yvonne Villoria on their sustainable technology farm, *Dem Dats Doin* (☎07/22470; ②), on the way to San Pedro Columbia, 2km from the turn-off on the San Antonio road – ask at the *TVIC* at the ferry dock in Punta Gorda.

THE CRYSTAL SKULL OF LUBAANTUN

Perhaps Lubantuun's most enigmatic find came in 1926, when the famous **Crystal Skull** was unearthed here. This skull, which is made from pure rock crystal, was apparently found beneath an altar by Anna Mitchell-Hedges, the adopted daughter of the British Museum expedition's leader, FA Mitchell-Hedges. By a stroke of luck the find happened to coincide with her seventeenth birthday, and the skull was then given to the local Indians, who in turn presented it to Anna's father as a token of their gratitude for the help he had given them. Today Anna Mitchell-Hedges still owns it. In London's Museum of Mankind there's another crystal skull which – according to Dr G M Morant, an anthropologist who examined both skulls in 1936 – is a copy of the one found at Lubaantun. He also concluded that both of the life-size crystal skulls are modelled on the same original human head but could give no answer as to their true age and origin. There is a similar, smaller crystal skull in the Musee de l'Homme in Paris.

Mystery and controversy still surround the original skull. It's possible that the "discovery" was a birthday gift for Anna, placed there by her father who had acquired it on his previous travels, although she strenuously denies the allegation. The label on the Museum of Mankind's skull is suitably vague: "Possibly from Mexico, age uncertain . . . resembles in style the Mixtec carving of fifteenth-century Mexico, though some lines on the teeth appear to be cut with a jeweller's wheel. If so it may have been made after the Spanish Conquest".

travel details

The Southern Highway doesn't have anything like the same number of buses running along it as the Northern and Western highways, and trips into the south will inevitably take a day or two. The main routes are listed below; other buses to the smaller villages are covered in the text.

Buses

Belize City to Dangriga (4hr) is best covered by *Z-Line*, from the same terminal as *Venus* in Magazine Rd, Belize City (☎502/79907). There are ten departures daily: 8am, 9am, 10am and noon, then hourly until 5pm with an extra service at 3.30pm.

Belize City to Punta Gorda (9hr). Again, the best service is *Z-Line* (Mon–Sat 8am, noon & 3pm, Sun 10am & 3pm); the 8am, noon and 3pm departures connect with a bus leaving Dangriga for Punta Gorda. *James* also operate the run, leaving from Pound Yard Bridge (Mon, Wed & Sat, 7am).

Belize City to Gales Point. Two daily *Z-Line* services (2hr), and two in the other direction.

Dangriga to Belize City. *Z-Line* has 10 daily buses from 8am–4.30pm; for **Placencia** (2hr) they leave daily at noon and 1pm – the 1pm service calls at **Hopkins** (1hr) and **Sittee River** (1hr 30min). To **Independence** there's a daily bus at 2.30pm (2hr), to **Punta Gorda** daily at noon, 4pm and 7pm (5hr).

Punta Gorda to Belize City. *Z-Line* at 5am, 9am and noon. *James* leaves on Sun at 6am, Tues and Fri at 11am, connecting with the ferry from Guatemala. To **Dangriga** *Z-Line* leaves daily at 5am and 11am. All buses between Dangriga and Punta Gorda stop at Independence/Mango Creek.

Placencia to Dangriga. Daily, 5am and 6am.

Independence to Dangriga. Daily at 6am.

Hopkins and Sittee River to Dangriga. Daily at 7am.

Flights

As tourism in the South is growing, there may well be more flights and more operators in the near future. At present, *Maya Airways* have flights from **Belize City to Dangriga** (45min), most continuing to **Placencia and Punta Gorda** (1hr). Flights from Punta Gorda to Belize City call at Placencia and Dangriga. *Tropic Air* also operate scheduled flights to Dangriga and Punta Gorda.

Ferries

The twice-weekly ferry from **Punta Gorda to Puerto Barrios** in Guatemala (3hr) leaves at 2pm on Tues and Fri. It returns on Tues and Fri at 8am. There's a daily skiff at 8.30am Tues and Fri, 9am other days.

PART FOUR

THE
CONTEXTS

HISTORY

Not until the early nineteenth century is it really possible to talk of Guatemala and Belize (or British Honduras) as we know them now. Their histories began to diverge, however, as early as the tenth century, with the collapse of the Classic Maya civilization. It's that break which has been regarded as crucial here. The later histories are dealt with separately: before that the area has to be considered as part of Mesoamerica, which includes Mexico and the rest of Central America. This definition is designed to exclude the North American Indians (whose culture remained largely nomadic), and to bunch together the pre-Columbian civilizations of their southern neighbours.

By far the most important of these as far as Guatemala and Belize are concerned are the **Maya**, whose culture began to emerge here as early as 2000 BC and whose cities were at the height of their power and glory between 300 and 900 AD.

BEGINNINGS

Delving into the early history of Central America archeologists are on uncertain ground, piecing together a rough idea on the basis of scattered archeological remains and a handful of written texts. Prior to the advent of Maya civilization very little is known about the area, and even the Maya remain fairly mysterious.

Set out here is a brief overview of many separate theories, none of which can claim to dominate the academic debate. Over the last few years the situation has, if anything, become even more confused, as excavations of important new sites (especially in Belize) throw up information that casts doubt on many accepted notions. At any moment our whole understanding could be overturned by new discoveries, and there is certainly still a great deal to learn.

PREHISTORY

The earliest inhabitants of the Americas are thought to have crossed the Bering land bridge from Siberia to Alaska during the Fourth Ice Age, around 60,000 years ago, when sea levels were considerably lower than they are today. Successive waves of Stone Age hunters, travelling south along an ice-free corridor, had reached Central and South America by 15,000 BC. The first recognizable culture, known as **Clovis**, had emerged by 10,000 BC. Worked stone tools, including spearpoints, blades and scrapers, dating from 9000 BC, have been found in the Guatemalan highlands. In northern Belize thousands of chert flakes, which may be man-made artefacts, discovered at the Richmond Hill site could be evidence of human occupation 20,000 years ago.

In Mesoamerica, an area defined as stretching from north-central Mexico through Central America to Panamá, the first settled pattern of development took place around 8000 BC, as a warming climate forced the hunter-gatherers to adapt to a different way of life. The glaciers were in retreat and the big game, which the hunters depended upon, became scarce due to the warmer, drier climate and possibly over-hunting. This period, in which the hunters turned to more intensive use of plant foods, is known as the **Archaic** and lasted until about 2000 BC. During this time the food plants vital to the subsequent development of agriculture, such as corn, beans, peppers, squash and probably maize, were domesticated.

In Belize, the subject of extensive investigation in the 1980s, there is evidence of Archaic sequences dating from 7500 BC until later than 2000 BC. An early language, known as Proto-Maya, was in use in the western highlands of Guatemala, and probably other places too. Recent research on ancient pollen samples indicates that 4000 years ago Petén was an area of savannahs and broad-leaved woodlands. The current theory is that tropical forest did not appear until the Classic period, by which time the Maya could more easily control its profuse growth.

THE EARLY MAYA

Somewhere between 2000 and 1500 BC we move into the **Preclassic**, a name used by archeologists to describe the earliest developments in the history of the **Maya**, marking the first phase on a long road of evolution and increasing sophistication which culminates with the Classic (300–900 AD).

The names given to archeological periods are often confusing. Current excavations seem to be pushing back the dates when the earliest breakthroughs were made, and the dates of each period vary according to what you read; but in general terms the tail end of the Archaic (5000–1500 BC) becomes the **Formative** or **Preclassic** (1500 BC–300 AD), in which the early Maya settled in villages, practised agriculture and began making pottery. Some of the earliest ceramics, found at Cuello in northern Belize, date from around 2000 BC (other artefacts from Cuello are dated as early as 2500 BC, making it the oldest Maya site yet found). Many of the temple mounds at Kaminaljuyú, on the outskirts of Guatemala City, are also Preclassic, although thorough excavation is impossible as the mounds are now largely covered by sprawling suburbs. Further evidence, from a site near Ocós on the Pacific coast of Guatemala, shows groups of between three and twenty family huts, some of which include small temples.

By the **Middle Preclassic** (1000–300 BC) similar pottery and artefacts, including red and orange jars, dishes of the *Mamon* style and stone *metates*, for grinding corn, are found throughout the Maya lands, from southern Guatemala to northern Yucatán. Temple mounds are still at their most basic and the entire culture remains village-based. However, it's thought that some kind of Maya language was spoken throughout the area and that there was a substantial increase in the population. Religion, practised from a very early date, may have provided the stimulus and social cohesion to build bigger towns and, as in all early

agricultural communities, food surpluses freed some to eventually become seers, priests and astronomers. However, the Middle Preclassic is primarily marked by the spread of stable village life, with little in the way of sophisticated cultural advances.

Elsewhere in Mesoamerica, however, big changes were taking place that were to have a far-reaching impact throughout the region. The first great culture to emerge was the **Olmec** civilization, originating in the coastal plain of Veracruz, in Mexico. The Olmecs, often regarded as the true ancestors of Maya culture, developed a complex polytheistic religion, an early writing system and a calendar known as the "Long Count", which was later adopted by the Maya.

Among the Maya, real advances in architecture came in the **Late Preclassic** (300 BC–300 AD), when the **Chicanel culture** dominated the northern and central areas. Large pyramids and temple platforms were built at Tikal, El Mirador, Río Azul, Kaminaljuyú and many other sites in Guatemala and Belize, in what amounted to an explosion of Maya culture. Traditionally, these early Maya were painted as peaceful peasant farmers led by astronomer-priests, but in fact these new cities were bloodthirsty, warring rivals. Trade was of vital importance in the Late Preclassic. Cerros, at the mouth of the New River in Belize, and Lamanai, on New River Lagoon, were great trading centres, probably continuing in this role right through the Classic and into the Postclassic period. The famous Maya corbelled arch (which was not a true arch, with a keystone, but consisted of two sides, each with stones overlapping until they eventually met, and thus could only span a relatively narrow gap) was developed in this period, and the whole range of buildings became more ambitious. The question of what sparked this phase of rapid development is a subject of much debate. Some archeologists argue that the area was injected with ideas from across the Pacific, while others see the catalyst as the Olmec culture from the Gulf of Mexico. Both groups agree, however, that writing and calendar systems spread south along the Pacific coast, which developed before the Petén area: in the archeological sites around the modern town of Santa Lucía Cotzumalguapa there is much evidence of Olmec-style carving.

Rivalling the developments on the Pacific coast was the city of **Kaminaljuyú**, on the site of the modern capital of Guatemala, which dominated the central highlands in the early Preclassic. The principal centre in Petén during this period was **El Mirador**, which reached a scale comparable to the later achievement at Tikal. El Mirador remains one of the least understood of the great Maya cities and its ruins will doubtless yield some important information on Preclassic Maya civilization.

THE CLASSIC MAYA

The development that separates the Late Preclassic from the early **Classic period** (300–900 AD) is the introduction of the Long Count calendar and a recognizable form of writing. This appears to have taken place by the fourth century AD and marks the beginning of the greatest phase of Maya achievement.

During the Classic period all the cities we now know as ruined or restored sites were built, almost always over earlier structures. Elaborately carved **stelae**, bearing dates and emblem-glyphs, were erected at regular intervals. These tell of actual rulers and of historical events in their lives – battles, marriages, dynastic succession and so on. As these dates have come to be deciphered they have provided confirmation (or otherwise) of archeological evidence and offered a major insight into the nature of Maya dynastic rule.

Developments in the Maya area were still powerfully influenced by events to the north. The overbearing presence of the Olmecs was replaced by that of **Teotihuacán**, which dominated Central Mexico during the early Classic period. Armed merchants, called *pochteca*, operated at this time, spreading the influence of Teotihuacán as far as Petén and the Yucatán. They brought new styles of ceramics and alternative religious beliefs and perhaps preceded a complete military invasion. Whatever happened around 400 AD, the overwhelming power of Teotihuacán radically altered life in Maya lands. Influence spread south, via the Pacific coast, first to Kaminaljuyú on the site of modern Guatemala City and thence to Petén, where Tikal's rise to power must have been helped by close links with Teotihuacán. Both cities prospered greatly: Kaminaljuyú was rebuilt in the style of Teotihuacán, and Tikal has a stela depicting a lord of Tikal on one side and a warrior from Teotihuacán on the other.

Exactly how the various centres related to one another is unclear, but it appears that large cities dominated specific regions though no city held sway throughout the Maya area. Broadly speaking the culture was made up of a federation of city states, bound together by a coherent religion and culture and supporting a sophisticated trade network. The cities jostled for power and influence, a struggle that occasionally erupted into open warfare.

Intense wars were fought as rival cities sought to dominate one another, with no ruler appearing to gain ascendancy for very long. There were clearly three or four main centres that dominated the region through an uncertain process of alliances. Tikal was certainly a powerful city, but at one time Caracol in Belize defeated Tikal, as shown by a Caracol ball-court marker. Detailed carvings on wooden lintels and stone monuments depict elaborately costumed lords trampling on captives and spilling their own blood at propitious festivals, staged according to the dictates of the intricate and precise Maya calendar. Copán and Quiriguá were certainly important centres in the southern area, while the cities of the highlands were still in their infancy.

At the height of Maya power, advances were temporarily halted by what is known as the **Middle Classic Hiatus**, a period during which there was little new building at Tikal and after which many smaller centres, once under the control of Tikal, became independent city states. The victory of Caracol over Tikal, some time around 550 AD, may have been a symptom or a cause of this, and certainly the collapse of Teotihuacán in the seventh century caused shock waves throughout the civilizations of Mesoamerica. In the Maya cities no stelae commemorating events were erected, and monuments and statues were defaced and damaged. In all likelihood the Maya centres suffered revolts, and warfare raged as rival lords strove to win political power.

However, as the new kings established dynasties, now free of Teotihuacán's military or political control, the Maya cities flourished as never before. Architecture, astronomy and art reached degrees of sophistication unequalled by any other pre-Columbian society. Trade prospered and populations grew: Tikal had an estimated 40,000 people. Many Maya centres were larger than contemporary Western European cities, then in their "Dark Ages".

The prosperity and grandeur of the **Late Classic** (600–800 AD) reached all across the Maya lands: from Bonampak and Palenque in the west, to Labná, Sayil, Calakmul and Uxmal in the north, Altun Ha and Cerros in the east, and Copán and Quiriguá in the south, as well as hundreds of smaller centres. Masterpieces of painted pottery and carved jade (their most precious material) were created, often to be used as funerary offerings. Shell, bone and, rarely, marble were also exquisitely carved; temples were painted in brilliant colours, inside and out. Most of the pigments have faded long ago, but vestiges remain, enabling experts to reconstruct vivid images of the appearance of the ancient cities.

THE MAYA IN DECLINE

The days of glory were not to last very long, however. By 750 AD political and social changes began to be felt; alliances and trade links broke down, wars increased and stelae recording periods of time were carved less frequently. Cities gradually became depopulated and new construction ceased in the central area after about 830 AD. Bonampak was abandoned before its famous murals could be completed, while many of the great sites along the River Usumacinta (now part of the border between Guatemala and Mexico) were occupied by militaristic outsiders.

The reason for the decline is not (and may never be) known. Probably, several factors contributed to the downfall of the Maya. The growth and demands of the unproductive elite may have led to a peasant revolt, while the increase in population put great strains on food production, possibly exhausting the fertility of the soil, and epidemics may have combined to cause the abandonment of city life. At the end of the Classic period there appears to have been strife and disorder throughout Mesoamerica. The power vacuum left by the departing elite could have been partially filled by Putun or Chontal Maya moving into Petén from Tabasco and Campeche in Mexico.

By the tenth century, the Maya had abandoned their central cities and those few Maya that remained were reduced to a fairly primitive state. But not all Maya cities were entirely deserted: those in northern Belize, in particular, survived to some degree, with Lamanai and other cities in the area remaining occupied throughout the **Postclassic** period (900 AD to Spanish Conquest); the Yucatán peninsula, which appears to have escaped the worst of the depopulation, was conquered by the militaristic Toltecs who came from central Mexico in 987 AD. The invaders imposed their culture on the Maya, possibly introducing human sacrifice and creating a hybrid of Classic Maya culture.

GUATEMALA SINCE MAYA TIMES

The decline of Maya civilization in the Petén lowlands meant a rapid depopulation of the heartland of the Maya, an event which prompted an influx of population into the surrounding areas, and in particular into the Yucatán peninsula in the north and the Guatemalan highlands to the south. These areas, formerly peripheral regions of relatively little development, now contained the last vestiges of Maya culture, and it's at this time that the Guatemala area began to take on some of the local characteristics which are still in evidence today. By the end of the Classic period there were small settlements throughout the highlands, usually built on open valley floors and supporting large populations with the use of terraced farming and irrigation. Little was to change in this basic village structure for several hundred years.

PRE-CONQUEST: THE HIGHLAND TRIBES

Towards the end of the thirteenth century, however, the great cities of the Yucatán, such as Chichén Itzá and Uxmal, which were now inhabited by groups of Toltec-Maya from the gulf coast of Mexico, were also abandoned. At around the same time there was an invasion of the central Guatemalan highlands, also by a group of **Toltec-Maya**, although whether they came from the Yucatán or from the Gulf of Mexico remains uncertain. Some argue that they travelled due south into the highlands along the Usumacinta and Chixoy river valleys, while others claim that they came from further west and entered the area via the Pacific coast, which has always been a popular route for invading armies. Their numbers were probably small but their impact was profound, and following their arrival life in the highlands was radically altered.

What once had been a relatively settled, peaceful and religious society became, under the influence of the Toltecs, fundamentally secular, aggressive and militaristic. The Toltec invaders were ruthlessly well organized and in no time at all they established themselves as a ruling elite, founding a series of competing empires. The greatest of these were the **Quiché**, who dominated the central area and had their capital, **Utatlán**, to the west of the modern town of Santa Cruz del Quiché. Next in line were the **Cakchiquel**, who were originally based to the south of the Quiché, around the modern town of Chichicastenango, but later moved their capital to **Iximché**. On the southern shores of Lake Atitlán the **Tzutujil** had their capital on the lower slopes of the San Pedro volcano. To the west the **Mam** occupied the area around the modern town of Huehuetenango, with their capital at **Zaculeu**, while the northern slopes of the Cuchumatanes were home to a collection of smaller groups such as the **Chuj**, the **Kanjabal**, and further to the east the **Aguatec** and the **Ixil**. The eastern highlands, around the modern city of Cobán, were home to the notoriously fierce **Achi** nation, with the **Kekchi** to their north, while around the modern site of Guatemala City the land was controlled by the **Pokoman**, with their capital at **Mixco Viejo**. Finally, along the Pacific coast the **Pipil**, a tribe that had also migrated from the north, occupied the lowlands.

The sheer numbers of these tribes give an impression of the extent to which the area was fragmented, and it's these same divisions, now surviving on the basis of language alone, that still shape the highlands today (see map on p.472).

The Toltec rulers probably controlled only the dominant tribes – the Quiché, the Tzutujil, the Mam and the Cakchiquel – while their lesser neighbours were still made up entirely of Indians indigenous to the area. Arriving in the later part of the thirteenth century, the Toltecs must have terrorized the local Quiché-Cakchiquel highlanders and gradually established themselves in a new, rigidly hierarchical society. They brought with them many northern traditions – elements of a Nahua-based language, new gods and an array of military skills – and fused these with local ideas. Many of the rulers' names are similar to those used in the Toltec heartland to the north, and they claimed to trace their ancestry to Quetzalcoatl, a mythical ruling dynasty from the Toltec city of Tula. Shortly after the Spanish Conquest the Quiché wrote an account of their history, the *Popol Vuh*, in which they lay claim to a Toltec pedigree, as do the Cakchiquel in their account, *The Annals of the Cakchiquel*.

The Toltec invaders were not content with overpowering just a tribe or two, so under the direction of their new rulers the Quiché began to expand their empire by conquering neighbouring tribes. Between 1400 and 1475 they embarked on a campaign of conquest that brought the Cakchiquel, the Mam and several other tribes under their control. At the height of their power around a million highlanders bowed to the word of the Quiché king. But in 1475 the man who had masterminded their expansion, the great Quiché ruler **Quicab**, died, and the empire lost much of its authority. The Cakchiquel were the first to break from the fold, anticipating the death of Quicab and moving south to a new and fortified capital, Iximché, in around 1470. Shortly afterwards the other tribes managed to escape the grip of Quiché control and assert their independence. For the next fifty years or so the tribes were in a state of almost perpetual conflict, fighting for access to the inadequate supplies of farmland. All the archeological remains from this era give evidence of this instability; gone are the valley-floor centres of pre-Toltec times, and in their place are fortified hilltop sites, surrounded by ravines and man-made ditches.

When the Spanish arrived, the highlands were in crisis. The population had grown so fast that it had outstripped the food supply, forcing the tribes to fight for any available land in order to increase their agricultural capacity. With a growing sense of urgency both the Quiché and the Cakchiquel had begun to encroach on the lowlands of the Pacific coast. The situation could hardly have been more favourable to the Spanish, who fostered this intertribal friction, playing one group off against another.

THE SPANISH CONQUEST

While the tribes of highland Guatemala were fighting it out amongst themselves their northern neighbours, in what is now Mexico, were confronting a new and ruthless enemy. In 1521 the Spanish conquistadors had captured the Aztec capital at Tenochtitlan and were starting to cast their net further afield. Amidst the horrors of the Conquest there was one man, **Pedro de Alvarado**, whose evilness stood out above the rest. He could hardly have been better suited to the job – ambitious, cunning, intelligent, ingenious, dashingly handsome and ruthlessly cruel.

In 1523 Cortes despatched Alvarado to Guatemala, entreating him to use the minimum of force "and to preach matters concerning our Holy Faith". His army included 120 horsemen, 173 horses, 300 soldiers and 200 Mexican Indian warriors, largely Tlaxcalans who had allied themselves with Cortes in the conquest of Mexico. Marching south they entered Guatemala along the Pacific coast, where they met with the first wave of resistance, a small army of Quiché warriors. These were no match for the Spaniards, who cut through their ranks with ease. From here Alvarado turned north, taking his troops up into the highlands and through a narrow mountain pass to the Quezaltenango valley, where they came upon the deserted city of **Xelaju**, a Quiché outpost.

Warned of the impending arrival of the Spanish, the Quiché had struggled to build an alliance with the other tribes, but old rivalries proved too strong and the **Quiché** army stood alone. Three days later, on a nearby plain, they met the Spaniards in open warfare. It's said that the invading army was confronted by some 30,000 Quiché warriors, led by **Tecún Umán** in a headdress of quetzal feathers. Despite the huge disparity in numbers, sling-shot and foot soldiers were no match for cavalry and gunpowder, and the Spaniards were once again able to wade through the Indian ranks. Legend has it that the battle was brought to a close when Alvarado met Tecún Umán in hand-to-hand conflict – and cut him down.

Accepting this temporary setback, the Quiché decided to opt for a more diplomatic solution and invited the Spaniards to their capital **Utatlán**, where they planned to trap and destroy them. But when Alvarado saw their city he grew suspicious and took several Quiché lords as prisoners. When hostilities erupted once again he killed the captives and had the city burnt to the ground.

Having dealt with the Quiché, Alvarado turned his attention to the other tribal groups. The **Cakchiquel**, recognizing the military superiority of the Spanish, decided to form some kind of alliance with them and as a result of this the Spaniards established their first headquarters, in 1523, alongside the Cakchiquel capital of **Iximché**. From here they ranged far and wide, overpowering the countless smaller tribes. Travelling east, Alvarado's army met the **Tzutujil** on the shores of Lake Atitlán. Here the first battle took place at a site near the modern village of Panajachel, and the second beneath the Tzutujil capital, at the base of the San Pedro volcano, where the Spaniards were helped by a force of Cakchiquel warriors who arrived on the scene in some 300 canoes. Moving on, the Spanish travelled south to the Pacific coast, where they overcame the **Pipil** before making their way back to Iximché.

In 1524 Alvarado sent his brother Gonzalo on an expedition against the **Mam**, who were conquered after a month-long siege during which they holed up in their fortified capital **Zaculeu**. In 1525 Alvarado himself set out to take on the **Pokoman**, at their capital **Mixco Viejo**, where he came up against another army of some 3000 warriors. Once again they proved no match for the well-disciplined Spanish ranks.

Despite this string of relatively easy gains it wasn't until well into the 1530s that Alvarado managed to assert control over the more remote parts of the highlands. Moving into the Cuchumatanes his forces were beaten back by the **Uspantec** and met fierce resistance from the Indians of the **Ixil**. And while Alvarado's soldiers were struggling to contain resistance in these isolated mountainous areas, problems also arose at the very heart of the campaign. In 1526 the Cakchiquel rose up against their Spanish allies, in response to demands for tribute; abandoning their capital the Indians moved into the mountains, from where they waged a guerrilla war against their former partners. As a result of this the Spanish were forced to abandon their base at Iximché, and moved instead to a site near the modern town of Antigua.

Here they established their first permanent capital, the city of **Santiago de los**

Caballeros, on St Cecilia's Day, November 22, 1527. For ten years Indians toiled in the construction of the new city, neatly sited at the base of the Agua volcano, putting together a cathedral, a town hall, and a palace for Alvarado. The land within the city was given out to those who had fought alongside him, and plots on the edge of town were allocated to his remaining Indian allies.

Meanwhile, one particularly thorny problem for the Spanish was presented by the **Achi** and **Kekchi** Indians, who occupied what are now the Verapaz highlands. Despite all his efforts Alvarado was unable to conquer either of these tribes, who fought fiercely against the invading armies. In the end he gave up on the area, naming it *Tierra de Guerra* and abandoning all hopes of controlling it. The situation was eventually resolved by the Church. In 1537 **Fray Bartolomé de Las Casas**, the "protector of the Indians", travelled into the area in a bid to persuade the locals to accept both Christianity and Spanish authority. Within three years the priests had succeeded where Alvarado's armies had failed, and the last of the highland tribes was brought under colonial control in 1540. Thus did the area earn its name of *Verapaz*, true peace.

Alvarado himself grew tired of the Conquest, disappointed by the lack of plunder, and his reputation for brutality began to spread. He was forced to return to Spain to face charges of treason, but returned a free man with a young wife at his side. Life in the New World soon sent his bride to an early grave and Alvarado set out once again, in search of the great mineral wealth that had eluded him in Guatemala. First he travelled south to Peru, where it's said that Pizarro paid him to leave South America. He then returned to Spain once again, where he married **Beatriz de la Cueva**, his first wife's sister, and the two of them made their way back to Guatemala, where he dropped off his new bride before setting sail for the Spice Islands. Along the way he stopped in Mexico, to put down an Indian uprising, and was crushed to death beneath a rolling horse.

From 1524 until his death in 1541 Alvarado had ruled Guatemala as a personal fiefdom, desperately seeking adventure and wealth and enslaving and abusing the local Indian population in order to finance his urge to explore. By the time of his death all the Indian tribes had been overcome, although local uprisings, which have persisted to this day, had already started to take place.

COLONIAL RULE

The early years of colonial rule were marked by a turmoil of uprisings and political wrangling, and while the death of Alvarado might have been expected to bring a degree of calm, it was in fact followed by fresh disaster. When his wife, Beatriz de la Cueva, heard of Alvarado's death she plunged the capital into a period of prolonged mourning. She had the entire palace painted black, both inside and out, and ordered the city authorities to appoint her as the new governor. Meanwhile, the area was swept by a series of storms, and on the night of September 10, 1541, it was shaken by a massive earthquake. The sides of the Agua volcano shuddered, undermining the walls of the cone and releasing its contents. A great wall of mud and water swept down the side of the cone, and the city of Santiago was buried beneath it.

The surviving colonial authorities moved up the valley to a new site, where a second **Santiago de los Caballeros** was founded in the following year. This new city served as the administrative headquarters of the **Audiencia de Guatemala**, which was made up of six provinces: Costa Rica, Nicaragua, San Salvador, Honduras, Guatemala and Chiapas (now part of Mexico). With Alvarado out of the way the authorities began to build a new society, re-creating the splendours of the homeland. Santiago was never endowed with the same wealth or freedom as Mexico City and Lima, but it was nevertheless the centre of political and religious power for two hundred years, accumulating a superb array of arts and architecture. By the mid-eighteenth century its population had reached some 80,000. Here colonial society was at its most developed, rigidly structured along racial lines with purebred Spaniards at the top, Indian slaves at the bottom, and a host of carefully defined racial strata in between. The city was regularly shaken by scandal, intrigue and earthquakes, and it was eventually destroyed in 1773 by the last of these, after which the capital was moved to its modern site.

Perhaps the greatest power in colonial Central America was the **Church**. The first religious order to reach Guatemala was the **Franciscans**, who arrived with Alvarado himself, and by 1532 the **Mercedarians** and **Dominicans** had followed suit, with the **Jesuits** arriving shortly after. **Francisco Marroquín**, the country's first bishop, rewarded these early arrivals with huge concessions, taking in both land and Indians, which later enabled them to earn fortunes from sugar, wheat and indigo, income boosted by the fact that they were exempt from tax. In later years a whole range of other orders arrived in Santiago, and religious rivalry became an important shaping force in the colony. The wealth and power of the Church fostered the splendour of the colonial capital while ruthlessly exploiting the Indians and their land. In Santiago alone there were some eighty churches, and alongside these were schools, convents, hospitals, hermitages, craft centres and colleges. The religious orders became the main benefactors of the arts, amassing a wealth of tapestry, jewels, sculpture and painting, and staging concerts, fiestas and endless religious processions. Religious persecution was at its worst between 1572 and 1580, when the office of the **Inquisition** set up in Santiago, seeking out those who had failed to receive the faith and dealing with them harshly. Not much is known about the precise nature of the Guatemalan inquisition, however, as no written records have survived.

By the eighteenth century the power of the Church had started to get out of control, and the Spanish kings began to impose taxes on the religious orders and to limit their power and freedom. The conflict between Church and State came to a head in 1767, when Carlos III banished the Jesuits from the Spanish colonies.

The Spanish must have been disappointed with their conquest of Central America as it offered none of the instant plunder that had been found in Mexico and Peru. They found small amounts of silver around the modern town of Huehuetenango and a few grains of gold in the rivers of Honduras, but nothing that could compare with the vast resources of Potosí (a huge silver mine in Bolivia) or highland Mexico. In Central America the **colonial economy** was based on agriculture. The coastal area produced cacao, tobacco, cotton and, most valuable of all, indigo; the highlands

were grazed with sheep and goats; and cattle, specially imported from Spain, were raised on coastal ranches. In the lowlands of Petén and the jungles of the lower Motagua valley, the mosquitoes and forests remained unchallenged, although here and there certain aspects of the forest were developed; chicle, the raw material of chewing gum, was bled from the sapodilla trees, as was sarsaparilla, used to treat syphilis.

At the heart of the colonial economy was the system of *repartamientos*, whereby the ruling classes were granted the right to extract labour from the Indian population. It was this that established the process of Indians being transported to the Pacific coast to work the plantations, a pattern that is still a tremendous burden for the Indians of today.

Meanwhile, in the capital it was graft and corruption that controlled the movement of money, with titles and appointments sold to the highest bidder. All of the colony's wealth was funnelled through the city, and it was only here that the monetary economy really developed.

The impact of the Conquest was perhaps at its most serious in the highlands, where the **Indian population** had their lives totally restructured. The first stage in this process was the *reduccion*, whereby scattered Indian communities were combined into new Spanish-style towns and villages. Between 1543 and 1600 some 700 new settlements were created, each based around a Catholic church. Ostensibly, the purpose of this was to enable the Church to work on its new-found converts, but it also had the effect of pooling the available labour and making its exploitation that much easier. The highland villages were still bound up in an ancient system of subsistence farming, although its pattern was now disturbed by demands for tribute.

Indian **social structures** were also profoundly altered by post-conquest changes. The great central authorities that had previously dominated were now eradicated, replaced by local structures based in the new villages. *Caciques* (local chiefs) and *Alcaldes* (mayors) now held the bulk of local power, which was bestowed on them by the Church. In the distant corners of the highlands, however, priests were few and far between, only visiting the villages from time to time. Those that they left in charge developed not only their own power structures but also their own religion, mixing the new with the old. By the start of the nineteenth century the Indian population had largely recovered from the initial impact of the Conquest, and in many places these local structures became increasingly important. In each village *Cofradía* (brotherhood) groups were entrusted with the care of saints, while *Principales*, village elders, held the bulk of traditional authority, a situation that still persists today. Throughout the highlands village uprisings became increasingly commonplace as the new indigenous culture became stronger and stronger.

Perhaps even more serious for the indigenous population than any social changes were the **diseases** that arrived with the conquistadors. Waves of plague, typhoid and fever swept through a population without any natural resistance to them. In the worst-hit areas the Indian population was cut by some 90 percent, and in many parts of the country their numbers were halved.

Two centuries of colonial rule totally reshaped the structure of Guatemalan society, giving it new cities, a new religion, a transformed economy and a racist hierarchy. Nevertheless, the impact of colonial rule was perhaps less marked than in many other parts of Latin America. Only two sizeable cities had emerged and the outlying areas had received little attention from the colonial authorities. While the indigenous population had been ruthlessly exploited and suffered enormous losses at the hands of foreign weapons and imported diseases, its culture was never eradicated. It simply absorbed the symbols and ideas of the new Spanish ideology, creating a dynamic synthesis that is neither Maya nor Catholic.

INDEPENDENCE

The racist nature of colonial rule had given birth to deep dissatisfaction amongst many groups in Central America. Spain's policy was to keep wealth and power in the hands of those born in Spain (*chapetones*), a policy that left growing numbers of Creoles (including those of Spanish blood born in Guatemala) and Mestizos (of mixed blood) resentful and hungry for power and change. (For the majority of the indigenous Indians, both power and wealth were way beyond their reach.) As the Spanish departed, Guatemalan politics were dominated by a struggle between **conservatives**, who sided with the Church and the Crown, and **liberals**, who advocated a secular and more egalitarian state. One result of the split was that independence was not a clean break, but was declared several times.

The spark, as throughout Spanish America, was Napoleon's invasion of Spain and the abdication of King Fernando VII. In the chaos that followed a liberal constitution was imposed on Spain in 1812 and a mood of reform swept through the colonies. At the time Central America was under the control of **Brigadier Don Gabino Gainza**, the last of the Captains General. His one concern was to maintain the status quo, in which he was strongly backed by the wealthy landowners and the church hierarchy. Bowing to demands for independence, but still hoping to preserve the power structure, Gainza signed a formal **Act of Independence** on September 15, 1821, enshrining the authority of the Church and seeking to preserve the old order under new leadership. Augustín de Iturbide, the short-lived emperor of newly independent Mexico, promptly sent troops to annex Guatemala to the Mexican empire, a union which was to last less than a year.

A second Declaration of Independence, in 1823, joined the Central American states in a loose **federation**, adopting a constitution modelled on that of the United States, abolishing slavery and advocating liberal reforms. The federation, however, was doomed by the struggle between the countries and within each of them. The first president of the federation was **General Manuel José Acre**, a Salvadorean, who fought bitterly with his party and then founded a government of his own. This prompted others to do the same and the liberals of Salvador, Honduras and Guatemala united under the leadership of **Francisco Morazon**, a Honduran general. Under his rule **Mariano Galvez** became the chief of state in Guatemala: religious orders were abolished, the death penalty done away with, and trial by jury, a general school system, civil marriage and the Lívingston law code were all instituted.

The liberal era, however, lasted little longer than the Mexican empire, and the reforming government was overthrown by a revolt from the mountains. Throughout the turmoil of independence, life in the highlands remained harsh, with the Indian population still bearing the burdens imposed on them by two centuries of colonial rule. In 1823 a cholera epidemic swept through the entire country, killing thousands and only adding to the misery of life in the mountains. Seething with discontent, the Indians were united behind an illiterate but charismatic leader, the 23-year-old **Rafael Carrera**, under whose command they marched on Guatemala City.

Carrera respected no authority other than that of the Church, and his immediate reforms swept aside the changes instituted by the liberal government. The religious orders were restored to their former position and traditional Spanish titles were reinstated. The conservatives had little in common with Carrera but they could see that he offered to uphold their position with a tremendous weight of popular support, and hence they sided with him. Under Carrera Guatemala fought a bitter war against Morazon and the federation, eventually establishing itself as an independent republic in 1847. Carrera's other great challenge came from the state of **Los Altos**, which included much of the western highlands and proclaimed itself an independent republic in defiance of him: it was a short-lived threat, however, and the state was soon brought back into the republic.

In 1865 Carrera died, at the age of 50, leaving the country ravaged by the chaos of his tyranny and inefficiency. He was succeeded by **Vicente Cerna**, another conservative, who was to rule for the next six years.

Meanwhile, the liberal opposition was gathering momentum yet again and 1867 saw the first **liberal uprising**, led by **Serpio Cruz**. His bid for power was unsuccessful but it inspired two young liberals, Justo Rufino Barrios and Francisco Cruz, to follow suit. In the next few years they mounted several other unsuccessful revolts, and in 1870 Serpio Cruz was captured and hanged.

RUFINO BARRIOS AND THE COFFEE BOOM

1871 marked a major turning point in Guatemalan politics. In that year Rufino Barrios and Marcia García Ganados set out from Mexico with an army of just 45 men, entering Guatemala via the small border town of Cuilco. The **liberal revolution** thus set in motion was an astounding success, the army growing by the day as it approached the capital, which was finally taken on June 30, 1871. Ganados took the helm of the new liberal administration but held the presidency for just a few years, surrounding himself with ageing comrades and offering only very limited reforms.

Meanwhile, out in the district of Los Altos, **Rufino Barrios**, now a local military commander, was infuriated by the lack of action. In 1872 he marched his troops to the capital and installed them in the San José barracks, demanding immediate elections. These were granted and he won with ease. Barrios was a charismatic leader with tyrannical tendencies (monuments throughout the country testify to his sense of his own importance) who regarded himself as the great reformer and was intent on making sweeping changes. Above all he was a man of action. His most immediate acts were classic liberal gestures: the restructuring of the education system and an attack on the Church. The University of San Carlos was secularized and modernized, while clerics were forbidden to wear the cloth and public religious processions were banned. The Church was outraged and excommunicated Barrios, which prompted him to expel the archbishop in retaliation.

The new liberal perspective, though, was instilled with a deep arrogance and Barrios would tolerate no opposition, regarding his own racial and economic outlook as absolute. In order to ensure the success of his reforms he developed an effective network of secret police and struggled to make the army increasingly professional. In later years he founded the *politecnica*, an academy for young officers, and the army became an essential part of his political power base.

Alongside all this Barrios set about reforming agriculture, in which he presided over a boom period, largely as a result of the cultivation of **coffee**. It was this more than anything else that distinguished the era and was to fundamentally reshape the country. When the liberals came to power coffee already accounted for half the value of the country's exports, and by 1884 the volume of output had increased five times. To foster this expansion Barrios founded a Ministry of Development, which extended the railway network (begun in 1880), established a national bank, and developed the ports of Champerico, San José and Iztapa to handle the growth in exports. Between 1870 and 1900 the volume of foreign trade increased twenty times.

All this had an enormous impact on Guatemalan **society**. Many of the new plantations were owned and run by German immigrants, and indeed the majority of the coffee eventually found its way to Germany. The newcomers soon formed a powerful elite, and although most of the Germans were later forced out of Guatemala (during World War II), their impact can still be felt: directly in the Verapaz highlands, and more subtly in the continuing presence of an extremely powerful clique, their wealth based on the income from plantation farming, who are still central to political life in Guatemala. The new liberal perspective maintained that foreign ideas were superior to indigenous ones, and while immigrants were welcomed with open arms the Indian population was still regarded as hopelessly inferior.

Indian society was also deeply affected by the needs of the coffee boom, and it was here that the new crop had the most damaging and lasting effect. Under the previous regime landowners had complained that the Indian population was reluctant to work on the plantations and that this endangered the coffee crop. Barrios was quick to respond to their needs and instituted a system of **forced labour**. In 1876 he ordered local political chiefs to make the necessary workers available: up to one-quarter of the male population could be despatched to work on the *fincas*; in addition to this the landowners continued to employ their old methods and debt peonage spread throughout the highlands. Conditions on the *fincas* were appalling and the Indian workforce was treated with utter contempt.

As a result of the coffee boom the Indians lost not only their freedom but also their land. From 1873 onwards the government began confiscating land that was either unused or communally owned, and selling it to the highest bidder. In some instances Indian villages were given small tracts of land taken from unproductive *fincas*, but in the vast majority of cases it was the Indians who lost their land to large coffee plantations. Huge amounts of land were seized, and land that had been communally owned for centuries was gobbled up by

the new wave of agribusiness. In many areas the villagers rose up in defiance, and there were significant **revolts** throughout the western highlands. In Momostenango some 500 armed men faced the authorities, only to find their village overrun by troops and their homes burnt to the ground. In Cantel troops shot all of the village officials, who were campaigning against plans to build a textile factory on their land. Throughout the latter years of the nineteenth and the early ones of the twentieth century, villages continued to rise up in defiance of demands on their land and labour. At the same time the loss of their most productive land forced the Indians to become dependent on seasonal labour, while attacks on their communities drove them into increasing introspection.

JORGE UBICO AND THE BANANA EMPIRE

Rufino Barrios was eventually killed in 1885 while fighting to re-create a unified Central America, and was succeeded by a string of short-lived, like-minded presidents. The next to hold power for any time was **Manuel Estrada Cabrera**, a stern authoritarian who restricted union organization and supported the interests of big business. He ruled from 1898 until he was overthrown in 1920, by which time he was on the verge of insanity.

Meanwhile, a new and exceptionally powerful player was becoming involved: the **United Fruit Company**, whose influence asserted itself over much of Central America in the early decades of the twentieth century and which was to exercise tremendous power over the next fifty years. The story of the United Fruit Company starts in Costa Rica, where a man named Minor Keith was contracted to build a railway from San José to the Pacific coast. Running short of money he was forced to plant bananas on land granted as part of the railway contract. The business proved so profitable that Keith merged his own Tropical Trading and Transport Company with his main rival The Boston Fruit company, to form the United Fruit Company.

The Company first moved into Guatemala in 1901, when it bought a small tract of land on which to grow bananas, and in 1904 it was awarded a contract to complete the railway from Guatemala City to Puerto Barrios. The company was also granted 100 feet on either side of the track, exempted from paying any tax for the next 99 years, and assured that the government wouldn't interfere with its activities. In 1912 ownership of the Pacific railway network fell to the company and, as it already controlled the main Caribbean port, this gave it a virtual monopoly over transport. It was around this time that large-scale banana cultivation really took off, and by 1934 United Fruit controlled a massive amount of land, exporting around 3.5 million bunches of bananas annually and reaping vast profits. In 1941 some 25,000 Guatemalans were employed in the banana industry.

The power of the United Fruit Company was by no means restricted to agriculture, and its influence was so pervasive that the company earned itself the nickname *El Pulpo*, "the octopus". Control of the transport network brought with it control of the coffee trade: by 1930 28 percent of the country's coffee output was handled by the company's Caribbean port, Puerto Barrios. During the 1930s it cost as much to ship coffee from Guatemala to New Orleans as it did from Río de Janeiro to New Orleans.

Against this background the power of the Guatemalan government was severely limited, with the influence of the United States increasing alongside that of the United Fruit Company. In 1919 Guatemala faced a financial crisis and President Cabrera was ousted by a coup the following year. He was replaced by **Carlos Herrera**, who represented the Union Party, a rare compromise between liberal and conservative politicians. Herrera refused to use the traditional weapons of tyranny and his reforms threatened to terminate United Fruit Company contracts. As a result of this Herrera was to last barely more than a year, replaced by **General José Maria Orellano** in December 1921. Orellano had no qualms about repressive measures and his minister of war, Jorge Ubico, killed some 290 opponents in 1926, the year in which Orellano died of a heart attack. His death prompted a bitter power struggle between Jorge Ubico, a fierce radical, and **Lazaro Chacon**, who won the day and was elected as the new liberal president. In the next few years indigenous farmers began to express their anger at the United Fruit Company monopoly, while the company demanded the renewal of longstanding contracts, squeezing Chacon from both sides. His rule came to an end in 1930, when he suffered a stroke.

The way was now clear for **Jorge Ubico**, a charismatic leader who was well connected with the ruling and land-owning elite. Ubico had risen fast through the ranks of local government as *jefe politico* in Alta Verapaz and Retalhuleu (greatly assisted by the patronage of his godfather Rufino Barrios), earning a reputation for efficiency and honesty. As president, however, he inherited financial disaster. Guatemala had been badly hit by the Depression, accumulating debts of some $5 million: in response Ubico fought hard to expand the export market for Guatemalan produce, managing to sign trade agreements that exempted local coffee and bananas from import duties in the United States. But increased trade with the great American power was only possible at the expense of traditional links with Europe.

Within Guatemala Ubico steadfastly supported the United Fruit Company and the interests of US business. This relationship was of such importance that by 1940 90 percent of all Guatemalan exports were being sold in the United States. Trade and diplomacy drew Guatemala ever closer to the United States, a relationship exemplified when Ubico, against his will, was forced to bow to US pressure for the expulsion of German landowners in the run-up to World War II.

Internally, Ubico embarked on a radical programme of reform, including a sweeping drive against corruption and a massive road-building effort, which bought him great popularity in the provinces. Despite his liberal pretensions, however, Ubico sided firmly with big business when the chips were down, always offering his assistance to the United Fruit Company and other sections of the land-owning elite. The system of debt peonage was replaced by the **vagrancy law**, under which all landless peasants were forced to work 150 days a year. If they weren't needed by the *fincas* then their labour was used in the road-building programme or some other public works scheme. The power of landowners was further reinforced by a 1943 law that gave them the power to shoot poachers and vandals, and in effect landowners were given total authority over their workforce. Throughout his period of office Ubico ignored the rights and needs of the peasant population, who were still regarded as ignorant and backward, and as a result of this there were continued uprisings in the late 1930s and early 1940s.

Internal security was another obsession that was to dominate Ubico's years in office, as he became increasingly paranoid. He maintained that he was a reincarnation of Napoleon and was fascinated by all aspects of the military: he operated a network of spies and informers whom he regularly used to unleash waves of repression, particularly in the run-up to elections. In 1934, when he discovered an assassination plan, 300 people were killed in just two days. To prevent any further opposition he registered all printing presses in the country and made discipline the cornerstone of state education.

But while Ubico tightened his grip on every aspect of government, the rumblings of opposition grew louder. In 1944 discontent erupted in a wave of student violence, and Ubico was finally forced to resign after 14 years of tyrannical rule. Power was transferred to **Juan Frederico Ponce Viades**, who attempted to continue in the same style, but by the end of the year he was also faced with open revolt, and finally the pair of them were driven into exile.

TEN YEARS OF "SPIRITUAL SOCIALISM"

The overthrow of Jorge Ubico released a wave of opposition that had been bottled up throughout his rule. Students, professionals and young military officers demanded democracy and freedom. It was a mood that was to transform Guatemalan politics and was so extreme a contrast to previous governments that the handover was dubbed **the 1944 revolution**.

Power was initially passed to a joint military and civilian junta, elections were planned, and in March 1945 a new constitution was instituted, extending suffrage to include all adults and prohibiting the president from standing for a second term of office. In the elections **Juan José Arevalo**, a teacher, won the presidency with 85 percent of the vote. His political doctrine was dubbed "spiritual socialism", and he immediately set about effecting much-needed structural reforms.

Under a new budget, a third of the government's income was allocated to social welfare, to be spent on the construction of schools and hospitals, a programme of immunization, and a far-reaching literacy campaign. The vagrancy laws were abolished, a national development agency was founded, and in 1947 a labour code was adopted, granting workers the right to strike and union representation.

The expulsion of German plantation owners during World War II had placed several large *fincas* in the hands of the state, and under Arevalo some of these were turned into cooperatives, while new laws protected tenant farmers from eviction. Other policies were intended to promote industrial and agricultural development: technical assistance and credit were made available to peasant farmers and there was some attempt to colonize Petén.

In Arevalo's final years the pace of reform slackened somewhat as he concentrated on consolidating the gains made in early years and evading various attempts to overthrow him. Despite his popularity Arevalo was still wary of the traditional elite: church leaders, old-school army officers and wealthy landowners all resented the new wave of legislation, and there were repeated coup attempts.

Elections were scheduled for 1950 and during the run-up the two main candidates were **Colonel Francisco Arana** and **Colonel Jacobo Arbenz**, both military members of the junta that had taken over at the end of the Ubico era. But in 1949 Arana, who was favoured by the right, was assassinated. Suspicion fell on Arbenz, who was backed by the peasant organizations and unions, but there was no hard proof. For the actual vote Arana was replaced by **Brigadier Ydigoras Fuentes**, an army officer from the Ubico years.

Arbenz won the election with ease, taking 65 percent of the vote, and declared that he would transform the country into an independent capitalist nation and raise the standard of living. But the process of "overthrowing feudal society and ending economic dependency" was to lead to a direct confrontation between the new government and the American corporations that still dominated the economy.

Aware of the size of the task that faced him, Arbenz enlisted the support of the masses, encouraging the participation of peasants in the programme of agrarian reform and inciting the militancy of students and unions. He also attempted to break the great monopolies, building a state-run hydroelectric plant to rival the American-owned generating company and a highway to compete with the railway to the Caribbean, and planning a new port alongside Puerto Barrios, which was still owned by the United Fruit Company. At the same time Arbenz began a series of suits against foreign corporations, seeking unpaid taxes. Internally, these measures aroused a mood of national pride, but they were strongly resented by the American companies whose empires were under attack.

The situation became even more serious with the **law of agrarian reform** passed in July 1952, which stated that idle and state-owned land would be distributed to the landless. Some of this land was to be rented out for a lifetime lease, but the bulk of it was handed over outright to the new owners, who were to pay a small percentage of its market value. The former owners of the land were to be compensated with government bonds, but the value of the land was calculated on the basis of the tax they had been paying, usually a fraction of its true value.

The new laws outraged landowners, despite the fact that they were given the right to appeal. Between 1953 and 1954 around 884,000 hectares were redistributed to the benefit of some 100,000 peasant families. It was the first time since the arrival of the Spanish that the government had responded to the needs of the indigenous population, although some studies suggest that the whole thing confused the Indians, who were unsure how to respond. The landowner most seriously affected by the reforms was the United Fruit Company, which only farmed around 15 percent of its land holdings, and lost about half of its property.

As the pace of reform gathered, Arbenz began to take an increasingly radical stance. In 1951 the Communist Party was granted legal status, and in the next election four party members were elected to the legislature. But the Arbenz government was by no means a communist government, although it remained staunchly anti-American.

In the United States the press repeatedly accused the new Guatemalan government of being a communist beach-head in Central America, and the US government attempted to intervene on behalf of the United Fruit Company. Allen Dulles, the new director of the CIA, happened also to be a member of the company's board.

In 1953 President Eisenhower finally approved plans to overthrow the government. The CIA set up a small military invasion of Guatemala to depose Arbenz and install an alternative administration more suited to their tastes. A rag-tag army of exiles and mercenaries was put together in Honduras, and on June 18, 1954, Guatemala City was bombed with leaflets demanding the resignation of Arbenz. Aware that the army would never support him, Arbenz had bought a boat-load of Czechoslovakian arms, hoping to arm the people; but the guns were intercepted by the CIA before they reached Puerto Barrios. On the night of June 18, Guatemala was strafed with machine-gun fire while the invading army, described by Arbenz as "a heterogeneous Fruit Company expeditionary force", was getting closer to the city by the hour.

On June 27 Arbenz declared that he was relinquishing the presidency to **Colonel Carlos Enrique Diaz**, the army chief of staff. And on July 3 John Peurifoy, the American Ambassador to Guatemala, flew the new government to Guatemala aboard a US Air Force plane. Guatemala's attempt to escape the clutches of outside intervention and bring about social change had been brought to an abrupt end.

COUNTER-REVOLUTION AND MILITARY RULE

Following the overthrow of Arbenz it was the army that rose to fill the power vacuum, and they were to dominate politics for the next thirty years, sending the country into a spiral of violence and economic decline. Since the time of Jorge Ubico the army had become increasingly professional and political, and now it began to receive increasing amounts of US aid, expanding its influence to include a wide range of public works and infrastructure projects.

In 1954 the American ambassador had persuaded a provisional government to accept **Castillo Armas** as the new president, and the gains of the previous ten years were immediately swept away. Hardest hit were the indigenous Indians — who had enjoyed the greatest benefits under the Arbenz administration — as *Ladino* rule was firmly reinstated. The constitution of 1945 was revoked and replaced by a more restrictive version; all illiterates were disenfranchised, left-wing parties were outlawed, and large numbers of unionists and agrarian reformers were simply executed. Restrictions placed on foreign investment were lifted and all the land that had been confiscated was returned to its previous owners. Meanwhile, Armas surrounded himself with old-style Ubico supporters, attempting to reinstate the traditional elite and drawing heavily on US assistance in order to develop the economy.

To lend a degree of legitimacy to the administration Armas held a referendum in which voters were given the chance to support his rule (though what else was on offer was never made clear). With or without popular support, however, the new government had only limited backing from the armed forces, and coup rumblings continued throughout his period of office, which was brought to a close in 1957, when he was shot by his own bodyguard.

The assassination was followed by several months of political turmoil, out of which **Ydigoras** (who had stood against Arbenz in 1954, but declined an offer to lead the CIA invasion) emerged as the next president, representing the National Democratic Renovation Party. Ydigoras was to rule for five years, a period that was marked by corruption, incompetence, outrageous patronage and economic decline caused by a fall in coffee prices, although as some compensation the formation of the Central American Common Market helped to boost light industry. The government was so disastrous that it prompted opposition even from within the ranks of the elite. In 1960 a group of young military officers, led by **Marcos Yon Sosa** and **Turcios Lima**, attempted, without success, to take control, while in 1962 a large section of the Congress withdrew its support from the government.

Ydigoras was eventually overthrown when Arevalo threatened to return to Guatemala and contest the 1963 elections, which he might well have won. The possibility of another socialist government sent shock waves through the establishment in both Guatemala and the United States, and John F. Kennedy gave the go ahead for another coup. In 1963 the army once more took control, under the leadership of **Perlata Azurdia**.

Perlata was president for just three years, during which he fiddled with the constitution and took his time in restoring the electoral process. Meanwhile, the authoritarian nature of his government came up against the first wave of armed resistance. Two failed coupsters from 1960, Turcios Lima and Marcos Yon Sosa, both army officers, took to the eastern highlands and waged a **guerrilla war** against the army. Trained in counter-insurgency by the US army in Panamá and both ín their early twenties, they began to attack local army posts. A second organization, FAR, emerged later that year, and the Guatemalan Labour Party (PGT) formed a shaky alliance with the guerrillas, attempting to represent their grievances in the political arena and advocating a return to Arevalo's rule.

Perlata finally lost control in the 1966 elections, which were won by **Julio Cesar Montenegro** of the centre-left *Partido Revolucionario*. Before taking office, however, Montenegro was forced to sign a pact with the military, obliging him to obey their instructions and giving the army a totally free hand in all affairs of national security. Montenegro was elected on July 1, and his first act was to offer an amnesty to the guerrillas: when this was rejected a ruthless counter-insurgency campaign swung into action (a pattern of events that was repeated in the early 1980s under Ríos Montt).

Under the command of **Colonel Carlos Arana Osorio**, "the Jackal of Zacapa", specially trained units, backed by US advisers, undermined peasant support for the guerrillas by terrorizing the local population. The guerrillas were soon forced to spend much of their time on the move, and further damage was done to the movement by the death of Turcios Lima, in a car crash. By the end of the decade the guerrilla movement had been virtually eradicated in the eastern highlands, and its activities, greatly reduced, shifted to Guatemala City.

Meanwhile, Montenegro declared his government to be "the third government of the revolution", aligning it with the socialist administrations of Arevalo and Arbenz. But despite the support of reformers, students, professionals and a large section of the middle classes, his hands were tied by the influence of the army. Above all else the administration was marked by the rise of political violence and the increasing power of an alliance between the army and the MLN, a right-wing political party. Political assassination became commonplace as "**death squads**" such as the *Mano Blanco* and *Ojo por Ojo* operated with impunity, killing peasant leaders, students, unionists and academics.

ECONOMIC DECLINE AND POLITICAL VIOLENCE

The history of Guatemala since 1970 has been dominated by electoral fraud and political violence. At the heart of the crisis is the injustice and inequality of Guatemalan society: for while the country remains fairly prosperous the benefits of its success never reach the poor, who are denied access to land, education or health care and are forced instead to work in the coastal plantations that fuel the capital's affluence. The victims of this system have little to lose, while the ruling elite refuse to concede any ground.

In the 1970 elections the power of the military and the far right (represented by the MLN and PID) was confirmed, and **Colonel Arana Osorio**, who had directed the counter-insurgency campaign in the east, was elected president. The turnout was under 50 percent, of which Arana polled just under half, giving him the votes of around 4 percent of the population (bearing in mind that only a small percentage was enfranchised).

Once in power he set about eradicating armed opposition, declaring that "if it is necessary to turn the country into a cemetery in order to pacify it, I will not hesitate to do so". The reign of terror, conducted by both the armed forces and the "death squads", reached unprecedented levels. Once again the violence was to claim the lives of students, academics, opposition politicians, union leaders and agrarian reformers. According to one estimate there were 15,000 political killings during the first three years of Arana's rule.

The next round of presidential elections was held in 1974, and was contended by a broad coalition of centre-left parties under the banner of the National Opposition Front (FNO), headed by General Efraín Ríos Montt. The campaign was marked by manipulation and fraud on the part of the right, who pronounced their candidate, **Kjell Laugerud**, as the winner. The result caused uproar, and for several days the situation was extremely tense. Ríos Montt was eventually persuaded to accept defeat and packed off to a diplomatic post in Spain, although many had hoped that reforming elements within the armed forces would secure his right to the presidency.

Meanwhile, the feared severity of the Laugerud regime never materialized and instead he began to offer limited reforms, incorporating Christian Democrats into his government. Greater tolerance was shown towards union organizations and the cooperative movement, and the government launched a plan for the colonization of Petén and the Northern Transversal Strip in an attempt to provide more land. The army, though, continued as ever to consolidate its authority, spreading its influence across a wider range of business and commercial interests and challenging Laugerud's moderation.

All of this was interrupted by a massive **earthquake** on February 4, 1976. The quake left around 23,000 dead, 77,000 injured and a million homeless. For the most part it was the homes of the poor, built from makeshift materials and on unstable ground, that suffered the most, while subsistence farmers were caught out just as they were about to plant their corn. On the Caribbean coast Puerto Barrios was almost totally destroyed and remained cut off from the capital for several months.

In the wake of the earthquake, during the process of reconstruction, fresh centres of regional control emerged on both sides of the political spectrum. The electoral process seemed to offer no respite from the injustice that was at the heart of Guatemalan society, and many of the victims felt the time had come to take action. A revived trade union organization championed the cause of the majority, while a new guerrilla organization, The Guerrilla Army of the Poor (EGP), emerged in the Ixil area, and army operations became increasingly ferocious. In 1977 President Carter suspended all military aid to Guatemala because of the country's appalling human rights record.

In the following year, 1978, Guatemala's elections were once again dominated by the army, who engineered a victory for **Brigadier General Fernando Lucas García**, who had served as defence minister in the Laugerud administration. The run-up to the elections was marred by serious disturbances in Guatemala City, after bus fares were doubled. Lucas García promised to bring the situation under control, and things took a significant turn for the worse as the new administration unleashed a fresh wave of violence. All opposition groups met with severe repression, as did journalists, trade unionists and academics. Conditions throughout the country were deteriorating rapidly, and the economy was badly affected by a fall in commodity prices, while several guerrilla armies were developing strongholds in the highlands.

As chaos threatened, the army resorted to extreme measures, and within a month there was a major massacre. In the village of **Panzos**, Alta Verapaz, a group of local people were cut down by soldiers when they arrived for a meeting — 100 were left dead. In Guatemala City the situation became so dangerous that political parties were driven underground. Two leading members of the Social Democrats, who were expected to win the next election, lost their lives in 1979. Once they were out of the way the government turned on the Christian Democrats, killing over 100 of their members and forcing **Vinicio Cerezo**, the party's leader, into hiding.

Throughout the Lucas administration the **army** became increasingly powerful and the death toll rose steadily. In rural areas the war against the guerrillas was reaching new heights as army casualties rose to 250 a month, and the demand for conscripts grew rapidly. The four main guerrilla groups had an estimated 6000 combatants and some 250,000 unarmed collaborators. Under the Lucas administration the horrors of **repression** were at their most intense, both in the highlands and in the cities. The victims again included students, journalists, academics, politicians, priests, lawyers, teachers, unionists, and above all peasant farmers, massacred in their hundreds. Accurate figures are impossible to calculate but it's estimated that around 25,000 Guatemalans were killed during the four years of the Lucas regime.

But while high-ranking officers became more and more involved in big business and political wrangling, the officers in the field began to feel deserted. Here there was growing discontent as a result of repeated military failures, inefficiency and a shortage of supplies, despite increased military aid from Israel.

RIOS MONTT

The 1982 elections were again manipulated by the far right, who ensured a victory for **Aníbal Guevara**. However, on March 23 a group of young military officers led a successful coup, which installed **General Efraín Ríos Montt** (who had been denied the post in 1974) as the head of a three-member junta. The coup leaders argued that they had been left with no option as the ruling elite had overridden the electoral process three times in the last eight years, and the takeover was supported by the majority of the opposition parties.

Ríos Montt was a committed Christian, a member of the *Iglesia del Verbo*, and throughout his rule Sunday-night television was dominated by presidential sermons. Above all he was determined to restore law and order, eradicate corruption, and defeat the guerrillas, with the ultimate aim of restoring "authentic democracy". Government officials were issued with identity cards inscribed with the words "I do not steal. I do not lie."

In the immediate aftermath of the coup things improved dramatically. Repression dropped overnight in the cities, a welcome relief after the turmoil of the Lucas regime. Corrupt police and army officers were forced to resign, and trade and tourism began to return.

However, in the highlands the war intensified, as Ríos Montt declared that he would defeat the guerrillas by Christmas. Throughout June they were offered **amnesty** if they turned themselves in to the authorities, but once the month had passed (and only a handful had accepted) the army descended on the highlands with renewed vigour. Montt had instituted a new "code of conduct" for the army, binding soldiers not to "take a pin from the villagers" and not to "make romantic overtures to the women of the region". The army set about destroying the guerrillas' infrastructure by undermining their support within the communíty. In those villages that had been "pacified" the local men were organized into Civil Defence Patrols (PACs), armed with ancient rifles, and told to patrol the countryside. Those who refused were denounced as "subversives". Thus the people of the villages were forced to take sides, caught between the attraction of guerrilla propaganda and the sheer brutality of the armed forces.

Ríos Montt's bizarre blend of stern morality and ruthlessness was as successful as it was murderous, and the army was soon making significant gains against the guerrillas. In late 1982 President Reagan, deciding that Ríos Montt had been given a "bum rap", restored American military aid. Meanwhile, the "state of siege" became a "state of alarm", under which special tribunals were given the power to try and execute suspects. By the middle of 1983 Ríos Montt was facing growing pressure from all sides. Leaders of the Catholic Church were outraged by the influx of evangelical preachers, while politicians, business people, farmers and professionals were angered by the lack of progress towards democratic rule, and landowners were frightened by rumours of land reform.

In August 1983 Ríos Montt was overthrown by yet another military coup, this one backed by a US government keen to see Guatemala set on the road to democracy. The new president was **General Mejía Víctores**, and although the death squads and disappearances continued, elections were held for an 88-member Constituent Assembly, which was given the task of drawing up a new constitution in preparation for presidential elections.

Under Víctores there was an upturn in the level of rural repression, though the process of reconstruction initiated by Ríos Montt continued. Internal refugees were rehoused in "model villages", where they were under the control of the army. Scarcely any money was available for rebuilding the devastated communities, and it was often widows and orphans who were left to construct their own homes. In the Ixil Triangle alone the war had displaced 60,000 people (72 percent of the population), and 9 model villages were built to replace 49 that had been destroyed. Nationwide a total of 440 villages had been destroyed and around 100,000 had lost their lives.

In 1985 presidential elections were held, the first free vote in Guatemala for thirty years.

CEREZO AND THE RETURN TO DEMOCRATIC RULE

The elections were won by **Vinicio Cerezo**, a Christian Democrat whose father had served in the Arbenz administration. Cerezo was by no means associated with the traditional ruling elite and had himself been the intended victim of several assassination attempts. His election victory was the result of a sweeping wave of popular support, and in the run-up to the election he offered a programme of reform that he claimed would rid the country of repression.

Once in office, however, Cerezo was aware that his room for manoeuvre was subject to severe limitations, and he declared that the army still held 75 percent of the power. From the outset he could promise little: "I'm a politician not a magician. Why promise what I cannot deliver? All I commit myself to doing is opening up the political space, giving democracy a chance."

Throughout his six-year rule Cerezo offered a **non-confrontational approach**, seeking above all else to avoid upsetting the powerful alliance of business interests, landowners and generals. To protect himself, he courted the support of a group of sympathetic officers, and with their aid survived several coup attempts. But the administration remained trapped in the middle; the right accused Cerezo of communist leanings, while the left claimed that he was evading his commitment to reform.

Political killings dropped off a great deal under civilian rule, although they by no means stopped. Murder was still a daily event in Guatemala in the late 1980s and the war between the army and the guerrillas still raged in remote corners of the highlands. In Guatemala City the death squads continued to operate freely. No one accused Cerezo of involvement in the killings but it was clear that they were often carried out by policemen or soldiers as the right continued to use violent repression to direct and control the political situation.

In many ways the Cerezo administration was a bitter disappointment to the Guatemalan people. Although these early years of civilian rule did create a breathing space, by the time the decade drew to a close it was clear that the army was still actively controlling political opposition. Having forsaken the role of government, the generals allowed Cerezo to take office, presenting an acceptable face to the world, but the army continued to control the countryside and the economy continued to serve a small but potent elite. By 1988 violence was again on the increase, and in the village of El Aguacate, in the department of Chimaltenango, 22 corpses were found in a shallow grave. Army and guerrillas have blamed each other for the massacre, by far the most serious under Cerezo's rule, but no real proof has emerged (which may in itself be an indication of official involvement). Urban killings and **"disappearances"** were also on the increase in the final years of Cerezo's rule. In February 1989 there were 220 killings, of which 82 were politically motivated. It now appears that the Cerezo administration failed to stem the tide of violence or to alter the country's distorted balance of power.

The country's leading **human rights organization**, The Mutual Support Group (GAM), hoped that civilian rule would present them with a chance to investigate the fate of the "disappeared" and to face up to the country's horrific recent history. Cerezo, however, chose to forget the past, and ongoing abuses went largely uninvestigated and unpunished. GAM's leaders, meanwhile, became victims of the death squads.

Nevertheless, the promise of civilian rule created a general thaw in the political climate, fostering the growth of numerous pressure groups and fresh demands for reform, making protests and strikes a regular feature of Guatemalan life. Real change, however, never materialized. Despite the fact that at least 65 percent of the population were still living below the official poverty line little was done to meet their needs in terms of education, health care or employment. The thirst for land reform reared its head once again, and under the leadership of Padre Andrés Girón, some 35,000 peasants demanded action. Girón's approach was direct. He accused business interests of "exploiting and killing our people. We want the south coast, that's where the wealth of Guatemala lies." Cerezo avoided the issue and in a bid to appease the business community steered clear of any significant tax reform or privatization policy. (Padre Girón was the intended victim of an assassination attempt.) The population became increasingly frustrated with the Cerezo regime; teachers, postal workers and farm labourers all came out on strike, demanding action on human rights and economic reform, while the threat of a military coup continued to restrict the government's room for manoeuvre.

Meanwhile, the economy was hit badly by falling commodity prices (most notably the price of coffee), further restricting the president's position. Despite the fact that Guatemalan income tax is among the lowest in the world, any move to increase tax receipts was met with bitter resistance from the land-owning classes. However, Cerezo did successfully negotiate a loan from the IMF and instituted a series of austerity measures designed to revitalize the economy after decades of decline.

Acknowledging that his greatest achievement had been to survive, Cerezo organized the country's first civilian transfer of power for thirty years in 1990.

THE 1990 ELECTIONS & THE SERRANO ADMINISTRATION

The **1990 elections** were dogged by controversy. The constitution prevented Cerezo from standing for re-election, while another former president, General Ríos Montt, who retained much popularity in the countryside, was prevented from running for office since he had previously come to power as the result of a military coup. In the end twelve candidates contested the election, and it was won by a former minister in the Ríos Montt government, **Jorge Serrano**. However, with a third of the population not registered to vote and an abstention rate of 56 percent, Serrano had the support of less than a quarter of the people.

An engineer and evangelical, Serrano emphasized his centre-right economic goals and attempted to negotiate a final solution to the country's thirty-year civil war. But once again the government appeared both uninterested and incapable of effecting any real reform. The level of human rights abuse remained high, death squad activity continued, the economy remained weak and the army was still a powerful force, using intimidation and murder to stamp out opposition. (Five hundred Guatemalans either disappeared or were killed in extrajudicial executions in 1992.)

Despite the fact that Guatemala remained one of the richest nations in the region **economic growth** was slow and the economy remained largely dependent on commodities, US aid and tourism. The Serrano administration, unable to act decisively, in 1993 faced a growing wave of strikes and protests following a series of price rises and wage freezes. Economic activity was still controlled by a tiny elite; 60 percent of the workforce were employed in agriculture and less than 2 percent of landowners owned more than 65 percent of the land, leaving some 85 percent of the population living in poverty, with little access to health care or education.

Nevertheless, Guatemala's dispossessed and poor continued to clamour for change. Out in the countryside the **indigenous population** became increasingly organized and influential, denouncing the continued bombardment of villages and rejecting the presence of the army and the system of civil patrols. Matters were brought into sharp focus in 1992, when Rigoberta Menchú was awarded the Nobel Peace Prize for her campaigning work on behalf of Guatemala's indigenous population. In spite of the efforts of the Serrano administration the country's civil war still rumbled on and three main guerrilla armies, united as the URNG, continued to confront the army. (The guerrillas were thought to have between 1000 and 3000 armed regulars, while the army numbered some 43,000.)

One of the most pressing problems for the indigenous people was the return of some 45,000 **refugees** who had been living in camps in Mexico. In January 1993 a first group of 2500 refugees returned home after more than a decade in Mexico, resettling in villages in the Ixcán region in the north of the department of Quiché. Prior to their return other villages in the area were bombarded and two were destroyed by the army after their inhabitants had fled, a move that was frighteningly reminiscent of the worst days of the country's civil war. As the remaining refugees started to make their way home, hardened by ten years in exile, their resettlement was a great test of how far Guatemala had come since those days. The refugees insisted upon their right to establish free civil communities, while the army argued that they were linked with guerrillas.

1993: SERRANO OUSTED

In **May 1993**, much to the surprise of the international community, President Serrano responded to a wave of popular protest with an *autogolpe* or **self-coup**. Suspending the constitution he stated that he would rule by decree. Following the example of Peru's President Fujimori, Serrano argued that the country was endangered by civil disorder and corruption. "I had to put a stop to it", he claimed, arguing that the drug mafia planned to take over Guatemala. Few were convinced, and the US responded by suspending its annual $67 million of aid.

Serrano's claims about the "drug mafia" masked a more self-serving purpose, that of holding onto power. Throughout the early part of 1993 his popularity was in steep decline; price rises met with violent protest, human rights abuses remained commonplace and negotiations with the guerrillas were deadlocked. As his former supporters deserted him Serrano was forced to rely increasingly upon the support of the army and it was the generals who backed and orchestrated the coup. However, within a couple of days they had decided that Serrano's fumbling wasn't really serving their purposes and on June 1 he was removed from office. Into his shoes stepped the Defence Minister, **General José Domingo Carcia Samayoa**, but in the face of further widespread protests, from both left and right, congress finally appointed **Ramiro de Leon Carpio**, the country's human rights ombudsman, as the new president.

In some ways the crisis drew back the curtains on Guatemala's flirtation with civilian rule to reveal that the army retained the controlling hand, although for the generals the coup had a bitter sting in its tail. Serrano, like Cerezo before him, was a useful front man, but certain key issues such as human rights, tax and land reform, remained unassailable. Guatemalan society maintained its hoplelessly imbalanced structure, dominated by an alliance of the army, big business and landowners, who allowed civilians to run the government so that they could get on with the more serious business of running the country. Coup rumblings reminded the presidents that the troops were waiting in the wings.

However, the generals clearly underestimated the force of popular protest and even they couldn't sustain Serrano or control the appointment of his successor. While the coup was going on Leon de Carpio's home was surrounded by troops. His subsequent appointment as president suggests that Serrano's backers themselves were replaced. One of Leon de Carpio's first moves was a reshuffle of the senior military command, although he rejected calls for revenge. In an interview with *El Pais* he said "My task is to attain stability . . . We are a people that has scarcely experienced democracy. It has arrived overnight, without us having the culture or education that goes with it. Couple that with the terrible violence rooted in this country and you see there is a lack of political consciousness. But we will come out ahead."

1996 AND THE ARRIVAL OF THE MODERNIZING RIGHT

In January 1996 Guatemalans went to the polls to elect a new president. Above all the elections demonstrated the country's increasing lack of faith in the electoral process, which had failed to bring any real change after the much-heralded return to civilian rule in 1986. As a result, some 63 percent of registered voters stayed at home and it was only a strong showing in Guatemala City that ensured Alvaro Arzú's success. Blond, blue-eyed and somewhat bland, **Arzú** represents Guatemala's so-called modernizing right. His party, the PAN or National Advancement Party, has strong oligarchic roots and is committed to private sector lead growth and the free market. Nevertheless, the early appointment of new defence, foreign and economic ministers does suggest a relatively progressive stance, which has Guatemala's left holding its breath in anticipation. Though on taking office the new president said "the clock has been turned back to zero", he also promised to lay the foundations for a freer and fairer country, to allow the full investigation of past human rights abuses and to disengage the barbarous military intelligence services from internal politics. Only time will tell whether he has the strength and commitment to bring about real improvements; for Guatemalans weary of such promises the situation and rhetoric may appear all too familiar. The cards are, as ever, heavily stacked against

progressive change: within weeks of his election Arzú faced a botched assassination attempt.

BELIZE SINCE THE DECLINE OF CLASSIC MAYA CIVILIZATION

From around 900 AD, and the break-up of Classic Maya civilization, the Belize area was largely independent, but it remains impossible to separate the early history of Belize from that of the surrounding areas of Petén in Guatemala or the Yucatán of Mexico, where small tribal groups fought bitterly to maintain their independence.

After the collapse of lowland Maya civilization in the ninth century and the invasion of the Toltecs in 987 AD, the Yucatán peninsula became the main centre of Maya political and social life. To the south, however, the Belize area was never entirely deserted and many of the cities here not only survived but prospered long after those in the Yucatán.

Relatively little is known of this period of decline. Chichén Itzá, the great centre in the Yucatán, was abandoned early in the thirteenth century, and thereafter power moved to Mayapan. This in turn declined in the fifteenth century and many of the inhabitants moved south into the jungles of Petén. In the years leading up to the Spanish Conquest the Yucatán and northern Belize consisted of over a dozen rival provinces, bound up in a cycle of competition and conflict.

THE FIRST EUROPEANS

The general assumption that Belize was practically deserted by the time Europeans arrived is now widely discredited. In fact the Maya towns and provinces, though no longer powerful city-states with far-reaching trade links, were still vigorously independent, as the Spanish found to their cost on several occasions.

The northern part of Belize, possibly reaching as far south as the Northern River, was part of the Maya province of **Chactemal**, later known as Chetumal. Its capital was not at the Mexican city of the same name, but probably a site now known as **Santa Rita**, in present-day Corozal. Chetumal was a wealthy province, producing cacao and honey and covering an area from Maskall in Belize to northern Lake Bacalar in Mexico. Trade, alliances and wars kept Chetumal in contact with surrounding Maya states up to and beyond the Spanish conquest of Aztec Mexico.

Further south the forests were thicker and the ridge of the Maya Mountains intruded across the land. To the Maya of Chetumal this area was known as *Dzuluinicob* – "land of foreigners". The capital of this province was **Tipu**, possibly located at Baking Pot on the Belize River or, more likely, at Negroman, on the Macal River south of San Ignacio. The Maya here controlled the upper Belize River valley and put up strenuous resistance to attempts by the Spanish to subdue and convert them. The struggle was to continue with simmering resentment until 1707 when the population of Tipu was forcibly removed to Lake Petén Itzá.

The first **Europeans** to set eyes on the mainland of Belize were the Spanish sailors Pinzon and de Solis in 1506 or 1508, on a voyage round the Bay of Honduras, but they didn't attempt a landing. In 1511 a small group of Spanish sailors, shipwrecked off Jamaica, managed to reach land on the southern coast of Yucatán. This first, accidental, contact between European and Maya was fatal for a number of the shipwrecked Spaniards: some became slaves, five were immediately sacrificed, and some escaped.

It is possible that at least one of the escapees regained contact with his fellow countrymen because when **Cortes** reached Yucatán in 1519 he knew of the existence of two survivors of the shipwreck, and sent for them once he had established his force on Cozumel. Geronimo de Aguilar immediately joined Cortes, but the other survivor, Gonzalo Guerrero, refused. (The archeologist Eric Thompson calls him the first European to make Belize his home.) Guerrero eventually married the daughter of Nachankan, the chief of Chetumal, and was to become a crucial military adviser to the Maya in their subsequent resistance to Spanish domination. Cortes, meanwhile, sailed north around Yucatán and into the Bay of Campeche to land at Veracruz: the destruction of the Aztec Empire promised greater glory and pillage.

In the early years of the Conquest few reports were made of contact with the Maya in the east, possibly because the Spanish had heard no stories of gold or treasure – their overriding obsession. In 1525 Cortes himself almost certainly passed through the extreme south of Belize on his epic march from Veracruz in Mexico to punish a rebellious subordinate in a recently established town on the Gulf of Honduras. The course of his march took Cortes and his retinue of 140 Spanish soldiers and 3000 Indians across the heartland of the Maya, which still contained many thriving towns and cities. They traversed largely unknown territory – jungles, swamps, tropical rivers and mountains, heading through Tabasco, Chiapas and Petén. Cortes was welcomed at Tayasal on Lake Petén Itzá by Can Ek, chief of the Itzá, who had heard of Cortes' cruelty in conquering the Aztecs and decided not to oppose him. The expedition continued southwards, to the valley of the Sarstoon River, the present boundary with Guatemala, either following that river to the coast or crossing it and following the Río Dulce. The destination was San Gil de Buena Vista at the mouth of the Río Dulce, the recently renamed and relocated Maya town of Nito, a Late Postclassic trading centre on the Río Dulce.

After pacifying the rebels Cortes sailed north to Mexico, without apparently realizing Yucatán was a peninsula. Despite previous expeditions, including landings on the island of Cozumel and the settlement of Salamanca on the mainland near Xelha, it was not until 1528, when Francisco de Montejo sailed south along the coast of Yucatán to Honduras, that the Spanish realized the Yucatán was not an island.

ATTEMPTED CONQUEST

At the time of the Conquest, the Maya of Yucatán and Belize were not united into a single empire. Postclassic society in the northern lowlands consisted of numerous city-states, constantly fighting each other or forming alliances to gain temporary advantage. The leaders of these provinces were accustomed to dealing with enemies and fighting to retain their independence, which is one reason why the Spanish found the Yucatán and Belize such a difficult area to subdue.

In Mexico and Peru it had proved relatively simple to capture and eventually kill the "living god", leader of a militaristic, unified and highly organized society, and replace him with an equally despotic Spanish ruler. However, here the situation was very different, similar in many ways to that in the highlands of Guatemala.

The first stage in the attempted conquest of Yucatán was the granting of permission by the Spanish crown to **Francisco de Montejo** to colonize "the islands of Cozumel and Yucatán". He established a small settlement at Salamanca, but this was not safe from attack, so in 1528 he sailed south to find a more secure location for a permanent Spanish colony. At the same time his lieutenant, **Alonso Davila**, was to lead an overland expedition to the south. Neither was particularly successful; Davila encountered hostile Maya after a short distance and Montejo was forced to turn away from Chetumal by Maya under the leadership of Gonzalo Guerrero.

A second attempt by Davila to found a town at Chetumal, in 1531, was also short-lived. On this occasion the Maya had abandoned the town, on the advice of Guerrero who realized they could not defeat the Spanish outright, and it was occupied by Davila and renamed **Villa Real**. This was the first attempt by Spain to conquer and settle the area later to become Belize. Once established, however, Davila and his troops were continually harassed by the Maya when searching for food and were driven out eighteen months later, fleeing south along the coast of Belize and eventually reaching Omoa in Honduras.

Montejo's vision of a vast province of the Spanish empire comprising the whole of Yucatán, Chiapas and Honduras was not to be fulfilled. His son, Montejo the Younger, completed the conquest of Yucatán, establishing the capital at **Mérida** in 1542. Montejo himself was occupied further south, in the sparsely settled, ill-defined area of Honduras. From 1535 to 1544 he was *Adelantado* of Yucatán and Governor of Honduras-Higueras, which would have included Belize. With the establishment of the *Audiencia de los Confines* in 1544 Montejo lost control of Honduras, but he still considered the area north of the Río Dulce to be part of Yucatán and within his domain. Expeditions he sent in 1546–47 to the Río Dulce were opposed by the Dominicans working there to peacefully convert the Maya,

and by 1549 he was forced to abandon the idea of a settlement, his authority restricted to Yucatán alone.

For some years after Montejo and Davila's unsuccessful attempts to conquer Chetumal, northern Belize remained independent. Chetumal regained its important trading links and was obviously also a powerful military force, in 1542 sending fifty war canoes 320km to Omoa in Honduras to assist local Indians in their fight against the Spanish.

Late in 1543, however, **Gaspar Pacheco**, his son Melchor and his nephew Alonso began another chapter in the sickeningly familiar tale of Spanish atrocities, advancing on Chetumal, destroying crops and food stores and ruthlessly slaughtering the Indians. In a letter to Spain, Fray Lorenzo de Bienvenida wrote: "Nero was not more cruel [than Alonso Pacheco]. He passed through and reached a province called Chetumal, which was at peace.... This captain with his own hands committed outrages: he killed many with the garrote, saying 'This is a good rod with which to punish these people'."

In 1544 the Pachecos had subdued Maya resistance sufficiently to found a town on Lake Bacalar and claim *encomienda* (tribute) from villages in Chetumal. It is likely that the Pachecos also conquered parts of the province of Dzuluinicob to the south, though there was strong opposition to Spanish control with uprisings in Yucatán and Chetumal. Tipu, for a time at least, was the centre of an alliance between Chetumal and Dzuluinicob, showing that there was still organized resistance to Spanish domination.

During the second half of the sixteenth century missions were established, including one at Lamanai, and the Spanish, with difficulty, strengthened their hold over northern Belize. The resentment that was always present beneath the surface, however, boiled over into total rebellion in 1638, forcing Spain to abandon the area of Chetumal and Tipu completely.

In the mid-seventeenth century the nearest permanent Spanish settlements to Belize were at Salamanca de Bacalar in Yucatán and Lake Izabal in Guatemala. Records are scarce but it is possible that the Maya of Belize were under some form of Spanish influence even if they were not under Spanish rule. Perhaps the determination of Maya resistance deterred Spain from attempting to colonize the area; perhaps the experience of cruelty and oppression that followed conquest caused the Maya to flee to inaccessible forests in an attempt to retain their independence. Repeated **expeditions** were mounted by friars and colonial leaders during the seventeenth century. One unsuccessful *entrada* led by Fray Fuensalida in 1641 attempted to convert the people of Tipu, but there was little, if any, Spanish contact until 1695, when a Spanish mission met Itzá leaders to discuss the **surrender of the Itzá**. The negotiations were fruitless and in 1697 Spanish forces attacked Tayasal (on Lake Petén Itzá), bringing Maya independence to an end, at least in theory.

Events didn't all go in favour of the Spanish even now. In the late seventeenth century Bacalar was abandoned after years of **Indian and pirate attacks**. Spain's forces were simply too stretched to cope with securing and administering the vast (and relatively gold-free) territory from Campeche to Honduras. English, and later British, trade and territorial ambitions in the sixteenth century focused on America, resulting in almost continuous conflict with Spain. The capture of Jamaica in 1655, after 150 years of Spanish rule, gave Britain a base in the Caribbean from which it could harass Spanish shipping and support the growth of its colonies.

THE ARRIVAL OF THE BRITISH

The failure of the Spanish authorities to clearly delineate the southern boundary of Yucatán subsequently allowed **buccaneers** (primarily British) to find refuge along the coast of Belize and ultimately led to Guatemala's claim to the territory of British Honduras and refusal to recognize Belize's independence. Had Spain effectively occupied the area between Yucatán and Honduras it is unlikely that British influence would have been allowed to become established. When Spain did take action on various occasions to expel the British settlers (Baymen), there was confusion over whether the captain-general of Yucatán or Guatemala maintained jurisdiction in the area. Consequently, the Baymen were able to return in the absence of any permanent Spanish outposts on the coast.

British incursions along the Bay of Honduras were first made by buccaneers, resting and seeking refuge after raids on Spanish ships and settlements. Some of the great Elizabethan sailors such as Raleigh, Hawkins and Drake may have landed on the coast of Belize, although there are no records to prove this. (Indeed records referring to settlements, even temporary camps, are scarce: while the dates of the establishment of other British colonies in the Caribbean are known, there was no attempt on the part of the British government to colonize Belize.)

Britain was not the only power interested in establishing colonies in this lucrative area of the Caribbean, with both **France** and the **Netherlands** keen to establish a foothold. Companies were set up to equip privateers, really government-sanctioned pirate ships, to raid the Spanish treasure fleets. Treasure wasn't always easy to come by and sometimes they would plunder the piles of logwood, cut and awaiting shipment to Spain.

In due course the cutting of **logwood** was to become an important industry in Belize. The wood itself, hard and extremely heavy, was worth £90–110 per ton and the trade was controlled by Spain. Back in Europe logwood was used in the expanding textile industry to dye woollens black, red and grey. Naturally, such an abundance of convertible wealth attracted the buccaneers, once they learned of its importance. By the mid-seventeenth century, and possibly as early as 1640, British buccaneers had settled on the coasts of Campeche and the Spanish Caribbean.

The signing of the **Godolphin Treaty** of 1670 between Britain and Spain recognized the right of Britain to own and occupy any territories already held in the Americas at that time. This acknowledgement by Spain was intended partly to control the activities of the buccaneers (already outlawed in a treaty of 1667) and partly to ease tension between the two powers in the face of increasing French might in Europe and the Caribbean. However, it was never intended that the treaty should legitimize the existing British settlements or the cutting of logwood on the coast from Mexico to Panamá, which Spain clearly regarded as its own domain.

Of course the logwood cutters did not simply go away and Spain's attitude to the trade was ambivalent, with local officials tending to ignore it. For the next 130 years **British settlements** on the western shore of the Caribbean periodically came under attack whenever Spain sought to defend its interests, but the settlements on the coasts of Campeche, Yucatán, Belize and the Mosquito Coast were on the periphery of much wider and, to the Great Powers of the period, more important issues. France and the Netherlands as well as Britain and Spain were building empires and competing for trade across the globe. The attention of the governments of these countries rarely rested upon the humid and insect-ridden swamps where the logwood cutters, who were becoming known as **Baymen**, worked and lived. Treaties were signed, edicts passed and the British government, while wishing to profit from the trade in logwood, preferred to avoid the question of whether or not the Baymen were British subjects. For the most part they were left to their own devices.

Life in the logwood camps was uncomfortable to say the least. Though the wood was mainly cut in the dry season, the men often had to wait until the rains to float it down the rivers to be stored for shipment. The Baymen lived in rough huts thatched with palmetto leaves, surviving on provisions brought by ships from Jamaica. These ships also brought rum, which the Baymen drank with relish whenever it was available; an English merchant (writing in 1726) reports: "Rum Punch is their Drink, which they'll sometimes sit several Days at . . . for while the Liquor is moving they don't care to leave it."

Though many of the cutters had "voluntarily" given up buccaneering, raiding of Spanish ships still occurred in the later years of the seventeenth century, only to be punished by Spain whenever it had the will and opportunity. An attack by Spain on settlers in the Bay of Campeche left the survivors imprisoned in Mexico and led to Belize becoming the main centre for logwood cutting. (Some cutters did return to Campeche but in further attacks in 1716 and 1735 Spain again destroyed the settlements.)

Attacks by Spanish forces, from both Yucatán and Petén, on the settlements in the Belize River valley occurred throughout the eighteenth century, with the Baymen being driven out on several occasions. Increasingly

though, Britain – at war with Spain from 1739 to 1748 (The War of Jenkins' Ear) and France from 1743 to 1748 (The War of Austrian Succession) – began to admit a measure of responsibility for the protection of the settlers. For the British there was little to lose.

In 1746, in response to requests from the Baymen, the governor of Jamaica sent troops to Belize, but this assistance didn't stop the Spanish laying waste to the settlement in 1747 and again in 1754. The **Paris Peace Treaty** of 1763 was the first (of many) to allow the British to cut logwood, but since it did not define boundaries the governor of Yucatán sent troops from Bacalar to ensure that the cutters confined themselves to the Belize River. The Baymen complained at this interference and in 1765 the commander-in-chief at Jamaica, Admiral Burnaby, visited Belize to ensure that the provisions of the treaty, vague though they were, were upheld. As so often in reports of naval officers concerning the condition of settlers, he found them in "a state of Anarchy and Confusion". The admiral decided the Baymen needed laws and regulations. His rules, known as **Burnaby's Code**, were a simple set of laws concerning the maintenance of justice in a remote and uncouth area where the British government did not care to become too closely involved. They gave authority to a bench of magistrates to hold quarterly courts with the power to impose fines, supported by a jury. The Baymen attached an importance to the Code (though they apparently rarely obeyed it) beyond that which Burnaby intended, and even voted to increase its scope a year later.

Decades of Spanish attacks had fostered in the settlers a spirit of defiance and self-reliance, and the realization that British rule was preferable to Spanish, as long as they could choose which of its institutions to accept.

THE BATTLE OF ST GEORGE'S CAYE

The **Battle of St George's Caye** was the culmination of over a century of antagonism, boundary disputes and mutual suspicion between the Spanish colonial authorities and the woodcutting (ex-buccaneering) Baymen. Relations were never secure: the Spanish feared raids on their treasure ships, and the Baymen feared being driven out of what was ostensibly Spanish territory.

In 1779 Spain (then allied with France on the side of the American colonies) had sent a fleet under the Commandant of Bacalar to Belize and captured all the inhabitants of St George's Caye, then the chief settlement of the Baymen, imprisoning them in Mérida and later Havana.

The Versailles Peace Treaty (1783) did little to resolve the question of the Bay settlement, but a convention signed three years later in London granted concessions to the Baymen. Logwood (and other timber) could be cut as far as the Sibun River, and St George's Caye could be inhabited though no plantations were to be established. The clause that rankled most with the independent-minded settlers was that no fortifications were allowed and no system of government could be established without approval from Madrid. True to their "turbulent and unsettled disposition", the Baymen ignored the strictures of the convention, cutting wood where they pleased and being generally unruly. After 1791 the settlement was without even the little-regarded authority of a superintendent appointed by the governor of Jamaica.

With the outbreak of war between Britain and Spain in 1796 the settlers appealed for help in their defence to Lord Balcarres, the governor of Jamaica. In spite of difficulties on his own territory, Balcarres sent a small amount of gunpowder and arms to the settlement and in December a **Lieutenant-Colonel Barrow** was despatched to Belize as superintendent, to command the settlers in the event of hostilities. Under the supervision of Colonel Barrow the settlers prepared for war, albeit grudgingly.

A vital **public meeting**, held on June 1, 1797, decided by 65 votes to 51 to defend the settlement rather than evacuate. A few companies of troops were sent from Jamaica and slaves were released from woodcutting to be armed and trained. The sloop **HMS Merlin** was stationed in the Bay, local vessels were armed, gun rafts built and an attack was expected at any time. Throughout the next year the mood of the defenders vacillated between aggression and despair. Martial law was imposed, all men of military age were ordered to Belize Town and buildings on St George's Caye were pulled down to prevent their use by the enemy. As late as August 1798, 53 of the

Baymen wrote to Barrow asking him for help in their request to Lord Balcarres that they be removed to safety in the Bahamas or Jamaica; the plea was ignored. The Baymen (and their slaves) would have to defend themselves with the scant resources at their disposal.

The available local support for *HMS Merlin* consisted of the sloops *Towser*, *Tickler* and *Mermaid*, with one gun each; and the schooners *Swinger* and *Teazer*, each armed with six four-pounders; and seven gun-flats (rafts) armed with one nine-pound gun each.

The **Spanish fleet** assembled by the governor of Yucatán, one Don Arturo O'Neill Tirone, sailed from Bacalar early in September. There were reported to be 32 vessels, including 16 heavily armed men-of-war and 2000 troops – on September 3, 1798, lookout boats north of Belize Town sighted them. The main body of the Spanish fleet remained in deep water beyond the reef while five ships attempted to force their way over Montego Caye Shoals, just north of St George's Caye. They were repulsed by the three sloops and the next day the Spanish tried again to force a passage, but again they were beaten back, this time withdrawing to the safety of the main fleet. That evening, September 4, stakes placed by the Spanish to mark the reefs and channels were removed by the defenders, who knew these waters well. Yet another attempt was mounted on September 5 to break through Montego Caye Shoals, and again it proved unsuccessful.

Colonel Barrow and Captain Moss of the *Merlin* correctly guessed the Spanish would now try to seize St George's Caye. The *Merlin* and part of the Baymen's tiny fleet sailed there on the evening of September 5, securing it just as twelve of the heaviest Spanish warships were attempting to do the same. The Spanish, frustrated by these setbacks, withdrew to their anchorage between Long Caye and Caye Chapel.

The next few days must have passed anxiously for both sides: the Spanish with their massive firepower severely restricted by the shallow water; and the Baymen with their small but highly manoeuvrable fleet, awaiting the impending attack. On the morning of **September 10, 1798**, fourteen of the largest Spanish ships sailed to within a mile and a half of St George's Caye. Five of these vessels, packed with troops, anchored to the east of the caye, while the other nine, armed with 18- and 24-pounder cannon and towing launches loaded with soldiers, formed a line abreast and began firing.

In the centre of the channel Captain Moss of HMS *Merlin* held his fire; the Spanish broadsides were falling short. At 1.30pm he gave the order to open fire. Guns blazing, the small fleet swept forward, wreaking havoc among the heavy and crowded Spanish warships. The battle was fast and furious, the Baymen's slaves at least as eager to fight the Spanish as their masters were. Although a dory was sent to Belize to summon Colonel Barrow to join in the fight and the troops immediately set off in any craft available, they arrived too late to take part in the action.

The Spanish fleet, already weakened by desertions and yellow fever, suffered heavy losses and fled in disorder to Caye Chapel. There they remained for five days, burying some of their dead on the island. On the morning of September 16 the Spanish sailed for Bacalar, defeated but still harassed by the Baymen, who captured a packet-boat that evening and took five prisoners.

Though a victory was won against almost overwhelming odds, the Battle of St George's Caye was not by itself decisive. No one in the Bay settlement was sure that the Spanish would not once again attempt to remove the Baymen by force. The legal status was as before: a settlement where the inhabitants could cut timber but did not constitute a territory of the British empire. Sovereign rights remained, nominally at least, with the Spanish crown, though it was never clear which of the neighbouring *Audiencias*, Mexico or Guatemala, had responsibility for implementing the numerous treaties and agreements between Britain and Spain.

In purely practical terms the power of the Spanish empire was waning while the British empire was consolidating and expanding. But in Belize the slaves were still slaves though they had fought valiantly alongside the Baymen: their owners expected them to go back to cutting mahogany. Emancipation came no earlier than elsewhere in the British empire.

In 1898, the centenary of the battle, on September 10, was established as a national holiday, St George's Caye Day, still jubilantly observed today.

SETTLERS AND SLAVES

The population of the Honduras settlements during the century following the arrival of the first buccaneers had never been more than a few hundred, their livelihoods dependent on the attitude of the adjacent Spanish colonies. In order to gain concessions from Spain favourable to the Belize settlement, Britain had agreed to relinquish claims to the Mosquito Shore (along the coasts of Honduras and Nicaragua, including the Bay Islands) in the **Convention of 1786**. Many of the aggrieved inhabitants displaced by the convention settled in Belize and by 1790 the population had reached over 2900, of whom over 2100 were slaves.

A report by a Spanish missionary in 1724 mentions the ownership of **slaves** by English settlers, and it is unlikely that slaves were brought in (from Jamaica and Bermuda) much before that time. Over the years the view that slavery in Belize was somehow less harsh than elsewhere has emerged. It's a misconception that may have arisen because of the differences between plantation slavery, as practised in the West Indies, and the mainly forest labour that Belize slaves were employed upon. A number of slave revolts from 1745 to 1820 show that relations between master and slave were not as amicable as some would like to believe. The Whites in the settlement, always vastly outnumbered by their slaves, feared rebellion at least as much as they feared attack by the Spanish, requesting help from Jamaica on several occasions. The biggest (and arguably most successful) revolt occurred in 1773 when six White men were murdered and at least eleven slaves escaped across the River Hondo, where they were promised asylum by the Spanish authorities. This was not a display of altruism on the part of the Spanish, since encouraging slaves to flee the Belize settlement was calculated to weaken its economy.

In spite of revolts, the nature of slavery in Belize was very different from that on the sugar plantations in the West Indies. The cutting of mahogany, which had overtaken logwood as the principal export by the 1760s, involved small gangs working in the forest on their own or on a fairly harmonious level with an overseer. The slaves were armed, with firearms in some cases, to hunt for food and for protection against Indians. Skills developed in searching for the trees, cutting them down and transporting them to the coast gave the slaves involved a status and position of trust that their masters depended upon for the continuation of their own way of life. Manumission, whereby a slave might purchase freedom or be freed as a gift or as a bequest in a will, was much more frequent in Belize than in the Caribbean islands, perhaps an indication of the greater informality of Belizean society. However, treatment could still be harsh and little protection was offered by the law. Owners could inflict up to 39 lashes or imprison their slaves, and if a slave was hanged for rebellion or assault the owner could be compensated for the loss of property.

Ironically, it was the Abolition Act of 1807, which made it illegal for British subjects to continue with the African slave trade but not to transport slaves from one British colony to another, that gave the settlers in Belize recognition as **British subjects**. If Belize was not a colony (which it clearly was not) then slaves could not be transported between Jamaica and the settlement. Superintendent Arthur, the British government's representative and upholder of the law in Belize, decided that the settlers in Belize were British subjects and as such forbidden to engage in the slave trade. The **Abolition Act of 1833** ended slavery throughout the British empire, and a special clause was written to include Belize.

As the gangs of woodcutters advanced further into the forests in search of mahogany, which was of increasing value in furniture-making, they came into contact with scattered bands of Maya. For centuries the Indians had been driven from their homelands, taking refuge from European settlers and missionaries. The Baymen, however, had no wish to colonize or convert the Maya, so there was little conflict in the early and mid-eighteenth century.

THE SETTLEMENT BECOMES A COLONY

The consolidation of British logging interests in the late eighteenth century led to grudging, tentative steps toward recognition from Spain. A form of British colonial government gradually became established, though the settlement did not achieve **colony status** until 1862. Since the 1730s the settlers had been electing magistrates at the Public Meeting which, in the democratic spirit of the time, gave only property-owning White males a vote. Free Coloured men were allowed to vote at the Public Meeting after 1808, though they had to prove five years' residence and own property worth £200 (against a White's one year and £100).

The **public meeting** had its origins in the early years of the settlement, as the need arose for a rudimentary form of government to bring order to the lawless and independent logwood cutters. At first informal, the meeting slowly assumed greater importance, and members voted to grant powers to the magistrates to hold courts and impose fines. Burnaby's Code in 1765 had reinforced and enlarged the jurisdiction of the magistrates and also allowed the laws passed to be enforced by the captain of a British naval ship. Frequently, visiting naval officers reported on the settlers' inability to keep the laws, generally finding Belize in disorder, even anarchy.

These early examples of Britain's acceptance of some form of responsibility to the settlers led to the appointment in 1784 of the first **superintendent**, Captain Despard, who took up his position in 1786. The office of superintendent, always held by an army officer, appears to have been a difficult one. They often faced an awkward, unsupportive public meeting, which wanted to run affairs in the settlement without "interference" from London. Gradually, though, during the first half of the nineteenth century, the powers of the superintendent grew, while those of the magistrates lessened. Magistrates, elected but unpaid, had traditionally shouldered the burden of public office, including the finance of the settlement – collecting taxes, deciding on expenditure and administering justice. The election of magistrates ceased in 1832, after which they were appointed by the superintendent with the approval of the Colonial Office. Progress towards an elected **Legislative Assembly**, along the lines of those in British colonies, was made, and the office of superintendent took on the role (though not the title) of a lieutenant-governor of a colony.

In 1854 a Legislative Assembly was finally formed, consisting of eighteen elected men and three appointees of the superintendent. A speaker was elected from among the Assembly and the beginnings of colonial-rule parliamentary democracy were established. The Assembly began petitioning for recognition as a colony, arguing that British Honduras, in fact if not in law, was already a British colony. Earl Grey, at the Colonial Office, supported the Assembly and Palmerston, British prime minister from 1855, agreed. On May 12, 1862, the settlements in Belize, with the boundaries that still exist today, became the **Colony of British Honduras**.

MEXICAN AND GUATEMALAN CLAIMS

After the Battle of St George's Caye in 1798 Spain continued to maintain her claim to the territory between the Hondo and Sarstoon rivers, and the **Treaty of Amiens** in 1802 required Britain to hand back to Spain the territory captured during the war. In spite of the longstanding occupation by the Baymen, who showed no sign of leaving, Spain took this to include Belize. But in the face of gathering difficulties in the Spanish empire, and Britain's decision to assist the settlers in their defence of the settlement, Spain's claim became increasingly unsupportable.

Independence, achieved by Mexico in 1821, signalled the end of the Spanish empire in the Americas. Guatemala, briefly ruled by Mexico following independence, became, in 1823, a part of the United Provinces of Central America, a loosely knit and inherently unstable federation consisting of the republics of El Salvador, Honduras, Nicaragua, Costa Rica and Guatemala. The federation was never recognized by Britain and it fell apart in 1839.

The years between the collapse of the Spanish empire in America and the close of the nineteenth century were filled with claim and counter-claim, treaties made and broken – a situation not entirely resolved today.

Mexico, in spite of years of internal strife, war with the United States in 1846, the Caste Wars of 1847 and a period of British, French and Spanish occupation in the 1860s, continued to claim British Honduras as an extension of Yucatán. This was unacceptable to the British government and eventually, after numerous diplomatic exchanges, an **Anglo-Mexican Treaty** was ratified in 1897. However, Mexico stated that should Guatemala revive any of its claims to British Honduras then Mexico would press a claim to the land north of the Sibun River.

Guatemala's claim has been the source of more belligerent disagreement with Britain, and there's no doubt that the British government shares much of the blame for the confusion. In treaty after treaty Britain regarded Belize as a territory under Spanish sovereignty, where British subjects had a right to cut timber. Long after Spain's expulsion from the area, Britain maintained the fiction of Spanish sovereignty, and the refusal to recognize Central America was to complicate relations with Guatemala following the dissolution of the federation.

Guatemala's claim to the territory of Belize rested upon the acceptance in international law of *uti possidetis* – the right of a colony which successfully gains independence from a colonial authority to inherit the rights and territory of that authority at the time of independence. This presumed that the entire territory of British Honduras (Belize) had been under Spanish control in 1821 and that the premise of *uti possidetis* was valid. The British position was that Spain hadn't effectively occupied Belize at the time of Guatemala's independence, and therefore Guatemala's claim was invalid.

In a vain attempt to reach a settlement Britain and Guatemala signed a treaty in 1859 which has been the subject of controversy ever since. This treaty, in the British view, settled the boundaries of Belize and Guatemala in their existing positions. Guatemala interpreted it differently – as a disguised treaty of cession of the territory outlined, not confirmation of the boundaries. With such a gulf of interpretation it's no wonder the dispute ground on for so many years, keeping international lawyers busy and several times threatening to erupt in war.

The most controversial clause of the treaty was the addition of Article 7 – the agreement to build a road between Belize City and Guatemala City. For various reasons the road was never built, but a route was surveyed in 1859 and a costing given of £100,000. The disputes were no nearer resolution when the settlement became the colony of British Honduras in 1862. An additional convention in 1863 failed because Guatemala was at war with El Salvador and by 1864 the British

Foreign Office was of the opinion that the convention was invalid because Guatemala had failed to ratify.

Throughout the 1860s Article 7 was the source of numerous exchanges between Britain and Guatemala, but the British government failed to vote any funds for construction of the road, claiming Guatemala had no intention of complying with the convention.

CASTE WARS AND INDIAN UPRISING

The terrible, bloody **Caste War** of Yucatán began with a Maya uprising at Valladolid in January 1847. The Indians, supplied with arms and ammunition from Belize, sacked the town and over the next year terror spread throughout the peninsula. From 1848, as Mexico sent troops to put down the rebellion, thousands of Maya and Mestizo refugees fled to Belize. Some returned but many stayed, increasing the population of Corozal and Orange Walk and clearing the land for agriculture.

The Santa Cruz Maya, occupying a virtually independent territory north of the Belizean border, were not subdued by Mexico until 1901, and the border between Belize and Mexico was fluid, with many refugees settling in Belize. Mexico's claim, in 1864, to the territory extending to the Sarstoon River enraged the Santa Cruz Maya, who resisted Mexico's attempts to defeat them, taking it to mean that Mexico intended to occupy the territory. British settlers were justifiably afraid of **Indian attack** which, when it came, was from the Icaiche, not the Santa Cruz.

The Icaiche, supported by Mexico and led by Marcus Canul, attacked a mahogany camp on the River Bravo in 1866, capturing dozens of prisoners, who were later ransomed. The Indian raids caused panic in Belize, appeals for help were sent to Jamaica and troops were sent for the defence of the colony. Even Canul's death in 1872 after a raid on Orange Walk did not put an end to the raids. Corozal became a military base and although the attacks lessened the danger wasn't over until the 1890s. The ruling class in Belize City was unwilling to vote funds for the defence of the northern areas under threat, while the British government objected to the cost of extra troops.

Partly as a result of arguments about raising finance, the Legislative Assembly dissolved itself in 1870 and was replaced by a **Legislative Council**. This enabled the British government to establish a Crown Colony form of government in 1871, in line with colonial policy throughout the West Indies. **Agriculture**, hitherto unimportant, began to play an increasing role in the economy. The arrival of Yucatecans, many of them small farmers, during the Caste Wars, and the introduction of new crops and forestry techniques, gradually changed the economic base.

TROUBLED TIMES: THE EARLY TWENTIETH CENTURY

By 1900, free for the moment from worries about external threats, Belize was an integral, though minor, colony of the British empire. The population in the census of 1901 was 37,500, of whom 28,500 were born in the colony.

Comfortable complacency set in; the economy stagnated and the predominantly White property owners could foresee no change to their rule. The workers in the forests and on the estates were mainly Black, the descendants of former slaves, known locally as "Creoles". Wages were low and employers maintained strict controls over their workers – up to three months' imprisonment for missing a day's work.

The start of **World War I** in 1914 caused a rush of volunteers to defend the empire and a limited period of prosperity began in Belize as demand for forest products increased. The troops from Belize, however, were not thought capable of fighting and instead were employed on river transport in British-held Mesopotamia. On their return in 1919, humiliated and disillusioned by their role, bitterness exploded into violence and the troops were joined by thousands of Belize City's population (including the police) in looting and rioting.

The status of workers had improved little over the last century and the Depression years of the 1930s brought extreme hardship. The mechanization of forestry in the 1920s caused even more unemployment, and a disastrous hurricane in 1931 compounded the misery. The disaster prompted workers to organize in 1934 after a relief programme initiated by the governor was a dismal failure. Their leader, Antonio Soberanis, was imprisoned after attempting to post mail for pickets at a sawmill who had been arrested.

The colonial government responded by passing restrictive laws, banning marches, and increasing the powers of the governor to deal with disturbances.

TOWARDS INDEPENDENCE

World War II again gave a boost to forestry and the opportunity for many Belizeans to work in Britain or on merchant ships. Conditions for the returning soldiers and workers at the end of the war were, however, no better than they had been at the end of World War I. Property and income qualifications limited the franchise to only 2.8 percent of the population by 1948, and political power lay with a wealthy elite who controlled the Executive Council, and with the governor, a Foreign Office appointee. The devaluation of the British Honduras dollar at the end of 1949 caused more hardship and reinforced the belief that Belize was manipulated for the benefit of the ruling class.

A cautious report on constitutional reform in 1951 only increased calls for "one person, one vote", and violent political incidents occurred during the 1952 **national strike**. A **new constitution**, based on the recommendations of the 1951 report, was approved and in 1954 elections were held in which all literate adults over the age of 21 could vote. These elections were won with an overwhelming majority by the **Peoples' United Party** (PUP), led by **George Price**. A semblance of ministerial government was introduced in 1955 but control of financial measures was retained by the governor, and the elected members of the Executive Council did not have a clear majority.

The delay in achieving independence was caused largely by Guatemala's still unresolved claim to Belize. In 1933 Guatemala had begun to renew what it saw as its claim under the 1859 Treaty. Various motives were involved, among them national pride and an attempt to focus attention away from problems at home. The claim took a more formal, potentially dangerous, turn in 1945 when "Belice" was declared an integral province of Guatemalan national territory.

In spite of the territorial dispute Belize was granted full **internal self-government** in 1964, intended after a relatively short time to lead to complete independence, as was the policy throughout the Commonwealth. The British government, through the governor, remained responsible for defence, foreign affairs and internal security. The Assembly became a bicameral system with a Senate, whose eight members were appointed by the governor after consultation, and a House of Representatives consisting entirely of elected members.

Meanwhile the **dispute with Guatemala** regained prominence: numerous meetings between Britain and Guatemala to solve the problem by diplomatic means got nowhere. Joint control was proposed, but this was unacceptable to Belize, as was any settlement involving concessions of Belizean territory. At least twice, in 1972 and 1977, Guatemala moved troops to the border and threatened to invade, but prompt British reinforcements, especially the deployment of Harrier jets, were an effective dissuasion. The situation remained tense but international opinion was gradually in favour of Belizean independence.

In 1975 the Non-Aligned Movement gave its full support for an independent Belize and in 1976 President Omar Torrijos of Panamá campaigned on Belize's behalf throughout Latin America. With the overthrow of Somoza in 1979 the Sandinista government of Nicaragua gave full support to Belize. The most important demonstration of worldwide endorsement of Belize's right to self-determination was the **UN resolution** passed in 1980, which demanded secure independence, with all territory intact, before the next session. This time 139 countries voted in favour, with none against.

Further negotiations with Guatemala began and some progress was made, but complete agreement could not be reached. Guatemala still insisted on some territorial concessions. On March 11, 1981, Britain, Guatemala and Belize released the "Heads of Agreement", a document listing subjects for future discussion, which would, they hoped, result in a peaceful solution of the longstanding dispute. Guatemala agreed to recognize the independence of Belize, on condition agreement was reached on points it considered vital to Guatemalan interests. These included "use and enjoyment" of certain cayes, free port facilities, cooperation in security and a non-aggression pact, but were not clearly specified.

Belize's response was that **independence** could not be delayed any longer and further negotiations could take place afterwards. Accordingly, on September 21, 1981, Belize became an independent country within the British Commonwealth, with Queen Elizabeth II as head of state. In a unique decision British troops were to remain in Belize, to ensure the territorial integrity of the new nation.

The government of Belize formed by the PUP with George Price as premier – he had held power through various constitutions and assemblies since 1954 – continued in power until the general election of 1984. Then thirty years of one-party domination came to an end as the United Democratic Party (UDP), led by **Manuel Esquivel**, began its first term in office. The new government encouraged private enterprise and foreign investment, policies which had some success in reducing foreign debt, but despite the introduction of high tariffs did not manage to stem the flow of imported luxury goods. The September **1989 general election** restored George Price and the PUP to power with the narrowest of margins, gaining 50.02 percent of votes cast.

THE 1990s: THE BORDER DISPUTE UNRESOLVED

In 1988 Guatemala and Belize established a Joint Commission to work towards a "just and honourable" solution to the border dispute. By August 1990, after a series of meetings between representatives of both countries, and at times Britain, it was agreed in principle that Guatemala would accept the existing borders of Belize. Another significant result of negotiations was Belize's admission to the Organization of American States in January 1991. And, in a classic case of history repeating itself, Britain agreed to provide £22.5 million worth of financial and technical assistance to improve road links between the two countries. Three hundred and fifty years of territorial dispute appeared to be coming to an end.

The only sticking point preventing full recognition by Guatemala was a geographical anomaly in the extreme south, where the territorial waters of Belize and Honduras formed a common boundary, making it theoretically possible for Guatemalan ships to be excluded from their own Caribbean ports. Thus there was an unprecedented flurry of diplomatic activity in the late summer of 1991 as steps were taken to secure recognition prior to the tenth anniversary of Belize's independence on September 21.

In August 1991 the **Maritime Areas Bill** was introduced into the Belize House of Representatives, which was to allow Guatemala access to the high seas by restricting Belize's territorial waters between the Sarstoon River and Ranguana Caye, 100km northeast. This measure proved acceptable to Guatemala's President Serrano and on September 11, 1991, just ten days before the anniversary celebrations, the governments of Belize and Guatemala established full diplomatic relations and agreed to exchange ambassadors at the earliest opportunity.

The air of euphoria soured somewhat during 1992 as opposition to President Serrano's controversial recognition of Belize became more vocal and was ultimately challenged in Guatemala's Constitutional Court. Eventually the court decided the president had not actually violated the constitution but it still referred several matters to Congress for ratification. On November 24, 1992, Congress (albeit with thirteen abstentions) conditionally approved the president's actions, authorizing him to continue negotiations with Belize. President Serrano's absence from the Central American heads of state meeting, held in Belize in February 1993, was further evidence that the decision to recognize Belize sat uneasily with factions inside Guatemala.

In June 1993, the overthrow of Guatemala's President Serrano, together with the decision to recall the British troops, convinced Premier George Price (who hoped to gain from divisions in the opposition UDP) that this was an opportune moment to call a snap **general election**. To the surprise of most commentators, the gamble failed, and Manuel Esquivel's United Democratic Party began their second period of office on July 2, 1993.

Serrano's eventual successor, Ramiro de Leon Carpio, attempted to disassociate himself from his predecessor's questionable treatment of Guatemala's constitutional position on Belize by reactivating the Belize Council, an advisory body to the foreign ministry, but Belize was never high enough on the agenda during his term in office. There was sabre rattling in Guatemala in 1994–5 when the Belize government tried to evict a few Guatemalan families who had cleared *milpas* in Belize, and again when Belize attempted to deport striking banana plantation workers from Stann Creek, assuming them to be Guatemalan immigrants, though in fact the majority were Honduran. Following the Guatemalan general election in 1996, the new government of Alvaro Arzú restated Guatemala's claim to Belizean territory but also claimed to be committed to ending the dispute by negotiation.

BELIZE'S ECONOMY

While agriculture is still the mainstay of Belize's economy, accounting for 25 percent of GDP, 75 percent of export earnings and 35 percent of employment, the service sector, led by a booming tourist industry, plays an increasingly important role. Sugar is the most valuable export, followed by bananas. Citrus and seafood products are fast being overtaken by the growing clothing industry. Tourist numbers increase every year, bringing in more than US$100 million annually in foreign exchange, though the industry remains dominated by foreign investors.

Previously the main source of tax revenue in Belize was the notoriously high import duties. These are being replaced with consumer taxes, principally VAT at 15 percent, levied on all goods and services at the point of sale.

CHRONOLOGY: THE MAYA

25,000 BC	**Paleo-Indian**	First waves of nomadic hunters from the north.
20,000 BC		Worked stone chips in northern Belize.
9000 BC		Stone tools in Guatemalan highlands.
7500 BC	**Archaic period**	Evidence of settled agricultural communiti throughout Mesoamerica, maize cultivated ar animals domesticated.
4500 BC	First Maya-speaking groups settle in western Guatemala, around Huehuetenango.	
2000 BC	First evidence of Maya settlement in Belize.	During this period the Maya began building th centres which developed into the great cities of th
1500 BC	**Preclassic or Formative period**	Classic period. Trade, of vital importance, increase and contact with the **Olmec** people of Mexic
	Divided into:	brought many cultural developments, including
	Early: 1500–1000 BC	calendar and new gods. **Kaminaljuyú** dominate
	Middle: 1000–300 BC	highland Guatemala, while **El Mirador** is the mo
	Late: 300 BC–300 AD	important city in the east.
1000BC		House platforms, pottery and middens at **Cuello**.
300 AD	**Classic period**	The central lowlands are thickly populated, wi
	Maya culture reaches its high point – introduc-	almost all the sites now known flourishing. In the Ear
	tion of the Long Count **calendar**, used to mark	Classic the influence of **Teotihuacán** was stron
	events on carved stelae and monuments.	client cities like **Kaminaljuyú** and **Tikal** were partic
		larly successful. Later, and especially after the fall
		Teotihuacán, more and more cities flourish: Tik
		remains important but is defeated in battle at lea:
		once by **Caracol**. The great buildings today associate
		with the Maya almost all date from the Classic period
900 AD	**Postclassic period**	Population decline and abandonment of many impo
	Decline of Classic civilizations in Mexico as well	tant Maya centres. Others, however, like **Lamana**
	as Guatemala and Belize, for reasons which	in Belize, do survive and indeed remain relativel
	remain unclear.	prosperous throughout the Postclassic period.
987 AD	**Toltec** invasion of Yucatán.	Toltec culture grafted onto Maya: possible Mexica influence on Maya in Guatemala and Belize.
c.1200	Cities of the Yucatán abandoned – major move- ment south of Toltec-Maya population. Toltecs come to dominate many of the Guatemalan high- land tribes.	In Belize many of the Maya cities continue to thriv while in Guatemala the village-based highland soc ety familiar today is developing.
1400–75	**Quiché** overrun much of highland Guatemala, conquering their rivals. After 1475 their power declines and tribes splinter again.	Quiché capital at **Utatlán**; Cakchiquel version a **Iximché**.
1519	**Cortes** lands in Mexico.	
1521	Aztec capital of Tenochtitlán falls to Spanish.	
1523	**Alvarado** arrives in Guatemala.	
1523–40	**Spanish Conquest** of Guatemala proceeds: first Spanish capital founded 1527.	Only sporadic advances in Belize area.

CHRONOLOGY: GUATEMALA AND BELIZE

1541	Alvarado dies; new capital founded at **Antigua**.	
1543		**Alonso Pacheco** brutally conquers Corozal area.
17th c.	**Colonial rule** is gradually established throughout Guatemala. Antigua is the capital of the whole of Central America. Power of the Church grows.	Spain claims sovereignty over Belize, but never effectively colonizes the area. British and other **pirates** use the coast as a refuge.
1697	Conquest of the Itzá at Tayasal on Lake Petén Itzá: the last of the independent Maya.	
18th c.	Colonial Guatemala remains a backwater, with no great riches for the Spanish.	**Conflict** between Spanish authorities and increasingly established settlers (Baymen): they are driven out several times but always return. First slaves arrive from Africa. Britain increasingly prepared to defend settlers' rights.
1798		**Battle of St George's Caye**; settlers defeat Spanish fleet with British aid.
1821	Mexico and Central America gain **independence** from Spain; Guatemala annexed by Mexico, then joins Central American Federation.	All sides claim Belize.
1832		First large influx of **Garifuna** from Roatan.
1847	Guatemala becomes republic independent of Central America under **Rafael Carrera**.	Caste Wars in Yucatán.
1850		Clayton Bulwer Treaty and other agreements aim to end dispute between Guatemala and Britain over Belize, but no real conclusion is reached.
1862		Belize officially becomes part of British Empire as Colony of **British Honduras**.
1867	First **liberal uprising** under Serpio Cruz.	
1871	Liberal revolution; **Rufino Barrios** becomes president. Start of coffee boom.	Status raised to **Crown Colony**.
1919		Belizean troops riot on return from World War I: start of nationalist sentiment which grows through the century.
1930	**Jorge Ubico** president – banana boom and height of **United Fruit Company** power.	
1944–54	"Spiritual Socialism" presidencies of Arevalo and Arbenz: ended by CIA-backed military **coup**.	
1949		British Honduras dollar devalued: resultant hardships strengthen anti-colonial feeling. **PUP** formed in 1950. Universal adult suffrage introduced.
1954	Castillo Armas president: the start of **military rule** and a series of military-backed dictators.	
1960s	First **guerrilla** actions, rapidly followed by repressive clampdowns and rise of **death squads** under Colonel Carlos Arana.	Guatemalan claims to Belize renewed, delaying independence. **Full internal self-government** granted 1964.
1970	**Colonel Arana Osorio** president.	
1974	Electoral fraud wins presidency for Kjell Laugerud.	
1976	**Earthquake** leaves 23,000 dead, million homeless.	
1978	**Lucas García** president, repression, thousands die.	
1981		
1982	**Ríos Montt** president: situation improves.	Belize becomes **independent**.
1984		
1986	**Vinicio Cerezo** elected: return to civilian rule though power of military remains great.	Manuel Esquivel and UDP elected.
1989		
1990	Jorge Serrano elected on less than 25 percent of vote.	
1991		George Price and PUP elected. Belize recognized by Guatemala in time for 10th anniversary of independence.
1993	Serrano ousted by generals – Kamiro de Leon appointed.	versary of independence.
1996	Alvaro Arzú and the PAN elected.	Manuel Esquivel re-elected in snap election

THE MAYA ACHIEVEMENT

For some three thousand years before the arrival of the Spanish, Maya civilization dominated Central America, leaving behind some of the most impressive and mysterious architecture in the entire continent. At their peak, around 300 AD, Maya cities were far larger and more elaborate than anything that existed in Europe at the time. Their culture was complex and sophisticated, fostering the highest standards of engineering, astronomy, stone-carving and mathematics, as well as an intricate writing system.

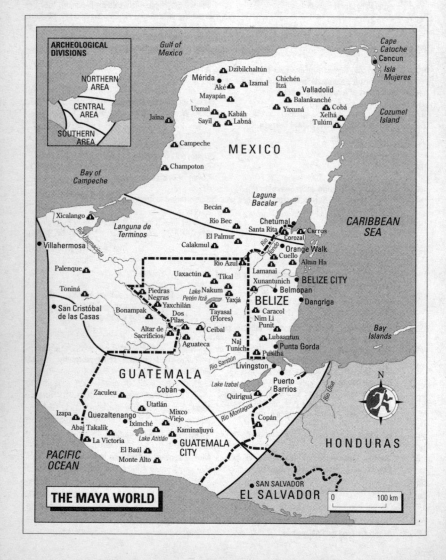

THE MAYA WORLD

To appreciate all this you have to see for yourself the remains of the great centres. Despite centuries of neglect and abuse they are still astounding, their main temples towering above the forest roof. Stone monuments, however, leave much of the story untold, and there is still a great deal that we have to learn about Maya civilization. What follows is the briefest of introductions to the subject, hopefully just enough to whet your appetite for the immense volumes that have been written on it.

MAYA SOCIETY

While the remains of the great Maya sites are a testament to the scale and sophistication of Maya civilization, they offer little insight into daily life in Maya times. To reconstruct the lives of ordinary people archeologists have turned to the smaller **residential groups** that surround the main sites, littered with the remains of household utensils, pottery, bones and farming tools. These groups are made up of simple structures made of poles and wattle-and-daub, each of which was home to a single family. The groups as a whole probably housed an extended family, who would have farmed and hunted together and may well have specialized in some trade or craft. The people living in these groups were the commoners, their lives largely dependent on agriculture. Maize, beans, cacao, squash, chillies and fruit trees were cultivated in raised and irrigated fields, while wild fruits were harvested from the surrounding forest. Much of the land was communally owned and groups of around twenty men worked in the fields together.

Maya **agriculture** was continuously adapting to the needs of the developing society, and the early practice of slash and burn was soon replaced by more intensive and sophisticated methods to meet the needs of a growing population. Some of the land was terraced, drained or irrigated in order to improve its fertility and ensure that fields didn't have to lie fallow for long periods, and the capture of water became crucial to the success of a site. The large cities, today hemmed in by the forest, were once surrounded by open fields, canals and residential compounds, while slash and burn agriculture probably continued in marginal and outlying areas. Agriculture became a specialized profession and a large section of the popu-

lation would have bought at least some of their food in markets, although all households still had a kitchen garden where they grew herbs and fruit.

Maize has always been the basis of the Maya **diet**, in ancient times as much as it is today. Once harvested it was made into *saka*, a corn-meal gruel, which was eaten with chilli as the first meal of the day. During the day labourers ate a mixture of corn dough and water, and we know that *tamales* were also a popular speciality. The main meal, eaten in the evenings, would have been similarly maize-based, although it may well have included meat and vegetables. As a supplement to this simple diet, deer, peccary, wild turkeys, duck, pigeons and quail were all hunted with bows and arrows or blowguns. The Maya also made use of dogs, both for hunting and eating. Fish were also eaten, and the remains of fish hooks and nets have been found in some sites, while there is evidence that those living on the coast traded dried fish far inland. As well as food, the forest provided firewood, and cotton was cultivated to be dyed with natural colours and then spun into cloth.

The main sites represent larger versions of the basic residential groups, housing the most powerful families and their assorted retainers. Beyond this these centres transcended the limits of family ties, taking on larger political, religious and administrative roles, and as Maya society developed they became small cities. The principal occupants were a small number of priestly rulers, but others included bureaucrats, merchants, warriors, architects and assorted craftsmen – an emerging middle class. At the highest level this **hierarchy** was controlled by a series of hereditary positions, with a single chief at its head.

The relationship between the cities and the land, drawn up along feudal lines, was at the heart of Maya life. The peasant farmers supported the ruling class by providing labour – building and maintaining the temples and palaces – food and other basic goods. In return the **elite** provided the peasantry with leadership, direction, protection and above all else the security of their knowledge of calendrics and supernatural prophecy. This knowledge was thought to be the basis of successful agriculture, and the priests were relied upon to divine the appropriate time to plant and harvest.

In turn, the sites themselves became organized into a hierarchy of power. At times a single city, such as Tikal or El Mirador, dominated vast areas, controlling all of the smaller sites, while at other times smaller centres operated independently. A complex structure of **alliances** bound the various sites together and there were periodic outbursts of open **warfare**. The distance between the larger sites averaged around 30km, and between these were myriad smaller settlements, religious centres and residential groups. The structure of these alliances can be traced in the use of emblem glyphs. Only those of the main centres are used in isolation, while the names of smaller sites are used in conjunction with those of their larger patrons. Trade and warfare between the large centres was commonplace as the cities were bound up in an endless round of competition and conflict.

THE MAYA CALENDAR

The cornerstone of all Maya thinking was an obsession with **time**. For both practical and mystical reasons the Maya developed a highly sophisticated understanding of arithmetics, calendrics and astronomy, all of which they believed gave them the power to understand and predict events. All great occasions were interpreted on the basis of the Maya calendar, and it was this precise understanding of time that gave the ruling elite its authority. The majority of carving, on temples and stelae, records the exact date at which rulers were born, ascended to power, and died.

The basis of all Maya **calculation** was the vigesimal counting system, which used multiples of twenty. All figures were written using a combination of three symbols – a shell to denote zero, a dot for one and a bar for five – which you can still see on many stelae. When calculating calendrical systems the Maya used a slightly different notation known as the head-variant system, in which each number from one to twenty was represented by a deity, whose head was used to represent the number.

When it comes to the Maya **calendar** things start to get a little more complicated as a number of different counting systems were used, depending on the reason the date was being calculated. The basic unit of the Maya calendar was the day, or *kin*, followed by the *uinal*, a group of twenty days roughly equivalent to our month; but at the next level things start to get more complex as the Maya marked the passing of time in three distinct ways. The **260-day almanac** (16 *uinals*) was used to calculate the timing of ceremonial events. Each day was associated with a particular deity that had strong influence over those born on that particular day. This calendar wasn't divided into months but had 260 distinct day names. (This system is still in use among the Cakchiquel Indians who name their children according to its structure and celebrate fiestas according to its dictates.) A second calendar, the so-called **"vague year"** or *haab*, was made up of 18 *uinals* and five *kins*, a total of 365 days, making it a close approximation of the solar year. These two calendars weren't used in isolation but operated in parallel so that once every 52 years the new day of the solar year coincided with the same day in the 260-day almanac, a meeting that was regarded as very powerful and marked the start of a new era.

Finally the Maya had another system for marking the passing of history, which is used on dedicatory monuments. The system, known as the **long count**, is based on the great cycle of 13 *baktuns* (a period of 5128 years). The current period dates from 3116 BC and is destined to come to an end on December 10, 2012. The dates in this system simply record the number of days that have elapsed since the start of the current great cycle, a task that calls for ten different numbers – recording the equivalent of years, decades, centuries etc. In later years the Maya sculptors obviously tired of this exhaustive process and opted instead for the short count, an abbreviated version.

ASTRONOMY

Alongside their fascination with time the Maya were interested in the sky and devoted much time and energy to unravelling its patterns. Several large sites such as Copán, Uaxactún and Chichén Itzá have **observatories** carefully aligned with solar and lunar sequences.

The Maya showed a great understanding of **astronomy** and with their 365-day "vague year" were just half a day out in their calculations of the solar year, while at Copán, towards the end of the seventh century AD, Maya astronomers had calculated the lunar cycle at 29.53020 days, not too far off our current esti-

MAYA TIME – THE UNITS

1 *kin* = 24 hours

20 *kins* = 1 *uinal*, or 20 days

18 *uinals* = 1 *tun*, or 360 days

20 *tuns* = 1 *katun*, or 7200 days

20 *katuns* = 1 *baktun*, or 144,000 days

20 *baktun* = 1 *pictun*, or 2,880,000 days

20 *pictuns* = 1 *calabtun*, or 57,600,000 days

20 *calabtuns* = 1 *kinchiltun*, or 1,152,000,000 days

20 *kinchiltuns* = 1 *alautun*, or 23,040,000,000 days

mate of 29.53059. In the Dresden Codex their calculations extend to the 405 lunations over a period of 11,960 days, as part of a pattern that set out to predict eclipses. At the same time they had calculated with astonishing accuracy the movements of Venus, Mars and perhaps Mercury. Venus was of particular importance to the Maya as they linked its presence with success in war, and there are several stelae that record the presence of Venus prompting the decision to attack.

RELIGION

Maya **cosmology** is by no means straightforward as at every stage an idea is balanced by its opposite and each part of the universe is made up of many layers. To the Maya this is the third version of the earth, the previous two having been destroyed by deluges. The current version is a flat surface, with four corners, each associated with a certain colour; white for north, red for east, yellow for south, and black for west, with green at the centre. Above this the sky is supported by four trees, each a different colour and species, which are also sometimes depicted as gods, known as *Bacabs*. At its centre the sky is supported by a ceiba tree. Above the sky is a heaven of thirteen layers, each of which has its own god, while the very top layer is overseen by an owl. Other attested models of the world include that of a turtle (the land) floating on the sea. However, it was the underworld, *Xibalda*, "The Place of Fright", which was of greater importance to most Maya, as it was in this direction that they passed after death, on their way to the place of

rest. The nine layers of hell were guarded by the "Lords of the Night", and deep caves were thought to connect with the underworld.

Woven into this universe the Maya recognized an incredible array of **gods**. Every divinity had four manifestations based upon colour and direction and many also had counterparts in the underworld and consorts of the opposite sex. In addition to this there was an extensive array of patron deities, each associated with a particular trade or particular class. Every activity from suicide to sex had its representative in the Maya pantheon.

RELIGIOUS RITUAL

The combined complexity of the Maya pantheon and calendar gave every day a particular significance, and the ancient Maya were bound up in a demanding **cycle of religious ritual**. The main purpose of ritual was the procurement of success by appealing to the right god at the right time and in the right way. As every event, from planting to childbirth, was associated with a particular divinity, all of the main events in daily life demanded some kind of religious ritual and for the most important of these the Maya staged elaborate ceremonies.

While each ceremony had its own format there's a certain pattern that binds them all. The correct day was carefully chosen by priestly divination, and for several days beforehand the participants fasted and remained abstinent. The main ceremony was dominated by the expulsion of all evil spirits, the burning of incense before the idols, a sacrifice (either animal or human), and blood-letting.

In divination rituals, used to foretell the pattern of future events or account for the cause of past events, the elite used various **drugs** to achieve altered states of consciousness. Perhaps the most obvious of these was alcohol, either made from fermented maize or a combination of honey and the bark of the balnche tree. Wild tobacco, which is considerably stronger than the modern domesticated version, was also smoked. The Maya also used a range of hallucinogenic mushrooms, all of which were appropriately named, but none more so than the *xibalbaj obox*, "underworld mushroom", and the *k'aizalah obox*, "lost judgement mushroom".

ARCHEOLOGY IN BELIZE

Like almost everything in Belize, archeology has made leaps and bounds in the last decade or so as researchers have unveiled a wealth of new material. What follows is written by Winnel Branche, Belize Museums Director, and illustrates the problems facing Belizean archeology as it emerges into the limelight, under siege from foreign expeditions and looters.

The ancient Maya sites of Belize have seen activity since the late nineteenth century. During these early times British amateur archeologists and both British and American museums kept up a lively interest in artefacts from these sites. Preservation of monuments was not yet "in" and techniques were far from subtle. In some cases dynamite was used to plunder the sites and Belizean artefacts often found their way, unmonitored, into museums and private collections worldwide.

Since 1894 the ancient monuments and antiquities of Belize have had loosely structured legislation to protect them, but it was not until 1952 that a civil servant was made responsible for archeology, and not until 1957 that a department was formed to excavate, protect and preserve these remains. Since then scientific excavation of hundreds of sites in Belize has been carried out, with prior agreement from the department of Archeology, by universities, museums and scientific institutions from the USA, Canada and, to a lesser extent, Britain.

The Belize Department of Archeology had grown from one member in 1957 to eight members of office staff by 1990. It monitors fieldwork and excavations carried out by foreign researchers in the country. It also performs small-scale salvage excavations in emergencies and is dedicated to the training of Belizeans to carry out all archeological work in the country. A vital task is to prevent looting activities, which have become rampant in recent years, but all these efforts are hampered by the lack of resources. The Department also carries out educational activities including lectures, slide shows and travelling exhibitions in an attempt to sensitize the public on this part of their heritage. The responsibility of maintaining archeological sites, especially those open to the public, falls to the Department, as has the safekeeping of the vast national collections in the absence of a museum in Belize. Since any immoveable man-made structure over 100 years old and any moveable man-made item over 150 years old are considered ancient monuments and artefacts respectively, the Department is also in charge of all the non-Maya historical and colonial remains.

There are now sixteen archeological research teams visiting Belize annually, illustrating the fact that the Maya of Belize were not on the fringe of the Maya civilization, as had previously been thought, but were in fact a core area of the Maya culture. Evidence has been found of extensive raised-field agriculture and irrigation canals in northern Belize, and the oldest known site so far found in the Maya world is at Cuello, near Orange Walk. Even Tikal in Guatemala, once thought to be the centre of power of the lowland Maya, is now known to have been toppled at least once by Caracol, perhaps the largest site in Belize.

There has been increased interest lately in ancient Maya maritime trade, with coastal sites and those on the cayes receiving more attention. In addition the extensive cave systems which form a network under inland Belize have shown much evidence of use by the Maya. In 1984 the longest cave system in Central America, containing the largest cave room in the western hemisphere, was discovered in Belize. It is known as the Chiquibul Cave System and exploration here has revealed areas of concentration of Maya artefacts.

With the wealth of Maya remains in the country, it is hardly surprising but most unfortunate that looting of sites and the sale of antiquities on the black market is increasing. In Belize all ancient monuments and antiquities are owned by the state, whether on private or government land or underwater. Residents are allowed to keep registered collections under licence, but the sale, purchase, import or export of antiquities is illegal and punishable under the law. Excavation and other scientific research can only be done with Department permission after agreement on conditions. While intended to prevent looting and destruction, this law is also meant to keep the remains intact and within the country so that Belizeans and visitors can see the evidence of this splendid heritage.

INDIAN GUATEMALA

A vital Indian culture is perhaps Guatemala's most unique feature. It's a strange blend of contradictions, and while the Indians themselves may appear quiet and humble, their costumes, fiestas and markets are a riot of colour, creativity and celebration. In many ways the Indians live in a world of their own, responding to local traditions and values and regarding themselves as Indians first and Guatemalans second.

It's generally accepted that indigenous Indians, the vast majority of whom live in the western highlands, make up about half of Guatemala's population, although it's extremely hard to define exactly who is an Indian. For the sake of the national census, people who consider themselves Indians are classed as such, regardless of their parentage. And when it comes to defining Indians as a

GUATEMALA:
INDIGENOUS LANGUAGES

N

BELIZE

MEXICO

Gulf of
Honduras

CHUJ
San Mateo
Ixtatán
JACALTECA   Solomá   IXIL
KANJOBAL   KEKCHÍ

Nebaj   Cobán

Huehuetenango   Aguacatán   USPANTECA   Tactic
                                POCOMCHI
                 Sta. Cruz   QUICHÉ
MAM   del Quiché
                 Totonicapán
San Marcos
Quezaltenango   Sololá   CAKCHIQUEL
                TZUTUJIL   Antigua   GUATEMALA CITY
                    Palín   POKOMAN

HONDURAS

PACIFIC OCEAN   EL SALVADOR

group, culture is more important than pedigree, as Indians define themselves through their relationships with their land, gods, villages and families. Holding aloof from the melting pot of modern Guatemalan society, Indians adhere instead to their traditional *costumbres*, codes of practice that govern every aspect of life.

As a result of this the only way to define Indian culture is by describing its main characteristics, acknowledging that all Indians will be a part of some of them, and accepting that many are neither Indian nor *Ladino*, but combine elements of both.

INDIAN CULTURE

When the Spanish set about destroying the Maya tribes of Guatemala they altered every aspect of life for the indigenous people, uprooting their social structures and reshaping their communities. Before the Conquest the bulk of the population had lived scattered in the hills, paying tribute to a tribal elite, and surviving through subsistence farming and hunting. Under Spanish rule they were moved into new **villages**, known as *reducciones*, where their homes were clustered around a church and a marketplace. Horizons shrank rapidly as allegiances became very localized and tribal structures were replaced by the village hierarchies that still dominate the highlands today.

For the last 450 years the Indian population has suffered repeated **abuse**, as the predominantly White elite have exploited Indian land and labour, regarding the Indians themselves as an expendable commodity. But within their own communities the Indians were left pretty much to themselves and developed an astoundingly introspective culture that is continually adapting to new threats, reshaping itself for the future. **Village life** has been insulated from the outside world and in many areas only a handful of the population speak fluent Spanish, the remainder speaking one of the 28 indigenous languages and dialects (see map on p.472). Today's Indian culture is a complex synthesis including elements of Maya, Spanish and modern American cultures.

The vast majority of the Indian population still live by **subsistence farming**, their homes either spread across the hills or gathered in small villages. The land is farmed using the *milpa* system to produce beans, chillies, maize and squash – which have been the staple diet for thousands of years. To the Indians land is sacred and the need to own and farm it is central to their culture, despite the fact that few of them can survive by farming alone. Most are now forced to migrate to the coast for several months a year, where they work in appalling conditions on the **plantations**, in order to supplement their income. In some villages the economy is boosted by a local **craft**: in Momostenango they produce wool and blankets, around Lake Atitlán the villagers make reed mats, in Cotzal and San Pablo la Laguna they make rope, while other villages specialize in market gardening, pottery, flowers or textiles.

Family life is also rigidly traditional with large families very much a part of Indian culture. Marriage customs vary from place to place but in general the groom is expected to pay the bride's parents, and the couple may well live with their in-laws. If things don't work out separation isn't a great problem and men often take more than one wife (nor is it totally unheard of for a woman to live with two men). A man's place is in the fields and a woman's in the home, where she cooks, tends to the children, and weaves. Authority within the village is usually given to men, although in the Ixil area women are involved in all decision making.

INDIAN RELIGION

Every aspect of Indian life – from the birth of a child to the planting of corn – is loaded with religious significance, based on a complicated **fusion of the Maya pantheon and the Catholic religion**. Christ and the saints have taken their place alongside *Dios Mundo*, the God of the World, and *Hurakan*, the Heart of Heaven. The two religions have merged to form a hybrid, in which the outward forms of Catholicism are used to worship the ancient pantheon, a compromise that was probably fostered by Spanish priests. The symbol of the cross, for example, was well known to the Maya, as used to signify the four winds of heaven, the four directions, and everlasting life. Today many of the deities have both Maya and Hispanic names, and are usually associated with a particular saint. All of the deities remain subordinate to a mighty and remote supreme being, and Christ takes a place in the upper echelons of the hierarchy.

For the Indians **God** is everywhere, bound up in the seasons, the mountains, the crops, the soil, the air and the sky. Every important event is marked by prayer and offerings, with disasters often attributed to divine intervention. Even more numerous than the gods are the **spirits** that are to be found in every imaginable object, binding together the universe. Each individual is born with a *nagual*, or spiritual counterpart, in the animal world, and his or her destiny is bound up with that particular animal. The spirits of dead ancestors are also ever-present and have to be looked after by each successive generation.

Traditionally, **worship** is organized by the community's religious hierarchy. All office-holders are male and throughout their lives they progress through the system, moving from post to post. The various posts are grouped into **cofradías**, ritual brotherhoods, each of which is responsible for a particular saint. Throughout the year the saint is kept in the home of an elder member, and on the appointed date, in the midst of a fiesta, it's paraded through the streets, to spend the next year somewhere else. The elder responsible for the saint will have to pay for much of the fiesta, including costumes, alcohol and assorted offerings, but it's a responsibility, or *cargo*, that's considered a great honour. In the traditional village hierarchy it's these duties that give the elders a prominent role in village life and through which they exercise their authority. Spending money on **fiestas** is really the only way that wealthy villagers can use their money in an acceptable way. (In some villages, such as Chichicastenango and Sololá, a *municipalidad indígena*, or Indian government, operates alongside the *cofradías*, and is similarly hierarchical. As men work their way up through the system they may well alternate between the civil and religious hierarchies.) The *cofradías* don't necessarily confine themselves to the traditional list of saints, and have been known to foster "evil" saints, such as San Simón or **Maximón**, a drinking, smoking *Ladino* figure, sometimes referred to as Judas or Pedro de Alvarado.

On a more superstitious level, personal religious needs are catered for by *brujos*, native priests who communicate with the gods and spirits. This is usually done on behalf of an individual client who's in search of a blessing, and often takes place at shrines and caves in the mountains, with offerings of *copal*, a type of incense, and alcohol. They also make extensive use of old Maya sites, and small burnt patches of grass litter many of the ruins in the highlands. *Brujos* are also credited with the ability to cast spells, predict the future and communicate with the dead. For specific medical problems Indians appeal to *zahorins*, who practise traditional medicine with a combination of invocation and herbs, and are closely associated with the *brujo* tradition.

Until the 1950s, when Catholic **missionaries** became active in the highlands, many Indians had no idea that there was a gulf between their own religion and orthodox Catholicism. To start with the missionaries drew most of their support from the younger generation, many of whom were frustrated by the rigidity of the village hierarchy. Gradually, this has eroded the authority of the traditional religious system, undermining the *cofradías*, disapproving of traditional fiestas, and scorning the work of the *brujos*. As a part of this the reforming movement *Catholic Action*, combining the drive for orthodoxy with an involvement in social issues, has also had a profound impact.

In the 1920s and 1930s the first Protestant missionaries, known as **evangelicos**, arrived in Guatemala, and their presence has also accelerated the decline of traditional religion. In the 1980s their numbers were greatly boosted by the influence of Ríos Montt, at a time when the Catholic Church was suffering severe repression. These days there are at least one hundred different sects in operation, backed by a huge injection of money from the US, and offering all sorts of incentives to fresh converts. But Indian religion is no stranger to oppression and despite the efforts of outsiders the *brujos* and *cofradías* are still in business, and fiestas remain drunken and vaguely pagan.

MARKETS AND FIESTAS

At the heart of the Indian economy is the **weekly market**, which remains central to life in the highlands and provides one of the best opportunities to see Indian life at close quarters. The majority of the Indian population still live by subsistence farming but spare a single day to gather together in the nearest village and trade their surplus produce. The market is as much a social occasion as an economic one and people come to talk, eat, drink, gossip and have a good time. In some places the action starts the night before with marimba music and heavy drinking.

On market day itself the village is filled by a steady flow of people, arriving by bus, on foot, or by donkey. In no time at all trading gets under way, and the plaza is soon buzzing with activity and humming with conversation, although raised voices are a rarity and the mood always subdued, with bargains struck after long and tortuous negotiations. Markets certainly don't operate in the way that "westerners" might expect and rival traders will happily set up alongside one another, more concerned about the day's conversation than the volume of trade.

The scale and atmosphere of markets varies from place to place. The country's largest is in San Francisco El Alto, on Friday, and draws traders from throughout the country. Other

REPRESSION OF THE INDIAN POPULATION

Throughout their history Guatemala's Indians have been severely victimized and exploited, but in the last two decades the situation has become increasingly serious, threatening the future of the entire indigenous population. Indians have always been the victims of racism, malnutrition and poor health care, suffering through the neglect of central government. However, Guatemala's undeclared civil war has increased their burden immeasurably. In 1983 Survival International published an account of the repression of the Indian population, which examined the way Indians were being selected for particularly brutal treatment. What follows is an extract from that report, which describes the situation at its very worst. Since then things have improved significantly:

Indians are reportedly bearing the brunt of the Guatemalan army's efforts to root out subversion. In May, *El Gráfico*, Guatemala's second largest newspaper, condemned the "genocide being carried out in the Indian regions of the country". A western European diplomat quoted on June 3 by the *New York Times* said, "Indians are systematically being destroyed as a group. . . . There is no break with the past." A priest in Huehuetenango told John Dinges in July that "the army is trying to kill every Indian alive". Guatemalan security forces do not always distinguish between innocent civilians and guerrillas, acknowledges General Ríos Montt. "Look, the problem of war is not just a question of who is shooting. For each one who is shooting there are ten behind him." His press secretary, Francisco Bianchi, adds: "The guerrillas won over many Indian collaborators. Therefore, the Indians were subversives, right? And how do you fight subversion? Clearly you had to kill Indians because they were collaborating with subversion. And then they say, "You're massacring innocent people." But they weren't innocent. They had sold out to subversion."

According to some reports, the government is also seeking to destroy once and for all the traditional Indian way of life. Measures are being aimed at the elimination of the several Indian languages still spoken in rural Guatemala. Young men conscripted into the army are stationed in regions where different languages are spoken and are forbidden to speak to each other in their own language. The army is said to aggressively discourage the use of Indian language by everyone else, whether in their own community or relocated in strategic hamlets (model villages). The Indians' distinctive traditional costume, which is such an important expression and symbol of their ethnic identity and pride, is taken from them and burned. The religious fiestas which used to be a feature of Indian life in rural Guatemala are forbidden with the claim that food prepared for these occasions will be given to the guerrillas. The musical instruments used in these fiestas are destroyed. The linkages between generations which permit and channel the transmission and continuation of cultural traditions are broken as the people are made orphans, losing their children, their parents, and their grandparents. Community solidarity is undermined by forcing men conscripted into the "civil patrols" to attack and kill their neighbours or fellow-villagers.

Not only are Indian customs, beliefs and traditions under attack but the economic and ecological basis for Indian existence is being destroyed. It is reported that when the army attacks an' Indian community, the people's houses, belongings and crops are burned and their domestic animals are killed or illegally confiscated. Rivers and streams, sources of drinking water, are said to be poisoned. In certain areas extensive pine forests are being burned down, in some cases set on fire by incendiary bombs thrown from helicopters.

famous ones are the Friday market in Sololá, and the Thursday and Sunday markets in Chichicastenango, but almost every village has its day. Some of the very best are in tiny, isolated hamlets, high in the mountains.

Once a year every village, however small, indulges in an orgy of celebration in honour of its patron saint — you'll find a list of them at the end of each chapter. These **fiestas** are a great swirl of dance, music, religion, fireworks, eating and outrageous drinking, and express the vitality of indigenous culture. They usually centre on religious processions, in which the image of the local patron saint is paraded through the streets, accompanied by the elders of the *cofradía*, who dress in full regalia. (All members of a *cofradía* usually have special ceremonial costumes, superbly woven and beautifully decorated.) The larger fiestas also involve funfairs and week-long markets. Traditional music is played with marimbas, drums and flutes; or professional bands may be hired, blasting out popular tunes through crackling PA systems.

Dance, too, is very much a part of fiestas, and incorporates routines and ideas that date from Maya times. Dance costumes are incredibly elaborate, covered in mirrors and sequins, and have to be rented for the occasion. Despite the cost, which is high by highland standards, the dancers see their role both as an obligation — to tradition and the community — and an honour. Most of the dances form an extension of some vague dramatic tradition where local history was retold in dance dramas, and are loosely based on historical events. The *Dance of the conquistadors* is one of the most popular, modelled on the *Dance of the Moors* and introduced by the Spanish as a re-enactment of the Conquest, although in some cases it's been instilled with a significance that can never have been intended by the Spanish. The dancers often see no connection with the Conquest, but dance instead to release the spirits of the dead, a function perhaps closer to Maya religion than Catholicism. The *Palo Volador*, a dramatic dance in which men swing perilously to the ground from a twenty-metre pole, certainly dates from the pre-Columbian era (these days you'll only see it in Cubulco, Chichicastenango and Joyabaj), as does the *Dance of the Deer*, while the *Dance of the Bullfight* and the *Dance of the Volcano* relate

incidents from the Conquest itself. Most of the dances do have steps to them, but the dancers are usually blind drunk and sway around as best they can in time to the music, sometimes tumbling over each other or even passing out — so don't expect to see anything too dainty.

INDIAN COSTUME

To outsiders the most obvious and impressive feature of Indian culture is the **hand-woven cloth** that's worn by the majority of the women and some of the men. This, like so much else in the Indian world, is not simply a relic of the past but a living skill, responding to new ideas and impulses and re-created by each generation.

Nevertheless, **weaving** is one of the oldest of Maya skills, and was practised for centuries before the arrival of the Spanish. We know that it was a highly valued skill, and the Maya goddess Ix Chel, "she of the rainbow", who presided over childbirth, divination and healing, is often depicted at her loom. In pre-Columbian times the majority of the Indian population probably wore long white cotton tunics, similar to those worn by the Lacandon Indians today. In the highlands it's a style that has been largely superseded, although in some villages, such as Soloma and San Mateo Ixtatán, the basic format is still the same, now embellished with magnificent embroidery. We also know, from Maya tombs and sculptures, that the nobility wore elaborate headdresses and heavily decorated cloth, using blues and reds created with vegetable dyes. Here it seems that tunics and robes were also the fashion of the day.

After the Conquest, the Indian nobility was virtually eradicated and the focus was shifted from large regional centres to small village communities. Meanwhile, silk and wool were introduced by the Spanish, as were a whole range of new dyes. Not much is known about the development of Indian costume in colonial times, and it's impossible to say when or why each village developed a distinctive style of dress. Some argue that the styles were introduced by the Spanish as a means of control, rather like the branding of sheep, while others claim that they developed naturally from the introspective nature of village culture. The truth is probably to be found somewhere between the two: we know that Spanish symbols were introduced into traditional costume designs, but that at times the Spanish had little influence over life in the villages.

WOMEN'S CLOTHING

Today there are around 150 villages where women still wear **traditional costume**, each with its own patterns, designs and colours. What little we know of their development shows that designs are constantly changing, adopting new patterns and ideas. The advent of literacy, a recent development in most areas, means that modern *huipiles* might include the word *escuela* (school), the name of the village, or even the words *Coca Cola*. Synthetic thread, including garish silvers and golds, has also been absorbed into many of the patterns, and as village society starts to open up, some designs, once specific to a single village, are coming to be used throughout the country.

Nevertheless, the basic style of the clothing worn by women has changed little since Maya times. The most significant development is simply that the **huipile**, which once hung loose, is now tucked into the skirt. Only in one or two places have the women added sleeves, or gathered their skirts, although in recent times young women have responded to outside influences and the latest generation of Indian costumes tend to emphasize the shape of the body. But in defiance of modern fashion Indian women still wear their hair in an assortment of bizarre styles, ranging from the halos of Santiago Atitlán to the pompoms of Aguacatán. Ceremonial *huipiles*, which are always the most spectacular, are still worn loose, in Maya style.

The basic element of an Indian woman's costume is the *huipile*, a loose-fitting blouse, normally woven by the women themselves on a back-strap loom. All *huipiles* are intricately decorated, either as a part of the woven pattern or with complex embroidery, and these designs are specific to each village. To protect the embroidery some women wear their *huipiles* inside out, saving the full splendour for market days. Ceremonial *huipiles*, reserved for fiestas, are usually more extravagant, often hanging low in the most traditional style. Under the *huipile* a skirt, or *corte*, is worn, and these are becoming increasingly standardized. Usually woven on a foot loom, it is a simple piece of cloth, up to five metres long, joined to

form a tube into which the women step. Most common are the *jaspeado cortes* woven on looms in Salcajá, San Francisco Totonicapán and Cobán by commercial weavers, and tie-dyed in universally worn patterns. In some cases there are distinct styles, but these tend to be used in a general region rather than in specific villages: the brilliant reds of Nebaj and Cajul, the yellows of San Pedro and San Marcos, and the blues of the Huehuetenango area, for example. To add individuality to their skirts the women decorate them with thin strips of coloured embroidery, known as *randa*. And to hold them up they use elaborate **sashes**, woven in superb colours and intricate patterns, and often including decorative tassels. Perhaps the most outlandish part of women's costume is the headdress, which varies widely and seems to have no connection with modern styles. The most famous of these are the halos of Santiago Atitlán – twelve-metre strips of cloth – while the turbans of Nebaj and Aguacatán are some of the finest. In addition to the cloth that they wear the women also weave **tzutes**, used to carry babies or food, and shawls that ward off the highland chill.

MEN'S CLOTHING

In the life of the Indian village men have had greater contact with the outside world, and as a result of this they have been more susceptible to change. From the outset their costume was influenced to a greater extent by the arrival of the Spanish, and today **men's traditional costume** is worn in only a few villages. The more traditional styles are generally reflected in ceremonial costume, while everyday clothes are heavily influenced by non-traditional "western" styles. If you're around for a fiesta you'll probably see some fantastic costumes worn by men who wear jeans every other day of the year.

On the whole even "traditional costumes" now have more in common with shirt and trousers than the ancient loose-hanging tunic. Nevertheless, men's costumes do include superb weaving and spectacular designs. Their jackets are particularly unusual, ranging from the superb reds of Nebaj, modelled on those worn by Spanish officers, to the ornate tuxedo-style of Sololá. (Those worn in Sololá seem to undergo regular changes, and the greys of late have now been superseded by a very ornate white version.) In the Cuchumatanes the men wear *capixays*, small ponchos made from wool, and in San Juan Atitlán these bear a remarkable similarity to monks' habits. Other particularly unusual features are the *ponchitos*, short woollen skirts, worn in Nahualá and San Antonio Palopo; the superbly embroidered shorts of Santiago Atitlán and Santa Catarina Palopo; and the cowboy-style shirts of Todos Santos. And although fewer men wear traditional costume the styles that remain are astonishingly diverse, their scarcity making them appear all the more outlandish. The *tzute*, a

ETHNIC BELIZE

Belize has a very mixed cultural background, with the two largest ethnic groups, Creoles and Mestizos, which together form 75 percent of the population, themselves the descendants of very different ancestors. **Creoles**, descended from Africans brought to the West Indies as slaves and early White settlers, comprise just under a third of the population. They make up a large proportion of the population of Belize City, with scattered settlements around the rest of the country. Creole is the common language in Belize, a form of English similar to that spoken in those parts of the West Indies that were once part of the British empire. Belizean Creole is currently undergoing a formalization similar to that taken by The Garifuna in the 1980s. A society has been formed to standardize written Creole and possibly produce a dictionary, and controversy rages in the press over whether or not Creole should become the country's official language and be taught in schools.

The largest group (44 percent) are **Mestizos**, descended from Amerindians and early Spanish settlers, who speak Spanish as their first language. They are mainly located in the north and on Ambergris Caye and Caye Caulker, with a sizeable population in Cayo. Many of the ancestors of the present population fled to Belize during the Caste Wars of the Yucatán. And in recent years, many thousands of refugees from conflicts and repression in El Salvador, Guatemala and Honduras have settled in Belize, probably adding permanently to the numbers of Spanish-speaking Mestizos.

The **Maya** in Belize are from three groups – the Yucatec, Mopan and Kekchi – and make up around 11 percent of the population. The Yucatecan Maya also entered Belize to escape the fighting in the Caste Wars and most were soon acculturated into the *Ladino* way of life as small farmers. The Mopan Maya came to Belize in the 1880s and settled in the hills of Toledo and the area of Benque Viejo in the west. The last group, the Kekchi, came from the area around Cobán in Guatemala to work in cacao plantations in southern Belize. Small numbers still arrive in Belize each year, founding new villages in the southern district of Toledo.

The **Caribs** or **Garifuna** (see p.413) live mainly in Dangriga and the villages on the south coast, such as Hopkins and Seine Bight. They form about 7 percent of the population. They are descended from shipwrecked and escaped slaves who mingled with the last of the Carib Indians on the island of St Vincent and eventually settled in Belize in the nineteenth century. A Garifuna dictionary, published by the National Garifuna Council, is available within the country.

Another group is the **East Indians**. They are relatively recent immigrants as apparently none of the earlier East Indians, brought as servants for the British administrators, left any descendants.

Since the 1980s, the arrival of an estimated 40,000 **Central American immigrants**, refugees from war and poverty, has boosted Belize's population to more than 200,000. Those granted refugee status were settled in camps, mostly in Cayo, and allowed to farm small plots, though many, especially the undocumented refugees, provide convenient cheap labour in citrus and banana plantations. The immigrants are tolerated, if not exactly welcomed – few countries could absorb a sudden 20 percent increase in population without a certain amount of turmoil – and the official policy is to encourage the refugees to integrate into Belizean society. Though there is no question of an enforced repatriation scheme, anyone wanting to return is supported. In 1995 only 57 people were voluntarily repatriated, while the vast majority chose to remain in Belize. The refugees are industrious agriculturists providing a a variety of crops for the domestic market. However, despite official tolerance they are often referred to as "aliens" and blamed for a disproportionate amount of crime. Their presence means that Spanish is now the most widely spoken first language, causing some Creoles to feel marginalized. Without doubt this recent Hispanic influence represents the greatest shift in Belize's demography for centuries.

piece of cloth worn either on the head or folded on the shoulder, is of particular significance, óften marking out an important member of the *cofradía*. In some villages the mayor, dressed in jeans and a T-shirt, will still wear a woven *tzute* on his shoulder as a symbol of office.

DESIGNS

The **designs** used in the traditional costume of both men and women are as diverse as the costumes themselves, an amazing collection of sophisticated patterns, using superb combinations of colour and shape. They include a range of animals, plants and people, as well as abstract designs, words and names. Many of them probably date from long before the Conquest: we know that the snake, the double-headed eagle, the sun and the moon were commonly used in Maya design, while the peacock, horse and chicken can only have been introduced after the arrival of the Spanish. The **quetzal** is perhaps the most universal feature and is certain to date from pre-conquest times, when the bird was seen as the spiritual protector of Quiché kings. The significance of the designs is as imprecise as their origins, although according to Lily de Jongh Osborne, an expert on Indian culture, designs once expressed the weaver's position within the social hierarchy, and could also indicate marital status. One particularly interesting design is the bat on the back of the jackets of Sololá, which dates back to the bat dynasty, among the last Cakchiquel rulers. In days gone by each level of the village hierarchy wore a different style of jacket, although today fashion is the prime consideration, and each generation is simply more outrageous than the last.

HUMAN RIGHTS IN GUATEMALA

Since the arrival of the Spanish, Guatemalan history has been character- ized by political repression and economic exploitation, involving the denial of the most basic human rights. A horrifying catalogue of events stretches across the last 450 years, but reached levels as barbaric as any previously seen in the late 1970s and the early 1980s. The chief victims have always been the indigenous Indians, generally regarded as backward, ignorant and dispensable. Today the story of Guatemalan repression is very much an unfinished history, despite the fact that the level of violence has declined signifi- cantly in the last few years.

THE EARLY YEARS

When **Pedro de Alvarado** arrived in Guatemala in 1523 he brought with him the notions of violent conquest and racist exploita- tion that have dominated the country to the present day. In the early years of the Conquest towns were burnt to the ground and huge numbers of Indians were massacred and enslaved. At the same time they had to contend with repeated epidemics that were to halve their numbers. Once the initial conquest was over the survivors were systematically herded into villages, deprived of their land, and forced to work in the new plantations: a pattern that seems all too familiar in modern Guatemala.

Equally familiar is the response of the indig- enous population, who rose in defiance. It took almost two centuries for their numbers to recover from the devastation of the Conquest, but by the start of the eighteenth century upris- ings were common. There were **Indian revolts** in 1708, 1743, 1760, 1764, 1770, 1803, 1817, 1818, 1820, 1838, 1839, 1898 and 1905, all of which met with severe repression.

Independence brought little change. Under **Rufino Barrios** (1873–85) the demands of coffee put fresh strains on the Indian popula- tion, as their land and labour were once again exploited for the benefit of foreign investors and the ruling elite. Under **Jorge Ubico** (1931–44) laws were introduced that obliged Indians to work on the plantations, and for the first time the government developed a network of spies and informers, giving it the capacity to deal directly with dissenting voices: a capacity it demonstrated in 1934, when Ubico discov- ered a plot to assassinate him and had some 300 people killed in just two days.

The most significant developments, at least in terms of human rights, came during the socialist governments of **Arevalo** and **Arbenz** (1945–55) which, for the first time, sought to meet the needs of the indigenous population. Local organizations such as unions and cooper- atives were free to operate, suffrage was extended to include all adults, health and schooling were expanded, and land was redis- tributed to the dispossessed. For the first time in the country's history the issues of inequality and injustice were taken by the horns.

However, in 1954 the government was over- thrown by a CIA-backed coup, which cleared the stage for military rule and ushered in the modern era of repression.

MILITARY RULE

Since the 1954 coup the army has dominated the government, operating in alliance with the land-owning elite and foreign business inter- ests to consolidate the power of the right. Large-scale repression wasn't to begin until the mid-1960s, but directly after the takeover the army began gathering the names of those who had been active under the socialist administra- tion. In association with the CIA they put together a list of some 70,000 people – a much-used reference source once the killing began.

The **guerrilla** movement, which developed out of an army revolt in 1960, was first active in the eastern highlands. Throughout the 1960s political violence was on the increase, aimed not just at the guerrillas, but at all political opponents and left-wing sympathizers. In the war against the guerrillas the army was unable to strike directly at its enemy and opted instead to eradicate their support in the community. Between 1966 and 1977 some 10,000 noncombatants were killed in a bid to destroy a guerrilla force that numbered no more than 500; and by the early 1970s the guerrillas were

EYEWITNESS TESTIMONY

The following account, of a massacre in San Francisco Nentón that took place on July 17, 1982, is one of the best documented of many such incidents during the Ríos Montt administration (see opposite). The events were related to a priest in a Mexican refugee camp by survivors; the account is taken from an Amnesty International report.

At 11am on Saturday 17 July the army arrived in San Francisco having passed through the nearby villages of Bulej and Yalambojoch. The army had previously visited the village on 24 June and had told the inhabitants that they could be killed if they were found not to be peacefully working in their homes and their fields. Soldiers had also said, however, that the villagers should not run away from the army, as it was there to defend them. On 17 July some 600 soldiers arrived on foot. A helicopter circled nearby and eventually landed. The military were accompanied by an ex-guerrilla, now in military uniform, who was apparently acting as the army's informer. The people were told to assemble for a discussion with the colonel. It was the first day on which the village's new civil defense patrol was to have begun its duties. Some of the survivors said that the patrol, of 21, was taken away shortly after the arrival of the army and had not been seen since. They are presumed dead.

According to testimonies collected by priests, the villagers first sensed they were in danger when a man who survivors said had been "tied up like a pig" was brought before them by the soldiers. They knew he had not been involved in anything, and yet saw that he was being "punished". They also saw how "angry" the commander appeared to be and began to fear for themselves. They were first asked to unload the soldiers' supplies from the helicopter, which they did. The men were then shut up in the courthouse to begin praying "to make peace with God", as they were about to suffer. A survivor described how: "We pray, 11 o'clock, 12 o'clock passes. By now, everyone has come into town and been shut up. At 1 o'clock, it began: a blast of gunfire at the women, there in the church. It makes so much noise. All the little children are crying."

This witness went on to tell how the women who survived the initial gunfire were taken off in small groups to different houses by soldiers where they were killed, many apparently with machetes. After they had been killed, the houses were set on fire. This witness and the others interviewed described a particularly atrocious killing they had seen, the murder of a child of about three. The child was disembowelled, as were several others, but kept screaming, until a soldier smashed his head with a pole, then swung him by his feet and threw him into a burning house. "Yes", said the witness, "yes, I saw it. Yes, I saw how they threw him away, threw him into the house."

The witness continued: "At 2 o'clock, they began with all the men. They ordered them out of the courthouse in small groups, and then blasted them with gunfire. It went on and on. They tied up the men's hands and then 'bang, bang'. We couldn't see, we could only hear the noise of the guns. The killing took place in the courtyard outside the courthouse, then they'd throw the bodies into the church. They killed the three old people with a blunt machete, the way you would kill sheep."

Another witness described how the old were killed: "The old people said, 'What have we done, no, we are tired and old. We're not thinking of doing anything. We're not strong. We can't do anything any more.' But they said, 'You're not worth anything any more, even if you're tired, get out of there.' They dragged them out, and knifed them. They stabbed and cut them as if they were animals and they were laughing when they killed them. They killed them with a machete that had no teeth. They put one man on the table and cut open his chest, the poor man, and he was still alive, and so they started to cut his throat. They cut his throat slowly. He was suffering a lot. They were cutting people under the ribs, and blood came rushing out and they were laughing." Another survivor continued: "When they got to the end, they killed six people in the courthouse. One was a military commissioner. They didn't care. They killed him there at his table with his three policemen."

"By now it was 6.30pm. It was getting dark outside. They threw a bomb into the corner of the courthouse. It was bloody, two were killed. How the blood ran! It ran all over me. Then they fired at the remaining bodies in the courthouse. Then they threw all the bodies in a heap. They dragged people by the feet, as if they were animals. They threw me on top of the dead bodies."

One witness ended his testimony: "Father my heart is so heavy with pain for the dead, because of what I have seen. I saw how my brothers died. All of them: friends, godparents, everyone, as we are all brothers. My heart will cry for them the rest of my life. But they had committed no crime. Nobody said: 'This is your crime. Here is the proof.' They just killed them, that's all. That's how death came."

A list of the dead was compiled in Mexico on September 5. It included 302 people, 92 of whom were under twelve, and the youngest less than two months old.

on the run, unable to mount attacks or add to their numbers.

In other parts of the country there was a brutal clampdown on a range of "suspect" organizations. In Guatemala City this campaign gave birth to the "**death squads**", put together by the right-wing MLN (National Liberation Movement) and the army. The first to emerge was *Mano Blanco*, who swore "to eradicate national renegades and traitors to the fatherland". Today the death squads have become a permanent feature of Guatemalan politics, and they were active throughout the 1960s, 1970s and 1980s, assassinating unionists, left-wing politicians and students. Victims were usually abducted by men in unmarked cars, and later their bodies were found, dumped by the roadside, mutilated and tortured. Between 1970 and 1974, 15,325 people "disappeared".

By 1975 the guerrilla movement was once again on the rise, as were peasant organizations, cooperatives and unions, all inspired by the move towards **liberation theology**, under which the Catholic Church began to campaign on social issues. The experience of 1954 proved to the Guatemalan people that their political options were severely restricted, and in the 1970s and 1980s they directed their energies towards grass-roots organization and eventually armed uprising. But in response to this the repression continued, and in 1976 Amnesty International stated that a total of 20,000 Guatemalans had been killed in the previous decade.

The closing years of the 1970s saw a rapid polarization of the situation that gave birth to a fresh wave of violence. The **guerrilla movements** were by now well established in many different parts of the country, as repression in the highlands drove increasing numbers to seek refuge in their ranks. At this stage there were four main organizations: the PGT (Guatemalan Workers Party), who operated in Guatemala City and on the Pacific coast; FAR (the Rebel Armed Forces), who fought throughout Petén; EGP (the Guerrilla Army of the Poor), who had several fronts in northern Quiché; and ORPA (Organization of People in Arms), who functioned in San Marcos and Quezaltenango.

The election of **Lucas García** in 1978 marked the onset of unprecedented mass repression. Once again the list of victims included left-wing politicians, labour leaders,

lawyers, priests, nuns, teachers, unionists, academics and students, all of whom were regarded as subversive. In the highlands the war against the guerrillas also reached a new intensity, as selective killings were replaced by outright massacres. Once again the army found itself pitched against an elusive enemy and resorted to indiscriminate killings in a bid to undermine peasant support for the guerrillas.

Repression was so widespread that human rights organizations found it almost impossible to keep track of the situation, although certain incidents still came to light. In 1980 36 bodies were found in a mass grave outside Comalapa; in early 1981 17 people were killed in Santiago Atitlán; and in April 1981 Oxfam estimated that 1500 Indians had been killed in Chimaltenango in the previous two months. Precise numbers are impossible to calculate, but according to some estimates 25,000 died during the first four years of the Lucas administration, the vast majority killed either by the security forces or by the death squads, which were often operated by off-duty soldiers or policemen and directed from an annexe of the National Palace.

RÍOS MONTT

In March 1982 Lucas was replaced by **General Efraín Ríos Montt**, and the situation improved significantly. The guerrillas were offered amnesty, death squad activity dropped off, and an office was set up to investigate the fate of the disappeared. But Ríos Montt had vowed to defeat the guerrillas by Christmas and in rural areas the level of violence did increase as the army began to make big gains in the fight against the guerrillas. In the early months of Ríos Montt's rule massacres were still commonplace as it took him some time to reshape the armed forces and provide an alternative to the brutal approach they had adopted under Lucas García. The campaign still claimed a heavy death toll, despite the downturn in indiscriminate slaughter. According to Amnesty International there were 2186 killings in the first four months of the new administration, and by now some 200,000 refugees had fled the country. Amnesty's report on the Ríos Montt administration (see box) is a catalogue of horror, though in many ways the events described were more typical of the Lucas García regime. However, its eyewitness accounts of army campaigns capture the full extent of repression in the highlands.

Under Ríos Montt the army campaign was much more successful and the guerrillas were driven into the remote corners of the highlands. Soldiers swept through the mountains, rounding up those who had fled from previous campaigns and herding them into refugee camps, while villagers were forced to defend their own communities in Civil Defence Patrols. Those who returned from the mountains were put to work by the army, who fed and "re-educated" them. Accounts of the army campaign under Ríos Montt are deeply divided. Some commentators see him as a significant reformer, who saved the rural population by transforming the approach of the army. On the other hand there are those who regard him as the most brutal of all Guatemala's rulers. Most Guatemalans, particularly those in the highlands, do seem to speak very highly of him and say that when he came to power he managed to put a stop to the indiscriminate violence which had plagued the country.

Ríos Montt was replaced by **Mejía Victores** in August 1983, and under the new administration there was a significant drop in the level of rural repression, although selective killings were still an everyday event. In 1984, however, the number of urban disappearances rose once again, with around fifty people abducted each month. In the highlands the process of reconstruction began. Guerrilla forces had dropped to around 1500, and although military campaigns continued, "model villages" were now being built to replace those that had been destroyed. Even so the conditions for refugees and survivors were still highly restricted and many large and impoverished communities are now made up entirely of widows and orphans.

Towards the end of 1985 the country faced its first free elections in thirty years, after a period that had seen 18 different administrations and cost the lives of 100,000 people. Another 38,000 had "disappeared", 440 villages had been destroyed, and 100,000 Guatemalans had fled to Mexico.

CIVILIAN RULE

In 1986 the election of **Vinicio Cerezo** as Guatemala's first civilian president for almost thirty years was widely regarded as a major opportunity to improve the human rights situation within the country. Cerezo himself had, on several occasions, come close to assassination, and members of his party, the Christian Democrats, have always been a favourite target of the death squads.

Following Cerezo's inauguration there was a marked decrease in the quantity of human rights violations although in a matter of months things started to deteriorate once again. Abductions, killings and intimidation remained widespread, with the victims drawn from the same groups as before. Between February 1986 and January 1987 there were at least 1000 killings, the vast majority attributable to "death squads". No one accused Cerezo of involvement in the murders, but it does seem that they were carried out by members of the security forces, which is a measure of his inability to control them.

In rural areas the level of violence dropped off significantly. With guerrilla forces estimated at 1000 to 3000, the army had little need to use the same heavy-handed tactics it had employed in the past. Many observers felt that the reduction in human rights abuse was simply a reflection of a more refined strategy by the army, who had already established control and could now use a more subtle but no less effective form of repression – killing selective targets rather than destroying entire communities. Abuses of the indigenous population remained common, and the Indians were often exploited and undernourished, with little access to education or health care. In many areas the indigenous population was forced to participate in civil patrols (despite assurances that they would have the option not to), which themselves became important in the system of repression and were responsible for intimidation, murder and abduction.

In 1988, just two years after the return to civilian rule, the level of violence began to increase sharply. Many people's worst fears were confirmed in November of that year when 22 bodies were found in a shallow grave near El Aguacate, a small village in the department of Chimaltenango. As yet there is no clear evidence to indicate who carried out the massacre, although recent testimonies do suggest that the army was responsible: they blame the guerrillas.

The killing continued throughout Cerezo's term in office and there was no real effort to either find the bodies of the disappeared – despite the pleas of their relatives – or to bring the guilty to trial. Cerezo himself remained preoccupied with holding onto power, fending off several coup attempts and trying to build some kind of power base. As president he adopted a nonconfrontational approach which not only ensured a reprieve for the guilty but also allowed the continued abuse of human rights. In his more candid moments Cerezo admitted that the continuing power of the army restricted his room for manoeuvre and argued that any investigation of past abuses would be impossible as he would have to put the entire army on trial.

INTO THE 1990s

In 1990 Cerezo handed the reins of power to **President Serrano**, but the situation remained bleak, with abductions, torture, intimidation and extrajudicial executions still commonplace. According to several US human rights groups, 500 Guatemalans were either "disappeared" or killed in extrajudicial executions in 1992 alone. That said, the administration was forced to tackle several high-profile cases, including the murder of street children and the assassinations of US citizen Michael Devine and the anthropologist Myrna Mack Chang, and for the first time members of the armed forces were convicted of human rights violations. A number of defiant local groups were very vocal in denouncing violations, particularly the Mutual Support Group (**GAM**), many of whose members and leaders were kidnapped and murdered. By contrast the government's Human Right Commission received over 1000 complaints of human rights violations and acted on none of them.

Meanwhile out **in the highlands** a number of new factors emerged. In December 1990 the people of Santiago Atitlán expelled the army from their village, after troops shot and killed thirteen people. In the wake of this incident a number of other villages called for army bases to be closed. The confidence of the Indian population was further boosted in 1992, when the Nobel Peace Prize was awarded to Rigoberta Menchú (see over), briefly focusing world attention on the plight of Guatemala's indigenous population. In early 1993 the first **refugees** began returning from Mexico to settle in the Ixcán region of northern Quiché. Their return provoked a fresh crisis in the countryside and the army bombarded nearby villages and resorted to familiar tactics to terrorize those returning. As more refugees have come home, the shortage of land and the uncertainty surrounding their future has provided additional tension and resulted in a fresh wave of human rights abuses by the armed forces. The most serious recent case was the massacre of eleven people (and the wounding of thirty more) by soldiers in the village of **Xamán** in Alta Verapaz on October 5, 1995. With more than 30,000 refugees wanting to return from camps in Mexico the new government will have to demonstrate a firm commitment to human rights to ensure that repatriation remains a realistic possibility for those still in exile.

For more information on human rights in Guatemala contact Amnesty International, 1 Easton St, London WC1X 0DW (☎0171/413 5500), or The Guatemalan Committee for Human Rights, 83 Margaret St, London W1N 7HB (☎0171/631 4200).

RIGOBERTA MENCHÚ AND THE NOBEL PEACE PRIZE

Five hundred years after Columbus reached the Americas the Nobel committee awarded their peace prize to **Rigoberta Menchú**, a 33-year-old Maya woman who has campaigned tirelessly for peace in Guatemala. In their official statement the Nobel committee described Menchú as "a vivid symbol of peace and reconciliation across ethnic, cultural and social dividing lines."

Within Guatemala, however, the honour provoked controversy. There can be little doubt that Menchú does have firm connections and deep sympathies with Guatemala's guerrillas, although after she was awarded the prize she distanced herself from the armed struggle. Nevertheless, many people argued that her support for armed uprising made her an inappropriate winner of a peace prize. A couple of days before the announcement the army's chief spokesman Captain Julio Yon Rivera said she "defamed the fatherland" although once the prize was awarded he claimed to have been expressing a personal opinion that was not the official view of the Guatemalan army. The foreign minister, Gonzalo Mendez Park, was equally dismissive, describing Menchú as "tied to certain groups that have endangered Guatemala".

Many others fear that the prize will be interpreted as a vindication of the guerrillas and will only serve to perpetuate the civil war. For those who seek peaceful solutions to Guatemala's problems, any gesture that appears to support the guerrillas is seen as a step backwards.

Menchú's own words, however, show her to be essentially a pacifst and suggest that her unspoken support for the guerrillas was very much a last resort. "For us, killing is something monstrous. And that's why we feel so angered by all the repression . . .. Even though the tortures and kidnappings had done our people a lot of harm, we shouldn't lose faith in change. This is when I began working in a peasant organization and went on to another stage of my life. There are other things, other ways."

Menchú's story is undeniably tragic and her account of it offers a real insight into the darkest years of Guatemalan history and their impact on the indigenous people. Born in the tiny hamlet of Chimel, in the hills north of Uspantán, Menchú is the sixth of nine children. By the age of eight she was working on the coastal plantations picking coffee, where one of her brothers died of malnutrition and her best friend died from pesticide poisoning. Her father was an activist who campaigned for the defence of Indian land, although his role within the community probably made the family an obvious target for repression. In 1979 one of Menchú's brothers was kidnapped by the army and burnt alive, along with several other prisoners. In early 1980 her father was part of a delegation of Indian leaders who peacefully occupied the Spanish embassy in Guatemala City in order to draw attention to their plight. The Guatemalan army, however, set fire to the building, killing all those inside. Three months later Menchú's mother was kidnapped by the army, raped, tortured and murdered.

In 1980 Menchú fled the country for Mexico, where she collaborated with a Venezuelan journalist to write her autobiography, *I, Rigoberta Menchú – An Indian Woman In Guatemala*, and campaigned tirelessly for the cause of indigenous people in Guatemala and throughout the Americas. Since leaving, Menchú has returned to Guatemala on a number of occasions, although she faces the constant threat of assassination.

Today Menchú remains the most visible international campaigner for the rights of Guatemala's indigenous people and provides a clear focus for what is a fairly diverse movement. Her role is both difficult and dangerous; in November 1995, when she was becoming heavily involved in the campaign for a proper investigation into the Xamán massacre, Menchú's nephew was abducted in Guatemala City. In an interview at the time, Menchú expressed her confidence in a gradual but important process of change. "In Guatemala human rights continue to be violated every day. You only have to look at the summaries every weekend to see the number of people killed. But on the other hand, the population is coping with the situation in an exemplary way. Every day the vote against fear is gathering strength and this is the foundation for change in the future. What has already changed is the participation of the population in human rights activism".

LANDSCAPE
AND WILDLIFE

Between them **Guatemala and Belize embrace an astonishingly diverse collection of environments**, ranging from the coral reefs of the Caribbean coast to the exposed central highlands of Guatemala, where the ground is often hard with frost. The wildlife of Central America is correspondingly varied; undisturbed forests provide a home to both temperate species from the north and tropical ones from the south, as well as a number of indigenous species found nowhere else in the world.

For the sake of organization this piece traces the landscape from south to north, Pacific to Caribbean, exploring each of the environments along the way.

THE PACIFIC COAST

Guatemala's **Pacific coastline** is marked by a thin strip of black volcanic sand, pounded by the surf. There are no natural harbours and boats have to take their chances in the breakers or launch from one of the piers (though the purpose-built Puerto Quetzal now takes large, ocean-going ships). The sea itself provides a rich natural harvest of shrimp, tuna, snapper and mackerel, most of which go for export. The coastal waters are also ideal for sport fishing. A couple of kilometres offshore, dorado, which grow to around forty pounds, are

plentiful, while further out there are marlin, sailfish, wahoo and skipjack.

The **beach** itself rises from the water to form a large sandbank, dotted with palm trees, behind which the land drops off into low-lying mangrove swamps and canals. In the east, from San José to the border, the **Chiquimulilla Canal** runs behind the beach for around 100km. For most of the way it's no more than a narrow strip of water, but here and there it fans out into swamps, creating a maze of waterways that are an ideal breeding ground for young fish, waterfowl and a range of small mammals. The sandy shoreline is an ideal nesting site for **sea turtles**, which occasionally emerge from the water, drag themselves up the beach and deposit a clutch of eggs before hauling their weight back into the water. At Monterrico, to the east of San José, a nature reserve protects a small section of the coastline for the benefit of the turtles, and with luck you might see one here. **The Monterrico Reserve** (p.206) is in fact the best place to see wildlife on the Pacific coast as it includes a superb mangrove swamp, typical of the area directly behind the beach, which you can easily explore by boat.

The **mangroves** are mixed in with water lilies, bulrushes and tropical hardwoods, amongst which you'll see **herons**, **kingfishers** and an array of **ducks** including **muscovies** and **white whistling ducks**. In the area around Monterrico flocks of **wood stork** are common, and you might also see the **white ibis** or the occasional **great jabiru**, a massive stork that nests in the area (and can also be seen in Belize). With real perseverance and a bit of luck you might also catch a glimpse of a **racoon**, **anteater** or **opossum**. Other birds that you might see almost anywhere along the coast include **plovers**, **coots** and **terns**, and a number of winter migrants including **white** and **brown pelicans**.

Between the shore and the foothills of the highlands, the **coastal plain** is an intensely fertile and heavily farmed area, where the volcanic and alluvial soils are ideal for sugar cane, cotton, palm oil, rubber plantations and cattle ranches. In recent years soya and sorghum, which require less labour, have been added to this list. Guatemala's coastal **agribusiness** is high cost and high yield: the soils are treated chemically and the crops regularly sprayed with a cocktail of pesticides, herbicides and fertilizers. There's little land that remains untouched by the hand of commercial agriculture so it's hard to imagine what this must once have looked like, but it was almost certainly very similar to Petén, a mixture of savannah and rainforest supporting a rich array of wildlife. These days it's only the swamps, steep hillsides and towering hedges that give any hint of its former glory, although beautiful flocks of white **snowy** and **cattle egrets** feed alongside the beef cattle.

Finally, one particularly interesting lowland species is the **opendula**, a large oriole which builds a long woven nest hanging from trees and telephone wires. They tend to nest in colonies and a single tree might support fifty nests. You'll probably notice the nests more than the birds, but they thrive throughout Belize and Guatemala.

THE BOCA COSTA

Approaching the highlands, the coastal plain starts to slope up towards a string of volcanic cones, and this section of well-drained hillside is known as the **Boca Costa**. The volcanic soils, high rainfall and good drainage conspire to make it ideal for growing **coffee**, and it's here that Guatemala's best crop is produced, with rows of olive-green bushes ranked beneath shady trees.

Where the land is unsuitable for coffee, lush tropical forest still grows, clinging to the hills. As you head up into the highlands, through deeply cleft valleys, you pass through some of this superb forest, dripping with moss-covered vines, bromeliads and orchids. The full value of this environment had remained unexplored for many years and the foundation of the **Faro Field Station**, on the southern slopes of the **Santiaguito** volcano, revealed an amazing, undisturbed ecosystem, protected by the threat of volcanic eruption. Over 120 species of bird have been sighted here, including some real rarities such as **solitary eagles**, **quetzals** and **highland guans**. The **azure-rumped tanager**, seen here in June 1988, hadn't previously been sighted in Guatemala since the mid-nineteenth century.

THE HIGHLANDS

The highlands proper begin with a chain of **volcanoes**. There are 33 in all, running in a direct line from the southwest to the northeast. Most can be climbed in five or six hours and the view from the top is always superb. The highest is **Tajamulco** (4210m), which marks the Mexican border, and there are also three active cones: **Fuego**, **Pacaya** and **Santiaguito**, all of which belch sulphurous fumes, volcanic ash, and the occasional fountain of molten rock. Beneath the surface their subterranean fires heat the bedrock and there are several places where spring water emerges at near boiling point, offering the luxury of a hot bath (for the best of these see Almolonga, p.156).

On this southern side of the central highlands there are two large lakes, set in superb countryside and hemmed in by volcanic peaks. Both tell a sad tale of environmental mismanagement. **Lake Amatitlán**, to the south of Guatemala City, is further down the road to contamination, its waters already blackened by pollution and its shores ringed with holiday homes. It remains a popular picnic spot for the capital's not so rich. Further to the west is **Lake Atitlán**, still spectacularly beautiful, with crystal blue waters. There are moves afoot to develop this lake along the lines of Amatitlán, and increasing tourist development threatens to damage the delicate ecological balance. The greatest damage so far was done by the introduction of the **black bass** in 1958, in a bid to create a sport fishery. The bass is a greedy, thuggish beast and in no time at all its presence had reshaped the food chain. Smaller fish were increasingly rare, as were crabs, frogs, insects and small mammals. Worst hit was the **Atitlán grebe**, a small, flightless water bird that was found nowhere else in the world. Young grebes were gobbled up by the hungry bass, and by 1965 just eighty of them survived. By 1984, falling water levels due to the 1976 earthquake, combined with tourist development of the lakeshore cut their numbers by another thirty, and today the bird is officially extinct. Meanwhile the beauty of Lake Atitlán remains under threat from overdevelopment, population growth and soil erosion.

On the northern side of the volcanic ridge are the **central valleys** of the highlands, a complex mixture of sweeping bowls, steep-sided valleys, open plateaux and jagged peaks. This central area is home to the vast majority of Guatemala's population and all the available land is intensely farmed, with hillsides carved into workable terraces and portioned up into a patchwork of small fields. Here the land is farmed by Indians using techniques that predate the arrival of the Spanish. The *milpa* is the mainstay of Indian farming practices: a field is cleared, usually by slash and burn, and is planted with maize as the main crop, with beans, chillies and squash grown beneath it at ground level. Traditionally, the land is rotated between *milpa* and pasture, and also left fallow for a while, but in some areas it's now under constant pressure, the fertility of the soil is virtually exhausted and only with the assistance of fertilizer can it still produce a worthwhile crop. The pressure on land is immense and each generation is forced to farm more marginal territory, planting on steep hillsides where exposed soil is soon washed into the valley below.

Some areas remain off-limits to farmers, however, and there are still vast tracts of the highlands that are **forested**. In the cool valleys of the central highlands pine trees dominate, intermixed with oak, cedar and fir, all of which occur naturally. To the south, on the volcanic slopes and in the warmth of deep-cut valleys, lush tropical forest thrives in a world kept permanently moist – similar in many ways to the forest of Verapaz, where constant rain fosters the growth of "high rainforest".

Heading on to the north the land rises to form several **mountain ranges**. The largest of these are the Cuchumatanes, a massive chain of granite peaks that reach a height of 3790m above the town of Huehuetenango. Further to the east there are several smaller ranges such as the Sierra de Chuacús, the Sierra de las Minas and the Sierra de Chama. The high peaks support stunted trees and open grassland, used for grazing sheep and cattle, but are too cold for maize and most other crops.

Birdlife is plentiful throughout the highlands; you'll see a variety of **hummingbirds**, flocks of screeching **parakeets**, **swifts**, **egrets** and the ever-present **vultures**. Slightly less commonplace are the **quails** and **wood partridges**, **white-tailed pigeons**, and several species of doves including the **little Inca** and the **white-winged dove**. Last but by no means least is the **quetzal**, which has been revered since Maya times. The male quetzal has fantastic green tail-feathers which snake behind it through the air as it flies: these have always been prized by hunters and even today the bird is very rare indeed. The only nature reserve in the highlands is the **Biotopo del Quetzal**, a protected area of high rainforest in the department of Baja Verapaz, where quetzals breed.

The highlands also support a number of small **mammals**, including foxes and small cats, although your chances of seeing these are very slim indeed.

THE RAINFORESTS OF PETÉN

To the north of the highlands the land drops away into the **rainforests** of Petén, a massive area that's miraculously undisturbed, although recent oil finds, guerrilla war and migrant settlers are all putting fresh strain on this ecological wonderland. A 1981 United Nations report predicted that Guatemala will lose a third of its forest by the end of the century, and a report by the Guatemalan Commission for the Environment, published in 1990, claimed the country had lost 40 percent of its forest cover in the last thirty years, prompting a significant drop in the amount of rainfall. The forest of Petén extends across the Mexican border, where it merges with the Lacandon rainforest, and into Belize, where it skirts around the lower slopes of the Maya Mountains, reaching to the Caribbean coast.

Ninety percent of Petén is still covered by **primary forest**, with a canopy that towers 50m above the forest floor, made up of hundreds of species of trees, including ceiba, mahogany, aguacate, ebony and sapodilla. The combination of a year-round growing season, plenty of moisture and millions of years of evolution have produced an environment that supports literally thousands of species of plants and trees. While temperate forests tend to be dominated by a single species – fir, oak or beech, say – it's diversity that characterizes the tropical forest. Each species is specifically adapted to fit into a particular ecological niche, where it receives a precise amount of light and moisture.

It's a biological storehouse that has yet to be fully explored although it has already yielded some astonishing **discoveries**. Steroid hormones, such as cortisone, and diosgenin, the active ingredient in birth control pills, were developed from wild yams found in these forests; and tetrodoxin, which is derived from a species of Central American frog, is an anesthetic 160,000 times stronger than cocaine.

Despite its size and diversity the forest is surprisingly **fragile**. It forms a closed system in which nutrients are continuously recycled and decaying plant matter fuels new growth. The forest floor is a spongy mass of roots, fungi, mosses, bacteria and micro-organisms, in which nutrients are stored, broken down with the assistance of insects and chemical decay, and gradually released to the waiting roots and fresh seedlings. The thick canopy prevents much light reaching the forest floor, ensuring that the soil remains damp but warm, a hotbed of chemical activity. The death of a large tree prompts a flurry of growth as new light reaches the forest floor, and in no time at all a young tree rises to fill the gap. But once the trees are removed the soil is highly vulnerable, deprived of its main source of fertility. Exposed to the harsh tropical sun and direct rainfall, an area of cleared forest soon becomes prone to flooding and drought. Recently cleared land will contain enough nutrients for four or five years of good growth, but soon afterwards its usefulness declines rapidly and within twenty years it will be almost completely barren. If the trees are stripped from a large area soil erosion will silt the rivers and parched soils disrupt local rainfall patterns.

However, **settlement** needn't mean the end of the rainforest, and in the past this area supported a huge population of Maya Indians, who probably numbered several million. (Although some archeologists argue that during Maya occupation Petén was a mixture of savannah and grassland, and that relatively recent climatic changes have enabled it to evolve into rainforest.) Only one small group of Indians, the Lacandon, still farm the forest using traditional methods. They allow the existing trees to point them in the right direction, avoiding areas that support mahogany, as they tend to be too wet, and searching out ceiba and ramon trees, which thrive in rich, well-drained soils. In April a patch of forest is burnt down and then, to prevent soil erosion, planted with fast-growing trees such as bananas and papaya, and with root crops to fix the soil. A few weeks later they plant their main crops: maize and a selection of others, from garlic to sweet potatoes. Every inch of the soil is covered in growth, a method that mimics the forest and thereby protects the soil. The same land is cultivated for three or four years and then allowed to return to its wild state, although they continue to harvest from the fruit-bearing plants and in due course return to the same area. The whole process is in perfect harmony with the forest, extracting only what it can afford to lose and ensuring that it remains fertile. Sadly, the Lacandon are a dying breed and the traditional farming practices are now used by very few. In their place are waves of new settlers, burning the forest and planting grass for cattle. Neither the cattle, the farmers or the forest will survive long under such a system.

In its undisturbed state the rainforest is still superbly beautiful and is home to an incredible range of wildlife. Amongst the birds the **ocellated turkey**, found only in Petén, is perhaps the most famous. But the forest is also home to **toucans**, **motmots**, several species of **parrots** including **Aztec** and **green parakeets**, and the endangered **scarlet macaw**, which is said to live to at least fifty. As in the highlands, **hummingbirds**, **buzzards** and **hawks** are all common. A surprising number of these can be seen fairly easily in the **Tikal National Park**, particularly if you hang around until sunset.

Amongst the mammals you'll find **jaguars** (referred to as *tigre* in Guatemala and *tiger* in Belize), **peccary** (a type of wild boar), **brocket deer**, **opossums**, **weasels**, **porcupines**, **pumas**, **ocelots**, **armadillos** and several different species of **monkey**, including **spiders** and **howlers**, which emit a chilling deep-throated roar. The massive **tapir** (mountain cow) plunder through the forests, and the river banks are occupied by tiny **ridge-backed turtles** and **crocodiles**, while **egrets** and **kingfishers** fish from overhanging branches. The rivers and lakes of Petén are correspondingly rich, packed with **snook**, **tarpon** and **mullet**.

THE MAYA MOUNTAINS

Heading east from the central part of Petén, the granite and limestone peaks of the **Maya Mountains** run northeast, straddling the border with **Belize**. This wild region, covered in dense forest and riddled with caves and underground rivers, has few permanent residents.

Almost all the Belize highlands are protected in a huge swathe of **national parks** and **forest reserves**, the most accessible of which are the **Mountain Pine Ridge** (p.398) and the **Cockscomb Basin Wildlife Sanctuary** (p.418), home of Belize's **jaguar preserve**. Technically, the vegetation here is **tropical moist forest**, classified by average temperatures of 24°C and annual rainfall of between 2000 and 4000mm. The flora and fauna are similar to those found in the tropical forests of Guatemala but are often more prolific since there's much less pressure on the land.

LOWLAND BELIZE

The forests of Petén extend into **north-western Belize**, where the generally low-lying land is broken by a series of roughly parallel **limestone escarpments**, with rivers draining either north to the River Hondo or south to the Belize River. Further east the plain is more open; pine savannah is interspersed with slow-flowing rivers and lagoons, providing spectacular **wetland habitats** that continue to the coast. The tiny village of Sarteneja is the only settlement between Belize City and Corozal on the east coast, an important area for **wading birds**, **crocodiles**, **turtles** and **manatee**.

Less space is given over to nature reserves in the north but those that exist protect viable areas, representative of the various habitats found here. In the west the **Rio Bravo Conservation Area** (p.341) protects a huge area of rainforest north of the village of Gallon Jug. In the centre **Crooked Tree Wildlife Sanctuary** (p.342) covers several freshwater lagoons, protecting over 200 bird species, including the nesting sites of the rare **jabiru stork**. South of here, at the **Bermudian Landing Baboon Sanctuary** (p.345), visitors can be almost guaranteed views of troops of **black howler monkeys**. Whilst there are no monkeys at **Shipstern Nature Reserve**, almost all the other mammals of Belize, including **jaguars**, **ocelot**, and **tapir**, can be found at this 9000-hectare site, a mosaic of coastal lagoon, hardwood forest and mangrove swamp.

In the south there's only a relatively narrow stretch of lowland between the Maya Mountains and the coast, but heavy rainfall ensures the growth of lush rainforest. Along the coast and navigable rivers much of the original forest has been logged; some is in varying stages of regrowth after hurricane damage, and around human settlements it has been replaced by patches of agricultural land and coconut plantations.

THE CARIBBEAN COASTLINE AND THE BARRIER REEF

Belize's most unique environment is its Caribbean coastline and offshore barrier reef, dotted with small islands and atolls. The shoreline is largely made up of mangrove swamps, which, like those on the Pacific coast of Guatemala, are an ideal marine nursery. Young **stingrays** cruise through the tangle of roots, accompanied by baby **black-tipped sharks**, **bonefish** and small **barracudas**. The basis of the food chain is the nutrient-rich mud, held in place by the mangroves, while the roots themselves are home to **oysters** and **sponges**. The dominant species of the coastal fringe is the **red mangrove**, although in due course it undermines its own environment by consolidating the sea bed until it becomes more suitable for the less salt-tolerant black and white mangroves. Mangroves play an important role in the Belizean economy, not merely as nurseries for commercial fish species but also for their stabilization of the shoreline and their ability to absorb the force of hurricanes. Each kilometre of mangrove shoreline is valued at several thousand dollars per year. The cutting down of mangroves, particularly on the cayes, exposes the land to the full force of the sea and can mean the end of a small and unstable island.

A boat journey along the **Burdon Canal Nature Reserve**, which connects the Belize and Sibun rivers, is a good introduction to the wildlife to be found in the **inland** mangrove forests. Out to sea, around half of Belize's cayes are mangrove cayes and are best explored in a small boat. In a canoe you can easily spot the **brown pelican**, **white ibis**, **roseate spoonbill** or even a **greater flamingo**. The tallest mangrove forests in Belize are found along the Temash River, in the recently designated **Sarstoon Delta Wildlife Sanctuary**, where the black mangroves reach heights of over 30m.

The mangrove swamps are also home to the **manatee**, an endangered species that looks rather like an overgrown seal. Manatees grow to 4m in length and can weigh as much as a ton, but are placid and shy, moving between the freshwater lagoons and the open sea. Unlike the seal, they are entirely aquatic. They were once common on the eastern seaboard of the United States but were hunted for their meat and their numbers are now dangerously low.

Heading out to sea you reach the barrier reef, the longest in the western hemisphere, an almost continuous chain of coral that stretches from Mexico to Guatemala, between fifteen and forty kilometres offshore. Beneath the water is a world of astounding beauty, where fish and coral come in every imaginable colour. The corals grow like an underwater forest, with fields of grass carpeting the sea bed, overshadowed by the larger coral formations that feed off plankton wafting past in the current. Among these you'll find the **chalice sponge**, which is a garish pink, the **fire coral**, with hundreds of tiny tentacles, the delicate **feather-star crinoid**, and the **apartment sponge**, a tall thin tube with lots of small holes in it. The fish, including **angel** and **parrot fish**, several species of **stingrays** and **sharks** (the most common the relatively harmless nurse shark), **conger** and **moray eels**, **spotted goatfish**, and even a small striped fish called the **sergeant-major**, are just as unusual. The reef and its islands are also home to **marlin, barracuda, dolphins** and American **salt-water crocodiles**.

For centuries the reef has been harvested by fishermen. In the past they caught manatees and turtles, but these days the **spiny lobster** and **queen conch** are the main catch, exported to the US. In the last two decades the fishing industry has been booming and the numbers of both of these have now gone into decline.

In an effort to protect endangered species, the **Hol Chan Marine Reserve** has been established on the southern tip of Ambergris Caye, a superb spot for snorkelling and diving. Belize's first "undersea park", this will soon be joined by others if the recently published Coastal Zone Management Plan is implemented.

Belize's three species of **sea turtles**, the **loggerhead**, the **green** and the **hawksbill**, occur throughout the reef, nesting on isolated beaches, but are infrequently seen as they are still hunted for food. Proposed changes in legislation should provide them with greater protection, however. As well as complete protection for the hawksbill turtle, the new laws will extend the closed season and limit the largest permitted size to 90cm. This last provision should give the older, sexually mature turtles a greater chance to breed.

Above the water the cayes are an ideal nesting ground for birds, providing protection from predators and surrounded by an inexhaustible food supply. At **Half Moon Caye**, right out on the eastern edge of the reef, there's a wildlife reserve designed to protect a breeding colony of 4000 **red-footed boobies**. Here you'll also see **frigate birds, ospreys, mangrove warblers** and **white-crowned pigeons**, amongst a total of 98 different species.

CONSERVATION IN BELIZE

Recent additions to Belize's already impressive network of national parks, nature reserves and wildlife sanctuaries now bring over 35 percent of the land under some form of legal protection, an amazing feat for a developing country with a population of only 200,000. With such enlightened strategies designed to safeguard the nation's biodiversity Belize is gaining recognition as the most conservation-conscious country in the Americas.

The success of these **nature reserves** and community wildlife sanctuaries (covered in detail in the relevant chapters) is due as much to the efforts of local communities to become involved in conservation as it is to governmental decisions. The variety of tropical land and marine ecosystems also makes Belize, in spite of its small size, increasingly a focus of scientific research. Over 70 percent of land is still forested, with large areas of undisturbed wilderness and a vitally important coral reef. There are 4000 species of flowering plants, 533 bird species (including the rare harpy eagle), all five species of cats found in the Americas, the largest population of manatees outside the US, sea and river turtles, crocodiles and snakes, and countless insect species.

The conservation of these natural resources is the main plank in the government's declared policy to make **"ecotourism"** the focus of development and marketing in the nation's tourism industry. Ideally this is a community-based form of tourism, inspired primarily by the wildlife and landscape of an area and showing respect for local cultures. The theory is that by practising small-scale, nonconsumptive use of the country's natural resources, visitors will be contributing financially both to the conservation of protected areas and to local communities; it is hoped that this will aid sustainable development not only locally but in Belize as a whole.

Conservation legislation in Belize originally focused on forest reserves established by the colonial government to provide areas for timber exploitation, not primarily for nature preservation. In 1928,

however, Half Moon Caye was established as a Crown Reserve to offer protection to the red-footed booby. Other bird and wildlife sanctuaries were established in the 1960s and 1970s, and in the period since independence the government has taken measures to increase the land available for wildlife protection. The passing of the National Parks Act in 1981 provided the legal basis for establishing national parks, natural monuments and reserves, and the Wildlife Protection Act of 1981 (extended in 1991) created closed seasons for various endangered species, including marine and freshwater turtles, lobster, conch and black coral. Belize's timber reserves have always been within the compass of the Forestry Department, which in 1990 created a Conservation Division, recognizing their own in-house expertise. A conservation officer will eventually be appointed to all of the forest reserves.

Another step in the right direction has been the 1992 **Environmental Protection Act**, which is intended to control pollution and promote environmental health by requiring companies to carry out an Environmental Impact Assessment before undertaking any proposed development. Low penalties for its contravention, though, compounded by the loosely worded definitions the act contains, may dull its impact. **Hunting**, which has long been a means of supplementing diet and income, remains a real problem in almost all reserves and protected lands; the most popular species include iguana, armadillo, deer and the gibnut, or *tepescuintle*, a large rodent sometimes seen on menus. Needless to say you should avoid ordering these creatures in restaurants.

At the time of writing a thorough overview of Belize's environmental and wildlife protection legislation is occuring. Known as the **National Protected Areas Systems Plan for Belize**, it recognizes that a viable plan cannot be established on nationally owned lands alone, but will need cooperation from many private landowners.

Various national and international **voluntary organizations** have been active in conservation in Belize for many years, building up experience by practical work and by attending and hosting environmental conferences. The organizations recently joined to present a united

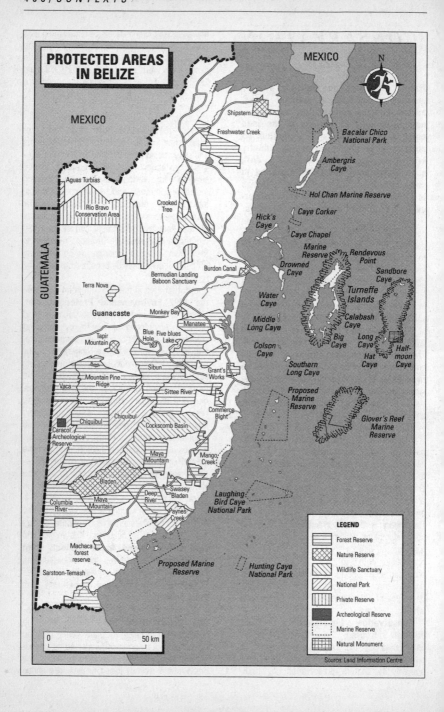

PROTECTED AREAS IN BELIZE

MEXICO

N

MEXICO

Shipstern

Freshwater Creek

Bacalar Chico National Park

Ambergris Caye

Aguas Turbias

Rio Bravo Conservation Area

Crooked Tree

Hol Chan Marine Reserve

Caye Corker

Hick's Caye

Caye Chapel

Marine Reserve

Rendevous Point

Drowned Caye

Sandbore Caye

Burdon Canal

Bermudian Landing Baboon Sanctuary

Turneffe Islands

Terra Nova

Water Caye

GUATEMALA

Guanacaste

Monkey Bay

Manatee

Middle Long Caye

Calabash Caye

Long Caye

Tapir Mountain

Blue Hole

Five blues Lake

Colson Caye

Big Caye

Half-moon Caye

Vaca

Mountain Pine Ridge

Sibun

Grant's Works

Southern Long Caye

Hat Caye

Sittee River

Chiquibul

Chiquibul

Commerce Bight

Proposed Marine Reserve

Caracol Archeological Reserve

Cockscomb Basin

Maya Mountain

Mango Creek

Glover's Reef Marine Reserve

Bladen

Swasey Bladen

Deep River

Laughing Bird Caye National Park

Columbia River

Maya Mountain

Paynes Creek

Machaca forest reserve

Proposed Marine Reserve

Hunting Caye National Park

Sarstoon-Temash

LEGEND

Forest Reserve

Nature Reserve

Wildlife Sanctuary

National Park

Private Reserve

Archeological Reserve

Marine Reserve

Natural Monument

Source: Land Information Centre

0   50 km

front known as the **Belize Association of Conservation NGO's (BANCONGO)** in order to more effectively present their cause to government. This unity has most recently been demonstrated in the total opposition, in conjunction with the local Maya community, to a logging operation in the Columbia River Forest reserve in Toledo which calls into question the government's entire environmental and conservation policies. However, the dramatic increase in the amount

of protected land has posed the question of how such protection is to be financed, the task of providing wardens and safeguarding all the reserve boundaries being clearly beyond the scope of the charitable and voluntary organizations. Several years of meetings between various nongovernmental organizations (NGOs) and the Belize government as to how the necessary funds should be raised has resulted in the

CONSERVATION ORGANIZATIONS IN BELIZE

The Belize Audubon Society, which was founded in 1969, is the oldest conservation organization in Belize and manages many of the country's reserves including Half Moon Caye and Guanacaste Park. Members receive a monthly newsletter about the progress of wildlife conservation in Belize. Call in at the office to find out how to get to the various nature reserves; the society will often be in radio contact with reserve managers. For details of membership contact *BAS*, PO Box 1001, 12 Fort St, Belize City (☎ 02/34987; fax 34985).

The Belize Zoo is becoming increasingly well known throughout the conservation world, especially so in Britain after Gerald Durrell's visit in 1989. In Belize the zoo encourages schoolchildren to understand the natural environment by visits and the Outreach Programme. The zoo is easy to reach from Belize City (see p.384), and if you wish to support its aims individual membership is avaiable. Write to Sharon Matola (the zoo's director), PO Box 474, Belize City (☎08/13004).

The Belize Center for Environmental Studies is a nonprofit organization established in 1988 to promote sustainable use of Belize's natural resources. It also acts as a coordinating agency for conservation groups in Belize and for anyone overseas interested in Belize's environment. Studies made by the Center evaluate threats to the environment, and use may be made of its facilities by scientists, students, researchers and other interested parties. The Center publishes a bimonthly newsletter and the *Center Environmental Quarterly*. For more information call at 55 Eve St, Belize City (☎02/45545), or write to PO Box 666, Belize City.

Coral Cay Conservation (CCC), established in 1989, is a nonprofit organization that provides scientific expertise and resources to the government of Belize and assists with the development

of initiatives for the protection and sustainable use of marine resources. One aim is to establish the country's second marine reserve at South Water Caye (p.415). Research for this, and for another proposed marine reserve around the Sapodilla Cayes in the south, is undertaken by teams of volunteer divers under the guidance of qualified marine scientists. A CCC Charitable Trust has been established to provide funds for training Belizeans in resource management skills. For information contact *Coral Cay Conservation*, 54 Clapham Park Rd, London SW4 7DE (☎0171/498 6248; fax 498 8447); Suite 124, 230 12th St, Miami Beach, FL 33139, USA (☎ & fax 305/534-7638); c/o *Australian Marine Conservation Society*, PO Box 49, Moorooka, QLD 4105, Australia (☎07/848 5235; fax 892 5814).

The Programme for Belize (PFB), initiated in 1988 by the Massachusetts Audubon Society and launched in Britain in 1989, manages over 250,000 acres in the Rio Bravo Conservation Area. The Programme has bought land, to be held in trust for the people of Belize, and is managing it for the benefit of wildlife. They always need donations/ suport to maintain protected areas. For more information contact 2 South Park St, Belize City (☎02/75616; fax 75635); John Burton, PO Box 99, Saxmundham, Suffolk IP 17 2LB, UK, or 208 Great South Rd, Lincoln MA 01773 (☎617/259-9500; fax 259-8899).

The World Wide Fund for Nature supports a number of projects in Belize, from the Community Baboon Sanctuary at Bermudian Landing to the Cockscomb Basin Jaguar Preserve (sponsored by Jaguar Cars). The *WWF Conservation Yearbook* contains an A–Z of Belizean wildlife. Contact 1250 24th St NW, Washington DC, 20037 USA (☎202/ 293-4800); 90 Eglinton Ave E, Toronto, Ontario M4P 2Z7, Canada (☎416/489-8800), or Panda House, Weyside Park, Godalming, Surrey GU7 1XR, UK (☎01483/26444).

Protected Areas Conservation Trust (PACT), an **exit tax** of Bz$47.50, payable at all departure points. The revenue is shared between the government departments and voluntary organizations responsible for conservation, according to a pre-arranged formula. National Park and archeological site entry fees have also been raised, and some new ones implemented, though tourism industry bodies are lobbying for lower rises than those planned.

The tourism industry is playing its part in raising environmental awareness; the recently formed **Belize Eco-Tourism Association (BETA)** is a small but growing number of hotels and lodges whose members agree to a code of ethics promot-ing sustainable tourism management. One of the agreed aims is to reduce (and eliminate) the use of disposable products from their businesses; if you're concerned about your hotel's impact on the environment ask if they're a member of BETA and if so, observe the level of compliance with the code.

Future moves could see the establishment of a **Biosphere Reserve** in Belize, under the UN Man and the Biosphere Programme. The Belize Barrier Reef has also been proposed as a natural candidate for nomination as a **World Heritage Site**. The benefits and drawbacks of these suggestions are currently under discussion.

MUSIC IN BELIZE

For such a tiny country, Belize enjoys an exceptional range of musical styles and traditions. Whether your tastes run to the ethereal harp melodies of the Maya or the up-tempo punta of the Garifuna, or to calypso, marimba, brukdown, soca or steelpan, Belize is sure to have something to suit. Some visitors still complain about the noisiness of Belizean society and the volume at which the music is played, but if you can get into it, it's one of the quickest ways to the heart of Belizeans and their culture.

ROOTS

Until the demise of the Maya civilization and the arrival of the Spanish, the indigenous **Maya** of Belize played a limited range of instruments drawn almost entirely from the flute and drum families. Drums were usually made from hollowed logs covered in goat skin. Rattles, gourd drums and the turtleshell provided further rhythmic accompaniment. Trumpets, flutes, bells, shells and whistles completed the instrumentation. Most music was ritual in character and could involve up to 800 dancers, although smaller ceremonial ensembles were more common. Sadly, the sounds of this now silent culture are no longer with us.

However, as befits a nation of immigrants, each new group arriving – the Europeans, the Creoles, the Mestizos and the Garifuna – brought with them new styles, vigour and variety which today inform and influence popular culture. The **Europeans** introduced much of the hardware and software for playing music: "Western" musical instruments and sheet music, record players and discs, and most recently cassettes, compact discs and massive sound systems. The Schottische, quadrille, polka and waltz can be counted amongst their strictly musical innovations. From **Africa** via Jamaica came a melange of West African rhythms and melodies which also brought drums and stringed instruments into the mix.

A new syncretic style, nurtured in the logging camps and combining "Western" instrumentation with specifically African inflections, emerged in the late nineteenth century under the name "**Brukdown**". With a twentieth-century line-up of guitar, banjo, accordion, drums and the jawbone of an ass, *brukdown* remains a potent reminder of past Creole culture. Although the style is slowly fading, there are still several bands playing in and around Belize City of which **Mr Peter's Boom and Chime** is the best. **Brad Patico**, an accomplished guitarist and singer, similarly does his best to keep alive the Creole folk song tradition, and from his base in Burrel Boom collects old material, composes new songs and performs regularly to highly appreciative audiences. More recently, the "African" elements in Creole music have been expressed through wider pan-Caribbean styles like calypso, reggae, soca and rap.

Calypso enjoyed a brief period of preeminence and is still usually associated with **Lord Rhaburn's Combo**. The band can still be found performing regularly at the *Big Apple* but live appearances by Rhaburn himself are increasingly rare. Most other bands copy current hits with one or two original compositions thrown in: Youth Connection, Gilharry 7, Santino's Messengers and Brother David (particularly the last) can all provide an excellent evening's entertainment.

Mestizo communities (including the Mopan Maya) in the north and west of the country continue to favour **marimba** ensembles comprising half a dozen men playing two large wooden xylophones, perhaps supported by a double bass and a drum kit. Up to half a dozen bands play regularly in the Cayo district: Elfigo

Panti, who doubles up as the knowledgeable tourist guide at Xunantunich, presides over the nation's pre-eminent marimba group – **Alma Belicena**. Orange Walk district boasts the country's sole brass band, playing a roots Mexican style, and just as leading marimba bands occasionally pop over from Flores in Guatemala, so too do Mexican **mariachi** bands occasionally appear. Nonetheless, traditional Mestizo music remains under threat as the youth turn to rock, rap and punta.

Davi Obi – better known as Bredda David – is the creator of **Cungo** Music (Creole for "let's go with the music"), a mixture of musical styles that includes the traditional Creole music of Belize and the pulsating drum rhythms of Africa.

PUNTA ROCK

If Maya, Mestizo and Creole styles retain only a fragile hold on popular musical consciousness, it is the **Garifuna** who have catapulted to centre-stage over the last decade with the invention and development of **punta rock**. Descended from Carib Indians and African slaves, the Garifuna arrived in Belize in the early nineteenth century having been forcefully exiled from St Vincent by the British. With a distinct language and a vibrant, living culture, the Garifuna suffered a century of discrimination in Belize before re-establishing their individuality in the cultural renaissance of the early 1980s.

The key musical developments were the amplification of several traditional drum rhythms, the addition of new instruments such as the turtleshell, and the almost universal aversion to singing in anything but Garifuna. The new mood was pioneered by singer, guitarist and artist **Pen Cayetano** in Dangriga. His drum, guitar and brass arrangements provided the springboard for a number of Dangriga-based electric bands such as Sound City, Black Choral, Sounds Incorporated, and above all **Andy Palacio**, whose satirical 1988 hit "Bikini Panti" remains a national favourite. The **Wariba-gabaga Drum and Dance troupe**, formed in 1964, remain the chief guardians of more orthodox arrangements and should on no account be missed when they perform in Dangriga. Other popular artists include Peter "Poots" Flores, Alvin Paine and Bella Caribe.

VENUES AND ARTISTS

Thursday evening is widely considered to mark the start of the weekend, and weekends are the best time to catch bands and other entertainment in **Belize City**. The *Big Apple*, *Shangri-La*, *Lumba Yaad* and the *Privateer* usually offer live music, while bigger venues like *Bird's Isle* and the *Civic Auditorium* often host longer variety bills. Most of the bigger hotels hire smaller outfits for residencies and special events and it would be a pity to leave Belize without hearing one of the several **one-man bands** which, with an array of electronic equipment and virtuoso keyboard skills, provide enjoyable dance music in less crowded settings. The most popular performers remain **Davonix**, **Steve Babb** and the talented **Magana**, while probably the most popular band in Belize today is the **Garifuna Kids**.

Caye Chapel offers live entertainment and beach barbecues on the last Saturday of every month, while neighbouring **San Pedro**, as the major tourist destination in Belize, guarantees some kind of entertainment throughout the tourist season. **Belmopan** is less well served. The *Bayman Inn*'s disco changes hands with a disruptive regularity while *Ed's Bar* in nearby Roaring Creek, despite its enjoyable dance-hall ambiance, can seldom guarantee a show. **San Ignacio**, capital of the Cayo district, presents far livelier options, and residents of Belmopan clearly prefer the west to Belize City when it comes to weekend fun. Bands regularly perform at the *San Ignacio Hotel*, *Cahal Pech Tavern* and the *Blue Angel*, while the delightful Obandos entertain guests at their family-owned resort at *Las Casitas*. **Pablo Collado**, of Benque Viejo, with two beautiful, evocative and much sought after flute and guitar instrumental albums, *Armonia en la Selva* and *Amancear,* to his credit, frequently plays at locations in Cayo; definitely worth getting to.

In **Dangriga**, the *Riverside Disco* provides regular live music while **Pen Cayetano and the Turtleshell Band** can sometimes be found playing in the street in front of the art studio on a Friday night. **Punta Gorda**, **Benque Viejo** and **Corozal** seldom offer live music, but on the other hand the more rural areas do occasionally come up trumps with unexpected and informal performances. Placencia, Hopkins, Succotz, Bullet Tree,

Ladyville, Burrell Boom, Consejo and Maskall all still entertain in the traditional way, and luck alone will determine whether anything is happening on the night you happen to be there.

The large tourist **hotels** usually have something on offer as well, and it is always worth checking the *Pelican* in Dangriga, *Victoria* in Orange Walk and the *Bellevue* and *Fort George* in Belize City.

SPECIAL EVENTS

Perhaps the best times to hear and see the full panoply of Belizean musical culture are the various **national events** which regularly punctuate the social calendar. Biggest and best are National Day (September 10) and Independence Day (September 21) – dates which mark almost two weeks of festivities as Belize City comes close to the spirit and atmosphere of Caribbean carnival. Street parades, floats, block parties, "jump-ups" and late-night revelry characterize what are known locally as "The Celebrations".

Garifuna Settlement Day falls on November 19 and brings huge crowds to Dangriga for a long weekend of late nights, rum and rhythm. Mestizo communities celebrate with a number of very Latin type **fiestas** – bands, funfairs, sports and competitions. These are usually held around Easter and are soon followed by the **National Agricultural Show** held just outside Belmopan, when up to 50,000 people gather over three days for things both agricultural and recreational. All the country's top bands will appear at some stage during the weekend.

Occasionally, the scene is further enlivened by visits from **Belizean musicians based in the States**. Los Angeles is the favourite destination for many Belizeans' bands like Chatuye, Jah Warriors, Poopa Curly and Sounds Incorporated usually try to come at least once a year; and Calypso Rose is a regular visitor.

RECORDINGS

On an official level, the government takes a lively interest in local arts with a revitalized Arts Council based at the Bliss Institute. *Radio Belize* does its best to promote local talent, but cable TV and pirate satellite stations steadily erode interest in local products.

Stonetree Records is a new and thriving music house established by *Cubola*, Belize's foremost publishing house, to provide a platform for Belizean music of all genres, from melodic Maya harps through the African-born beat of punta and cungo to experimental fusion by such artists as Ivan Duran, founder of Free Access.

Other groups, like Brother David, Messengers and Sounds Incorporated, have also produced good local cassettes, and there are some signs that local record shops are beginning to respect the rights of musicians to also earn a living.

Of course there are those who do not fit into any of the tidy categories outlined above. Both the **Police Band** and the **Belize Defence Force Band** perform regularly and creditably. The **All-Stars Steel Band** plough a lonely furrow but are well received wherever they play. There are also a number of small **jazz** outfits and some very gifted up-and-coming **female vocalists**. But on a national level, punta still holds sway and there is no question, given the richness of their traditional musical repertoire, that the Garifuna will continue to develop new styles for decades to come. For their part, several young musicians are now experimenting with more traditional Mestizo melodies and rhythms. Mestizo rock, anyone?

Ronnie Graham and Cindy Carlson

BOOKS

In the past Guatemala and Belize never inspired a great deal of literature; but in recent years the political turmoil has spawned a boom in books about Guatemala, while Belizean independence prompted a handful of new Belizean histories. Politics overshadows almost all books about Guatemala, and most travel accounts deal with Central America as a whole, offering only a small slice of Belize or Guatemala.

Many of the books listed below are very difficult to find outside the US, though they may be imported by specialist bookshops. Useful sources include the *Interhemispheric Education Research Center* in the US (☎505/842-8288; fax 246-1601) and the *Latin American Bureau*, 1 Amwell St, London EC1R 1UL (☎0171/278 2829; fax 278 0165). Where a book is put out by a specialist publisher and may be particularly difficult to track down, we have named the publisher in parentheses after the title, along with the country of publication. O/p means a book is out of print.

THE SPANISH CONQUEST

Anthony Daniels *Sweet Waist of America*. A delight to read. Daniels takes a refreshingly even-handed approach to Guatemala and comes up with a fascinating cocktail of people and politics, discarding the stereotypes that litter most books on Central America. The book also includes some interesting interviews with prominent characters from Guatemala's recent history.

Thomas Gage *Travels in the New World*. Unusual account of a Dominican friar's travels through Mexico and Central America between 1635 and 1637, including some fascinating insights into colonial life as well as some great attacks on the greed and pomposity of the Catholic Church abroad.

Aldous Huxley *Beyond the Mexique Bay*. Huxley's travels, in 1934, took him from Belize through Guatemala to Mexico, swept on by his fascination for history and religion, and sprouting bizarre theories on the basis of everything he sees. There are some great descriptions of Maya sites and Indian culture, with superb one-liners summing up people and places.

Patrick Marnham *So far from God . . . .* A saddened and vaguely right-wing account of Marnham's travels through the Americas from the United States to Panamá (missing out Belize). Dotted with amusing anecdotes and interesting observations, the book was researched in 1984, and its description of Guatemala is dominated by the reign of terror. The Paraxtut massacre, mentioned by Marnham, has since been unmasked as a fabrication.

Jonathan Evans Maslow *Bird of Life, Bird of Death*. Again travel and political comment are merged as Maslow sets out in search of the quetzal, using the bird's uncertain future as a metaphor for contemporary Guatemala and contrasting this with the success of the vulture. It's a sweeping account, very entertaining, but more concerned with impressing the reader than representing the truth. A great yarn, set in a country that's larger than life in every possible way, but in the end a naive and stereotypical image of Central American horror.

Jeremy Paxman *Through the Volcanoes*. Similar in many ways to Patrick Marnham's book, this is another political travel account investigating the turmoil of Central America and finding solace in the calm of Costa Rica. Paxman's travels take him through all seven of the republics, including Belize, and he offers a good overview of the politics and history of the region.

Nigel Pride *A Butterfly Sings to Pacaya*. The author, accompanied by his wife and four-year-old son, travels south from the US border in a Jeep, heading through Mexico, Guatemala and Belize. A large section of the book is set in Maya areas and illustrated by the author's drawings of landscapes, people and animals. Though the travels took place nearly twenty years ago the pleasures and privations they experience rarely appear dated: the description of the climb of the Pacaya volcano is one of the highlights of the book.

John Lloyd Stephens *Incidents of Travel in Central America, Chiapas, and Yucatán.* Stephens was a classic nineteenth-century traveller. Acting as American ambassador to Central America, he indulged his own enthusiasm for archeology; while the republics fought it out among themselves he was wading through the jungle stumbling across ancient cities. His journals, told with superb Victorian pomposity punctuated with sudden waves of enthusiasm, make great reading. Some editions include fantastic illustrations by Catherwood of the ruins overgrown with tropical rainforest.

Paul Theroux *The Old Patagonian Express.* An epic train journey from Boston to Patagonia that takes in a couple of miserable train trips in Guatemala. Theroux doesn't have much time for Guatemalans, dismissing them as unhelpful and taciturn, but as usual, his way with words paints a vivid picture. See p.43 for a taster.

Ronald Wright *Time Among the Maya.* A vivid and sympathetic account of travels from Belize through Guatemala, Chiapas and Yucatán, meeting the Maya of today and exploring their obsession with time. The book's twin points of interest are the ancient Maya and the recent violence. An encyclopedic bibliography offers ideas for exploration in depth, and the author's knowledge is evident in the superb historical insight he imparts through the book. Certainly one of the best travel books on the area.

FICTION, AUTOBIOGRAPHY AND POETRY

Miguel Angel Asturias *Hombres de Maiz.* Guatemala's most famous author, Asturias is deeply indebted to Guatemalan history and culture in his work. "Men of Maize" is generally regarded as his masterpiece, classically Latin American in its magic realist style, and bound up in the complexity of Indian culture. His other works include *El Señor Presidente,* a grotesque portrayal of social chaos and dictatorial rule, based on Asturias's own experience; *El Papa Verde,* which explores the murky world of the United Fruit Company; and *Weekend en Guatemala,* describing the downfall of the Arbenz government. Asturias died in 1974, after he had won the Nobel prize for literature.

Paul Bowles *Up Above the World.* Paul Bowles is at his chilling, understated best in this novel based on experiences of Guatemala in the late 1930s. **Jane Bowles** used the same visit for her fiction in *A Guatemalan Idyll* and other tales, recently republished in *Everything is Nice: Collected Stories of Jane Bowles.*

Zee Edgell *Beka Lamb.* A young girl's account of growing up in Belize in the 1950s, in which the problems of adolescence are described alongside those of the Belizean independence movement. The book also explores everyday life in the colony, describing the powerful structure of matriarchal society and the influence of the Catholic Church. Her latest book, *In Times Like These,* is a semi-autobiographical account of personal and political intrigue set in the months leading up to Belize's independence.

Zoila Ellis *On Heroes, Lizards and Passion* (Cubola Productions, Belize). Seven short stories written by a Belizean woman with a deep understanding of her country's people and their culture.

Francisco Goldman *The Long Night of White Chickens.* Drawing on the stylistic complexity of Latin American fiction, this novel tells the tale of a young Guatemalan orphan who flees to the US and works as a maid. When she finally returns home she is murdered. It's an interesting and ambitious story flavoured with all the bitterness and beauty of Guatemala's natural and political landscape.

Felicia Hernandez *Those Ridiculous Years* (Cubola Productions, Belize). A short autobiographical book about growing up in Dangriga in the 1960s.

Norman Lewis *The Volcano Above Us.* Vaguely historical novel published in 1957 that pulls together all the main elements of Guatemala's recent history. The image that it summons is one of depressing drudgery and eternal conflict, set against a background of repression and racism. In the light of what's happened since it has a certain prophetic quality, and remains gripping despite its miserable conclusions.

Victor Perera *Rites: A Guatemalan Boyhood.* Autobiographical account of a childhood in Guatemala City's Jewish community. It may not cast much light on the country, but it's an interesting read, pulling together an unusual combination of cultures.

Rodrigo Rey Rosa *Dust on her Tongue; The Beggar's Knife*. Two collections of stories by a young Guatemalan writer, translated by Paul Bowles. The tales are brutal and lyrical, concerned, as Bowles comments, with "a present-day Central America troubled by atavistic memories of its sanguinary past". Recommended.

Shots From The Heart (Cubola Productions, Belize). Slim anthology of the work of three young Belizean poets: Yasser Musa, Kiren Shoman and Simone Waight. Evocative imagery and perceptive comment relate experiences of a changing society.

GUATEMALAN HISTORY, POLITICS & HUMAN RIGHTS

Tom Barry *Guatemala A Country Guide* (The Resource Centre, Albuquerque, UK and US). A comprehensive and concise account of the political, social and economic situation in Guatemala, with a mild left-wing stance. Currently the best source for a good overview of the situation.

Philip Berryman *Christians in Guatemala's Struggle* (Catholic Institute for International Relations, UK/Orbis Books, US). Well informed and written slim volume, covering 1944–84. Even if you're not particularly interested in the Christian angle, it offers a concise account of the political situation, seen through the eyes of the oppressed. It includes a great deal of information about the development of opposition to the oligarchy, particularly union organization.

George Black *Garrison Guatemala*. An account of the militarization of Guatemalan politics up to 1982. Black's condemnation is total: the conflict in Guatemala is seen as a battle to the death, with armed uprising the only possible solution and the probable outcome.

Jim Handy *Gift of the Devil*. The best modern history of Guatemala, concise and readable with a sharp focus on the Indian population and the brief period of socialist government. Don't expect too much detail on the distant past, which is only explored in order to set the modern reality in some kind of context, but if you're interested in the history of Guatemalan brutality then this is the book to read. By no means objective, it sets out to expose the development of oppression and point the finger at those who oppress.

Margaret Hooks *Guatemalan Women Speak* (Catholic Institute for International Relations, UK). An interesting collection of interviews with Guatemalan women, ranging from the wife of a *finca* owner to an impoverished highland Indian. The book embraces a wide range of topics, including work, family, sexuality, politics and religion, and gives voice to a seldom heard perspective on the nation's problems.

George Lovell *Conquest and Survival in Colonial Guatemala* (McGill Queen's University Press, US). Very localized in its area of study, this book sets out to examine in intimate detail the rise and fall of the indigenous population in the Cuchumatanes from 1500 to 1821.

Victor Montejo *Testimony: Death of a Guatemalan Village*. Yet another horrifying account of murder and destruction. In this case it's the personal testimony of a school teacher, describing the arrival of the army in a small highland village and the killing that follows.

James Painter *Guatemala: False Hope, False Freedom*. Another deeply depressing analysis of the situation in Guatemala today. First published in 1988, and revised in 1989, it deals with the failure of civilian rule. It also includes an investigation into the roots of inequality and a summary of the main forces that help perpetuate it. Read it alongside Jean-Marie Simon's book.

Mario Payeras *Days of the Jungle*. A slim volume originally written under the auspices of the EGP, one of Guatemala's main guerrilla armies. In this sense it's unique, as the voice of the guerrillas is rarely heard. Here one of their number tells of the early days of the organization, as they enter Guatemala through the jungles of the northwest and attempt to establish contacts amongst the local population. There are, however, serious doubts about the accuracy of the story in the book.

Jean-Marie Simon *Eternal Spring – Eternal Tyranny*. Of all the books on human rights in Guatemala, this is the one that speaks with blinding authority and the utmost clarity. Combining the highest standards in photography with crisp text, there's no attempt to persuade you – the facts are allowed to speak for themselves, which they do with amazing strength. If you want to know what happened in Guatemala over the last twenty years or so there is no better book. Again Simon clearly takes sides, aligning herself with the revolutionary left: there's no mention of any abuses committed by the guerrillas.

Stephen Schlesinger and Stephen Kinzer *Bitter Fruit: The Untold Story of the American Coup In Guatemala* (o/p). As the title says, this book traces the American connection in the 1954 coup, delving into the murky water of United Fruit Company politics and proving that the invading army received its orders from the White House.

Guatemala in Rebellion. Fascinating historical snippets and eyewitness accounts tracing Guatemalan history from the arrival of the Spanish to 1983, in which the people involved are allowed to speak for themselves. They range from conquistadors to priests and indigenous peoples.

Guatemala: A Country Study Published by the US army, this is a comprehensive overview of Guatemala, taking in everything from soil types to Indian languages. The style is dry, but the information superb.

BELIZEAN HISTORY AND POLITICS

Nigel Bolland *Colonialism and Resistance in Belize* (Cubola Productions, Belize). Perhaps the most academic text on Belizean history, adopting a staunchly Marxist stance, and sweeping away many of the myths and much of the romance that surrounds the history of Belize.

Gerald S Koop *Pioneer Years in Belize*. History of the Mennonites in Belize, written in a style as stolid and practical as the lives of the pioneers themselves. A good read nonetheless.

William David Setzekon *A Profile of the New Nation of Belize, formerly British Honduras*. An approachable, easy-going Belize history.

Assad Shoman *Thirteen Chapters of a History of Belize*. A long overdue and superb treatment of the country's history written by a Belizean who's not afraid to examine colonial myths with a detailed and rational analysis. It's a school textbook, but the style will not alienate non-student readers. Shoman, active in politics both before and since independence, also wrote *Party Politics in Belize*, which, less than one hundred pages long, is nevertheless a highly detailed account of the development of party politics in the country.

The Baymen's Legacy – A Portrait of Belize City and **A History of Belize – A Nation in the Making**. Straightforward and simple historical accounts, possibly written for use in schools and available within Belize.

CENTRAL AMERICAN POLITICS

Tom Barry *Central America Inside Out*. Well-informed background reading on the entire region. By the same author, *Inside Guatemala* and the excellent *Inside Belize* (InterHemispheric Education Resource Center/ LAB) are two in a series of up-to-date guides covering the history, politics, ecomomy and society of Central America. Packed with accessible facts and analysis.

James Dunkerley *Power in the Isthmus*. Detailed account of Central American politics that excludes Belize and Panamá. Nevertheless, it offers a good summary of the contemporary situation, albeit in turgid academic style.

Ralph Lee Woodward Jr *Central America: A Nation Divided*. More readable than the above, this is probably the best book for a general summary of the Central American situation, despite its daft title.

INDIGENOUS CULTURE

Linda Asturias de Barrios *Comalapa: Native Dress and its Significance* (Ixchel Museum, Guatemala). Only available in Guatemala, this is a work of skilled academic research, investigating weaving skills and their place within modern Indian communities.

Krystyna Deuss *Indian Costumes from Guatemala* (K Deuss, UK, o/p). A rather sketchy survey of the traditional costumes worn in Guatemala, but still the best introduction to the subject.

Byron Foster *Spirit Possession in the Garifuna Community of Belize* (Cubola Productions, Belize). The only offering on indigenous culture in Belize is by no means comprehensive. There's little background on Garifuna culture, though the main focus of the book is the experience of spirit possession, which is described by several Garifuna from southern Belize.

Guisela Mayen de Castellanos *Tzute and Hierarchy in Sololá* (Ixchel Museum, Guatemala). Only available within Guatemala, this is a detailed and academic account of Indian costume and the complex hierarchy that it embodies. Somewhat dry in its approach, but the research is superb and some of the information is fascinating.

Rigoberta Menchú *I, Rigoberta Menchú – An Indian Woman in Guatemala*. Unusual and fascinating account of life in the highlands, tracing the abuse of the Indian population and the rising tide of violence. It includes a chilling description of the military campaign and of the power and complexity of Indian culture, homing in on the enormous gulf between *Ladinos* and Indians. In 1992 Rigoberta Menchú was awarded the Nobel Peace Prize for her work in promoting the cause of indigenous people (see p.490).

Hans Namuth *Los Todos Santeros*. Slendid book of black and white photographs taken in the village of Todos Santos, to the north of Huehuetenango. The book was inspired by the work of anthropologist Maud Oakes – see below.

Maud Oakes, *Beyond the Windy Place; The Two Crosses of Todos Santos* An anthropologist who spent many years in the Mam-speaking village of Todos Santos, north of Huehuetenango. Oakes' studies of life in the village were published in the 1940s and 1950s and still make fascinating reading.

The Popol Vuh The great poem of the Quiché, written shortly after the Conquest and intended to preserve the tribe's knowledge of its history. It's an amazing swirl of ancient mythological characters and their wandering through the Quiché highlands, tracing Quiché ancestry back to the beginning. There are several versions on offer and many of them are very half-hearted, including only a few lines from the original. The best version is translated by Dennis Tedlock and published by Touchstone in the US.

James D Sexton (ed) *Son of Tecún Umán; Campesino*. Two excellent autobiographical accounts originally written by an anonymous Indian from somewhere on the south side of Lake Atitlán. The books give a real impression of life inside a modern Indian village, bound up in poverty, local politics and a mixture of Catholicism and superstition, and avoiding the stereotyping that usually characterizes description of the Indian population. The earlier of the two is *Son of Tecún Umán*, which takes us from 1972–77, while the second account,

Campesino, leads up to 1982 and includes the worst years of political violence. Both books make fascinating reading. *Casa Andinista*, in Antigua, Guatemala, sometimes has copies.

Philip Werne *The Maya of Guatemala* (Minority Rights Group, UK). A short study of repression and the Indians of Guatemala. Published in October 1989 and somewhat out of date, it is interesting nonetheless.

ARCHEOLOGY

Carmack *Quichean Civilization*. Thorough study of the Quiché and their history, drawing on archeological evidence and accounts of the Conquest. A useful insight into the structure of highland society at the time of the Conquest.

Michael Coe *The Maya*. Now in its fifth edition, this clear and comprehensive introduction to Maya archeology is certainly the best on offer. Coe has also written several more weighty, academic volumes. His *Breaking the Maya Code*, a very personal history of the decipherment of the glyphs, owes much to the fact that Coe was present at many of the most important meetings leading to the breakthrough. While his pointed criticism of J Eric Thompson – much of whose work he describes as burdened with "irrelevant quotations", and his role in the decipherment of the Maya script as "entirely negative" – may provoke controversy, this book demonstrates that the glyphs did actually reproduce Maya speech.

William Coe *Tikal: A Handbook to the Ancient Maya Ruins*. Superbly detailed account of the site, usually available at the ruins. The detailed map of the main area is essential for in-depth exploration.

Charles Gallenkamp *Maya*. Perhaps a touch over-the-top on the sensational aspects of Maya archeology, this is nonetheless another reasonable introduction to the subject. An overview of the history of Maya archeology, the book takes you through the process of unravelling the complexity of the Maya world.

Orellana *The Tzutujil Mayas*. Another study of highland tribes. This one goes into greater depth when it comes to events since the Conquest.

Linda Schele and David Freidel *A Forest of Kings: The Untold Story of the Ancient Maya*. The authors, in the forefront of the "new archeology", have been personally responsible for decoding many of the glyphs. This book, in conjunction with *The Blood of Kings*, by Linda Schele and Mary Miller, shows that far from being governed by peaceful astronomer-priests, the ancient Maya were ruled by hereditary kings, lived in populous, aggressive city-states, and engaged in a continuous entanglement of alliances and war. *The Maya Cosmos*, by Schele, Freidel and Joy Parker is more difficult to read, dense with copious notes, but continues to examine Maya ritual and religion in a unique and far-reaching way.

Robert Sharer *The Ancient Maya.* If you really want to dig deep try this weighty account of Maya civilization, now in its fourth edition. More concerned with being scientifically accurate than readable, it's a long, dry account, but if you can spare the time you'll end up well informed.

J Eric S Thompson *The Rise and Fall of the Maya Civilization.* A major authority on the ancient Maya, Thompson has produced many academic studies. This is one of the more approachable. He is also the author of a very interesting study of Belizean history in the first two centuries of Spanish colonial rule, *The Maya of Belize – Historical Chapters Since Columbus* (Cubola Productions, Belize). It's an interesting investigation into a little-studied area of Belizean history and casts some light on the tribes that weren't immediately conquered by the Spanish.

Warlords and Maize Men (Cubola Publications, Belize). Subtitled "A Guide to the Maya Sites of Belize" and written by various experts, this is an excellent handbook to fifteen of the most accessible sites in Belize compiled by the *Association for Belizean Archeology* and the Belizean government's Department of Archeology.

WILDLIFE AND THE ENVIRONMENT

Rosita Arvigo with Nadia Epstein *Sastun.* A rare glimpse into the life and work of a Maya *curandero*, the late Elijio Panti of San Antonio, Belize. Dr Arvigo has ensured the survival of many generations of accumulated healing knowledge, and this book is a testimony both to her perseverance in becoming accepted by Mr Panti and the cultural wisdom of the indige-

nous people. Arvigo has also written and co-authored several other books on traditional medicine in Belize, including *Rainforest Remedies*.

Louise H Emmons *Neotropical Rainforest Mammals*, illustrated by Francois Feer. Highly informative, with colour illustrations, written by experts for non-scientists. Local and scientific names are given, along with plenty of interesting snippets.

Carol Farnetti Foster and John R Meyer *A Guide to the Frogs and Toads of Belize.* Great book with plenty of photos and text to help you identify the many anurans you'll see – and hear – in Belize.

Steve Howe and Sophie Webb *The Birds of Mexico and Northern Central America.* A tremendous work, the result of years of research, this is the definitive book on the region's birds. Essential for all serious birders.

John C Kricher *A Neotropical Companion.* Subtitled "An Introduction to the Animals, Plants and Ecosystems of the New World Tropics", this contains an amazing amount of valuable information for nature lovers. Researched mainly in Central America, so there's plenty that's directly relevant.

Alan Rabinowitz *Jaguar.* Written by a US zoologist studying jaguars for the New York Zoological Society in the early 1980s and living with a Maya family in the Cockscomb Basin, Belize. Rabinowitz was instrumental in the establishment of the Jaguar Reserve in 1984.

Smith, Trimm and Wayne *The Birds of Tikal.* This is sadly all that's on offer for budding ornithologists in Guatemala, but we should be thankful for small mercies. The book can usually be bought at Tikal.

The Jungles of Central America. Glossy trip through the wildernesses of Central America. By no means a comprehensive account of the region's wildlife but a good read nonetheless, with several useful sections on Guatemala and Belize.

GUIDES, OLD AND NEW

Kirk Barrett *Belize by Kayak.* The most detailed book on this increasingly popular activity. Not widely available; contact *Reef Link Kayaking*, 3806 Cottage Grove, Des Moines, Iowa, US.

Bruce Hunter *A Guide to Ancient Maya Ruins* (University of Oklahoma Press, UK and US). The only guide that focuses exclusively on Maya ruins, this offers an account of all the most important sites in Mexico, Guatemala and Belize. Many of the more obscure ruins are ignored, but it's well worth reading.

Emory King *Emory King's Driving Guide to Belize.* Worth a look if you're travelling around. The maps are perhaps a little too sketchy for complete accuracy but the book is typically Belizean: laid-back and easy-going. Emory King is something of a celebrity in Belize and has also written a humorous description of family life in Belize: *Hey Dad This is Belize.* These and other books written by him are only available in Belize.

Barbara Balchin de Koose *Antigua for You* (Watson, Guatemala). The latest in a long line of guides focusing on Guatemala's most popular tourist city, this book gives a very good and comprehensive account of the colonial architectural wonders, but not much else.

Trevor Long and Elizabeth Bell *Antigua Guatemala.* Published in Guatemala, this is the best guide to Antigua, replacing an older version by Mike Shawcross which is now out of print. The book is available from several shops in Antigua.

Ned Middleton *Diving in Belize.* The most readable book on the subject, expertly written and illustrated with excellent photographs taken by the author. Covers in detail all the atolls and many of the reefs and individual dive sites. Includes a section on Mexico's Banquo Chinchorro, just north of Belize.

Lily de Jongh Osborne *Four Keys to Guatemala* (1939, o/p). One of the best guides to Guatemala ever written, including a short piece on every aspect of the country's history and culture. Osborne also wrote a good book on arts and crafts produced in Indian Guatemala. Sadly, both of these books are now out of print.

Carlos E. Prahl Redondo *Guia de los Volcanes de Guatemala* (Club Andino Guatemalteco). A very comprehensive and systematic account of the nation's 37 volcanoes and how to get to the top of them, put together by a local teacher.

A SINGLE COOKBOOK

Copeland Marks *False Tongues and Sunday Bread: A Guatemalan and Maya Cookbook.* Having travelled in Guatemala and suffered the endless onslaught of beans and tortillas, you may be surprised to find that the country has an established culinary tradition. Copeland Marks, an American food writer, has spent years unearthing the finest Guatemalan recipes, from hen in chocolate sauce to the standard black beans. The book is a beautifully bound celebration of Guatemalan food as it should be.

LANGUAGE

Guatemala and Belize take in a bewildering collection of languages, probably numbering thirty in all, but fortunately for the traveller there are two that dominate – Spanish and English.

CREOLE

Creole may sound like English from a distance and as you listen to a few words you'll think that their meaning is clear, but as things move on you'll soon realize that complete comprehension is just out of reach. It's a beautifully warm and relaxed language, typically Caribbean, and loosely based on English but including elements of Spanish and Indian languages. Written Creole is a little easier to get to grips with, but it's hardly ever used. There is one compensation – almost anyone who can speak Creole can also speak English.

Just to give you a taste of Belizean Creole here are a couple of simple phrases:

Bad ting neda gat owner – Bad things never have owners.
Better belly bus dan good bikkle waste – It's better that the belly bursts than good victuals go to waste.
Cow no business eena haas gylop – Cows have no business in a horse race.

If you're after more of these then get yourself a copy of *Creole Proverbs of Belize*, which is usually available in Belize City.

SPANISH

The Spanish spoken in both Guatemala and Belize has a strong Latin American flavour to it,

and if you're used to the dainty intonation of Madrid or Granada then this may come as something of a surprise. Gone is the soft s, replaced by a crisp and clear version. If you're new to Spanish it's a lot easier to pick up than the native version. Everywhere you'll find people willing to make an effort to understand you, eager to speak to passing gringos.

The rules of **pronunciation** are pretty straightforward and, once you get to know them, strictly observed. Unless there's an accent, words ending in d, l, r and z are **stressed** on the last syllable, all others on the second last. All **vowels** are pure and short.

A somewhere between the "A" sound of back and that of father.

E as in get.

I as in police.

O as in hot.

U as in rule.

C is soft before E and I, hard otherwise: *cerca* is pronounced serka.

G works the same way, a guttural "H" sound (like the *ch* in loch) before E or I, a hard G elsewhere – *gigante* becomes higante.

H is always silent.

J the same sound as a guttural G: *jamon* is pronounced hamon.

LL sounds like an English Y: *tortilla* is pronounced torteeya.

N is as in English unless it has a tilde (accent) over it, when it becomes NY: *mañana* sounds like manyana.

QU is pronounced like an English K.

R is rolled, RR doubly so.

V sounds more like B, *vino* becoming beano.

X is slightly softer than in English – sometimes almost SH – *Xela* is pronounced shela.

Z is the same as a soft C, so *cerveza* becomes servesa.

Over the page is a list of a few essential words and phrases (and see p.32 for food lists), though if you're travelling for any length of time a dictionary or phrase book is obviously a worthwhile investment – some specifically Latin American ones are available. If you're using a **dictionary**, remember that in Spanish CH, LL, and Ñ count as separate letters and are listed after the Cs, Ls, and Ns respectively.

A SPANISH LANGUAGE GUIDE

BASICS

Yes, No	*Si, No*	Open, Closed	*Abierto/a, Cerrado/a*
Please, Thank you	*Por favor, Gracias*	With, Without	*Con, Sin*
Where, When	*Donde, Cuando*	Good, Bad	*Buen(o)/a, Mal(o)/a*
What, How much	*Qué, Cuanto*	Big, Small	*Gran(de), Pequeño/a*
Here, There	*Aqui, Alli*	More, Less	*Mas, Menos*
This, That	*Este, Eso*	Today, Tomorrow	*Hoy, Mañana*
Now, Later	*Ahora, Mas tarde*	Yesterday	*Ayer*

GREETINGS AND RESPONSES

Hello, Goodbye	*Ola, Adios*	Not at all/You're welcome	*De nada*
Good morning	*Buenos días*		
Good afternoon/night	*Buenas tardes/noches*	Do you speak English?	*¿Habla (usted) Ingles?*
See you later	*Hasta luego*	I don't speak Spanish	*(No) Hablo Español*
Sorry	*Lo siento/disculpeme*	My name is . . .	*Me llamo . . .*
Excuse me	*Con permiso/perdón*	What's your name?	*¿Como se llama usted?*
How are you?	*¿Como está (usted)?*	I am English/	*Soy/Ingles(a)/*
I (don't) understand	*(No) Entiendo*	Australian	*Australiano(a).*

NEEDS – HOTELS AND TRANSPORT

I want	*Quiero*	Left, right, straight on	*Izquierda, derecha, derecho*
I'd like	*Quisiera*		
Do you know . . . ?	*¿Sabe . . . ?*	Where is . . . ?	*¿Donde esta . . . ?*
I don't know	*No se*	. . . the bus station	*. . . el terminal de camionetas*
There is (is there)?	*(¿)Hay(?)*		
Give me . . .	*Deme . . .*	. . . the train station	*. . . la estación de ferrocarriles*
(one like that)	*(uno asi)*		
Do you have . . . ?	*¿Tiene . . . ?*	. . . the nearest bank	*. . . el banco mas cercano*
. . . the time	*. . . la hora*		
. . . a room	*. . . un cuarto*	. . . the post office	*. . . el correo/la oficina de correos*
. . . with two beds/ double bed	*. . . con dos camas/ cama matrimonial*	. . . the toilet	*. . . el baño/ sanitario*
It's for one person (two people)	*Es para una persona (dos personas)*	Where does the bus to . . . leave from?	*¿De donde sale la camioneta para . . . ?*
. . . for one night (one week)	*. . . para una noche (una semana)*	Is this the train for Puerto Barrios?	*¿Es este el tren para Puerto Barrios?*
It's fine, how much is it?	*¿Está bien, cuanto es?*	I'd like a (return) ticket to . . .	*Quisiera un boleto (de ida y vuelta) para . . .*
It's too expensive	*Es demasiado caro*		
Don't you have anything cheaper?	*¿No tiene algo más barato?*		
Can one . . . ?	*¿Se puede . . . ?*	What time does it leave (arrive in . . .)?	*¿A qué hora sale (llega en . . .)?*
. . . camp (near) here?	*¿ . . . acampar aqui (cerca)?*	What is there to eat?	*¿Qué hay para comer?*
Is there a hotel nearby?	*¿Hay un hotel aquí cerca?*	What's that?	*¿Qué es eso?*
How do I get to . . . ?	*¿Por donde se va a . . . ?*	What's this called in Spanish?	*¿Como se llama este en Español?*

NUMBERS AND DAYS

1	un/uno/una	20	veinte	1990	mil novocientos
2	dos	21	veintiuno		noventa
3	tres	30	treinta	1991	...y uno
4	cuatro	40	cuarenta	first	primero/a
5	cinco	50	cincuenta	second	segundo/a
6	seis	60	sesenta	third	tercero/a
7	siete	70	setenta		
8	ocho	80	ochenta	Monday	lunes
9	nueve	90	noventa	Tuesday	martes
10	diez	100	cien(to)	Wednesday	miercoles
11	once	101	ciento uno	Thursday	jueves
12	doce	200	doscientos	Friday	viernes
13	trece	201	doscientos uno	Saturday	sabado
14	catorce	500	quinientos	Sunday	domingo
15	quince	1000	mil		
16	diez y seis	2000	dos mil		

PHRASEBOOKS AND DICTIONARIES

Any good Spanish phrasebook or dictionary should see you through in Guatemala, but specifically Latin American ones are a help. The *University of Chicago Dictionary of Latin-American Spanish* is a good all-rounder, while *Mexican Spanish: A Rough Guide Phrasebook*, has a menu reader, rundown of colloquialisms and a number of cultural tips that are relevant to many of the Latin American countries, including Guatemala.

GLOSSARY

AGUARDIENTE Raw alcohol made from sugar cane.

AGUAS Bottled fizzy drinks.

ALDEA Small settlement.

ALTIPLANO Highland area of central Guatemala.

ATOL Drink usually made from maize dough, cooked with water, salt, sugar and milk. Can also be made from rice.

BARRANCA Steep-sided ravine.

BARRIO Slum or shantytown.

BAYMAN Early White settler in Belize.

BOCA COSTA Western slopes of the Guatemalan highlands, prime coffee-growing country.

CAKCHIQUEL Indigenous highland tribe occupying an area between Guatemala City and Lake Atitlán.

CAMIONETA Second-class bus. In other parts of Latin America the same word means a small truck or van.

CANTINA Local hard-drinking bar.

CAYE or **CAY** Belizean term for a small island.

CHICLE Sapodilla tree sap from which chewing gum is made.

CLASSIC Period during which ancient Maya civilization was at its height, usually given as 300–900 AD.

COFRADÍA Religious brotherhood dedicated to the protection of a particular saint. These groups form the basis of religious and civil hierarchy in traditional highland society and combine Catholic and pagan practices.

COMEDOR Basic Guatemalan restaurant, usually with just one or two things on the menu, always the cheapest places to eat.

CORRIENTE Another name for a second-class bus.

CORTE Traditional Guatemalan skirt.

COSTUMBRE Guatemalan word for traditional customs of the highland Maya, usually of religious and cultural significance. The word often refers to traditions which owe more to paganism than to Catholicism.

METATE Flat stone for grinding maize into flour.

MILPA Maize field, usually cleared by slash and burn.

MLN *Movimiento de Liberacion Nacional* (National Liberation Movement). Right-wing political party in Guatemala.

NATURAL Another term for an indigenous person.

PENSIÓN Simple hotel.

PGT *Partido Guatemalteco de Trabajadores* (Guatemalan Labour Party, also known as the Guatemalan Communist Party).

PIPIL Indigenous tribal group which occupied much of the Pacific coast at the time of the Conquest, but no longer survives.

PLANTATION Farm (in Belize), similar to *milpa* in Guatemala.

POSTCLASSIC Period between the decline of Maya civilization and the arrival of the Spanish, 900–1530 AD.

PRECLASSIC Archeological era preceding the blooming of Maya civilization, usually given as 1500 BC–300 AD.

PULLMAN Fast and comfortable bus, usually an old Greyhound.

PUP People's United Party (Belize).

QUICHÉ Largest of the highland Maya tribes, centred on the town of Santa Cruz del Quiché.

SIERRA Mountain range.

STELA Freestanding carved monument. Most are of Maya origin.

TECÚN UMÁN Last king of the Quiché tribe.

TIENDA Shop.

TRAJE Traditional costume.

TZUTE Headcloth or scarf worn as a part of traditional Indian costume.

TZUTUJIL Indigenous tribal group occupying the land to the south of Lake Atitlán.

UDP United Democratic Party (Belize).

URNG *Unidad Revolucionaria Nacional Guatemalteca* (Guatemalan National Revolutionary Unity).

USAC *Universidad de San Carlos* (National University of San Carlos, Guatemala).

CREOLE Belizean term used to describe those of Afro-Caribbean descent and the version of English that they speak.

DCG *Democracia Cristiana Guatemalteca* (Guatemalan Christian Democratic Party).

EFECTIVO Cash.

EGP *Ejercito Guerrillero de los Pobres* (Guerrilla Army of the Poor). A Guatemalan guerrilla group operating in the Ixil triangle and Ixcán areas.

EVANGELICO Christian evangelist or fundamentalist, often missionaries. Name given to numerous Protestant sects seeking converts in Central America.

FAR *Fuerzas Armadas Rebeldes* (Revolutionary Armed Forces). Another Guatemalan guerrilla group, operating mainly in Petén.

FINCA Plantation-style farm.

GLYPH Element in Maya writing and carving, roughly the equivalent of a letter or numeral.

GRINGO Any White person, not necessarily a term of abuse.

HOSPEDAJE Another name for a small basic hotel.

HUIPILE Woman's traditional blouse, usually woven or embroidered.

INDIGENA Indigenous person/Indian.

INGUAT Guatemalan tourist board.

I.V.A. Guatemalan sales tax of 10 percent.

IXIL Highland tribe grouped around the three towns of the Ixil triangle – Nebaj, Chajul and San Juan Cotzal.

KEKCHI Tribal group based in the Cobán area and Verapaz highlands.

LADINO A vague term – at its most specific defining someone of mixed Spanish and Indian blood, but more commonly used to describe a person of "Western" culture, or one who dresses in "Western" style, be they of Indian or mixed blood.

LENG Slang for *centavo*.

MAM Maya tribe occupying the west of the western highlands, the area around Huehuetenango.

MARIACHI Mexican musical style popular in Guatemala.

MARIMBA Xylophone-like instrument used in traditional Guatemalan music, also used by the Belizean Maya.

MAYA General term for the tribe who inhabited Guatemala, Honduras, southern Mexico and Belize since the earliest times, and still do.

MESTIZO Person of mixed Indian and Spanish blood, though like the term *Ladino* it has more cultural than racial significance.

INDEX

direct orders from

Amsterdam	1-85828-086-9	£7.99	US$13.95	CAN$16.99
Andalucia	1-85828-094-X	8.99	14.95	18.99
Australia	1-85828-141-5	12.99	19.95	25.99
Bali	1-85828-134-2	8.99	14.95	19.99
Barcelona	1-85828-106-7	8.99	13.95	17.99
Berlin	1-85828-129-6	8.99	14.95	19.99
Brazil	1-85828-102-4	9.99	15.95	19.99
Britain	1-85828-208-X	12.99	19.95	25.99
Brittany & Normandy	1-85828-126-1	8.99	14.95	19.99
Bulgaria	1-85828-183-0	9.99	16.95	22.99
California	1-85828-181-4	10.99	16.95	22.99
Canada	1-85828-130-X	10.99	14.95	19.99
Corsica	1-85828-089-3	8.99	14.95	18.99
Costa Rica	1-85828-136-9	9.99	15.95	21.99
Crete	1-85828-132-6	8.99	14.95	18.99
Cyprus	1-85828-182-2	9.99	16.95	22.99
Czech & Slovak Republics	1-85828-121-0	9.99	16.95	22.99
Egypt	1-85828-075-3	10.99	17.95	21.99
Europe	1-85828-159-8	14.99	19.95	25.99
England	1-85828-160-1	10.99	17.95	23.99
First Time Europe	1-85828-210-1	7.99	9.95	12.99
Florida	1-85828-184-4	10.99	16.95	22.99
France	1-85828-124-5	10.99	16.95	21.99
Germany	1-85828-128-8	11.99	17.95	23.99
Goa	1-85828-156-3	8.99	14.95	19.99
Greece	1-85828-131-8	9.99	16.95	20.99
Greek Islands	1-85828-163-6	8.99	14.95	19.99
Guatemala	1-85828-189-X	10.99	16.95	22.99
Hawaii: Big Island	1-85828-158-X	8.99	12.95	16.99
Hawaii	1-85828-206-3	10.99	16.95	22.99
Holland, Belgium & Luxembourg	1-85828-087-7	9.99	15.95	20.99
Hong Kong	1-85828-187-3	8.99	14.95	19.99
Hungary	1-85828-123-7	8.99	14.95	19.99
India	1-85828-104-0	13.99	22.95	28.99
Ireland	1-85828-179-2	10.99	17.95	23.99
Italy	1-85828-167-9	12.99	19.95	25.99
Kenya	1-85828-192-X	11.99	18.95	24.99
London	1-85828-117-2	8.99	12.95	16.99
Mallorca & Menorca	1-85828-165-2	8.99	14.95	19.99
Malaysia, Singapore & Brunei	1-85828-103-2	9.99	16.95	20.99
Mexico	1-85828-044-3	10.99	16.95	22.99
Morocco	1-85828-040-0	9.99	16.95	21.99
Moscow	1-85828-118-0	8.99	14.95	19.99
Nepal	1-85828-190-3	10.99	17.95	23.99
New York	1-85828-171-7	9.99	15.95	21.99

Pacific Northwest	1-85828-092-3	9.99	14.95	19.99
Paris	1-85828-125-3	7.99	13.95	16.99
Poland	1-85828-168-7	10.99	17.95	23.99
Portugal	1-85828-180-6	9.99	16.95	22.99
Prague	1-85828-122-9	8.99	14.95	19.99
Provence	1-85828-127-X	9.99	16.95	22.99
Pyrenees	1-85828-093-1	8.99	15.95	19.99
Rhodes & the Dodecanese	1-85828-120-2	8.99	14.95	19.99
Romania	1-85828-097-4	9.99	15.95	21.99
San Francisco	1-85828-185-7	8.99	14.95	19.99
Scandinavia	1-85828-039-7	10.99	16.99	21.99
Scotland	1-85828-166-0	9.99	16.95	22.99
Sicily	1-85828-178-4	9.99	16.95	22.99
Singapore	1-85828-135-0	8.99	14.95	19.99
Spain	1-85828-081-8	9.99	16.95	20.99
St Petersburg	1-85828-133-4	8.99	14.95	19.99
Thailand	1-85828-140-7	10.99	17.95	24.99
Tunisia	1-85828-139-3	10.99	17.95	24.99
Turkey	1-85828-088-5	9.99	16.95	20.99
Tuscany & Umbria	1-85828-091-5	8.99	15.95	19.99
USA	1-85828-161-X	14.99	19.95	25.99
Venice	1-85828-170-9	8.99	14.95	19.99
Wales	1-85828-096-6	8.99	14.95	18.99
West Africa	1-85828-101-6	15.99	24.95	34.99
More Women Travel	1-85828-098-2	9.99	14.95	19.99
Zimbabwe & Botswana	1-85828-041-9	10.99	16.95	21.99
Phrasebooks				
Czech	1-85828-148-2	3.50	5.00	7.00
French	1-85828-144-X	3.50	5.00	7.00
German	1-85828-146-6	3.50	5.00	7.00
Greek	1-85828-145-8	3.50	5.00	7.00
Italian	1-85828-143-1	3.50	5.00	7.00
Mexican	1-85828-176-8	3.50	5.00	7.00
Portuguese	1-85828-175-X	3.50	5.00	7.00
Polish	1-85828-174-1	3.50	5.00	7.00
Spanish	1-85828-147-4	3.50	5.00	7.00
Thai	1-85828-177-6	3.50	5.00	7.00
Turkish	1-85828-173-3	3.50	5.00	7.00
Vietnamese	1-85828-172-5	3.50	5.00	7.00
Reference				
Classical Music	1-85828-113-X	12.99	19.95	25.99
Internet	1-85828-198-9	5.00	8.00	10.00
Jazz	1-85828-137-7	16.99	24.95	34.99
Rock	1-85828-201-2	17.99	26.95	35.00
World Music	1-85828-017-6	16.99	22.95	29.99

NORTH SOUTH TRAVEL

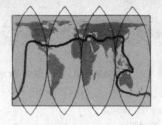

DISCOUNT FARES

PROFITS TO CHARITIES

- North South Travel is a friendly, competitive travel agency, offering discount fares world-wide.
- North South Travel's profits contribute to community projects in the developing world.
- We have special experience of booking destinations in Africa, Asia and Latin America.
- Clients who book through North South Travel include exchange groups, students and independent travellers, as well as charities, church organisations and small businesses.

To discuss your booking requirements: contact Brenda Skinner between 9am and 5pm, Monday to Friday, on (01245) 492 882: Fax (01245) 356 612, any time. Or write to: North South Travel Limited, Moulsham Mill Centre, Parkway, Chelmsford, Essex CM2 7PX, UK

Help us to help others – Your travel can make a difference

Our Holidays Their Homes

Exploring New Destinations?
Ever wondered what that means to the locals?
Ever seen things you're uncomfortable with?
Ever thought of joining Tourism Concern?

Tourism Concern is the only independent British organisation seeking ways to make tourism just, participatory and sustainable · world-wide.

For a membership fee of only £15 (£8 unwaged) UK, £25 overseas, you will support us in our work, receive our quarterly magazine, and learn about what is happening in tourism around the world.

We'll help find answers to the questions.

Tourism Concern, Southlands College, Wimbledon Parkside, London SW19 5NN UK Tel: 0181-944 0464 Fax: 0181-944 6583.